The Unfinished Nation

A CONCISE HISTORY
OF THE AMERICAN PEOPLE

Volume Two: From 1865

The Unfinished Nation

A CONCISE HISTORY
OF THE AMERICAN PEOPLE

Volume Two: From 1865

Second Edition

Alan Brinkley

Columbia University

OVERTURE
BOOKS

The McGraw-Hill Companies, Inc.

New York St. Louis San Francisco Auckland Bogotá Caracas
Lisbon London Madrid Mexico City Milan Montreal New Delhi
San Juan Singapore Sydney Tokyo Toronto

McGraw-Hill

A Division of The **McGraw·Hill** *Companies*

THE UNFINISHED NATION: A Concise History of the American People
Volume Two: From 1865

This book is printed on acid-free paper.

2 3 4 5 6 7 8 9 0 DOCDOC 9 0 9 8 7

ISBN 0-07-008218-9 (Vol. Two)

This book was set in Janson by ComCom, Inc.
R. R. Donnelley & Sons Company was printer and binder.
Maps were prepared by David Lindroth Inc.
Cover design by Wanda Kossak.

Publisher: Jane Vaicunas
Sponsoring Editor: Lyn Uhl
Editing Manager: Larry Goldberg
Design Manager: Joseph A. Piliero
Production Supervisor: Elizabeth J. Strange
Photo Editor: Elyse Rieder

Cover photo: *Music in the Plaza,* 1920. By John Sloan. Museum of Fine Arts,
Museum of New Mexico, Santa Fe, New Mexico. The full image is reproduced
on the back cover.

Library of Congress Cataloging-in-Publication Data

Brinkley, Alan.
    The unfinished nation : a concise history of the American people /
Alan Brinkley.—2nd ed.
        p.   cm.
    "Overture books."
    Includes bibliographical references and index.
    ISBN 0-07-008219-7.—ISBN 0-07-008216-2 (pbk.)
    ISBN 0-07-008217-0 (Vol. One)—ISBN 0-07-008218-9 (Vol. Two)
    1. United States—History. I. Title.
E178.1.B827   1997
973—dc20   96-1210

Contents

AMERICAN VOICES

DEBATING THE PAST

APPENDICES

List of Illustrations

List of Maps

Preface

The story of the American past, which is the subject of this book, has undergone a remarkable transformation in recent decades. The past itself has not changed, of course; but the way Americans understand it has changed dramatically. And in the wake of those changes have come both new forms of presentation and bitter controversies.

On the one hand, history is becoming more visible to more people than ever before as a part of American popular culture. Historical museums and exhibitions have multiplied; popular writing on history—both in novels and in nonfiction—has grown in popularity; history is a constant presence on television, in films, and, increasingly, on the Internet; it is a major element in theme parks and even shopping malls. At the same time, historical scholarship has become the source of increasing debate—both among historians themselves and among national politicians, some of whom have attacked the historical profession for what they claim is an excessively critical view of the American past.

The growing prominence of American history in popular culture and the increasing controversy over its meaning are to a large degree a result of the same things. In turbulent and confusing times, people have naturally looked to their past for guidance and reassurance—and for a reminder of what they believe was a better era. But those same times have encouraged historians to look to the past to understand the tensions and contests that preoccupy us today. In the process, they have reinterpreted much of it. As the population of the United States has become ever more diverse and as groups that once stood outside the view of scholarship thrust themselves into its center, historians have set out to reveal the immense and, until relatively recently, inadequately understood complexity of their country's past. The result has been the slow emergence of a richer and fuller history of the United States, but also a more fragmented, contentious, and controversial one. That history offers a picture of a highly diverse people. It also provides a picture of a great nation.

Threading one's way through the many, conflicting demands of contemporary scholars and contemporary readers is no easy task. But I have tried in this book to find an acceptable middle ground between the claims of diversity and the claims of unity. The United States is, indeed, a nation of many cultures. We cannot understand its history without understanding the experiences of all the different groups that have shaped American society, without understanding the particular worlds that have developed within it based on region, religion, class, ideology, race, gender, and ethnicity.

But the United States is more than just a collection of different cultures. It is also a nation. And as important as understanding its diversity is understanding the forces that have drawn it together and allowed it to survive and flourish despite division. The United States has constructed a remarkably stable and enduring political system that touches the lives of all Americans. It has developed an immense, highly productive national economy that affects the working and consuming lives of virtually everyone. It has created a mass popular culture that colors the experiences and assumptions of almost all the American people, and the people of much of the rest of the world as well. One can admire these unifying forces for their contributions to America's considerable success as a nation, or condemn them for the ways they have contributed to inequality, injustice, and failure. But no one proposing to understand the history of the United States can afford to ignore them.

In the great historical narratives of the nineteenth and early twentieth centuries, the story of America moved smoothly and triumphantly from one clearly defined era to another, focusing on great events and great men and tracing the rise of national institutions. The late twentieth century has produced a different narrative, with frequent, sometimes jarring, changes of focus and direction. It devotes attention to private as well as public events, to failure as well as success, to difference as well as to unity. And yet it remains, in the end, a narrative, a story—newly complicated, perhaps, by our understanding of the many worlds of historical experience that once eluded us—but even more remarkable and compelling for those complications.

This second edition of *The Unfinished Nation* continues the effort to tell this newer story of America for students of history and for general readers in a single, reasonably concise volume. Those familiar with the first edition will notice a number of important changes: Chapters 7 through 11 have been thoroughly reorganized to allow for a more extended and coherent discussion of antebellum American society and culture and to permit a considerable expansion of the treatment of the Old South and slavery. Chapter 15 has been restructured to link an extended description of the New South to the account of the Reconstruction process, which did much to shape it. Chapter 16 is now devoted entirely to the history of the trans-Mississippi West in the late nineteenth century and offers a considerably expanded treatment of the history of that region. And there is a new final chapter (34) which contains an account of events since the publication of the first edition and a major reorganization and expansion of the discussion of contemporary society and culture.

There are other important changes as well. Throughout the book, I have given considerably expanded attention to the American West (beginning with an extended discussion of early Spanish settlement in what is now the American Southwest and continuing to the rise of the modern "Sunbelt"). I have substantially increased the coverage of Hispanic Americans and Asian Americans. There is much new material from recent scholarship in women's history. There is a greatly expanded discussion of the complicated social and cultural history of the 1950s, a new section on the origins of the Vietnam War and a much-expanded discussion of the conflict itself, and a new section on the rise of the right in the 1960s and 1970s. There are also new illustrations and maps, two new essays on "Debating the Past," and illustrated time lines covering significant events in each chapter.

The result, I hope, is a book that will serve to introduce readers to enough different approaches to and areas of American history to make them aware of its extraordinary richness and diversity. I hope it will also give readers some sense of the shared experiences of Americans.

The title of this book, *The Unfinished Nation*, is meant to suggest several things. It is a reminder of America's exceptional diversity: of the degree to which, despite all the many efforts to build a single, uniform definition of the meaning of American nationhood, that meaning remains contested and diverse. It is a reference to the centrality of change in American history: to the way in which the nation has continually transformed itself and to how it continues to do so in our own time. And it is a description of the writing of American history itself, of the way historians are engaged in a continuing, ever unfinished, process of asking new questions of the past.

Many people contributed to this book: Lyn Uhl, Larry Goldberg, Elizabeth Strange, Kathy Bendo, Elyse Rieder, Irving Tullar, Wanda Kossak, and Wanda Lubelska at McGraw-Hill; my research assistants Thad Russell, Charlie Forcey, and Dave Ekbladh; Yanek Mieczkowski, who prepared the time lines; and several anonymous scholars who commented on the first edition and alerted me to various errors and omissions. The reviewers of the second edition made helpful suggestions and comments: Stacy Cole, Ohlone College; Randy Kelly, Community College of Allegheny; Chana Lee, Indiana University; and Ronald Petrin, Oklahoma State University. The reviewers of the text's supplements also made useful contributions: Gisela Ables, Houston Community College; Carla Joy, Red Rocks Community College; Susan Hult, Houston Community College; and Joseph Stout,

Oklahoma State University. I am grateful to them all. I will also be grateful to any readers who wish to offer comments, criticisms, and corrections as I prepare future editions. Suggestions can be sent to me in care of the Department of History, Columbia University, New York, NY 10027; I will respond to them as fully and constructively as I can.

ALAN BRINKLEY

The
Unfinished
Nation

A CONCISE HISTORY
OF THE AMERICAN PEOPLE

Volume Two: From 1865

CHAPTER FIFTEEN

Reconstruction and the New South

The Problems of Peacemaking ∼ *Radical Reconstruction*
The South in Reconstruction ∼ *The Grant Administration*
The Abandonment of Reconstruction ∼ *The New South*

EW PERIODS IN the history of the United States have produced as much bitterness or created such enduring controversy as the era of Reconstruction—the years following the Civil War during which Americans attempted to reunite their shattered nation. Those who lived through Reconstruction viewed it in sharply different ways. To many white Southerners, it was a vicious and destructive experience—a period when vindictive Northerners inflicted humiliation and revenge on the prostrate South and unnecessarily delayed a genuine reunion of the sections. Northern defenders of Reconstruction, in contrast, argued that their policies were the only way to prevent unrepentant Confederates from restoring Southern society as it had been before the war; without forceful federal intervention, there would be no way to forestall the reemergence of a backward aristocracy and the continued subjugation of former slaves—no way, in other words, to prevent the same sectional problems that had produced the Civil War in the first place.

To most African Americans at the time, and to many people of all races since, Reconstruction was notable for other reasons. Neither a vicious tyranny, as white Southerners charged, nor a thoroughgoing reform, as many Northerners claimed, it was, rather, a small but important first step in the effort to secure civil rights and economic power for the former slaves. Reconstruction did not provide African Americans with either the legal protections or the material resources to assure them anything like real equality. And when it came to an end in the late 1870s—as a result of an economic crisis, a lack of political will in the North, and organized, at times violent, resistance by white Southerners—the freed slaves found themselves abandoned by the federal government to face a system of economic peonage and

419

TIME LINE

1863	1864	1865	1866	1867
Lincoln announces Reconstruction plan	Lincoln vetoes Wade-Davis bill	Lincoln assassinated; Johnson becomes president Freedmen's Bureau established Joint Committee on Reconstruction established	Republicans gain in congressional elections	Congressional Reconstruction begins

1868	1869	1872	1873	1875
Grant elected president	Congress passes 15th Amendment	Grant reelected	Panic and depression	"Whiskey ring" scandal

1877	1883	1890s	1895	1896
Hayes wins disputed election Compromise of 1877 ends Reconstruction	Supreme Court upholds segregation	Jim Crow laws in South	Atlanta Compromise	*Plessy* v. *Ferguson*

legal subordination. For the remainder of the nineteenth century, those black men and women who continued to live in what came to be known as the New South had little power to resist their oppression.

And yet for all its shortcomings, Reconstruction did help African Americans create institutions and legal precedents that helped them survive and that ultimately, well into the twentieth century, became the basis of later efforts to win freedom and equality.

THE PROBLEMS OF PEACEMAKING

In 1865, when it became clear that the war was almost over, no one in Washington knew quite what to do. Abraham Lincoln could not negotiate a treaty with the defeated government; he continued to insist that the Confederate government had no legal right to exist. Yet neither could he simply readmit the Southern states into the Union as if nothing had happened.

The Aftermath of War and Emancipation

The South after the Civil War was a desolate place. Towns had been gutted, plantations burned, fields neglected, bridges and railroads destroyed. Many white Southerners—stripped of their slaves through emancipation and stripped of the capital they had invested in now worthless Confederate bonds and currency—had almost no personal property. More than 258,000 Confederate soldiers had died in the war, and thousands more returned home wounded or sick. Many families had to rebuild their fortunes without the help of adult males. Some white Southerners faced starvation and homelessness.

If conditions were bad for Southern whites, they were far worse for Southern blacks—the 4 million men and women now emerging from

CHARLESTON, 1865 Not until 1864 did substantial fighting and destruction begin to take place in the urban South. But in the last year of the war, several major cities (and many towns and smaller communities) experienced devastation at the hands of the Northern armies—among them Richmond, Atlanta, and (as seen here) Charleston.

bondage. As soon as the war ended, hundreds of thousands of them—young and old, many of them ill and feeble—left the plantations in search of a new life in freedom. But most had nowhere to go, and few had any possessions except the clothes they wore.

Despite the disarray of Southern society, almost everyone faced the future with some very clear aspirations. For blacks and whites alike, Reconstruction became a struggle to define the meaning of freedom. But the former slaves and the defeated whites had very different conceptions of what freedom meant.

For African Americans, freedom meant above all an end to slavery. But it also meant acquiring rights and protections that would enable them to live as free people, just as whites did. Some blacks believed the only way to secure freedom was to have the government take land away from white people, who owned virtually all of it, and give it to black people, who owned virtually none. Others asked only for legal equality, confident that they could advance successfully in American society once the formal obstacles to their advancement disappeared. But whatever their particular demands, virtually all former slaves were united in their desire for independence from white control. Throughout the post–Civil War South, African Americans separated themselves from white institutions—pulling out of white-controlled churches and establishing their own, creating clubs and societies for their own people, in some cases starting their own schools.

For most white Southerners, freedom meant something very different. It meant the ability to control their own destinies without interference from the North or the federal government. And in the immediate aftermath of the war, they attempted to exercise this version of freedom by trying to restore their society to its antebellum form. When these white Southerners fought for what they considered freedom, they were fighting above all to preserve local and regional autonomy and white supremacy.

The federal government kept troops in the South to preserve order and protect the freedmen. And in March 1865, Congress established the Freedmen's Bureau, an agency of the army directed by General Oliver O. Howard. The Freedmen's Bureau distributed food to millions of former slaves. It established schools, staffed by missionaries and teachers who had been sent to the South by Freedmen's Aid Societies and other private and church groups in the North. It made a modest effort to settle blacks on lands of their own. (The bureau also offered considerable assistance to poor whites, many of whom were similarly destitute and homeless after the war.) But the Freedmen's Bureau was not a permanent solution. It had authority to operate for only one year, and it was, in any case, far too small to deal effectively with the enormous problems facing Southern society. By the time the war ended, other proposals for reconstructing the defeated South were emerging.

Plans for Reconstruction

Most Democrats favored a Reconstruction process that would readmit the former Confederate states to the Union quickly and painlessly. (That was in part because the Democratic Party had the most to gain from the readmission of the South, most of whose voters were likely to be Democrats.) But control of Reconstruction remained largely in the hands of the Republicans, who had substantial majorities in both houses of Congress. And the Republicans were divided in their approach to the issue. Conservatives within the party insisted that the South accept the abolition of slavery, but they proposed few other conditions for the readmission of the seceded states. The Radicals, led by Representative Thaddeus Stevens of Pennsylvania and Senator Charles Sumner of Massachusetts, urged a much harsher course, including disenfranchising large numbers of Southern whites, protecting black civil rights, and confiscating the property of wealthy white Southerners who had aided the Confederacy and distributing the land among the freedmen. There was also a group of Republican Moderates, who rejected the most stringent demands of the Radicals but supported extracting at least some concessions from the South on black rights.

President Lincoln's sympathies lay with the Moderates and Conservatives of his party. He favored a lenient Reconstruction policy, and he believed that Southern Unionists (mostly former Whigs) could become the nucleus of new, loyal state governments in the South. Lincoln announced his Reconstruction plan in December 1863, more than a year before the war ended. It offered a general amnesty to white Southerners—other than high officials of the Confederacy—who would pledge an oath of loyalty to the government and accept the elimination of slavery. When 10 percent of a state's total number of voters in 1860 took the oath, those loyal voters could set up a state government. Lincoln also proposed extending suffrage to those blacks who were educated, owned property, and had served in the Union army. Three Southern states—Louisiana, Arkansas, and Tennessee, all under Union occupation—reestablished loyal governments under the Lincoln formula in 1864.

The Radical Republicans were outraged at the mildness of Lincoln's program and refused to admit representatives from the three "reconstructed"

ABRAHAM LINCOLN Lincoln was the subject of many
photographic portraits, of which this one, by
Mathew Brady, is one of the most famous.

states to Congress. In July 1864, they pushed their own plan through Congress in the form of the Wade-Davis Bill. It called for the president to appoint a provisional governor for each conquered state. When a majority (not Lincoln's 10 percent) of the white males of a state pledged their allegiance to the Union, the governor could summon a state constitutional convention, whose delegates were to be elected by voters who had never borne arms against the United States (again, a major departure from Lincoln's plan). The new state constitutions would be required to abolish slavery, disenfranchise Confederate civil and military leaders, and repudiate debts accumulated by the state governments during the war. Only then would Congress readmit the states to the Union. Like the president's proposal, the Wade-Davis Bill left up to the states the question of political rights for blacks.

Congress passed the bill a few days before it adjourned in 1864, and Lincoln disposed of it with a pocket veto. His action enraged the Radical leaders, and the pragmatic Lincoln realized he would have to accept at least some of the Radical demands. In the first weeks of 1865, he began to move toward a new approach to Reconstruction.

The Death of Lincoln

What plan he might have produced no one can say. On the night of April 14, 1865, Lincoln and his wife attended a play at Ford's Theater in Washington. As they sat in the presidential box, John Wilkes Booth, an actor obsessed with aiding the Southern cause, entered the box from the rear and shot Lincoln in the head. Early the next morning, the president died.

The circumstances of Lincoln's death earned him immediate martyrdom. They also produced something close to hysteria throughout the North, especially because it quickly became clear that Booth had been the leader of a conspiracy. One of his associates shot and wounded Secretary of State William Seward on the night of the assassination, and another abandoned at the last moment a scheme to murder Vice President Andrew Johnson. Booth himself escaped on horseback into the Maryland countryside, where, on April 26, he was cornered by Union troops and shot to death in a blazing barn. Eight other people were convicted by a military tribunal of participating in the conspiracy (at least two of them on the basis of virtually no evidence). Four were hanged.

To many Northerners, however, the murder of the president seemed evidence of an even greater conspiracy—one masterminded and directed by the unrepentant leaders of the defeated South. Militant Republicans exploited such suspicions relentlessly in the ensuing months, ensuring that Lincoln's death would help doom his plans for a relatively easy peace.

Johnson and "Restoration"

Leadership of the Moderates and Conservatives fell to Lincoln's successor, Andrew Johnson of Tennessee, who was not well suited, either by circumstance or personality, for the task. A Democrat until he had joined the Union ticket with Lincoln in 1864, he became president at a time of growing partisan passions. And Johnson himself was an intemperate and tactless man, filled with resentments and insecurities.

Johnson revealed his plan for Reconstruction—or "Restoration," as he preferred to call it—soon after he took office, and he implemented it during the summer of 1865 when Congress was in recess. Like Lincoln, he offered some form of amnesty to Southerners who would take an oath of allegiance. In most other respects, however, his plan resembled that of the Wade-Davis Bill. The president appointed a provisional governor in each state and charged him with inviting qualified voters to elect delegates to a constitutional convention. In order to win readmission to Congress, a state had to revoke its ordinance of secession, abolish slavery and ratify the Thirteenth Amendment, and repudiate Confederate and state war debts—essentially the same terms as in Wade-Davis.

By the end of 1865, all the seceded states had formed new governments—some under Lincoln's plan, some under Johnson's—and awaited congressional approval of them. But Radicals in Congress vowed not to recognize the Johnson governments, just as they had previously refused to recognize the Lincoln regimes, for by now, Northern opinion had become more hostile toward the South than it had been a year earlier when Congress passed the Wade-Davis Bill. Delegates to the Southern conventions had angered much of the North by their apparent reluctance to abolish slavery and by their refusal to grant suffrage to any blacks. Southern states had elected prominent Confederate leaders to represent them in Congress, among them Alexander H. Stephens, former vice president of the Confederacy, who was selected as a United States senator from Georgia.

RADICAL RECONSTRUCTION

Reconstruction under Johnson's plan—often known as "presidential Reconstruction"—continued only until Congress reconvened in December 1865. At that point, Congress refused to seat the representatives of the "restored" states and created a new Joint Committee on Reconstruction to frame a Reconstruction policy of its own. The period of "congressional" or "Radical" Reconstruction had begun.

The Black Codes

Meanwhile, events in the South were driving Northern opinion in even more radical directions. Throughout the South in 1865 and early 1866, state legislatures were enacting sets of laws known as the Black Codes, designed to give whites substantial control over former slaves. The codes authorized local officials to apprehend unemployed blacks, fine them for vagrancy, and hire them out to private employers to satisfy the fine. Some of the codes forbade blacks to own or lease farms or to take any jobs other than as plantation workers or domestic servants. To many Northerners, and to most African Americans, the Black Codes represented a return to slavery in all but name.

Congress first responded to the Black Codes by passing an act extending the life of the Freedmen's Bureau and widening its powers. The bureau could now establish special courts, which could nullify work agreements forced on freedmen under the Black Codes. Then, in April, Congress passed the first Civil Rights Act, which declared blacks to be citizens of the United States and gave the federal government power to intervene in state affairs to protect the rights of citizens. Johnson vetoed both the Freedmen's Bureau and Civil Rights Acts, but Congress overrode him.

The Fourteenth Amendment

In April 1866, the Joint Committee on Reconstruction proposed a new amendment to the Constitution, which Congress approved in early summer and sent to the states for ratification. Eventually, it became one of the most important of all the provisions in the Constitution.

The Fourteenth Amendment offered the first constitutional definition of American citizenship. Everyone born in the United States, and everyone naturalized, was automatically a citizen and entitled to all the "privileges and immunities" guaranteed by the Constitution, including equal protection of the laws by both the state and national governments. There could be no other requirements for citizenship. The amendment also imposed penalties—reduction of representation in Congress and in the electoral college—on states that denied suffrage to any adult male inhabitants. (The wording reflected the prevailing view in Congress and elsewhere that the franchise was properly restricted to men.) Finally, it prohibited former members of Congress or other former federal officials who had aided the Confederacy from holding any state or federal office unless two-thirds of Congress voted to pardon them.

Congressional Radicals offered to readmit to the Union any state whose legislature ratified the Fourteenth Amendment. Only Tennessee did so. All the other former Confederate states, along with Delaware and Kentucky, refused to do so. That denied the amendment the necessary approval of three-fourths of the states and temporarily derailed it.

But in the meantime, the Radicals were growing more confident and determined. Bloody race riots in New Orleans and other Southern cities—riots in which blacks were the principal victims—were among the events that strengthened their hand. In the 1866 congressional elections, Johnson actively campaigned for Conservative candidates, but he did his own cause more harm than good with his intemperate speeches. The voters returned an overwhelming majority of Republicans, most of them Radicals, to Congress. In the Senate, there were now 42 Republicans to 11 Democrats; in the House, 143 Republicans to 49 Democrats. (The South remained largely unrepresented in both chambers.) Congressional Republicans, who until this point had served mainly as an obstacle to the president's plans for Reconstruction, were now strong enough to produce a plan of their own.

The Congressional Plan

The Radicals passed three Reconstruction bills early in 1867 and overrode Johnson's vetoes of all of them. These bills established finally, nearly two years after the end of the war, a coherent plan for Reconstruction.

Under the congressional plan, Tennessee, which had ratified the Fourteenth Amendment, was promptly readmitted. But Congress rejected the Lincoln-Johnson governments of the other ten Confederate states and, instead, combined those states into five military districts. A military commander governed each district and had orders to register qualified voters (defined as all adult black males and those white males who had not participated in the rebellion). Once registered, voters would elect conventions to prepare new state constitutions, which had to include provisions for black suffrage. Once voters ratified the new constitutions, they could elect state governments. Congress had to approve a state's constitution, and the state legislature had to ratify the Fourteenth Amendment. Once that happened, and once enough states ratified the amendment to make it part of the Constitution, then the former Confederate states could be restored to the Union.

By 1868, seven of the ten former Confederate states (Arkansas, North Carolina, South Carolina, Louisiana, Alabama, Georgia, and Florida) had fulfilled these conditions (including ratification of the Fourteenth Amendment, which now became part of the Constitution) and were readmitted to the Union. Conservative whites held up the return of Virginia and Texas until 1869 and Mississippi until 1870. By then, Congress had added an additional requirement for readmission—ratification of another constitutional amendment, the Fifteenth, which forbade the states and the federal government to deny suffrage to any citizen on account of "race, color, or previous condition of servitude." Several Northern and border states refused to approve the Fifteenth Amendment, and it was adopted only with the support of the three Southern states that had to ratify it in order to be readmitted to the Union.

To stop the president from interfering with their plans, the congressional Radicals passed two remarkable laws of dubious constitutionality in 1867. One, the Tenure of Office Act, forbade the president to remove civil officials, including members of his own cabinet, without the consent of the Senate. The principal purpose of the law was to protect the job of Secretary of

A CELEBRATION OF RECONSTRUCTION The celebrated
cartoonist Thomas Nast—best known for his savage
caricatures of machine politicians in New York's Tammany
Hall—drew this celebratory, and optimistic, image of
Reconstruction not long after the end of the
Civil War: a classical goddess restoring the former
Confederate states to their rightful place within symbolic
fasces that represented union. In fact, the Reconstruction
process proved much more difficult than this hopeful
image suggested.

War Edwin M. Stanton, who was the only Lincoln appointee still in Johnson's cabinet and who was cooperating with the Radicals. The other law, the
Command of the Army Act, prohibited the president from issuing military
orders except through the commanding general of the army (General Grant),
whose headquarters were to be in Washington and who could not be relieved
or assigned elsewhere without the consent of the Senate.

The congressional Radicals also took action to stop the Supreme Court from interfering with their plans. In 1866, the Court had declared in the case of *Ex parte Milligan* that military tribunals were unconstitutional in places where civil courts were functioning, a decision that seemed to threaten the system of military government the Radicals were planning for the South. Radicals in Congress immediately proposed several bills that would require two-thirds of the justices to support any decision overruling a law of Congress, would deny the Court jurisdiction in Reconstruction cases, would reduce its membership to three, and would even abolish it. The justices apparently took notice. Over the next two years, the Court refused to accept jurisdiction in any cases involving Reconstruction (and the congressional bills concerning the Court never passed).

The Impeachment of the President

President Johnson had long since ceased to be a serious obstacle to the passage of Radical legislation, but he was still the official charged with administering the Reconstruction programs. As such, the Radicals believed, he remained a serious impediment to their plans. Early in 1867, they began looking for a way to get rid of him. Under the Constitution, Congress could impeach a President and remove him from office only for "high crimes or misdemeanors," so Republicans were seeking a basis for such charges. Johnson finally gave them what they considered a plausible reason for impeachment when he dismissed Secretary of War Stanton despite Congress's refusal to agree, thus deliberately violating the Tenure of Office Act in hopes of testing the law before the courts. Elated Radicals in the House quickly impeached the president on eleven charges and sent the case to the Senate for trial. Nine counts dealt with the violation of the Tenure of Office Act. The others charged Johnson with slandering Congress and not enforcing the Reconstruction Acts.

The trial before the Senate lasted throughout April and May 1868. The Radicals put heavy pressure on all the Republican senators, but the Moderates (who were losing faith in the Radical program) vacillated. On the first three charges to come to a vote, seven Republicans joined the twelve Democrats to support acquittal. The vote was 35 to 19, one short of the constitutionally required two-thirds majority. After that, the Radicals dropped the impeachment campaign.

THE SOUTH IN RECONSTRUCTION

When white Southerners spoke bitterly in later years of the effects of Reconstruction, they referred most frequently to the governments Congress imposed on them—governments that were, they claimed, both incompetent and corrupt, that saddled the region with enormous debts, and that trampled on the rights of citizens. When black Southerners and their defenders condemned Reconstruction, in contrast, they spoke of its failure to guarantee to freedmen even the most elemental rights of citizenship—a failure that resulted in a new and cruel system of economic subordination.

The Reconstruction Governments

In the ten states of the South that were reorganized under the congressional plan, approximately one-fourth of the white males were at first excluded from voting or holding office, which produced black majorities among voters in South Carolina, Mississippi, and Louisiana (where blacks were also a majority of the population) and in Alabama and Florida (where they were not). But federal officials soon lifted most suffrage restrictions so that nearly all white males could vote. After that, Republicans could maintain control only with a combination of black and white support.

Critics labeled Southern white Republicans with the derogatory terms "scalawags" and "carpetbaggers." Many of the "scalawags" were former Whigs who had never felt comfortable in the Democratic Party or farmers who lived in remote areas where there had been little or no slavery; most of these Republicans hoped the party's program of internal improvements would help end their economic isolation. The "carpetbaggers" were white men from the North, most of them veterans of the Union army who looked on the South as a new frontier, more promising than the West. They had settled there at war's end as hopeful planters, businessmen, or professionals.

The most numerous Republicans in the South were the black freedmen, most of whom had no previous experience in politics and tried, therefore, to build institutions through which they could learn to exercise their power. In several states, African-American voters held their own conventions to chart their future course. One such "colored convention," as Southern whites called it, assembled in Alabama in 1867 and announced: "We claim exactly the same rights, privileges and immunities as are enjoyed by white men— we ask nothing more and will be content with nothing less." The black churches freedmen created after emancipation, when they withdrew from the white-dominated churches they had been compelled to attend under slavery, also helped give them unity and political self-confidence.

African Americans played a significant role in the politics of the Reconstruction South. They served as delegates to the constitutional conventions. They held public offices of practically every kind. Between 1869 and 1901, twenty blacks served in the United States House of Representatives, two in the Senate. They served, too, in state legislatures and in various other state offices. Southern whites complained loudly (both at the time and for generations to come) about "Negro rule" during Reconstruction, but no such thing ever actually existed in any of the states. No black man was ever elected governor of a Southern state (although P. B. S. Pinchback, the African-American lieutenant governor of Louisiana, was acting governor briefly). Blacks never controlled any of the state legislatures (although African Americans did once win a majority of seats in South Carolina's lower house). In the South as a whole, the percentage of black officeholders was always far lower than the percentage of blacks in the population.

The record of the Reconstruction governments is mixed. Critics at the time and later denounced them for corruption and financial extravagance, and there is some truth to both charges. Officeholders in many states enriched themselves through graft and other illicit activities. State budgets expanded to hitherto unknown totals, and state debts soared to previously undreamed-of heights. But the corruption in the South, real as it was, was hardly unique to the Reconstruction governments. Corruption had been rife in some antebellum and Confederate governments, and it was at least as rampant in the Northern states. In some of the Southern state governments, moreover, corruption continued and even grew worse after the end of Reconstruction.

The large state expenditures of the Reconstruction years were huge only in comparison with the meager budgets of the antebellum era. They represented an effort to provide the South with desperately needed services that antebellum governments had never offered: public education, public works programs, poor relief, and other costly new commitments. There were, to be sure, graft and extravagance in Reconstruction governments; there were also positive and permanent accomplishments.

Perhaps the most important of those accomplishments was a dramatic improvement in Southern education—an improvement that benefited both whites and blacks. In the first years of Reconstruction, much of the impetus for educational reform in the South came from outside groups—from the Freedmen's Bureau, from Northern private philanthropic organizations, from the many Northern white women who traveled to the South to teach in freedmen's schools—and from African Americans themselves. Over the opposition of many Southern whites, who feared that education would give blacks "false notions of equality," these reformers established a large network of schools for former slaves—4,000 schools by 1870, staffed by 9,000 teachers (half of them black), teaching 200,000 students (about 12 percent of the total school-age population of the freedmen). In the 1870s, Reconstruction governments began to build a comprehensive public school system in the South. By 1876, more than half of all white children and about 40 percent of all black children were attending schools in the South (although almost all such schools were racially segregated). Several black "academies," offering more advanced education, also began operating. Gradually, these academies grew into an important network of black colleges and universities.

Landownership

The most ambitious goal of the Freedmen's Bureau, and of some Republican Radicals in Congress, was to reform landownership in the South. The effort failed. By June 1865, the bureau had settled nearly 10,000 black families on their own land—most of it drawn from abandoned plantations in areas occupied by the Union armies. By the end of that year, however, Southern plantation owners were returning and demanding the restoration of their property. President Johnson supported their demands, and the government eventually returned most of the confiscated lands to their original white owners. Congress never had much stomach for the idea of land redistribution, and the experiment quickly died.

Even so, the distribution of landownership in the South changed considerably in the postwar years. Among whites, there was a striking decline in landownership, from 80 percent before the war to 67 percent by the end of Reconstruction. Some whites lost their land because of unpaid debt or increased taxes; some left the marginal lands they had owned to move to more fertile areas, where they rented. Among blacks, during the same period, the proportion who owned land rose from virtually none to more than 20 percent.

Still, most blacks, and a growing minority of whites, did not own their own land during Reconstruction, and some who acquired land in the 1860s had lost it by the 1890s. Instead, they worked for others in one form or another. Many black agricultural laborers—perhaps 25 percent of the total—simply worked for wages. Most, however, became tenants of white landowners—that is, they worked their own plots of land and paid their landlords either a fixed rent or a share of their crop (hence the term "sharecropping").

AFTER SLAVERY Although most freed slaves remained agricultural laborers after Emancipation, a considerable number moved off the land in search of new occupations and new homes. For many, that meant living for some time without stable employment or a permanent home. This photograph from the late 1860s shows a group of former slaves at a county almshouse in the South.

The new system represented a repudiation by blacks of the gang-labor system of the antebellum plantation, in which slaves had lived and worked together under the direction of a master. As tenants and sharecroppers, blacks enjoyed at least a physical independence from their landlords and had the sense of working their own land, even if in most cases they could never hope to buy it. But tenantry also benefited landlords in some ways, relieving them of the cost of purchasing slaves and of any responsibility for the physical well-being of their workers.

Incomes and Credit

In some respects, the postwar years were a period of remarkable economic progress for African Americans in the South. When the material benefits they had received under slavery are calculated as income, prewar blacks had earned about a 22 percent share of the profits of the plantation system. By the end of Reconstruction, they were earning 56 percent. Measured another way, the per capita income of blacks rose 46 percent between 1857 and

1879, while the per capita income of whites declined 35 percent. This represented one of the most significant redistributions of income in American history.

But those figures tell only part of the story. The black share of profits was increasing, but the total profits of Southern agriculture were declining—a result of the dislocations of the war and a reduction in the world market for cotton. And while African Americans were earning a greater return on their labor than they had under slavery, they were also working less. Women and children were less likely to labor in the fields than they had been in the past. Adult men tended to work shorter days. In all, the black labor force worked about one-third fewer hours during Reconstruction than it had been compelled to do under slavery—a reduction that brought the working schedule of blacks roughly into accord with that of white farm laborers. Nor did the income redistribution of the postwar years lift many blacks out of poverty. Black per capita income rose from about one-quarter of white per capita income to about one-half in the first few years after the war. After this initial increase, it rose hardly at all.

For blacks and poor whites alike, whatever gains there might have been as a result of land and income redistribution were often overshadowed by the ravages of the crop-lien system. Few of the traditional institutions of credit in the South—the "factors" and banks—returned after the war. In their stead emerged a new system of credit, centered in large part on local country stores—some of them owned by planters, others owned by independent merchants. Blacks and whites, landowners and tenants—all depended on these stores for such necessities as food, clothing, seed, and farm implements. And since farmers do not have the same steady cash flow as other workers, customers usually had to rely on credit from these merchants in order to purchase what they needed. Most local stores had no competition (and went to great lengths to ensure that things stayed that way). As a result, they were able to set interest rates as high as 50 or 60 percent. Farmers had to give the merchants a lien (or claim) on their crops as collateral for the loans (thus the term "crop-lien system," generally used to describe Southern farming in this period). Farmers who suffered a few bad years in a row, as many did, could become trapped in a cycle of debt from which they could never escape.

One effect of this burdensome credit system was that some blacks who had acquired land during the early years of Reconstruction gradually lost it as they fell into debt. So, to a lesser extent, did white small landowners. Another was that Southern farmers became almost wholly dependent on cash crops—and most of all on cotton—because only such marketable commodities seemed to offer any possibility of escape from debt. The relentless planting of cotton contributed to an exhaustion of the soil. The crop-lien system, in other words, was not only helping to impoverish small farmers; it was also contributing to a general decline in the Southern agricultural economy.

The African-American Family in Freedom

One of the most striking features of the black response to Reconstruction was the effort to build or rebuild family structures and to protect them from the interference they had experienced under slavery. A major reason for the rapid departure of so many blacks from plantations was the desire to find lost relatives and reunite families. Thousands of African Americans wandered through the South looking for husbands, wives, children, or other relatives from whom they had been separated. Former slaves rushed to have their marriages, previously without legal standing, sanctified by church and law. Black families resisted living in the former slave quarters and moved instead to small cabins scattered widely across the countryside, where they could enjoy at least some privacy.

Within the black family, the definition of male and female roles quickly came to resemble that within white families. Many women and children ceased working in the fields. Such work, they believed, was a badge of slavery. Instead, many women restricted themselves largely to domestic tasks—cooking, cleaning, gardening, raising children, attending to the needs of their husbands. Still, economic necessity often compelled black women to engage in income-producing activities: working as domestic servants, taking in laundry, or helping their husbands in the fields. By the end of Reconstruction, half of all black women over the age of sixteen were working for wages. And unlike white working women, most black female income earners were married.

THE GRANT ADMINISTRATION

Exhausted by the political turmoil of the Johnson administration, American voters in 1868 yearned for a strong, stable figure to guide them through the troubled years of Reconstruction. They did not find one. Instead, they turned trustingly to General Ulysses S. Grant, the hero of the war and, by 1868, a revered national idol. Grant was a disastrous president. During his two terms in office, he faced problems that would have taxed the abilities of a master of statecraft. Grant, however, had few political skills and little vision.

The Soldier President

Grant could have had the nomination of either party in 1868. But believing that Republican Reconstruction policies were more attuned to public opinion than the Democratic alternatives, he accepted the Republican nomination. The Democrats nominated former governor Horatio Seymour of New York. The campaign was a bitter one, and Grant's triumph was surprisingly narrow. He carried twenty-six states to Seymour's eight, but his popular majority was a scant 310,000 votes. Without the 500,000 black Republican voters in the South, he would have had a minority of the popular vote.

Grant entered the White House with no political experience, and his performance was clumsy and ineffectual from the start. Except for Hamilton Fish, whom Grant appointed secretary of state and who served for eight years with great distinction, most members of the cabinet were as inept as the president. Grant relied chiefly, and increasingly, on the machine leaders in the party—the group most ardently devoted to the spoils system; consequently, his administration used the spoils system even more blatantly than most of his predecessors. The result was the emergence of a growing sentiment among reformers and others for a civil service system, which would fill many government positions on "merit" and not through patronage. Grant also attracted the hostility of many of his fellow Republicans, particularly as Northerners grew disillusioned with the Radical Reconstruction policies Grant continued to support. Some Republicans suspected, correctly, that there was also corruption in the Grant administration itself.

By the end of Grant's first term, therefore, members of a substantial faction of the party—who referred to themselves as Liberal Republicans—had come to oppose what they called "Grantism." In 1872, hoping to prevent Grant's reelection, they bolted the party and nominated their own presidential candidate: Horace Greeley, veteran editor and publisher of the New York *Tribune*. The Democrats, somewhat reluctantly, named Greeley their candidate as well, hoping that the alliance with the Liberals would enable them to defeat Grant. But the effort was in vain. Grant won a substantial victory, polling 286 electoral votes and 3,597,000 popular votes to Greeley's 66 and 2,834,000. Three weeks later, apparently crushed by his defeat, Greeley died.

The Grant Scandals

During the 1872 campaign, the first of a series of political scandals came to light that would plague Grant and the Republicans for the next eight years.

It involved the French-owned Crédit Mobilier construction company, which had helped build the Union Pacific Railroad. The heads of Crédit Mobilier had used their positions as Union Pacific stockholders to steer large fraudulent contracts to their construction company, thus bilking the Union Pacific (and the federal government, which provided large subsidies to the railroad) of millions. To prevent investigations, the directors had given Crédit Mobilier stock to key members of Congress. But in 1872, Congress did conduct an investigation, which revealed that some highly placed Republicans—including Schuyler Colfax, now Grant's vice president—had accepted stock.

One dreary episode followed another in Grant's second term. Benjamin H. Bristow, Grant's third Treasury secretary, discovered that some of his officials and a group of distillers operating as a "whiskey ring" were cheating the government out of taxes by filing false reports. Then a House investigation revealed that William W. Belknap, secretary of war, had accepted bribes to retain an Indian-post trader in office (the so-called Indian ring). Other, lesser scandals added to the growing impression that "Grantism" had brought rampant corruption to government.

The Greenback Question

Compounding Grant's, and the nation's, problems was the financial crisis known as the Panic of 1873. It began with the failure of a leading investment banking firm, Jay Cooke and Company, which had invested too heavily in postwar railroad building. There had been panics before—in 1819, 1837, and 1857—but this was the worst one yet. The depression it produced lasted four years.

Debtors now pressured the government to inflate the value of their currency, which would have made it easier for them to pay their debts. More specifically, they urged the government to redeem federal war bonds with greenbacks, paper currency of the sort printed during the Civil War, which would increase the amount of money in circulation. But Grant and most Republicans wanted a "sound" currency—based solidly on gold reserves—which would favor the interests of banks and other creditors.

The greenback question would not go away. There was approximately $356 million in paper currency issued during the Civil War that was still in circulation. And in 1873, when the Supreme Court ruled in *Knox* v. *Lee* that greenbacks were legal, the Treasury issued more in response to the panic. The following year, Congress voted to raise the total further. But Grant, under pressure from eastern financial interests, vetoed the measure.

In 1875, Republican leaders in Congress, in an effort to crush the greenback movement for good, passed the Specie Resumption Act. This law provided that after January 1, 1879, the greenback dollars, whose value constantly fluctuated, would be redeemed by the government and replaced with new certificates, firmly pegged to the price of gold. The law satisfied creditors, who had worried that debts would be repaid in paper currency of uncertain value. But "resumption" made things more difficult for debtors, because the gold-based money supply could not easily expand. As a result, money became scarcer.

In 1875, the "greenbackers," as the inflationists were called, formed their own political organization: the National Greenback Party. It was active in the next three presidential elections, but it failed to gain widespread support. It did, however, keep the money issue alive. The question of the proper composition of the currency was to remain one of the most controversial and enduring issues in late-nineteenth-century American politics.

Republican Diplomacy

The Johnson and Grant administrations achieved their greatest successes in foreign affairs. The accomplishments were the work not of the presidents themselves, who displayed little aptitude for diplomacy, but of two outstanding secretaries of state: William H. Seward, who had served Lincoln and who remained in office until 1869; and Hamilton Fish, who served throughout the two terms of the Grant administration.

An ardent expansionist, Seward acted with as much daring as the demands of Reconstruction politics and the Republican hatred of President Johnson would permit. Seward accepted a Russian offer to sell Alaska to the United States for $7.2 million, despite criticism from many who considered Alaska a useless frozen wasteland and derided it as "Seward's Folly." In 1867, Seward also engineered the American annexation of the tiny Midway Islands, west of Hawaii.

Hamilton Fish was also a firm and decisive diplomat. His first major challenge was resolving a longstanding controversy with England. Many Americans believed that the British government had violated the neutrality laws during the Civil War by permitting English shipyards to build ships (among them the *Alabama*) for the Confederacy. American demands that England pay for the damage these vessels had caused became known as the "Alabama claims." In 1871, after a number of failed efforts, Fish forged an agreement, the Treaty of Washington, which provided for international arbitration and in which Britain expressed regret for the escape of the *Alabama* from England.

THE ABANDONMENT OF RECONSTRUCTION

As the North grew increasingly preoccupied with its own political and economic problems, interest in Reconstruction began to wane. The Grant administration continued to protect Republican governments in the South, although less because of any interest in helping the freedmen than because of a desire to prevent the reemergence of a strong Democratic Party in the region. But even the presence of federal troops was not enough to prevent white Southerners from overturning the Reconstruction regimes. By the time Grant left office, Democrats had taken back (or, as white Southerners liked to put it, "redeemed") seven of the governments of the former Confederate states.

For three other states—South Carolina, Louisiana, and Florida—the end of Reconstruction had to wait for the withdrawal of the last federal troops in 1877, a withdrawal that was the result of a long process of political bargaining and compromise at the national level.

The Southern States "Redeemed"

In the states where whites constituted a majority—the states of the upper South—overthrowing Republican control was relatively simple. By 1872, all but a handful of Southern whites had regained suffrage. Now a clear majority, they needed only to organize and elect their candidates.

In other states, where blacks were a majority or the populations of the two races were almost equal, whites used intimidation and violence to undermine the Reconstruction regimes. Secret societies—the Ku Klux Klan, the Knights of the White Camellia, and others—used terrorism to frighten or physically bar blacks from voting or otherwise exercising citizenship. Paramilitary organizations—the Red Shirts and White Leagues—armed themselves to "police" elections and worked to force all white males to join the Democratic Party and to exclude all blacks from meaningful political activity. Strongest of all, however, was the simple weapon of economic pressure. Some planters refused to rent land to Republican blacks; storekeepers refused to extend them credit; employers refused to give them work.

In the meantime, Southern blacks were losing the support of many of their former advocates in the North. After the adoption of the Fifteenth Amendment in 1870, some reformers convinced themselves that their long campaign in behalf of black people was now over, that with the vote blacks ought to be able to take care of themselves. Former Radical leaders such as Charles Sumner and Horace Greeley now began calling themselves Liberals, cooperating with the Democrats, and at times outdoing even the Democrats in denouncing what they viewed as black-and-carpetbag misgovernment. Within the South itself, many white Republicans joined the Liberals and moved into the Democratic Party.

The Panic of 1873 further undermined support for Reconstruction. In the congressional elections of 1874, the Democrats won control of the House of Representatives for the first time since 1861. Grant took note of the changing temper of the North and reduced the use of military force to prop up the Republican regimes that were still standing in the South.

By the end of 1876, only three states were left in the hands of the Republicans—South Carolina, Louisiana, and Florida. In the state elections that year, Democrats (after using terrorist tactics) claimed victory in all three. But the Republicans claimed victory as well and were able to remain in office because of the presence of federal troops. If the troops were to be withdrawn, the last of the Republican regimes would fall.

The Compromise of 1877

Grant had hoped to run for another term in 1876, but most Republican leaders—shaken by recent Democratic successes, afraid of the scandals with which Grant was associated, and worried about the president's failing health—resisted. Instead, they sought a candidate not associated with the problems of the Grant years, one who might entice Liberals back and unite the party again. They settled on Rutherford B. Hayes, a former Union army officer and congressman, three times governor of Ohio, and a champion of civil service reform. The Democrats united behind Samuel J. Tilden, the reform governor of New York, who had been instrumental in overthrowing the corrupt Tweed Ring of New York City's Tammany Hall.

Although the campaign was a bitter one, there were few differences of principle between the candidates, both of whom were conservatives committed to moderate reform. The November election produced an apparent Democratic victory. Tilden carried the South and several large Northern states, and his popular margin over Hayes was nearly 300,000 votes. But disputed returns from Louisiana, South Carolina, Florida, and Oregon, whose electoral votes totaled 20, threw the election in doubt. Tilden had undisputed claim to 184 electoral votes, only one short of the majority. But Hayes could still win if he managed to receive all 20 disputed votes.

The Constitution had established no method to determine the validity of disputed returns. It was clear that the decision lay with Congress, but it was not clear with which house or through what method. (The Senate was

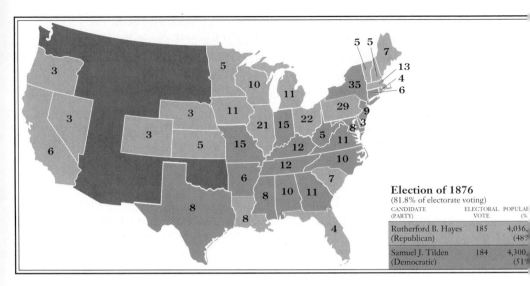

Election of 1876
(81.8% of electorate voting)

CANDIDATE (PARTY)	ELECTORAL VOTE	POPULAR (%
Rutherford B. Hayes (Republican)	185	4,036, (48%
Samuel J. Tilden (Democratic)	184	4,300, (51%

Republican, and the House was Democratic.) Members of each party naturally supported a solution that would yield them the victory.

Finally, late in January 1877, Congress tried to break the deadlock by creating a special electoral commission to judge the disputed votes. The commission was to be composed of five senators, five representatives, and five justices of the Supreme Court. The congressional delegation would consist of five Republicans and five Democrats. The Court delegation would include two Republicans, two Democrats, and the only independent, Justice David Davis. But when the Illinois legislature elected Davis to the United States Senate, the justice resigned from the commission. His seat went instead to a Republican justice. The commission voted along straight party lines, 8 to 7, awarding every disputed vote to Hayes. Congress accepted the verdict on March 2. Two days later, Hayes was inaugurated.

Behind the resolution of the deadlock, however, lay a series of elaborate compromises among leaders of both parties. When a Democratic filibuster threatened to derail the commission's report, Republican Senate leaders met secretly with Southern Democratic leaders to work out terms by which the Democrats would support Hayes. As the price of their cooperation, the Southern Democrats (among them some former Whigs) exacted several pledges from the Republicans: the appointment of at least one Southerner to the Hayes cabinet, control of federal patronage in their areas, generous internal improvements, federal aid for the Texas and Pacific Railroad, and withdrawal of the troops. Many powerful Southern Democrats supported industrializing the region. They believed that Republican programs of federal support for business would aid their region more than the states' rights policies of the Democrats.

In his inaugural address, Hayes announced that the South's most pressing need was the restoration of "wise, honest, and peaceful local self-government"—a signal that he planned to withdraw the troops and let white Democrats take over the state governments. The statement, and Hayes's subsequent actions, supported the widespread charges that he was paying off the South for acquiescing in his election and strengthened those who referred to him as "His Fraudulency." But the election had already created such bitterness that there was probably nothing Hayes could have done to mollify his critics, not even his promise to serve only one term.

The president and his party hoped to build up a "new Republican" organization in the South drawn from Whiggish conservative white groups and committed to modest support for black rights. But all such efforts failed. Although many white Southern leaders sympathized with Republican economic policies, resentment of Reconstruction was so deep that supporting the party was politically impossible. The "solid" Democratic South, which would survive until the mid-twentieth century, was taking shape. And the withdrawal of federal troops was a signal that the national government was giving up its attempt to control Southern politics and to improve the lot of blacks in Southern society.

The Legacy of Reconstruction

Reconstruction made important contributions to the efforts of former slaves to achieve dignity and equality in American life. There was a significant redistribution of income, from which blacks benefited. There was a more limited but not unimportant redistribution of landownership, which enabled some former slaves to acquire property. There was both a relative and an absolute improvement in the economic circumstances of most blacks. Perhaps most of all, there was a large, and largely successful, effort by blacks themselves to carve out a society and culture of their own within the American South, to create or strengthen their own institutions, and to convince themselves that they were, indeed, no longer slaves.

Nor was Reconstruction as disastrous an experience for Southern white elites as most believed at the time. Within little more than a decade after the end of a devastating war, the white South had regained control of its own institutions and, to a great extent, restored its traditional ruling class to power. Former Confederate leaders received no severe punishments. The federal government imposed no drastic economic reforms on the region, and indeed few lasting political changes of any kind other than the abolition of slavery. Not many conquered peoples have fared as well.

But Reconstruction was also notable for its limitations. For in those years the United States failed in its first serious effort to resolve its oldest and deepest social problem—the problem of race. What was more, the experience so disappointed, disillusioned, and embittered white Americans that it would be nearly a century before they would try again in any serious way. Why did this great assault on racial injustice not achieve more? In part, it was because of the weaknesses and errors of the people who directed it. But in greater part, it was because attempts to produce solutions ran up against conservative obstacles so deeply embedded in the nation's life that they could not be dislodged: among them, a profound respect for private property and free enterprise and a pervasive belief among many of even the most liberal whites that African Americans were inherently inferior. Given the odds confronting them, therefore, African Americans had reason for considerable pride in the gains they were able to make during Reconstruction. And future generations could be grateful for two great charters of freedom—the Fourteenth and Fifteenth Amendments to the Constitution—which, although widely ignored at the time, would one day serve as the basis for a "Second Reconstruction" that would renew the drive to bring freedom to all Americans.

THE NEW SOUTH

The agreement between southern Democrats and northern Republicans that helped settle the disputed election of 1876 was supposed to be the first step toward developing a stable, permanent Republican Party in the South. In that respect, at least, it failed. In the years following the end of Reconstruction, white southerners established the Democratic Party as the only viable political organization for the region's whites. Even so, the South did change in the years after Reconstruction in some of the ways the framers of the Compromise of 1877 had hoped.

The "Redeemers"

By the end of 1877—after the last withdrawal of federal troops—every southern state government had been "redeemed." That is, political power had been restored to white Democrats. Many white southerners rejoiced at the restoration of what they liked to call "home rule." But in reality, political power in the region was soon more restricted than at any time since the Civil War. Once again, the South fell under the control of a powerful, conservative oligarchy, whose members were known variously as the "Redeemers" or the "Bourbons."

In some places, this post-Reconstruction ruling class was much the same as the ruling class of the antebellum period. In Alabama, for example, the old planter elite—despite challenges from new merchant and industrial forces—retained much of its former power and continued largely to dominate the state for decades. In other areas, however, the Redeemers constituted a genuinely new ruling class. They were merchants, industrialists, railroad developers, and financiers. Some of them were former planters, some of them northern immigrants who had been absorbed into the region's life, some of them ambitious, upwardly mobile white southerners from the region's lower social tiers. They combined a commitment to "home rule" and social conservatism with a commitment to economic development.

The various Bourbon governments of the New South behaved in many respects quite similarly. Conservatives had complained that the Reconstruction governments fostered widespread corruption, but the Redeemer regimes were, if anything, even more awash in waste and fraud. (In this, they were little different from governments in every region of the country.) At the same time, virtually all the new Democratic regimes lowered taxes, reduced spending, and drastically diminished state services. One state after another eliminated or reduced its support for public school systems.

Industrialization and the "New South"

Many white southern leaders in the post-Reconstruction era hoped to see their region become the home of a vigorous industrial economy, a "New South." Henry Grady, editor of the *Atlanta Constitution*, and other prominent spokesmen for a New South seldom challenged white supremacy, but they did advocate other important changes in southern values. Above all, they promoted the virtues of thrift, industry, and progress—qualities that prewar southerners had often denounced in northern society.

New South enthusiasts helped southern industry expand dramatically in the years after Reconstruction and become a more important part of the region's economy than ever before. Most visible was the growth in textile manufacturing, which increased ninefold in the last twenty years of the century. In the past, southern planters had usually shipped their cotton out of the region to manufacturers in the North or in Europe. Now textile factories appeared in the South itself—many of them drawn to the region from New

England by the abundance of water power, the ready supply of cheap labor, the low taxes, and the accommodating conservative governments. The tobacco-processing industry, similarly, established an important foothold in the region. In the lower South, and particularly in Birmingham, Alabama, the iron (and, later, steel) industry grew rapidly. By 1890, the southern iron and steel industry represented nearly a fifth of the nation's total capacity.

Railroad development also increased substantially in the post-Reconstruction years—at a rate far greater than that of the nation at large. Between 1880 and 1890, trackage in the South more than doubled. And the South took a major step toward integrating its transportation system with that of the rest of the country when, in 1886, it changed the gauge (width) of its trackage to correspond with the standards of the North. No longer would it be necessary for cargoes heading into the South to be transferred from one train to another at the borders of the region.

Yet southern industry developed within strict limits, and its effects on the region were never even remotely comparable to the effects of industrialization on the North. The southern share of national manufacturing doubled in the last twenty years of the century, but it was still only 10 percent of the total. The region's per capita income increased 21 percent in the same period, but average income in the South was still only 40 percent of that in the North; in 1860 it had been more than 60 percent. And even in those industries where development had been most rapid—textiles, iron, railroads—much of the capital had come from, and many of the profits thus flowed to, the North.

The growth of industry in the South required the region to recruit a substantial industrial work force for the first time. From the beginning, a high percentage of the factory workers (and an especially high percentage of textile workers) were women. Heavy male casualties in the Civil War had helped create a large population of unmarried women who desperately needed employment. Factories also hired entire families, many of whom moved into towns from failed farms. Hours were long (often as much as twelve hours a day), and wages were far below the northern equivalent; indeed, one of the greatest attractions of the South to industrialists was that employers were able to pay workers there as little as one-half what northern workers received. Life in most mill towns was rigidly controlled by the owners and managers of the factories. They rigorously suppressed attempts at protest or union organization. Company stores sold goods to workers at inflated prices and issued credit at exorbitant rates (much like country stores in agrarian areas), and mill owners ensured that no competitors were able to establish themselves in the community.

Some industries, such as textiles, offered virtually no opportunities to

African-American workers. Others—tobacco, iron, and lumber, for example—did provide some employment for blacks, usually the most menial and lowest-paid positions. Some mill towns, therefore, were places where the black and white cultures came into close contact. That contributed less to the growth of racial harmony than to the determination of white leaders to take additional measures to protect white supremacy.

Tenants and Sharecroppers

Despite significant growth in southern industry, the region remained primarily agrarian. The most important economic reality in the post-Reconstruction South, therefore, was the impoverished state of agriculture. The 1870s and 1880s saw an acceleration of the process that had begun in the immediate postwar years: the imposition of systems of tenantry and debt peonage on much of the region; the reliance on a few cash crops rather than on a diversified agricultural system; and increasing absentee ownership of valuable farmlands. During Reconstruction, perhaps a third or more of the farmers in the South were tenants; by 1900 the figure had increased to 70 percent. That was in large part the result of the crop-lien system that had emerged in the aftermath of the Civil War. Farmers who owned their own land often lost it as merchants seized it for payment of debts. Farmers who rented could never accumulate enough capital to buy land.

Tenantry, which now dominated Southern agriculture, took several forms. Farmers who owned tools, equipment, and farm animals—or who had the money to buy them—usually paid an annual cash rent for their land. But many farmers (including most black ones) had no money or equipment at all. Landlords would supply them with land, a crude house, a few tools, seed, and sometimes a mule. In return, the farmers would promise the landlord a large share of the annual crop. After paying their landlords and their local furnishing merchants (who were often the same people), these "sharecroppers" seldom had anything left to sell on their own.

The crop-lien system was particularly devastating to southern blacks, few of whom owned their own land to begin with. These economic difficulties were compounded by social and legal discrimination, which in the post-Reconstruction era began to take new forms and to inspire new responses.

African Americans and the New South

The "New South creed" was not the property of whites alone. Many African Americans were attracted to the vision of progress and self-improvement as well. Some blacks succeeded in elevating themselves into a distinct middle class—even if one far less prosperous than the white middle class. These were former slaves (and, as the decades passed, their offspring) who managed to acquire property, establish small businesses, or enter professions.

This rising group of African Americans believed strongly that education was vital to the future of their people. With the support of northern missionary societies and, to a far lesser extent, a few southern state governments, they expanded the network of black colleges and institutes that had taken root during Reconstruction into an important educational system.

The chief spokesman for this commitment to education, and for a time the most prominent spokesman for black people as a whole, was Booker T. Washington, founder and president of the Tuskegee Institute in Alabama. Born into slavery, Washington had worked his way out of poverty after acquiring an education (at Virginia's Hampton Institute). He urged other blacks to follow the same road to self-improvement.

Washington's message was both cautious and hopeful. African Americans should attend school, learn skills, and establish a solid footing in agriculture and the trades. Industrial, not classical, education should be their goal. Blacks should, moreover, refine their speech, improve their dress, and adopt habits of thrift and personal cleanliness; they should, in short, adopt the standards of the white middle class. Only thus, he claimed, could they win the respect of the white population, the prerequisite for any larger social gains.

In a famous speech in Georgia in 1895, Washington outlined a controversial philosophy of race relations that became widely known as the Atlanta Compromise. Blacks, he said, should forgo agitating for political rights and concentrate on self-improvement and preparation for equality. If blacks were ever to win the rights and privileges of citizenship, they must first show that they were "prepared for the exercise of these privileges." Washington offered a powerful challenge to those whites who wanted to discourage African Americans from acquiring an education or winning any economic gains. But his message was also intended to assure whites that blacks would not challenge the system of segregation, which southern governments were in the process of creating.

The Birth of Jim Crow

Few white southerners had ever accepted the idea of racial equality. That the former slaves acquired any legal and political rights at all after emancipation was in large part the result of their own efforts and critical federal support. That outside support all but vanished after 1877. Federal troops withdrew. Congress lost interest. And the Supreme Court effectively stripped the Fourteenth and Fifteenth Amendments of much of their significance. In the so-called civil rights cases of 1883, the Court ruled that the Fourteenth Amendment prohibited state governments from discriminating against people because of race but did not restrict private organizations or individuals from doing so. Thus railroads, hotels, theaters, and the like could legally practice segregation.

Eventually, the Court also validated state legislation that institutionalized the separation of the races. In *Plessy* v. *Ferguson* (1896), a case involving a Louisiana law that required separate seating arrangements for the races on railroads, the Court held that separate accommodations did not deprive blacks of equal rights if the accommodations were equal, a decision that survived for years as part of the legal basis of segregated schools. In *Cumming* v. *County Board of Education* (1899), the Court ruled that communities could establish schools for whites only even if there were no comparable schools for blacks.

Even before these decisions, white southerners were working to separate the races to the greatest extent possible. One illustration of this movement from subordination to segregation was black voting rights. In some states, disfranchisement had begun almost as soon as Reconstruction ended. But in other areas, black voting continued for some time after Reconstruction—largely because conservative whites believed they could control the black electorate and use it to beat back the attempts of poor white farmers to take control of the Democratic Party.

In the 1890s, however, franchise restrictions became much more rigid. During those years, some small white farmers began to demand complete black disfranchisement—both because of racial prejudice and because they objected to the black vote being used against them by the Bourbons. At the same time, many members of the conservative elite began to fear that poor whites might unite politically with poor blacks to challenge them. They too began to support further franchise restrictions.

In devising laws to disfranchise black males (black females, like white women, had never voted), the southern states had to find ways to evade the Fifteenth Amendment, which prohibited states from denying anyone the right to vote because of race. Two devices emerged before 1900 to accomplish this goal. One was the poll tax or some form of property qualification; few blacks were prosperous enough to meet such requirements. Another was the "literacy" or "understanding" test, which required voters to demonstrate an ability to read and to interpret the Constitution. Even those African

Americans who could read had a hard time passing the difficult test white officials gave them. The laws affected poor white voters as well as blacks. By the late 1890s, the black vote had decreased by 62 percent, the white vote by 26 percent. The Supreme Court proved as compliant in upholding the disfranchising laws as it was in dealing with the civil rights cases.

Laws restricting the franchise and segregating schools were only part of a network of state and local statutes—known as the Jim Crow laws—that by the first years of the twentieth century had institutionalized an elaborate system of segregation reaching into almost every area of southern life. Blacks and whites could not ride together in the same railroad cars, sit in the same waiting rooms, use the same washrooms, eat in the same restaurants, or sit in the same theaters. Blacks had no access to many public parks, beaches, picnic areas; they could not be patients in many hospitals. Much of the new legal structure did no more than confirm what had already been widespread social practice in the South since well before the end of Reconstruction. But the Jim Crow laws also stripped blacks of many of the modest social, economic, and political gains they had made in the more fluid atmosphere of the late nineteenth century. They served, too, as a means for whites to retain control of social relations between the races in the rapidly growing cities and towns of the South, where traditional patterns of subjugation were more difficult to preserve than in the countryside.

More than legal efforts were involved in this process. The 1890s witnessed a dramatic increase in white violence against blacks, which, along with the Jim Crow laws, served to inhibit black agitation for equal rights. The worst such violence—lynching of blacks by white mobs, either because the victims were accused of crimes or because they had seemed somehow to violate their proper station—reached appalling levels. In the nation as a whole in the 1890s, there was an average of 187 lynchings each year, more than 80 percent of them in the South. The vast majority of victims were black. Those involved in lynchings often saw their actions as a legitimate form of law enforcement, and some victims of lynchings had in fact committed crimes. But lynchings were also a means by which whites controlled the black population through terror and intimidation.

The rise of lynchings shocked the conscience of many white Americans in a way that other forms of racial injustice did not. In 1892 Ida B. Wells, a committed black journalist, launched what became an international antilynching movement with a series of impassioned articles after the lynching of three of her friends in Memphis, Tennessee, her home. The movement gradually gathered strength in the first years of the twentieth century, attracting substantial support from whites in both the North and South (par-

LYNCH MOB, 1893 White Southerners sometimes traveled many miles to watch a lynching, such as this one of a black man accused of killing a three-year-old white girl. More common than these large public lynchings, however, were less conspicuous vigilante murders by small groups of whites.

ticularly from white women). Its goal was a federal antilynching law, which would allow the national government to do what state and local governments in the South were generally unwilling to do: punish those responsible for lynchings.

But the substantial southern white opposition to lynchings stood as an exception to the general white support for suppression of African Americans. Indeed, just as in the antebellum period, the shared commitment to white supremacy helped dilute class animosities between poorer whites and the Bourbon oligarchies. Economic issues tended to play a secondary role to race in southern politics, distracting people from the glaring social inequalities that afflicted blacks and whites alike. The commitment to white supremacy, in short, was a burden for poor whites as well as for blacks.

D E B A T I N G   T H E   P A S T

Reconstruction

EBATE OVER THE nature of Reconstruction has been unusually intense, not only among historians but among much of the larger public as well. Indeed, few issues in American history have raised such deep and enduring passions.

Beginning in the late nineteenth century and continuing well into the twentieth, a relatively uniform and highly critical view of Reconstruction prevailed among historians—a reflection of a broad consensus among white Americans about the inferiority of blacks and of a yearning in both the North and the South for sectional reconciliation. William A. Dunning's *Reconstruction, Political and Economic* (1907) was the principal scholarly expression of this prevailing view. Dunning portrayed Reconstruction as a corrupt and oppressive outrage imposed on a prostrate South by a vindictive group of Northern Republican radicals. Unscrupulous carpetbaggers flooded the South and plundered the region. Ignorant African Americans were thrust into political offices for which they were unfit. Reconstruction governments were awash in corruption and compiled enormous levels of debt. The Dunning interpretation dominated several generations of historical scholarship. It also helped shape such popular images of Reconstruction as those in the novel and film *Gone with the Wind*.

Among historians, at least, the Dunning interpretation gradually lost credibility in the face of a series of challenges. W. E. B. Du Bois, the great African-American scholar, offered one of the first alternative views in *Black Reconstruction* (1935). To Du Bois, Reconstruction was an effort by freed blacks (and their white allies) to create a more democratic society in the

South, and it was responsible for many valuable social innovations. In the early 1960s, John Hope Franklin and Kenneth Stampp, building on a generation of work by other scholars, published new histories of Reconstruction that also radically revised the Dunning interpretation. Reconstruction, they argued, was a genuine, if flawed, effort to solve the problem of race in the South. The Reconstruction governments were not perfect, but they were bold experiments in interracial politics. Congressional radicals were not saints, but they were genuinely concerned with protecting the rights of former slaves. Reconstruction had brought important, if temporary, progress to the South and had created no more corruption there than governments were creating in the North at the same time. What was tragic about Reconstruction, the revisionists claimed, was not what it did to Southern whites but what it failed to do for Southern blacks. It was, in the end, too weak and too short-lived to guarantee African Americans genuine equality.

In more recent years, some historians have begun to question the assessment of the first revisionists that, in the end, Reconstruction accomplished relatively little. Leon Litwack argued in *Been in the Storm So Long* (1979) that former slaves used the protections Reconstruction offered them to carve out a certain level of independence for themselves within southern society: strengthening churches, reuniting families, and resisting the efforts of white planters to revive the gang labor system.

Eric Foner's *Reconstruction: America's Unfinished Revolution* (1988) also emphasized how far African Americans moved toward freedom and independence in a short time, how much of lasting value they were able to accomplish despite imposing obstacles, and how important they were in shaping the execution of Reconstruction policies. Reconstruction, he argues, "can only be judged a failure" as an effort to secure "blacks' rights as citizens and free laborers." But it "closed off even more oppressive alternatives. . . . The post-Reconstruction labor system embodied neither a return to the closely supervised gang labor of antebellum days, nor the complete dispossession and immobilization of the black labor force and coercive apprenticeship systems envisioned by white Southerners in 1865 and 1866. Nor were blacks, as in twentieth-century South Africa, barred from citizenship, herded into labor reserves, or prohibited by law from moving from one part of the country to another. . . . The doors of economic opportunity that had opened could never be completely closed."

CHAPTER SIXTEEN

The Conquest of the Far West

The Societies of the Far West ∼ *The Changing Western Economy*
The Dispersal of the Tribes   ∼   *The Rise and Decline of the Western Farmer*

hrough much of the first half of the nineteenth century, relatively few English-speaking Americans considered moving into the vast and presumably arid lands west of the Mississippi River. By the mid-1840s, however, migrants from the eastern regions of the nation had settled in the West in substantial numbers. Farmers, ranchers, and miners all found opportunity in the western lands. By the end of the Civil War, the West had become legendary in the eastern states. No longer the Great American Desert, it was now the "frontier": an empty land awaiting settlement and civilization; a place of wealth, adventure, opportunity, and untrammeled individualism.

In fact, the real West of the mid-nineteenth century bore little resemblance to its popular image. It was a diverse land, with many different regions, many different climates, many different stores of natural resources. And it was extensively populated, with a number of well-developed societies and cultures. The English-speaking migrants of the late nineteenth century did not find an empty, desolate land. They found Indians, Mexicans, French and British Canadians, Asians, and others, some of whose families had been living in the West for generations.

The Anglo-American settlers tried, with considerable success, to conquer and disperse many of the peoples already living in the region, but they were never able to make the West theirs alone. Almost everything the Anglo-Americans did and built reflected the influence of the other cultures of the region. Nevertheless, English-speaking Americans transformed the West by connecting it with, and making it part of, the growing capitalist economy of the East. And despite their self-image as rugged individualists, they relied heavily on assistance from the federal government—land grants, subsidies, and military protection—as they developed the region.

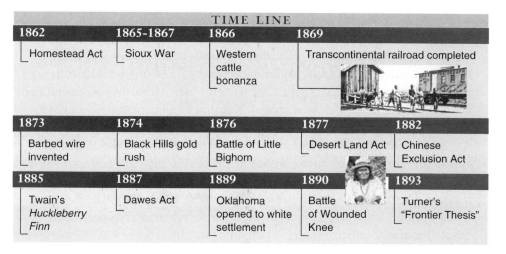

TIME LINE			
1862	**1865-1867**	**1866**	**1869**
Homestead Act	Sioux War	Western cattle bonanza	Transcontinental railroad completed
1873	**1874**	**1876**	**1877** **1882**
Barbed wire invented	Black Hills gold rush	Battle of Little Bighorn	Desert Land Act Chinese Exclusion Act
1885	**1887**	**1889**	**1890** **1893**
Twain's *Huckleberry Finn*	Dawes Act	Oklahoma opened to white settlement	Battle of Wounded Knee Turner's "Frontier Thesis"

THE SOCIETIES OF THE FAR WEST

The Far West—the region beyond the Mississippi River into which millions of Anglo-Americans moved in the years after the Civil War—was in fact many lands. It contained some of the most arid territory in the United States, and some of the wettest and lushest. It contained the flattest plains and the highest mountains. And it contained many peoples.

The Western Tribes

The largest and most important western population group before the great American migration was the Indian tribes. Some were members of eastern tribes—Cherokee, Creek, and others—who had been forcibly resettled west of the Mississippi to "Indian Territory" (later Oklahoma) and elsewhere before the Civil War. But most were members of tribes indigenous to the West.

The western tribes had developed a number of patterns of civilization. More than 300,000 Indians (among them the Serrano, Chumash, Pomo, Maidu, Yurok, and Chinook) had lived on the Pacific Coast before the arrival of Spanish settlers, supporting themselves through a combination of fishing, foraging, and simple agriculture. Disease and dislocation decimated the tribes, but in the mid-nineteenth century 150,000 Indians remained—some living within the Hispanic society the Spanish and Mexican settlers had created, many still living within their own tribal communities.

The Pueblos of the Southwest had long lived largely as farmers and had established permanent settlements there even before the Spanish arrived in the seventeenth century. The Pueblos grew corn; they built towns and cities of adobe houses; they practiced elaborate forms of irrigation; and they participated in trade and commerce. In the eighteenth and nineteenth centuries, their intimate relationship with the Spanish (later Mexicans) produced, in effect, an alliance against the Apaches, Navajos, and Commanches of the region.

The most widespread Indian groups in the West were the Plains Indians. They were, in fact, many different tribal and language groups. Some lived more or less sedentary lives as farmers; others were highly nomadic hunters. Despite their differences, however, the tribes shared some traits. Their cultures were based on close, extended family networks and on an intimate relationship with nature. Women's roles were largely domestic and artistic: raising children, cooking, gathering roots and berries, preparing hides, and tending fields and gardens in those places where bands remained settled long enough to raise crops. Men worked as hunters and traders and supervised religious and military life. Most of the Plains Indians practiced a religion centered on a belief in the spiritual power of the natural world—of plants and animals and the rhythms of the days and the seasons.

Many of the Plains tribes—including some of the most powerful tribes in the Sioux nation—subsisted largely through hunting buffalo. Riding small but powerful horses, the tribes moved through the grasslands following the herds. Permanent settlements were rare. When a band halted, it constructed tepees as temporary dwellings; when it departed, it left the landscape almost completely undisturbed.

The buffalo, or bison, which the Indians so relentlessly pursued, provided the economic basis for the Plains Indians' way of life. The flesh of the large animal was their principal source of food, and its skin supplied materials for clothing, shoes, tepees, blankets, robes, and utensils. "Buffalo chips"—dried manure—provided fuel; buffalo bones became knives and arrow tips; buffalo tendons formed the strings of bows.

The Plains Indians were proud and aggressive warriors, schooled in warfare from their frequent (and usually brief) skirmishes with rival tribes. By the early nineteenth century, the Sioux had become the most powerful tribe in the Missouri River valley and had begun expanding west and south until they dominated much of the plains and were the most important military force in the region.

The Plains warriors proved to be the most formidable foes white settlers encountered. But they also suffered from several serious weaknesses. One was the inability of the various tribes (and often even of the bands within tribes) to unite against white aggression. Not only were they seldom able to draw together a coalition large enough to counter white power; they were also frequently distracted from their battles with whites by conflicts among the tribes themselves. And at times, tribal warriors faced white forces who were being assisted by guides and even fighters from other, usually rival, tribes.

Even so, some tribes were at times able to overcome their divisions and unite effectively. By the mid-nineteenth century, for example, the Sioux, Arapaho, and Cheyenne had forged a powerful alliance that dominated the northern plains. The more important weaknesses of the western tribes in their contest with white society were, in fact, ecological and economic. Indians were tragically vulnerable to eastern infectious diseases. Smallpox epidemics, for example, decimated the Pawnees in Nebraska in the 1840s and many of the California tribes in the early 1850s. And the tribes were, of course, at a considerable disadvantage in any long-term battle with an economically and industrially advanced people. They were, in the end, outmanned and outgunned.

Hispanic New Mexico

For centuries, much of the Far West had been part of, first, the Spanish Empire and, later, the Mexican Republic. When the United States acquired its new lands there in the 1840s, it acquired many Mexican residents at the same time.

In New Mexico, the centers of Spanish-speaking society were the farming and trading communities the Spanish had established in the seventeenth century. Descendants of the original Spanish settlers (and more recent migrants from Mexico) lived alongside the Pueblo Indians and some American traders and engaged primarily in cattle and sheep ranching. When the United States acquired title to New Mexico in the aftermath of the Mexican War, General Stephen Kearny—who had commanded the American troops in the region during the conflict—tried to establish a territorial government there. He drew most of the officials from among the approximately 1,000 Anglo-Americans in the region, ignoring the over 50,000 Hispanics. There were widespread fears among Hispanics and Indians alike that the new American rulers of the region would confiscate their lands and otherwise threaten their societies. In 1847, Taos Indians rebelled; they killed the new governor and other Anglo-American officials before being subdued by United States Army forces. New Mexico remained under military rule for three years, until the United States finally organized a territorial government there in 1850.

Even without its former political power, Hispanic society in New Mexico survived and even grew in the face of the expansion of Anglo-American settlement in the Southwest. The United States Army finally did what the Hispanic residents had been unable to accomplish for 200 years: it broke the power of the Navajo, Apache, and other tribes that had long prevented the residents of New Mexico from expanding their society and commerce. The defeat of the tribes led to substantial Hispanic migration into other areas of the Southwest and as far north as Colorado. Most of the expansion involved peasants and small tradespeople who were looking for land or new opportunities for commerce.

The Anglo-American presence in the Southwest grew rapidly once the railroads established lines into the region in the 1880s and early 1890s. With the railroads came extensive new ranching, farming, and mining. The expansion of economic activity in the region attracted a new wave of Mexican immigrants—perhaps as many as 100,000 by 1900—who moved across the border (which was unregulated until World War I) in search of work. But unlike the earlier Hispanic residents of the Southwest, the new immigrants entered a society in which the best opportunities were now reserved for Anglo-Americans. The English-speaking proprietors of the new enterprises restricted most Mexicans to the lowest-paying and least stable jobs.

Hispanic California and Texas

In California, Spanish settlement began in the eighteenth century with a string of Christian missions along the Pacific coast. The missionaries and the soldiers who accompanied them gathered most of the coastal Indians into their communities, some forcibly and some by persuasion. The Indians were targets of the evangelizing efforts of the missionaries, who baptized over 50,000 of them. They were also a labor force for the flourishing and largely self-sufficient economies the missionaries created; the Spanish forced most of these laborers into a state of servitude little different from slavery.

In the 1830s, after the new Mexican government began reducing the power of the church, the mission society largely collapsed. In its place emerged a secular Mexican aristocracy, which controlled a chain of large estates (some of them former missions) in the fertile lands west of the Sierra mountains. For them, the arrival of Anglo-Americans before and after the Civil War was disastrous. So vast were the numbers of English-speaking immigrants that the *californios* (as the Hispanic residents of the region were known) had little power to resist the onslaught. English-speaking prospectors organized to exclude them, sometimes violently, from the mines during the gold rush. Many *californios* also lost their lands—either through corrupt business deals or through outright seizure (sometimes with the help of the courts and often through simple occupation by squatters).

In the southern areas of California, where there were at first fewer English-speaking migrants, some Mexican landowners managed to hang on for a time. The booming Anglo communities in the north of the state created a large market for the cattle that southern *rancheros* were raising. But a combination of reckless expansion, growing indebtedness, and a severe drought in the 1860s devastated the Mexican ranching culture. By the 1880s, the Hispanic aristocracy in California had largely ceased to exist.

Increasingly, Mexicans and Mexican Americans became part of the lower end of the state's working class, clustered in barrios in Los Angeles or elsewhere or laboring as migrant farmworkers. Even small Hispanic landowners who managed to hang on to their farms found themselves unable to raise livestock, as the once-communal grazing lands fell under the control of powerful Anglo ranchers.

A similar pattern occurred in Texas. After the territory joined the United States, many Mexican landowners lost their land—some as a result of fraud and coercion, some because even the most substantial Mexican ranchers could not compete with the enormous Anglo-American ranching kingdoms that were emerging. In 1859, angry Mexicans, led by the rancher Juan Cortina, raided the jail in Brownsville and freed all the Mexican prisoners inside. But such resistance had little long-term effect. As in California, Mexicans in southern Texas (who constituted nearly three-quarters of the population there) became an increasingly impoverished working class relegated largely to unskilled farm or industrial labor.

The Chinese Migration

At the same time that ambitious or impoverished Europeans were crossing the Atlantic in search of opportunities in the New World, many Chinese were crossing the Pacific in hopes of better lives than they could expect in their own poverty-stricken land. Not all came to the United States. Many Chinese moved to Hawaii, Australia, Latin America, South Africa, and even the Caribbean—some as "coolies" (indentured servants whose condition was close to slavery).

A few Chinese traveled to the American West even before the gold rush, but after 1848 the flow increased dramatically. By 1880, more than 200,000 Chinese had settled in the United States, mostly in California, where they constituted nearly a tenth of the population. Almost all came as free laborers. For a time, white Americans welcomed the Chinese as a conscientious, hardworking people. Very quickly, however, white opinion turned hostile—in part because the Chinese were so industrious and successful that some white Americans began considering them rivals, even threats.

In the early 1850s, large numbers of Chinese immigrants worked in the gold mines. Many of them were well-organized, hardworking prospectors, and for a time some of them enjoyed considerable success. But opportunities for Chinese to prosper in the mines were fleeting. In 1852, the California legislature began trying to exclude the Chinese from gold mining by enacting a "foreign miners" tax (which also helped exclude Mexicans). Gradually, the effect of the discriminatory laws, the hostility of white miners, and the declining profitability of the surface mines drove most Chinese out of prospecting.

As mining declined as a source of wealth and jobs for the Chinese, railroad employment grew. Beginning in 1865, over 12,000 Chinese found work building the transcontinental railroad. In fact, Chinese workers formed 90 percent of the labor force of the Central Pacific and were mainly responsible for construction of the western part of the new road. The company preferred them to white workers because they worked hard, made few demands, and accepted relatively low wages.

Work on the Central Pacific was arduous and often dangerous, and the company made few concessions to the difficult conditions. In the winter, many Chinese tunneled into snow banks at night to create warm sleeping areas for themselves, even though such tunnels frequently collapsed, suffocating those inside. In the spring of 1866, 5,000 Chinese railroad workers rebelled against the terrible conditions of their work and went on strike demanding higher wages and a shorter workday. The company isolated them, surrounded them with strikebreakers, and starved them into submission. The strike failed, and most of the workers returned to their jobs.

In 1869 the transcontinental railroad was completed. Thousands of Chinese were now out of work. Some moved into agricultural work, usually in menial positions. Increasingly, however, the Chinese flocked to cities. By 1900, nearly half the Chinese population of California lived in urban areas. By far the largest single Chinese community was in San Francisco. Much of community life there, and in other "Chinatowns" throughout the West, revolved around organizations—usually formed by people from the same clan or community in China—that functioned as something like benevolent societies and filled many of the roles that political machines often served in immigrant communities in eastern cities. They were often led by prominent

CHINESE WORKERS ON THE UNION PACIFIC RAILROAD The Union Pacific Railroad, which moved east from California en route to its meeting with the Central Pacific in Utah, was one of the great engineering feats of the nineteenth century. It was also one of the largest employers of its day, and the captains of the project made heavy use of Chinese laborers—because they accepted low wages, because they worked reliably and hard, and because they seldom complained about the arduous conditions under which they were often forced to live.

merchants. (In San Francisco, the leading merchants—known as the "Six Companies"—often worked together to advance their interests in the larger community of the city and state.) These organizations became, in effect, employment brokers, unions, arbitrators of disputes, defenders of the community against outside persecution, and dispensers of social services. They also organized the elaborate festivals and celebrations that were such a conspicuous and important part of life in Chinatowns.

Other Chinese organizations were secret societies, known as "tongs." And some of the tongs were violent criminal organizations, involved in the opium trade and prostitution. Few people outside the Chinese communities were aware of their existence, except when rival tongs engaged in violent conflict (or "tong wars"), as occurred frequently in San Francisco in the 1880s.

In San Francisco and other western cities, the Chinese usually occupied the lower rungs of the employment ladder. Many worked as common laborers, servants, and unskilled factory hands. Some established their own small businesses, especially laundries. They moved into this business not because of experience—there were few commercial laundries in China—but because laundries could be started with very little capital and required only limited command of English. By the 1890s, Chinese constituted over two-thirds of all the laundry workers in California, many of them in shops they themselves owned and ran.

During the earliest Chinese migrations to California, virtually all the relatively small number of women who made the journey did so because they had been sold into prostitution in China. As late as 1880, nearly half the Chinese women in California were prostitutes. Gradually, however, the number of Chinese women increased (both through immigration and birth), and Chinese men in America became more likely to seek companionship in families.

Anti-Chinese Sentiments

As Chinese communities grew larger and more conspicuous in western cities, anti-Chinese sentiment among white residents became increasingly virulent. In fact, next to the Indians, the Chinese probably suffered the most intense persecution from white Americans in the West. Anti-Chinese activities, some of them violent, reflected the resentment of many white workers toward Chinese laborers for accepting low wages and thus undercutting union members. As the political value of attacking the Chinese grew in California, the Democratic Party took up the call. So did the Workingmen's Party of California—created in 1878 by Denis Kearney, an Irish immigrant—which gained significant political power in the state in large part on the basis of its hostility to the Chinese. By the mid-1880s, anti-Chinese agitation and violence had spread up and down the Pacific Coast and into other areas of the West—combining economic and racist resentments.

In 1882, Congress responded to the political pressure and the growing violence by passing the Chinese Exclusion Act, which banned Chinese immigration into the United States for ten years and barred Chinese already in the country from becoming naturalized citizens. Congress renewed the law for another ten years in 1892 and made it permanent in 1902. It had a dramatic effect on the Chinese population, which declined by more than 40 percent in the forty years after the act's passage.

Migration from the East

The great wave of new settlers in the West from the eastern United States after the Civil War followed important earlier migrations. But the scale of the postwar migration dwarfed everything that had preceded it. In previous decades, the settlers had come in thousands. Now they came in millions, spreading throughout the vast western territories—into empty and inhabited lands alike. Most of the new settlers were from the established Anglo-American societies of the eastern United States, but substantial numbers—over 2 million between 1870 and 1900—were foreign-born immigrants from Europe: Scandinavians, Germans, Irish, Russians, Czechs, and others.

They came to the West for many reasons. Settlers were attracted by gold and silver deposits, by the shortgrass pasture for cattle and sheep, and ultimately by the sod of the plains and the meadowlands of the mountains, which they discovered were suitable for farming or ranching. The completion of the great transcontinental railroad line in 1869, and the construction of the many subsidiary lines that spread out from it, encouraged settlement. So did the land policies of the federal government. The Homestead Act of 1862 permitted settlers to buy plots of 160 acres for a small fee if they occupied the land they purchased for five years and improved it.

Supporters of the Homestead Act believed it would create new markets and new outposts of commercial agriculture for the nation's growing economy. But a unit of 160 acres, while ample in much of the East, was too small for the grazing and grain farming of the Great Plains. Although over 400,000 homesteaders stayed on Homestead Act claims long enough to gain title to their land, a much larger number abandoned the region before the end of the necessary five years, unable to cope with the bleak life and the economic hardships on the windswept plains.

Not for the last time, beleaguered westerners looked to the federal government for solutions to their problems. In response to their demands, Congress increased the homestead allotments. The Timber Culture Act (1873) permitted homesteaders to receive grants of 160 additional acres if they planted 40 acres of trees on them. The Desert Land Act (1877) provided that claimants could buy 640 acres at $1.25 an acre provided they irrigated part of their holdings within three years. These and other laws ultimately made it possible for individuals to acquire as much as 1,280 acres of land at little cost. Some enterprising settlers got much more. Fraud ran rampant in the administration of the acts. Lumber, mining, and cattle companies, by employing "dummy" registrants and using other illegal devices, seized millions of acres of the public domain.

Political organization followed on the heels of settlement. By the close of the 1860s, territorial governments were in operation in the new provinces of Nevada, Colorado, Dakota, Arizona, Idaho, Montana, and Wyoming. Statehood rapidly followed. Nevada became a state in 1864, Nebraska in

1867, and Colorado in 1876. In 1889, North and South Dakota, Montana, and Washington won admission; Wyoming and Idaho entered the next year. Congress denied Utah statehood until its Mormon leaders convinced the government in 1896 that polygamy (the practice of men taking several wives) had been abandoned. At the turn of the century, only Arizona, New Mexico, and Oklahoma—all with small white populations—remained outside the Union.

THE CHANGING WESTERN ECONOMY

Among many other things, the new wave of Anglo-American settlement transformed the economy of the Far West. The new American settlers tied the West firmly to the growing industrial economy of the East (and of much of the rest of the world).

Labor in the West

As commercial activity increased, many farmers, ranchers, and miners found it necessary to recruit a paid labor force—not an easy task for those far away from major population centers and unable or unwilling to hire Indian workers. The labor shortage of the region led to higher wages for some workers than were typical in most areas of the East. But working conditions were often arduous, and job security was almost nonexistent. Once a railroad was built, a crop harvested, a herd sent to market, a mine played out, hundreds and even thousands of workers could find themselves suddenly unemployed. Competition from Chinese immigrants, whom employers could usually hire for considerably lower wages than they had to pay whites, also forced some Anglo-Americans out of work.

Even more than in many parts of the East, the western working class was highly multiracial. English-speaking whites worked alongside African Americans and immigrants from southern and eastern Europe, as they did in the East. Even more, they worked with Chinese, Filipinos, Mexicans, and Indians. But the work force was highly stratified along racial lines. In almost every area of the western economy, white workers (whatever their ethnicity) occupied the upper tiers of employment: management and skilled labor. The lower tiers—unskilled and often arduous work in the mines, on the railroads, or in agriculture—consisted overwhelmingly of nonwhites.

This dual labor system rested in part on a set of racial myths—arguments for the inherent inferiority of nonwhite workers. Such myths served the interests of employers, because it helped keep the work force divided. But many white workers embraced them too. That was in part because the myths supported a system that reserved whatever mobility there was largely for whites. Poor whites in the American South often believed they had more in common with wealthy planters than they did with black workers. Similarly in the West, white laborers—when forced to choose sides—often supported white bosses over nonwhite fellow workers.

The western economy was, however, no more a single entity than the economy of the East. In the late nineteenth century, the region produced three major industries, each with a distinctive history and distinctive characteristics: mining, ranching, and commercial farming.

The Arrival of the Miners

The first economic boom in the Far West came in mining. The life span of the mining boom was relatively brief. It began in earnest around 1860 (although there had, of course, been some earlier booms, most notably in California), and it flourished until the 1890s. And then it abruptly declined.

News of a gold or silver strike in an area would start a stampede reminiscent of the California gold rush of 1849, followed by several stages of settlement. Individual prospectors would exploit the first shallow deposits of ore largely by hand, with pan and placer mining. After these surface deposits dwindled, corporations moved in to engage in lode or quartz mining, which dug deeper beneath the surface. Then, as those deposits dwindled, commercial mining either disappeared or continued on a restricted basis, and ranchers and farmers moved in and established a more permanent economy.

The first great mineral strikes (other than the California gold rush) occurred just before the Civil War. In 1858, gold was discovered in the Pike's Peak district of what would soon be the territory of Colorado; the following year, 50,000 prospectors stormed in from California, the Mississippi Valley, and the East. Denver and other mining camps blossomed into "cities" overnight. Almost as rapidly as it had developed, the boom ended. Later, the discovery of silver near Leadville supplied a new source of mineral wealth.

While the Colorado rush of 1859 was still in progress, news of another strike drew miners to Nevada. Gold had been found in the Washoe district, but the most valuable ore in the great Comstock Lode (first discovered in 1858 by Henry Comstock) and other veins was silver. The first prospectors to reach the Washoe fields came from California, and from the beginning, Californians dominated the settlement and development of Nevada. In a remote desert without railroad transportation, the territory produced no supplies of its

COLORADO BOOM TOWN After a prospector discovered silver nearby in 1890, miners flocked to the town of Creede, Colorado. For a time in the early 1890s, 150 to 300 people arrived there daily. Although the town was located in a canyon so narrow that there was room for only one street, buildings sprouted rapidly to serve the growing community. Like other such boom towns, however, Creede's prosperity was short-lived. In 1893 the price of silver collapsed, and by the end of the century, Creede was almost deserted.

own, and everything—from food and machinery to whiskey and prostitutes—had to be shipped from California to Virginia City, Carson City, and other roaring camp towns. When the first placer (or surface) deposits ran out, Californian and eastern capitalists bought the claims of the pioneer prospectors and began to use the more difficult process of quartz mining, which enabled them to retrieve silver from deeper veins. For a few years these outside owners reaped tremendous profits; from 1860 to 1880 the Nevada lodes yielded bullion worth $306 million. After that, the mines quickly played out.

The next important mineral discoveries came in 1874, when gold was found in the Black Hills of southwestern Dakota Territory. Prospectors swarmed into the area, then (and for years to come) accessible only by stagecoach. Like the others, the boom flared for a time, until surface resources faded and corporations took over from the miners. One enormous company, the Homestake, came to dominate the fields. The Dakotas, like other boom areas of the mineral empire, ultimately developed a largely agricultural economy.

Although the gold and silver discoveries generated the most popular excitement, in the long run other, less glamorous natural resources proved more important to the development of the West. The great Anaconda copper mine launched by William Clark in 1881 marked the beginning of an industry that would remain important to Montana for many decades. In other areas, mining operations had significant success with lead, tin, quartz, and zinc.

Life in the mining boomtowns had a hectic tempo and a gaudy flavor unknown in any other part of the Far West. A speculative spirit, a mood of heady optimism, gripped almost everyone and dominated every phase of community activity. And while very few of the prospectors and miners ever "struck it rich," there was at least some truth to the popular belief that mining provided opportunities for sudden wealth. The "bonanza kings"—the miners who did become enormously wealthy off a strike—were much more likely to have come from modest or impoverished backgrounds than the industrial tycoons of the East.

The conditions of mine life in the boom period—the presence of precious minerals, the vagueness of claim boundaries, the cargoes of gold being shipped out—attracted to the camps outlaws and "bad men," operating as individuals or gangs. When the situation became intolerable in a community, those members interested in order began enforcing their own laws through vigilance committees, an unofficial system of social control used earlier in California. Vigilantes were unconstrained by the legal system, and they often imposed their notion of justice arbitrarily and without regard for any form of due process. Some vigilantes continued to operate as private "law" enforcers even after the creation of regular governments.

Men greatly outnumbered women in the mining towns, and younger men in particular had difficulty finding female companions of comparable age. Those women who did gravitate to the new communities often came with their husbands, and their activities were generally (although not always) confined to the same kinds of domestic tasks that eastern women performed. Single women, or women whose husbands were earning no money, did work for wages at times, as cooks, laundresses, and tavern keepers. And in the sexually imbalanced mining communities, there was always a ready market for prostitutes.

The thousands of people who flocked to the mining towns in search of quick wealth and failed to find it often remained as wage laborers in corporate mines after the boom period, working in almost uniformly terrible conditions. In the 1870s, before technological advances eliminated some of the dangers, one worker in every thirty was disabled in the mines, and one in every eighty was killed. That rate fell later in the nineteenth century, but mining remained one of the most dangerous and arduous working environments in the United States.

The Cattle Kingdom

A second important element of the changing economy of the Far West was cattle ranching. The open range—the vast grasslands of the public domain—provided a huge area on the Great Plains where cattle raisers could graze their herds free of charge and unrestricted by the boundaries of private farms. The railroads gave birth to the range-cattle industry by giving it access to markets. Eventually, the same railroads ended it by bringing farmers to the plains and thus destroying the open range.

The western cattle industry was Mexican and Texan by ancestry. Long before citizens of the United States entered the Southwest, Mexican ranchers had developed the techniques and equipment that the cattlemen and cowboys of the Great Plains later employed: branding (a device known in all frontier areas where stock was grazing in common areas), roundups, roping, and the gear of the herders—their lariats, saddles, leather chaps, and spurs. Americans in Texas adopted these methods and carried them to the northernmost ranges of the cattle kingdom. Texas also had the largest herds of cattle in the country. From Texas, too, came the small, muscular horses (broncos and mustangs) that enabled cowboys to control the herds.

At the end of the Civil War, an estimated 5 million cattle roamed the Texas ranges. Eastern markets were offering fat prices for steers in any condition, and the challenge facing the cattle industry was getting the animals from the range to the railroad centers. Early in 1866, some Texas cattle ranchers began driving their combined herds, some 260,000 head, north to Sedalia, Missouri, on the Missouri Pacific Railroad. The caravan suffered heavy losses. But the drive proved that cattle could be driven to distant markets and pastured along the trail, and that they would even gain weight during the journey. This earliest of the "long drives," in other words, established the first, tentative link between the isolated cattle breeders of west Texas and the booming urban markets of the East. It laid the groundwork for the explosion of the industry—for the creation of the "cattle kingdom."

With the precedent of the long drive established, the next step was to find an easier route through more accessible country. Market facilities grew up at Abilene, Kansas, on the Kansas Pacific Railroad, and for years the town reigned as the railhead of the cattle kingdom. But by the mid-1870s, agricultural development in western Kansas was eating away at the open-range

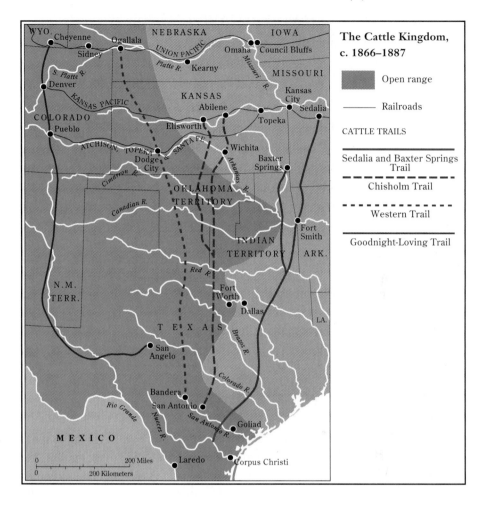

The Cattle Kingdom, c. 1866–1887

Open range

Railroads

CATTLE TRAILS

Sedalia and Baxter Springs Trail

Chisholm Trail

Western Trail

Goodnight-Loving Trail

land. Cattlemen had to develop other trails and other market outlets. As the railroads began to reach farther west, Dodge City and Wichita in Kansas, Ogallala and Sidney in Nebraska, Cheyenne and Laramie in Wyoming, and Miles City and Glendive in Montana all began to rival Abilene as major centers of stock herding.

There had always been an element of risk and speculation in the open-range cattle business. At any time, "Texas fever"—a disease transmitted to cattle by parasite-carrying ticks—might decimate a herd. Rustlers and Indians frequently seized large numbers of animals. But as settlement of the plains increased, new forms of competition joined these traditional risks. Sheep breeders from California and Oregon brought their flocks onto the range to compete for grass. Farmers ("nesters") from the East threw fences around their claims, blocking trails and breaking up the open range. A series of "range wars"—between sheepmen and cattlemen, between ranchers and farmers—erupted out of the tensions between these competing groups. Some of the wars resulted in significant loss of life and extensive property damage.

Accounts of the lofty profits to be made in the cattle business—it was said that an investment of $5,000 would return $45,000 in four years—tempted eastern, English, and Scottish capital to the plains. Increasingly, the structure of the cattle economy became corporate; in one year, twenty corporations with a combined capital of $12 million were chartered in Wyoming. The result of this frenzied, speculative expansion was that the ranges, already severed and shrunk by the railroads and the farmers, became overstocked. There was not enough grass to support the crowding herds or sustain the long drives. Two severe winters, in 1885–1886 and 1886–1887, with a searing summer between them, stung and scorched the plains. Hundreds of thousands of cattle died; streams and grass dried up; princely ranches and costly investments disappeared in a season.

The open-range industry never recovered; the long drive disappeared for good. Railroads displaced the trail as the route to market for livestock. But established cattle ranches—with fenced-in grazing land and stocks of hay for winter feed—survived, grew, and prospered, eventually producing more beef than ever.

Although the cattle industry was overwhelmingly male in its early years, there were always a few women involved in ranching and driving. And as ranching became more sedentary, the presence of women greatly increased. By 1890, more than 250,000 women owned ranches or farms in the western states (many of them as proxies for their husbands or fathers, but some in their own right). Indeed, the region provided women with many opportunities that were closed to them in the East—including the opportunity to participate in politics. Wyoming was the first state in the Union to guarantee woman suffrage.

THE DISPERSAL OF THE TRIBES

Having imagined the West as a "virgin land" awaiting civilization by white people, many Americans tried to force the region to match their image of it. That meant, above all, ensuring that the Indian tribes would not remain obstacles to the spread of white society.

White Tribal Policies

The traditional policy of the federal government was to regard the tribes simultaneously as independent nations (with which the United States could negotiate treaties) and as wards of the president (who would exercise paternalistic authority over the Indians). The concept of Indian sovereignty had supported the government's attempt before 1860 to erect a permanent frontier between whites and Indians and to reserve the region west of the bend of the Missouri River as a permanent Indian country separated from the rest of the United States. But the belief in tribal sovereignty, and the treaties or agreements with the Indians, were not strong enough to withstand the pressure of white settlers eager for access to Indian lands. The history of relations between the United States and the Native Americans was, therefore, one of nearly endless broken promises—as the national government used its allegedly paternalistic responsibilities to abrogate treaties and seize Indian lands.

By the early 1850s, the idea of establishing one great enclave in which many tribes could live gave way, in the face of white demands for access to lands in Indian Territory, to a new reservations policy, known as "concentration." In 1851, the government assigned each tribe its own defined reservation, confirmed by separate treaties—treaties often illegitimately negotiated with unauthorized "representatives" chosen by whites, people known sarcastically as "treaty chiefs." The new arrangement had many benefits for whites and few for the Indians. It divided the tribes from one another and made them easier to control. It allowed the government to force tribes into scattered locations and to take over the most desirable lands for white settlement. But it did not survive as the basis of Indian policy for long.

In 1867, in the aftermath of a series of bloody conflicts, Congress established the Indian Peace Commission, composed of both soldiers and civilians, to recommend a new and presumably permanent Indian policy. The commission recommended replacing the "concentration" policy with a new one. The government would move all the Plains tribes into two large reservations—one in Indian Territory (Oklahoma), the other in the Dakotas. At a series of meetings with the tribes, government agents cajoled, bribed, and tricked representatives of the Arapaho, Cheyenne, Sioux, and other tribes into agreeing to treaties establishing the new reservations.

But this "solution" worked little better than previous ones. Part of the problem was the way in which the government administered the reservations it had established. White management of Indian matters was entrusted to the Bureau of Indian Affairs, located in the Department of the Interior. The

BUFFALO HIDES The appetite for buffalo hides in the urban East grew rapidly in the late nineteenth century, creating an incentive for hunters to decimate the massive herds. This photograph shows 40,000 buffalo hides pile up in a yard in Dodge City, Kansas, in 1878. Within a few years after that, the buffalo herds were almost extinct.

bureau was responsible for distributing land, making payments, and supervising the shipment of supplies. Its record was abysmal. The bureau's agents in the West, products of political patronage, were often men of extraordinary incompetence and dishonesty. But even the most honest and diligent agents were generally ill-prepared for their jobs. The poor and usually corrupt administration of the reservations was one reason for the constant conflicts between the tribes and the whites who were surrounding them.

But the problem was also a result of the relentless slaughtering by whites of the buffalo herds that supported the tribes' way of life. Even in the 1850s, whites had been killing buffalo at a rapid rate to provide food and supplies for the large bands of migrants traveling to the gold rush in California. After the Civil War, white demand for buffalo hides (especially in the East) became a national phenomenon. Professional and amateur hunters, even casual visitors shooting from passing trains, swarmed over the plains killing the huge animals. Some Indian tribes (notably the Blackfeet) also began killing large numbers of buffalo to sell in the booming new market. The buffalo suffered too from the ecological changes white settlement brought to the region—the reduction and in some areas virtual disappearance of the open plains on which the buffalo depended. The southern herd was virtually exterminated by 1875, and within a few years the smaller northern herd had met the same fate. In 1865, there had been at least 15 million buffalo; a decade later, fewer than a thousand of the great beasts survived. By destroying the buffalo herds, whites were destroying the Indians' source of food and supplies and their ability to resist the white advance. They were also inadvertently contributing to a climate in which Indian warriors felt the need to fight to preserve their way of life.

The Indian Wars

There was almost incessant fighting between whites and Indians from the 1850s to the 1880s, as Indians struggled against the growing threats to their civilizations. Indian warriors, usually traveling in raiding parties of thirty to forty men, attacked wagon trains, stagecoaches, and isolated ranches, often in retaliation for earlier attacks on them by whites. As the United States Army became more deeply involved in the fighting, the tribes began to focus more of their attacks on white soldiers.

At times, this small-scale fighting escalated into something close to a war. During the Civil War, the eastern Sioux in Minnesota, cramped on a small reservation and exploited by corrupt white agents, suddenly rebelled. Led by Little Crow, they killed more than 700 whites before being subdued by a force of regulars and militiamen. Thirty-eight of the Indians were hanged, and the tribe was exiled to the Dakotas.

At the same time, fighting flared up in eastern Colorado, where the Arapaho and Cheyenne were coming into conflict with white miners settling in the region. Bands of Indians attacked stagecoach lines and settlements in an effort to regain territory they had lost. In response to these incidents, whites called up a large territorial militia, and the army issued dire threats of retribution. The governor urged all friendly Indians to congregate at army posts for protection before the army began its campaign. One Arapaho and Cheyenne band under Black Kettle, apparently in response to the invitation, camped near Fort Lyon on Sand Creek in November 1864. Some members of the party were warriors, but Black Kettle believed he was under official protection and exhibited no hostile intention. Nevertheless, Colonel J. M. Chivington, apparently encouraged by the army commander of the district, led a volunteer militia force—largely consisting of unemployed miners, many of whom were apparently drunk—to the unsuspecting camp and massacred 133 people, 105 of them women and children. Black Kettle himself escaped the Sand Creek massacre. But four years later, in 1868, he and his Cheyennes, some of whom were now at war with the whites, were caught on the Washita River, near the Texas border, by Colonel George A. Custer. White troops killed the chief and his people.

At the end of the Civil War, white troops stepped up their wars against the western Indians on several fronts. The most serious and sustained conflict was in Montana, where the army was attempting to build a road, the Bozeman Trail, to connect Fort Laramie, Wyoming, to the new mining centers. The western Sioux resented this intrusion into the heart of their buffalo range. Led by one of their great chiefs, Red Cloud, they so harried the soldiers and the construction party—among other things, burning the forts that were supposed to guard the route—that the road could not be used.

But it was not only the United States military that harried the tribes. It was also unofficial violence by white vigilantes who engaged in what became known as "Indian hunting." In California, in particular, tracking down and killing Indians became for some whites a kind of sport. Sometimes the killing was in response to Indian raids on white communities. But considerable numbers of whites were committed to the goal of literal "elimination" of the tribes whatever their behavior, a goal that rested on the belief in the essential inhumanity of Indians and the impossibility of white society's coexisting with them. In California, civilians killed close to 5,000 Indians between 1850 and 1880—one of many factors (disease and poverty being the more important) that reduced the Indian population of the state from 150,000 before the Civil War to 30,000 in 1870.

The treaties negotiated in 1867 brought a temporary lull to many of the conflicts. But new forces soon shattered the peace again. In the early 1870s, more waves of white settlers, mostly miners, began to penetrate some of the lands in Dakota Territory supposedly guaranteed to the tribes in 1867. At the same time, the federal government, responding to the recommendations of a commission, decided that it would no longer recognize the tribes as independent entities and would no longer negotiate with tribal chiefs. This step was intended to undermine the collective nature of Indian life and to force the Indians to assimilate into white culture—a goal cherished by many white reformers, who believed that only through assimilation could the Indians achieve genuine "civilization."

Indian resistance flared anew, this time with even greater strength. In the northern plains, the Sioux rose up in 1875 and left their reservation. When white officials ordered them to return, bands of warriors gathered in Montana and united under two great leaders: Crazy Horse and Sitting Bull. Three army columns set out to round them up and force them back onto the reservation. With the expedition, as colonel of the famous Seventh Cavalry, was the colorful and controversial George A. Custer. At the Battle of the Little Bighorn in southern Montana in 1876—perhaps the most famous of all conflicts between whites and Indians—an unprecedentedly large army of up to 4,000 tribal warriors surprised Custer and part of his regiment, surrounded them, and killed every man.

But the Indians did not have the political organization or the supplies to keep their troops united. Soon the warriors drifted off in bands to elude pursuit or search for food, and the army ran them down singly and returned them to Dakota. The power of the Sioux—and of their proud leaders, Crazy Horse and Sitting Bull—soon collapsed. They accepted defeat and life on reservations.

One of the most dramatic episodes in Indian history occurred in Idaho in 1877. The Nez Percé were a small and relatively peaceful tribe, some of whose members had managed to live unmolested in Oregon into the 1870s without ever signing a treaty with the United States. But under pressure from white settlers, the government forced them to move into a reservation that another branch of the tribe had accepted by treaty in the 1850s. With no realistic prospect of resisting, the Indians began the journey to the reservation; but on the way, several younger Indians, drunk and angry, killed four white settlers.

The leader of the band, Chief Joseph, persuaded his followers to flee from the expected retribution. American troops pursued and attacked them, only to be driven off in a battle at White Bird Canyon. After that, the Nez Percé scattered in several directions and became part of a remarkable chase. Joseph moved with 200 men and 350 women, children, and old people in an effort to reach Canada and take refuge with the Sioux there. Pursued by four columns of American soldiers smarting from their defeat at White Bird Canyon, the Indians covered 1,321 miles in seventy-five days, repelling or evading the army time and again. They were finally caught just short of the Canadian boundary. Some escaped and slipped across the border; but Joseph and most of his followers, weary and discouraged, finally gave up. "Hear me, my chiefs," Joseph said after meeting with the American general Nelson Miles. "I am tired. My heart is sick and sad. From where the sun now stands, I will fight no more forever." He surrendered, and the Nez Percé were shipped from one place to another for several years; in the process, many of them died of disease and malnutrition (although Joseph himself lived until 1908).

The last Indians to maintain organized resistance against the whites were the Chiricahua Apaches, who fought intermittently from the 1860s to the late 1880s. The two ablest chiefs of this fierce tribe were Mangas Colorados and Cochise. Mangas was murdered during the Civil War by white

A M E R I C A N   V O I C E S

Two Indian Leaders Face Conquest

CHIEF JOSEPH SURRENDERS, 1877

I am tired of fighting. The old men are all dead. [My brother] who led the young men is dead. It is cold, and we have no blankets. The little children are freezing to death. My people, some of them, have run away to the hills. No one knows where they are. I want to have some time to look for my children. Maybe I shall find them among the dead.

Hear me, my chiefs. From where the sun now stands, I will fight no more forever.

SITTING BULL SPEAKS OF LIFE ON THE SIOUX RESERVATION, 1883

Whatever you wanted of me I have obeyed. The Great Father sent me word that whatever he had against me in the past had been forgiven and thrown aside, and I accepted his promises and came in [the reservation]. And he told me not to step aside from the white man's path, and I am doing my best to travel in that path. I sit here and look around me now, and I see my people starving. We want cattle to butcher. That is the way you live, and we want to live the same way. When the Great Father told me to live like his people, I told him to send me six teams of mules, because that is the way the white people make a living. I asked for a horse and buggy for my children; I was advised to follow the ways of the white man, and that is why I asked for those things.

THE SURRENDER OF GERONIMO The great Apache warrior Geronimo (front row, third from right) sits with members of his diminished band after surrendering to United States troops in 1886. The two men at front row, left, are Geronimo's half brothers. The young boy at front row, right, is his son.

soldiers who tricked him into surrendering, and in 1872 Cochise agreed to peace in exchange for a reservation that included some of the tribe's traditional land. But Cochise died in 1874, and his successor, Geronimo—unwilling to bow to white pressures to assimilate—fought on for more than a decade longer, establishing bases in the mountains of Arizona and Mexico and leading warriors in intermittent raids against white outposts. With each raid, however, the number of warring Apaches dwindled, as some warriors died and others drifted away to the reservation. By 1886, Geronimo's plight was hopeless. His band consisted of only about 30 people, including women and children, while his white pursuers numbered perhaps 10,000. Geronimo recognized the odds and surrendered, an event that marked the end of formal warfare between Indians and whites.

The Apache wars were the most violent of all the Indian conflicts, perhaps because the tribes were now the most desperate. But it was the whites who committed the most flagrant and vicious atrocities. In 1871, for example, a mob of white miners invaded an Apache camp, slaughtered over a hundred Indians, and captured children, whom they sold as slaves to rival tribes. On other occasions, white troops murdered Indians who responded to invitations to peace conferences, once killing them with poisoned food.

Nor did the brutality end with the conclusion of the Apache wars. Another tragic encounter occurred in 1890 as a result of a religious revival among the Sioux—a revival that itself symbolized the catastrophic effects of the white assaults on Indian civilization. The Sioux were by now aware that their culture and their glories were irrevocably fading; some were also near starvation because corrupt government agents had reduced their food rations. As other tribes had done in trying times in the past, many of these Indians turned to a prophet who led them in a religious revival.

This time the prophet was Wovoka, a Paiute who inspired a fervent spiritual awakening that began in Nevada and spread quickly to the plains. The new revival emphasized the coming of a messiah, but its most conspicuous feature was a mass, emotional "Ghost Dance," which inspired ecstatic visions that many participants believed were genuinely mystical. Among these visions were images of a retreat of white people from the plains and a restoration of the great buffalo herds. White agents on the Sioux reservation watched the dances in bewilderment and fear; some believed they might be the preliminary to hostilities.

On December 29, 1890, the Seventh Cavalry (which had once been Custer's regiment) tried to round up a group of about 350 cold and starving Sioux at Wounded Knee, South Dakota. Fighting broke out in which about 40 white soldiers and more than 300 of the Indians, including women and children, died. An Indian may well have fired the first shot, but the battle soon turned into a one-sided massacre, as the white soldiers turned their new machine guns on the Indians and mowed them down in the snow.

The Dawes Act

Even before the Ghost Dance and the Wounded Knee tragedy, the federal government had moved to destroy forever the tribal structure that had always been the cornerstone of Indian culture. Reversing its policy of nearly fifty years of creating reservations in which the tribes would be isolated from white society, Congress abolished the practice by which tribes owned reservation lands communally. Some supporters of the new policy believed they were acting for the good of the Indians, whom they considered a "vanishing race" in need of rescue by white society. But the action was frankly designed to force Indians to become landowners and farmers, to abandon their collective society and culture and become part of white civilization.

The Dawes Severalty Act of 1887 (usually known simply as the Dawes Act) provided for the gradual elimination of most tribal ownership of land and the allotment of tracts to individual owners: 160 acres to the head of a family, 80 acres to a single adult or orphan, 40 acres to each dependent child. Adult owners were given United States citizenship, but unlike other citizens, they could not gain full title to their property for twenty-five years (supposedly to prevent them from selling the land to speculators). The act applied to most of the western tribes.

In applying the Dawes Act, the Bureau of Indian Affairs relentlessly promoted the idea of assimilation that lay behind it. Not only did agents of the bureau try to move Indian families onto their own plots of land; they also took Indian children away from their families and sent them to boarding schools run by whites, where they believed the young people could be educated to abandon tribal ways. They also moved to stop Indian religious rituals and encouraged the spread of Christianity and the creation of Christian churches on the reservations.

Few Indians were prepared for this wrenching change. In any case, white administration of the Dawes Act was so corrupt and inept that ultimately the government simply abandoned most efforts to enforce it. Much of the reservation land, therefore, was never distributed to individual owners. Congress attempted to speed assimilation with the Burke Act of 1906, but Indians continued to resist.

THE RISE AND DECLINE
OF THE WESTERN FARMER

The arrival of the miners, the empire building of the cattle ranchers, the dispersal of the Indian tribes—all served as a prelude to the decisive phase of white settlement of the Far West. Even before the Civil War, farmers had begun moving into the plains region, challenging the dominance of the ranchers and the Indians and occasionally coming into conflict with both. By the 1870s, what was once a trickle had become a deluge. Farmers poured into the plains and beyond, enclosed land that had once been hunting territory for Indians and grazing territory for cattle, and established a new agricultural region.

For a time in the late 1870s and early 1880s, the new western farmers flourished, enjoying the fruits of an agricultural economic boom comparable in many ways to the booms that eastern industry periodically enjoyed. Beginning in the mid-1880s, however, the boom turned to bust, and the western agricultural economy began a long, steady decline.

Farming on the Plains

Many factors combined to produce the surge of western agricultural settlement, but the most important was the railroads. Before the Civil War, the Great Plains had been accessible only through a difficult journey by wagon. But beginning in the 1860s, a great new network of railroad lines developed, spearheaded by the transcontinental route Congress had authorized and subsidized in 1862. They made huge new areas of settlement accessible.

The building of the transcontinental line—completed in 1869 when the two lines met at Promontory Point, Utah—was a dramatic and monumental achievement. But while this first transcontinental line captured the public imagination, the construction of subsidiary lines in the following years proved of greater importance to the West. State governments, imitating Washington, subsidized railroad development by offering direct financial aid, favorable loans, and more than 50 million acres of land (on top of the 130 million acres the federal government had already provided). Although built and operated by private corporations, the railroads were in many respects public projects.

The railroads spurred agricultural settlement by making access to the Great Plains easier. But the railroad companies also actively promoted settlement, both to provide themselves with customers for their services and to increase the value of their vast landholdings. The companies set rates so low for settlers that almost anyone could afford the trip west. And they sold much of their land at very low prices and with liberal credit to prospective settlers.

Contributing further to the great surge of white agricultural expansion was a pronounced but temporary change in the climate of the Great Plains. For several years in succession, beginning in the 1870s, rainfall in the plains states was well above average. White Americans now rejected the old idea that the region was the Great American Desert. Some even claimed that cultivation of the plains actually encouraged rainfall.

Even under the most favorable conditions, farming on the plains presented special problems. First was the problem of fencing. Farmers had to enclose their land, if for no other reason than to protect it from the herds of the open-range cattlemen. But materials for traditional wood or stone fences were unavailable, and in any case, such fences would be ineffective as barriers to cattle. In the mid-1870s, however, two Illinois farmers, Joseph H. Glidden and I. L. Ellwood, solved this problem by developing and marketing barbed wire, which became standard equipment on the plains and revolutionized fencing practices all over the country and the world.

The second problem was water. Water was scarce even when rainfall was above average. After 1887, a series of dry seasons began, and lands that had been fertile now returned to semidesert. Some farmers dealt with the problem by using deep wells pumped by steel windmills, or by turning to what was called dryland farming (a system of tillage designed to conserve moisture in the soil by covering it with a dust blanket), or by planting drought-resistant crops. In many areas of the plains, however, only large-scale irrigation could save the endangered farms. But irrigation projects of the necessary magnitude required government assistance, and neither the federal nor the state governments were prepared to fund the projects.

Most of the people who moved into the region had previously been farmers in the Middle West, the East, or Europe. In the booming years of the early 1880s, with land values rising, the new farmers had no problem obtaining extensive and easy credit and had every reason to believe they would soon be able to retire their debts. But the arid years of the late 1880s—during which crop prices were falling while production was becoming more expensive—changed that prospect. Tens of thousands of farmers could not pay their debts and were forced to abandon their farms. There was, in effect, a reverse migration: white settlers moving back east, sometimes turning once-flourishing communities into desolate ghost towns. Those who remained continued to suffer from falling prices (for example, wheat, which had sold for $1.60 a bushel at the end of the Civil War, dropped to 49 cents in the 1890s) and persistent indebtedness.

Commercial Agriculture

American farming by the late nineteenth century no longer bore very much relation to the comforting image many Americans continued to cherish. The sturdy, independent farmer of popular myth was being replaced by the commercial farmer—attempting to do in the agricultural economy what industrialists were doing in the manufacturing economy.

Commercial farmers were not self-sufficient and made no effort to become so. They specialized in cash crops which they sold in national or world markets. They did not often make their own household supplies or grow their own food but bought them from merchants. This kind of farming, when it was successful, raised farmers' living standards. But it also made them dependent on bankers and interest rates, railroads and freight rates, national and European markets, world supply and demand. And unlike the capitalists of the industrial order, they could not regulate their production or influence the prices of what they sold.

Between 1865 and 1900, agriculture became an international business. Farm output increased dramatically, not only in the United States but in Brazil, Argentina, Canada, Australia, New Zealand, Russia, and elsewhere. At the same time, modern forms of communication and transportation—the telephone, the telegraph, steam navigation, railroads—were creating new markets around the world for agricultural goods. American commercial farmers, constantly opening new lands, produced much more than the domestic market could consume; they relied on the world market to absorb their surplus, but in that market they faced major competition. Cotton farmers depended on export sales for 70 percent of their annual income, wheat farmers for 30 to 40 percent; but the volatility of the international market put them at great risk. Beginning in the 1880s, worldwide overproduction led to a drop in prices for most agricultural goods and hence to great economic distress for many of the more than 6 million American farm families. By the 1890s, 27 percent of the farms in the country were mortgaged; by 1910, 33 percent. In 1880, 25 percent of all farms had been operated by tenants; by 1910, the proportion had grown to 37 percent. Commercial farming made some people fabulously wealthy. But the farm economy as a whole was suffering a significant decline relative to the rest of the nation.

The Farmers' Grievances

American farmers were painfully aware that something was wrong. But few yet understood the implications of national and world overproduction. Instead, they concentrated their attention and anger on more immediate, more comprehensible—and no less real—problems: inequitable freight rates, high interest charges, and an inadequate currency.

The farmers' first and most burning grievance was against the railroads. In many cases, the railroads charged higher rates for farm goods than for other goods, and higher rates in the South and West than in the Northeast. Railroads also controlled elevator and warehouse facilities in buying centers and charged arbitrary storage rates.

Farmers also resented the institutions controlling credit—banks, loan companies, insurance corporations. Since sources of credit in the West and South were few, farmers had to take loans on whatever terms they could get, often at interest rates of from 10 to 25 percent. Many farmers had to pay these loans back in years when prices were dropping and currency was becoming scarce. As a result, expansion of the currency became an increasingly important issue to farmers.

A third grievance concerned prices—both the prices farmers received for their products and the prices they paid for goods they bought. Farmers sold their products in a competitive world market over which they had no control and of which they had no advance knowledge. A farmer could plant a large crop at a moment when its price was high and find that by the time of the harvest the price had declined. Farmers' fortunes rose and fell in response to unpredictable forces. But many farmers became convinced (often with some reason) that "middlemen"—speculators, bankers, regional and local agents—were conspiring with one another to fix prices so as to benefit themselves at the growers' expense. Many farmers also came to believe (again, not entirely without reason) that manufacturers in the East were colluding to keep the prices of farm goods low and the prices of industrial goods high. Although farmers sold their crops in a competitive world market, they bought manufactured goods in a domestic market protected by tariffs and dominated by trusts and corporations.

The Agrarian Malaise

These economic difficulties produced a series of social and cultural resentments. In part, this was a result of the isolation of farm life. Farm families in some parts of the country—particularly in the prairie and plains regions, where large farms were scattered over vast areas—were virtually cut off from the outside world. During the winter months and spells of bad weather, the loneliness and boredom could become nearly unbearable. Many farmers lacked access to adequate education for their children, to proper medical facilities, to recreational or cultural activities, to virtually anything that might give them a sense of being members of a community. Older farmers felt the sting of watching their children leave the farm for the city. They felt the humiliation of being ridiculed as "hayseeds" by the new urban culture that was coming to dominate American life.

The result of this sense of isolation and obsolescence was a growing malaise among many farmers, a discontent that would help create a great national political movement in the 1890s. It found reflection, too, in the literature that emerged from rural America. Writers in the late nineteenth century might romanticize the rugged life of the cowboy and the western miner. For the farmer, however, the image was usually different. Hamlin Garland, for example, reflected the growing disillusionment in a series of novels and short stories. In the past, Garland wrote in the introduction to his novel *Jason Edwards* (1891), the agrarian frontier had seemed to be "the Golden West, the land of wealth and freedom and happiness. All of the associations called up by the spoken word, the West, were fabulous, mythic, hopeful." Now, however, the bright promise had faded. The trials of rural life were crushing the human spirit. "So this is the reality of the dream!" a character in Jason Edwards exclaims. "A shanty on a barren plain, hot and lone as a desert. My God!" Once, sturdy yeoman farmers had viewed themselves as the backbone of American life. Now they were becoming painfully aware that their position was declining in relation to the rising urban-industrial society to the east.

D E B A T I N G   T H E   P A S T

The Frontier and the West

HE EMERGENCE OF the history of the American West as an important field of scholarship can be traced to the paper Frederick Jackson Turner delivered at a meeting of the American Historical Association in 1893: "The Significance of the Frontier in American History." The "Turner thesis," or "frontier thesis," as his argument became known, shaped both popular and scholarly views of the West for two generations.

Turner stated his thesis simply. The settlement of the West by white Americans—"the existence of an area of free land, its continuous recession, and the advance of American settlement westward"—was the central story of the nation's history. The process of westward expansion had transformed a desolate and savage land into modern civilization. It had also continually renewed American ideas of democracy and individualism.

In the first half of the twentieth century, virtually everyone who wrote about the West echoed at least part of Turner's argument. Ray Allen Billington's *Westward Expansion* (1949), the standard textbook in the field for decades, was almost wholly consistent with the Turnerian model. In *The Great Plains* (1931) and *The Great Frontier* (1952), Walter Prescott Webb similarly emphasized the bravery and ingenuity of white settlers in the Southwest.

Serious efforts to displace the Turner thesis as the explanation of western American history began after World War II. In *Virgin Land* (1950), Henry Nash Smith examined many of the same heroic images of the West that Turner and his disciples had presented; but he treated those images less as descriptions of reality than as myths. Earl Pomeroy challenged Turner's notion of the West as a place of individualism, innovation, and democratic renewal. "Conservatism, inheritance, and continuity bulked at least as large," he claimed. Howard Lamar, in *Dakota Territory, 1861–1889* (1956) and *The Far Southwest* (1966), emphasized the highly diverse characters of different areas of the West and thus challenged the Turnerian idea that a distinctive western environment shaped the western experience.

(continued on next page)

The western historians who began to emerge in the late 1970s launched an even more emphatic attack on the Turner thesis and the idea of the "frontier." Echoing the interest of other historians in issues of race, gender, ethnicity, and culture, "new" western historians such as Richard White, Patricia Nelson Limerick, William Cronon, Donald Worster, Peggy Pascoe, and many others challenged the Turnerians on a number of points.

Turner saw the nineteenth-century West as "free land" awaiting the expansion of Anglo-American settlement and American democracy. The "new western historians" have rejected the concept of an empty "frontier" and emphasize, instead, the elaborate and highly developed civilizations (Native American, Hispanic, mixed-blood, and others) that already existed in the region. White, English-speaking Americans, they have argued, did not so much settle the West as conquer it. And Anglo-Americans in the West continue to share the region not only with the Indians and Hispanics who preceded them there, but also with African Americans, Asians, Latin Americans, and others who flowed into the West at the same time they did.

The Turnerian West was a place of heroism, triumph, and above all progress, dominated by the feats of brave white men. The West the new historians describe is a less triumphant (and less masculine) place in which bravery and success coexist with oppression, greed, and failure; in which decaying ghost towns, bleak Indian reservations, impoverished barrios, and ecologically devastated landscapes are as characteristic of western development as great ranches, rich farms, and prosperous cities; and in which women are as important as men in shaping the societies that emerged.

To Turner and his disciples, the nineteenth-century West was a place where rugged individualism flourished and replenished American democracy. The new scholars consider that belief a self-serving myth. Western "pioneers" were never self-sufficient. The region was inextricably tied to a national and international capitalist economy. Westerners depended on government-subsidized railroads for access to markets, federal troops for protection from Indians, and (later) government-funded dams and canals for irrigating their fields and sustaining their towns.

And while Turner defined the West as a process—a process of settlement that came to an end with the "closing of the frontier" in the late nineteenth century—the new historians see the West as a region. Its history does not end in 1890. It continues into our own time.

CHAPTER SEVENTEEN

Industrial Supremacy

Sources of Industrial Growth ∼ *Capitalism and Its Critics*
The Ordeal of the Worker

ITH A STRIDE that astonished statisticians, the conquering hosts of business enterprise swept over the continent; twenty-five years after the death of Lincoln, America had become, in the quantity and value of her products, the first manufacturing nation of the world. What England had accomplished in a hundred years, the United States had achieved in half the time." So wrote the historians Charles and Mary Beard in the 1920s, expressing the amazement many Americans felt when they considered the remarkable expansion of their industrial economy in the late nineteenth century.

In fact, America's rise to industrial supremacy was not as sudden as such observers suggested. The nation had been building a manufacturing economy since early in the nineteenth century; industry was well established before the Civil War. But Americans were clearly correct in observing that the accomplishments of the last three decades of the nineteenth century overshadowed all the earlier progress. Those years witnessed nothing less than the transformation of the nation.

The remarkable growth did much to increase the wealth and improve the lives of many Americans. But such benefits were far from equally shared. While industrial titans and a growing middle class were enjoying a prosperity without precedent in the nation's history, workers, farmers, and others were experiencing an often painful ordeal that slowly edged the United States toward a great economic and political crisis.

SOURCES OF INDUSTRIAL GROWTH

Many factors contributed to the growth of American industry: abundant raw materials; a large and growing labor supply; a surge in technological innovation; the emergence of a talented, ambitious, and often ruthless group of

TIME LINE				
1859	**1866**	**1870**	**1873**	**1876**
First oil well drilled	National Labor Union founded	Rockefeller founds Standard Oil	Carnegie Steel founded	Bell invents telephone
	First transatlantic cable		Economic panic	

1877	**1879**	**1881**	**1886**	**1887**	**1892**
Nationwide railroad strike	Edison invents electric light bulb	American Federation of Labor founded	Haymarket bombing	Bellamy's *Looking Backward*	Homestead Steel strike

1893	**1899**	**1901**	**1903**	**1914**	
Depression begins	Pullman strike	Morgan creates U.S. Steel	Wright brothers' airplane flight	Ford introduces factory assembly lines	

entrepreneurs; a federal government eager to assist the growth of business; and a great and expanding domestic market for the products of manufacturing.

Industrial Technology

The rapid emergence of new technologies, together with the discovery of new materials and productive processes, was one of the principal sources of late-nineteenth-century industrial growth.

Some of the most important innovations were in communications. In 1866, Cyrus W. Field laid a transatlantic telegraph cable to Europe. During the next decade, Alexander Graham Bell developed the first commercially useful telephone; and by the 1890s, the American Telephone and Telegraph Company, which handled his interests, had installed nearly half a million telephones in American cities. Other inventions that speeded the pace of business organization were the typewriter (by Christopher L. Sholes in 1868), the cash register (by James Ritty in 1879), and the calculating or adding machine (by William S. Burroughs in 1891).

Among the most revolutionary innovations was the introduction in the 1870s of electricity as a source of light and power. Among the pioneers of electric lighting were Charles F. Brush, who devised the arc lamp for street illumination, and Thomas A. Edison, who invented the incandescent lamp (or light bulb), which could be used for both street and home lighting. Edison and others designed improved generators and built large power plants to furnish electricity to whole cities. By the turn of the century, electric power was becoming commonplace in street railway systems, in the elevators of urban skyscrapers, in factories, and increasingly in offices and homes.

A process by which iron could be transformed into steel—a much more durable and versatile material—had been discovered simultaneously in the 1850s by an Englishman, Henry Bessemer, and an American, William Kelly. (The process consisted of blowing air through molten iron to burn out the impurities.) After the Civil War, the new process transformed the metal industry. In 1868, the New Jersey ironmaster Abram S. Hewitt introduced from Europe another method of making steel—the open-hearth process. These techniques made possible the production of steel in great quantities and large dimensions, for use in the manufacture of locomotives, steel rails, and girders for the construction of tall buildings.

The steel industry emerged first in western Pennsylvania and eastern Ohio, a region where iron ore and coal were abundant and where there was already a flourishing iron industry. Pittsburgh quickly became the center of the steel world. But the industry was growing so fast that new sources of ore were soon necessary. The upper peninsula of Michigan, the Mesabi range in Minnesota, and the area around Birmingham, Alabama, became important ore-producing centers by the end of the century, and new centers of steel production grew up near them: Cleveland, Detroit, Chicago, and Birmingham, among others.

The oil industry emerged in the late nineteenth century largely in response to the steel industry's need for lubrication for its machines. (Not until later did oil become important primarily for its potential as a fuel.) The existence of petroleum reserves in western Pennsylvania had been common knowledge for some time. Not until the 1850s, however, after Pennsylvania businessman George Bissell showed that the substance could be burned in lamps and that it could also yield such products as paraffin, naphtha, and lubricating oil, was there any sense of its commercial value. Bissell raised money to begin drilling; and in 1859, Edwin L. Drake, one of Bissell's employees, established the first oil well near Titusville, Pennsylvania, which was soon producing 500 barrels of oil a month. Demand for petroleum grew quickly, and promoters soon developed other fields in Pennsylvania, Ohio, and West Virginia. By the 1870s, oil had advanced to fourth place among the nation's exports.

Other great innovations were emerging by the beginning of the twentieth century. The Italian inventor Guglielmo Marconi was taking the first steps toward the development of radio in the 1890s. The Wright brothers launched the first airplane flight at Kitty Hawk, North Carolina, in 1903. Other inventors were developing the automobile. As early as the 1870s, designers in France, Germany, and Austria—inspired by the success of railroad engines—had begun to develop an "internal combustion engine," which used the expanding power of burning gas to drive pistons; and with this new engine, they created the first automobiles.

The American automobile industry developed rapidly soon thereafter. Charles and Frank Duryea built the first gasoline-driven motor vehicle in America in 1903. Three years later, Henry Ford produced the first of the famous cars that would bear his name. By 1910, the industry had become a major force in the economy, and the automobile was beginning to reshape

THE ASSEMBLY LINE AT FORD Henry Ford helped revolutionize automobile manufacturing when he introduced the moving assembly line, pictured here, to his plants in Dearborn, Michigan. Manufacturers all over the world followed his example, and in many places—among them the Soviet Union—the modern science of mass production came to be known as "Fordism."

American social and cultural life. In 1895, there were only four automobiles on the American highways. By 1917, there were nearly 5 million.

The Science of Production

Central to the growth of the automobile and other industries were changes in the techniques of production. By the turn of the century, many industrialists were embracing the new principles of "scientific management," often known as "Taylorism" after its leading theoretician, Frederick Winslow Taylor. Taylor himself, and his many admirers, argued that scientific management was a way to manage human labor to make it compatible with the demands of the machine age. But scientific management was also a way to increase the employer's control of the workplace, to make working people less independent. Taylor urged employers to reorganize the production process by subdividing tasks. This would speed up production; it would also make workers more interchangeable (less skilled, less in need of training) and thus diminish a manager's dependence on any particular employee. If properly managed by trained experts, he claimed, workers using modern machines could perform simple tasks at much greater speed, greatly increasing productive efficiency.

The most important change in production technology in the industrial era was the emergence of mass production and, along with it, the moving assembly line, which Henry Ford introduced in his automobile plants in 1914. This revolutionary technique cut the time for assembling a chassis from twelve and a half hours to one and a half hours. It enabled Ford to raise the wages and reduce the hours of his workers while cutting the base price of his Model T from $950 in 1914 to $290 in 1929. It became a standard for many other industries.

Railroad Expansion and the Corporation

But the principal agent of industrial development in the late nineteenth century was the expansion of the railroads. Railroads were the nation's primary method of transportation and gave industrialists access to distant markets and distant sources of raw materials. They were the nation's largest businesses and created new forms of corporate organization that served as models for other industries. And they were America's biggest investors, stimulating economic growth through their own enormous expenditures on construction and equipment.

Total railroad trackage increased dramatically in the last forty years of the nineteenth century: from 30,000 miles in 1860 to 193,000 in 1900. Subsidies from federal, state, and local governments (along with foreign loans and investments) were vital to this expansion, which required far more capital than private entrepreneurs could raise by themselves. Equally important was the emergence of great railroad combinations, many of them dominated by one or two individuals. The achievements (and excesses) of these tycoons—Cornelius Vanderbilt, James J. Hill, Collis R. Huntington, and others—became symbols to much of the nation of concentrated economic power. But railroad development was less significant for the individual barons it created than for its contribution to the growth of a new institution: the modern corporation.

There had been various forms of corporations in America since colonial times, but the modern corporation emerged as a major force only after the Civil War. By then, railroad magnates and other industrialists realized that their great ventures could not be financed by any single person, no matter how wealthy, or even by any single group of partners.

Under the laws of incorporation passed in many states in the 1830s and 1840s, business organizations could raise money by selling stock to members of the public; after the Civil War, one industry after another began doing so. What made the stocks more appealing than they had been in the past was that investors now had only "limited liability"—that is, they risked only the amount of their investments; they were not liable for any debts the corporation might accumulate beyond that point. The ability to sell stock to a broad public made it possible for entrepreneurs to gather vast sums of capital and undertake great projects.

The Pennsylvania and other railroads were among the first to adopt the new corporate form of organization. But incorporation quickly spread beyond the railroad industry. In steel, the central figure was Andrew Carnegie, a Scottish immigrant who had worked his way up from modest beginnings and in 1873 opened his own steelworks in Pittsburgh. Soon he dominated the industry. With his associate Henry Clay Frick, he bought up coal mines and leased part of the Mesabi iron range in Minnesota, operated a fleet of ore ships on the Great Lakes, and acquired railroads. Ultimately, he controlled the processing of his steel from mine to market. He financed his vast undertakings not only out of his own profits but out of the sale of stock. Then, in 1901, he sold out for $450 million to the banker J. Pierpont Morgan, who merged the Carnegie interests with others to create the giant United States Steel Corporation—a $14 billion enterprise that controlled almost two-thirds of the nation's steel production.

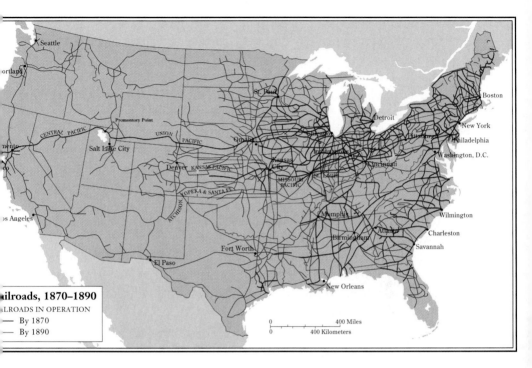

Railroads, 1870–1890

RAILROADS IN OPERATION
— By 1870
— By 1890

0 ____ 400 Miles
0 ____ 400 Kilometers

There were similar developments in other industries. Gustavus Swift developed a relatively small meatpacking company into a great national corporation. Isaac Singer patented a sewing machine in 1851 and created I. M. Singer and Company—one of the first modern manufacturing corporations.

Large, national business enterprises needed more systematic administrative structures than the limited, local ventures of the past. As a result, corporate leaders introduced a set of managerial techniques—the genesis of modern business administration—that relied on systematic division of responsibilities, a carefully designed hierarchy of control, careful cost-accounting procedures, and perhaps above all a new breed of business executive: the "middle manager," who formed a layer of command between workers and owners. Efficient administrative capabilities helped make possible another major feature of the modern corporation: consolidation.

Businessmen created large, consolidated organizations primarily through two methods. One was "horizontal integration"—the combining of a number of firms engaged in the same enterprise into a single corporation. The consolidation of many different railroad lines into one company was an example. Another method, which became popular in the 1890s, was "vertical integration"—the taking over of all the different businesses on which a company relied for its primary function. Carnegie Steel, which came to control not only steel mills but mines, railroads, and other enterprises, was an example of vertical integration.

The most celebrated corporate empire of the late nineteenth century was John D. Rockefeller's Standard Oil, a great combination created through both horizontal and vertical integration. Shortly after the Civil War, Rockefeller launched a refining company in Cleveland and immediately began trying to eliminate his competition. Allying himself with other wealthy capitalists, he proceeded methodically to buy out competing refineries. In 1870, he formed the Standard Oil Company of Ohio, which in a few years had acquired twenty of the twenty-five refineries in Cleveland, as well as plants in Pittsburgh, Philadelphia, New York, and Baltimore.

So far, Rockefeller had expanded only horizontally. But soon he began expanding vertically as well. He built his own barrel factories, terminal warehouses, and pipelines. Standard Oil owned its own freight cars and developed its own marketing organization. By the 1880s, Rockefeller had established such dominance within the petroleum industry that to much of the nation he served as the leading symbol of monopoly. He controlled access to 90 percent of the nation's refined oil.

Rockefeller and other industrialists saw consolidation as a way to cope with what they believed was the greatest curse of the modern economy: "cutthroat competition." Most businessmen claimed to believe in free enterprise and a competitive marketplace, but in fact they feared that substantial competition could spell instability and ruin for all. A successful enterprise, many capitalists believed (but did not say), was one that could eliminate or absorb its competitors.

As the movement toward combination accelerated, new vehicles emerged to facilitate it. The railroads began with so-called pool arrangements—informal agreements among various companies to stabilize rates and divide markets (arrangements that would, in later years, be known as cartels). But if even a few firms in an industry were unwilling to cooperate (as was almost always the case), the pool arrangements collapsed.

The failure of the pools led to new techniques of consolidation. At first, the most successful such technique was the creation of the "trust"—pioneered by Standard Oil in the early 1880s and perfected by the banker J. P. Morgan. Over time, the word "trust" became a popular term for describing any great economic combination, but the trust was in fact a particular kind of organization. Under a trust agreement, stockholders in individual corporations transferred their stocks to a small group of trustees in exchange for shares in the trust itself. Owners of trust certificates often had no direct control over the decisions of the trustees; they simply received a share of the profits of the combination. The trustees themselves, on the other hand, might literally own only a few companies but could exercise effective control over many.

In 1889, the state of New Jersey helped produce a third form of consolidation by changing its laws of incorporation to permit companies to buy up other companies. Other states soon followed. That made the trust unnecessary and permitted actual corporate mergers. Rockefeller, for example, quickly relocated Standard Oil in New Jersey and created there what became known as a "holding company"—a central corporate body that would buy up the stock of various members of the Standard Oil trust and establish direct, formal ownership of the corporations in the trust.

By the end of the nineteenth century, as a result of corporate consolidation, 1 percent of the corporations in America were able to control more than 33 percent of the manufacturing. A system of economic organization was emerging that lodged enormous power in the hands of very few men—the great bankers of New York such as J. P. Morgan, industrial titans such as Rockefeller (who himself gained control of a major bank), and others.

The industrial giants of the era were clearly responsible for substantial economic growth. They were also creating the basis for one of the greatest public controversies of their era: a raging debate over concentrated economic and political power that continued well into the twentieth century.

CAPITALISM AND ITS CRITICS

The rise of big business was not without its critics. Farmers and workers saw in the growth of the new corporate power centers a threat to notions of a republican society in which wealth and authority were widely distributed. Middle-class critics pointed to the corruption that the new industrial titans seemed to produce in their own enterprises and in local, state, and national politics. The growing criticisms challenged the captains of industry to create a defense of the new corporate economy.

Survival of the Fittest

The new rationale for capitalism rested squarely on an older ideology of individualism. The new industrial economy, its defenders argued, was not shrinking opportunities for individual advancement. It was expanding those opportunities. It was providing every individual with a chance to succeed and attain great wealth.

There was an element of truth in such claims, but only a small element. Before the Civil War there had been few millionaires in America; by 1892 there were more than 4,000. Some of them—Carnegie, Rockefeller, and a few others—were in fact what almost all millionaires claimed to be: "self-made men." But most of the new business tycoons had begun their careers from positions of comfort, privilege, and wealth. Nor was their rise to power and prominence always a result simply of hard work and ingenuity, as they liked to claim. It was also a result of ruthlessness and, at times, rampant corruption.

Nevertheless, most tycoons continued to claim that they had attained their wealth and power through hard work, acquisitiveness, and thrift—the traditional virtues of Protestant America. Those who succeeded, they argued, deserved their success, and those who failed had earned their failure through their own laziness, stupidity, or carelessness. Such assumptions became the basis of a popular social theory of the late nineteenth century: Social Darwinism, the application to human society of Charles Darwin's laws of evolution and natural selection among species. Just as only the fittest survived in the process of evolution, the Social Darwinists argued, so in human society only the fittest individuals survived and flourished in the marketplace.

The English philosopher Herbert Spencer was the first and most important proponent of this theory. Society, he argued, benefited from the elimination of the unfit and the survival of the strong and talented. Spencer's teachings found prominent supporters among American intellectuals, most notably William Graham Sumner of Yale, who promoted similar ideas in lectures, articles, and a famous 1906 book, *Folkways*. Sumner did not agree with everything Spencer wrote, but he did share Spencer's belief that individuals must have absolute freedom to struggle, to compete, to succeed, or to fail.

Social Darwinism appealed to corporate leaders because it seemed to legitimize their success and confirm their virtues. It was not, however, an ideology that had very much to do with the realities of the corporate economy. At the same time that businessmen were celebrating the virtues of competition and the free market, they were making active efforts to protect themselves from competition and to replace the natural workings of the marketplace with control by great combinations. Vicious competitive battle—which Spencer and Sumner celebrated and called a source of healthy progress—was in fact the very thing that American businessmen most feared and tried to eliminate.

The Gospel of Wealth

Some businessmen attempted to temper the harsh philosophy of Social Darwinism with a gentler, if in some ways equally self-serving, idea: the "gospel of wealth." People of great wealth, advocates of this idea argued, had not only great power but great responsibilities. It was their duty to use their riches to advance social progress. Andrew Carnegie elaborated on the creed in his 1901 book, *The Gospel of Wealth*, in which he wrote that people of wealth should consider all revenues in excess of their own needs as "trust funds" to be used for the good of the community. Carnegie was only one of many great industrialists who devoted large parts of their fortunes to philanthropic works.

The notion of private wealth as a public blessing existed alongside another popular concept: the notion of great wealth as something available to all. Russell H. Conwell, a Baptist minister, became the most prominent spokesman for the idea by delivering one lecture, "Acres of Diamonds," more than 6,000 times between 1880 and 1900. Conwell told a series of stories, which he claimed were true, of individuals who had found opportunities for extraordinary wealth in their own backyards. (One such story involved a modest farmer who discovered a vast diamond mine in his own fields in the course of working his land.) Most of the millionaires in the country, Conwell claimed (inaccurately), had begun on the lowest rung of the economic ladder and had worked their way to success. Every industrious individual had the chance to do likewise.

Horatio Alger was the most famous promoter of the success story. Alger was originally a minister in a small town in Massachusetts but was driven from his pulpit as a result of a scandal connected to his active, but hidden, homosexuality. He moved to New York, where he wrote his celebrated novels: *Ragged Dick*, *Tom the Bootblack*, *Sink or Swim*, and many others, more than 100 in all, which together sold more than 20 million copies. The titles and characters varied, but the story and message were invariably the same: a poor boy from a small town went to the big city to seek his fortune. By work, perseverance, and luck, he became rich.

Alternative Visions

Alongside the celebrations of competition, the justifications for great wealth, and the legitimization of the existing order stood a group of alternative philosophies, challenging the corporate ethos and at times capitalism itself.

One such philosophy emerged in the work of the sociologist Lester Frank Ward. Ward was a Darwinist, but he rejected the application of Darwinian laws to human society. In *Dynamic Sociology* (1883) and other books, he argued that civilization was not governed by natural selection but by human intelligence, which was capable of shaping society as it wished. In contrast to Sumner, who believed that state intervention to remodel the environment was futile, Ward thought that an active government engaged in positive planning was society's best hope.

Other Americans skeptical of the laissez-faire ideas of the Social Darwinists adopted more radical approaches to reform. Some dissenters found a home in the Socialist Labor Party, founded in the 1870s and led for many years by Daniel De Leon, an immigrant from the West Indies. Although De Leon attracted a modest following in the industrial cities, the party never became a major political force and never polled more than 82,000 votes. A dissident faction of De Leon's party, eager to forge stronger ties with organized labor, broke away and in 1901 formed the more enduring American Socialist Party.

Other radicals gained a wider following. One of the most influential was the California writer and activist Henry George. His angrily eloquent *Progress and Poverty*, published in 1879, became one of the best-selling nonfiction works in American publishing history. George blamed social problems on the ability of a few monopolists to grow wealthy as a result of rising land values. An increase in the value of land, he claimed, was not a result of any effort by the owner. It was an "unearned increment," produced by the growth of society around the land. Such profits were rightfully the property of the community. And so George proposed a "single tax" on land, to replace all other taxes, which would return the increment to the people. The tax, he argued, would destroy monopolies, distribute wealth more equally, and eliminate poverty. Single-tax societies sprang up in many cities, and in 1886, George, with the support of labor and the socialists, narrowly missed being elected mayor of New York.

Rivaling George in popularity was Edward Bellamy, whose utopian novel *Looking Backward*, published in 1888, sold more than 1 million copies. It described the experiences of a young Bostonian who went into a hypnotic sleep in 1887 and awoke in the year 2000 to find a new social order in which want, politics, and vice were unknown. The new society had emerged through a peaceful, evolutionary process: the large trusts of the late nineteenth century had continued to grow in size and to combine with one another until ultimately they formed a single, great trust, controlled by the government, which distributed the abundance of the industrial economy equally among all the people. "Fraternal cooperation" had replaced competition. Class divisions had disappeared. Bellamy labeled the philosophy behind this vision "nationalism," and his work inspired the formation of more than 160 Nationalist Clubs to propagate his ideas.

The Problems of Monopoly

Relatively few Americans shared the views of those who questioned capitalism itself. But as time went on, a growing number of people were becoming deeply concerned about a particular, glaring aspect of capitalism: the growth of monopoly.

By the end of the century, a wide range of groups had begun to assail monopoly and economic concentration. Workers, farmers, consumers, small manufacturers, conservative bankers and financiers, advocates of radical change—all joined the attack. They blamed monopoly for creating artificially

THE FEAR OF MONOPOLY As corporate organizations grew ever larger in the late nineteenth century, the fear of "monopoly power" became a potent force in American life. This cartoon from the political magazine *Puck* suggests something of the horror with which many Americans viewed the rise of monopoly and the tyranny they believed monopoly power exercised over the nation.

high prices. And they blamed it for America's highly unstable economy, which, beginning in 1873, fluctuated erratically, producing severe recessions every five or six years.

Adding to the resentment of monopoly was the emergence of a new class of enormously and conspicuously wealthy people, whose lifestyles became an affront to those struggling to stay afloat in the erratic economy. According to one estimate early in the century, 1 percent of the families in the United States controlled nearly 88 percent of the nation's assets. Some of the wealthy—Andrew Carnegie, for example—lived relatively modestly and donated large sums to philanthropic causes. Others, however, lived in almost grotesque luxury. Observing them were the four-fifths of the American people who lived modestly, and at least 10 million people who lived below the commonly accepted poverty line.

THE ORDEAL OF THE WORKER

The American working class was both a beneficiary and a victim of the growth of industrial capitalism. Most workers in the late nineteenth century experienced a real rise in their standard of living. But they did so at the cost of arduous and often dangerous working conditions, diminishing control over their own work, and a growing sense of powerlessness.

The Immigrant Work Force

The industrial work force expanded dramatically in the late nineteenth century as demand for factory labor grew. The source of that expansion was a massive migration into industrial cities—immigration of two sorts. The first was the continuing flow of rural Americans into factory towns and cities—people disillusioned with or bankrupted by life on the farm and eager for new economic and social opportunities. The second was the great wave of immigration from abroad (primarily from Europe, but also from Asia, Canada, and other areas) in the decades following the Civil War—an influx greater than that of any previous era. The 25 million immigrants who arrived in the United States between 1865 and 1915 were more than four times the number who had arrived in the fifty years before.

In the 1870s and 1880s, most of the immigrants came from the nation's traditional sources: England, Ireland, and northern Europe. By the end of the century, however, the major sources of immigrants had shifted, with large numbers of southern and eastern Europeans (Italians, Poles, Russians,

Greeks, Slavs, and others) moving into the country and into the industrial work force.

The new immigrants were coming to America in part to escape poverty and oppression in their homelands. But they were also lured to the United States by expectations of new opportunities. Some such expectations were unrealistic, the result of false promises. Railroads tried to lure immigrants into their western landholdings by distributing misleading advertisements overseas. Industrial employers actively recruited immigrant workers under the Labor Contract Law, which—until its repeal in 1885—permitted them to pay for the passage of workers in advance and deduct the amount later from their wages. Even after the repeal of the law, employers continued to encourage the immigration of unskilled laborers, often with the assistance of foreign-born labor brokers, such as the Greek and Italian *padrones*, who recruited work gangs of their fellow nationals.

The arrival of these new groups introduced heightened ethnic tensions into the dynamics of the working class. Low-paid Poles, Greeks, and French Canadians began to displace higher-paid British and Irish workers in the textile factories of New England. Italians, Slavs, and Poles emerged as a major source of labor for the mining industry, traditionally dominated by native workers or northern European immigrants. Chinese and Mexicans competed with Anglo-Americans and African Americans in mining, farmwork, and factory labor in California, Colorado, and Texas.

Wages and Working Conditions

At the turn of the century, the average income of the American worker was $400 to $500 a year—below the $600 figure that many believed was the minimum required to maintain a reasonable level of comfort. Nor did workers have much job security. All were vulnerable to the boom-and-bust cycle of the industrial economy, and some lost their jobs because of technological advances or because of the cyclical or seasonal nature of their work. Even those who kept their jobs could find their wages suddenly and substantially cut in hard times. Few workers, in other words, were ever very far from poverty.

American laborers faced a wide array of other hardships as well. For first-generation workers accustomed to the patterns of agrarian life, there was a difficult adjustment to the nature of modern industrial labor: the performance of routine, repetitive tasks, often requiring little skill, on a strict and monotonous schedule. To skilled artisans whose once-valued tasks were now performed by machines, the new system was impersonal and demeaning. Factory laborers worked ten-hour days, six days a week; in the steel industry they worked twelve hours a day. Industrial accidents were frequent and severe.

Women and Children at Work

The decreasing need for skilled work in factories induced many employers to increase the use of women and children, whom they could hire for lower wages than adult males. By 1900, 20 percent of all manufacturing workers were women, and 20 percent of all women (well over 5 million) were wage earners. Women worked in all areas of industry, even in some of the most arduous jobs. Most women, however, worked in a few industries where unskilled and semiskilled machine labor (as opposed to heavy manual labor) prevailed. The textile industry remained the largest single industrial employer of women. (Domestic service remained the most common female occupa-

CHILD LABOR Many working-class children of the early twentieth century found employment as "breaker boys," picking pieces of slate out of piles of coal. The coal dust was often so thick that they could hardly see one another, as this Lewis Hine photograph suggests.

tion overall.) Women worked for wages well below the minimum necessary for survival (and well below the wages paid to men working the same jobs).

At least 1.7 million children under sixteen years of age were employed in factories and fields, more than twice the number of thirty years before; 10 percent of all girls aged ten to fifteen, and 20 percent of all boys, held jobs. Under public pressure, thirty-eight states passed child labor laws in the late nineteenth century. But 60 percent of child workers were employed in agriculture, which was typically exempt from the laws. And even for children employed in factories, the laws merely set a minimum age of twelve years and a maximum workday of ten hours, standards that employers often ignored in any case.

Emerging Unionization

Laborers attempted to fight back against such conditions by adopting one of the same tactics their employers had used so effectively: creating large combinations—national unions. By the end of the century, however, their efforts had met with little success.

There had been craft unions in America, representing small groups of skilled workers, since well before the Civil War. Alone, however, individual unions could not hope to exert significant power in the economy. And during the recession years of the 1870s, unions faced the additional problem of widespread public hostility. When labor disputes with employers turned bitter and violent, as they occasionally did, much of the public instinctively blamed the workers (or the "radicals" and "anarchists" they believed were influencing the workers) for the trouble, rarely the employers. Particularly alarming to middle-class Americans was the emergence of the "Molly Maguires," in the anthracite coal region of western Pennsylvania. This militant labor organization occasionally used violence and even murder in its battle with coal operators. Much of the violence attributed to the Molly Maguires, however, was deliberately instigated by informers and agents employed by the mine owners, who wanted a pretext for ruthless measures suppressing unionization.

Excitement over the Molly Maguires paled beside the near hysteria that gripped the country during the railroad strike of 1877, which began when the eastern railroads announced a 10 percent wage cut and which soon expanded into something approaching a class war. Strikers disrupted rail service from Baltimore to St. Louis, destroyed equipment, and rioted in the streets of Pittsburgh and other cities. State militias were called out, and in July President Hayes ordered federal troops to suppress the disorders in West Virginia. In

Baltimore, eleven demonstrators died and forty were wounded in a conflict between workers and militiamen. In Philadelphia, the state militia killed twenty people when the troops opened fire on thousands of workers and their families who were attempting to block the railroad crossings. In all, over 100 people died before the strike finally collapsed several weeks after it had begun. The great railroad strike was America's first major, national labor conflict, and it illustrated that disputes between labor and capital could no longer be localized in the increasingly national economy.

The Knights of Labor

The first major effort to create a genuinely national labor organization was the founding in 1869 of the Noble Order of the Knights of Labor, under the leadership of Uriah S. Stephens. Membership was open to all who "toiled," a definition that included all workers, most business and professional people, and virtually all women—whether they worked in factories, as domestic servants, or in their own homes. The only excluded groups were lawyers, bankers, liquor dealers, and professional gamblers. The Knights of Labor was loosely organized, without much central direction. Its program was similarly vague. Although its leaders championed an eight-hour workday and the abolition of child labor, they were more interested in long-range reform of the economy. The Knights hoped to replace the "wage system" with a new "cooperative system," in which workers would themselves control a large part of the economy.

For several years, the Knights remained a secret fraternal organization. But in the late 1870s, under the leadership of Terence V. Powderly, the order moved into the open and entered a period of spectacular expansion. By 1886, it claimed a total membership of over 700,000, including some militant elements that the moderate leadership could not always control. Local unions or assemblies associated with the Knights launched a series of railroad and other strikes in the 1880s in defiance of Powderly's wishes. Their failure helped discredit the organization. By 1890, the membership of the Knights had shrunk to 100,000. A few years later, the organization disappeared altogether.

The AFL

Even before the Knights began to decline, a rival association based on a very different organizational concept appeared. In 1881, representatives of a number of craft unions formed the Federation of Organized Trade and

Labor Unions of the United States and Canada. Five years later, this body took the name it has borne ever since, the American Federation of Labor (AFL), and it soon became the most important labor group in the country.

Rejecting the Knights' idea of one big union for everybody, the Federation was an association of essentially autonomous craft unions and represented mainly skilled workers. Samuel Gompers, the powerful leader of the AFL, accepted the basic premises of capitalism; his goal was simply to secure for the workers he represented a greater share of capitalism's material rewards. The AFL concentrated on labor's immediate objectives: wages, hours, and working conditions. While it hoped to attain its ends by collective bargaining, it was ready to use strikes if necessary.

As one of its first objectives, the AFL demanded a national eight-hour workday and called for a general strike if the goal was not achieved by May 1, 1886. On that day, strikes and demonstrations for a shorter workday took place all over the country, most of them staged by AFL unions but a few by more radical groups.

In Chicago, a center of labor and radical strength, a strike was already in progress at the McCormick Harvester Company. City police had been harassing the strikers, and labor and radical leaders called a protest meeting at Haymarket Square. When the police ordered the crowd to disperse, someone threw a bomb that killed seven policemen and injured sixty-seven others. The police, who had killed four strikers the day before, fired into the crowd and killed four more people. Conservative, property-conscious Americans—frightened and outraged—demanded retribution, even though no one knew who had thrown the bomb. Chicago officials finally rounded up eight anarchists and charged them with murder, on the grounds that their statements had incited whoever had hurled the bomb. All eight scapegoats were found guilty after a remarkably injudicious trial. Seven were sentenced to death. One of them committed suicide, four were executed, and two had their sentences commuted to life imprisonment.

To most middle-class Americans, the Haymarket bombing was an alarming symbol of social chaos and radicalism. "Anarchism" now became in the public mind a code word for terrorism and violence, even though most anarchists were relatively peaceful visionaries dreaming of a new social order. For the next thirty years, the specter of anarchism remained one of the most frightening concepts in the American imagination. It was a constant obstacle to the goals of the AFL and other labor organizations, and it did particular damage to the Knights of Labor. However much they tried to distance themselves from radicals, labor leaders were always vulnerable to accusations of anarchism, as the violent strikes of the 1890s occasionally illustrated.

The Homestead Strike

The Amalgamated Association of Iron and Steel Workers, which was affiliated with the American Federation of Labor, was the most powerful trade union in the country. Its members were skilled workers, in great demand by employers, and thus had long been able to exercise significant power in the workplace. In the mid-1880s, however, demand for skilled workers was in decline as new production methods changed the steelmaking process. In the Carnegie system, which was coming to dominate the steel industry, the union was able to maintain a foothold in only one of the corporation's three major factories—the Homestead plant near Pittsburgh.

By 1890, Carnegie and his chief lieutenant, Henry Clay Frick, had decided that the Amalgamated "had to go" even at Homestead. Over the next two years, they repeatedly cut wages at Homestead. At first, the union acquiesced, aware that it was not strong enough to wage a successful strike.

BREAKING THE HOMESTEAD STRIKE, 1892 State militiamen enter Homestead, Pennsylvania, to put an end to the Amalgamated union's violent strike by opening the Carnegie-owned steel plant to strikebreaking workers. This double photograph forms a "stereograph," which, when viewed through a special lens (a "stereoscope"), gave the impression of a three-dimensional scene.

But in 1892, when the company stopped even discussing its decisions with the union and gave it two days to accept another wage cut, the Amalgamated called for a strike.

Frick abruptly shut down the plant and called in 300 guards from the Pinkerton Detective Agency to enable the company to hire nonunion workers. The hated Pinkertons were well-known strikebreakers, and their presence alone was often enough to incite workers to violence. They approached the plant by river, on barges, on July 6, 1892. The strikers poured gasoline on the water, set it on fire, and then met the Pinkertons at the docks with guns and dynamite. A pitched battle broke out. After several hours of fighting, which brought death to three guards and ten strikers and injuries to many others, the Pinkertons surrendered and were escorted roughly out of town.

But the workers' victory was temporary. The governor of Pennsylvania, at the company's request, sent the state's entire National Guard contingent, some 8,000 men, to Homestead. Production resumed, with strikebreakers now protected by troops. And public opinion turned against the strikers when a radical made an attempt to assassinate Frick. Slowly, workers drifted back to their jobs, and finally—four months after the strike began—the Amalgamated surrendered. By 1900, every major steel plant in the Northeast had broken with the Amalgamated, which now had virtually no power to resist. Its membership shrank from a high of 24,000 in 1891 (two-thirds of all eligible steelworkers) to fewer than 7,000 a decade later.

The Pullman Strike

A dispute of greater magnitude and equal bitterness, if less violence, was the Pullman strike in 1894. The Pullman Palace Car Company manufactured sleeping and parlor cars for railroads, which it built and repaired at a plant near Chicago. There the company constructed a 600-acre town, Pullman, and rented its trim, orderly houses to the employees. George M. Pullman, owner of the company, saw the town as a model—a solution to the problems of industrial workers; he referred to the workers as his "children." But many residents chafed at the regimentation (and the high rents). In the winter of 1893–1894, the Pullman Company slashed wages by about 25 percent, citing its own declining revenues in the depression. At the same time, Pullman refused to reduce rents in its model town, which were 20 to 25 percent higher than those for comparable accommodations in surrounding areas. Workers went on strike and persuaded the militant American Railway Union, led by Eugene V. Debs, to support them by refusing to handle Pullman cars and equipment. Within a few days thousands of railroad workers in twenty-seven states and territories were on strike, and transportation from Chicago to the Pacific Coast was paralyzed.

Most state governors responded readily to appeals from strike-threatened businesses; but the governor of Illinois, John Peter Altgeld, was a man with demonstrated sympathies for workers and their grievances. He refused to call out the militia to protect employers now. Bypassing Altgeld, railroad operators asked the federal government to send regular army troops to Illinois, using the pretext that the strike was preventing the movement of mail on the trains. In July 1894, President Grover Cleveland, over Altgeld's objections, ordered 2,000 troops to the Chicago area. A federal court issued an injunction forbidding the union to continue the strike. When Debs and his associates defied it, they were arrested and imprisoned. With federal troops protecting the hiring of new workers and with the union leaders in a federal jail, the strike quickly collapsed.

Sources of Labor Weakness

The last decades of the nineteenth century were years in which labor, despite its occasionally militant organizing efforts, made few real gains. Industrial wages rose hardly at all. Labor leaders won a few legislative victories—the abolition by Congress in 1885 of the Contract Labor Law; the establishment by Congress in 1868 of an eight-hour day on public works projects and in 1892 of the same workday for government employees; and state laws governing hours of labor and safety standards and establishing systems for compensating workers injured on the job. But many such laws were not enforced. There were widespread strikes and protests, and many other working-class forms of resistance, large and small, but few real gains. The end of the century found most workers with less political power and less control of the workplace than they had had forty years before.

Workers failed to make greater gains for many reasons. The principal labor organizations represented only a small percentage of the industrial work force; the AFL, the most important, excluded unskilled workers, who were emerging as the core of the industrial work force, and along with them most women, blacks, and recent immigrants. Divisions within the work force contributed further to union weakness. Tensions among different ethnic and racial groups kept laborers divided.

Another source of labor weakness was the shifting nature of the work force. Many immigrant workers came to America intending to remain only briefly, to earn some money and then return home. The assumption that they had no long-range future in the country, even if that assumption was often inaccurate, eroded their willingness to organize. Other workers—natives and immigrants alike—were in constant motion, moving from one job to another, one town to another, seldom in a single place long enough to establish any institutional ties or exert any real power.

Above all, perhaps, workers made few gains in the late nineteenth century because of the strength of the forces arrayed against them. They faced corporate organizations of vast wealth and power, which were generally determined to crush any efforts by workers to challenge their prerogatives. And as the Homestead and Pullman strikes suggest, the corporations usually had the support of local, state, and federal authorities, who were willing to send in troops to "preserve order" and crush labor uprisings on demand.

Despite the creation of new labor unions, despite a wave of strikes and protests that in the 1880s and 1890s reached startling proportions, workers in the late nineteenth century failed on the whole to create successful organizations or to protect their interests in the way the large corporations managed to do. In the battle for power within the emerging industrial economy, almost all the advantages seemed to lie with capital.

Test

CHAPTER EIGHTEEN

The Age of the City

The New Urban Growth ∼ *Society and Culture in Urbanizing America*
High Culture in the Urban Age

HE INDUSTRIALIZATION AND commercialization of America changed the face of society in countless ways. No change was more profound, however, than the growing size and influence of cities. Having begun its life as a primarily agrarian republic, the United States in the late nineteenth century was becoming an urban nation—with a culture increasingly shaped and dominated by its cities.

THE NEW URBAN GROWTH

The great movement of people from the countryside to the city was not unique to the United States. It was occurring simultaneously throughout much of the Western world in response to industrialization and the factory system. But America, a society with little experience of great cities, found urbanization particularly jarring. The city attracted people because it offered conveniences, entertainments, and cultural experiences unavailable in rural communities. But it attracted people most of all because it offered more and better-paying jobs than were available in the countryside. Whatever the reasons, the urban population of America increased sevenfold in the half-century after the Civil War. And in 1920, the census revealed that for the first time, a majority of the American people lived in "urban" areas—defined as communities of 2,500 people or more.

Natural increase accounted for only a small part of the urban growth. Urban families experienced a high rate of infant mortality, a declining fertility rate, and a high death rate from disease. Without immigration, cities would have grown relatively slowly.

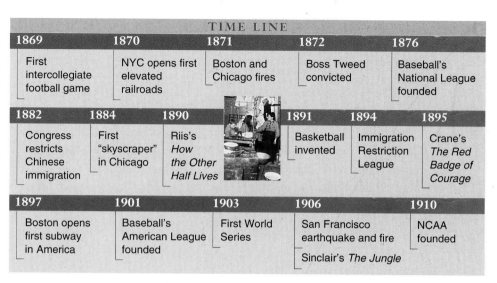

TIME LINE				
1869	**1870**	**1871**	**1872**	**1876**
First intercollegiate football game	NYC opens first elevated railroads	Boston and Chicago fires	Boss Tweed convicted	Baseball's National League founded
1882	**1884**	**1890**	**1891**	**1894**	**1895**
Congress restricts Chinese immigration	First "skyscraper" in Chicago	Riis's *How the Other Half Lives*	Basketball invented	Immigration Restriction League	Crane's *The Red Badge of Courage*
1897	**1901**	**1903**	**1906**	**1910**
Boston opens first subway in America	Baseball's American League founded	First World Series	San Francisco earthquake and fire Sinclair's *The Jungle*	NCAA founded

The Migrations

The late nineteenth century was an age of unprecedented geographical mobility, as Americans left the declining agricultural regions of the East at a dramatic rate. Some of those who left were moving to the newly developing farmlands of the West. But almost as many were moving to the cities of the East and the Midwest.

Among those leaving rural America for industrial cities in the 1880s were southern blacks. They were escaping the poverty, debt, violence, and oppression they faced in the South. They were also seeking new opportunities in cities—opportunities that were limited but usually an improvement over what they left behind. Factory jobs for blacks were rare and professional opportunities almost nonexistent. Urban blacks tended to work as cooks, janitors, and domestic servants, as well as in other service occupations. Since many such jobs were considered women's work, black women often outnumbered black men in the cities. By the end of the nineteenth century, there were substantial black communities (10,000 people or more) in over thirty cities.

The most important source of urban population growth in the late nineteenth century, however, was the arrival of great numbers of new immigrants from abroad. Some came from Canada, Latin America, and—particularly on the West Coast—China and Japan. But the greatest number came from Europe. After 1880, the flow of new arrivals began to include large numbers of people from southern and eastern Europe. By the 1890s, more than half of all immigrants came from these new regions, as opposed to fewer than 2 percent in the 1860s.

In earlier years, most new immigrants from Europe (particularly Germans and Scandinavians) had arrived with at least some money and education. Most of them had headed west—either to be farmers or to work as businessmen, professionals, or skilled laborers in midwestern cities such as St. Louis, Cincinnati, and Milwaukee. But the new immigrants of the late nineteenth century generally lacked the capital to buy farmland and lacked the education to establish themselves in professions. So, like similarly poor Irish immigrants before the Civil War, they settled overwhelmingly in industrial cities, where they occupied largely unskilled jobs.

The Ethnic City

By 1890, most of the population of the major urban areas consisted of immigrants: 87 percent of the population in Chicago, 80 percent in New York, 84 percent in Milwaukee and Detroit. (London, the largest industrial city in Europe, had by contrast a population that was 94 percent native.)

Equally striking was the diversity of the new immigrant populations. In other countries experiencing heavy immigration in this period, most of the new arrivals were coming from one or two sources. But in the United States, no single national group dominated. In the last four decades of the nineteenth century, substantial groups arrived from Italy, Germany, Scandinavia, Austria, Hungary, Russia, Great Britain, Ireland, Poland, Greece, Canada, Japan, China, Holland, Mexico, and other nations. In some towns, a dozen different ethnic groups might find themselves living in close proximity to one another.

Most of the new immigrants were rural people, and their adjustment to city life was often a painful one. To help ease the transition, many national groups formed close-knit ethnic communities within the cities: neighborhoods (often called "immigrant ghettoes") that attempted to re-create in the New World many of the features of the Old. Some ethnic neighborhoods consisted of people who had migrated to America together from the same province, town, or village. Even when the population was more diverse, however, the community offered newcomers much that was familiar. They could find newspapers and theaters in their native languages, stores selling their native foods, and church and fraternal organizations that provided links with their national pasts. Many immigrants also maintained close ties with their native countries. They stayed in touch with relatives who had remained be-

A M E R I C A N   V O I C E S

ANZIA YEZIERSKA

A Jewish Immigrant Strains Against the Past

 FOR SEVENTEEN YEARS I had stood [my father's] preaching and his bullying. But now all the hammering hell that I had to listen to since I was born cracked my brain. His heartlessness to Mother, his pitiless driving away Bessie's only chance to love, bargaining away Fania to a gambler and Mashah to a diamond-faker—when they each had the luck to win lovers of their own—all these tyrannies crashed over me. Should I let him crush me as he crushed them? No. This is America, where children are people. . . .

Blindly, I grabbed my things together into a bundle. I didn't care where I was going or what was to become of me. Only to break away from my black life. Only not to hear Father's preaching voice again. . . .

As I came through the door with my bundle, Father caught sight of me. "What's this?" he asked. "Where are you going?"

"I'm going back to work, in New York. . . . I've got to live my own life. It's enough that Mother and the others lived for you. . . . Thank God, I'm not living in olden times. Thank God I'm living in America! You made the lives of the other children. I'm going to make my own life!"

"You blasphemer!" His hand flung out and struck my cheek. "Denier of God! I'll teach you respect for the law!"

I leaped back and dashed for the door. The Old World had struck its last on me.

SOURCE: Selections from *Bread Givers* by Anzia Yezierska, copyright © 1925 by Doubleday, copyright renewed 1952 by Anzia Yezierska, transferred to Louise Levitas Henriksen in 1970. Reprinted by permission of Persea Books, Inc.

hind. Some (perhaps as many as a third in the early years) returned to their homelands after a relatively short time; others helped bring the rest of their families to America.

The cultural cohesiveness of the ethnic communities clearly eased the pain of separation from the immigrants' native lands. What role it played in helping immigrants become absorbed into the economic life of America is a more difficult question to answer. It is clear that some ethnic groups (Jews and Germans in particular) advanced economically more rapidly than others (for example, the Irish). One explanation is that, by huddling together in ethnic neighborhoods, immigrant groups tended to reinforce the cultural values of their previous societies. When those values were particularly well suited to economic advancement—as was, for example, the high value Jews placed on education—ethnic identification may have helped members of a group to improve their lots. When other values predominated—maintaining community solidarity, strengthening family ties, preserving order—progress could be less rapid.

But other factors were at least as important in determining how well immigrants fared. Immigrants who aroused strong racial prejudice among native-born whites—most notably African Americans, Asians, and Mexicans—found it very difficult to advance whatever their talents. Those who arrived with a valuable skill or with some capital did better than those who did not. And over time, those who lived in cities where people of their own nationality came to predominate—for example, the Irish in New York and Boston, or the Germans in Milwaukee—gained an advantage as they learned to exert their political power.

Assimilation and Exclusion

Despite the many differences among the various immigrant communities, virtually all groups had certain things in common. Most immigrants shared the experience of living in cities (and of adapting from a rural past to an urban present). Most were young; the majority of newcomers were between fifteen and forty-five years old. And in most foreign-born immigrant communities, the strength of ethnic ties had to compete against another powerful force: the desire for assimilation.

Many of the new arrivals had come to America with romantic visions of the New World. And however disillusioning they might find their first contact with the United States, they usually retained the dream of becoming true "Americans." Second-generation immigrants were particularly likely to attempt to break with the old ways, to assimilate themselves completely into what they considered the real American culture. Some even looked with contempt on parents and grandparents who continued to defend traditional ethnic habits and values. Young women, in particular, sometimes rebelled against parents who tried to arrange (or prevent) marriages or who opposed women entering the workplace.

Assimilation was not, of course, entirely a matter of choice. Native-born Americans encouraged it, both deliberately and inadvertently, in countless ways. Public schools taught children in English, and employers often insisted that workers speak English on the job. Most stores sold mainly American products, forcing immigrants to adapt their diets, clothing, and lifestyles to American norms. Church leaders were often native-born Americans or more assimilated immigrants who encouraged their parishioners to adopt American ways. Some even reformed their religion to make it more compatible with the norms of the new country. Reform Judaism, imported from Germany in the late nineteenth century, was an effort by American Jewish leaders (as it had been by German ones) to make their faith less "foreign" to the dominant culture of a largely Christian nation.

The arrival of these vast numbers of new immigrants, and the way many of them clung to old ways and created distinctive communities, provoked fear and resentment among some native-born Americans in much the same way earlier arrivals had done. Some people reacted against the immigrants out of generalized fears and prejudices, seeing in their "foreignness" the source of all the disorder and corruption of the urban world. Native laborers were also often incensed by the willingness of the immigrants to accept lower wages and to take over the jobs of strikers.

The rising nativism provoked political responses. In 1887, Henry Bowers, a self-educated lawyer obsessed with a hatred of Catholics and foreigners, founded the American Protective Association, a group committed to stopping immigration. By 1894, membership in the organization reportedly reached 500,000, with chapters throughout the Northeast and Midwest. That same year, five Harvard alumni founded a more genteel organization—the Immigration Restriction League—in Boston. They proposed screening immigrants through literacy tests and other standards, to separate the "desirable" from the "undesirable."

Even before the rise of these new organizations, politicians were struggling with the "immigration question." In 1882 Congress had responded to strong anti-Asian sentiment in California and elsewhere and excluded the Chinese. In the same year, Congress denied entry to "undesirables"—

convicts, paupers, the mentally incompetent—and placed a tax of 50 cents on each person admitted. Later legislation of the 1890s enlarged the list of those barred from immigrating and increased the tax.

But these laws kept out only a small number of aliens, and more ambitious restriction proposals made little progress in Congress. That was because immigration was providing a cheap and plentiful labor supply to the rapidly growing economy, and many argued that America's industrial (and indeed agricultural) development would be impossible without it.

The Urban Landscape

The city was a place of remarkable contrasts. It had homes of almost unimaginable size and grandeur and hovels of indescribable squalor. It had conveniences unknown to earlier generations and problems that seemed beyond the capacity of society to solve. Both the attractions and the problems were a result of the stunning pace at which cities were growing. The expansion of the urban population helped spur important new technological and industrial developments. But the rapid growth also produced misgovernment, poverty, congestion, filth, epidemics, and great fires. The rate of growth was simply too fast for planning and building to keep pace.

One of the greatest problems was providing housing for the thousands of new residents who were pouring into the cities every day. For the prosperous, housing was seldom a worry. The availability of cheap labor and the increasing accessibility of tools and materials reduced the cost of building in the late nineteenth century and permitted anyone with even a moderate income to afford a house. Some of the richest urban residents lived in palatial mansions in the heart of the city. Many of the moderately well-to-do took advantage of less expensive land on the edges of the city and settled in new suburbs, linked to the downtowns by trains or streetcars.

Most urban residents, however, could not afford either to own a house in the city or to move to the suburbs. Instead, they stayed in the city centers and rented. Landlords tried to squeeze as many rent-paying residents as possible into the smallest available space. In Manhattan, for example, the average population density in 1894 was 143 people per acre—a rate higher than that of the most crowded cities of Europe (Paris had 127 per acre, Berlin 101) and far higher than that of any other American city then or since. In the cities of the South—Charleston, New Orleans, Richmond—poor blacks lived in crumbling former slave quarters. In Boston, immigrants moved into cheap three-story wooden houses ("triple deckers"), many of them decaying fire hazards. In Baltimore and Philadelphia, the new arrivals crowded into narrow brick row houses. And in New York and many other cities, they lived in tenements.

The word "tenement" had originally referred simply to a multiple-family rental building, but by the late nineteenth century it had become a term for slum dwellings only. The first tenements, built in 1850, had been hailed as a great improvement in housing for the poor. But most were, in fact, miserable places, with many windowless rooms, little or no plumbing or heating, and often a row of privies in the basement. Jacob Riis, a Danish immigrant and New York newspaper reporter and photographer, shocked many middle-class Americans with his sensational (and some claimed sensationalized) descriptions and pictures of tenement life in his 1890 book, *How*

A NEW YORK TENEMENT, 1910 This photograph of a woman and her children in a rear tenement bedroom was meant to illustrate the crowding and squalor of urban immigrant life. The photographer was Lewis Hine, who from 1907 to 1914 worked for a government committee investigating child labor and whose efforts to expose social conditions helped spur legislative action.

the Other Half Lives. But the solution reformers often adopted was simply to raze slum dwellings without building any new housing to replace them.

Urban growth posed monumental transportation challenges. Old downtown streets were often too narrow for the heavy traffic that was beginning to move over them. Most were without a hard, paved surface and resembled either a sea of mud or a cloud of dust, depending on the weather. But it was not simply the conditions of the streets that impeded urban transportation. It was the numbers of people who needed to move every day from one part of the city to another, numbers that mandated the development of mass transportation. Streetcars drawn on tracks by horses had been introduced into some cities even before the Civil War. But the horsecars were not fast enough, so many communities developed new forms of mass transit. In 1870, New York opened its first elevated railway, whose noisy, filthy steam-powered trains moved rapidly above the city streets on massive iron structures. New York, Chicago, San Francisco, and other cities also experimented with cable cars, towed by continuously moving underground cables. Richmond, Virginia, introduced the first electric trolley line in 1888, and in 1897 Boston opened the first American subway. At the same time, cities were developing new techniques of road and bridge building. One of the great technological marvels of the 1880s was the completion of the Brooklyn Bridge in New York—a dramatic steel-cable suspension span designed by John A. Roebling.

Cities were growing upward as well as outward. In Chicago, the construction of the first modern "skyscraper"—by later standards a relatively modest building, ten stories high—launched a new era in urban architecture. Once builders perfected the technique of constructing tall buildings with cast iron and then steel beams, and once other inventors produced the electric elevator, no obstacle remained to even higher buildings.

Strains of Urban Life

The increasing congestion of the city and the absence of adequate public services produced serious hazards. One was fire. In one major city after another, fires destroyed large downtown areas. Chicago and Boston suffered "great fires" in 1871. Other cities—among them Baltimore and San Francisco, where a tremendous earthquake produced a catastrophic fire in 1906—experienced similar disasters. The great fires were terrible experiences, but they were also important events in the development of the cities involved. They encouraged the construction of fireproof buildings and the development of professional fire departments. They also forced cities to rebuild at a time when new technological and architectural innovations were available. Some of the modern, high-rise downtowns of American cities arose out of the rubble of great fires.

An even greater hazard than fire was disease, especially in poor neighborhoods with inadequate sanitation facilities. But an epidemic that began in a poor neighborhood could (and often did) spread easily into other neighborhoods as well. Few municipal officials recognized the relationship of improper sewage disposal and water contamination to such epidemic diseases as typhoid fever and cholera; many cities lacked adequate systems for disposing of human waste until well into the twentieth century.

Above all, perhaps, the expansion of the city spawned widespread and often desperate poverty. Despite the rapid growth of urban economies, the sheer number of new residents ensured that many people would be unable to earn enough for a decent subsistence. Public agencies and private philanthropic organizations offered some relief. But they were generally dominated by middle-class people who believed that too much assistance would breed dependency and that poverty was the fault of the poor themselves.

Poverty and crowding naturally bred crime and violence. The American murder rate rose rapidly in the late nineteenth century (even as such rates were declining in Europe), from 25 murders for every million people in 1880 to over 100 by the end of the century. The rising crime rates encouraged many cities to develop larger and more professional police forces. But police forces themselves could spawn corruption and brutality, particularly since jobs on them were often filled through political patronage.

Americans and Europeans alike reacted to the city with marked ambivalence. It was a place of strong allure and great excitement. Yet it was also a place of alienating impersonality, a new feeling of anonymity, a different kind of work with which the individual could feel only limited identification. To some, it was also a place of degradation and exploitation. Theodore Dreiser's novel *Sister Carrie* (1900) exposed one troubling aspect of urban life: the plight of single women (like Dreiser's heroine, Carrie) who moved from the countryside into the city and found themselves without any means of support. Carrie first took an exhausting and ill-paying job in a Chicago shoe factory; then she drifted into a life of "sin," exploited by predatory men. Many women were experiencing in reality the dilemmas Carrie experienced in fiction. Living in conditions of extreme poverty and hardship, some moved into prostitution—which, degrading and dangerous as it was, produced a livelihood and some sense of community for desperate people.

The Machine and the Boss

Newly arrived immigrants, many of whom could not speak English, were much in need of institutions to help them adjust to American urban life. For many residents of the inner cities, the principal source of assistance was the political "machine."

The urban machine was one of America's most distinctive political institutions. It owed its existence to the power vacuum that the chaotic growth of cities (and the very limited growth of governments) had created. It was also a product of the potential voting power of large immigrant communities. Any politician who could mobilize that power stood to gain enormous influence or public office. And so there emerged a group of "urban" bosses, themselves often of foreign birth or parentage. Many were Irish, because they spoke English and because some had previous political experience from the long Irish struggle against the English at home.

The principal function of the political boss was simple: to win votes for his organization. That meant winning the loyalty of his constituents. To do so, a boss might provide them with occasional relief—a basket of groceries or a bag of coal. He might step in to save those arrested for petty crimes from jail. When he could, he found work for the unemployed. Above all, he rewarded many of his followers with patronage: with jobs in city government or in such city agencies as the police (which the machine's elected officials often controlled); with jobs building or operating the new transit systems; and with opportunities to rise in the political organization itself.

Machines were also vehicles for making money. Politicians enriched themselves and their allies through various forms of graft and corruption. Some of it might be fairly open—what George Washington Plunkitt of New York's Tammany Hall called "honest graft." For example, a politician might discover in advance where a new road or streetcar line was to be built, buy land near it, and sell it at a profit to the city or to developers when property values rose as a result of the construction. There was also covert graft. Officials received kickbacks from contractors in exchange for contracts to build streets, sewers, public buildings, and other projects, and they sold franchises for the operation of such public utilities as street railways, waterworks, and electric light and power systems. The most famously corrupt city boss was William M. Tweed, boss of New York City's Tammany Hall in the 1860s and 1870s, whose extravagant use of public funds on projects that paid kickbacks to the organization finally landed him in jail in 1872.

Middle-class critics cited corruption as the principal characteristic of the machine, but it was also notable for other things. Political organizations contributed to modernizing city infrastructures, to expanding the role of government, and to creating stability in a political and social climate that otherwise would have lacked a center.

Several factors made boss rule possible. One was the power of immigrant voters, who were less concerned with middle-class ideas of political morality than with obtaining the services that machines provided and reformers did not. Another was the link between the political organizations and many wealthy, prominent citizens who profited from their dealings with bosses and resisted efforts to overthrow them.

The urban machine was not without competition. Reform groups frequently mobilized public outrage at the corruption of the bosses and often succeeded in driving machine politicians from office. Tammany, for example, saw its candidates for mayor and other high city offices lose almost as often as they won in the last decades of the nineteenth century. But the reform organizations typically lacked the permanence of the machine, and more often than not, their power faded after a few years.

SOCIETY AND CULTURE IN URBANIZING AMERICA

For urban middle-class Americans, the last decades of the nineteenth century were a time of dramatic advances. Indeed, it was in those years that a distinctive middle-class culture began to exert a powerful influence over the whole of American life. Other groups in society advanced less rapidly, or not at all, but almost no one was unaffected by the rise of the new urban, consumer culture.

The Rise of Mass Consumption

The growth of American industry could not have occurred without the expansion of markets for the goods being produced. Much of the emerging mass market for industrial goods consisted of the increasingly wealthy middle class. But much of it also consisted of less affluent people who consumed more because mass production and mass distribution were making consumer goods less expensive.

Incomes were rising for almost everyone in the industrial era, although at highly uneven rates. The most conspicuous result of the new economy was the creation of vast fortunes, but perhaps the most important result for society as a whole was the growth and increasing prosperity of the middle class. The salaries of clerks, accountants, middle managers, and other "white-collar" workers rose by an average of a third between 1890 and 1910—and in some parts of the middle class, much higher. Doctors, lawyers, and other professionals, for example, experienced a particularly dramatic increase in both the prestige and the profitability of their professions. Working-class incomes rose too in those years, although from a much lower base and often more slowly. The iron and steel industries saw workers' hourly wages increase by a third between 1890 and 1910; but industries with large female work forces—shoes, textiles, and paper—saw more modest increases, as did almost all industries in the South. Wages for African Americans, Mexicans, and Asians also tended to rise more slowly than those for other workers.

The new mass market was also a result of the development of affordable products and the creation of new merchandising techniques, which made many consumer goods available to a mass market for the first time. A good example of such changes was the emergence of ready-made clothing. In the early nineteenth century, most Americans had made their own clothing—usually from cloth they bought from merchants, at times from fabrics they spun and wove themselves. The invention of the sewing machine and the spur that the Civil War (and its demand for uniforms) gave to the manufacture of clothing helped create an enormous industry devoted to producing ready-made garments. By the end of the century, virtually all Americans bought their clothing from stores. Partly as a result, much larger numbers of people became concerned with personal style. Interest in women's fashion, for example, had once been a luxury reserved for the relatively affluent. Now middle-class and even working-class women could strive to develop a distinctive style of dress.

Buying and preparing food also became a critical part of the new consumerism. The development and mass production of tin cans in the 1880s created a large new industry devoted to packaging and selling canned food and condensed milk. Refrigerated railroad cars made it possible for perishables—meats, vegetables, dairy products, and other foodstuffs—to be transported over long distances without spoiling. Artificially frozen ice enabled many households to afford iceboxes. Among other things, the changes meant improved diets and better health. Life expectancy rose six years in the first two decades of the twentieth century.

Changes in marketing also altered the way Americans bought goods. New "chain stores" could usually offer a wider array of goods at lower prices than the small local stores with which they competed. The Atlantic and Pacific Tea Company (the A & P) began a national network of grocery stores

THE DEPARTMENT STORE, C. 1892 This detail from an advertisement shows an interior cross section of the Abraham and Straus department store in Brooklyn, New York. Early department stores boasted not just of the variety of their merchandise but also of the almost magical consumer world they created.

in the 1870s. F. W. Woolworth built a chain of dry goods stores. Sears and Roebuck established a large market for its mail-order merchandise by distributing an enormous catalog each year. Even people in remote rural areas could order its products.

In larger cities, the emergence of great department stores helped transform buying habits and turn shopping into a more alluring and glamorous activity. Marshall Field in Chicago created one of the first American department stores—a place deliberately designed to produce a sense of wonder and excitement. Similar stores emerged in New York, Brooklyn, Boston, Philadelphia, and other cities.

The rise of mass consumption had particularly dramatic effects on American women, who were generally the primary consumers within families. Women's clothing styles changed much more rapidly and dramatically than those of men. Women generally bought and prepared food for their families, so the availability of new food products changed not only the way everyone ate but the way women shopped and cooked. Canning and refrigeration meant greater variety in the diet. It also meant that food did not always have to be purchased on the day it was eaten. The consumer economy also produced new employment opportunities for women as salesclerks in department stores and as waitresses in rapidly proliferating restaurants. And it spawned the creation of a new movement in which women were to play a vital role: the consumer protection movement. The National Consumers

League, formed in the 1890s under the leadership of Florence Kelley, attempted to mobilize the power of women as consumers to force retailers and manufacturers to improve wages and working conditions.

Leisure and Sport

Closely related to the growth of consumption was a growing interest in leisure time, which for many people was increasing rapidly. Members of the urban middle and professional classes had large blocks of time during which they were not at work—evenings, weekends, even paid vacations. Working hours in many factories declined, from an average of nearly seventy hours a week in 1860 to under sixty in 1900. Even farmers found that the mechanization of agriculture gave them more free time. The lives of many Americans were becoming more compartmentalized, with clear distinctions between work and leisure that had not existed in the past. The change produced a search for new forms of recreation and entertainment.

Among the most important responses to this search was the rise of organized spectator sports, and especially baseball, which by the end of the century was well on its way to becoming the "national pastime." A game much like baseball—known as "rounders" and derived from cricket—had enjoyed limited popularity in Great Britain in the early nineteenth century. Versions of the game began to appear in America in the early 1830s, well before Abner Doubleday supposedly "invented" baseball. (Doubleday, in fact, had almost nothing to do with the creation of baseball and actually cared little for sports. Alexander Cartwright, a member of a New York City baseball club, defined many of the rules and features of the game as we know it today in the 1840s.)

By the end of the Civil War, interest in the game had grown rapidly. More than 200 amateur or semiprofessional teams and clubs existed, many of which joined a national association and proclaimed a set of standard rules. As the game grew in popularity, it offered opportunities for profit. The first salaried team, the Cincinnati Red Stockings, was formed in 1869. Other cities soon fielded professional teams, and in 1876 the teams banded together in the National League. A rival league, the American Association, soon appeared. It eventually collapsed, but in 1901 the American League emerged to replace it. And in 1903, the first modern World Series was played, in which the American League Boston Red Sox beat the National League Pittsburgh Pirates. By then, baseball had become an important business and a great national preoccupation (at least among men), attracting paying crowds at times as large as 50,000.

Baseball had great appeal to working-class males. The second most popular game, football, appealed at first to a more elite segment of the male population, in part because it originated in colleges and universities. The first intercollegiate football game in America occurred between Princeton and Rutgers in 1869, and soon the game began to become entrenched as part of collegiate life. Early intercollegiate football bore only an indirect relation to the modern game; it was more similar to what is now known as rugby. By the late 1870s, however, the game was becoming standardized and was taking on the outlines of its modern form.

Basketball was invented in 1891 at Springfield, Massachusetts, by Dr. James A. Naismith, a Canadian working as athletic director for a local college. Boxing, which had long been a disreputable activity concentrated primarily among the urban lower classes, became by the 1880s a more popular and in some places more reputable sport.

The major spectator sports of the era were activities open almost exclusively to men. But a number of other sports were emerging in which women became important participants. Golf and tennis seldom attracted crowds in the late nineteenth century, but both experienced a rapid increase in participation among relatively wealthy men and women. Bicycling and croquet also enjoyed widespread popularity in the 1890s among women as well as men. Women's colleges introduced their students to more strenuous sports as well—track, crew, swimming, and (beginning in the late 1890s) basketball—challenging the once-prevalent notion that vigorous exercise was dangerous to women.

Leisure and Popular Culture

Other forms of popular entertainment developed in the cities in response to the large potential markets there. Many ethnic communities maintained their own theaters, in which immigrants heard the music of their homelands and listened to comedians making light of their experiences in the New World. Urban theaters also introduced some of the most distinctively American entertainment forms: the musical comedy, which evolved gradually from the comic operettas of European theater; and vaudeville, a form of theater adapted from French models, which remained the most popular urban entertainment in the first decades of the twentieth century. Even saloons and small community theaters could afford to offer their customers vaudeville, which consisted of a variety of acts (musicians, comedians, magicians, jugglers, and others) and was, at least in the beginning, inexpensive to produce. As the economic potential of vaudeville grew, some promoters—most prominently Florenz Ziegfeld of New York—staged much more elaborate spectacles.

Vaudeville was also one of the few entertainment media open to black performers. They brought to it elements of the minstrel shows they had earlier developed for black audiences in the late nineteenth century. Some minstrel singers (including the most famous, Al Jolson) were whites wearing heavy makeup (or "blackface"), but most were black. Entertainers of both races performed music based on the gospel and folk tunes of the plantation and on the jazz and ragtime of black urban communities. Performers of both races also tailored their acts to prevailing white prejudices, ridiculing blacks by acting out demeaning stereotypes.

The most important form of mass entertainment (until the invention of radio and television), and the one that reached most widely across the nation, was the movies. Thomas Edison and others had created the technology of the motion picture in the 1880s. Soon after that, short films became available to individual viewers watching peepshows in pool halls, penny ar-

A NICKELODEON An early movie theater, with musicians providing a live accompaniment to a silent film. The first feature-length sound picture (or "talkie"), *The Jazz Singer*, appeared in 1927.

cades, and amusement parks. Soon, larger projectors made it possible to project the images onto big screens, which permitted substantial audiences to see films in theaters. By 1900, Americans were becoming attracted in large numbers to these early movies—usually plotless films of trains or waterfalls or other spectacles designed mainly to show off the technology. The great D. W. Griffith carried the motion picture into a new era with his silent epics—*The Birth of a Nation* (1915), *Intolerance* (1916), and others—which introduced serious (if notoriously racist) plots and elaborate productions to filmmaking. Motion pictures were the first truly mass entertainment medium—one that reached all areas of the country and most groups in the population.

Particularly striking about popular entertainment in the late nineteenth and early twentieth centuries was its public quality. Many Americans spent their leisure time in places where they would find not only entertainment but also other people. Thousands of working-class New Yorkers flocked to the amusement park at Coney Island, for example, not just for the rides and shows but for the excitement of the crowds, as did the thousands who spent evenings in dance halls, vaudeville houses, and concert halls. More affluent New Yorkers enjoyed afternoons in Central Park, where a principal attraction was seeing other people (and being seen by them). Moviegoers were attracted not just by the movies themselves but by the energy of the audiences at the lavish "movie palaces" that began to appear in cities in the early twentieth century, just as sports fans were drawn by the crowds as well as by the games.

Mass entertainment did not usually bridge differences of class or race; there were relatively few places where people of widely diverse backgrounds gathered together. When members of different classes or races did meet in public spaces—as they did, for example, in city parks—there was often considerable conflict over what constituted appropriate public behavior. Elites in New York City, for example, tried to prohibit anything but quiet, "genteel" activities in Central Park, while working-class people wanted to use the public spaces for sports and entertainments. But even divided by class, new forms of popular entertainment helped sustain a vigorous public culture.

Not all popular entertainment, however, involved public events. Many Americans amused themselves privately by reading novels and poetry. The so-called dime novels, cheaply bound and widely circulated, became popular after the Civil War, with detective stories, tales of the "Wild West," sagas of scientific adventure (such as the Tom Swift stories), and novels of "moral uplift" (among them those of Horatio Alger). Publishers also distributed sentimental novels of romance, which developed a large audience among women, as did books about animals and about young children growing up. Louisa May Alcott's *Little Women*, most of whose readers were women, sold more than 2 million copies.

Mass Communications

Urban-industrial society created a vast market for news and information. And so American publishing and journalism experienced an important change in the decades following the Civil War. Between 1870 and 1910, the circulation of daily newspapers increased nearly ninefold (from under 3 million to more than 24 million), a rate three times as great as the rate of population increase. And while standards varied widely from one paper to another, American journalism was developing the beginnings of a professional identity. Salaries of reporters increased; many newspapers began separating the reporting of news from the expression of opinion; and newspapers themselves became important businesses.

One striking change was the emergence of national press services, which made use of the telegraph to supply papers throughout the country with news and features and which contributed, as a result, to a standardization of the product. By the turn of the century important newspaper chains had emerged as well. The most powerful was owned by William Randolph Hearst, who by 1914 controlled nine newspapers and two magazines. Hearst and rival publisher Joseph Pulitzer helped popularize what became known as "yellow journalism"—a deliberately sensational, even lurid, style of reporting presented in bold graphics, designed to reach a mass audience uninterested in the sober, detailed reporting of more traditional newspapers.

Another major change occurred in the nature of American magazines. Beginning in the 1880s, a new kind of magazine appeared, designed to achieve a mass circulation. One of the pioneers in this field was Edward W. Bok, who took over the *Ladies' Home Journal* in 1899 and, by targeting a mass female audience, built the circulation of the journal to over 700,000.

HIGH CULTURE IN THE URBAN AGE

In addition to the important changes in popular culture that accompanied the rise of cities and industry, there were profound changes in the realm of "high culture"—in the ideas and activities of intellectuals and elites. Even the idea of a distinction between "highbrow" and "lowbrow" culture was largely new to the industrial era. In the early nineteenth century, most cultural activities had attracted people of widely varying backgrounds and targeted people of all classes. By the late nineteenth century, however, elites were developing a cultural and intellectual life quite separate from the popular amusements of the urban masses.

The Literature of Urban America

The high culture of late-nineteenth-century America was shaped profoundly by the growth of industry and the rise of the city. Some writers and artists—the local-color writers of the South, for example, and Mark Twain, in such novels as *Huckleberry Finn* and *Tom Sawyer*—responded to the new civilization by evoking an older, more natural world. But others grappled directly with the modern, urban order.

One of the strongest impulses in late-nineteenth- and early-twentieth-century American literature was the effort to re-create urban social reality. This trend toward realism found an early voice in Stephen Crane, who—although best known for his novel of the Civil War, *The Red Badge of Courage* (1895)—created a sensation in 1893 when he published *Maggie: A Girl of the Streets*, a grim picture of urban poverty and slum life. Theodore Dreiser, Frank Norris, and Upton Sinclair—whose 1906 novel, *The Jungle*, inspired federal legislation with its exposure of abuses in the meatpacking industry—were similarly drawn to social issues as themes. Kate Chopin, a southern writer who explored the oppressive features of traditional marriage, encountered widespread public abuse (and in some places formal bans) after publication of her shocking novel, *The Awakening*, in 1899. It described a young wife and mother who abandoned her family in search of personal fulfillment. William Dean Howells, in *The Rise of Silas Lapham* and other works, described what he considered the shallowness and corruption in ordinary American lifestyles.

Other critics of American society responded to the new civilization not by attacking it but by withdrawing from it. The historian Henry Adams published an autobiography in 1906, *The Education of Henry Adams*, which portrayed a man disillusioned with and unable to relate to his society, even though he continued to live in it. The novelist Henry James lived the major part of his adult life in England and Europe and produced a series of coldly realistic novels—*The American* (1877), *Portrait of a Lady* (1881), *The Ambassadors* (1903), and others—that showed his ambivalence about the merits of both American and European civilization.

Art in the Age of the City

American art through most of the nineteenth century had been overshadowed by the art of Europe. By 1900, however, a number of American artists, although some continued to study and even live in Europe, broke from the Old World traditions and experimented with new styles. Winslow Homer was vigorously American in his paintings of New England maritime life and other native subjects. James McNeil Whistler was one of the first western artists to appreciate the beauty of Japanese color prints and to introduce Oriental themes into American and European art.

By the first years of the new century, some American artists were turning decisively away from the traditional academic style (a style perhaps best

EDWARD HOPPER, *AUTOMAT* Edward Hopper was one of a growing group of American painters in the early twentieth century who chose to chronicle not the world of wealth and power, the characteristic subject of earlier artists, but the harsh, gritty world of the modern city. Hopper's work was distinctive for its evocation of the loneliness of urban life. This 1927 painting of a scene in an "automat" in New York City is characteristic of his work.

exemplified in America by the brilliant portraitist John Singer Sargent). Instead, many younger painters were exploring the same grim aspects of modern life that were becoming the subject of American literature. Members of the so-called Ashcan School produced work startling in its naturalism and stark in its portrayal of the social realities of the era. John Sloan portrayed the dreariness of American urban slums; George Bellows caught the vigor and violence of his time in paintings and drawings of prizefights; Edward Hopper explored the starkness and loneliness of the modern city. The Ashcan artists were also among the first Americans to appreciate expressionism and abstraction; and they showed their interest in new forms in 1913 when they helped stage the famous "Armory Show" in New York City, which displayed works of the French postimpressionists and of some American moderns.

The work of these and other artists marked the beginning in America of an artistic movement known as modernism, a movement that had counterparts in many other areas of cultural and intellectual life as well. Rejecting the heavy reliance on established forms that characterized the "genteel tradition" of the nineteenth-century art world, modernists embraced new subjects and new forms. The genteel tradition emphasized the "dignified" and "elevated" aspects of civilization (and glorified the achievements of gifted elites); modernism gloried in the ordinary, even the coarse. The genteel tradition placed great importance on respect for the past and maintenance of "standards"; modernism looked to the future and gloried in the new. Eventually, modernism developed strict orthodoxies of its own. But in its early stages, it seemed to promise an escape from rigid, formal traditions and an unleashing of individual creativity.

The Impact of Darwinism

The single most profound intellectual development in the late nineteenth century was the widespread acceptance of the theory of evolution, associated most prominently with the English naturalist Charles Darwin. Darwinism argued that the human species had evolved from earlier forms of life (and most immediately from simian creatures similar to apes) through a process of "natural selection." History, Darwinism suggested, was not the working out of a divine plan, as most Americans had always believed. It was a random process dominated by the fiercest or luckiest competitors.

The theory of evolution met widespread resistance at first from educators, theologians, and even many scientists. By the end of the century, however, the evolutionists had converted most members of the urban professional and educated classes. Even many middle-class Protestant religious leaders had accepted the doctrine, making significant alterations in theology to accommodate it. Evolution had become enshrined in schools and universities; virtually no serious scientist any longer questioned its basic validity. Unseen by most urban Americans at the time, however, the rise of Darwinism was contributing to a deep schism between the new, cosmopolitan culture of the city—which was receptive to new ideas such as evolution—and the more traditional, provincial culture of some rural areas—which remained wedded to fundamentalist religious beliefs and older values. Thus the late nineteenth century saw not only the rise of a liberal Protestantism in tune with new scientific discoveries but also the beginning of an organized Protestant fundamentalism, which would make its presence felt politically in the 1920s and beyond.

Darwinism helped spawn other new intellectual currents. There was the Social Darwinism of William Graham Sumner and others, which industrialists used so enthusiastically to justify their favored position in American life. But there were also more sophisticated philosophies, among them a doctrine that became known as "pragmatism," which reflected Darwinism's rejection of inherited ideas and its emphasis on scientific research. William James, a Harvard psychologist (and brother of the novelist Henry James), was the most prominent publicist of the new theory, although earlier intellectuals such as Charles S. Peirce and later ones such as John Dewey were also important to its development and dissemination. According to the pragmatists, modern society should rely for guidance not on inherited ideals and moral principles but on the test of scientific inquiry. No idea or institution (not even religious faith) was valid, they claimed, unless it worked, unless it stood the test of experience.

A similar concern for scientific inquiry was intruding into the social sciences and challenging traditional orthodoxies. Sociologists such as Edward A. Ross and Lester Frank Ward urged applying the scientific method to the solution of social and political problems. Historians such as Frederick Jackson Turner and Charles Beard argued that economic factors more than spiritual ideals had been the governing force in historical development. John Dewey proposed a new approach to education that placed less emphasis on the rote learning of traditional knowledge and more on a flexible, democratic approach to schooling, one that enabled students to acquire knowledge that would help them deal with the realities of their society.

The implications of Darwinism also promoted the growth of anthropology and encouraged some scholars to begin examining other cultures—

most significantly, perhaps, the culture of American Indians—in new ways. Some white Americans began to look at Indian society as a coherent culture with its own norms and values that were worthy of respect and preservation, even though they were different from those of white society.

Toward Universal Schooling

A society increasingly dependent on specialized skills and scientific knowledge was, of course, a society with a high demand for education. The late nineteenth century, therefore, was a time of rapid expansion and reform of American schools and universities.

One example was the spread of free public primary and secondary education. In 1860, there were only 100 public high schools in the entire United States. By 1900, the number had reached 6,000 and by 1914 over 12,000. By 1900, compulsory school attendance laws were in effect in thirty-one states and territories. But education was still far from universal. Rural areas lagged far behind urban-industrial ones in funding public education. And in the South, many blacks had access to no schools at all.

Educational reformers sought to provide educational opportunities to the Indian tribes as well, in an effort to "civilize" them and help them adapt to white society. In the 1870s, reformers recruited small groups of Indians to attend Hampton Institute (a primarily black college). In 1879 they organized the Carlisle Indian Industrial School in Pennsylvania. Like many black colleges, Carlisle emphasized the kind of practical "industrial" education that Booker T. Washington had urged on blacks. Ultimately, however, these reform efforts failed, partly because of inadequate funding and commitment and partly because the venture itself—the effort to remove Indians from their traditional surroundings and transform them into members of white society—was unpopular with its intended beneficiaries.

Colleges and universities were also proliferating rapidly in the late nineteenth century. They benefited particularly from the Morrill Land Grant Act of the Civil War era, by which the federal government had donated land to states for the establishment of colleges. After 1865, states in the South and West took particular advantage of the law. In all, sixty-nine "land-grant" institutions were established in the last decades of the century—among them the state university systems of California, Illinois, Minnesota, and Wisconsin. Other universities benefited from millions of dollars contributed by business and financial tycoons. Rockefeller, Carnegie, and others gave generously to such schools as Columbia, Chicago, Harvard, Northwestern,

Princeton, Syracuse, and Yale. Other philanthropists founded new universities or reorganized older ones and perpetuated their family names—Vanderbilt, Johns Hopkins, Cornell, Duke, Tulane, and Stanford.

Education for Women

The post–Civil War era saw, too, an important expansion of educational opportunities for women, although such opportunities continued to lag far behind those available to men and were almost without exception denied to black women.

Most public high schools accepted women readily, but opportunities for higher education were fewer. At the end of the Civil War, only three American colleges were coeducational. In the years after the war, many of the land-grant colleges and universities in the Midwest and such private universities as Cornell and Wesleyan began to admit women along with men. But coeducation was less crucial to women's education in this period than was the creation of a network of women's colleges. Mount Holyoke in central Massachusetts had begun its life in 1836 as a "seminary" for women; it became a full-fledged college in the 1880s, at about the same time that entirely new female institutions were emerging: Vassar, Wellesley, Smith, Bryn Mawr, Wells, and Goucher. A few of the larger private universities created separate colleges for women on their campuses (Barnard at Columbia and Radcliffe at Harvard, for example). Proponents of women's colleges saw the institutions as places where female students would not be treated as "second-class citizens" by predominantly male student bodies and faculties.

The female college was part of an important phenomenon in the history of modern American women: the emergence of distinctive women's communities. Most faculty members and many administrators were women (usually unmarried). And the life of the college produced a spirit of sorority and commitment among educated women that had important effects in later years, as women became the leaders of many reform activities. Most female college graduates ultimately married, but they married at a more advanced age than their noncollege counterparts. A significant minority, perhaps over 25 percent, did not marry at all, but devoted themselves to careers. The growth of female higher education clearly became for some women a liberating experience, persuading them that they had roles to perform in their rapidly changing urban-industrial society other than as wives and mothers.

CHAPTER NINETEEN

From Stalemate to Crisis

The Politics of Equilibrium ~ *The Agrarian Revolt*
The Crisis of the 1890s

THE ENORMOUS CHANGES America was experiencing in the late nineteenth century strained not only the nation's traditional social arrangements but its political institutions as well. Industrialization and urbanization were responsible for considerable progress and substantial achievements. They also produced disorder and despair. Gradually, Americans began to look to government for leadership in their search for stability and social justice.

Yet American government during much of this period was ill equipped to deal with the new challenges confronting it. In the face of unprecedented dilemmas, it responded with apparent passivity and confusion. Its leaders, for the most part, seemed political mediocrities. The issues with which it was concerned generally had little to do with the nation's most important problems. Rather than taking active leadership of America's dramatic transformation, the American political system for nearly two decades after the end of Reconstruction (a period sometimes described by a phrase Mark Twain coined for it, "the Gilded Age") was locked in a rigid stalemate—watching the remarkable changes that were occurring in the nation and doing relatively little to affect them. The result was a set of problems and grievances that festered and grew without any natural outlet. It was not surprising, under the circumstances, that in the 1890s the United States entered a period of national crisis.

THE POLITICS OF EQUILIBRIUM

To modern eyes, the nature of the American political system in the late nineteenth century appears in many ways paradoxical. The two political parties enjoyed a strength and stability during those years that neither was ever to

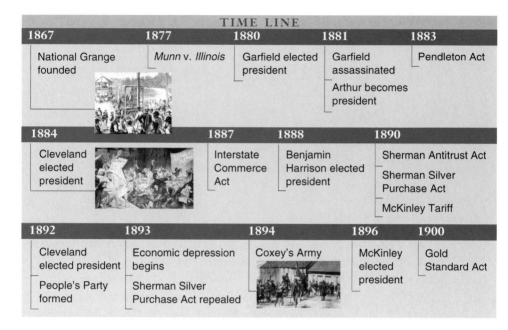

TIME LINE

1867	1877	1880	1881	1883
National Grange founded	*Munn* v. *Illinois*	Garfield elected president	Garfield assassinated Arthur becomes president	Pendleton Act

1884	1887	1888	1890
Cleveland elected president	Interstate Commerce Act	Benjamin Harrison elected president	Sherman Antitrust Act Sherman Silver Purchase Act McKinley Tariff

1892	1893	1894	1896	1900
Cleveland elected president People's Party formed	Economic depression begins Sherman Silver Purchase Act repealed	Coxey's Army	McKinley elected president	Gold Standard Act

know again. And yet the federal government, which the two parties were struggling to control, was doing relatively little of importance. In fact, most Americans in those years engaged in political activity not because of an interest in particular issues but because of broad regional, ethnic, or religious sentiments. Party loyalty had less to do with positions on public policy than with the way Americans defined themselves socially and culturally.

The Party System

The most striking feature of the late-nineteenth-century party system was its remarkable stability. From the end of Reconstruction until the late 1890s, the electorate was divided almost precisely evenly between the Republicans and the Democrats. Loyalties fluctuated almost not at all. Sixteen states were solidly and consistently Republican, and fourteen states (most of them in the South) were solidly and consistently Democratic. Only five states (the most important of them New York and Ohio) were usually in doubt, and their voters generally decided the results of national elections, often on the basis of voter turnout. The Republican Party captured the presidency in all but two of the elections of the era, but the party was not really as dominant as those victories suggest. In the five presidential elections beginning in

1876, the average popular-vote margin separating the Democratic and Republican candidates was 1.5 percent. The congressional balance was similarly stable, with the Republicans generally controlling the Senate and the Democrats generally controlling the House.

As striking as the balance between the parties was the intensity of public loyalty to them. In most of the country, Americans viewed their party affiliations with a passion and enthusiasm that is difficult for later generations to understand. Voter turnout in presidential elections between 1860 and 1900 averaged over 78 percent of all eligible voters (as compared with only slightly over 50 percent in the 1980s and 1990s). Even in nonpresidential years, from 60 to 80 percent of the voters turned out to cast ballots for congressional candidates. Large groups of potential voters were disfranchised in these years: women in most states; almost all blacks and many poor whites in the South. But for adult white males outside the South, there were few franchise restrictions. The remarkable turnout represented a genuinely mass-based politics.

What explains this extraordinary loyalty to the two political parties? It was not, certainly, because the parties took distinct positions on important public issues. They did so rarely. Party loyalties reflected other factors. Region was perhaps the most important. To white southerners, loyalty to the Democratic Party was a matter of unquestioned faith. It was the vehicle by which they had triumphed over Reconstruction, the vehicle by which they preserved white supremacy. To many northerners, white and black, Republican loyalties were equally intense for the opposite reason. The party of Lincoln remained what it had been during the Civil War: a bulwark against slavery and treason.

Religious and ethnic differences also shaped party loyalties. The Democratic Party attracted most of the Catholic voters, most of the recent immigrants, and most of the poorer workers; those three groups, of course, often overlapped. The Republican Party appealed to northern Protestants, citizens of old stock, and much of the middle class; those groups, too, had considerable overlap. Among the few substantive issues on which the parties took clearly different stands were matters connected with immigrants. Republicans tended to support measures restricting immigration and to favor temperance legislation, which many believed would help discipline immigrant communities. Catholics and immigrants viewed such proposals as assaults on them and their cultures and opposed them; the Democratic Party followed their lead.

Party identification, then, was usually more a reflection of cultural inclinations than a calculation of economic interest. Individuals might affiliate with a party because their parents had done so, or because it was the party of their region, their church, or their ethnic group. Most clung to their party loyalties with great persistence and passion.

The National Government

One reason the two parties managed to avoid substantive issues was that the federal government (and for the most part state and local governments as well) did relatively little. The government in Washington was responsible for delivering the mails, for maintaining a national military, for conducting foreign policy, and for collecting tariffs and taxes. It had few other responsibilities and few institutions with which it could have undertaken additional responsibilities even if it had chosen to do so.

There was one significant exception. From the end of the Civil War to the early twentieth century, the federal government administered a system of annual pensions for Union Civil War veterans who had retired from work and for their widows. At its peak, this pension system was making payments to a majority of the male citizens (black and white) of the North and to many women as well. Some reformers hoped to make the system permanent and universal; they pressured the government to create a system of old-age pensions for all Americans. But their efforts failed. That was in part because the Civil War pension system was awash in party patronage and corruption. Other reformers—believers in "good government"—saw elimination of the pension system as a way to fight graft, corruption, and party rule. When the Civil War generation died out, the pension system died with it.

In most other respects, the United States in the late nineteenth century was a society without a modern, national government. The most powerful national political institutions were the two political parties (and the bosses and machines that dominated them) and the federal courts. The national leaders of both parties were primarily concerned not with policy but with office—with winning elections and controlling patronage.

Presidents and Patronage

The power of party bosses had an important effect on the power of the presidency. The office had great symbolic importance, but its occupants were unable to do very much except distribute government appointments. A new president and his tiny staff had to make almost 100,000 appointments (most of them in the post office, the only really large government agency); and even in that function, presidents had limited latitude, since they had to avoid offending the various factions within their own parties.

Sometimes that proved impossible, as the presidency of Rutherford B. Hayes (1877–1881) demonstrated. By the end of his term, two groups—the Stalwarts, led by Roscoe Conkling of New York, and the Half-Breeds, captained by James G. Blaine of Maine—were competing for control of the Republican Party and threatening to split it. The dispute between the Stalwarts and the Half-Breeds was characteristic of the political battles of the era. It had little basis in substance. Rhetorically, the Stalwarts favored traditional, professional machine politics, while the Half-Breeds favored reform. In fact,

REVOLT AMONG REPUBLICANS Many Republican reformers, believers in "good government," were aghast when their party nominated James G. Blaine for president in 1884. Blaine, a former Speaker of the House, U.S. senator, and secretary of state, was the leader of the "Half-Breed" faction of the party, the faction that claimed to support cautious reform. But he was controversial even among reformers after a long career of wily political maneuvering and because of the scandals that continually attached themselves to his name. This cartoon by Joseph Keppler in the political magazine *Puck* shows Republican leaders responding with horror to "the writing on the wall," and to the dire consequences they believed would follow the nomination of Blaine. Blaine himself, at left, hides behind the *New York Herald-Tribune*, the principal organ of the reformers and a critic of Blaine.

both groups were mainly interested in a larger share of the patronage pie. Hayes tried to satisfy both and ended up satisfying neither.

The battle over patronage overshadowed all else during Hayes's unhappy presidency. His one important substantive initiative—an effort to create a civil service system—attracted no support from either party. And his early announcement that he would not seek reelection only weakened him further. He had virtually no power in Congress. The Democrats controlled the House throughout his presidency and the Senate during the last two years of his term. And Senate Republicans, led by Roscoe Conkling, opposed his efforts to defy the machines in making appointments. (His popularity with politicians in Washington was not enhanced by the unwillingness of his wife, a temperance advocate widely known as "Lemonade Lucy," to permit alcoholic beverages to be served in the White House.) Hayes's presidency was a study in frustration.

The Republicans managed to retain the presidency in 1880 in part because they managed to agree on a ticket that included a Stalwart and a Half-Breed. After a long convention deadlock, they nominated James A. Garfield, a veteran congressman from Ohio and a Half-Breed, for president and Chester A. Arthur of New York, a Stalwart and Conkling henchman, for vice president. The Democrats nominated General Winfield Scott Hancock, a minor Civil War commander with no national following. Benefiting from the end of the recession of 1879, Garfield won a decisive electoral victory, although his popular-vote margin was very thin. The Republicans also captured both houses of Congress.

Garfield began his presidency by trying to defy the Stalwarts in his appointments and by showing support for civil service reform. He soon found himself embroiled in an ugly public quarrel with both Conkling and other Stalwarts. It was never resolved. On July 2, 1881, only four months after his inauguration, Garfield was shot twice while standing in the Washington railroad station by an apparently deranged gunman (and unsuccessful office seeker) who shouted, "I am a Stalwart and Arthur is president now!" Garfield lingered for nearly three months but finally died, a victim as much of inept medical treatment as of the wounds themselves.

Chester A. Arthur, who succeeded Garfield, had spent a political lifetime as a devoted, skilled, and open spoilsman and a close ally of Roscoe Conkling. But on becoming president, he tried—like Hayes and Garfield before him—to follow an independent course and even to promote reform, aware no doubt that the Garfield assassination had to some degree discredited the traditional spoils system. To the dismay of the Stalwarts, Arthur kept most of Garfield's appointees in office and supported civil service reform, aware that the legislation was likely to pass whether he supported it or not. In 1883, Congress passed the first national civil service measure, the Pendleton Act, which required that some federal jobs be filled by competitive written examinations rather than by patronage. Relatively few offices fell under civil service at first, but its reach extended steadily so that by the mid-twentieth century most federal employees were civil servants.

Cleveland, Harrison, and the Tariff

In the unsavory election of 1884, the Republican candidate for president was Senator James G. Blaine of Maine—known to his adoring admirers as "the Plumed Knight" but to thousands of other Americans as a symbol of seamy party politics. A group of disgruntled "liberal Republicans," known derisively by their critics as the "mugwumps," announced they would bolt the party and support an honest Democrat. Rising to the bait, the Democrats nominated Grover Cleveland, the "reform" governor of New York. He differed from Blaine on no substantive issues but had acquired a reputation as an enemy of corruption.

In a campaign filled with personal invective, what may have decided the election was the last-minute introduction of a religious controversy. Shortly before the election, a delegation of Protestant ministers called on Blaine in New York City; their spokesman, Dr. Samuel Burchard, referred to the Democrats as the party of "rum, Romanism, and rebellion." Blaine was slow to repudiate Burchard's indiscretion, and Democrats quickly spread the news that Blaine had tolerated a slander on the Catholic Church. Cleveland's narrow victory was probably a result of an unusually heavy Catholic vote for the Democrats in New York. Cleveland won 219 electoral votes to Blaine's 182; his popular margin was only 23,000.

Grover Cleveland was respected, if not often liked, for his stern and righteous opposition to politicians, grafters, pressure groups, and Tammany Hall. He had become famous as the "veto governor," as an official who was not afraid to say no. He was the embodiment of an era in which few Americans believed the federal government could, or should, do very much. Cleveland had always doubted the wisdom of protective tariffs (taxes on imported goods designed to protect domestic producers). The existing high rates, he believed, were responsible for the annual surplus in federal revenues, which was tempting Congress to pass "reckless" and "extravagant" legislation, which he frequently vetoed. In December 1887, therefore, he asked Congress to reduce the tariff rates. Democrats in the House approved a tariff reduction, but Senate Republicans defiantly passed a bill of their own actually raising the rates. The resulting deadlock made the tariff an issue in the election of 1888.

The Democrats renominated Cleveland and supported tariff reductions. The Republicans settled on former senator Benjamin Harrison of Indiana, who was obscure but respectable (and the grandson of President William Henry Harrison); and they endorsed protection. The campaign was the first since the Civil War to involve a clear question of economic difference between the parties. It was also one of the most corrupt (and one of the closest) elections in American history. Harrison won an electoral majority of 233 to 168, but Cleveland's popular vote exceeded Harrison's by 100,000.

Changing Issues

Benjamin Harrison's record as president was little more substantial than that of his grandfather, who had died a month after taking office. Harrison had few visible convictions, and he made no effort to influence Congress. And yet during Harrison's passive administration, public opinion was beginning to force the government to confront some of the pressing social and economic issues of the day. Most notably, perhaps, sentiment was rising in favor of legislation to curb the power of trusts.

By the mid-1880s, fifteen western and southern states had adopted laws prohibiting combinations that restrained competition. But corporations found it easy to escape limitations by incorporating in states such as New Jersey and Delaware that offered them special privileges. If antitrust legislation was to be effective, its supporters believed, it would have to come from the national government. Responding to growing popular demands, both houses of Congress passed the Sherman Antitrust Act in July 1890, almost without dissent. Most members of Congress saw the act as a largely symbolic measure, one that would help deflect public criticism but was not likely to have any real effect on corporate power. And for over a decade after its passage, the Sherman Act—indifferently enforced and steadily weakened by the courts—had virtually no impact. As of 1901, the Justice Department had instituted many antitrust suits against unions, but only fourteen against business combinations; there had been few convictions.

The Republicans were more interested, however, in the issue they believed had won them the 1888 election: the tariff. Representative William McKinley of Ohio and Senator Nelson W. Aldrich of Rhode Island drafted the highest protective measure ever proposed to Congress. Known as the McKinley Act, it became law in October 1890. But Republican leaders apparently misinterpreted public sentiment, for the party suffered a stunning reversal in the 1890 congressional election. The Republicans' substantial Senate majority was slashed to 8; in the House, the party retained only 88 of the 323 seats. McKinley himself was among those who went down to defeat. Nor were the Republicans able to recover in the course of the next two years. In the presidential election of 1892, Benjamin Harrison once again supported protection; Grover Cleveland, renominated by the Democrats, once again opposed it. A new third party, the People's Party, with James B. Weaver as its candidate, advocated more substantial economic reform. Cleveland won 277 electoral votes to Harrison's 145 and had a popular margin of 380,000. Weaver showed some significant strength, but still ran far behind. For the first time since 1878, the Democrats won a majority of both houses of Congress.

The policies of Cleveland's second term were much like those of his first—devoted to minimal government and hostile to active efforts to deal with social or economic problems. Again, he supported a tariff reduction, which the House approved but the Senate weakened. Cleveland denounced the result but allowed it to become law as the Wilson-Gorman Tariff. It included only a few, very modest reductions.

But public pressure was growing in the 1880s for other reforms, among them regulation of the railroads. Farm organizations in the Midwest (most notably the Grangers) had persuaded several state legislatures to pass regulatory legislation in the early 1870s. But in 1886, the Supreme Court—in *Wabash, St. Louis, and Pacific Railway Co.* v. *Illinois*, known as the *Wabash* case—ruled one of the Granger Laws in Illinois unconstitutional. According to the Court, the law was an attempt to control interstate commerce and thus infringed on the exclusive power of Congress. Later, the courts limited the powers of the states to regulate commerce even within their own boundaries.

Effective railroad regulation, it was now clear, could come only from the federal government. Congress grudgingly responded to public pressure in 1887 with the Interstate Commerce Act, which banned discrimination in rates between long and short hauls, required that railroads publish their rate schedules and file them with the government, and declared that all interstate rail rates must be "reasonable and just"—although the act did not define what that meant. A five-person agency, the Interstate Commerce Commission (ICC), was to administer the act. But it had to rely on the courts to enforce its rulings. For almost twenty years after its passage, the Interstate Commerce Act—which was, like the Sherman Act, haphazardly enforced and narrowly interpreted by the courts—was without much practical effect.

The agitation over the tariff, the trusts, and the railroads was a sign that the dramatic changes in the American economy were creating problems that much of the public considered too important and dangerous to ignore. But the federal government lacked both the will and the institutional capacity to respond effectively to those problems. The effort to create a government capable of doing more would dominate much of American public life in the coming decades. That effort first became visible in a dramatic dissident movement that helped shatter the political equilibrium the nation had experienced for the previous twenty years.

THE AGRARIAN REVOLT

No group watched the performance of the federal government in the 1880s with more dismay than American farmers. Isolated from the urban-industrial society that was beginning to dominate national life, suffering from a long, painful economic decline, afflicted with a sense of obsolescence, rural Americans were keenly aware of the problems of the modern economy and particularly eager for government assistance in dealing with them. The result was the emergence of one of the most powerful movements of political protest in American history: what became known as Populism.

The Grangers

Farmers had been making efforts to organize politically for several decades before the 1880s. The first major farm organization had its origins shortly after the Civil War in a tour through the South by a minor Agriculture Department official, Oliver H. Kelley, who became appalled by what he considered the isolation and drabness of rural life. In 1867 he left the government and helped found the National Grange of the Patrons of Husbandry, from which emerged a network of local organizations. At first, the Granges simply tried to teach new scientific agricultural techniques and attempted to create a feeling of community, to relieve the loneliness of rural life. But when the depression of 1873 caused a sharp decline in farm prices, membership rapidly increased and the direction of the organization changed. Granges in the Midwest began to organize marketing cooperatives, which would allow farmers to circumvent the hated middlemen. And they promoted political action to curb the monopolistic practices of the railroads and warehouses. The Granges succeeded for a time both in creating an impressive network of farm cooperatives and in putting effective pressure on state legislatures. At their peak, their supporters controlled the legislatures in

A MEETING OF THE GRANGE, 1873 The Grange attracted broad and enthusiastic support from midwestern farmers in the 1870s. They were attracted by the political message of its leaders, who championed the cause of farmers against railroads, food processors, and others whom they charged with exploiting agricultural producers. But farmers liked the Grange, too, as a social organization—as a vehicle through which men and women who lived much of their lives in relative isolation could gather together. This sketch depicts a great Grange meeting in Edwardsville, Illinois.

most of the midwestern states. The result was the Granger Laws of the early 1870s, by which many states imposed strict regulations on railroad rates and practices. But the destruction of the new regulations by the courts, combined with the political inexperience of many Grange leaders and the return of prosperity in the late 1870s, produced a dramatic decline in the power of the association by the end of the decade.

The Alliances

The successor to the Granges as the leading vehicle of agrarian protest began to emerge even before the Granger movement had faded. As early as 1875, farmers in parts of the South (most notably in Texas) were banding together in so-called Farmers' Alliances. By 1880, the Southern Alliance had more than 4 million members; and a comparable Northwestern Alliance was taking root in the plains states and the Midwest and developing ties with its southern counterpart.

Like the Granges, the Alliances formed cooperatives and other marketing mechanisms. They established stores, banks, processing plants, and other facilities for their members—to free them from dependence on the hated "furnishing merchants" who kept so many farmers in debt. Some Alliance leaders, however, saw the movement in larger terms: as an effort to build a new society in which economic competition might give way to cooperation. Alliance lecturers traveled throughout rural areas lambasting the concentrated power of the great corporations and financial institutions.

Although the Alliances quickly became far more widespread than the Granges had ever been, they suffered from similar problems. Their cooperatives did not always work well, partly because the market forces operating against them were sometimes too strong to be overcome and partly because the cooperatives themselves were often mismanaged. These economic frustrations helped push the movement into a new phase at the end of the 1880s: the creation of a national political organization.

In 1889, the Southern and Northwestern Alliances, despite continuing differences between them, agreed to a loose merger. The next year the Alliances held a national convention at Ocala, Florida, and issued the so-called Ocala Demands, which were, in effect, a party platform. In the 1890 off-year elections, candidates supported by the Alliances won partial or complete control of the legislatures in twelve states. They also won six governorships, three seats in the Senate, and approximately fifty in the House of Representatives. Many of the successful Alliance candidates were simply Democrats who had benefited—often passively—from Alliance endorsements. But dissident farmers drew enough encouragement from the results to contemplate further political action, including forming a party of their own.

Alliance leaders discussed plans for a third party at meetings in Cincinnati in May 1891 and St. Louis in February 1892—meetings attended by many northern Alliance members, a smaller but still significant number of Southern Alliance leaders, and representatives of the fading Knights of Labor, whom some farm leaders hoped to bring into the coalition. Then, in July 1892, 1,300 exultant delegates poured into Omaha, Nebraska, to proclaim the creation of the new party, approve an official set of principles, and nominate candidates for the presidency and vice presidency. The new organization's official name was the People's Party, but the movement was more commonly referred to as Populism.

The election of 1892 demonstrated the potential power of the new movement. The Populist presidential candidate—James B. Weaver of Iowa, a former Greenbacker—polled more than 1 million votes, 8.5 percent of the total, and carried six mountain and plains states for 22 electoral votes. Nearly 1,500 Populist candidates won election to state legislatures and local offices. The party elected three governors, five senators, and ten congressmen. It could also claim the support of many Republicans and Democrats in Congress who had been elected by appealing to Populist sentiment.

The Populist Constituency

Already, however, there were signs of the limits of Populist strength. Populism had great appeal to farmers, and particularly to small farmers with little long-range economic security—people whose operations were only minimally mechanized, if at all, who relied on one crop, and who had little access to credit. But Populism failed to move much beyond that group. Its leaders made energetic efforts to include labor within the coalition. In addition to courting the Knights of Labor, the new party added a labor plank to its platform—calling for shorter hours for workers and restrictions on immigration, and denouncing the use of private detective agencies as strikebreakers in labor disputes. But Populism never attracted any substantial labor support, in part because the economic interests of labor and the interests of farmers were often at odds.

In the South in particular, white Populists struggled with the question of accepting African Americans in the party, since their numbers and their poverty made them potentially valuable allies. And indeed there was an important black component to the movement—a network of "Colored Alliances" that by 1890 numbered over 1.25 million members. But most white Populists were willing to accept the assistance of blacks only as long as it was clear that whites would remain indisputably in control. When southern conservatives began to attack the Populists for undermining white supremacy, the interracial character of the movement quickly faded.

Populist Ideas

The reform program of the Populists was spelled out first in the Ocala Demands of 1890 and then, even more clearly, in the Omaha platform of 1892. It proposed a system of "subtreasuries," which would replace and strengthen the cooperatives with which the Granges and Alliances had been experimenting for years. The national government would establish a network of warehouses, where farmers could deposit their crops. Using those crops as collateral, growers could then borrow money from the government at low rates of interest and wait for the price of their goods to go up before selling them. In addition, the Populists called for the abolition of national banks, which they believed were dangerous institutions of concentrated power; the end of absentee ownership of land; the direct election of United States senators (which would weaken the power of conservative state legislatures); and other devices to improve the ability of the people to influence the political process. They called as well for regulation and (after 1892) government ownership of railroads, telephones, and telegraphs. And they demanded a system of government-operated postal savings banks, a graduated income tax, the inflation of the currency, and, later, the remonetization of silver.

Some Populists were openly anti-Semitic. Others were anti-intellectual, antieastern, and antiurban. But bigotry was not the dominant force behind Populism. The movement was a serious and often intelligent effort to find solutions to real problems. Populists emphatically rejected the laissez-faire orthodoxies of their time, the idea that the rights of ownership are absolute. Populism was less a critique of industrialization or capitalism than a challenge, one of the most powerful such challenges of the era, to what the Populists considered the brutal and chaotic way in which the economy was developing. Progress and growth should continue, they urged, but it should be strictly defined by the needs of individuals and communities.

THE CRISIS OF THE 1890S

The rising agrarian protest was only one of many indications of the national political crisis emerging in the 1890s. There was a severe depression, which began in 1893. There was widespread labor unrest and violence, culminating in the tumultuous strikes of 1894. There was the continuing failure of either major party to respond to the growing distress. And there was the rigid conservatism of Grover Cleveland, who took office for the second time just at the moment that the economy collapsed. Out of this growing sense of crisis came some of the most heated political battles in American history, culminating in the dramatic campaign of 1896, which many Americans came to believe would determine the future of the nation.

The Panic of 1893

The Panic of 1893 precipitated the most severe depression the nation had ever experienced. It began in March 1893, when the Philadelphia and Reading Railroads declared bankruptcy, unable to meet demands for payment by British banks from which they had borrowed large sums. Two months later, the National Cordage Company failed as well. Together, the two corporate failures triggered a collapse of the stock market. And since many of the major New York banks were heavy investors in the market, a wave of bank failures soon began. That caused a contraction of credit, which meant that many of the new, aggressive businesses that had recently begun operations soon went bankrupt because they were unable to secure the loans they needed.

There were other, longer-range causes of the financial collapse. Depressed prices in agriculture since 1887 had weakened the purchasing power of farmers, the largest group in the population. Depression conditions that had begun earlier in Europe were resulting in a loss of American markets abroad and a withdrawal by foreign investors of gold invested in the United States. Railroads and other major industries had expanded too rapidly, well beyond market demand. The depression reflected, too, the degree to which all parts of the American economy were now interconnected, the degree to which failures in one area affected all other areas. And the depression showed how dependent the economy was on the health of the railroads, which remained the nation's most powerful corporate and financial institutions. When the railroads suffered, as they did beginning in 1893, everything suffered.

Once the panic began, its effects spread with startling speed. Within six months, more than 8,000 businesses, 156 railroads, and 400 banks failed. Already low agricultural prices tumbled further. Up to 1 million workers, 20 percent of the labor force, lost their jobs—the highest level of unemployment in American history to that point, a level comparable to that of the Great Depression of the 1930s. The depression was unprecedented not only in its severity but also in its persistence. Although there was slight improvement beginning in 1895, prosperity did not fully return until after 1898.

The depression produced widespread social unrest, not least among the enormous numbers of unemployed workers. In 1894, Jacob S. Coxey, an Ohio businessman and Populist, began advocating an inflation of the currency and a massive public works program to create jobs for the unemployed. When it became clear that his proposals were making no progress in Congress, Coxey organized a march of the unemployed (known as "Coxey's Army") to Washington to present his demands to the government. Congress took no action on the demands.

There were major labor upheavals as well during the decade—of which the Homestead and Pullman strikes were only the most prominent exam-

COXEY'S ARMY Jacob S. Coxey's "army" of the unemployed marches toward Washington in 1894 to demand relief from the federal government. Although several thousand people started out from various parts of the country to join the army, only about 400 actually reached the Capitol. The protest disbanded after Coxey and several others were arrested for "trespassing" on the grounds of the United States Capitol.

ples. (See pp. 506–508.) To many middle-class Americans, the worker unrest was a sign of dangerous social instability, even perhaps a revolution. Labor radicalism—some of it real, much of it imagined by the frightened middle class—was seldom far from the public mind, heightening the general sense of crisis.

The Silver Question

Debate over the causes of the depression centered increasingly on the currency. Populists, and many others, blamed the crisis on an inadequate supply of money. Conservatives blamed it on a lack of commitment to a "sound currency." The "money question," therefore, became one of the burning issues of the era.

The currency issue is a complicated and confusing one, and it has often been difficult for later generations to understand the enormous passions the controversy aroused. The heart of the debate was over what would form the basis of the dollar, what would lie behind it and give it value. Today, the value of the dollar rests on little more than public confidence in the government. But in the nineteenth century, most people assumed that currency was worthless if there was not something concrete behind it—precious metal (specie), which holders of paper money could collect if they presented their currency to a bank or to the Treasury.

During most of its existence as a nation, the United States had recognized two metals—gold and silver—as a basis for the dollar, a formula known as "bimetallism." In the 1870s, however, that had changed. The official ratio of the value of silver to the value of gold for purposes of creating currency (the "mint ratio") was 16 to 1: sixteen ounces of silver equaled one ounce of gold. But the actual commercial value of silver (the "market ratio") was much higher than that. Owners of silver could get more by selling it for manufacture into jewelry and other objects than they could by taking it to the mint for conversion to coins. So they stopped taking it to the mint, and the mint stopped coining silver.

In 1873, Congress passed a law that seemed simply to recognize the existing situation by officially discontinuing silver coinage. Few objected at the time. But later in the 1870s, the market value of silver fell well below the official mint ratio of 16 to 1. (Sixteen ounces of silver, in other words, were now worth less, not more, than one ounce of gold.) Silver was suddenly available for coinage again, and it soon became clear that Congress had foreclosed a potential method of expanding the currency. Before long, many Americans concluded that a conspiracy of big bankers had been responsible for the "demonetization" of silver, and they referred to the law as the "Crime of '73."

Two groups of Americans were especially determined to undo the "Crime of '73." One consisted of silver-mine owners and their allies, now understandably eager to have the government take their surplus silver and pay them much more than the market price. The other group consisted of discontented farmers, who wanted an increase in the quantity of money—an inflation of the currency—as a means of raising the prices of farm products and easing payment of the farmers' debts. The inflationists demanded that the government return at once to "free silver"—that is, to the "free and unlimited coinage of silver" at the old ratio of 16 to 1. In 1893, Congress responded weakly to these demands with the Sherman Silver Purchase Act of 1893, which required the government to purchase (but not coin) silver and pay for it in gold. That provided some relief to silver miners, but it did nothing to expand the currency.

At the same time, the nation's gold reserves were steadily dropping. And the Panic of 1893 intensified the demands on those reserves. President Cleveland believed that the chief cause of the weakening gold reserves was the Sherman Silver Purchase Act. Early in his second administration, therefore, Congress responded to his request and repealed the act—although only after a bitter and divisive battle that helped create a permanent split in the Democratic Party. The president's gold policy had aligned the southern and western Democrats in a solid phalanx against him and his eastern followers. Only substantial Republican support had allowed the bill to pass.

By now, both sides had invested the currency question with great symbolic and emotional importance. Supporters of the gold standard considered its survival essential to the honor and stability of the nation. Because the supply of gold was limited, a gold-based currency would be assured of stable, long-term value. Supporters of free silver were equally passionate. They considered the gold standard an instrument of tyranny and silver an instrument of liberation. The issue achieved an intensity rarely seen in the politics of the era, culminating in the tumultuous presidential election of 1896.

"A Cross of Gold"

Republicans, watching the failure of Cleveland and the Democrats to deal effectively with the depression, were confident of success in 1896. Party leaders, led by the Ohio boss Marcus A. Hanna, settled on former congressman William McKinley, author of the 1890 tariff act and now governor of Ohio, as the party's presidential candidate. The tariff, they believed, should be the principal issue in the campaign. But their platform also opposed the free coinage of silver except by agreement with the leading commercial nations (which everyone realized was unlikely). Thirty-four delegates from the mountain and plains states walked out in protest and joined the Democratic Party.

The Democratic convention of 1896 was unusually tumultuous. Southern and western delegates, eager for a way to compete with the populists, were determined to seize control of the party from conservative easterners and incorporate some Populist demands—among them free silver—into the Democratic platform. They wanted as well to nominate a pro-silver candidate. The divided platform committee presented two reports to the convention. The majority report, the work of westerners and southerners, called for tariff reduction, an income tax, "stricter control" of trusts and railroads, and—most prominently—free silver. The minority report, the product of the party's eastern wing, echoed the Republican platform by opposing the free coinage of silver except by international agreement. The debate over the two competing platforms dominated the convention.

Defenders of the gold standard seemed to prevail in the debate, until the final speech. Then William Jennings Bryan, a handsome, thirty-six-year-old congressman from Nebraska, already well known as an effective orator, mounted the podium to address the convention. His great voice echoed through the hall as he delivered a defense of free silver that became one of the most famous political speeches in American history. The closing passage sent his audience into something close to a frenzy: "If they dare to come out in the open and defend the gold standard as a good thing, we will fight them to the uttermost. Having behind us the producing masses of this nation and the world, supported by the commercial interests, the laboring interests and the toilers everywhere, we will answer their demand for a gold standard by saying to them: 'You shall not press down upon the brow of labor this crown of thorns; you shall not crucify mankind upon a cross of gold.' " It became known as the "Cross of Gold" speech.

In the glow of Bryan's speech, the convention voted to adopt the pro-silver platform. Perhaps more important, the agrarians embraced Bryan as their leader. The following day, Bryan (as he had eagerly, and not entirely

WILLIAM JENNINGS BRYAN Bryan addresses a crowd late in his career, displaying the flamboyant oratorical style that characterized his public life from the beginning. The poster at the lower left of the platform shows him as he appeared in the 1890s, when, as a young congressman from Nebraska, he became known as the "Boy Orator of the Platte" and the leader of the national free-silver movement.

secretly, hoped) was nominated for president on the fifth ballot. He remains the youngest man ever nominated for president by a major party.

The choice of Bryan and the nature of the Democratic platform created a quandary for the Populists. They had expected both major parties to adopt conservative programs and nominate conservative candidates, leaving the Populists to represent the growing forces of protest. But now the Democrats had stolen much of their thunder. The Populists faced the choice of naming their own candidate and splitting the protest vote or endorsing Bryan and losing their identity as a party. The Populists supported the free-silver cause, but without Bryan's passion; they considered other issues more important. Many Populists argued that "fusion" with the Democrats—who had endorsed free silver but ignored the other, more important Populist demands—would destroy their party. But the majority concluded that there was no viable alternative. Amid considerable acrimony, the convention voted to support Bryan. In a feeble effort to maintain their independence, the Populists repudiated the Democratic nominee for vice president and chose their own, Tom Watson of Georgia.

The Conservative Victory

The campaign of 1896 produced desperation among conservatives. The business and financial community, frightened beyond reason at the prospect of a Bryan victory, contributed lavishly to the Republican campaign, which may have spent as much as $7 million, as compared with the Democrats' $300,000. From his home at Canton, Ohio, McKinley conducted a dignified "front-porch" campaign before pilgrimages of the Republican faithful, customary behavior in an age when many Americans considered it undignified to campaign too openly for the presidency.

Bryan showed no such restraint. He became the first presidential candidate in American history to stump the country systematically, to appear in villages and hamlets—indeed, the first to say frankly to the voters that he wanted to be president. He traveled 18,000 miles (mostly in the West and South) and addressed an estimated 5 million people. But Bryan may have done himself more harm than good. His revivalistic, camp-meeting style pleased old-stock Protestants, but it alienated many of the immigrant Catholics and other ethnics who normally voted Democratic. Employers, meanwhile, warned workers that a Bryan victory would cost them their jobs, thus intimidating many traditional Democrats into supporting McKinley or not voting at all.

On election day, McKinley polled 271 electoral votes to Bryan's 176 and

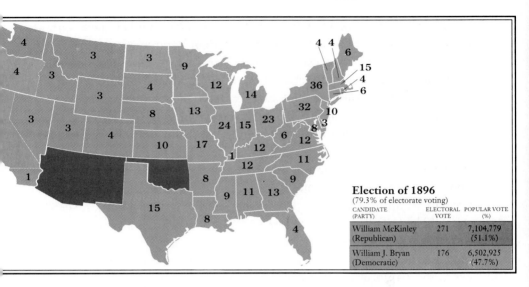

Election of 1896
(79.3% of electorate voting)

CANDIDATE (PARTY)	ELECTORAL VOTE	POPULAR VOTE (%)
William McKinley (Republican)	271	7,104,779 (51.1%)
William J. Bryan (Democratic)	176	6,502,925 (47.7%)

received 51.1 percent of the popular vote to Bryan's 47.7. Bryan carried only those areas of the South and West where miners or struggling staple farmers predominated. The Democratic program, like that of the Populists, had been too narrow to win a national election.

For the Populists and their allies, the election results were a disaster. They had gambled everything on their "fusion" with the Democratic Party and lost. Within months of the election, the People's Party began to dissolve. Never again would American farmers unite so militantly to demand economic reform. And never again would so large a group of Americans raise so forceful a protest against the nature of the industrial economy.

McKinley and Prosperity

The administration of William McKinley, which began in the aftermath of turmoil, saw a return to relative calm. The labor and agrarian protests that had dominated the early 1890s subsided; the depression began to ease; and the McKinley administration shrewdly committed itself to a reassuring stability.

McKinley and his allies worked actively and energetically on only one issue, one on which they knew virtually all Republicans were agreed: the need for higher tariff rates. Within weeks of McKinley's inauguration, the administration won approval of the Dingley Tariff, raising duties to the highest point in American history. The administration dealt more gingerly with the explosive silver question (an issue McKinley himself had never considered very important in any case). McKinley sent a commission to Europe to explore the possibility of a silver agreement with Great Britain and France. As he and everyone else anticipated, the effort produced no agreement. The Republicans then enacted the Currency, or Gold Standard, Act of 1900, which confirmed the nation's commitment to the gold standard.

And so the "battle of the standards" ended in victory for the forces of conservatism. Economic developments at the time seemed to vindicate them. Prosperity returned beginning in 1898. Foreign crop failures sent United States farm prices surging upward, and American business entered another cycle of booming expansion. Prosperity and the gold standard, it seemed, were closely allied.

But while the free-silver movement had failed, it had raised an important question for the American economy. In the quarter-century before 1900, the countries of the Western world had experienced a spectacular growth in productive facilities and population. Yet the supply of money had not kept pace with economic progress, because the supply was tied to gold and the amount of gold had remained practically constant. Had it not been for a dramatic increase in the gold supply in the late 1890s (a result of new techniques for extracting gold from low-content ores and the discovery of huge new gold deposits in Alaska, South Africa, and Australia), Populist predictions of financial disaster might in fact have proved correct. In 1898, two and a half times as much gold was produced as in 1890, and the currency supply was soon inflated far beyond anything Bryan and the free-silver forces had proposed.

By then, however, Bryan—like many other Americans—was becoming engaged with another major issue: the nation's growing involvement in world affairs and its increasing flirtation with imperialism.

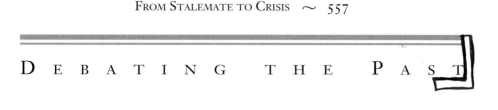

D E B A T I N G   T H E   P A S T

Populism

THE SCHOLARLY DEBATES over the nature of Populism have tended to reflect a larger debate over the nature of popular mass movements. To some historians, mass uprisings seem dangerous and potentially antidemocratic; and to them, the Populist movement has usually appeared ominous. To others, such insurgency is evidence of a healthy democratic resistance to oppression; and to them, Populism has generally seemed more appealing.

The latter view shaped the first, and for many years the only, general history of Populism: John D. Hicks's *The Populist Revolt* (1931). Reflecting the influence of Frederick Jackson Turner, Hicks portrayed Populism as an expression of the healthy, democratic sentiments of the West. (He paid relatively little attention to the South.) Populists were reacting rationally and constructively to the harsh impact of eastern industrial growth on agrarian society, and they were proposing potentially valuable reforms to restrict the power of the new financial titans. Populism was, he wrote, "the last phase of a long and perhaps a losing struggle—the struggle to save agricultural America from the devouring jaws of industrial America."

In the early 1950s, scholars sensitive to the nature of European fascism and contemporary communism took a more suspicious view of mass popular politics and a more hostile view of Populism. The leading figure in this reinterpretation was Richard Hofstadter. In *The Age of Reform* (1955), he conceded that the Populists had genuine grievances and advanced some sensible reforms. But he concentrated on revealing what he called the "soft" and "dark" sides of the movement. Populism, Hofstadter claimed, rested on a romanticized and obsolete vision of the role of farmers in American society. And it was permeated with bigotry and ignorance.

(continued on next page)

Hofstadter's harsh portrait inspired a series of spirited challenges. Norman Pollack, beginning in 1962, argued that the agrarian revolt rested not on nostalgic and romantic concepts but on a sophisticated and even radical vision of reform. A year later, Walter T. K. Nugent attempted to show that Populists were not bigoted, that they not only tolerated but welcomed Jews and other minorities into their party. And in 1976, Lawrence Goodwyn published *Democratic Promise*, the first full-scale history of the Populist movement since Hicks's study forty-five years earlier. Goodwyn described Populism as a "cooperative crusade," battling against the "coercive potential of the emerging corporate state." It was offering a genuine alternative to the inequities of modern, corporate capitalism; and it was promoting that alternative by developing an intensely democratic popular movement.

At the same time that historians were debating the meaning of Populism, they were also arguing over who the Populists were. Hicks, Hofstadter, and Goodwyn, for all their many disagreements, shared a belief that Populists were victims of economic distress—usually one-crop farmers in economically marginal regions victimized by drought and debt. Others, however, have suggested that this description is, if not wrong, at least inadequate. Sheldon Hackney maintained in 1969 that Populists in Alabama were not only economically troubled but socially rootless, "only tenuously connected to society by economic function, by personal relationships, by stable community membership, by political participation, or by psychological identification with the South's distinctive myths." Peter Argersinger, Stanley Parsons, James Turner, and others have similarly suggested that Populists tended to be people who were socially and even geographically isolated. Steven Hahn's 1983 study *The Roots of Southern Populism* described the poor farmers of "upcountry" Georgia who became Populists as people almost entirely unconnected to the modern capitalist economy. They were reacting not simply to the distress of being "left behind," but also to a real economic threat to their way of life from the intrusion into their world of a new commercial order of which they were not a part and from which they were unlikely to benefit.

There has, finally, been continuing disagreement over whether Populism has survived into the twentieth century—whether it is part of an enduring political language used by such later popular leaders as Huey Long, George Wallace, or even Ross Perot, or whether the idea of Populism has meaning only in reference to the insurgents of the 1890s.

CHAPTER TWENTY

The Imperial Republic

Stirrings of Imperialism ∼ *War with Spain*
The Republic as Empire

HE AMERICAN REPUBLIC had been an expansionist nation since the earliest days of its existence. Throughout the first half of the nineteenth century, as the population of the United States grew and pressed westward, the government, through purchase or conquest, had continually acquired new lands: the trans-Appalachian West, the Louisiana Territory, Florida, Texas, Oregon, California, New Mexico, Alaska. It was the nation's "Manifest Destiny," many Americans believed, to expand into new realms.

In the last years of the nineteenth century, with little room left for territorial growth on the North American continent, expansionism moved into a new phase. In the past, the nation had generally annexed land adjacent to its existing boundaries; American citizens could move there relatively easily, and the new lands could ultimately become states of the Union. But the expansionism of the 1890s, the new Manifest Destiny, involved acquiring possessions separate from the continental United States: distant island territories, many thickly populated, most of which were unlikely to attract massive settlement from America, few of which were expected to become states of the Union. The United States was joining England, France, Germany, and others in the great imperial drive that was, by the end of the century, to bring much of the nonindustrial world under the control of the industrial powers of the West.

STIRRINGS OF IMPERIALISM

For over two decades after the Civil War, the United States expanded geographically hardly at all. By the 1890s, however, some Americans were ready—indeed, eager—to resume the course of Manifest Destiny that had

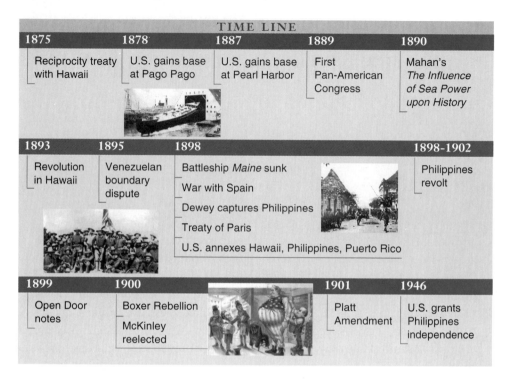

inspired their ancestors to wrest an empire from Mexico in the expansionist 1840s.

The New Manifest Destiny

Several developments helped shift American attention to lands across the seas. The experience of subjugating the Indian tribes had established a precedent for exerting colonial control over dependent peoples. The supposed "closing of the frontier," widely heralded by Frederick Jackson Turner and others in the 1890s, produced fears that natural resources would soon dwindle and that alternative sources must be found abroad. The depression that began in 1893 encouraged some businessmen to look for new markets abroad. The bitter social protests of the time—the Populist movement, the free-silver crusade, the bloody labor disputes—led some politicians to urge a more aggressive foreign policy as an outlet for frustrations that would otherwise destabilize domestic life.

Foreign trade was becoming increasingly important to the American economy in the late nineteenth century. The nation's exports had totaled about $392 million in 1870; by 1900, the figure had reached $1.4 billion. Many Americans began to argue that colonies could expand overseas markets further. Americans were, moreover, well aware of the imperialist fever that was raging through Europe. It was leading the major powers to partition most of Africa among themselves and to turn covetous eyes on the Far East and the feeble Chinese Empire. Some Americans feared that their nation would soon be left out, that the Europeans would seize all these potential markets for themselves.

Scholars and others found a philosophic justification for expansionism in Charles Darwin's theories. They contended that nations or "races," like biological species, struggled constantly for existence and that only the fittest could survive. For strong nations to dominate weak ones was, therefore, in accordance with the laws of nature. (This was an application to world affairs of the same strained reinterpretation of Darwinism that industrialists and

LAUNCHING THE *MAINE*, 1889 The battleship *Maine* played a major role in American military history when it blew up in the harbor of Havana, Cuba, in 1898, and helped precipitate the Spanish-American War. But it was also significant as part of the growing naval strength the United States was developing in the late nineteenth century. This engraving from *Harper's Weekly* portrays the launching of the *Maine* from the New York Navy Yard in November 1889.

others had been applying to domestic economic affairs in the form of Social Darwinism.)

The ablest and most effective apostle of imperialism was Alfred Thayer Mahan, a captain and later admiral in the navy. Mahan's thesis—presented in *The Influence of Sea Power upon History* (1890) and other works—was simple: Countries with sea power were the great nations of history; the greatness of the United States, bounded by two oceans, would rest on naval power. Effective sea power required, among other things, colonies. Mahan believed America should, at the least, acquire defensive bases in the Caribbean and the Pacific and take possession of Hawaii and other Pacific islands.

Mahan feared that the United States did not have a large enough navy to play the great role he envisioned. But during the 1870s and 1880s, the government launched a shipbuilding program that by 1898 had moved the United States to fifth place among the world's naval powers, and by 1900 to third.

Hemispheric Hegemony

James G. Blaine, who served as secretary of state in the Republican administrations of the 1880s, led the early efforts to expand American influence into Latin America, where, Blaine believed, the United States must look for markets for its surplus goods. In October 1889, he helped organize the first Pan-American Congress, which attracted delegates from nineteen nations. The delegates agreed to create the Pan-American Union, a weak international organization located in Washington that served as a clearinghouse for distributing information to the member nations. But they rejected Blaine's more substantive proposals: an inter-American customs union and arbitration procedures for hemispheric disputes.

The second Cleveland administration took a similarly lively interest in Latin America. In 1895, it supported Venezuela in a dispute with Great Britain over the boundary between Venezuela and British Guiana. When the British ignored American demands that the matter be submitted to arbitration, Secretary of State Richard Olney charged that Britain was violating the Monroe Doctrine. When Britain still did not act, Cleveland created a special commission to determine the boundary line; if Britain resisted the commission's decision, he insisted, the United States should be willing to go to war to enforce it. As war talk raged throughout the country, the British government finally realized that it had stumbled into a genuine diplomatic crisis and agreed to arbitration.

Hawaii and Samoa

The islands of Hawaii in the mid-Pacific had been an important way station for American ships in the China trade since the early nineteenth century. By the 1880s, officers of the expanding United States Navy were looking covetously at Pearl Harbor on the island of Oahu as a possible permanent base for American ships. Pressure for an increased American presence in Hawaii was emerging from another source as well: the growing number of Americans who had settled on the islands and who had gradually come to dominate their economic and political life.

In doing so, the Americans were wresting authority away from the leaders of an ancient civilization. Settled by Polynesian people beginning in about 1500 B.C., Hawaii had developed an agricultural and fishing society in which different islands (and different communities on the same islands), each with its own chieftain, lived more or less self-sufficiently. When the first Americans arrived in Hawaii in the 1790s on merchant ships from New England, there were perhaps a half-million people living there.

Battles among rival communities were frequent, as ambitious chieftains tried to consolidate power over their neighbors. In 1810, after a series of such battles, King Kamehameha I established his dominance over the other chieftains on Hawaii. He welcomed American traders and helped them develop a thriving trade between Hawaii and China, from which the natives profited along with the merchants. But Americans soon wanted more than trade. Missionaries began settling there in the early nineteenth century, and in the 1830s, William Hooper, a Boston trader, became the first of many Americans to buy land and establish a sugar plantation on the islands.

The arrival of these merchants, missionaries, and planters was devastating to native Hawaiian society. The newcomers inadvertently brought infectious diseases to which the Hawaiians, like the American Indians before them, were tragically vulnerable. By the mid-nineteenth century, more than half the native population had died. By the turn of the century, disease had cut the population by more than half again. But the Americans brought other incursions as well. Missionaries worked to replace native religion with Christianity. Other white settlers introduced liquor, firearms, and a commercial economy, all of which eroded the traditional character of Hawaiian society. By the 1840s, American planters had spread throughout the islands; and an American settler, G. P. Judd, had become prime minister of Hawaii under King Kamehameha III, who had agreed to establish a constitutional monarchy. Judd governed Hawaii for over a decade.

In 1887, the United States negotiated a treaty with Hawaii that permitted it to open a naval base at Pearl Harbor. By then, growing sugar for export to America had become the basis of the Hawaiian economy—as a result of an 1875 agreement allowing Hawaiian sugar to enter the United States duty-free. The American-dominated sugar plantation system displaced native Hawaiians from their lands and relied heavily for workers on Asian immigrants, whom the Americans considered more reliable and more docile than the natives. Indeed, finding adequate labor, and keeping it under control, was the principal concern of many planters. Some deliberately sought to create a mixed-race work force (Chinese, Japanese, native Hawaiian, Filipinos, Portuguese, and others) as a way to keep the workers divided and unlikely to challenge them.

Native Hawaiians did not accept these changes without protest. In 1891, they elevated a powerful nationalist to the throne: Queen Liliuokalani, who set out to challenge the growing American control of the islands. But she remained in power only two years. In 1890, the United States had eliminated the 1875 exemption from tariffs for Hawaiian sugar planters. The result was devastating to the economy of the islands, and American planters concluded that the only way for them to recover was to become part of the United States (and hence exempt from its tariffs). In 1893 they staged a revolution and called on the United States for protection. After the American minister ordered marines from a warship in Honolulu harbor to go ashore to aid the rebels, the queen yielded her authority.

A provisional government, dominated by Americans (who constituted less than 5 percent of the population of the islands), immediately sent a delegation to Washington to negotiate a treaty of annexation. President Harrison signed an annexation agreement in February 1893, just before leaving office. But the Senate, controlled by Democrats after the 1892 election, refused to ratify the treaty, and Grover Cleveland, the new president, refused to support it. Debate over the annexation of Hawaii continued until 1898, when the Republicans, back in power, approved the agreement.

Three thousand miles south of Hawaii, the Samoan islands had also long served as a way station for American ships in the Pacific trade. As American commerce with Asia increased, business groups in the United States regarded Samoa with new interest, and the American navy began eyeing the Samoan harbor at Pago Pago. In 1878, the Hayes administration extracted a treaty from Samoan leaders for an American naval station at Pago Pago. It bound the United States to arbitrate any differences between Samoa and other nations. Clearly, the United States now expected to have a voice in Samoan affairs.

But Great Britain and Germany were also interested in the islands, and they too secured treaty rights from the native princes. For the next ten years the three powers jockeyed for dominance in Samoa, playing off one native ruler against another and coming dangerously close to war. Finally, the three powers agreed to create a tripartite protectorate over Samoa, with the native chiefs exercising only nominal authority. The three-way arrangement failed to halt the intrigues and rivalries of its members, and in 1899, the United States and Germany divided the islands between them, compensating Britain with territories elsewhere in the Pacific. The United States retained the harbor at Pago Pago.

WAR WITH SPAIN

Imperial ambitions had thus begun to stir within the United States well before the late 1890s. But a war with Spain in 1898 turned those stirrings into overt expansionism. The war transformed America's relationship to the rest of the world, and it left the nation with a far-flung overseas empire.

Controversy over Cuba

The Spanish-American War emerged out of events in Cuba, which along with Puerto Rico represented virtually all that remained of Spain's once-extensive American empire. Cubans had been resisting Spanish rule intermittently since at least 1868, when they began a long but ultimately unsuccessful fight for independence. Many Americans had sympathized with the Cubans during that ten-year struggle, but the United States did not intervene.

In 1895, the Cubans rose up again. (Although their goal was an end to Spanish misrule, the island's problems were now in part a result of the Wilson-Gorman Tariff of 1894, whose high duties on sugar had prostrated Cuba's important sugar economy by cutting off exports to the United States, the island's principal market.) This rebellion produced a ferocity on both sides that horrified Americans. The Cubans deliberately devastated the island to force the Spaniards to leave. The Spanish, commanded by General Valeriano Weyler (known in the American press as "Butcher" Weyler), confined civilians in certain areas to hastily prepared concentration camps, where they died by the thousands, victims of disease and malnutrition. The Spanish had used equally savage methods during the earlier struggle in Cuba without shocking American sensibilities. But the revolt of 1895 was reported more fully and floridly by American newspapers, and particularly by the new "yellow press" of William Randolph Hearst and Joseph Pulitzer, who were engaged in a ruthless circulation war with each other in New York City and elsewhere. In their effort to play to popular sentiment, they gave the impression that all the cruelties were being perpetrated by the Spaniards.

A growing population of Cuban émigrés in the United States—centered in Florida, New York, Philadelphia, and Trenton, New Jersey—gave extensive support to the Cuban Revolutionary Party (whose headquarters was in New York) and helped publicize its leader, José Martí, who was killed in Cuba in 1895. Later, Cuban Americans formed other clubs and associations to support the cause of *Cuba Libre* (Free Cuba). In some areas of the country, their efforts were as important as those of the yellow journalists in generating popular support for the revolution. The mounting storm of indignation against Spain did not persuade President Cleveland to intervene in the conflict. He proclaimed American neutrality and tried to stop the agitation by Cuban refugees in New York City. But when McKinley became president in 1897, he took a stronger stand. He formally protested Spain's "uncivilized and inhuman" conduct, causing the Spanish government (fearful of American intervention) to recall Weyler, modify the concentration policy, and grant the island a qualified autonomy. At the end of 1897, with the insurrection losing ground, it seemed that American involvement in the war might be averted.

But whatever chances there were for a peaceful settlement vanished as a result of two dramatic incidents in February 1898. The first occurred when a Cuban agent in Havana stole a private letter written by Dupuy de Lôme, the Spanish minister in Washington, and turned it over to the American press. It described McKinley as a weak man and "a bidder for the admiration of the crowd." This was no more than what many Americans, including some Republicans, were saying about their president (Assistant Secretary of the Navy Theodore Roosevelt once described McKinley as having "no more backbone than a chocolate eclair"). But coming from a foreigner, it created intense popular anger. Dupuy de Lôme promptly resigned.

While excitement over the de Lôme letter was still high, the American battleship *Maine* blew up in Havana harbor with a loss of more than 260 people. The ship had been ordered to Cuba in January to protect American lives and property against possible attacks by Spanish loyalists. Many Americans assumed that the Spanish had sunk the ship, particularly when a naval court of inquiry reported that an external explosion by a submarine mine had caused the disaster. (Later evidence suggested that the disaster was actually the result of an accidental explosion inside one of the engine rooms.) War hysteria swept the country, and Congress unanimously appropriated $50 million for military preparations. "Remember the *Maine!*" became a national chant for revenge.

McKinley still hoped to avoid a conflict. But others in his administration (including Theodore Roosevelt) were clamoring for war. In March 1898, the president asked Spain to agree to an armistice, negotiations for a permanent peace, and an end to the concentration camps. Spain agreed to stop the fighting and eliminate the concentration camps, but it refused to negotiate with the rebels and reserved the right to resume hostilities at its discretion. That satisfied neither public opinion nor Congress. A few days later, McKinley asked for and, on April 25, received a congressional declaration of war.

"A Splendid Little War"

Secretary of State John Hay called the Spanish-American conflict "a splendid little war," an opinion that most Americans—with the exception of many of the enlisted men who fought in it—seemed to share. Declared in April, it was over in August. That was in part because Cuban rebels had already greatly weakened the Spanish resistance, which made the American intervention in many respects little more than a "mopping up" exercise. Only 460 Americans were killed in battle or died of wounds, although some 5,200 perished of disease: malaria, dysentery, and typhoid, among others. Casualties among Cuban insurgents, who continued to bear the brunt of the struggle, were much higher.

Yet the American war effort was not without difficulties. United States soldiers faced serious supply problems: a shortage of modern rifles and ammunition, uniforms too heavy for the warm Caribbean weather, inadequate medical services, and skimpy, almost indigestible food. The regular army numbered only 28,000 troops and officers, most of whom had experience in quelling Indian outbreaks but none in larger-scale warfare. That meant that, as in the Civil War, the United States had to rely heavily on National Guard units, organized by local communities and commanded for the most part by local leaders without military experience. The entire mobilization process was conducted with remarkable inefficiency.

There were also racial conflicts. A significant proportion of the American invasion force consisted of black soldiers. Some were volunteer troops

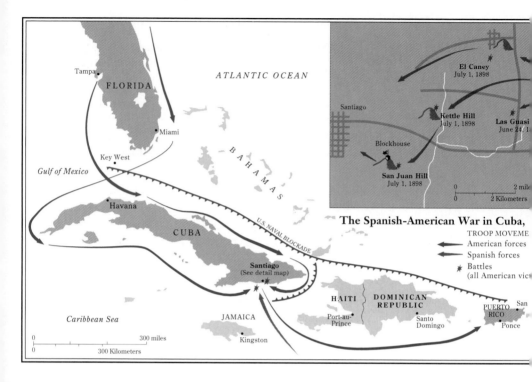

The Spanish-American War in Cuba,

TROOP MOVEME
← American forces
← Spanish forces
✳ Battles
(all American victo

put together by black communities (although some governors refused to allow the formation of such units). Others were members of the four black regiments in the regular army, who had been stationed on the frontier to defend white settlements against Indians and were now transferred east to fight in Cuba. As the black soldiers traveled through the South toward the training camps, they chafed at the rigid segregation to which they were subjected and occasionally openly resisted the restrictions. Black soldiers in Georgia deliberately made use of a "whites only" park; in Florida, they beat a soda-fountain operator for refusing to serve them; in Tampa, white provocations and black retaliation led to a night-long riot that left thirty wounded.

Racial tensions continued in Cuba itself, where African Americans played crucial roles in some of the important battles of the war (including the famous charge at San Juan Hill) and won many medals. Nearly half the Cuban insurgents fighting with the Americans were black, but unlike their American counterparts they were fully integrated into the rebel army. (Indeed, one of the leading insurgent commanders, Antonio Maceo, was a black man.) The sight of black Cuban soldiers fighting alongside whites as equals gave African Americans a stronger sense of the injustice of their own position.

Seizing the Philippines

No agency in the American military had clear authority over strategic planning. Only the navy had worked out an objective, but its objective had little to do with freeing Cuba. Assistant Secretary of the Navy Theodore Roosevelt was an ardent imperialist, an active proponent of war, and a man uninhibited by the fact that he was a relatively lowly figure in the military chain of command. Roosevelt unilaterally strengthened the navy's Pacific squadron and instructed its commander, Commodore George Dewey, to attack Spanish naval forces in the Philippines, a colony of Spain, in the event of war.

Immediately after war was declared, Dewey sailed for the Philippines. On May 1, 1898, he steamed into Manila Bay and completely destroyed the aging Spanish fleet there. Only one American sailor died in the battle (of heatstroke), and George Dewey, immediately promoted to admiral, became the first hero of the war. Several months later, after the arrival of an American expeditionary force, the Spanish surrendered the city of Manila itself. In the rejoicing over Dewey's victory, few Americans paused to note that the character of the war was changing. What had begun as a war to free Cuba was becoming a war to seize Spain's colonies.

The Battle for Cuba

Cuba, however, remained the principal focus of American military efforts. At first, the American commanders planned a long period of training before actually sending troops into combat. But when a Spanish fleet under Admiral Pascual Cervera slipped past the American navy into Santiago harbor, on the southern coast of Cuba, plans changed quickly. The American Atlantic fleet quickly bottled Cervera up in the harbor. And the army's commanding general, Nelson A. Miles, hastily altered his strategy and ordered a force of 17,000 to leave Tampa in June to attack Santiago. Both the departure from Florida and the landing in Cuba were scenes of fantastic incompetence. It took five days for the relatively small army to get ashore, and that was with the enemy offering no opposition.

General William R. Shafter, the American commander in Cuba, moved toward Santiago, which he planned to surround and capture. On the way he met and defeated Spanish forces at Las Guasimas and, a week later, in two simultaneous battles, El Caney and San Juan Hill. At the center of the fighting (and on the front pages of the newspapers) during all these engagements was a cavalry unit known as the Rough Riders. Nominally commanded by General Leonard Wood, its real leader was Colonel Theodore Roosevelt,

THE ROUGH RIDERS Theodore Roosevelt, center, poses with some of the Rough Riders after their famous charge in the Battle of San Juan Hill. The brigade had an unofficial anthem: "Rough, rough, we're the stuff. We want to fight, and we can't get enough."

who had resigned from the Navy Department to get into the war and who had struggled with an almost desperate fury to ensure that his regiment made it to the front before the fighting ended. Roosevelt rapidly emerged as a hero of the conflict. His fame rested in large part on his role in leading a bold, if perhaps reckless, charge up Kettle Hill (a charge that was a minor part of the larger battle for the adjacent San Juan Hill) directly into the face of Spanish guns. Roosevelt himself emerged unscathed, but nearly a hundred of his soldiers were killed or wounded. He remembered the battle as "the great day of my life."

Although Shafter was now in position to assault Santiago, his army was so weakened by sickness that he feared he might have to abandon his position, particularly as the commander of the American naval force blockading Santiago refused to enter the harbor because of mines. Disaster seemed imminent. But unknown to the Americans, the Spanish government had by now decided that Santiago was lost and had ordered Cervera to evacuate. On July 3, even though he knew the effort was hopeless, Cervera tried to escape the harbor. The waiting American squadron destroyed his entire fleet. On July

16, the commander of the Spanish ground forces in Santiago surrendered. At about the same time, an American army landed in Puerto Rico and occupied it against virtually no opposition. On August 12, the United States accepted an end to the war when Spain signed an armistice recognizing Cuban independence, ceding Puerto Rico to the United States, and accepting American occupation of Manila until the two nations reached a final agreement on the Philippines.

Puerto Rico and the United States

The annexation of Puerto Rico produced relatively little controversy in the United States—ironically, since of all the territory America acquired as a result of the Spanish-American War, Puerto Rico would be the most important to the nation's future.

The island of Puerto Rico had been a part of the Spanish Empire since Ponce de León arrived there in 1508, and it had contained Spanish settlements since the founding of San Juan in 1521. The native people of the island, the Arawaks, disappeared almost entirely as a result of infectious diseases, Spanish brutality, and poverty. Puerto Rican society developed, therefore, with a Spanish ruling class and a large African work force for the coffee and sugar plantations that came to dominate its economy.

As Puerto Rican society became increasingly distinctive, resistance to Spanish rule began to emerge, just as it had emerged in Cuba. Uprisings occurred intermittently beginning in the 1820s; the most important of them—the so-called Lares Rebellion—was, like the others, effectively crushed by the Spanish in 1868. But the growing resistance did prompt some reforms: the abolition of slavery in 1873, representation in the Spanish parliament, and other changes. Demands for independence continued to grow, and in 1898, in response to political pressure organized by Luis Muñoz Rivera, Spain granted the island a degree of independence. But before the changes had any chance to take effect, control of Puerto Rico shifted to the United States.

American military forces occupied the island during the war. They remained in control until 1900, when the Foraker Act ended military rule and established a formal colonial government: an American governor, a two-chamber legislature (the members of the upper chamber appointed by the United States, the members of the lower elected by the Puerto Rican people). The United States could amend or veto any legislation the Puerto Ricans passed. Agitation for independence continued. And in 1917, under pressure to clarify the relationship between Puerto Rico and America, Congress passed the Jones Act, which declared Puerto Rico to be United States territory and made all Puerto Ricans American citizens.

The Puerto Rican sugar industry flourished as it took advantage of the American market that was now open to it without tariffs. As in Hawaii, Americans began establishing large sugar plantations on the island and hired natives to work them; many of the planters did not even live in Puerto Rico. The growing emphasis on sugar as a cash crop and the transformation of many Puerto Rican farmers into paid laborers led to a reduction in the growing of food for the island. Puerto Ricans became increasingly dependent on imported food and hence increasingly a part of the international commercial economy. When international sugar prices were high, Puerto Rico did well. When they dropped, the island's economy sagged, pushing the many plantation workers—already desperately poor—into destitution. Unhappy with the instability, the poverty among natives, and the American threat to Hispanic culture, many Puerto Ricans continued to agitate for independence. Others, however, began to envision closer relations with the United States, even statehood.

The Debate over the Philippines

If the annexation of Puerto Rico produced relatively little controversy, the annexation of the Philippines occasioned a long and impassioned debate. Controlling a nearby Caribbean island fit reasonably comfortably into America's sense of itself as the dominant power in the Western Hemisphere. Controlling a large and densely populated territory thousands of miles away seemed different and, to many Americans, more ominous.

McKinley claimed to be reluctant to support annexation. But, according to his own accounts, he emerged from an "agonizing night of prayer" convinced that there were no acceptable alternatives. Returning the Philippines to Spain would be "cowardly and dishonorable," he claimed. Turning the islands over to another imperialist power (France, Germany, or Britain) would be "bad business and discreditable." Granting them independence would be irresponsible; the Filipinos were "unfit for self government." The only solution was "to take them all and to educate the Filipinos, and uplift and Christianize them, and by God's grace do the very best we could by them." Growing popular support for annexation and the pressure of the imperialist leaders of his party undoubtedly helped him reach this decision of conscience.

The Treaty of Paris, signed in December 1898, brought a formal end to the Spanish-American War. It confirmed the terms of the armistice concerning Cuba, Puerto Rico, and Guam. But American negotiators startled the Spanish by demanding that they cede the Philippines to the United States. The Spanish objected briefly, but an American offer of $20 million for the islands softened their resistance. They accepted all the American terms.

In the United States Senate, however, resistance was fierce. During debate over ratification of the treaty, a powerful anti-imperialist movement arose throughout the country to oppose acquisition of the Philippines. Among the anti-imperialists were some of the nation's wealthiest and most influential figures: Andrew Carnegie, Mark Twain, Samuel Gompers, Senator John Sherman, and others. Their motives were various. Some believed simply that imperialism was immoral, a repudiation of America's commitment to human freedom. Some feared "polluting" the American population by introducing "inferior" Asian races into it. Industrial workers feared being undercut by a flood of cheap laborers from the new colonies. Conservatives feared that the large standing army and entangling foreign alliances they thought imperialism would require would threaten American liberties. Sugar growers and others feared unwelcome competition from the new territories. The Anti-Imperialist League, established by upper-class Bostonians, New Yorkers, and others late in 1898 to fight against annexation, attracted a widespread following in the Northeast and waged a vigorous campaign against ratification of the Paris treaty.

Favoring ratification was an equally varied group. There were the exuberant imperialists such as Theodore Roosevelt, who saw the acquisition of empire as a way to reinvigorate the nation, to keep alive what they considered the healthy, restorative influence of the war. Some businessmen saw opportunities in the Philippines and believed annexation would position the United States to dominate the Oriental trade. And most Republicans saw partisan advantages in acquiring valuable new territories through a war fought and won by a Republican administration. Perhaps the strongest argument in favor of annexation, however, was the apparent ease with which it could be accomplished. The United States, after all, already possessed the islands.

When anti-imperialists warned of the danger of acquiring heavily populated territories whose people might have to become citizens, the imperialists had a ready answer: The nation's longstanding policies toward Indians—treating them as dependents rather than as citizens—had created a precedent for annexing land without absorbing people. Senator Henry Cabot

Lodge of Massachusetts, one of the leading imperialists in Congress, made the point explicitly:

> The other day . . . a great Democratic thinker announced that a Republic can have no subjects. He seems to have forgotten that this Republic not only has held subjects from the beginning, . . . but [that we have] acquired them by purchase. . . . [We] denied to the Indian tribes even the right to choose their allegiance, or to become citizens.

The fate of the treaty remained in doubt for weeks, until it received the unexpected support of William Jennings Bryan. Bryan was a fervent anti-imperialist who hoped to move the issue out of the Senate and make annexation the subject of a national referendum in 1900, when he expected to be the Democratic presidential candidate again. Bryan persuaded a number of anti-imperialist Democrats to support the treaty so as to set up the 1900 debate. The Senate ratified it finally on February 6, 1899.

But Bryan miscalculated. If the election of 1900 was in fact a referendum on the Philippines, as Bryan tried to make it, it proved beyond doubt that the nation had decided in favor of imperialism. Once again, Bryan ran against McKinley, and once again, McKinley won—even more decisively than in 1896. It was not only the issue of the colonies, however, that ensured McKinley's victory. The Republicans were the beneficiaries of growing national prosperity—and also of the colorful personality of their vice presidential candidate, Colonel Theodore Roosevelt, the hero of San Juan Hill.

THE REPUBLIC AS EMPIRE

The new American empire was a small one by the standards of the great imperial powers of Europe. But it created large problems. It embroiled the United States in the politics of both Europe and the Far East in ways the nation had always tried to avoid in the past. It also drew Americans into a brutal war in the Philippines.

Governing the Colonies

Three of the new American dependencies—Hawaii, Alaska, and Puerto Rico—presented relatively few problems. They received territorial status (and their residents American citizenship) relatively quickly: Hawaii in 1900, Alaska in 1912, and Puerto Rico (in stages) by 1917. The navy took control

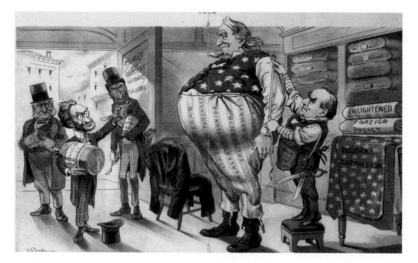

"MEASURING UNCLE SAM FOR A NEW SUIT," BY J. S. PUGHE, IN *PUCK* MAGAZINE, 1900 President William McKinley is approvingly depicted here as a tailor, measuring his client for a suit large enough to accommodate the new possessions the United States obtained in the aftermath of the Spanish-American War. The cartoon tries to link this expansion with earlier, less controversial ones such as the Louisiana Purchase.

of Guam and Tutuila. The United States had also acquired some of the smallest, least populated Pacific islands; it simply left them alone.

Cuba was a thornier problem. American military forces, commanded by General Leonard Wood, remained there until 1902 to prepare the island for independence. They built roads, schools, and hospitals; reorganized the legal, financial, and administrative systems; and introduced medical and sanitation reforms. But the United States was also laying the basis for years of American economic domination of the island. When Cuba drew up a constitution that made no reference to the United States, Congress responded by passing the Platt Amendment in 1901 and pressuring Cuba into incorporating the amendment's terms into its constitution. The Platt Amendment barred Cuba from making treaties with other nations (thus, in effect, giving the United States effective control of Cuban foreign policy); it gave the United States the right to intervene in Cuba to preserve independence, life, and property; and it required Cuba to permit American naval stations on its territory. The amendment left Cuba only nominally independent politically. And American capital, which quickly took over the island's economy, made the new nation an American economic appendage as well. American investors poured into Cuba, buying up plantations, factories, railroads, and refineries. Absentee American ownership of many of the island's most important resources was the source of resentment and agitation for decades. Resistance to "Yankee imperialism" produced intermittent revolts against the Cuban government—revolts that at times prompted United States military intervention. American troops occupied the island from 1906 to 1909 after one such rebellion; they returned again in 1912, to suppress a revolt by black plantation workers. As in Puerto Rico and Hawaii, sugar production—spurred by access to the American market—increasingly dominated the island's economy and subjected it to the same cycle of booms and busts that so plagued other sugar-producing appendages of the United States economy.

The Philippine War

Americans did not like to think of themselves as imperial rulers in the European mold. Yet like other imperial powers, the United States soon discovered—as it had discovered at home in its relations with the Indians—that subjugating another people required more than ideals; it also required strength and at times brutality. That, at least, was the lesson of the American experience in the Philippines, where American forces soon became engaged in a long and bloody war with insurgent forces fighting for independence.

The conflict in the Philippines is the least remembered of all American wars. It was also one of the longest (it lasted from 1898 to 1902) and one of the most vicious. It involved 200,000 American troops and resulted in 4,300 American deaths, nearly ten times the number who had died in combat in the Spanish-American War. The number of Filipinos killed in the conflict is still in dispute, but it seems likely that at least 50,000 natives (and perhaps many more) died. The American occupiers faced guerrilla tactics in the Philippines very similar to those the Spanish occupiers had faced prior to 1898 in Cuba. And they soon found themselves drawn into the same pattern of brutality that had outraged so many Americans when Weyler had used them in the Caribbean.

The Filipinos had been rebelling against Spanish rule even before 1898. And as soon as they realized the Americans had come to stay, they rebelled against them as well. Ably led by Emilio Aguinaldo, who claimed to head the legitimate government of the nation, Filipinos harried the American army of occupation from island to island for more than three years. At first, American commanders believed the rebels had only a small popular following. But by early 1900, General Arthur MacArthur, an American commander in the islands (and the father of General Douglas MacArthur), was writing: "I have been reluctantly compelled to believe that the Filipino masses are loyal to Aguinaldo and the government which he heads."

To MacArthur and others, that was not a reason to moderate American tactics or conciliate the rebels. It was a reason to adopt more severe measures. Gradually, the American military effort became more systematically vicious and brutal. Captured Filipino guerrillas were treated not as prisoners of war but as murderers. Most were summarily executed. On some islands, entire communities were evacuated—the residents forced into concentration camps while American troops destroyed their villages, farms, crops, and livestock. A spirit of savagery grew among American soldiers, who came to view the Filipinos as almost subhuman and at times seemed to take pleasure in killing almost arbitrarily.

By 1902, reports of the brutality and of the American casualties had soured the American public on the war. But by then, the rebellion had largely exhausted itself and the occupiers had established control over most of the islands. The key to their victory was the March 1901 capture of Aguinaldo, who later signed a document in which he urged his followers to stop fighting and declared his own allegiance to the United States. (Aguinaldo then re-

WAR IN THE PHILIPPINES American troops take possession of a war-scarred village in the Philippines during the long, bloody conflict that followed the U.S. annexation of the islands after the Spanish-American War.

tired from public life and lived quietly until 1964.) Fighting continued in some places for another year, and the war revived intermittently until as late as 1906; but American possession of the Philippines was now secure.

In the summer of 1901, the military transferred authority over the islands to William Howard Taft, who became the first civilian governor. Taft announced that the American mission in the Philippines was to prepare the islands for independence, and he gave the Filipinos broad local autonomy. The Americans also built roads, schools, bridges, and sewers; instituted major administrative and financial reforms; and established a public health system. Filipino self-rule slowly increased. But not until July 4, 1946, did the islands finally gain their independence.

The Open Door

The acquisition of the Philippines greatly increased the already strong American interest in Asia. Americans were particularly concerned about the future of China, with which the United States already had an important trading relationship and which was now so enfeebled that it provided a tempting target for exploitation by stronger countries. By 1900, England, France, Germany, Russia, and Japan were beginning to carve up China among themselves, pressuring the Chinese government for "concessions" that gave them effective economic control over various regions. In some cases, they simply seized Chinese territory and claimed it as their own "spheres of influence." Many Americans feared the process would soon cut them out of the China trade altogether.

Eager for a way to protect American interests in China without risking war, McKinley issued a statement in September 1898 saying the United States wanted access to China but no special advantages there: "Asking only the open door for ourselves, we are ready to accord the open door to others." Later, Secretary of State John Hay translated the president's words into policy when he addressed identical messages—which became known as the "Open Door notes"—to England, Germany, Russia, France, Japan, and Italy. He asked them to approve three principles: Each nation with a "sphere of influence" in China was to respect the rights and privileges of other nations in its sphere; Chinese officials were to continue to collect tariff duties in all spheres (the existing tariff favored the United States); and nations were not to discriminate against other nations in levying port dues and railroad rates within their own spheres. Together, these principles would allow the United States to trade freely with the Chinese without fear of interference and without having to become militarily involved in the region.

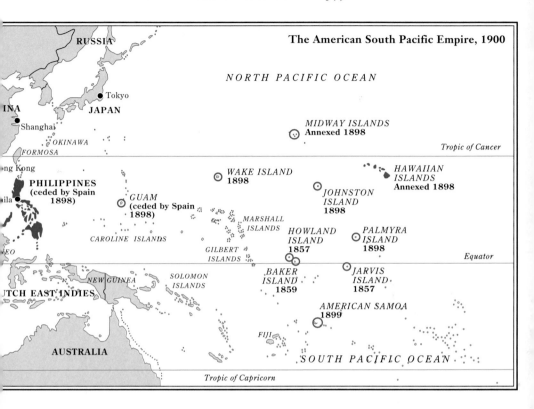

The American South Pacific Empire, 1900

But the Open Door proposals were coolly received in Europe and Japan. Russia openly rejected them; each of the other powers claimed to accept them in principle but to be unable to act unless all the other powers agreed. Hay refused to consider this a rebuff. He announced that all the powers had accepted the principles of the Open Door and that the United States expected them to observe those principles. But unless the United States was willing to resort to war, it could not prevent any nation that wanted to violate the Open Door from doing so.

No sooner had the diplomatic maneuvering over the Open Door ended than the Boxers, a secret Chinese martial-arts society, launched a revolt against foreigners in China. The climax of the Boxer Rebellion was a siege of the entire foreign diplomatic corps in the British embassy in Beijing (Peking). The imperial powers (including the United States) sent an international expeditionary force into China to rescue the diplomats. In August 1900, it fought its way into Beijing and broke the siege.

McKinley and Hay had agreed to American participation so as to secure a voice in the settlement of the uprising and to prevent the partition of China. Hay now won support for his Open Door approach from England and Germany and then induced the other participating powers to accept compensation from the Chinese for the damages the Boxer Rebellion had caused. Chinese territorial integrity survived at least in name, and the United States retained access to its lucrative trade.

A Modern Military System

The war with Spain had revealed glaring deficiencies in the American military system. The army had exhibited the greatest weaknesses, but the entire military organization had failed to coordinate its efforts. Had the United States been fighting a more powerful nation, disaster might have resulted. After the war, McKinley appointed Elihu Root, an able New York corporate lawyer, as secretary of war to supervise a major overhaul of the armed forces. (Root was one of the first of several generations of attorney-statesmen who moved easily between public and private roles and became the core of what later came to be called the American "foreign policy establishment.") Between 1900 and 1903, Root created a new military system.

The Root reforms enlarged the regular army from 25,000 to a maximum of 100,000. They established federal command of the National Guard, ensuring that never again would the nation fight a war with volunteer regiments over which the federal government had only limited control. They sparked the creation of a system of officer training schools, including the Army Staff College (later the Command and General Staff School) at Fort Leavenworth, Kansas, and the Army War College in Washington, D.C. And in 1903, they established a general staff (now known as the Joint Chiefs of Staff) to act as military advisers to the secretary of war. As a result of the new reforms, the United States entered the twentieth century with something resembling a modern military system. The country would make substantial use of it in the turbulent century to come.

CHAPTER TWENTY-ONE

The Rise of Progressivism

The Progressive Impulse ∼ *Women and Reform*
The Assault on the Parties ∼ *Sources of Progressive Reform*
Crusades for Order and Reform

WELL BEFORE THE TURN of the century, many Americans had become convinced that the rapid industrialization and urbanization of their society had created intolerable problems—that the nation's most pressing need was to impose order on the growing chaos and to curb industrial society's most glaring injustices. In the early years of the new century, that outlook acquired a name: progressivism.

Not even those who called themselves progressives could always agree on what the word "progressive" really meant. Indeed, more than one historian has suggested that the word ultimately came to mean so many different things to so many different people that it ceased to mean anything at all. Yet if progressivism was a phenomenon of great scope and diversity, it was also one that rested on an identifiable set of central assumptions. It was, first, an optimistic vision. Progressives believed, as their name implies, in the idea of progress. They believed that society was capable of improvement, even of something close to perfection, and that continued growth and advancement were the nation's destiny. But progressives believed, too, that growth and progress could not continue to occur recklessly, as they had in the late nineteenth century. The "natural laws" of the marketplace, and the doctrines of laissez faire and Social Darwinism that celebrated those laws, were not sufficient to create the order and stability that the growing society required. Purposeful human intervention was necessary to solve the nation's problems. Progressives did not always agree on the form that intervention should take, but most believed that government should play an important role in the process.

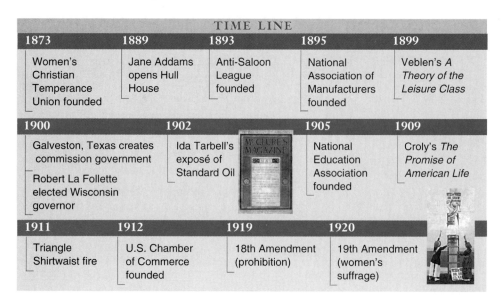

TIME LINE				
1873	**1889**	**1893**	**1895**	**1899**
Women's Christian Temperance Union founded	Jane Addams opens Hull House	Anti-Saloon League founded	National Association of Manufacturers founded	Veblen's *A Theory of the Leisure Class*
1900	**1902**		**1905**	**1909**
Galveston, Texas creates commission government Robert La Follette elected Wisconsin governor	Ida Tarbell's exposé of Standard Oil		National Education Association founded	Croly's *The Promise of American Life*
1911	**1912**	**1919**	**1920**	
Triangle Shirtwaist fire	U.S. Chamber of Commerce founded	18th Amendment (prohibition)	19th Amendment (women's suffrage)	

THE PROGRESSIVE IMPULSE

Beyond these central premises, progressivism flowed outward in a number of different directions. One powerful impulse was the spirit of "antimonopoly," the fear of concentrated power and the urge to limit and disperse authority and wealth. A second progressive impulse was a belief in the importance of social cohesion: the belief that individuals are not autonomous but part of a great web of social relationships, that the welfare of any single person is dependent on the welfare of society as a whole. And a third progressive impulse was a belief in organization and efficiency: the belief that social order was a result of intelligent social organization and rational procedures for guiding social and economic life. These varied reform impulses were not entirely incompatible with one another. Many progressives made use of all these ideas at times as they tried to restore order and stability to their turbulent society.

The Muckrakers and the Social Gospel

Among the first to articulate the new spirit of reform was a group of crusading journalists who began in the late nineteenth and early twentieth centuries to direct public attention toward social, economic, and political injustices. They became known as the "muckrakers" after Theodore Roosevelt accused one of them of raking up muck through his writings. They were committed to exposing scandal, corruption, and injustice to public view.

At first, their major targets were the trusts and particularly the railroads, which the muckrakers considered dangerously powerful and deeply corrupt. Exposés of the great corporate organizations began to appear as early as the 1860s, when Charles Francis Adams, Jr., and others uncovered corruption among the railroad barons. Decades later, Ida Tarbell produced a scorching study of the Standard Oil trust, keeping the issue of corporate power alive. By the turn of the century, however, many muckrakers were turning their attention to government and particularly to the urban political machines. The most influential, perhaps, was Lincoln Steffens, a reporter for *McClure's Magazine.* His portraits of "machine government" and "boss rule";

MCCLURE'S MAGAZINE, May 1903 *McClure's* was the leading outlet for a form of journalism known as "muckraking," which exposed social and economic scandals in the hope of promoting reform. This issue contains articles by two of the leading muckrakers, Lincoln Steffens and Ida Tarbell.

his exposures of "boodlers" in cities as diverse as St. Louis, Minneapolis, Cleveland, Cincinnati, Chicago, Philadelphia, and New York; his tone of studied moral outrage (as reflected in the title of his series and of the book that emerged from it, *The Shame of the Cities*)—all helped arouse sentiment for urban political reform. The muckrakers reached the peak of their influence in the first decade of the twentieth century. They investigated governments, labor unions, and corporations. They explored the problems of child labor, immigrant ghettoes, prostitution, and family disorganization. They denounced waste and destruction of natural resources, the subjugation of women, even occasionally the oppression of blacks.

The moralistic tone of the muckrakers' exposés reflected one important aspect of emerging progressive sentiment: a sense of outrage at social and economic injustice. That outrage, combined with a humanitarian sense of social responsibility, helped produce one of the central missions of many reformers: the pursuit of "social justice." A clear expression of that concern was the rise of what became known as the "Social Gospel." By the early twentieth century, it had become a powerful movement within American Protestantism (and, to a lesser extent, within American Catholicism and Judaism) to redeem the nation's cities. The Salvation Army, which began in England but soon spread to the United States, was a Christian social welfare organization with a vaguely military structure. By 1900, it had recruited 3,000 "officers" and 20,000 "privates" and was offering both material aid and spiritual service to the urban poor. In addition, many ministers, priests, and rabbis left traditional parish work to serve in the troubled cities. Charles Sheldon's *In His Steps* (1898), the story of a young minister who abandoned a comfortable post to work among the needy, sold more than 15 million copies and established itself as the most successful novel of the era. The engagement of religion with reform helped bring to progressivism a powerful moral impulse and a concern for the plight of some of society's most impoverished and degraded people.

The Settlement House Movement

One of the strongest elements of progressive thought was the belief that the environment shaped individual development. Social Darwinists such as William Graham Sumner had argued that people's fortunes reflected their inherent "fitness" for survival. Most progressive theorists disagreed. Ignorance, poverty, even criminality, they argued, were not the result of inherent moral or genetic failings or of the workings of providence. They were, rather, the effects of an unhealthy environment. To elevate the distressed,

AMERICAN VOICES

JANE ADDAMS

First Days at Hull House

FROM THE FIRST it seemed understood that we were ready to perform the humblest neighborhood services. We were asked to wash the newborn babies, and to prepare the dead for burial, to nurse the sick, and to "mind the children." Occasionally these neighborly offices unexpectedly uncovered ugly human traits. . . . a little Italian bride of fifteen sought shelter with us one November evening, to escape her husband who had beaten her every night for a week when he returned home from work, because she had lost her wedding ring; two of us officiated quite alone at the birth of an illegitimate child because the doctor was late in arriving, and none of the honest Irish matrons would "touch the likes of her." . . .

We were . . . early impressed with the curious isolation of many of the immigrants; an Italian woman once expressed her pleasure in the red roses that she saw at one of our receptions in surprise that they had been "brought so fresh all the way from Italy." She would not believe for an instant that they had been grown in America. . . . Her conception of America had been the untidy street in which she lived and had made her long struggle to adapt herself to American ways.

But in spite of some untoward experiences, we were constantly impressed with the uniform kindness and courtesy we received. Perhaps these first days laid the simple human foundations which are certainly essential for continuous living among the poor: . . . the conviction . . . that the things which make men alike are finer and better than the things that keep them apart, and that these basic likenesses, if they are properly accentuated, easily transcend the less essential differences of race, language, creed, and tradition.

SOURCE: Jane Addams, *Twenty Years at Hull House* (New York: The Macmillan Company, 1910), pp. 88–89.

therefore, required an improvement of the conditions in which the distressed lived.

Nothing produced more distress, many reformers believed, than the crowded immigrant neighborhoods of American cities. One response to the problems of such communities, borrowed from England, was the settlement house. The most famous, and one of the first, was Hull House, which opened in 1889 in Chicago as a result of the efforts of Jane Addams. It became a model for more than 400 similar institutions throughout the nation. Staffed by members of the educated middle class, settlement houses sought to help immigrant families adapt to the language and customs of their new country. Settlement houses avoided the condescension and moral disapproval of earlier philanthropic efforts. But they generally embodied a belief that middle-class Americans had a responsibility to impart their own values to immigrants. Even the word "settlement" suggested as much: middle-class people "settling" in the inner city and bringing civilization to the urban frontier.

Central to the settlement houses were the efforts of college women. Indeed, the movement became a training ground for many important female leaders of the twentieth century, among them Eleanor Roosevelt. The settlement houses also helped spawn another important institution of reform: the profession of social work—a profession in which women were to play an important role. The professional social worker combined a compassion for the poor with a commitment to the values of bureaucratic progressivism: scientific study, efficient organization, reliance on experts.

The Allure of Expertise

As the emergence of the social work profession suggests, progressives involved in humanitarian efforts often placed high value on knowledge and expertise. Even nonscientific problems, they believed, could be analyzed and solved scientifically. Many reformers came to believe that only enlightened experts and well-designed bureaucracies could create the stability and order America needed.

This belief found expression in many ways, among them through the writings of a new group of scholars and intellectuals. Unlike the Social Darwinists of the nineteenth century, these theorists were no longer content with merely justifying the existing industrial system. They spoke instead of the creation of a new civilization, one in which the expertise of scientists and engineers could be brought to bear on the problems of the economy and society. Among the most influential was the social scientist Thorstein Veblen.

Harshly critical of the industrial tycoons of the late nineteenth century—the "leisure class," as he satirically described them in his first major work, *A Theory of the Leisure Class* (1899)—Veblen proposed instead a new economic system in which power would reside in the hands of highly trained engineers. Only they, he argued, could fully understand the "machine process" by which modern society must be governed.

In practical terms, the impulse toward expertise and organization helped produce the idea of scientific management, or "Taylorism." (See p. 491.) It encouraged the development of modern mass-production techniques and, above all, the assembly line. It inspired a revolution in American education and the creation of a new area of inquiry—social science, the use of scientific techniques in the study of society and its institutions. It produced a generation of bureaucratic reformers concerned with the structure of organizations and committed to building new political and economic institutions capable of managing a modern society. It also helped create a movement toward organization among the expanding new group of middle-class professionals.

The Professions

The late nineteenth century saw a dramatic expansion in the number of Americans engaged in administrative and professional tasks. Industries needed managers, technicians, and accountants as well as workers. Cities required commercial, medical, legal, and educational services. The new technology required scientists and engineers, who, in turn, required institutions and instructors to train them. By the turn of the century, the people performing these services had come to constitute a distinct social group—what some have called a new middle class.

The new middle class placed a high value on education and individual accomplishment. By the early twentieth century, its millions of members were building organizations and establishing standards to secure their position in society. As their principal vehicle, they created the modern, organized professions. The idea of professionalism had been a frail one in America even as late as 1880. But as the demand for professional services increased, so did the pressures for reform.

Among the first to respond was the medical profession. Throughout the 1890s, doctors who considered themselves trained professionals began forming local associations and societies. In 1901, they reorganized the American Medical Association (AMA) into a national professional society. By 1920, nearly two-thirds of all American doctors were members. The AMA quickly called for strict, scientific standards for admission to the practice of medicine, with doctors themselves serving as protectors of the standards. State and local governments responded by passing new laws that required the licensing of all physicians and that restricted licenses to those practitioners approved by the profession.

There was similar movement in other professions. By 1916, lawyers in all forty-eight states had established professional bar associations, virtually all of which had succeeded in creating central examining boards, composed of lawyers, to regulate admission to the profession. Increasingly, aspiring lawyers found it necessary to enroll in graduate programs, and the nation's law schools accordingly expanded greatly, both in numbers and in the rigor of their curricula. Businessmen supported the creation of schools of business administration and created their own national organizations: the National Association of Manufacturers in 1895 and the United States Chamber of Commerce in 1912. Even farmers, long the symbol of the romantic spirit of individualism, responded to the new order by forming, through the National Farm Bureau Federation, a network of agricultural organizations designed to spread scientific farming methods, teach sound marketing techniques, and lobby for the interests of their members.

Among the chief purposes of the new professionalism was guarding entry into the professions. This was only partly an effort to defend the professions from the untrained and incompetent. The admission requirements also protected those already in the professions from excessive competition and lent prestige and status to the professional label. Some professions used their entrance requirements to exclude blacks, women, immigrants, and other "undesirables" from their ranks. Others used them simply to keep the numbers down, to ensure that demand for the services of existing members would remain high.

Women and the Professions

American women found themselves excluded—both by custom and by active barriers of law and prejudice—from most of the emerging professions. But a substantial number of middle-class women—particularly those emerging from the new women's colleges and from the coeducational state universities—nevertheless entered professional careers.

A few women managed to establish themselves as physicians, lawyers, engineers, scientists, and corporate managers. Several leading medical schools admitted women, and about 5 percent of all American physicians were female in 1900 (a proportion that remained unchanged until the 1960s).

SETTLEMENT HOUSE WORKERS Nurses from the Henry Street settlement in New York leave their headquarters to begin their visits to the homes of poor immigrants in lower Manhattan. This photograph dates from the early 1900s.

Most, however, turned by necessity to those professions that society considered suitable for women. Settlement houses and social work provided two "appropriate" professional outlets for women. The most important, however, was teaching. Indeed, in the late nineteenth century, more than two-thirds of all grammar-school teachers were women, and perhaps 90 percent of all professional women were teachers. For educated black women, in particular, teaching was often the only professional opportunity they could hope to find. The existence of segregated black schools in the South created a substantial market for African-American teachers.

Women also dominated other professional activities. Nursing had become primarily a women's field around the time of the Civil War, when it was still considered a menial occupation, akin to domestic service. But by the early twentieth century, it too was adopting professional standards. Prospective nurses generally needed certification from schools of nursing and could not simply learn on the job. Women also found opportunities as librarians, another field beginning to define itself in professional terms. And many women entered academia—often studying at predominantly male institutions that permitted women to earn advanced degrees, among them the University of Chicago, MIT, and Columbia—and finding professional opportunities in the new and expanding women's colleges.

The "women's professions" had much in common with other professions: the value they placed on training and expertise, the creation of professional organizations and a professional "identity," the monitoring of admission to professional work. But they also had distinctive qualities. Careers such as teaching, nursing, and library work were "helping" professions. They involved working primarily with other women or with children. Their activities occurred in places that seemed different from the offices that dominated the predominantly male business and professional worlds; such places as schools, hospitals, and libraries had a vaguely "domestic" or "feminine" image, which enabled men (and, indeed, most women) to reconcile the idea of female professional work with prevailing ideas about the proper role of women in society.

WOMEN AND REFORM

The prominent role of women in reform movements is one of the most striking features of progressivism. Women became important reformers even though they could not vote in most states, seldom held office, and had footholds in only a few professions. But their relative insulation from political and professional life in some ways enhanced their ability to wield influence, for it enabled them to tie their causes to the idea of a nonpartisan, nurturing culture uncontaminated by economic or political interests.

The "New Woman"

The phenomenon of the "new woman," widely remarked upon at the time, was a product of the social and economic changes of the era. By the end of the nineteenth century, almost all income-producing activity had moved out of the home and into the factory or the office. At the same time, many women were having fewer children, and their children were beginning school at earlier ages and spending more time there. For wives and mothers who did not work for wages, home and family were less all-consuming. Hence more and more women began looking for activities outside the home.

There were also more women who lived outside traditional families altogether. Some educated women shunned marriage entirely, believing that only by remaining single could they play the roles they envisioned in the public world; approximately 10 percent of all American women in the last decades of the nineteenth century never married—a high proportion of them middle-class women. Single women were among the most prominent female reformers of the time. Some of these women lived alone. Others lived with other women, often in long-term relationships—some of them secretly romantic—that were known at the time as "Boston marriages." The divorce rate also rose rapidly in the late nineteenth century, from one divorce for every twenty-one marriages in 1880 to one in nine by 1916; women initiated the great majority of them.

Higher levels of education also contributed to the prominence of women in reform activities. The proliferation of women's colleges and of coeducational public universities in the late nineteenth century produced the first generation of women in which significant numbers had education above the high-school level. (See p. 534.) The new colleges also helped create female communities, within which women could find support for their ambitions and companionship for their activities.

There was no single profile for the "new woman." But a growing number of American women at the beginning of the twentieth century were defining their lives in ways that included a substantial amount of activity outside the home, and they were deriving from their identity as women a set of distinctive concerns that defined—and limited—their public activities.

The Clubwomen

In the vanguard of progressive social reforms was a large network of women's clubs, which proliferated rapidly beginning in the 1880s and 1890s. The women's clubs began largely as cultural organizations to provide middle- and upper-class women with an outlet for their intellectual energies. In 1892, when women formed the General Federation of Women's Clubs to coordinate the activities of local organizations, there were more than 100,000 members in nearly 500 clubs. By 1917, there were over 1 million members.

By the early twentieth century, the clubs were becoming less concerned with cultural activities and more concerned with making a contribution to social reform. Much of what they did was uncontroversial: planting trees;

supporting schools, libraries, and settlement houses; building hospitals and parks. But clubwomen also supported such controversial measures as child labor laws, worker compensation, pure food and drug legislation, occupational safety, reforms in Indian policy, and—beginning in 1914—woman suffrage. Because many club members were from wealthy families, some organizations had substantial funds at their disposal to make their influence felt.

Black women occasionally joined clubs dominated by whites. But African Americans also formed clubs of their own, some of which affiliated with the General Federation, but more of which became part of the independent National Association of Colored Women. They modeled themselves on their white counterparts, but some black clubs took positions on issues of particular concern to blacks. Some crusaded against lynching and called for congressional legislation to make lynching a federal crime. Others protested aspects of segregation.

The women's club movement raised few overt challenges to prevailing assumptions about the proper role of women in society. But, like the limited movement of women into professions, it did represent an important effort by women to extend their influence beyond the traditional female sphere within the home and the family. Few clubwomen were willing to accept the arguments of such committed feminists as Charlotte Perkins Gilman, who in her 1898 book, *Women and Economics*, argued that the traditional definition of sexual roles was exploitive and obsolete. The club movement, rather, allowed women to define a space for themselves in the public world without openly challenging the existing, male-dominated order.

But the importance of the club movement did not lie simply in what it did for middle-class women. It lay also in what those women did for the working-class people they attempted to help. The women's club movement was an important force in winning passage of state (and ultimately federal) laws that regulated the conditions of woman and child labor, that established government inspection of workplaces, that regulated the food and drug industries, and that applied new standards to urban housing. In many of these efforts, the clubwomen formed alliances with such other women's groups as the Women's Trade Union League, founded in 1903 by female union members and upper-class reformers and committed to persuading women to join unions.

Woman Suffrage

Perhaps the largest single reform movement of the progressive era, indeed one of the largest in American history, was the fight for woman suffrage— a movement that attracted support from both women and men. It was the culmination of many decades of struggle by women to obtain basic political rights. But it was also the product of forces peculiar to the early twentieth century.

It is sometimes difficult for today's Americans to understand why the suffrage (or right-to-vote) issue could have become the source of such enormous controversy in the early twentieth century. But at the time, suffrage seemed to many of its critics a very radical demand—in part because of the rationale some of its supporters used to advance it. Throughout the late nineteenth century, many suffrage advocates presented their views in terms of "natural rights," arguing that women deserved the same rights as men—including, first and foremost, the right to vote. Elizabeth Cady Stanton, for example, wrote in 1892 of woman as "the arbiter of her own destiny. . . . if we are to consider her as a citizen, as a member of a great nation, she must have the same rights as all other members." A woman's role as "mother, wife, sister, daughter" was "incidental" to her larger role as a part of society.

This was an argument that boldly challenged the views of many men (and even many women) who believed that society required a distinctive female "sphere" in which women would serve first and foremost as wives and mothers. And so a powerful antisuffrage movement emerged, which challenged this apparent threat to the existing social order. There were antisuffrage organizations, newspapers, and political crusades. Antisuffragists associated suffrage with divorce, promiscuity, and neglect of children. Throughout much of the late nineteenth century, they effectively stymied most efforts by women to gain the vote.

The suffrage movement began to overcome this opposition and to win some substantial victories in the first years of the twentieth century. That was in part because suffragists were becoming better organized and more politically sophisticated than their opponents. Under the leadership of Anna Howard Shaw, a Boston social worker, and Carrie Chapman Catt, a journalist from Iowa, the National American Woman Suffrage Association grew from a membership of about 13,000 in 1893 to over 2 million in 1917. The involvement of such well-known and widely admired women as Jane Addams gave added respectability to the cause.

But the movement also gained strength because many of its most prominent leaders began to justify suffrage in "safer," less threatening ways. Suffrage, some supporters began to argue, would not challenge the "separate sphere" in which women resided. It would allow women to bring their special and distinct virtues more widely to bear on society's problems. It was, they claimed, precisely because women occupied a distinct sphere—because as mothers and wives and homemakers they had special experiences and spe-

SUFFRAGISTS Suffrage activists hang posters along the boardwalk in the beachfront town of Long Branch, New Jersey. Twenty-nine states had permitted women at least some access to the ballot before ratification of the Nineteenth Amendment in 1920. New Jersey was not one of them.

cial sensitivities to bring to public life—that woman suffrage could make such an important contribution to politics. In particular, many suffragists argued that enfranchising women would help the temperance movement, by giving its largest group of supporters a political voice. Some suffrage advocates claimed that once women had the vote, war would become a thing of the past, since women would—through their maternal instincts and their calming, peaceful influence—help curb the natural belligerence of men. That was one reason why World War I gave the final, decisive push to the movement for suffrage.

Not all suffragists narrowed their arguments. Among working-class, immigrant, and black women in particular, suffrage continued to generate substantial support precisely because it seemed so radical, because it promised to reshape the role of women and reform the social order. But among members of the middle class, the separation of the suffrage movement from more radical feminist goals, and its association with other reform causes of concern to many Americans, helped it gain widespread support.

The principal triumphs of the suffrage movement began in 1910. That year, Washington became the first state in fourteen years to extend suffrage to women. California joined it a year later, and in 1912 four other western states did the same. In 1913, Illinois became the first state east of the Mississippi to embrace woman suffrage. And in 1917 and 1918, New York and Michigan—two of the most populous states in the Union—gave women the vote. By 1919, thirty-nine states had granted women the right to vote in at least some elections; fifteen had allowed them full participation. In 1920, finally, suffragists won ratification of the Nineteenth Amendment, which guaranteed political rights to women throughout the nation.

To some feminists, however, the victory seemed less than complete. Alice Paul, the head of the militant National Woman's Party (founded in 1916), never accepted the relatively conservative "separate sphere" justification for suffrage. She argued that the Nineteenth Amendment alone would not be sufficient to protect women's rights. Women needed more: a constitutional amendment that would provide clear, legal protection for their rights and would prohibit all discrimination on the basis of sex. But Alice Paul's argument found limited favor even among many of the most important leaders of the recently triumphant suffrage crusade.

THE ASSAULT ON THE PARTIES

Sooner or later, most progressive goals required the involvement of government. Only government, reformers agreed, could effectively counter the powerful private interests that threatened the nation. But American government at the dawn of the new century was, progressives believed, poorly adapted to perform their ambitious tasks. At every level, political institutions were outmoded, inefficient, and corrupt. Before society could be effectively reformed, it would be necessary to reform government itself. In the beginning, at least, many progressives believed that such reform should start with an assault on the domination of government and politics by the political parties, which they thought had become corrupt, undemocratic, and reactionary.

Early Attacks

Attacks on party dominance had been frequent in the late nineteenth century. Greenbackism and Populism, for example, had been efforts to break the hammerlock with which the Republicans and Democrats controlled public life. The Independent Republicans (or mugwumps) had attempted to challenge the grip of partisanship, and former mugwumps became important supporters of progressive political reform activity in the 1890s and later.

The early assaults enjoyed some success. In the 1880s and 1890s, for example, most states adopted the secret ballot. Prior to that, the political parties themselves had printed ballots (or "tickets") with only the party's candidates listed, which they distributed to their supporters, who then simply went to the polls to deposit the tickets in the ballot box. The old system had made it possible for bosses to monitor the voting behavior of their constituents; it had also made it very difficult for voters to "split" their tickets—to vote for candidates of different parties for different offices. The new ballot—printed by the government and distributed at the polls, where it was filled out and deposited in secret—helped chip away at the power of the parties over the voters. (It also excluded many illiterate and non-English-speaking voters.)

By the late 1890s, critics of the parties were expanding their goals. Party rule could be broken, they believed, in one of two ways. It could be broken by increasing the power of the people, by permitting them to circumvent partisan institutions and express their will directly at the polls. Or it could be broken by placing more power in the hands of nonpartisan, nonelective officials, insulated from political life. Reformers promoted measures that moved along both those paths.

Municipal Reform

Many progressives believed the impact of party rule was most damaging in the cities. Municipal government, therefore, became the first target of those working for political reform. Muckraking journalists such as Lincoln Steffens were especially successful in arousing public outrage at corruption and incompetence in city politics.

The muckrakers struck a responsive chord among a powerful group of urban middle-class progressives. For several decades after the Civil War, most "respectable" citizens of the nation's large cities had avoided participation in municipal government. Viewing politics as a debased and demeaning activity, they shrank from contact with the "vulgar" elements who were coming to dominate public life. By the end of the century, however, a new generation of activists—some of them members of old aristocratic families, others newly part of the middle class—were taking a revived interest in government.

They faced a formidable array of opponents. In addition to challenging the powerful city bosses and their entrenched political organizations, they were attacking a large group of special interests: saloon owners, brothel keepers, businessmen who had established lucrative relationships with the urban machines and viewed reform as a threat to their profits, and many influential newspapers, which ridiculed the reformers as naïve do-gooders. Finally, there was the great constituency of urban working people, many of them recent immigrants, for whom the machines were a source of needed jobs and services. Gradually, however, the reformers gained in political strength—in part because of their own growing numbers, in part because of the failures of the existing political leadership. And in the first years of the twentieth century, they began to score some important victories.

An early and influential success came in Galveston, Texas, where the old city government proved completely unable to deal with the effects of a destructive tidal wave in 1900. Capitalizing on public dismay, reformers (many of them local businessmen) won approval of a new city charter that replaced the mayor and council with an elected, nonpartisan commission. In 1907, Des Moines, Iowa, adopted its own version of the commission plan, and other cities soon followed.

Another approach to reform, similarly motivated by the desire to remove city government from the hands of the parties, was the city-manager plan (first adopted in Staunton, Virginia, in 1908), by which elected officials hired an outside expert—often a professionally trained business manager or engineer—to take charge of the government. The city manager would presumably remain untainted by the corrupting influence of politics. By the end of the progressive era, almost 400 cities were operating under commissions, and another 45 employed city managers.

In most urban areas, and in the larger cities in particular, the enemies of party had to settle for less absolute victories. Some cities made the election of mayors nonpartisan (so that the parties could not choose the candidates) or moved them to years when no presidential or congressional races were in progress (to reduce the influence of the large turnouts that party organizations produced on such occasions). Reformers tried to make city-council members run at large so as to limit the influence of ward leaders and district bosses. They tried to strengthen the power of the mayor at the expense of the city council, on the assumption that reformers were more likely to get a sympathetic mayor elected than to win control of the entire council.

Statehouse Progressivism

But the assault on boss rule in the cities often did not produce results satisfying to reformers. Consequently, many progressives turned to state government as an agent for reform. These state-level progressives, like their municipal counterparts, considered existing state governments unfit to provide reform. They looked with particular scorn on state legislatures, whose ill-paid, relatively undistinguished members were, they believed, generally incompetent, often corrupt, and almost always controlled by party bosses. Many reformers began looking for ways to circumvent the legislatures (and the party bosses who controlled them) by increasing the power of the electorate.

Two of the most important changes were innovations first proposed by Populists in the 1890s: the initiative and the referendum. The initiative allowed reformers to circumvent state legislatures altogether by submitting new legislation directly to the voters in general elections. The referendum provided a method by which actions of the legislature could be returned to the electorate for approval. By 1918, more than twenty states had enacted one or both of these reforms.

The direct primary and the recall were, similarly, efforts to limit the power of parties and improve the quality of elected officials. The primary election was an attempt to take the selection of candidates away from the bosses and give it to the people. (In the South, it was also a device for excluding African Americans from voting.) The recall gave voters the right to remove a public official from office through a special election, which could be called after a sufficient number of citizens had signed a petition. By 1915 every state in the nation had instituted primary elections for at least some offices. The recall encountered more strenuous opposition, but some states adopted it as well.

Reform efforts proved most effective in states that elevated vigorous and committed politicians to positions of leadership. In New York, Governor Charles Evans Hughes exploited progressive sentiment to create a commission to regulate public utilities. In California, Governor Hiram Johnson promoted reforms to limit the political power of the Southern Pacific Railroad. In New Jersey, Woodrow Wilson, the Princeton University president who was elected governor in 1910, used executive leadership to win reforms designed to end New Jersey's widely denounced position as the "mother of trusts."

But the most celebrated state-level reformer was Robert M. La Follette of Wisconsin. Elected governor in 1900, he helped turn his state into what reformers across the nation described as a "laboratory of progressivism." The Wisconsin progressives won approval of direct primaries, initiatives, and referendums. They regulated railroads and utilities. They passed laws to regulate the workplace and provide compensation for laborers injured on the job. They instituted graduated taxes on inherited fortunes, and they nearly doubled state levies on railroads and other corporate interests. Ultimately, La Follette would find himself overshadowed by other national progressive leaders. In the early years of the century, however, few men were as effective in publicizing the message of reform. None was as successful in bending state government to that goal.

Parties and Interest Groups

The reformers did not, of course, eliminate parties from American political life. But they did diminish the parties' centrality. Evidence of that came from, among other things, the decline in voter turnout. In the late nineteenth century, up to 81 percent of eligible voters routinely turned out for national elections. In the early twentieth century, while turnout remained very high by today's standards, the figure declined markedly. In the presidential election of 1900, 73 percent of the electorate voted. By 1912, the figure had dropped to about 59 percent. Never again did voter turnout reach as high as 70 percent.

At the same time that parties were declining, other power centers were emerging to compete with them: what have become known as "interest groups." Beginning late in the nineteenth century and accelerating rapidly in the twentieth, new organizations emerged, outside the party system, that were designed to pressure government to do the bidding of their members: professional organizations; trade associations, representing particular businesses and industries; labor organizations; farm lobbies; and many others. Social workers, the settlement house movement, women's clubs, and others learned to operate as interest groups to advance their demands. A new pattern of politics, in which many individual interests organized to influence government directly rather than operating through party structures, was emerging. It would become the characteristic form of American politics in the twentieth century.

SOURCES OF PROGRESSIVE REFORM

Middle-class reformers, most of them from the East, dominated the public image and much of the substance of progressivism in the late nineteenth and early twentieth centuries. But they were not alone in seeking to improve social conditions. Working-class Americans, African Americans, westerners, even party bosses also played crucial roles in advancing some of the important reforms of the era.

Labor, the Machine, and Reform

Although the American Federation of Labor, and its leader Samuel Gompers, remained largely aloof from many of the reform efforts of the time (reflecting Gompers's firm belief that workers should not rely on government to improve their lot), some unions nevertheless played important roles in reform battles. In San Francisco, for example, workers in the Building Trades Council spearheaded the formation of the new Union Labor Party, committed to a program of reform almost indistinguishable from that of middle-class and elite progressives in the city. Between 1911 and 1913, in significant part because of the new party's efforts, California passed a child labor law, a workmen's compensation law, and a limitation on working hours for women. Union pressures contributed to the passage of similar laws in many other states as well.

One result of the assault on the parties was a change in the party organizations themselves, which attempted to adapt to the new realities so as to preserve their influence. Some party machines emerged from the progressive era almost as powerful as they had entered it. This was largely because bosses themselves recognized that they must change in order to survive. Thus they sometimes allowed their machines to become vehicles of social reform. One example was New York's Tammany Hall, the nation's oldest and most notorious city machine. Its astute leader, Charles Francis Murphy, began in the early years of the century to fuse the techniques of boss rule with some of the concerns of social reformers. Murphy did nothing to challenge the fundamental workings of Tammany Hall. But Tammany began to take an increased interest in state and national politics, which it had traditionally scorned; and it used its political power on behalf of legislation to improve working conditions, protect child laborers, and eliminate the worst abuses of the industrial economy.

In 1911, a terrible fire swept through the factory of the Triangle Shirtwaist Company in New York; 146 workers, most of them women, died. Many of them had been trapped inside the burning building because management had locked the emergency exits to prevent malingering. For the next three years, a state commission studied not only the background of the fire but the general condition of the industrial workplace. It was responding to intense public pressure from women's groups and New York City labor unions—and to less-public pressure from Tammany Hall. By 1914, the commission had issued a series of reports calling for major reforms in the conditions of modern labor.

The report itself was a classic progressive document, based on the testimony of experts, filled with statistics and technical data. Yet when its recommendations reached the New York legislature, its most effective supporters were not middle-class progressives but two Tammany Democrats from working-class backgrounds: Senator Robert F. Wagner and Assemblyman Alfred E. Smith. With the support of Murphy and the backing of other Tammany legislators, they steered through a series of pioneering labor laws that imposed strict regulations on factory owners and established effective mechanisms for enforcement.

Western Progressives

The American West produced some of the most notable progressive leaders of the time: Hiram Johnson of California, George Norris of Nebraska, William Borah of Idaho, and others—almost all of whom spent at least some of their political careers in the United States Senate. That was because for western states, the most important target of reform energies was not state or local governments, which had relatively little power, but the federal government, which exercised a kind of authority in the West that it had never possessed in the East.

Many of the most important issues to the future of the West required action above the state level. Disputes over water, for example, almost always involved rivers and streams that crossed state lines. More significant, perhaps, the federal government exercised enormous power over the lands and resources of the western states and provided substantial subsidies to the region in the form of land grants and support for railroad and water projects. Huge areas of the West remained (and still remain) public lands, controlled by Washington—a far greater proportion than in any states east of the Mississippi; and much of the growth of the West was (and continues to be) a result of federally funded dams and water projects.

Because so much authority in the region rested in federal bureaucracies which state and local governments could not control, political parties in most of the West were relatively weak. That was one reason why western states could move so quickly and decisively to embrace reforms that parties did not like: the initiative, the referendum, the recall, direct primaries. It is also why aspiring politicians were much quicker to look to Washington as a place from which they could influence the future of their region.

African Americans and Reform

One social question that received relatively little attention from white progressives was race. But among African Americans themselves, the progressive era produced some significant challenges to existing racial norms.

African Americans faced greater obstacles than any other group in challenging their own oppressed status and seeking reform. That was one reason why so many embraced the message of Booker T. Washington in the late nineteenth century, to "put down your bucket where you are," to work for immediate self-improvement rather than long-range social change. Not all blacks, however, were content with this approach. And by the turn of the century a powerful challenge was emerging—to the philosophy of Washington and, more important, to the entire structure of race relations. The chief spokesman for this new approach was W. E. B. Du Bois, a Harvard-trained sociologist and historian with a more expansive view than Washington of the future of his race.

In *The Souls of Black Folk* (1903), Du Bois launched an open attack on Washington's "Atlanta Compromise," which urged blacks to postpone efforts to achieve political equality and concentrate on self-improvement. Du Bois accused Washington of encouraging white efforts to impose segregation and of unnecessarily limiting the aspirations of his race. Rather than content themselves with education at the trade and agricultural schools, Du Bois advocated, talented blacks should accept nothing less than a full university education. They should aspire to the professions. They should, above all, fight for immediate progress on civil rights, not simply wait for them to be granted as a reward for patient striving. In 1905, Du Bois and a group of his supporters met at Niagara Falls—on the Canadian side of the border because no hotel on the American side of the Falls would have them—and launched what became known as the Niagara Movement. Four years later, after a race riot in Springfield, Illinois, they joined with white progressives sympathetic to their cause to form the National Association for the Advancement of Colored People (NAACP). In the years that followed, the new organization led the drive for equal rights, using as its principal weapon lawsuits in the federal courts.

W. E. B. DU BOIS AT HIS DESK Although W. E. B. Du Bois, unlike Booker T. Washington, never developed a large popular following, he was the acknowledged leader of the black elite in the late nineteenth and early twentieth centuries. He was the first African American to earn a doctorate at Harvard University, and he published a number of distinguished works of history and sociology during his long career. He also served as editor of *The Crisis*, the newspaper of the NAACP (which he had helped to found). He died in 1963, at the age of ninety-five.

The NAACP was not a radical, or even an egalitarian, organization. It relied, rather, on the efforts of the most intelligent and educated members of the black race, the "talented tenth" as Du Bois called them. And it stressed not so much the elevation of all blacks from poverty and oppression as the opportunity for exceptional blacks to gain positions of full equality. Ultimately, its members believed, such efforts would benefit all blacks. By creating a trained elite, blacks would in effect be creating a leadership group capable of fighting for the rights of the race as a whole.

CRUSADES FOR ORDER AND REFORM

Reformers directed many of their energies at the political process. But they also crusaded on behalf of what they considered moral issues. There were campaigns to eliminate alcohol from national life, to curb prostitution, to regulate divorce. There were efforts to restrict immigration and to curb the power of monopoly in the industrial economy. There were crusades to resolve what many considered longstanding injustices, of which the most prominent was the campaign for woman suffrage. Proponents of each of those reforms believed that success would help regenerate society as a whole.

The Temperance Crusade

Many progressives considered the elimination of alcohol from American life a necessary step in restoring order to society. Workers in settlement houses and social agencies abhorred the effects of drinking on working-class families: scarce wages vanished as workers spent hours in saloons; drunkenness spawned violence, and occasionally murder, within urban families. Women, in particular, saw alcohol as a source of some of the greatest problems of working-class wives and mothers, and hoped through temperance to reform abusive or irresponsible male behavior and thus improve women's lives. Employers regarded alcohol as an impediment to industrial efficiency; workers often missed time on the job because of drunkenness or, worse, came to the factory intoxicated and performed their tasks sloppily and dangerously. Critics of economic privilege denounced the liquor industry as one of the nation's most sinister trusts. And political reformers, who looked on the saloon (correctly) as one of the central institutions of the machine, saw an attack on drinking as part of an attack on the bosses. Out of such varied sentiments emerged the temperance movement.

Temperance had been a major reform movement before the Civil War, mobilizing large numbers of people (and particularly large numbers of women) in a crusade with strong religious overtones. Beginning in the 1870s, it experienced a major resurgence. As in the antebellum years, it was a movement led and supported primarily by women. In 1873, temperance advocates formed the Women's Christian Temperance Union (WCTU), led after 1879 by Frances Willard. By 1911, it had 245,000 members and had become the largest single women's organization in American history to that point. The WCTU publicized the evils of alcohol and the connection between drunkenness and family violence, unemployment, poverty, and disease. In 1893, the Anti-Saloon League joined the temperance movement and, along with the WCTU, began to press for a specific legislative solution: the legal abolition of saloons. Gradually, that demand grew to include the complete prohibition of the sale and manufacture of alcoholic beverages.

Despite substantial opposition from immigrant and working-class voters, pressure for prohibition grew steadily through the first decades of the new century. By 1916, nineteen states had passed prohibition laws. But since the consumption of alcohol was actually increasing in many unregulated areas, temperance supporters were beginning to advocate national prohibition. American entry into World War I, and the moral fervor it unleashed, provided the last push to the advocates of prohibition. In 1917, with the support of rural fundamentalists who opposed alcohol on moral and religious grounds, progressive advocates of prohibition steered through Congress a constitutional amendment embodying their demands. Two years later, after ratification by every state in the nation except Connecticut and Rhode Island (with large populations of Catholic immigrants opposed to prohibition), the Eighteenth Amendment became law, to take effect in January 1920.

Immigration Restriction

Virtually all reformers agreed that the growing immigrant population had created social problems, but there was wide disagreement on how best to respond. Some progressives believed that helping the new residents adapt to American society was the proper approach. Others argued that efforts at assimilation had failed and that the only solution was to limit the flow of new arrivals.

In the first decades of the century, the arguments of this second, more pessimistic, group gradually gained strength; and pressure grew to close the nation's gates. New scholarly theories, appealing to the progressive respect for expertise, argued that the introduction of immigrants into American society was diluting the purity of the nation's racial stock. The spurious "science" of eugenics spread the belief that human inequalities were hereditary and that immigration was contributing to the multiplication of the unfit. A special federal commission of "experts," chaired by Senator William P. Dillingham of Vermont, issued an elaborate report filled with statistics and scholarly testimony. It argued that the newer immigrant groups—largely southern and eastern Europeans—had proved themselves less assimilable than earlier immigrants. Immigration, the report implied, should be restricted by nationality. Even many people who rejected racial arguments supported limiting immigration as a way to solve such urban problems as overcrowding, unemployment, strained social services, and social unrest.

The combination of these concerns gradually won for the nativists the support of some of the nation's leading progressives: Theodore Roosevelt, Senator Henry Cabot Lodge, and others. Powerful opponents—employers who saw immigration as a source of cheap labor, immigrants themselves, and the immigrants' political representatives—managed to block the restriction movement for a time. But by the beginning of World War I (which itself effectively blocked immigration temporarily), the nativist tide was clearly rising.

The Dream of Socialism

At no time in the history of the United States to that point, and in few times after it, did radical critiques of the capitalist system attract more support than in the period between 1900 and 1914. Although never a force to rival, or even seriously threaten, the two major parties, the Socialist Party of America grew during the progressive era into a force of considerable strength. In the election of 1900, it had attracted the support of fewer than 100,000 voters; in 1912, its durable leader and perennial presidential candidate, Eugene V. Debs, received nearly 1 million ballots. Strongest in urban immigrant communities (particularly among Germans and Jews), it attracted the loyalties, too, of a substantial number of Protestant farmers in the South and Midwest. Socialists won election to over 1,000 state and local offices. And they had the support at times of such intellectuals as Lincoln Steffens, the crusader against municipal corruption, and Walter Lippmann, the brilliant young journalist and social critic. Florence Kelley, Frances Willard, and other women reformers were attracted to socialism because of its support for pacifism and labor militancy.

Virtually all socialists agreed on the need for basic structural changes in the economy, but they differed widely on the extent of those changes and the tactics necessary to achieve them. Some endorsed the radical goals of European Marxists (a complete end to capitalism and private property); others envisioned a more moderate reform that would allow small-scale private enterprise to survive but would nationalize major industries. Militant groups within the party favored direct, even revolutionary action. Most conspicuous was the radical labor union the Industrial Workers of the World (IWW), whose members were known to their opponents as "Wobblies." Under the leadership of William ("Big Bill") Haywood, the IWW advocated a single union for all workers, making it one of the few labor organizations of its time committed to organizing the unskilled, and abolition of the "wage slave" system; it rejected political action in favor of strikes—especially the general strike. The Wobblies were widely believed to have been responsible for the dynamiting of railroad lines and power stations and other acts of terror, although evidence of their actual participation in such activities is slim.

More moderate socialists, who advocated peaceful change through political struggle, dominated the party. They emphasized a gradual education of the public to the need for change and patient efforts within the system to achieve it. But by the end of World War I, because the party had refused to support the war effort and because of a growing wave of antiradicalism that subjected the socialists to enormous harassment and persecution, socialism was in decline as a significant political force.

Decentralization and Regulation

Many reformers agreed with the socialists that the greatest threat to the nation's economy was excessive centralization of power and concentration of wealth, but they retained a faith in the possibilities of reform within a capitalist system. Rather than nationalize basic industries, they hoped to restore the economy to a more human scale. Few envisioned a return to a society of small, local enterprises; some consolidation, they recognized, was inevitable. They did, however, argue that the federal government should work to break up the largest combinations and enforce a balance between the need for bigness and the need for competition. This viewpoint came to be identified particularly closely with Louis D. Brandeis, a brilliant lawyer and later a justice of the Supreme Court, who spoke and wrote widely (most notably in his 1913 book, *Other People's Money*) about the "curse of bigness."

Other progressives were less enthusiastic about the virtues of competition. More important to them was efficiency, which they believed economic concentration encouraged. What government should do, they argued, was not fight "bigness" but guard against abuses of power by large institutions. It should distinguish between "good trusts" and "bad trusts," encouraging the good while disciplining the bad. Since economic consolidation was destined to remain a permanent feature of American society, continuing oversight by a strong, modernized government, led by a strong president, was essential. One of the most important spokesmen for this emerging "nationalist" position was Herbert Croly, whose 1909 book, *The Promise of American Life*, became an influential progressive document.

Opinions varied widely on how to achieve economic order. But increasingly, attention focused on some form of coordination of the industrial economy. To some, that meant businesses themselves should learn new ways of cooperation and self-regulation; some of the most energetic "progressive" reformers of the period, in fact, were businessmen searching for ways to bring order to their own troubled world. To others, the solution was for government to play a more active role in regulating and planning economic life. One of those who came to endorse that position (although not fully until after 1910) was Theodore Roosevelt, who became for a time the most powerful symbol of the reform impulse at the national level.

D E B A T I N G　　T H E　　P A S T

Progressivism

NTIL THE EARLY 1950s, most historians seemed to agree on the central characteristics of early twentieth-century progressivism. It was just what many progressives themselves had said it was: a movement by the "people" to curb the power of "special interests." More specifically, it was a protest by an aroused citizenry against the excessive power of urban bosses, corporate moguls, and corrupt elected officials.

In 1951, George Mowry began the process of challenging these assumptions by examining progressives in California and describing them as a small, privileged elite of business and professional figures: people who considered themselves the natural leaders of society and who were trying to recover their fading influence from the new capitalist institutions that had displaced them. Progressivism was not, in other words, a popular, democratic movement; it was the effort of a displaced elite to restore its authority. Richard Hofstadter expanded on this idea in *The Age of Reform* (1955) by describing reformers as people afflicted by "status anxiety," fading elites suffering not from economic but from psychological discontent.

The Mowry-Hofstadter argument soon encountered a range of challenges. In 1963, Gabriel Kolko published his influential study *The Triumph of Conservatism*, in which he rejected both the older "democratic" view of progressivism and the newer "status-anxiety" view. Progressive reform, he argued, was not an effort to protect the people from the corporations; it was, rather, a vehicle through which corporate leaders used the government to protect themselves from competition. Regulation, Kolko argued, was "invariably controlled by the leaders of the regulated industry and directed towards ends they deemed acceptable or desirable."

A more moderate reinterpretation came from historians embracing what would later be called the "organizational" approach to twentieth-century

American history. First Samuel Hays, in *The Response to Industrialism* (1957), and then Robert Wiebe, in *The Search for Order* (1967), portrayed progressivism as a broad effort by businessmen, professionals, and other middle-class people to bring order and efficiency to political and economic life. In the new industrial society, economic power was increasingly concentrated in large, national organizations, while social and political life remained centered primarily in local communities. Progressivism, Wiebe argued, was the effort of a "new middle class"—a class tied to the emerging national economy—to stabilize and enhance its position in society by bringing those two worlds together.

In the 1970s and 1980s, scholarship on progressivism moved in so many different directions that some historians came to despair of finding any consistent meaning in the term. Much of the new scholarship focused on discovering new groups among whom "progressive" ideas and efforts flourished. Historians found evidence of progressivism in the rising movement by consumers to define their interests; in the growth of reform movements among African Americans; in the changing nature of urban political machines; and in the political activism of working people and labor organizations. Particularly influential was the effort to reveal the crucial role of women in promoting reform as a way of protecting their interests within a rapidly changing domestic sphere or of expanding their role in the public world.

Other scholars attempted to identify progressivism with broad changes in the structure and culture of politics. Richard McCormick, writing in 1981, argued that the crucial change in the "progressive era" was the decline of political parties and the corresponding rise of interest groups working for particular social and economic goals. Progressivism, he and others have suggested, was not so much a coherent "movement" as part of the broader process by which Americans adapted their political and social systems to the realities of the modern industrial age. At the same time, many historians were arguing that the role of women in progressive efforts helped determine the nature of early-twentieth-century reform, that women not only dominated many reform activities but shaped them to serve what they perceived to be the interests of their gender.

The search for the "essence" of progressivism will undoubtedly continue. But the scholarship of recent decades suggests that the real answer to the nature of progressive reform may be a recognition of its enormous diversity.

CHAPTER TWENTY-TWO

The Battle for National Reform

Theodore Roosevelt and the Progressive Presidency
The Troubled Succession ~ Woodrow Wilson and the New Freedom
The "Big Stick": America and the World, 1901–1917

EFFORTS TO REFORM the industrial economy encountered repeated frustrations at the state and local levels. The great combinations were national in scope, and reformers gradually concluded that only national action could effectively control their power. Beginning early in the twentieth century, they began to look to the federal government.

But just as at the state and local levels, the national government—mired in partisan politics—seemed poorly suited to serve as an agent of reform. Progressives attempted to make it more responsive to their demands. Some reformers, for example, urged an end to the system by which state legislatures elected the members of the United States Senate; they proposed instead a direct popular election, which they believed would force the Senate to react more directly to public demands. The Seventeenth Amendment, passed by Congress in 1912 and ratified by the states in 1913, provided for that change.

But even a reformed Congress, progressives believed, could not be expected to provide the kind of coherent leadership their agenda required. Congress was too clumsy, too divided, too tied to local, parochial interests. If the federal government was truly to fulfill its mission, most reformers agreed, it would require leadership from the one office capable of providing "modern," "efficient" leadership: the presidency.

THEODORE ROOSEVELT AND THE PROGRESSIVE PRESIDENCY

To a generation of progressive reformers, Theodore Roosevelt was more than an admired public figure; he was an idol. No president before and few after attracted such attention and devotion. Yet for all his popularity among

TIME LINE

1901	1902	1903	1904
McKinley assassinated	Northern Securities antitrust case	Department of Commerce and Labor created	Roosevelt Corollary
Theodore Roosevelt becomes president			Panamanian independence
Hay-Pauncefote Treaty			Roosevelt elected

1906	1908	1909	1912
Hepburn Railroad Regulation Act	Taft elected president	Payne-Aldrich Tariff	Wilson elected president
Meat Inspection Act		U.S. troops in Nicaragua	

1913	1914	1916
16th Amendment (income tax)	Federal Trade Commission Act	U.S. troops in Mexico
17th Amendment (direct election of U.S. senators)	Panama Canal opened	
Federal Reserve Act	U.S. troops in Haiti	

reformers, Roosevelt was in many respects decidedly conservative. He earned his extraordinary popularity less because of the extent of his reforms than because of his ebullient public personality and because he brought to his office a broad conception of its powers and invested the presidency with something of its modern status as the center of national political life.

The Accidental President

When President William McKinley suddenly died in September 1901, the victim of an assassination, Roosevelt (who had been elected vice president less than a year before) was only forty-two years old, the youngest man ever to assume the presidency. Already, however, he had achieved a reputation within the Republican Party as something of a wild man. Party leaders sensed his independence and despaired of controlling him. Mark Hanna, who had warned McKinley against selecting Roosevelt as his running mate, exclaimed, "Now look, that damned cowboy is president of the United States!" But Roosevelt as president never openly rebelled against the leaders of his party. He became, rather, a champion of cautious, moderate change.

Roosevelt envisioned the federal government not as the agent of any particular interest but as a mediator of the public good, with the president at its center. This attitude found expression in Roosevelt's policies toward the great industrial combinations. He was not opposed to the principle of economic concentration, but he acknowledged that consolidation produced dangerous abuses of power. He allied himself, therefore, with those progressives who urged regulation (but not destruction) of the trusts.

At the heart of Roosevelt's policy was his desire to win for government the power to investigate the activities of corporations and publicize the results. The pressure of educated public opinion, he believed, would alone eliminate most corporate abuses. Government could legislate solutions for those that remained.

Roosevelt engaged in a few highly publicized efforts to break up combinations, among them a 1902 suit against a great new railroad combination in the Northwest, the Northern Securities Company. But he was not a trustbuster at heart, and his occasional use of antitrust law did not mark any serious effort to reverse the prevailing trend toward economic concentration.

A similar commitment to establishing the government as an impartial regulatory mechanism shaped Roosevelt's policy toward labor. In the past, federal intervention in industrial disputes had almost always meant action on behalf of employers. Roosevelt was willing to consider labor's position as well. When a bitter 1902 strike by the United Mine Workers against the anthracite coal industry dragged on long enough to endanger coal supplies for the coming winter, Roosevelt asked both the operators and the miners to accept impartial federal arbitration; and he threatened to dispatch federal troops to seize the mines when the owners refused. They soon relented. Arbitrators awarded the strikers a 10 percent wage increase and a nine-hour day. Despite such episodes, Roosevelt viewed himself as no more the champion of labor than of management. On several occasions, he ordered federal troops to intervene in strikes on behalf of employers.

Reform was not Roosevelt's main priority during his first years as president. He was principally concerned with winning an election in his own right, which meant not antagonizing the conservative Republican Old Guard. By early 1904, Roosevelt had all but neutralized his opposition within the party. He won its presidential nomination with ease. And in the general election, where he faced a pallid conservative Democrat, Alton B. Parker, he captured over 57 percent of the popular vote and lost no states outside the South.

The Square Deal

During the 1904 campaign, Roosevelt boasted that he had worked in the anthracite coal strike to provide everyone with a "square deal." In his second term, he set out to extend this square deal further, although some of his efforts were more symbolic than substantive. One of his first targets was the powerful railroad industry. The Interstate Commerce Act of 1887, establishing the Interstate Commerce Commission (ICC), had been an early effort to regulate the industry, but over the years the courts had sharply limited its influence. The Hepburn Railroad Regulation Act of 1906 sought to restore some regulatory authority to the government by giving the ICC authority to inspect the books of railroad companies, a relatively modest expansion of its power.

Roosevelt also pressured Congress to enact the Pure Food and Drug Act, which restricted the sale of dangerous or ineffective medicines but had very modest enforcement mechanisms. When Upton Sinclair's powerful novel *The Jungle* appeared in 1906, featuring appalling descriptions of conditions

MAKING SAUSAGES The shockingly unsanitary conditions by which meatpackers (such as those shown here in the Chicago stockyards) made sausages inspired Upton Sinclair's novel *The Jungle*, which in turn precipitated federal legislation, the Meat Inspection Act of 1906, establishing government inspection of meat products.

in the meatpacking industry, Roosevelt insisted on passage of the Meat Inspection Act, which ultimately helped eliminate many diseases once transmitted in impure meat. Starting in 1907, he proposed even more stringent measures: an eight-hour day for workers, broader compensation for victims of industrial accidents, inheritance and income taxes, regulation of the stock market, and others. He also started openly to criticize conservatives in Congress and the judiciary, who were obstructing these programs. The result was not only a general stalemate in Roosevelt's reform agenda but a widening gulf between the president and the conservative wing of his party.

Roosevelt's aggressive policies on behalf of conservation contributed to that gulf. A lifelong sportsman and naturalist, he had long been concerned about the unchecked exploitation of America's natural resources and its remaining wilderness. Using executive powers, he limited private development on millions of acres of undeveloped government land by adding them to the previously modest national forest system. When conservatives in Congress restricted his authority over public lands in 1907, Roosevelt and his chief forester, Gifford Pinchot, worked furiously before the bill became law to

Establishment of National Parks and Forests

seize all the forests and many of the water power sites still in the public domain.

Roosevelt was the first president to take an active interest in the new and struggling American conservation movement, and his policies had a lasting effect on national environmental policies. More than most public figures, he was sympathetic to the concerns of the naturalists—those within the movement committed to protecting the natural beauty of the land. But Roosevelt's policies more often favored another faction within the conservation movement—those who believed in carefully managed development. That was in part a result of the influence of Pinchot, the first director of the National Forest Service, who supported rational and efficient human use of the wilderness.

The Old Guard may have opposed Roosevelt's efforts to extend government control over vast new lands. But they eagerly supported another important aspect of Roosevelt's natural resource policy: public reclamation and irrigation projects. In 1902, the president backed the Newlands Reclamation Act, which provided federal funds for the construction of dams, reservoirs, and canals in the West—projects to open new lands for cultivation and, years later, to provide cheap electric power. It was the beginning of many years of federal aid for irrigation and power development in the western states.

Despite the flurry of reforms Roosevelt was able to enact, the government still had relatively little control over the industrial economy. That became clear in 1907, when a serious recession began. Conservatives blamed Roosevelt's "mad" economic policies for the disaster. And while the president, naturally (and correctly), disagreed, he nevertheless acted quickly to reassure business leaders that he would not interfere with their private recovery efforts.

The great financier J. P. Morgan helped construct a pool of the assets of several important New York banks to prop up shaky financial institutions. The key to the arrangement, Morgan told the president, was the purchase by U.S. Steel of the shares of the Tennessee Coal and Iron Company, currently held by a threatened New York bank. He would, he insisted, need assurances that the purchase would not prompt antitrust action. Roosevelt tacitly agreed, and the Morgan plan proceeded. Whether or not as a result, the panic soon subsided.

Roosevelt loved being president, and many people assumed he would run for the office again in 1908 despite the longstanding tradition of presidents' serving no more than two terms. But the Panic of 1907, combined with Roosevelt's growing "radicalism" during his second term, so alienated conservatives in his own party that he might have had difficulty winning the Republican nomination for another term despite his great popularity. In 1904, moreover, he had made a public promise to step down four years later. And so, after nearly eight energetic years in the White House, during which he had transformed the role of the presidency in American government, Theodore Roosevelt, fifty years old, retired from public life—briefly.

THE TROUBLED SUCCESSION

William Howard Taft, who assumed the presidency in 1909, had been Theodore Roosevelt's most trusted lieutenant and his hand-picked successor; progressive reformers believed him to be one of their own. But Taft had also been a restrained and moderate jurist, a man with a punctilious regard for legal process; conservatives expected him to abandon Roosevelt's aggressive use of presidential powers. By seeming acceptable to almost everyone, Taft won election to the White House in 1908 with almost ridiculous ease. He received his party's nomination virtually uncontested. His victory in the general election in November—over William Jennings Bryan, running forlornly for the Democrats for the third time—was a foregone conclusion. Taft entered the White House on a wave of good feeling.

Four years later, however, Taft would leave office the most decisively defeated president of the twentieth century, his party deeply divided and the government in the hands of a Democratic administration for the first time in twenty years. Taft's failure was a result in part of his own character and style: his cautious, limited use of presidential powers; his failure to match Roosevelt's personal dynamism. (Contributing to Taft's image as a less than vigorous man was his enormous weight, which at times rose to 350 pounds.) More significant, however, was that having come into office as the darling of progressives and conservatives alike, he soon found that he could not please both groups. Gradually he found himself, without really intending it, pleasing the conservatives and alienating the progressives.

Taft and the Progressives

Taft's first problem arose in the opening months of the new administration, when he called Congress into special session to lower protective tariff rates, an old progressive demand. But the president made no effort to overcome the opposition of the congressional Old Guard, arguing that it would violate the constitutional doctrine of separation of powers if he were to intervene in legislative matters. The result was the feeble Payne-Aldrich Tariff, which reduced tariff rates scarcely at all and in some areas actually raised them. Progressives resented the president's passivity and were suspicious of his motives.

A sensational controversy broke out late in 1909 that helped destroy Taft's popularity with reformers for good. Many progressives had been unhappy when Taft replaced Roosevelt's secretary of the interior, James R. Garfield, an aggressive conservationist, with Richard A. Ballinger, a more conservative corporate lawyer. Suspicion of Ballinger grew when he attempted to invalidate Roosevelt's removal of nearly 1 million acres of forests and mineral reserves from the public lands available for private development.

In the midst of this mounting concern, Louis Glavis, an Interior Department investigator, charged the new secretary with having once connived to turn over valuable public coal lands in Alaska to a private syndicate for personal profit. Glavis took the evidence to Gifford Pinchot, still head of the Forest Service and a critic of Ballinger's policies. Pinchot took the charges to the president. Taft investigated them and decided they were groundless. But Pinchot was not satisfied, particularly after Taft fired Glavis for his part in the episode. He leaked the story to the press and asked Congress to investigate the scandal. The president discharged him for insubordination, and the congressional committee appointed to study the controversy, dominated by Old Guard Republicans, exonerated Ballinger. But progressives throughout the country supported Pinchot. The controversy aroused as much public passion as any dispute of its time; and when it was over, Taft had alienated the supporters of Roosevelt completely and, it seemed, irrevocably.

The Return of Roosevelt

During most of these controversies, Theodore Roosevelt was far away: on a long hunting safari in Africa and an extended tour of Europe. To the American public, however, Roosevelt remained a formidable presence. His return to New York in the spring of 1910 was a major public event.

Roosevelt insisted that he had no plans to reenter politics, but his resolve lasted less than a week. Politicians began flocking immediately to his Long Island home for conferences. Roosevelt took an active role in several New York political controversies, and within a month, he announced that he would embark on a national speaking tour before the end of the summer. Furious with Taft, he was becoming convinced that he alone was capable of reuniting the Republican Party.

ROOSEVELT AT OSAWATOMIE Roosevelt's famous speech at Osawatomie, Kansas, in 1910 was the most radical of his career and openly marked his break with the Taft administration and the Republican leadership.

The real signal of Roosevelt's decision to assume leadership of Republican reformers came in a speech he gave on September 1, 1910, in Osawatomie, Kansas. In it he outlined a set of principles, which he labeled the "New Nationalism," that made clear he had moved a considerable way from the cautious conservatism of the first years of his presidency. He argued that social justice was possible only through the vigorous efforts of a strong federal government whose executive acted as the "steward of the public welfare." Those who thought primarily of property rights and personal profit "must now give way to the advocate of human welfare." He supported graduated income and inheritance taxes, workers' compensation for industrial accidents, regulation of the labor of women and children, tariff revision, and firmer regulation of corporations.

Spreading Insurgency

The congressional elections of 1910 provided further evidence of how far the progressive revolt had spread. In primary elections, conservative Republicans suffered defeat after defeat while almost all the progressive incumbents were reelected. In the general election, the Democrats, who were now offering progressive candidates of their own, won control of the House of Representatives for the first time in sixteen years and gained strength in the Senate. Reform sentiment seemed clearly on the rise. But Roosevelt still denied any presidential ambitions and claimed that his real purpose was to pressure Taft to return to progressive policies. Two events, however, changed his mind. The first was an antitrust decision by the Taft administration. On October 27, 1911, the administration announced a suit against U.S. Steel, charging, among other things, that the 1907 acquisition of the Tennessee Coal and Iron Company had been illegal. Roosevelt had approved that acquisition in the midst of the 1907 panic, and he was enraged by the implication that he had acted improperly.

But Roosevelt was reluctant at first to become a candidate for president, largely because Senator Robert La Follette, the great Wisconsin progressive, had been working since 1911 to secure the presidential nomination for himself. But La Follette's candidacy stumbled in February 1912. Exhausted, and distraught over the illness of a daughter, he appeared to suffer a nervous breakdown during a speech in Philadelphia. Roosevelt announced his candidacy on February 22.

T. R. Versus Taft

La Follette retained some diehard support. But for all practical purposes, the campaign for the Republican nomination had now become a battle between Roosevelt, the champion of the progressives, and Taft, the candidate of the conservatives. Roosevelt scored overwhelming victories in all thirteen presidential primaries. Taft, however, remained the choice of most party leaders, whose preference was decisive.

The battle for the nomination at the Chicago convention revolved around an unusually large number of contested delegates: 254 in all. Roosevelt needed fewer than half the disputed seats to clinch the nomination. But the Republican National Committee, controlled by the Old Guard, awarded all but 19 of them to Taft. At a rally the night before the convention opened, Roosevelt addressed 5,000 cheering supporters and announced that if the party refused to seat his delegates, he would continue his own candidacy outside the party. "We stand at Armageddon," he told the roaring crowd, "and we battle for the Lord." The next day, he led his supporters out of the convention, and out of the party. The convention then quietly nominated Taft on the first ballot.

Roosevelt summoned his supporters back to Chicago in August for another convention, this one to launch the new Progressive Party and nominate himself as its presidential candidate. Roosevelt approached the battle feeling, as he put it, "fit as a bull moose" (thus giving his new party an enduring nickname). But by then, he was aware that his cause was virtually hopeless. That was partly because many of the insurgents who had supported him during the primaries refused to follow him out of the Republican Party. It was also because of the man the Democrats had nominated for president.

WOODROW WILSON
AND THE NEW FREEDOM

The 1912 presidential contest was not simply one between conservatives and reformers. It was also one between two brands of progressivism that reflected two different views of America's future. And it was one that matched the two most important national leaders of the early twentieth century in unequal contest.

Woodrow Wilson

Reform sentiment had been gaining strength within the Democratic as well as the Republican Party in the first years of the century. At the 1912 Democratic convention in Baltimore in June, Champ Clark, the conservative Speaker of the House, was unable to assemble the necessary two-thirds majority because of progressive opposition. Finally, on the forty-sixth ballot, Woodrow Wilson, the governor of New Jersey and the only genuinely progressive candidate in the race, emerged as the party's nominee.

Wilson had risen to political prominence by an unusual path. He had been a professor of political science at Princeton until 1902, when he was named president of the university. Elected governor of New Jersey in 1910, he demonstrated a commitment to reform that he had already displayed as a university president, and during his two years in the statehouse, he earned a national reputation for winning passage of progressive legislation. As a presidential candidate in 1912, Wilson presented a progressive program that came to be called the "New Freedom." Wilson's New Freedom differed from Roosevelt's New Nationalism most clearly in its approach to economic policy and the trusts. Roosevelt believed in accepting economic concentration and using government to regulate and control it. Wilson seemed to side with those who (like Brandeis) believed that bigness was both unjust and inefficient, that the proper response to monopoly was not to regulate it but to destroy it.

The 1912 presidential campaign was something of an anticlimax. William Howard Taft, resigned to defeat, delivered a few desultory, conservative speeches and then lapsed into silence. Roosevelt campaigned energetically (until a gunshot wound from a would-be assassin forced him to the sidelines during the last weeks before the election), but he failed to draw any significant numbers of Democratic progressives away from Wilson. In November, Roosevelt and Taft split the Republicans; Wilson held onto most Democrats and won. He polled only a plurality of the popular vote: 42 percent, compared with 27 percent for Roosevelt, 23 percent for Taft, and 6 percent for the socialist Eugene Debs. But in the electoral college, Wilson won 435 of the 531 votes. Roosevelt had carried only six states, Taft two, Debs none.

The Scholar as President

Wilson was a bold and forceful president. More than William Howard Taft, more even than Theodore Roosevelt, he concentrated the powers of the executive branch in his own hands. He exerted firm control over his cabinet, and he delegated real authority only to those whose loyalty to him was beyond question. Perhaps the clearest indication of his style of leadership was the identity of his most powerful adviser: Colonel Edward M. House, an intelligent and ambitious Texan who held no office and whose only claim to authority was his personal intimacy with the president.

In legislative matters, Wilson skillfully used his position as party leader to weld together a coalition that would support his program. Democratic majorities in both houses of Congress made his task easier. Wilson's first triumph as president was the fulfillment of an old Democratic (and progressive) goal: a substantial lowering of the protective tariff. The Underwood-Simmons Tariff, passed in a special session of Congress that Wilson summoned shortly after his inauguration, provided cuts substantial enough, progressives believed, to introduce real competition into American markets and thus to help break the power of trusts. It passed easily in the House, and despite Senate efforts to weaken its provisions, the bill survived more or less intact. To make up for the loss of revenue under the new tariff, Congress approved a graduated income tax, which the recently adopted Sixteenth Amendment to the Constitution now permitted. This first modern income tax imposed a 1 percent tax on individuals and corporations earning over $4,000, with rates ranging up to 6 percent on incomes over $500,000.

Wilson held Congress in session through the summer to work on a major reform of the American banking system: the Federal Reserve Act,

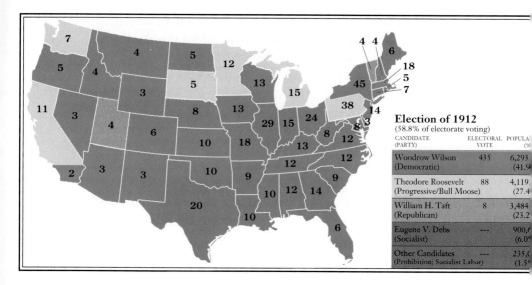

Election of 1912
(58.8% of electorate voting)

CANDIDATE (PARTY)	ELECTORAL VOTE	POPULA (%
Woodrow Wilson (Democratic)	435	6,293 (41.9
Theodore Roosevelt (Progressive/Bull Moose)	88	4,119 (27.4
William H. Taft (Republican)	8	3,484 (23.2
Eugene V. Debs (Socialist)	---	900,C (6.0⁴
Other Candidates (Prohibition; Socialist Labor)	---	235,C (1.5⁴

which Congress passed and which the president signed on December 23, 1913. It was the most important piece of domestic legislation of Wilson's administration. The Federal Reserve Act created twelve regional banks, each to be owned and controlled by the individual banks of its district. The regional Federal Reserve banks would hold a certain percentage of the assets of their member banks in reserve; they would use those reserves to support loans to private banks at an interest (or "discount") rate that the Federal Reserve system would set; they would issue a new type of paper currency—Federal Reserve notes—which would become the nation's basic medium of trade and would be backed by the government. Most important, perhaps, they would serve as central institutions able to shift funds quickly to troubled areas—to meet increased demands for credit or to protect imperiled banks. Supervising and regulating the entire system was a national Federal Reserve Board, whose members were appointed by the president. All "national" banks were required to join the system; smaller banks were encouraged to do the same. Nearly half the nation's banking resources were represented in the system within a year, and 80 percent by the late 1920s.

In 1914, turning to the central issue of his 1912 campaign, Wilson proposed two measures to deal with the problem of monopoly. In the process, he revealed how his own approach to the issue was beginning to change. There was a proposal to create a federal agency through which the government would help business police itself—in other words, a regulatory commission of the type Roosevelt had advocated in 1912. There were, in addition, proposals to strengthen the government's power to prosecute and dismantle the trusts—a decentralizing approach more characteristic of Wilson's campaign. The two measures took shape, ultimately, as the Federal Trade Commission Act and the Clayton Antitrust Act.

The Federal Trade Commission Act created a regulatory agency that would help businesses determine in advance whether their actions would be acceptable to the government. The agency would also have authority to launch prosecutions against "unfair trade practices," which the law did not define, and it would have wide power to investigate corporate behavior. The act, in short, increased the government's regulatory authority significantly. Wilson signed it happily. But he seemed to lose interest in the Clayton Antitrust Bill and did little to protect it from conservative assaults, which greatly weakened it. The vigorous legal pursuit of monopoly that Wilson had promised in 1912 never materialized. The future, he had apparently decided, lay with government supervision.

Retreat and Advance

By the fall of 1914, Wilson believed that the program of the New Freedom was essentially complete and that agitation for reform would now subside. He refused to support the movement for national woman suffrage. Deferring to southern Democrats, and reflecting his own southern background, he condoned the reimposition of segregation in the agencies of the federal government (in contrast to Theodore Roosevelt, who had ordered the elimination of many such barriers). When congressional progressives attempted to enlist his support for new reform legislation, he dismissed their proposals as unconstitutional or unnecessary.

The congressional elections of 1914, however, shattered the president's complacency. Democrats suffered major losses in the House of Representatives, and voters who in 1912 had supported the Progressive Party began returning to the Republicans. Wilson would not be able to rely on a divided opposition when he ran for reelection in 1916. By the end of 1915, therefore, Wilson had begun to support a second flurry of reforms. In January 1916, he appointed Louis Brandeis to the Supreme Court, making him not only the first Jew but the most advanced progressive to serve there. Later, he supported a measure to make it easier for farmers to receive credit and one creating a system of workers' compensation for federal employees.

Much of this renewed effort at reform suggested that Wilson had moved even closer to the New Nationalism. He was sponsoring measures that expanded the role of the national government in important ways, giving it new instruments by which it could regulate the economy and help shape the nation's economic and social structure. In 1916, for example, Wilson supported the Keating-Owen Act, the first federal law regulating child labor. The measure prohibited the shipment of goods produced by underage children across state lines, thus giving an expanded importance to the constitutional clause assigning Congress the task of regulating interstate commerce. (It would be some years before the Supreme Court would uphold this interpretation of the clause; the Court invalidated the Keating-Owen Act in 1918.) The president similarly supported measures that used federal taxing authority as a vehicle for legislating social change. After the Court struck down Keating-Owen, a new law attempted to achieve the same goal by imposing a heavy tax on the products of child labor. (The Court later struck it down too.) And the Smith-Lever Act of 1914 demonstrated another way in which the federal government could influence local behavior; it offered matching federal grants to states that agreed to support agricultural extension education.

THE "BIG STICK": AMERICA AND THE WORLD, 1901–1917

American foreign policy during the progressive years reflected many of the same impulses that were motivating domestic reform. But more than that, it reflected the nation's new sense of itself as a world power with far-flung economic and political interests.

Roosevelt and "Civilization"

Theodore Roosevelt was well suited, both by temperament and by ideology, for an activist foreign policy. He believed in the value and importance of using American power in the world (a conviction he once described by citing the proverb, "Speak softly, but carry a big stick"). But he had two different standards for using that power.

Roosevelt believed that an important distinction existed between the "civilized" and "uncivilized" nations of the world. "Civilized" nations, as he defined them, were predominantly white and Anglo-Saxon or Teutonic; "uncivilized" nations were generally nonwhite, Latin, or Slavic. But racism was only partly the basis of the distinction. At least as important was economic development. He believed, therefore, that Japan, a rapidly industrializing society, had earned admission to the ranks of the civilized.

Civilized nations were, by Roosevelt's definition, producers of industrial goods; uncivilized nations were suppliers of raw materials and markets. There was, he believed, an economic relationship between the two parts that was vital to both of them. A civilized society, therefore, had the right and duty to intervene in the affairs of a "backward" nation to preserve order and stability—for the sake of both nations. That belief was one important reason for Roosevelt's early support of the development of American sea power. By 1906, the American navy had attained a size and strength surpassed only by that of Great Britain (although Germany was fast gaining ground).

Protecting the "Open Door" in Asia

Roosevelt considered the "Open Door" vital for maintaining American trade in the Pacific and for preventing any single nation from establishing dominance there. He looked with alarm, therefore, at the military rivalries involving Japan, Russia, Germany, and France in Asia.

In 1904 the Japanese staged a surprise attack on the Russian fleet at Port Arthur in southern Manchuria, a province of China that both Russia and Japan hoped to control. Roosevelt, hoping to prevent either nation from becoming dominant there, agreed to a Japanese request to mediate an end to the conflict. Russia, faring badly in the war, had no choice but to agree. At a peace conference in Portsmouth, New Hampshire, in 1905, Roosevelt extracted from the embattled Russians a recognition of Japan's territorial gains and from the Japanese an agreement to cease the fighting and expand no further. At the same time, he negotiated a secret agreement with the Japanese to ensure that the United States could continue to trade freely in the region. Roosevelt won the Nobel Peace Prize in 1906 for his work in ending the Russo-Japanese War. But in the years that followed, relations between the United States and Japan steadily deteriorated. Having destroyed the Russian fleet at Port Arthur, Japan now emerged as the preeminent naval power in the Pacific and soon began to exclude American trade from many of the territories it controlled.

It did not help matters that in 1906 the school board of San Francisco voted to segregate the city's Asian schoolchildren in separate schools or that, a year later, the California legislature attempted to pass a law limiting the immigration of Japanese laborers into the state. Anti-Asian riots in California and inflammatory stories in the Hearst papers about the "Yellow Peril" further fanned resentment in Japan. The president persuaded the San Francisco school board to rescind its edict in return for a Japanese agreement to stop the flow of agricultural immigrants into California. Then, lest the Japanese government construe his actions as a sign of weakness, Roosevelt sent sixteen battleships of the new American navy (known as the "Great White Fleet") on an unprecedented voyage around the world that included a call on Japan—to remind the Japanese of the potential might of the United States.

The Iron-Fisted Neighbor

Roosevelt took a particular interest in events in what he (and most other Americans) considered the nation's special sphere of interest: Latin America. Unwilling to share trading rights, let alone military control, with any other nation, Roosevelt embarked on a series of ventures in the Caribbean and South America. He established a pattern of American intervention in the region that would long survive his presidency.

Crucial to Roosevelt's thinking was an incident early in his administration. In 1902, the financially troubled government of Venezuela began to renege on debts to European bankers. Naval forces of Britain, Italy, and Germany blockaded the Venezuelan coast in response. Then German ships began to bombard a Venezuelan port amid rumors that Germany planned to establish a permanent base in the region. Roosevelt used the threat of American naval power to pressure the German navy to withdraw.

The incident helped persuade Roosevelt that European intrusions into Latin America could result not only from aggression but from instability or irresponsibility (such as defaulting on debts) within the Latin American nations themselves. As a result, in 1904 he announced what came to be known as the "Roosevelt corollary" to the Monroe Doctrine. The United States, he claimed, had the right not only to oppose European intervention in the Western Hemisphere but to intervene itself in the domestic affairs of its neighbors if those neighbors proved unable to maintain order and national sovereignty on their own.

The immediate motivation for the Roosevelt corollary, and the first opportunity for using it, was a crisis in the Dominican Republic. A revolution had toppled its corrupt and bankrupt government in 1903, but the new regime proved no better able than the old to make good on the country's $22 million in debts to European nations. Using the rationale provided by the Roosevelt corollary, Roosevelt established, in effect, an American receivership, assuming control of Dominican customs and distributing 45 percent of the revenues to the Dominicans and the rest to foreign creditors. This arrangement lasted, in one form or another, for more than three decades.

In 1902, the United States granted political independence to Cuba, but

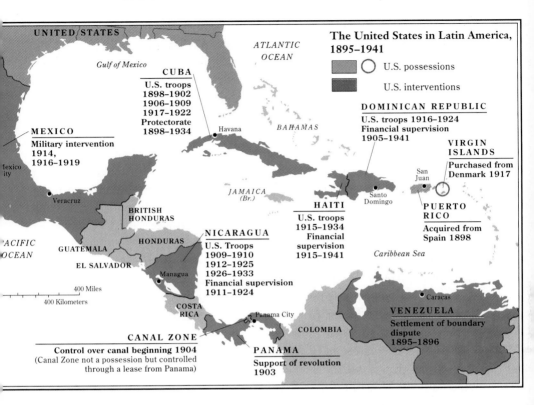

The United States in Latin America, 1895–1941

U.S. possessions
U.S. interventions

UNITED STATES

ATLANTIC OCEAN

Gulf of Mexico

CUBA
U.S. troops
1898–1902
1906–1909
1917–1922
Protectorate
1898–1934

MEXICO
Military intervention
1914,
1916–1919

Mexico City

Veracruz

BAHAMAS

Havana

DOMINICAN REPUBLIC
U.S. troops 1916–1924
Financial supervision
1905–1941

VIRGIN ISLANDS
Purchased from
Denmark 1917

San Juan

Santo Domingo

PUERTO RICO
Acquired from
Spain 1898

JAMAICA (Br.)

HAITI
U.S. troops
1915–1934
Financial
supervision
1915–1941

Caribbean Sea

BRITISH HONDURAS

NICARAGUA
U.S. Troops
1909–1910
1912–1925
1926–1933
Financial supervision
1911–1924

HONDURAS

GUATEMALA

EL SALVADOR

Managua

PACIFIC OCEAN

400 Miles
400 Kilometers

COSTA RICA

CANAL ZONE
Control over canal beginning 1904
(Canal Zone not a possession but controlled
through a lease from Panama)

Panama City

PANAMA
Support of revolution
1903

COLOMBIA

VENEZUELA
Settlement of boundary
dispute
1895–1896

Caracas

only after the new government had agreed to the so-called Platt Amendment (named after Senator Thomas Platt of Pennsylvania) to its constitution. The amendment gave the United States the right to prevent any foreign power from intruding into the new nation. In 1906, when domestic uprisings seemed to threaten the internal stability of the island, Roosevelt reasoned that America must intervene to "protect" Cuba from possible intervention by others. American troops landed in Cuba, quelled the fighting, and remained there for three years.

The Panama Canal

The most celebrated accomplishment of Roosevelt's presidency was the construction of the Panama Canal. Linking the Atlantic and the Pacific by creating a channel through Central America had been an unfulfilled dream of many nations since the mid-nineteenth century. Roosevelt was determined to achieve it.

The first step was the 1901 Hay-Pauncefote Treaty between America and Britain, canceling an 1850 pact in which the two nations had agreed to construct any such canal together. The United States was now free to act alone. The next step was to choose a site for the canal. At first, Roosevelt and many others favored a route across Nicaragua, which would permit a sea-level canal requiring no locks. But they soon turned instead to the narrow Isthmus of Panama in Colombia, the site of an earlier, failed effort by a French company to construct a channel. Although the Panama route was not at sea level (and would thus require locks), it was shorter than the one in Nicaragua. And construction was already about 40 percent complete. When the French company lowered the price for its holdings from $109 million to $40 million, the United States chose Panama.

Roosevelt dispatched John Hay, his secretary of state, to negotiate an agreement with Colombian diplomats in Washington that would allow construction to begin without delay. Under heavy American pressure, the Colombian chargé d'affaires, Tomas Herrán, unwisely signed an agreement giving the United States perpetual rights to a six-mile-wide "canal zone" across Colombia; in return, the United States would pay Colombia $10 million and an annual rental of $250,000. The treaty produced outrage in the Colombian senate, which refused to ratify it. Colombia then sent a new representative to Washington with instructions to demand at least $20 million from the Americans plus a share of the payment to the French.

Roosevelt was furious and began to look for ways to circumvent the Colombian government. Philippe Bunau-Varilla, chief engineer of the French canal project, was a ready ally. In November 1903, he helped organize and finance a revolution in Panama. There had been many previous revolts, all of them failures. But this one had the support of the United States. Roosevelt landed troops from the U.S.S. *Nashville* in Panama to "maintain order." Their presence prevented Colombian forces from suppressing the rebellion, and three days later Roosevelt recognized Panama as an independent nation. The new Panamanian government quickly agreed to the terms the Colombian senate had rejected. Work on the canal proceeded rapidly, and it opened in 1914.

Taft and "Dollar Diplomacy"

Like his predecessor, William Howard Taft worked to advance the nation's economic interests overseas. But he showed little interest in Roosevelt's larger vision of world stability. Taft's secretary of state, the corporate attorney Philander C. Knox, worked aggressively to extend American investments into less developed regions. Critics called his policies "Dollar Diplomacy."

The Taft-Knox foreign policy faced its severest test, and encountered its greatest failure, in the Far East. Ignoring Roosevelt's tacit 1905 agreement with Japan to limit American involvement in Manchuria, the new administration responded to pressure from American bankers and moved aggressively to increase America's economic influence in the region. In particular, Knox worked to include the United States in a consortium of Western powers formed to build railroads in China; and when the Europeans agreed, he went further and tried to exclude the Japanese from any role in Manchuria's railroads. When Japan responded by forming a loose alliance with Russia, the entire railroad project quickly collapsed.

In the Caribbean, the new administration continued and even expanded upon Roosevelt's policies of limiting European and expanding American influence in the region. That meant, Taft and Knox believed, not only preventing disorder but establishing a significant American economic presence there—replacing the investments of European nations with investments from the United States. But Dollar Diplomacy also had a more violent side. When a revolution broke out in Nicaragua in 1909, the administration quickly sided with the insurgents (who had been inspired to revolt by an

OPENING THE PANAMA CANAL The Panama Canal, the greatest engineering feat of the early twentieth century and one of the most notable achievements of Theodore Roosevelt's presidency, opened to shipping in 1913. This photograph shows the Tugboat *Gatun*, the first ship to travel through the canal to the Atlantic, in one of the canal's great locks.

American mining company) and sent American troops into the country to seize the customs houses. As soon as peace was restored, Knox encouraged American bankers to offer substantial loans to the new government, thus increasing Washington's financial leverage over the country. When the new pro-American government faced an insurrection less than two years later, Taft again landed American troops in Nicaragua, this time to protect the existing regime. The troops remained there for more than a decade.

Diplomacy and Morality

Woodrow Wilson entered the presidency with relatively little interest or experience in international affairs. Yet he faced international challenges of a scope and gravity unmatched by those of any president before him. Although the greatest test of Wilsonian diplomacy did not occur until World War I, many of the qualities that he would bring to that ordeal were evident in his foreign policy from his first moments in office, and particularly in his dealings with Latin America.

Having already seized control of the finances of the Dominican Republic in 1905, the United States established a military government there in 1916 when the Dominicans refused to accept a treaty that would have made the country a virtual American protectorate. The military occupation lasted eight years. In Haiti, which shares the island of Hispaniola with the Dominican Republic, Wilson landed the marines in 1915 to quell a revolution in the course of which a mob had murdered an unpopular president. American military forces remained in the country until 1934, and American officers drafted the new Haitian constitution adopted in 1918. When Wilson began to fear that the Danish West Indies might be about to fall into the hands of Germany, he bought the colony from Denmark and renamed it the Virgin Islands. Concerned about the possibility of European influence in Nicaragua, he signed a treaty with that country's government ensuring that no other nation would build a canal there and winning for the United States the right to intervene in Nicaragua's internal affairs to protect American interests. In all of these actions, Wilson was displaying an approach to Latin America very similar to the approaches of Roosevelt and Taft.

But Wilson's view of America's role in the Western Hemisphere (and the world) was not entirely similar to the views of his predecessors. That became clear in his dealings with Mexico. For many years, under the friendly auspices of the corrupt dictator Porfirio Díaz, American businessmen had been establishing an enormous economic presence in Mexico. In 1910, however, Díaz had been overthrown by the popular leader Francisco Madero, who promised democratic reform but who also seemed hostile to American businesses in Mexico. The United States quietly encouraged a reactionary general, Victoriano Huerta, to depose Madero early in 1913, and the Taft administration, in its last weeks in office, prepared to recognize the new Huerta regime and welcome back a receptive environment for American investments in Mexico. Before it could do so, however, the new government murdered Madero, and Woodrow Wilson took office in Washington. The new president instantly announced that he would never recognize Huerta's "government of butchers."

The conflict dragged on for years. At first, Wilson hoped that simply by refusing to recognize Huerta he could help topple the regime and bring to power the opposing Constitutionalists, led by Venustiano Carranza. But when Huerta, with the support of American business interests, established a full military dictatorship in October 1913, the president became more assertive. He pressured the British to stop supporting Huerta. Then he offered to send American troops to assist Carranza. Carranza, aware that such an open alliance with the United States would undermine his popular support in Mexico, declined the offer, but he did secure the right to buy arms in the United States.

In April 1914, a minor naval incident provided the president with an excuse for more open intervention. An officer in Huerta's army briefly arrested several American sailors from the U.S.S. *Dolphin* who had gone ashore in Tampico. The men were immediately released, but the American admiral—unsatisfied with the apology he received—demanded that the Huerta forces fire a twenty-one-gun salute to the American flag as a public display of penance. The Mexicans refused. Wilson used the trivial incident as a pretext for seizing the Mexican port of Veracruz.

Wilson had envisioned a bloodless action, but in a clash with Mexican troops in Veracruz, the Americans killed 126 of the defenders and suffered 19 casualties of their own. Now at the brink of war, Wilson began to look for a way out. His show of force, however, had helped strengthen the position of the Carranza faction, which captured Mexico City in August and forced Huerta to flee the country. At last, it seemed, the crisis might be over.

But Wilson was not yet satisfied. He reacted angrily when Carranza refused to accept American guidelines for the creation of a new government, and he briefly considered throwing his support to still another aspirant to leadership: Carranza's erstwhile lieutenant Pancho Villa, who was now leading a rebel army of his own. When Villa's military position deteriorated, however, Wilson abandoned him and finally, in October 1915, granted preliminary recognition to the Carranza government. By now, however, he had

PANCHO VILLA AND HIS SOLDIERS In 1913, when this photograph was taken, Pancho Villa (second from right) was still on good terms with the government of Woodrow Wilson, which viewed him as a fighter for democracy in Mexico. Three years later, Wilson declared Villa a "bandit" and sent American troops into Mexico in a futile effort to capture him.

created yet another crisis. Villa, angry at what he considered an American betrayal, retaliated in January 1916 by taking sixteen American mining engineers from a train in northern Mexico and shooting them. Two months later, he led his soldiers (or "bandits," as the United States preferred to call them) across the border into Columbus, New Mexico, where they killed seventeen more Americans. His goal, apparently, was to destabilize relations between Wilson and Carranza and provoke a war between them, which might provide him with an opportunity to improve his own declining fortunes.

With the permission of the Carranza government, Wilson ordered General John J. Pershing to lead an American expeditionary force across the Mexican border in pursuit of Villa. The American troops never found Villa, but they did engage in two ugly skirmishes with Carranza's army, in which forty Mexicans and twelve Americans died. Again, the United States and Mexico stood at the brink of war. But at the last minute, Wilson drew back. He quietly withdrew American troops from Mexico, and in March 1917, he at last granted formal recognition to the Carranza regime. By now, however, Wilson's attention was turning elsewhere—to the far greater international crisis engulfing the European continent and ultimately much of the world.

CHAPTER TWENTY-THREE

America and the Great War

The Road to War ～ *"War Without Stint"*
The Search for a New World Order ～ *A Society in Turmoil*

HE GREAT WAR, as it was known to a generation unaware that another, greater war would soon follow, began quietly in August 1914 when Austria-Hungary invaded the tiny Balkan nation of Serbia. Within weeks, however, it had grown into a conflagration engaging the armies of most of the major nations of Europe and shattering forever the delicate balance of power that had maintained a general peace on the Continent since the early nineteenth century. Americans looked on with horror as the war became the most savage in history and as it dragged on, murderously and inconclusively, for two and a half years. But Americans also believed at first that the conflict had little to do with them. They were wrong. After nearly three years of attempting to affect the outcome of the conflict without becoming embroiled in it, the United States formally entered the war in April 1917.

THE ROAD TO WAR

The causes of the war in Europe have been the subject of continued debate for nearly eighty years. But it is clear that the European nations had by 1914 created an unusually precarious international system that careened into war very quickly on the basis of what most historians agree was a minor series of provocations.

The Collapse of the European Peace

The major powers of Europe were organized by 1914 in two great, competing alliances. The "Triple Entente" linked Britain, France, and Russia. The "Triple Alliance" united Germany, the Austro-Hungarian Empire, and

TIME LINE

1914	1915	1916	1917
World War I begins	*Lusitania* torpedoed Wilson supports preparedness	Wilson reelected	German unrestricted submarine warfare U.S. enters World War I Selective Service Act War Industries Board created

1918	1919	1920	1927
Sedition Act Wilson's Fourteen Points Armistice ends war Paris Peace Conference	Senate rejects Treaty of Versailles Race riots (in Chicago and other cities) Steel strike and other labor actions	19th Amendment ratified Palmer Raids and Red Scare Harding elected president	Sacco and Vanzetti executed

Italy. The chief rivalry, however, was not between the two alliances but between the great powers that dominated them: Great Britain and Germany—the former long established as the world's most powerful colonial and commercial nation, the latter ambitious to expand its own empire and become at least Britain's equal.

The Anglo-German rivalry may have been the most important underlying source of the tensions that led to World War I, but it was not the immediate cause of its outbreak. The conflict emerged most directly out of a controversy involving nationalist movements within the Austro-Hungarian Empire. On June 28, 1914, the Archduke Franz Ferdinand, heir to the throne of the tottering empire, was assassinated while paying a state visit to Sarajevo. Sarajevo is the capital of Bosnia, then a province of Austria-Hungary, which Slavic nationalists wished to annex to neighboring Serbia; the archduke's assassin was a Serbian nationalist.

This local controversy quickly escalated through the workings of the system of alliances that the great powers had constructed. Germany supported Austria-Hungary's decision to launch a punitive assault on Serbia. The Serbians called on Russia to help with their defense. The Russians began mobilizing their army on July 30. Things quickly careened out of control. By August 3, Germany had declared war on both Russia and France and had invaded Belgium in preparation for a thrust across the French border. On

August 4, Great Britain—ostensibly to honor its alliance with France, but more importantly to blunt the advance of its principal rival—declared war on Germany. Russia and the Austro-Hungarian Empire formally began hostilities on August 6. Within months, Italy, the Ottoman Empire (Turkey), and other, smaller nations all joined the fighting. By early 1915, virtually the entire European continent (and part of Asia) was embroiled in a major war.

Wilson's Neutrality

Wilson called on his fellow citizens in 1914 to remain "impartial in thought as well as deed." But that was impossible, for several reasons. For one thing, many Americans were not, in fact, genuinely impartial. Some sympathized with the German cause (German Americans, because of affection for Germany; Irish Americans, because of hatred of Britain). Many more (including Wilson himself) sympathized with Britain. Lurid reports of German atrocities in Belgium and France, skillfully exaggerated by British propagandists, strengthened the hostility of many Americans toward Germany.

Economic realities also made it impossible for the United States to deal with the belligerents on equal terms. The British had imposed a naval blockade on Germany to prevent munitions and supplies from reaching the enemy. As a neutral, the United States had the right, in theory, to trade with Germany. A truly neutral response to the blockade would be either to defy it or to stop trading with Britain as well. But while the United States could survive an interruption of its relatively modest trade with the Central Powers (Germany, the Austro-Hungarian Empire, and the Ottoman Empire), it could not easily weather an embargo on its much more extensive trade with the Allies (Britain, France, Italy, and Russia), particularly when war orders from Britain and France soared after 1914, helping produce one of the greatest economic booms in the nation's history. So America tacitly accepted the blockade of Germany and continued trading with Britain. By 1915, the United States had gradually transformed itself from a neutral power into the arsenal of the Allies.

The Germans, in the meantime, were resorting to a new and, in American eyes, barbaric tactic: submarine warfare. Unable to challenge British domination on the ocean's surface, Germany began early in 1915 to use the newly improved submarine to try to stem the flow of supplies to England. Enemy vessels, the Germans announced, would be sunk on sight. Months later, on May 7, 1915, a German submarine sank the British passenger liner *Lusitania* without warning, causing the deaths of 1198 people, 128 of them

Americans. The ship was, it later became clear, carrying not only passengers but munitions; but most Americans considered the attack an unprovoked act.

Wilson angrily demanded that Germany promise not to repeat such outrages and that the Central Powers affirm their commitment to neutral rights (among which, he implausibly insisted, was the right of American citizens to travel on the nonmilitary vessels of belligerents). The Germans finally agreed to Wilson's demands, but tensions between the nations continued to grow. Early in 1916, in response to an announcement that the Allies were now arming merchant ships to sink submarines, Germany proclaimed that it would fire on such vessels without warning. A few weeks later, it attacked the unarmed French steamer *Sussex*, injuring several American passengers. Again, Wilson demanded that Germany abandon its "unlawful" tactics; again, the German government relented.

Preparedness Versus Pacifism

Despite the president's increasing bellicosity in 1916, he was still far from ready to commit the United States to war. One obstacle was American domestic politics. Facing a difficult battle for reelection, Wilson could not ignore the powerful factions that continued to oppose intervention.

The question of whether America should make military and economic preparations for war provided a preliminary issue over which pacifists and interventionists could debate. Wilson at first sided with the antipreparedness forces, denouncing the idea of an American military buildup as needless and provocative. As tensions between the United States and Germany grew, however, he changed his mind. In the fall of 1915, he endorsed an ambitious proposal by American military leaders for a large and rapid increase in the nation's armed forces. By midsummer 1916, armament for a possible conflict was well under way.

Still, the peace faction wielded considerable political strength, as became clear at the Democratic convention in the summer of 1916. The convention became almost hysterically enthusiastic when the keynote speaker, enumerating Wilson's accomplishments, punctuated his list of the president's diplomatic achievements with the chant, "What did we do? What did we do? . . . We didn't go to war! We didn't go to war!" That speech helped produce one of the most prominent slogans of Wilson's reelection campaign: "He kept us out of war." During the campaign, Wilson did nothing to discourage those who argued that the Republican candidate, the progressive New York governor Charles Evans Hughes, was more likely than he to lead the nation into war. Wilson ultimately won reelection by one of the smallest margins for an incumbent in American history: fewer than 600,000 popular votes and only 23 electoral votes. The Democrats retained a precarious control over Congress.

A War for Democracy

The election was behind him. Tensions between the United States and Germany remained high. But Wilson still required a justification for American intervention that would unite public opinion and satisfy his own sense of morality. In the end, he created that rationale himself. The United States, Wilson insisted, had no material aims in the conflict. The nation was, rather, committed to using the war as a vehicle for constructing a new world order, one based on the same progressive ideals that had motivated a generation of reform efforts in America. In a speech before a joint session of Congress in January 1917, he presented a plan for a postwar order in which the United

WOODROW WILSON ASKING FOR WAR Wilson appears before a joint session of Congress on April 2, 1917, and asks for a declaration of war against Germany and its allies in Europe. His impassioned speech did not persuade everyone. Debate over the resolution consumed nearly four days, and when it was over 56 members of Congress continued to oppose it.

States would help maintain peace through a permanent league of nations—a "peace without victory." These were, Wilson believed, goals worth fighting for if there was sufficient provocation. That provocation came quickly.

In January, after months of bloody but inconclusive warfare in the trenches of France, the military leaders of Germany decided on one last dramatic gamble to achieve victory. They would launch a series of major assaults on the enemy's lines in France. At the same time, they would begin unrestricted submarine warfare (against American as well as Allied ships) to cut Britain off from vital supplies. Then, on February 25, the British gave Wilson an intercepted telegram from the German foreign minister, Arthur Zimmermann, to the government of Mexico. It proposed that in the event of war between Germany and the United States, the Mexicans should join with Germany against the Americans. In return, they would regain their "lost provinces" in the north (Texas and much of the rest of the American Southwest) when the war was over. Widely publicized by British propagandists and in the American press, the Zimmermann telegram inflamed public opinion and helped build up popular sentiment for war.

Wilson drew additional comfort from another event, in March 1917. A revolution in Russia toppled the reactionary czarist regime and replaced it with a new, republican government. The United States would now be spared the embarrassment of allying itself with a despotic monarchy. The war for a progressive world order could proceed untainted.

On the rainy evening of April 2, two weeks after German submarines had torpedoed three American ships, Wilson appeared before a joint session of Congress and asked for a declaration of war. Even then, opposition remained. For four days, pacifists in Congress carried on their futile struggle. When the declaration of war finally passed on April 6, fifty representatives and six senators had voted against it.

"WAR WITHOUT STINT"

Armies on both sides in Europe were decimated and exhausted by the time of Woodrow Wilson's declaration of war. The German offensives of early 1917 had failed to produce an end to the struggle, and French and British counteroffensives had accomplished little beyond adding to the appalling casualties. The Allies looked desperately to the United States for help. Wilson, who had called on the nation to wage war "without stint or limit," was eager to oblige.

The Military Struggle

American intervention had its most immediate effect on the conflict at sea. By the spring of 1917, Great Britain was suffering such vast losses from attacks by German submarines—one of every four ships setting sail from British ports never returned—that its ability to continue receiving vital supplies from across the Atlantic was in question. Within weeks of joining the war the United States had begun to alter the balance. A fleet of American destroyers aided the British navy in its assault on the U-boats. Other American warships escorted merchant vessels across the Atlantic. Americans also helped plant antisubmarine mines in the North Sea. The results were dramatic. Sinkings of Allied ships had totaled nearly 900,000 tons in the month of April 1917; by December, the figure had dropped to 350,000; by October 1918, it had declined to 112,000.

Many Americans had hoped that providing naval assistance alone would be enough to turn the tide in the war, but it quickly became clear that a major commitment of American ground forces would be necessary as well to shore up the tottering Allies. Britain and France had few remaining reserves. By early 1918, Russia had withdrawn from the war altogether. After the Bol-

LONGPONT, FRANCE, 1918 American soldiers lead German prisoners-of-war through the streets of a French town shortly before the end of World War I. The devastation was typical of many areas of France where heavy fighting occurred.

shevik Revolution in November 1917 toppled the republican regime created the previous March, the new communist government, led by V. I. Lenin, negotiated a hasty and costly peace with the Central Powers, thus freeing German troops to fight on the western front.

But the United States did not have a large enough standing army to provide the necessary ground forces in 1917. Some (including Theodore Roosevelt, who hoped to raise and lead a regiment himself, much as he had done in the Spanish-American War) urged a voluntary recruitment process. The president, however, decided that only a national draft could provide the needed men. Despite protests, he won passage of the Selective Service Act in mid-May. The draft brought nearly 3 million men into the army; another 2 million joined various branches of the armed services voluntarily.

The engagement of these forces in combat was brief but intense. Not until the spring of 1918 were significant numbers of American troops available for battle. Eight months later, the war was over. Under the command of General John J. Pershing, the American troops joined the existing Allied forces in turning back a series of new German assaults. In early June, they assisted the French in repelling a bitter German offensive at Château-Thierry, near Paris. Six weeks later, the American Expeditionary Force (AEF) helped turn away another assault, at Rheims, farther south. By July 18, the German advance had been halted, and the Allies were beginning a successful offensive of their own. On September 26, an American fighting force of over 1 million soldiers advanced against the Germans in the Argonne Forest as part of a 200-mile attack that lasted nearly seven weeks. By the end of October, the force had helped push the Germans back toward their own border and had cut the enemy's major supply lines to the front.

Faced with an invasion of their own country, German military leaders now began to seek an armistice—an immediate cease-fire that would, they hoped, serve as a prelude to negotiations among the belligerents. Pershing wanted to drive on into Germany itself; but other Allied leaders, after first insisting on terms that made the agreement (in their eyes at least) little different from a surrender, accepted the German proposal. On November 11, 1918, more than four years after it began, the Great War shuddered to a close.

Organizing the Economy for War

By the time the war ended, the federal government had appropriated $32 billion for expenses directly related to the conflict. This was a staggering sum at the time. The entire federal budget had seldom exceeded $1 billion be-

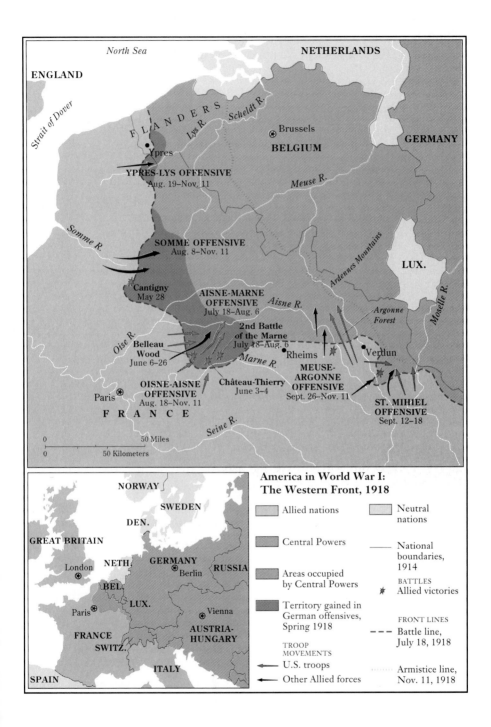

America in World War I:
The Western Front, 1918

fore 1915, and the nation's entire gross national product had been only $35 billion as recently as 1910. To raise the money, the government relied on two devices. First, it launched a major drive to solicit loans from the American people by selling "Liberty Bonds" to the public. By 1920, the sale of bonds, accompanied by elaborate patriotic appeals, had produced $23 billion. At the same time, new taxes were bringing in an additional sum of nearly $10 billion—some from levies on the "excess profits" of corporations, much from new, steeply graduated income and inheritance taxes that ultimately rose as high as 70 percent in some brackets.

An even greater challenge was organizing the economy to meet war needs. The administration tried two very different approaches. In 1916, Wilson established the Council of National Defense, composed of members of his cabinet, and the Civilian Advisory Commission, which set up local defense councils in every state and locality. Economic mobilization, according to this first plan, was to rest on a large-scale dispersal of power to local communities.

But this early administrative structure soon proved completely unworkable, and members of the Council of National Defense urged a more centralized approach. Instead of dividing the economy geographically, they proposed dividing it functionally by organizing a series of planning bodies, each to supervise a specific sector of the economy. Thus one agency would control transportation, another agriculture, another manufacturing. The administrative structure that slowly emerged from such proposals was dominated by a series of "war boards," one to oversee the railroads (led by Secretary of the Treasury William McAdoo), one to supervise fuel supplies (largely coal), another to handle food (a board that helped elevate to prominence the brilliant young engineer and business executive Herbert Hoover). The boards were not without weaknesses, but they generally succeeded in meeting essential war needs without paralyzing the domestic economy.

At the center of the effort to rationalize the economy was the War Industries Board (WIB), an agency created in July 1917 to coordinate government purchases of military supplies. Casually organized at first, it stumbled badly until March 1918, when Wilson restructured it and placed it under the control of the Wall Street financier Bernard Baruch. From then on, the board wielded powers greater (in theory at least) than any government agency had ever possessed. Baruch decided which factories would convert to the production of which war materials, and he set prices for the goods they produced. When materials were scarce, Baruch decided to whom they should go. When corporations were competing for government contracts, he chose

WOMEN WORKERS DURING WORLD WAR I With much of the male work force fighting overseas, women moved into occupations that in other times would have been considered unsuitable for them. One such occupation, pictured here, was delivering huge blocks of ice daily to households to be used (in this age before electric refrigeration) in wooden iceboxes.

among them. He was, it seemed, providing the centralized regulation of the economy that some progressives had long urged.

In reality, the vaunted efficiency of the WIB was something of a myth. The agency was, in fact, plagued by mismanagement and inefficiency and was less responsible for the nation's ability to meet its war needs than the sheer extent of American resources and productive capacities. Nor was the WIB in any real sense an example of state control of the economy. Baruch viewed himself, openly and explicitly, as a partner of business; and within the WIB, businessmen themselves—the so-called dollar-a-year men, who took paid leave from their corporate jobs and worked for the government for a token salary—supervised the affairs of the private economy. Rather than working to restrict private power and limit corporate profits, as many progressives had urged, the government was working to enhance the private sector through a mutually beneficial alliance.

This link between the public and the private sectors extended, although in very different form, to labor. The National War Labor Board, established in April 1918, served as the final mediator of labor disputes. It pressured industry to grant important concessions to workers: an eight-hour day, the maintenance of minimal living standards, equal pay for women doing equal work, recognition of the right of unions to organize and bargain collectively. In return, it insisted that workers forgo strikes and that employers not engage in lockouts. Membership in labor unions increased by more than 1.5 million between 1917 and 1919.

The effort to organize the economy for war produced some spectacular accomplishments: Hoover's efficient organization of food supplies, McAdoo's success in establishing state control of the railroads, and others. In some areas, however, progress was so slow that the war was over before many of the supplies ordered for it were ready. Even so, many leaders of both government and industry emerged from the experience convinced of the advantages of a close, cooperative relationship between the public and the private sectors. Some hoped to continue and extend the wartime experiments in the peacetime world.

The Search for Social Unity

The idea of unity—not only in the direction of the economy but in the nation's social purpose—had been the dream of many progressives for decades. To them, the war seemed to offer an unmatched opportunity for the United States to close ranks behind a great common cause. In the process, they hoped, society could achieve a lasting sense of collective purpose. In fact, however, the search for unity produced considerable repression.

Government leaders were painfully aware that public sentiment about American involvement in the war had been divided before April 1917 and remained so even after the declaration of war. Many believed that a crucial prerequisite for victory was uniting public opinion behind the war effort. The government approached that task in several ways.

The most conspicuous of its efforts was a vast propaganda campaign aimed at drumming up enthusiasm for the conflict. It was orchestrated by the Committee on Public Information (CPI), under the direction of the Denver journalist George Creel. The CPI supervised the distribution of over 75 million pieces of printed material and controlled much of the information available for newspapers and magazines. Creel encouraged journalists to exercise "self-censorship" when reporting war news, and most journalists—fearful of more coercive measures—complied by covering the war largely as the government wished. The CPI attempted at first to distribute only the "facts," believing that the truth would speak for itself. By 1918, however, government-distributed posters and films were offering lurid (and exaggerated) portrayals of the savagery of the Germans.

The government also soon began efforts to suppress dissent. CPI-financed advertisements in magazines appealed to citizens to report to the authorities any evidence among their neighbors of disloyalty, pessimism, or yearning for peace. The Espionage Act of 1917 gave the government new tools with which to combat spying, sabotage, or obstruction of the war effort (crimes that were often broadly defined). More repressive were two measures of 1918: the Sabotage Act of April 20 and the Sedition Act of May 16. These bills expanded the meaning of the Espionage Act to make illegal any public expression of opposition to the war; in practice, they allowed officials to prosecute anyone who criticized the president or the government.

The most frequent targets of the new legislation (and one of the reasons for its enactment in the first place) were such anticapitalist groups as the Socialist Party and the Industrial Workers of the World (IWW). Unlike their counterparts in Europe, American socialists had not dropped their opposition to the war after their country had decided to join it. Many Americans had favored the repression of socialists and radicals even before the war; the wartime policies now made it possible to move against them with full legal sanction. Eugene V. Debs, the humane leader of the Socialist Party and an opponent of the war, was sentenced to ten years in prison in 1918. (A pardon by President Warren G. Harding ultimately won his release in 1921.) Big Bill Haywood and members of the IWW were especially energetically prosecuted. Only by fleeing to the Soviet Union did Haywood avoid a long imprisonment. In all, more than 11,500 people were arrested in 1918 for the crime of criticizing the government.

State and local governments, corporations, universities, and private citizens contributed as well to the climate of repression. Vigilante mobs sprang up to "discipline" those who dared challenge the war. A cluster of citizens' groups emerged to mobilize "respectable" members of their communities to root out disloyalty. The most frequent victims of such activities were immigrants: Irish Americans, because of their historic animosity toward the British and because some had, before 1917, expressed hopes for a German victory; Jews, because many had expressed opposition to the anti-Semitic policies of the Russian government, until 1917 one of the Allies; and others.

The greatest target of abuse was the German-American community. Its members had unwittingly contributed to their plight. In the first years of the war in Europe, some had openly advocated American assistance to the Central Powers, and many had opposed United States intervention on behalf of the Allies. But while most German Americans supported the American war effort once it began, public opinion turned bitterly hostile. A campaign to purge society of all things German quickly gathered speed, at times assuming ludicrous forms. Performances of German music were frequently banned. German books were removed from the shelves of libraries. Courses in the German language were dropped from school curricula. Germans were routinely fired from jobs in war industries, lest they "sabotage" important tasks. Some were fired from positions entirely unrelated to the war, among them Karl Muck, the German-born conductor of the Boston Symphony Orchestra. Many Americans came to agree with the belief of the eminent psychologist G. Stanley Hall that "there is something fundamentally wrong with the Teutonic soul."

THE SEARCH FOR A NEW WORLD ORDER

Woodrow Wilson had led the nation into war promising a just and stable peace at its conclusion. Even before the armistice, he was preparing to lead the fight for what he considered a democratic postwar settlement—for a set of war aims resting on a vision of a new world order that became known as Wilsonian internationalism.

The Fourteen Points

On January 8, 1918, Wilson appeared before Congress to present the principles for which he claimed the nation was fighting. He grouped the war aims under fourteen headings, widely known as the Fourteen Points. They fell into three broad categories. First, Wilson's proposals contained a series of eight specific recommendations for adjusting postwar boundaries and for establishing new nations to replace the defunct Austro-Hungarian and Ottoman Empires. Those recommendations reflected his belief in the right of all peoples to self-determination. Second, there was a set of five general principles to govern international conduct in the future: freedom of the seas, open covenants instead of secret treaties, reductions in armaments, free trade, and impartial mediation of colonial claims. Finally, there was a proposal for a "League of Nations" that would help implement these new principles and territorial adjustments and resolve future controversies.

There were serious flaws in Wilson's proposals. For example, he provided no formula for deciding how to implement the "national self-determination" he promised for subjugated peoples. Nevertheless, Wilson's international vision quickly came to enchant not only much of his own generation (in both America and Europe) but members of generations to come. It reflected his belief, strongly rooted in the ideas of progressivism, that the world was as capable of just and efficient government as were individual nations—that once the international community accepted certain basic principles of conduct, and once it constructed modern institutions to implement them, the human race could live in peace.

Wilson was confident, as the war neared its end, that popular support would enable him to win Allied approval of his peace plan. There were, however, ominous signs both at home and abroad that his path might be more difficult than he expected. In Europe, leaders of the Allied powers were preparing to resist him even before the armistice was signed. Britain and France in particular, having suffered terrible losses and having developed great bitterness toward Germany as a result, were in no mood for a benign and generous peace. David Lloyd George, the British prime minister, had campaigned for reelection in 1918 by calling for the execution of Kaiser Wilhelm II.

At the same time, Wilson was encountering problems at home. In 1918, with the war almost over, Wilson unwisely appealed to the American voters to support his peace plans by electing Democrats to Congress in the November elections. Days later, the Republicans captured majorities in both houses. Domestic economic troubles, more than international issues, had been the most important factor in the voting; but because of the president's ill-timed appeal, the results damaged his ability to claim broad popular support for his peace plans.

The leaders of the Republican Party, in the meantime, were developing their own reasons for opposing Wilson. Many were angry that he had tried to make the 1918 balloting a referendum on his war aims, especially since many Republicans had been supporting the Fourteen Points. Wilson further antagonized them when he refused to appoint any important Republicans to the negotiating team that would represent the United States at the peace conference in Paris.

But the president considered such matters unimportant. There would be only one member of the American negotiating team with any real authority: Wilson himself. And once he had produced a just and moral treaty, he believed, the weight of world and American opinion would compel his enemies to support him.

The Paris Peace Conference

Wilson arrived in Europe to a welcome such as few men in history have experienced. To the war-weary people of the Continent, he was nothing less than a savior, the man who would create a new and better world. When he entered Paris on December 13, 1918, he was greeted, some claimed, by the largest crowd in the history of France. The conference itself, however, proved less satisfying.

The principal figures in the negotiations were the leaders of the victorious Allied nations: David Lloyd George, the prime minister of Great Britain; Georges Clemenceau, the president of France; Vittorio Orlando, the prime minister of Italy; and Wilson, who hoped to dominate them all.

From the beginning, the atmosphere of idealism Wilson had sought to create competed with a spirit of national self-interest. There was also a pervasive sense of unease about the unstable situation in eastern Europe and the threat of communism. Russia, whose new Bolshevik government was still fighting "White" counterrevolutionaries, was unrepresented in Paris; but the radical threat it seemed to pose to Western governments was never far from the minds of the delegates. Wilson himself had sent American troops into Russia in 1918, allegedly to protect Czech forces trapped there, but really, many believed, to support the anti-Bolshevik forces in the civil war.

In this tense and often vindictive atmosphere, Wilson was unable to win approval of many of the broad principles he had espoused: freedom of the seas, which the British refused even to discuss; free trade; "open covenants openly arrived at" (the Paris negotiations themselves were often conducted in secret). His pledge of "national self-determination" for all peoples suffered numerous assaults. Economic and strategic demands were constantly coming into conflict with the principle of cultural nationalism.

Where the treaty departed most conspicuously from Wilson's ideals was on the question of reparations. When the conference began, the president opposed demanding reparations from the defeated Central Powers. The other Allied leaders, however, insisted on them, and slowly Wilson gave way and accepted the principle of reparations, the specific sum to be set later by a commission. The final amount, established in 1921, was less than some earlier demands but far more than the crippled German economy could absorb.

Wilson did manage to win some important victories in Paris in setting boundaries and dealing with former colonies. But his most visible triumph, and the one of most importance to him, was the creation of a permanent international organization to oversee world affairs and prevent future wars. On January 25, 1919, the Allies voted to accept the "covenant" of the League of

Nations; and with that, Wilson believed, the peace treaty was transformed from a disappointment into a success. Any mistakes and inequities that had emerged from the peace conference, he was certain, the League could correct later.

The Ratification Battle

Wilson was well aware of the political obstacles awaiting him at home. Many Americans, accustomed to their nation's isolation from Europe, questioned the wisdom of this major new commitment to internationalism. Others had serious reservations about specific features of the treaty and the covenant. After a brief trip to Washington in February 1919, during which he listened to harsh objections to the treaty from members of the Senate and others, he returned to Europe and insisted on certain modifications in the covenant (limiting America's obligations to the League) to satisfy his critics. The changes were not enough to mollify his opponents, but Wilson refused to go further.

Wilson presented the Treaty of Versailles (which took its name from the former royal palace outside Paris where the final negotiating sessions had taken place) to the Senate on July 10, 1919. But members of the Senate had many objections to the treaty. Some—the so-called irreconcilables, many of them Western isolationists—opposed the agreement in principle. But many other opponents, with less fervent convictions, were principally concerned with constructing a winning issue for the Republicans in 1920. Most notable of these was Senator Henry Cabot Lodge of Massachusetts, the powerful chairman of the Foreign Relations Committee, who loathed the president. ("I never thought I could hate a man as I hate Wilson," Lodge once said.) He used every possible tactic to obstruct, delay, and amend the treaty.

Public sentiment clearly favored ratification, so at first Lodge could do little more than play for time. Gradually, however, Lodge's general opposition to the treaty crystallized into a series of "reservations"—amendments to the League covenant further limiting American obligations to the organization. Wilson might still have won approval at this point if he had agreed to some relatively minor changes in the language of the treaty. But the president refused to yield. The United States had a moral obligation, he claimed, to respect the terms of the agreement precisely as they stood. When he realized the Senate would not budge, he decided to appeal to the public.

He embarked on a grueling, cross-country speaking tour to arouse public support for the treaty. For more than three weeks, he traveled over 8,000 miles by train, speaking as often as four times a day, resting hardly at all. Finally, he reached the end of his strength. After speaking at Pueblo, Colorado, on September 25, 1919, he collapsed with severe headaches. Canceling the rest of his itinerary, he rushed back to Washington, where, a few days later, he suffered a major stroke. For two weeks, he was close to death; for six weeks more, he was so seriously ill that he could conduct virtually no public business. His wife and his doctor formed an almost impenetrable barrier around him, shielding the president from any official pressures that might impede his recovery and preventing the public from receiving any accurate information about the gravity of his condition.

Wilson ultimately recovered enough to resume a limited official schedule, but he was essentially an invalid for the remaining eighteen months of his presidency. His left side was partially paralyzed; more important, his mental and emotional state was unstable. His condition only intensified what had already been his strong tendency to view public issues in moral terms and to resist any attempts at compromise. When the Foreign Relations Committee finally sent the treaty to the Senate, recommending nearly fifty amendments and reservations, Wilson refused to consider any of them. When the full Senate voted in November to accept fourteen of the reservations, Wilson gave stern directions to his Democratic allies: they must vote only for a treaty with no changes whatsoever; any other version must be defeated. On November 19, 1919, forty-two Democrats, following the president's instructions, joined thirteen Republican "irreconcilables" to reject the amended treaty. When the Senate voted on the original version without any reservations, thirty-eight senators, all but one a Democrat, voted to approve it; fifty-five voted no.

There were sporadic efforts to revive the treaty over the next few months. But Wilson's opposition to anything but the precise settlement he had negotiated in Paris remained too formidable an obstacle to surmount. He was, moreover, becoming convinced that the 1920 national election would serve as a "solemn referendum" on the League. By now, however, public interest in the peace process had begun to fade—partly as a reaction against the tragic bitterness of the ratification fight, but more in response to a series of other crises.

A SOCIETY IN TURMOIL

Even during the Paris Peace Conference, many Americans were concerned less about international matters than about turbulent events at home. Some of this unease was a legacy of the almost hysterical social atmosphere of the war years; some of it was a response to issues that surfaced after the armistice.

The Unstable Economy

The war ended sooner than almost anyone had anticipated, and without warning, without planning, the nation lurched into the difficult task of economic reconversion. At first, the boom continued. But the postwar prosperity rested largely on the lingering effects of the war (government deficit spending continued for some months after the armistice) and on sudden, temporary demands (a booming market for scarce consumer goods at home and a strong market for American products in the war-ravaged nations of Europe). The postwar boom was accompanied, moreover, by raging inflation, a result in part of the sudden abandonment of wartime price controls. Through most of 1919 and 1920, prices rose at an average of more than 15 percent a year.

Finally, late in 1920, the economic bubble burst as many of the temporary forces that had created it disappeared and as inflation began killing the market for consumer goods. Between 1920 and 1921, the gross national product declined nearly 10 percent; 100,000 businesses went bankrupt; 453,000 farmers lost their land; and nearly 5 million Americans lost their jobs.

Well before this severe recession began, there was a dramatic increase in labor unrest. The raging inflation of 1919 wiped out the modest wage gains workers had achieved during the war; many laborers were worried about job security as hundreds of thousands of veterans returned to the work force; arduous working conditions—such as the twelve-hour day in the steel industry—continued to be a source of discontent. Employers aggravated the resentment by using the end of the war (and the end of government controls) to rescind benefits they had been forced to concede to workers in 1917 and 1918—most notably recognition of unions. The year 1919, therefore, saw an unprecedented wave of strikes—more than 3,600 in all, involving over 4 million workers. In January, a walkout by shipyard workers in Seattle, Washington, evolved into a general strike that brought the entire city to a virtual standstill. In September, there was a strike by the Boston police force, which was demanding recognition of its union in the wake of substantial layoffs and wage cuts. Seattle had remained generally calm; but with its police off the job, Boston erupted in violence and looting.

These and other strikes aroused widespread middle-class hostility to the unions, a hostility that played a part in defeating the greatest strike of 1919: a steel strike that began in September, when 350,000 steelworkers in several midwestern cities demanded an eight-hour day and recognition of their union. The steel strike was long and bitter and climaxed in a riot in Gary,

Indiana, in which eighteen strikers were killed. Steel executives managed to keep most plants running with nonunion labor, and public opinion was so hostile to the strikers that the AFL timidly repudiated them. By January, the strike had collapsed.

The wave of strikes was a reflection of the high expectations workers had in the aftermath of a war that they believed had been fought, in part, to secure their rights. It was also a reflection of the power of the forces arrayed against them. An official of the War Labor Board, observing the dismal postwar experience of unions, said in 1919: "The workers of the Allied world have been told that they were engaged in a democracy. . . . They are asking now, 'Where is that democracy for which we fought?' "

The Demands of African Americans

The black men who had served in the armed forces during the war (367,000 of them) came home in 1919 and marched down the main streets of the industrial cities with other returning troops. And then (in New York and other cities) they marched again through the streets of black neighborhoods such as Harlem, led by jazz bands, cheered by thousands of African Americans, who believed that the glory of black heroism in the war would make it impossible for white society ever again to treat African Americans as less than equal citizens.

In truth, the fact that black soldiers had fought in the war had almost no impact at all on white attitudes. But it did have a profound effect on black attitudes: it accentuated African-American bitterness—and increased blacks' determination to fight for their rights. Veterans expected a reward for their service. But for many other American blacks, the war raised expectations in other ways. Nearly half a million migrated from the rural South to industrial cities (often enticed by northern "labor agents," who offered them free transportation) in search of the factory jobs the war was rapidly generating. This was the beginning of what became known as the "Great Migration." Within a few years, the nation's racial demographics were transformed; suddenly there were large black communities crowding into northern cities, in some of which very few African Americans had lived in the past. Just as black soldiers expected their military service to enhance their social status, so black factory workers regarded their move north as an escape from racial prejudice and an opportunity for economic gain.

By 1919, however, the racial climate had become savage and murderous. In the South, there was a sudden increase in lynchings: more than seventy blacks, some of them war veterans, died at the hands of white mobs in 1919 alone. In the North, black factory workers faced widespread layoffs as returning white veterans displaced them from their jobs. Black veterans found no significant new opportunities. And as whites became convinced that black workers with lower wage demands were hurting them economically, animosity grew rapidly.

Wartime riots in East St. Louis and elsewhere were a prelude to a summer of much worse racial violence in 1919. In Chicago, a black teenager swimming in Lake Michigan on a hot July day happened to drift toward a white beach. Whites on shore allegedly stoned him unconscious; he sank and drowned. Angry blacks gathered in crowds and marched into white neighborhoods to retaliate; whites formed even larger crowds and roamed into black neighborhoods shooting, stabbing, and beating passersby and destroying homes and properties. For more than a week, Chicago was virtually at war. In the end, 38 people died—15 whites and 23 blacks—and 537 were injured; over 1,000 people were left homeless. The Chicago riot was the worst but not the only racial violence during the so-called red summer of 1919; in all, 120 people died in such racial outbreaks in the space of little more than three months.

Racial violence, and even racially motivated urban riots, were not new. But the 1919 riots were different in one respect: they did not just involve white people attacking blacks; they also involved blacks fighting back. The NAACP signaled this change by urging blacks not just to demand government protection but also to retaliate, to defend themselves. The poet Claude McKay, one of the major figures of what would shortly be known as the Harlem Renaissance, wrote a poem after the Chicago riot called "If We Must Die": "Like men we'll face the murderous cowardly pack. Pressed to the wall, dying, but fighting back."

At the same time, a black Jamaican, Marcus Garvey, began to attract a wide following in the United States, mostly among poor urban blacks, with his ideology of black nationalism. Garvey encouraged African Americans to reject assimilation into white society and develop pride in their own race and culture (which was, he claimed, superior to that of white society). His United Negro Improvement Association (UNIA) launched a chain of black-owned grocery stores and pressed for the creation of other black businesses. Eventually, Garvey began urging his supporters to leave America and return to Africa, where they could create a new society of their own. In the 1920s, the Garvey movement experienced explosive growth for a time. It began to decline, however, after Garvey was indicted in 1923 on charges of business

MARCUS GARVEY, 1924 Garvey attracted a broad
following in the early 1920s with his message of black
nationalism and self-help. He often dressed in
semimilitary regalia and organized meetings and parades
with a vaguely martial tone. His influence declined after
he was convicted of fraud for misuse of funds he had
raised to launch an African-American steamship
company. He served a short term in jail and in 1927 was
deported to his native Jamaica, where he died in 1940 in
relative obscurity.

fraud. He was deported to Jamaica two years later. But the allure of black nationalism, which he helped make visible to millions of African Americans, survived in black culture long after Garvey himself was gone.

The Red Scare

Much of the public considered the industrial warfare and the racial violence in 1919 a frightening omen of instability and radicalism. This was in part because other evidence emerging at the same time also seemed to suggest the existence of a radical menace. After the Russian Revolution of November 1917, communism was no longer simply a theory; it was now the basis of an important regime. Concerns about the communist threat grew in 1919 when the Soviet government announced the formation of the Communist International (or Comintern), whose purpose was to export revolution around the world.

In America, meanwhile, there were, in addition to the great number of imagined radicals, a modest number of real ones. These small groups of radicals were presumably responsible for a series of bombings in the spring of 1919 that produced great national alarm. In April, the post office intercepted several dozen parcels addressed to leading businessmen and politicians that were triggered to explode when opened. Two months later, eight bombs exploded in eight cities within minutes of one another, suggesting a nationwide conspiracy. One of them damaged the façade of United States Attorney General A. Mitchell Palmer's home in Washington.

In response to these and other provocations, what became known as the Red Scare began. Nearly thirty states enacted new peacetime sedition laws imposing harsh penalties on those who promoted revolution; some 300 people went to jail as a result. There were spontaneous acts of violence against supposed radicals in some communities, and more calculated efforts by universities and other institutions to expel radicals from their midst. But the greatest contribution to the Red Scare came from the federal government. On New Year's Day, 1920, Attorney General A. Mitchell Palmer and his ambitious young assistant, J. Edgar Hoover, orchestrated a series of raids on alleged radical centers throughout the country and arrested more than 6,000 people. The Palmer Raids had been designed to uncover huge caches of weapons and explosives; they netted a total of three pistols. Most of those arrested were ultimately released, but about 500 who were not American citizens were summarily deported.

The ferocity of the Red Scare soon abated, but its effects lingered well into the 1920s, most notably in the celebrated case of Sacco and Vanzetti.

In May of 1920, two Italian immigrants, Nicola Sacco and Bartolomeo Vanzetti, were charged with the murder of a paymaster in Braintree, Massachusetts. The case against them was questionable and suffused with nativist prejudices and fears; but because both men were confessed anarchists, they faced a widespread public presumption of guilt. They were convicted and sentenced to death. Over the next several years, public support for Sacco and Vanzetti grew to formidable proportions. But all requests for a new trial or a pardon were denied. On August 23, 1927, amid widespread protests around the world, Sacco and Vanzetti, still proclaiming their innocence, died in the electric chair.

The Retreat from Idealism

On August 26, 1920, the Nineteenth Amendment, guaranteeing women the right to vote, became part of the Constitution. To the woman suffrage movement, this was the culmination of nearly a century of struggle. To many progressives, who had seen the inclusion of women in the electorate as a way of bolstering their political strength, it seemed to promise new support for reform. Yet the passage of the Nineteenth Amendment marked not the beginning of an era of progressive reform but the end of one.

Economic problems, labor unrest, racial tensions, and the intensity of the antiradicalism they helped create—all combined in the years immediately following the war to produce a general sense of disillusionment. That became particularly apparent in the election of 1920. Woodrow Wilson wanted the campaign to be a referendum on the League of Nations, and the Democratic candidates, Governor James M. Cox of Ohio and Assistant Secretary of the Navy Franklin D. Roosevelt, dutifully tried to keep Wilson's ideals alive. The Republican presidential nominee, however, offered a different vision. He was Warren Gamaliel Harding, an obscure Ohio senator whom party leaders had chosen as their nominee confident that he would do their bidding once in office. Harding offered no ideals, only a vague promise of a return, as he later phrased it, to "normalcy." He won in a landslide. The Republican ticket received 61 percent of the popular vote and carried every state outside the South. The party made major gains in Congress as well. To many Americans it seemed that, for better or worse, a new era had begun.

CHAPTER TWENTY-FOUR

The New Era

The New Economy ∼ *The New Culture*
A Conflict of Cultures ∼ *Republican Government*

HE 1920S ARE OFTEN remembered as an era of affluence, conservatism, and cultural frivolity: the Roaring Twenties, the age of what Warren G. Harding once called "normalcy." In reality, however, the decade was a time of significant, even dramatic social, economic, and political change. It was an era in which the American economy not only enjoyed spectacular growth but developed new forms of organization. It was a time in which American popular culture reshaped itself to reflect the increasingly urban, industrial, consumer-oriented society of the United States. And it was a decade in which American government, for all its apparent conservatism, experimented with new approaches to public policy that helped pave the way for the important period of reform that was to follow. That was why contemporaries liked to refer to the 1920s as the "New Era"—an age in which America was becoming a modern nation.

At the same time, however, the decade saw the rise of a series of spirited and at times effective rebellions against the modern developments that were transforming American life. The intense cultural conflicts that characterized the 1920s were evidence of how much of American society remained unreconciled to the modernizing currents of the New Era.

THE NEW ECONOMY

After the recession of 1921–1922, the United States began a long period of almost uninterrupted prosperity and economic expansion. Less visible at the time, but equally significant, was the survival (and even the growth) of severe inequalities and imbalances.

TIME LINE

1914–1920	1920	1922	1923
Great Migration of blacks to North	Prohibition begins Harding elected president	Lewis's *Babbitt* Motion Picture Association founded	Harding dies; Coolidge becomes president Harding administration scandals revealed Ku Klux Klan membership peaks

1924	1925	1927	1928	1929
National Origins Act passed Coolidge elected president	Fitzgerald's *The Great Gatsby* Scopes Trial	Lindbergh's solo transatlantic flight First sound motion picture, *The Jazz Singer*	Hoover elected president	Faulkner's *The Sound and the Fury*

Economic Growth and Organization

No one could deny the remarkable, some believed miraculous, feats of the American economy in the 1920s. The nation's manufacturing output rose by more than 60 percent during the decade. Per capita income grew by a third. Inflation was negligible. A mild recession in 1923 interrupted the pattern of growth; but when it subsided early in 1924, the economy expanded with even greater vigor than before.

The economic boom was a result of many things, but one of the most important causes was technology, and the great industrial expansion it made possible. The automobile industry, as a result of the development of the assembly line and other innovations, now became one of the most important industries in the nation. It stimulated growth in other, related industries as well. Auto manufacturers purchased the products of steel, rubber, glass, and tool companies. Auto owners bought gasoline from the oil corporations. Road construction in response to the proliferation of motor vehicles became an important industry. The increased mobility that the automobile made possible increased the demand for suburban housing, fueling a boom in the construction industry.

Other new industries benefiting from technological innovations contributed as well to the economic growth. Radio became a booming concern within a few years of its commercial debut in 1920. The motion picture industry expanded dramatically, especially after the introduction of sound in 1927. Aviation, electronics, home appliances, plastics, synthetic fibers, aluminum, magnesium, oil, electric power, and other industries fueled by technological advances—all grew dramatically and spurred the economic boom.

Large sectors of American business were accelerating their drive toward national organization and consolidation. Certain industries—notably those such as steel and automobiles, dependent on large-scale mass production—seemed naturally to move toward concentrating production in a few large firms. Others—industries less dependent on technology and less susceptible to great economies of scale—proved resistant to consolidation, despite the efforts of many businessmen to promote it.

Some industries less prone to domination by a few great corporations attempted to stabilize themselves not through consolidation but through cooperation. An important vehicle was the trade association—a national organization created by various members of an industry to encourage coordination in production and marketing techniques. But trade associations worked best in the mass-production industries that had already succeeded in limiting competition through consolidation. In more decentralized industries, such as cotton textiles, their effectiveness was limited.

The strenuous efforts by industrialists throughout the economy to find ways to curb competition through consolidation or cooperation reflected a strong fear of overcapacity. Even in the booming 1920s, industrialists remembered how too-rapid expansion and overproduction had helped produce recessions in 1893, 1907, and 1920. The great, unrealized dream of the New Era was to find a way to stabilize the economy so that such collapses would never occur again.

Workers in an Age of Capital

The remarkable economic growth was accompanied by a continuing, and in some areas even increasing, maldistribution of wealth and purchasing power. More than two-thirds of the American people in 1929 lived at no better than what one major study described as the "minimum comfort level." Half of those languished at or below the level of "subsistence and poverty." Large segments of society, unable to organize, were without power to protect their economic interests.

American labor experienced both the successes and the failures of the 1920s as much as any other group. On the one hand, most workers saw their standard of living rise during the decade; many enjoyed greatly improved working conditions and other benefits. Some employers in the 1920s, eager to avoid disruptive labor unrest and forestall the growth of unions, adopted paternalistic techniques that came to be known as "welfare capitalism."

THE STEAMFITTER Lewis Hine was among the first
American photographers to recognize his craft as an art. In
this carefully posed photograph from the mid-1920s, Hine
made a point that many other artists were making in other
media: The rise of the machine could serve human beings,
but might also bend them to its own needs.

Henry Ford, for example, shortened the workweek, raised wages, and instituted paid vacations. By 1926, nearly 3 million industrial workers were eligible for at least modest pensions on retirement. When labor grievances surfaced despite these efforts, workers could voice them through the so-called
company unions that were emerging in many industries—workers' councils
and shop committees, organized by the corporations themselves. But welfare capitalism, in the end, gave workers no real control over their own
fates. Company unions were feeble vehicles. And welfare capitalism survived
only as long as industry prospered. After 1929, with the economy in crisis,
the entire system collapsed.

Welfare capitalism affected only a relatively small number of workers
in any case. Most laborers worked for employers interested primarily in

keeping their labor costs low. Workers as a whole, therefore, received wage increases that were proportionately far below the growth of the economy as a whole. Unskilled workers, in particular, saw their wages increase hardly at all—by only a little over 2 percent between 1920 and 1926. At the end of the decade, the average annual income of a worker remained below $1,500 a year when $1,800 was considered necessary to maintain a minimally decent standard of living. Only by relying on the earnings of several family members at once could many working-class families make ends meet.

The New Era was a bleak time for labor organization, in part because many unions themselves were relatively conservative and failed to adapt to the realities of the modern economy. The American Federation of Labor (led by the cautious William Green) remained wedded to the concept of the craft union, in which workers were organized on the basis of particular skills. The AFL sought peaceful cooperation with employers, without strikes. In the meantime, the number of unskilled industrial workers, many of them recent immigrants from southern or eastern Europe, was rising rapidly. They received little attention from the craft unions.

But whatever the weaknesses of the unions, the strength of the corporations was the principal reason for the absence of effective labor organization in the 1920s. After the turmoil of 1919, corporate leaders worked hard to spread the doctrine that unionism was somehow subversive, that a crucial element of democratic capitalism was the protection of the "open shop" (a shop in which no worker could be required to join a union). The crusade for the open shop, euphemistically titled the "American Plan," became a pretext for a harsh campaign of union busting across the country. As a result, union membership fell from more than 5 million in 1920 to under 3 million in 1929.

Women and Minorities in the Work Force

A growing proportion of the work force consisted of women, who were concentrated in what have since become known as "pink-collar" jobs—low-paying service occupations with many of the same problems as manufacturing employment. Large numbers of women worked as secretaries, salesclerks, and telephone operators and in other nonmanual service capacities. Because technically such positions were not industrial jobs, the AFL and other labor organizations were uninterested in organizing these workers. Similarly, the half-million African Americans who had migrated from the rural South into the cities during the Great Migration after 1914 had few opportunities for union representation. The skilled crafts represented in the AFL often worked actively to exclude blacks from their trades and organizations. Most blacks, however, worked in jobs in which the AFL took no interest at all—as janitors, dishwashers, garbage collectors, domestics, and other service capacities. A. Philip Randolph's Brotherhood of Sleeping Car Porters was one of the few important unions dominated and led by African Americans.

In the West and the Southwest, the ranks of the unskilled included considerable numbers of Asians and Hispanics, few of them organized, most actively excluded from white-dominated unions. In the wake of the Chinese Exclusion Acts, Japanese immigrants increasingly took the place of the Chinese in menial jobs in California, despite the continuing hostility of the white population. They worked on railroads, construction sites, and farms and in many other low-paying workplaces. Some Japanese managed to escape the ranks of the unskilled by forming their own small businesses or setting themselves up as truck farmers; and many of the Issei (Japanese immigrants) and Nisei (their American-born children) enjoyed significant economic success—so much so that California passed laws in 1913 and 1920 to make it more difficult for them to buy land. Other Asians—most notably Filipinos—also swelled the unskilled work force and generated considerable hostility. Anti-Filipino riots in California beginning in 1929 helped produce legislation in 1934 virtually eliminating immigration from the Philippines.

Mexican immigrants formed a major part of the unskilled work force throughout the Southwest and California. Nearly half a million Mexicans entered the United States in the 1920s, more than any other national group, increasing the total Mexican population to over a million. Most lived in California, Texas, Arizona, and New Mexico; and by 1930, most lived in cities. Large Mexican barrios—usually raw urban communities, often without even such basic services as plumbing and sewerage—grew up in Los Angeles, El Paso, San Antonio, Denver, and many other cities and towns. Some of the residents found work locally in factories and shops; others traveled to mines or did migratory labor on farms but returned to the cities between jobs. Mexican workers, too, faced hostility and discrimination from the Anglo population of the region, but there were few efforts actually to exclude them. Employers in the relatively underpopulated West needed this ready pool of low-paid, unskilled, and unorganized workers.

The Plight of the Farmer

Like industry, American agriculture in the 1920s was embracing new technologies for increasing production. The number of tractors on American farms, for example, quadrupled during the 1920s, helping to open 35 million new acres to cultivation. Agricultural production was increasing in other parts of the world as well. But the demand for agricultural goods was not rising as fast as production. The result was substantial surpluses, a disastrous decline in food prices, and a severe drop in farmers' income beginning early in the 1920s. More than 3 million people left agriculture altogether in the course of the decade. Of those who remained, many lost ownership of their lands and had to rent instead from banks or other landlords.

In response, some farmers began to demand relief in the form of government price supports. One price-raising scheme in particular came to dominate agrarian demands: the idea of "parity." Under parity, corn, for example, would bring a price that bore the same relation to the prices of all goods that it had in the period 1909–1913 (a good time for farmers.) Its purpose was to ensure that farmers would earn back at least their production costs no matter how the national or world agricultural market might fluctuate. Champions of parity urged high tariffs against foreign agricultural goods and a government commitment to buy surplus domestic crops at parity and sell them abroad at whatever the market would bring.

The legislative expression of the demand for parity was the McNary-Haugen Bill, named after its two principal sponsors in Congress and introduced repeatedly between 1924 and 1928. In 1926, Congress (where farm interests enjoyed disproportionate influence) approved a bill requiring parity for grain, cotton, tobacco, and rice, but President Coolidge vetoed it. In 1928, the bill won congressional approval again, only to succumb to another presidential veto.

THE NEW CULTURE

The increasingly urban and consumer-oriented culture of the 1920s helped Americans in all regions to live their lives and perceive their world in increasingly similar ways. That same culture exposed them to a new set of values that reflected both the prosperity and complexity of the modern economy. But the new mass culture could not, of course, erase the continuing, and indeed increasing, diversity of the United States. That culture reached Americans divided by region, race, religion, gender, and class, and they responded to the cultural messages they received in very different ways.

Consumerism and Communications

The United States of the 1920s was a consumer society—a society in which increasing numbers of men and women could afford more than simply what was necessary to survive. Many more people than ever before could buy items not just because of need but for convenience and pleasure. Middle-class families purchased electric refrigerators, washing machines, and vacuum cleaners. People wore wristwatches and smoked cigarettes. Women purchased cosmetics and mass-produced fashions. Above all, Americans bought automobiles. By the end of the decade, there were more than 30 million cars on American roads.

No group was more aware of the emergence of consumerism (or more responsible for creating it) than the advertising industry. The first advertising and public relations firms (N. W. Ayer and J. Walter Thompson) had

THE ELECTRIC REFRIGERATOR The development of new appliances for the home was an important part of the boom in the production and sale of consumer goods in the 1920s. Executives of the Delcom Light Company, a subsidiary of General Motors, pose here in front of the first Frigidaire electric refrigerator as it is readied for shipping from Dayton, Ohio, in 1921.

appeared well before World War I, but in the 1920s, partly as a result of techniques pioneered by wartime propaganda, advertising came of age. Publicists no longer simply conveyed information; they sought to identify products with a particular lifestyle. They also encouraged the public to absorb the values of promotion and salesmanship and to admire those who were effective "boosters" and publicists. One of the most successful books of the 1920s was *The Man Nobody Knows*, by advertising executive Bruce Barton. It portrayed Jesus Christ as not only a religious prophet but also a "super salesman." Barton's message, a message apparently in tune with the new spirit of the consumer culture, was that Jesus had been a man concerned with living a full and rewarding life in this world and that twentieth-century men and women should be concerned with doing the same.

The advertising industry could never have had the impact it did without the emergence of new vehicles of communication that made it possible

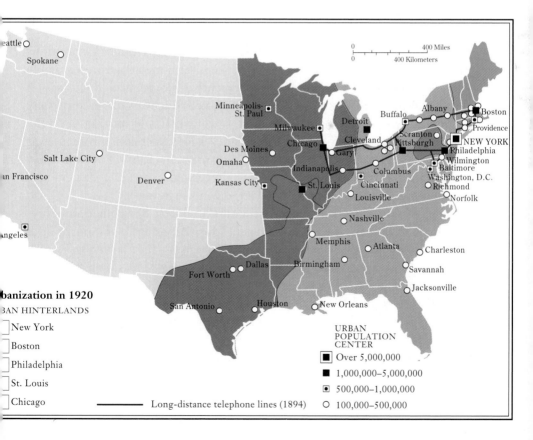

Urbanization in 1920
URBAN HINTERLANDS
☐ New York
☐ Boston
☐ Philadelphia
☐ St. Louis
☐ Chicago

URBAN POPULATION CENTER
■ Over 5,000,000
■ 1,000,000–5,000,000
▣ 500,000–1,000,000
○ 100,000–500,000

—— Long-distance telephone lines (1894)

to reach large audiences quickly and easily. Newspapers were being absorbed into national chains. Mass-circulation magazines—*Collier's, Ladies' Home Journal,* the *Saturday Evening Post, Time, Reader's Digest,* and others—attracted broad, national audiences. The movies were becoming an ever more popular and powerful form of mass communication; over 100 million people saw films in 1930, as compared with 40 million in 1922.

The most important communications vehicle, however, was the only one truly new to the 1920s: radio. The first commercial radio station in America, KDKA in Pittsburgh, began broadcasting in 1920, and the first national radio network, the National Broadcasting Company, was formed in 1927. By 1923, there were more than 500 radio stations, covering virtually every area of the country; by 1929, more than 12 million families owned radio sets.

Women in the New Era

College-educated women were no longer pioneers in the 1920s. There were now two and even three generations of graduates of women's or coeducational colleges and universities, and some were making their presence felt in professional areas that in the past women had rarely penetrated. Still, professional opportunities for women remained limited by society's assumptions about what were suitable occupations for them. Although there were notable success stories about female business executives, journalists, doctors, and lawyers, most professional women remained confined to such traditionally "feminine" fields as fashion, education, social work, and nursing or to the lower levels of business management. The "new professional woman" was a vivid and widely publicized image in the 1920s. In reality, however, most employed women were nonprofessional, lower-class workers. Middle-class women, in the meantime, remained largely in the home.

Yet the 1920s constituted a new era for middle-class women nonetheless. In particular, the decade saw a redefinition of motherhood. Shortly after World War I, an influential group of psychologists—the "behaviorists," led by John B. Watson—began to challenge the long-held assumption that women had an instinctive capacity for motherhood. Maternal affection was not, they claimed, sufficient preparation for child rearing. Instead, mothers should rely on the advice and assistance of experts and professionals: doctors, nurses, and trained educators in nursery schools and kindergartens.

For many middle-class women, these changes devalued what had been an important and consuming activity. Many attempted to compensate by devoting new attention to their roles as wives and companions. A woman's relationship with her husband assumed a greatly enhanced importance. And many women now openly considered their sexual relationships with their husbands not simply as a means of procreation, as earlier generations had been taught to do, but an important and pleasurable experience in its own right, as the culmination of romantic love.

One result was growing interest in birth control. The pioneer of the American birth-control movement, Margaret Sanger, began her career as a promoter of the diaphragm and other birth-control devices out of a concern for working-class women; she believed that large families were among the major causes of poverty and distress in poor communities. By the 1920s (partly because she had limited success in persuading working-class women to accept her teachings), she was becoming more concerned with and more effective in persuading middle-class women to see the benefits of birth control. Nevertheless, some birth control devices remained illegal in many states (and abortion remained illegal nearly everywhere).

The new, more secular view of womanhood had effects on women beyond the middle class as well. Some women concluded that in the New Era it was no longer necessary to maintain a rigid, Victorian female "respectability." They could smoke, drink, dance, wear seductive clothes and makeup, and attend lively parties. Those assumptions became the basis of the "flapper"—the modern woman whose liberated lifestyle found expression in dress, hairstyle, speech, and behavior. The flapper lifestyle had a particular impact on lower-middle-class and working-class single women, who were flocking to new jobs in industry and the service sector. (The young, middle-class, "Bohemian" women most often associated with the flapper image were, in fact, imitating a style that emerged among this larger group.) At night, such women flocked to clubs and dance halls in search of excitement and companionship.

Despite all the changes, most women remained highly dependent on men—both in the workplace and in the home—and relatively powerless when men exploited that dependence. The realization that the "new woman" was as much myth as reality inspired some American feminists to continue their crusade for reform. The National Woman's Party, under the leadership of Alice Paul, pressed on with its campaign for the Equal Rights Amendment, although it found little support in Congress (and met continued resistance from other feminist groups). Nevertheless, women's organizations and female political activities grew in many ways in the 1920s. Responding to the suffrage victory, women organized the League of Women Voters and the women's auxiliaries of both the Democratic and Republican Parties. Female-dominated consumer groups grew rapidly and increased the range and energy of their efforts.

Women activists won an apparent triumph in 1921 when they helped secure passage of a measure in keeping with the traditional feminist goal of securing "protective" legislation for women: the Sheppard-Towner Act. It provided federal funds to states to establish prenatal and child health-care programs. From the start, however, it produced controversy. Alice Paul and her supporters opposed the measure, complaining that it classified all women as mothers. Margaret Sanger complained that the new programs would discourage birth-control efforts. More important, the American Medical Association fought Sheppard-Towner, warning that it would introduce untrained outsiders into the health-care field. In 1929, Congress terminated the program.

The Disenchanted

Many artists and intellectuals coming of age in the 1920s were experiencing a disenchantment with modern America so fundamental that they were often able to view it only with contempt. As a result, they adopted a role different from that of most intellectuals of earlier eras. Rather than trying to influence and reform their society, they isolated themselves from it. At the heart of their disaffection was a sense of personal alienation, a belief that contemporary America no longer provided the individual with avenues by which he or she could achieve personal fulfillment.

One result of this alienation was a series of savage critiques of modern society by a wide range of writers, some of whom were known as the "debunkers." Among them was the Baltimore journalist H. L. Mencken, who delighted in ridiculing everything Americans held dear: religion, politics, the arts, even democracy itself. Sinclair Lewis, the first American to win a Nobel Prize in literature, published a series of savage novels—*Main Street* (1920), *Babbitt* (1922), *Arrowsmith* (1925), and others—in which he lashed out at one aspect of modern bourgeois society after another. Intellectuals of the 1920s claimed to reject the "success ethic" that they believed dominated American life (even though many of them hoped for—and a few achieved—commercial and critical success on their own terms). The novelist F. Scott Fitzgerald, for example, attacked the American obsession with material success in *The Great Gatsby* (1925).

Some artists and intellectuals expressed their disillusionment by leaving America to live in France, making Paris for a time a center of American artistic life. Others moved to the southwestern United States—to the art colonies at Taos and Santa Fe, New Mexico—attracted by the cultural and geographical distinctiveness of the region. Some adopted hedonistic lifestyles,

A M E R I C A N V O I C E S

LANGSTON HUGHES

I, Too (1926)

I, too, sing America.

I am the darker brother.
They send me to eat in the kitchen
When company comes,
But I laugh,
And eat well,
And grow strong.

Tomorrow,
I'll be at the table
When company comes.
Nobody'll dare
Say to me,
'Eat in the kitchen,'
Then.

Besides,
They'll see how beautiful I am
And be ashamed—

I, too, am America.

SOURCE: From *Collected Poems* by Langston Hughes. Copyright © 1994 by the Estate of Langston Hughes. Reprinted by permission of Alfred A. Knopf, Inc.

involving alcohol, drugs, casual sex, and wild parties. Most of these young men and women, however, believed the only real refuge from the travails of modern society was art. Only art, they argued, could allow them full individual expression; only the act of creation could offer them fulfillment.

Whether or not they found that fulfillment, they produced an extraordinary body of work. The roster of important American writers active in the 1920s may have no equal in any other period: Ernest Hemingway, Fitzgerald, Lewis, Thomas Wolfe, John Dos Passos, Ezra Pound, T. S. Eliot, Gertrude Stein, Edna Ferber, William Faulkner, and Eugene O'Neill.

To some intellectuals, the solution to contemporary problems lay neither in escapism nor in progressivism but in an exploration of their own cultural or regional origins. In New York City, a new generation of black intellectuals created a flourishing African-American culture widely described as the "Harlem Renaissance." The Harlem poets, novelists, and artists drew heavily from their African roots in an effort to prove the richness of their own racial heritage and to provide a basis for a cultural and political challenge to racial injustice. The poet Langston Hughes captured much of the spirit of the movement in a single sentence: "I am a Negro—and beautiful." Other black writers in Harlem and elsewhere—James Weldon Johnson, Countee Cullen, Zora Neale Hurston, Claude McKay, Alain Locke—as well as black artists and musicians helped to establish a thriving, and at times highly politicized, culture rooted in the historical legacy of their race.

A CONFLICT OF CULTURES

The modern, secular culture of the 1920s did not go unchallenged. It grew up alongside an older, more traditional culture, with which it continually and often bitterly competed. The older culture expressed the outlook of generally less affluent, less urban, more provincial Americans—men and women who continued to revere traditional values and customs and who feared and resented modernist threats to their way of life. The result of their fears was a series of harsh cultural controversies.

Prohibition

When the prohibition of the sale and manufacture of alcohol went into effect in January 1920, it had the support of most members of the middle class and most of those who considered themselves progressives. Within a year, however, it had become clear that the "noble experiment," as its defenders called it, was not working well. Prohibition did substantially reduce drinking in most parts of the country. But it also produced conspicuous and growing violations that made the law an almost immediate source of disillusionment and controversy.

The government hired only 1,500 agents to enforce prohibition, and in many places they received little help from local law enforcement agencies. Before long, it was almost as easy to acquire illegal alcohol in many parts of the country as it had once been to acquire legal alcohol. And since an enormous, lucrative industry was now barred to legitimate businessmen, organized-crime figures took it over.

Many middle-class progressives who had originally supported prohibition soon soured on the experiment. But an enormous constituency of provincial, largely rural, Protestant Americans continued vehemently to defend it. To them, prohibition had always meant more than stopping drinking. It represented the effort of an older America to maintain its dominance in a society in which they were becoming relatively less powerful. Drinking, which they associated with the modern city and with Catholic immigrants, became a symbol of the new culture they believed was displacing them.

As the decade proceeded, opponents of prohibition (or "wets," as they came to be known) gained steadily in influence. Not until 1933, however, when the Great Depression added weight to their appeals, were they finally able effectively to challenge the "drys" and win repeal of the Eighteenth Amendment.

Nativism and the Klan

The fear of immigrants that many prohibitionists expressed found other expressions as well. Agitation for a curb on foreign immigration to the United States had begun in the nineteenth century, and as with prohibition, it had gathered strength in the years before the war largely because of the support of middle-class progressives. Such concerns had not been sufficient in the first years of the century to win passage of curbs on immigration; but in the years immediately following the war, when immigration began to be associated with radicalism, popular sentiment on behalf of restriction grew rapidly.

In 1921, Congress passed an emergency immigration act, establishing a quota system by which annual immigration from any country could not exceed 3 percent of the number of persons of that nationality who had been in the United States in 1910. The new law cut immigration from 800,000 to 300,000 in any single year, but the nativists remained unsatisfied. The National Origins Act of 1924 banned immigration from east Asia entirely, a measure clearly directed against Japan, since Chinese immigration was already illegal. It also reduced the quota for Europeans from 3 to 2 percent. The quota would be based, moreover, not on the 1910 census, but on the census of 1890, a year in which there had been far fewer southern and eastern Europeans in the country. What immigration there was, in other words, would heavily favor northwestern Europeans—people of "Nordic" or "Teutonic" stock. Five years later, a further restriction set a rigid limit of 150,000 immigrants a year. In the years that followed, immigration officials seldom permitted even half that number actually to enter the country.

But the nativism of the 1920s extended well beyond restricting immigration. To defenders of an older, more provincial America, the growth of large communities of foreign peoples, alien in their speech, their habits, and their values, came to seem a direct threat to their own embattled way of life. Among other things, this provincial nativism helped instigate the rebirth of the Ku Klux Klan as a major force in American society. The first Klan, founded during Reconstruction, had died in the 1870s. But in 1915, a new group of white southerners met on Stone Mountain near Atlanta and established a modern version of the society. Nativist passions had swelled in Georgia and elsewhere in response to the case of Leo Frank, a Jewish factory manager in Atlanta convicted in 1914 (on very flimsy evidence) of murdering a female employee; a mob stormed Frank's jail and lynched him. The premiere (also in Atlanta) of D. W. Griffith's film *The Birth of a Nation*, which glorified the early Klan, also helped inspire white southerners to join a new one.

At first the new Klan, like the old, was largely concerned with intimidating blacks. After World War I, however, concern about blacks gradually became secondary to concern about Catholics, Jews, and foreigners. At that point, membership in the Klan expanded rapidly and dramatically, not just in the small towns and rural areas of the South but in industrial cities in the North and Midwest. By 1924, there were reportedly 4 million members, and the largest state Klan was not in the South but in Indiana. Beginning in 1925, a series of scandals involving the organization's leaders precipitated a slow but steady decline in the Klan's influence.

Most Klan units (or "klaverns") tried to present their members as patriots and defenders of morality, and some did nothing more menacing than stage occasional parades and rallies. Often, however, the Klan also operated as a brutal, even violent, opponent of "alien" groups and as a defender of traditional, fundamentalist morality. Klansmen systematically terrorized blacks, Jews, Catholics, and foreigners. At times, they did so violently, through public whipping, tarring and feathering, arson, and lynching. What the Klan feared, however, was not simply "foreign" or "racially impure" groups; it was anyone who posed a challenge to traditional values. Klansmen persecuted not only immigrants and blacks but those white Protestants they considered guilty of irreligion, sexual promiscuity, or drunkenness. The Ku Klux Klan, in short, was fighting not just to preserve racial homogeneity but to defend its definition of traditional culture against what its members believed to be the values and morals of modernity.

Religious Fundamentalism

Another cultural controversy of the 1920s was the result of a bitter conflict over the place of religion in contemporary society. By 1921, American Protestantism was already divided into two warring camps. On one side stood the modernists: mostly urban, middle-class people who were attempting to adapt religion to the teachings of modern science and to the realities of their modern, secular society. On the other side stood the fundamentalists: provincial, largely (although far from exclusively) rural men and women fighting to preserve traditional faith and to maintain the centrality of religion in American life. The fundamentalists insisted the Bible was to be interpreted literally. Above all, they opposed the teachings of Charles Darwin, who had openly challenged the biblical story of the Creation.

By the mid-1920s, to the great alarm of modernists, fundamentalism was gaining political strength in some states with its demands for legislation to forbid the teaching of evolution in the public schools. In Tennessee in March 1925, the legislature actually adopted a measure making it illegal for any public school teacher "to teach any theory that denies the story of the divine creation of man as taught in the Bible."

When the fledgling American Civil Liberties Union (ACLU) offered free counsel to any Tennessee educator willing to defy the law and become the defendant in a test case, a twenty-four-year-old biology teacher in the town of Dayton, John T. Scopes, agreed to have himself arrested. And when the ACLU decided to send the famous attorney Clarence Darrow to defend Scopes, the aging William Jennings Bryan (now an important fundamentalist spokesman) announced that he would travel to Dayton to assist the prosecution. Journalists from across the country flocked to Tennessee to cover

DARROW AND BRYAN IN DAYTON Although the Scopes trial was chiefly significant for the issues it raised, it attracted national attention in 1925 at least as much because of its two celebrated attorneys: Clarence Darrow, the best-known defense attorney in America and a personification of the modern, skeptical, secular intellect; and William Jennings Bryan, the great political leader who had become, in the last years of his life, an ardent defender of Christian fundamentalism.

the trial, which opened in a circuslike atmosphere. Scopes had, of course, clearly violated the law; and a verdict of guilty was a foregone conclusion, especially when the judge refused to permit "expert" testimony by evolution scholars. Scopes was fined $100, and the case was ultimately dismissed in a higher court because of a technicality. Nevertheless, Darrow scored an important victory for the modernists by calling Bryan himself to the stand to testify as an "expert on the Bible." In the course of the cross-examination, which was broadcast by radio to much of the nation, Darrow made Bryan's stubborn defense of biblical truths appear foolish and finally tricked Bryan into admitting the possibility that not all religious dogma was subject to only one interpretation.

The Scopes trial put fundamentalists on the defensive and discouraged many of them from participating openly in politics. But it did not resolve the conflict between fundamentalists and modernists. Four other states soon proceeded to pass antievolution laws of their own, and the issue continued to smolder for decades.

The Democrats' Ordeal

The anguish of provincial Americans attempting to defend an embattled way of life proved particularly troubling to the Democratic Party, which was seriously debilitated during the 1920s as a result of tensions between its urban and rural factions. More than the Republicans, the Democrats consisted of a diverse coalition of interest groups, linked to the party more by local tradition than common commitment. Among those interest groups were prohibitionists, Klansmen, and fundamentalists on one side and Catholics, urban workers, and immigrants on the other.

In 1924, the tensions between them proved devastating. At the Democratic National Convention in New York that summer, a bitter conflict broke out over the platform when the party's urban wing attempted to win approval of planks calling for the repeal of prohibition and a denunciation of the Klan. Both planks narrowly failed. More serious was a deadlock in the balloting for a presidential candidate. Urban Democrats supported Alfred E. Smith, the Irish Catholic Tammanyite who had risen to become a progressive governor of New York; rural Democrats backed William McAdoo, Woodrow Wilson's Treasury secretary (and son-in-law), later to become a senator from California, who had skillfully positioned himself to win the support of southern and western delegates suspicious of Tammany Hall and modern urban life. For 103 ballots, the convention dragged on, until finally both Smith and McAdoo withdrew and the party settled on a compromise: the corporate lawyer John W. Davis.

A similar schism plagued the Democrats again in 1928, when Al Smith finally secured his party's nomination for president after another acrimonious but less prolonged battle. He was not, however, able to unite his divided party—in part because of widespread anti-Catholic sentiment, especially in the South, and in part because of Smith's own conspicuous New York provincialism. He was the first Democrat since the Civil War not to carry the entire South. Elsewhere, although he did well in large cities, he carried no states at all except Massachusetts and Rhode Island. Smith's opponent, and the victor in the presidential election, was a man who perhaps more than any other personified the modern, prosperous, middle-class society of the New Era: Herbert Hoover. The business civilization of the 1920s, with its new institutions, fashions, and values, continued to arouse the animosity of large portions of the population, but the majority of the American people appeared to have accepted and approved it.

REPUBLICAN GOVERNMENT

For twelve years, beginning in 1921, both the presidency and the Congress rested in the hands of the Republican Party—a party in which the power of reformers had greatly dwindled. For most of those years, the federal government enjoyed a warm and supportive relationship with the American business community. Yet the government of the New Era was more than the passive, pliant instrument that critics often described. It attempted to serve in many respects as an active agent of economic change.

Harding and Coolidge

Nothing seemed more clearly to illustrate the unadventurous character of 1920s politics than the characters of the two men who served as president during most of the decade: Warren G. Harding and Calvin Coolidge.

Harding was elected to the presidency in 1920, having spent many years in public life doing little of note. An undistinguished senator from Ohio, he had received the Republican presidential nomination as a result of an agreement among leaders of his party, who considered him, as one noted, a "good second-rater." Harding appointed capable men to the most important cabinet offices; he attempted to stabilize the nation's troubled foreign policy; and he displayed on occasion a vigorous humanity, as when he pardoned socialist Eugene V. Debs in 1921. But even as he attempted to rise to his office, he seemed baffled by his responsibilities, as if he recognized his own unfitness. "I am a man of limited talents from a small town," he reportedly told friends on one occasion. "I don't seem to grasp that I am President." Harding's intellectual limits were compounded by personal weaknesses: his penchant for gambling, illegal alcohol, and attractive women. Unsurprisingly, perhaps, Harding soon found himself delegating much of his authority to others: to members of his cabinet, to political cronies, to Congress, to party leaders.

Harding realized the importance of capable subordinates in an administration in which the president himself was reluctant to act. But he lacked the strength to abandon the party hacks who had helped create his political success. One of them, Harry Daugherty, the Ohio party boss principally responsible for his meteoric political ascent, he appointed attorney general. Another, New Mexico Senator Albert B. Fall, he made secretary of the interior. Members of the so-called Ohio Gang filled important offices throughout the administration.

Unknown to the public (and perhaps also to Harding), Daugherty, Fall, and others were engaged in fraud and corruption. The most spectacular scandal involved the rich naval oil reserves at Teapot Dome, Wyoming, and Elk Hills, California. At the urging of Fall, Harding transferred control of those reserves from the Navy Department to the Interior Department. Fall then secretly leased them to two wealthy businessmen and received in return nearly half a million dollars in "loans" to ease his private financial troubles. Fall was ultimately convicted of bribery and sentenced to a year in prison; Harry Daugherty barely avoided a similar fate for his part in another scandal.

In the summer of 1923, only months before Senate investigations and press revelations brought the scandals to light, a tired and depressed Harding left Washington for a speaking tour in the West and a visit to Alaska. In Seattle late in July, he suffered severe pain, which his doctors wrongly diagnosed as food poisoning. A few days later, in San Francisco, he died. He had suffered two major heart attacks.

In many ways, Calvin Coolidge, who succeeded Harding in the presidency, was utterly different from his predecessor. Where Harding was genial, garrulous, and debauched, Coolidge was dour, silent, even puritanical. And while Harding was, if not perhaps personally corrupt, then at least tolerant of corruption in others, Coolidge seemed honest beyond reproach. In other ways, however, Harding and Coolidge were similar figures. Both took an essentially passive approach to their office.

Like Harding, Coolidge had risen to the presidency on the basis of few substantive accomplishments. Elected governor of Massachusetts in 1919, he had won national attention with his laconic response to the Boston police strike that year: "There is no right to strike against the public safety." That was enough to make him his party's vice presidential nominee in 1920. Three years later, after Harding's death, he took the oath of office from his father, a justice of the peace, by the light of a kerosene lamp.

If anything, Coolidge was even less active as president than Harding, partly as a result of his conviction that government should interfere as little as possible in the life of the nation. He proposed no significant legislation and took little part in the running of the nation's foreign policy. In 1924, he received his party's presidential nomination virtually unopposed. Running against John W. Davis, he won a comfortable victory: 54 percent of the popular vote and 382 of the 531 electoral votes. Robert La Follette, the candidate of the reincarnated Progressive Party, received 16 percent of the popular vote but carried only his home state of Wisconsin. Coolidge probably could have won renomination and reelection in 1928. Instead, in characteristically laconic fashion, he walked into a press room one day and handed each reporter a slip of paper containing a single sentence: "I do not choose to run for president in 1928."

Government and Business

The story of Harding and Coolidge themselves, however, is only a part—and by no means the most important part—of the story of their administrations. However passive the New Era presidents may have been, much of the federal government was working effectively and efficiently during the 1920s to adapt public policy to the widely accepted goal of the time: helping business and industry operate with maximum efficiency and productivity. The close relationship between the private sector and the federal government that had been forged during World War I continued. Secretary of the Treasury Andrew Mellon, a wealthy steel and aluminum tycoon, devoted himself to working for substantial reductions in taxes on corporate profits and personal incomes and inheritances. Largely because of his efforts, Congress cut them all by more than half. Mellon also worked closely with President Coolidge after 1924 on a series of measures to trim dramatically the already modest federal budget. The administration even managed to retire half the nation's World War I debt.

The most prominent member of the cabinet was Commerce Secretary Herbert Hoover, who considered himself, and was considered by others, a notable progressive. During his eight years in the Commerce Department, Hoover constantly encouraged voluntary cooperation in the private sector as the best avenue to stability. But the idea of voluntarism did not require that the government remain passive; on the contrary, public institutions, Hoover believed, had a duty to play an active role in creating the new, cooperative order. Above all, Hoover became the champion of the concept of business "associationalism"—a concept that envisioned the creation of national organizations of businessmen in particular industries. Through these trade associations, private entrepreneurs could, Hoover believed, stabilize their industries and promote efficiency in production and marketing.

The probusiness policies of the Republican administrations were not without their critics. In Congress, progressive reformers of the old school continued to criticize the monopolistic practices of big business, to attack

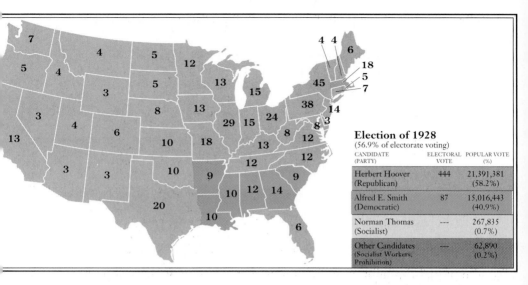

Election of 1928
(56.9% of electorate voting)

CANDIDATE (PARTY)	ELECTORAL VOTE	POPULAR VOTE (%)
Herbert Hoover (Republican)	444	21,391,381 (58.2%)
Alfred E. Smith (Democratic)	87	15,016,443 (40.9%)
Norman Thomas (Socialist)	---	267,835 (0.7%)
Other Candidates (Socialist Workers; Prohibition)	---	62,890 (0.2%)

government's alliance with the corporate community, and to decry social injustices. Occasionally, they were able to mobilize enough support to win congressional approval of progressive legislation, most notably the McNary-Haugen plan for farmers and an ambitious proposal to use federal funds to develop public electric power projects on the Tennessee River at Muscle Shoals. But the progressive reformers lacked the power to override the presidential vetoes that their bills almost always received.

Some progressives derived encouragement from the election of Herbert Hoover—widely regarded as the most progressive member of the Harding and Coolidge administrations—to the presidency in 1928. Hoover easily defeated Al Smith, the Democratic candidate. And he entered office promising bold new efforts to solve the nation's remaining economic problems. But Hoover had few opportunities to prove himself. Less than a year after his inauguration, the nation plunged into the severest and most prolonged economic crisis in its history—a crisis that brought many of the optimistic assumptions of the New Era crashing down and launched the nation into a period of unprecedented social innovation and reform.

The Great Depression

The Coming of the Depression ∼ *The American People in Hard Times*
The Ordeal of Herbert Hoover

E IN AMERICA TODAY," Herbert Hoover proclaimed in August 1928, not long before his election to the presidency, "are nearer to the final triumph over poverty than ever before in the history of any land. The poorhouse is vanishing from among us." Only fifteen months later, those words would return to haunt him, as the nation plunged into the severest and most prolonged economic depression in its history—a depression that continued in one form or another for a full decade, not only in the United States but throughout much of the world. The Depression was a traumatic experience for individual Americans, who faced unemployment, the loss of land and other property, and in some cases homelessness and starvation. It also placed great strains on the political and social fabric of the nation.

THE COMING OF THE DEPRESSION

The sudden financial collapse in 1929 came as an especially severe shock because it followed so closely a period in which the New Era seemed to be performing another series of economic miracles—miracles that seemed most clearly evident in the remarkable performance of the stock market.

In February 1928, stock prices began a steady ascent that continued, with only a few temporary lapses, for a year and a half. Between May 1928 and September 1929, the average price of stocks rose over 40 percent. The stocks of the major industrials—the stocks that were used to determine the Dow Jones Industrial Average—doubled in value in that same period. Trading mushroomed from 2 or 3 million shares a day to over 5 million, and at times to as many as 10 or 12 million. There was, in short, a widespread specula-

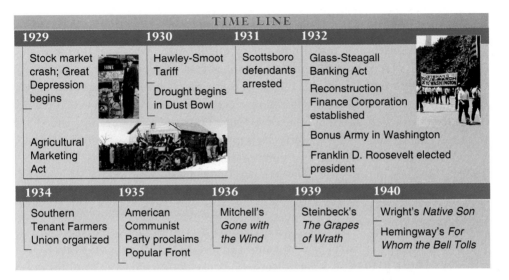

TIME LINE			
1929	**1930**	**1931**	**1932**
Stock market crash; Great Depression begins	Hawley-Smoot Tariff Drought begins in Dust Bowl	Scottsboro defendants arrested	Glass-Steagall Banking Act Reconstruction Finance Corporation established
Agricultural Marketing Act			Bonus Army in Washington Franklin D. Roosevelt elected president
1934	**1935**	**1936**	**1939**	**1940**
Southern Tenant Farmers Union organized	American Communist Party proclaims Popular Front	Mitchell's *Gone with the Wind*	Steinbeck's *The Grapes of Wrath*	Wright's *Native Son* Hemingway's *For Whom the Bell Tolls*

tive fever that grew steadily more intense, particularly once brokerage firms began encouraging the mania by offering absurdly easy credit to those buying stocks.

The Great Crash

In the autumn of 1929, the market began to fall apart. On October 21 and again on October 24, there were alarming declines in stock prices, in both cases followed by a temporary recovery. But on October 29, "Black Tuesday," all efforts to save the market failed. Sixteen million shares of stock were traded; the industrial index dropped 43 points (or nearly 10 percent), wiping out all the gains of the previous year; stocks in many companies became virtually worthless. Within a month stocks had lost half their September value, and despite occasional, short-lived rallies, they continued to decline for several years after that. In July 1932, the industrial index—which had stood at 452 in September 1929—bottomed out at 58. The market did not fully recover for over a decade.

Popular folklore has established the stock market crash as the beginning, and even the cause, of the Great Depression. But although October 1929 might have been the most visible early sign of the crisis, the Depression had earlier beginnings and more important causes.

Causes of the Depression

Economists, historians, and others have argued for decades about the causes of the Great Depression. But most agree on several things. They agree, first, that what is remarkable about the crisis is not that it occurred; periodic recessions are a normal feature of modern economies. What is remarkable is that it was so severe and that it lasted so long. The important question, therefore, is not so much why there was a depression but why it was such a bad one. Most observers agree, too, that a number of different factors account for the severity of the crisis, even if there is considerable disagreement about which was the most important.

One of those factors was a lack of diversification in the American economy in the 1920s. Prosperity had depended excessively on a few basic industries, notably construction and automobiles. In the late 1920s, those industries began to decline. Expenditures on construction fell from $11 billion to under $9 billion between 1926 and 1929. Automobile sales fell by more than a third in the first nine months of 1929. Newer industries were emerging to take up the slack—among them petroleum, chemicals, and plastics—but had not yet developed enough strength to compensate for the decline in other sectors.

A second important factor was the maldistribution of purchasing power and, as a result, a weakness in consumer demand. As industrial and agricultural production increased, the proportion of the profits going to farmers, workers, and other potential consumers was too small to create an adequate market for the goods the economy was producing. Even in 1929, after nearly a decade of economic growth, more than half the families in America lived on the edge of or below the minimum subsistence level—too poor to buy the goods the industrial economy was producing.

A third major problem was the credit structure of the economy. Farmers were deeply in debt—their land was mortgaged, and crop prices were too low to allow them to pay off what they owed. Small banks, especially those tied to the agricultural economy, were in constant trouble in the 1920s as their customers defaulted on loans; many of them failed. Large banks were in trouble too. Although most American bankers were very conservative, some of the nation's biggest banks were investing recklessly in the stock market or making unwise loans. When the market crashed and the loans went bad, some banks failed and others made the crisis worse by contracting the already scarce credit and calling in loans that borrowers could not pay.

A fourth factor contributing to the Depression was America's position in international trade. Late in the 1920s, European demand for American goods began to decline. That was partly because European industry and agriculture were becoming more productive and partly because some European nations were having financial difficulties of their own and could not afford to buy goods from overseas. But it was also because the European economy was being destabilized by the international debt structure that had emerged in the aftermath of World War I.

The international debt structure, therefore, was a fifth factor contributing to the Depression. When the war came to an end in 1918, all the European nations that had been allied with the United States owed large sums of money to American banks, sums much too large to be repaid out of their shattered economies. That was one reason why the Allies had insisted (over Woodrow Wilson's objections) on reparation payments from Germany and Austria. Reparations, they believed, would provide them with a way to pay off their own debts. But Germany and Austria were themselves in economic trouble after the war; they were no more able to pay the reparations than the Allies were able to pay their debts.

The American government refused to forgive or reduce the debts. Instead, American banks began making large loans to European governments, which used them to pay off their earlier loans. Thus debts (and reparations) were being paid only by piling up new and greater debts. In the late 1920s, and particularly after the American economy began to weaken in 1929, the European nations found it much more difficult to borrow money from the United States. At the same time, American protective tariffs—many raised to their highest level ever by the Hawley-Smoot Tariff of 1930—were making it difficult for them to sell their goods in American markets. Without any source of foreign exchange with which to repay their loans, they began to default. The collapse of the international credit structure was one of the reasons the Depression spread to Europe (and grew much worse in America) after 1931.

Progress of the Depression

The stock market crash of 1929 did not so much cause the Depression, then, as help trigger a chain of events that exposed larger weaknesses in the American economy. During the next three years, the crisis grew steadily worse.

The most serious problem at first was the collapse of much of the banking system. Over 9,000 American banks either went bankrupt or closed their doors to avoid bankruptcy between 1930 and 1933. Depositors lost over $2.5 billion in deposits. Partly as a result of these banking closures, the nation's money supply fell, according to some measurements, by more than a third between 1930 and 1933. The declining money supply meant a decline in purchasing power, and thus deflation. Manufacturers and merchants began reducing prices, cutting back on production, and laying off workers. Some economists argue that a severe depression could have been avoided if the Federal Reserve system had acted responsibly. But late in 1931, in a misguided effort to build international confidence in the dollar, it raised interest rates, which contracted the money supply even further and hastened the demise of many banks and corporations.

The collapse was both rapid and devastating. The American gross national product plummeted from over $104 billion in 1929 to $76.4 billion in 1932—a 25 percent decline in three years. In 1929, Americans had spent $16.2 billion to promote capital growth; in 1933, they invested only a third of a billion. The consumer price index declined 25 percent between 1929 and 1933; the wholesale price index, 32 percent. Gross farm income dropped from $12 billion to $5 billion in four years. By 1932, according to the relatively crude estimates of the time, 25 percent of the American work force was unemployed. (Some believe the figure was even higher.) For the rest of the decade, unemployment averaged nearly 20 percent, never dropping

SELLING APPLES, NEW YORK CITY In the fall of 1931 and again in the fall of 1932, large numbers of unemployed took to selling apples on the streets of major cities and became in the process a popular symbol of economic despair.

below 15 percent. Up to another one-third of the work force was "underemployed"—experiencing major reductions in wages, hours, or both.

THE AMERICAN PEOPLE IN HARD TIMES

Someone asked the British economist John Maynard Keynes in the 1930s whether he was aware of any historical era comparable to the Great Depression. "Yes," Keynes replied. "It was called the Dark Ages, and it lasted 400 years." The Depression did not last 400 years. It did, however, bring unprecedented despair to the economies of the United States and much of the Western world. And it had far-reaching effects on American society and culture.

Unemployment and Relief

The suffering extended into every area of society. In the industrial Northeast and Midwest, cities were becoming virtually paralyzed by unemployment. Cleveland, Ohio, for example, had an unemployment rate of 50 percent in 1932; Akron, 60 percent; Toledo, 80 percent. Unemployed workers walked through the streets day after day looking for jobs that did not exist. An increasing number of families were turning to state and local public relief systems, just to be able to eat. But those systems, which in the 1920s had served only a small number of indigents, were totally unequipped to handle the new demands being placed on them. In many cities, therefore, relief simply collapsed. Private charities attempted to supplement the public relief efforts, but the problem was far beyond their capabilities as well. State governments felt pressure to expand their own assistance to the unemployed; but tax revenues were declining along with everything else, and state leaders balked at placing additional strains on already tight budgets.

In rural areas conditions were in many ways worse. Farm income declined by 60 percent between 1929 and 1932. A third of all American farmers lost their land. In addition, a large area of agricultural settlement in the Great Plains was suffering from a catastrophic natural disaster: one of the worst droughts in the history of the nation. Beginning in 1930, the region, which came to be known as the "Dust Bowl" and which stretched north from Texas into the Dakotas, experienced a steady decline in rainfall and an accompanying increase in heat. The drought continued for a decade, turning what had once been fertile farm regions into virtual deserts. It is a measure of how productive American farmers were and how depressed the market for agricultural goods had become that even with these disastrous conditions, the farm economy continued through the 1930s to produce far more than American consumers could afford to buy.

Many farmers, like many urban unemployed, left their homes in search of work. In the South, in particular, many dispossessed farmers—black and white—simply wandered from town to town, hoping to find jobs or hand-outs. Hundreds of thousands of families from the Dust Bowl (often known as "Okies," since many came from Oklahoma) traveled to California and other states, where they found conditions little better than those they had left. Owning no land of their own, many worked as agricultural migrants, traveling from farm to farm picking fruit and other crops at starvation wages.

African Americans and the Depression

Most African Americans had not shared very much in the prosperity of the previous decade. They now experienced more unemployment, homelessness, malnutrition, and disease than they had in the past, and more than most whites experienced.

As the Depression began, over half of all black Americans still lived in the South. Most were farmers. The collapse of prices for cotton and other staple crops left some with no income at all. Many left the land altogether—either by choice or because they had been evicted by landlords who no longer found the sharecropping system profitable. Some migrated to southern cities. But there, unemployed whites believed they had first claim to what work there was, and some now began to take positions as janitors, street cleaners, and domestic servants, displacing the blacks who formerly occupied those jobs. By 1932, over half the blacks in the South were without employment. And what limited relief there was went almost invariably to whites first.

Unsurprisingly, therefore, many black southerners—perhaps 400,000 in all—left the South in the 1930s and journeyed to the cities of the North. There they generally found less blatant discrimination. But conditions were in most respects little better than those in the South. In New York, black unemployment was nearly 50 percent. In other cities, it was higher. Two million African Americans—half the total black population of the country—were on some form of relief by 1932.

Traditional patterns of segregation and disfranchisement in the South survived the Depression largely unchallenged. But a few particularly notorious examples of racism did attract the attention of the nation. The most celebrated was the Scottsboro case. In March 1931, nine black teenagers were taken off a freight train in northern Alabama (in a small town near Scotts-boro) and arrested for vagrancy and disorder. Later, two white women who had also been riding the train accused them of rape. In fact, there was over-whelming evidence, medical and otherwise, that the women had not been raped at all; they may have made their accusations out of fear of being ar-rested themselves. Nevertheless, an all-white jury in Alabama quickly con-victed all nine of the "Scottsboro boys" (as they were known to both friends and foes) and sentenced eight of them to death.

The Supreme Court overturned the convictions in 1932, and a series of new trials began that gradually attracted national attention. The Interna-tional Labor Defense, an organization associated with the Communist Party, came to the aid of the accused youths and began to publicize the case. The trials continued throughout the 1930s. Although the white southern juries who sat on the case never acquitted any of the defendants, all of the accused eventually gained their freedom—four because the charges were dropped, four because of early paroles, and one because he escaped. The last of the Scottsboro defendants did not leave prison until 1950.

The Depression was a time of important changes in the role and behavior of leading black organizations. The NAACP, for example, began to work diligently to win a position for blacks within the emerging labor movement, supporting the formation of the Congress of Industrial Organizations and helping break down racial barriers within labor unions. Partly as a result of such efforts, more than half a million blacks were able to join labor unions. In the steelworkers union, for example, African Americans constituted about 20 percent of the membership.

Hispanics and Asians in Depression America

Similar patterns of discrimination confronted many Mexicans and Mexican Americans. The Hispanic population of the United States had been grow-ing steadily since early in the century, largely in California and other areas of the Southwest through massive immigration from Mexico (which was specifically excluded from the immigration restriction laws of the 1920s). Chicanos (as Mexican Americans are sometimes known) filled many of the same menial jobs there that blacks had traditionally filled in other regions. Some farmed small, marginal tracts. Some became agricultural migrants, traveling from region to region harvesting fruit, lettuce, and other crops. Even during the prosperous 1920s, it had been a precarious existence. The Depression made things significantly worse. As in the South, unemployed whites in the Southwest demanded jobs held by Hispanics, jobs that whites had previously considered beneath them. Thus Mexican unemployment rose quickly to levels far higher than those for whites. Some Mexicans were, in effect, forced to leave the country by officials who arbitrarily removed them from relief rolls or simply rounded them up and transported them across the border. Perhaps half a million Chicanos left the United States for Mexico, many involuntarily, in the first years of the Depression.

Those who remained faced persistent discrimination. Most relief programs excluded Mexicans from their rolls or offered them benefits far below those available to whites. Hispanics generally had limited access to American schools. Many hospitals refused them admission. Unlike African Americans, who had established certain educational and social facilities of their own in response to discrimination, Hispanics generally had nowhere to turn. Even many who possessed American citizenship found themselves treated like foreigners.

There were, occasionally, signs of organized resistance by Mexican Americans themselves, most notably in California, where some formed a union of migrant farmworkers. But harsh repression by local growers and the public authorities allied with them prevented such organizations from having much impact. As a result, many Hispanics, like many African-American farmworkers, began to migrate to cities such as Los Angeles, where they lived in a poverty comparable to that of urban blacks in the South and Northeast.

For Asian Americans, too, the Depression reinforced longstanding patterns of discrimination and economic marginalization. In California, where the largest Japanese-American and Chinese-American populations were, even educated Asians had always found it difficult, if not impossible, to move into mainstream professions. Japanese-American college graduates often found themselves working in family fruit stands; 20 percent of all people of Japanese descent in Los Angeles worked at such stands at the end of the 1930s. For those who found jobs (usually poorly paid) in the industrial or service economy, employment was precarious; like blacks and Hispanics, they often lost jobs to white Americans desperate for work—jobs that a few years earlier the whites would not have considered. Japanese farmworkers, like Chicano farmworkers, suffered from the increasing competition for even these low-paying jobs from white migrants from the Great Plains.

In California, younger Japanese Americans tried to challenge the obstacles facing them through politics. They organized Japanese American Democratic Clubs in several cities, which worked for, among other things, laws protecting racial and ethnic minorities from discrimination. At the same time, some Japanese-American businessmen and professionals tried to overcome obstacles by encouraging members of their communities to become more assimilated, more "American." They formed the Japanese American Citizens League in 1930 to promote their goals. By 1940, it had nearly 6,000 members.

Chinese Americans fared no better. The overwhelming majority worked, as they had for many years, in Chinese-owned laundries and restaurants. Those who moved outside the Asian community could rarely find jobs above the entry level. Chinese women, for example, might find work as stock girls in department stores but almost never as salesclerks. Educated Chinese men and women could hope for virtually no professional opportunities outside the world of the Chinatowns.

Women and Families in the Great Depression

The economic crisis served in many ways to strengthen the widespread belief that a woman's proper place was in the home. Most men and many women believed that with employment so scarce, what work there was should go to men. There was a particularly strong belief that no woman whose husband was employed should accept a job. Indeed, from 1932 until 1937, it was illegal for more than one member of a family to hold a federal civil service job.

But the widespread assumption that married women, at least, should not work outside the home did not stop them from doing so. Both single and married women worked in the 1930s, despite public condemnation of the practice, because they or their families needed the money. In fact, the largest new group of female workers consisted of precisely those people who, according to popular attitudes, were supposed to be leaving the labor market: wives and mothers. By the end of the Depression, 25 percent more women were working than had been doing so at the beginning. This occurred despite considerable obstacles. Professional opportunities for women declined because unemployed men began moving into professions such as teaching and social work that had previously been considered women's fields. Female industrial workers were more likely to be laid off or to experience wage reductions than their male counterparts. But white women also had certain advantages in the workplace. The nonprofessional jobs that women traditionally held—salesclerks, stenographers, and other service positions—were less likely to disappear than the predominantly male jobs in heavy industry.

Black women enjoyed few such advantages. In the South, in particular, they suffered massive unemployment because of a great reduction of domestic service jobs. As many as half of all black working women lost their jobs in the 1930s. Even so, at the end of the 1930s, 38 percent of black women were employed, as compared with 24 percent of white women. That was because black women—both married and unmarried—had always been more likely to work than white women, less out of preference than out of economic necessity.

For American feminists, the Depression years were, on the whole, a time of frustration. Although economic pressures pushed more women into the work force, those same pressures helped to erode the frail support feminists had won in the 1920s for the idea of women becoming economically and professionally independent. In the difficult years of the 1930s, such aspirations seemed to many to be less important than dealing with economic hardship. By the end of the 1930s, American feminism had reached its lowest ebb in nearly a century.

The economic hardships of the Depression years placed great strains on American families. Middle-class families that had become accustomed in the 1920s to a steadily increasing standard of living now found themselves plunged suddenly into uncertainty, because of unemployment or the reduction of incomes among those who remained employed. Some working-class families too had achieved a precarious prosperity in the 1920s and saw their gains disappear in the 1930s.

Such circumstances caused many families to change the way they lived. Some women returned to sewing clothes for themselves and their families and to preserving their own food. Others engaged in home businesses such as taking in laundry or boarders. Many households expanded to take in relatives (grandparents, grandchildren, and others) who needed assistance.

But the Depression also worked to erode the strength of many family units. There was a decline in the divorce rate, but largely because divorce was now too expensive for some. More common was the informal breakup of families, particularly the desertion of families by unemployed men trying to escape the humiliation of being unable to earn a living. The marriage rate and the birth rate both declined for the first time since the early nineteenth century.

Values and Culture

Prosperity and industrial growth had done much to shape American values in the 1920s. Mainstream culture, at least, had celebrated affluence and consumerism and had stressed the importance of personal gratification through both. Many Americans assumed, therefore, that the experience of hard times would have profound effects on the nation's social values. In general, however, American social values seemed to change relatively little in response to the Depression. Rather, many people responded to hard times by redoubling their commitment to familiar ideas and goals.

No assumption would seem to have been more vulnerable to erosion during the Depression than the belief that the individual was in control of his or her own fate, that anyone displaying sufficient talent and industry could become a success. And in some respects, the economic crisis did work to undermine the traditional "success ethic" in America. Many people began to look to government for assistance; many learned to blame corporate moguls, international bankers, "economic royalists," and others for their distress. Yet the Depression did not destroy the success ethic.

The survival of the ideals of work and individual advancement was evident in many ways, not least in the reactions of those most traumatized by the Depression: conscientious working people who suddenly found themselves without employment. Some expressed anger and struck out at the economic system. Many, however, seemed to blame themselves. That was one reason why the effects of the Depression were sometimes hard to see: many of the unemployed tended to hide themselves, unwilling to display to the world what they considered their own personal failure. At the same time, millions responded eagerly to reassurances that they could, through their own efforts, restore themselves to prosperity and success. Dale Carnegie's *How to Win Friends and Influence People* (1936), a self-help manual preaching individual initiative, was one of the best-selling books of the decade.

Not all Americans, of course, responded to the crisis of the Depression so passively. Among the many people who saw the hard times as evidence of deep-rooted social injustice were many artists and intellectuals. There was, for example, a broad effort to dramatize the problem of rural poverty and to use it as an indictment of the failures of the economic system. Among those engaged in this effort were a group of documentary photographers, many of them employed by the federal Farm Security Administration in the late 1930s, who traveled through the South recording the nature of agricultural life. Men such as Roy Stryker, Walker Evans, Arthur Rothstein, and Ben Shahn and women such as Margaret Bourke-White and Dorothea Lange produced memorable studies of farm families and their surroundings, studies designed to show the savage impact of a hostile environment on its victims.

Many writers, similarly, turned away from the personal concerns of the 1920s and devoted themselves to exposés of social injustice. Erskine Caldwell's *Tobacco Road* (1932), which later became a long-running play, was an exposé of poverty in the rural South. James Agee's *Let Us Now Praise Famous*

AUCTIONING OFF A FARM Farm auctions such as this one, photographed in 1940 near Hastings, Nebraska, by the Farm Security Administration photographer Arthur Rothstein, were common sights in rural America during the Great Depression. Even after New Deal farm programs improved the fortunes of the agricultural economy as a whole, many small farmers continued to face debts they could not pay and hence foreclosure on their lands.

Men (1941), with photographs by Walker Evans, was a careful, nonjudgmental description of the lives of three poor rural families in the South. Richard Wright, a major African-American novelist, exposed the plight of residents of the urban ghetto in *Native Son* (1940). John Steinbeck's *The Grapes of Wrath* (1939) portrayed the trials of a migrant family in California, concluding with an open call for collective social action against injustice.

But the cultural products of the 1930s that attracted the widest popular audiences were those that diverted attention away from the Depression. The two most powerful instruments of popular culture in the 1930s—radio and the movies—provided mostly light and diverting entertainment. Although radio stations occasionally carried socially and politically provocative programs, the staple of broadcasting was escapism: comedies such as *Amos 'n Andy*, adventures such as *Superman*, *Dick Tracy*, and *The Lone Ranger*, and other entertainment programs. Hollywood continued to exercise tight control over its products through its resilient censor Will Hays, who ensured that most movies carried only safe, conventional messages. A few films, such as the adaptation of *The Grapes of Wrath* (1940), did explore political themes. Director Frank Capra provided a muted social message in several of his comedies—*Mr. Deeds Goes to Town* (1936), *Mr. Smith Goes to Washington* (1939), and *Meet John Doe* (1941)—which celebrated the virtues of the small town and the decency of the common people in contrast to the selfish, corrupt values of the city and the urban rich. Gangster films and westerns celebrated violence and implicitly glamorized resistance to authority. More often, however, the commercial films of the 1930s were deliberately and explicitly escapist: lavish musicals and "wacky" comedies designed to divert audiences from their troubles and, very often, satisfy their fantasies about quick and easy wealth.

The Allure of the Left

For some Americans—intellectuals, artists, workers, African Americans, and others who became disenchanted for various reasons with the prevailing values of American life—the Depression produced a commitment, for a time at least, to radical politics.

The importance of the 1936 Spanish Civil War to many American intellectuals was a good example of how the left produced a sense of commitment and purpose in individual lives. The battle against the Spanish fascists of Francisco Franco (who was receiving support from Hitler and Mussolini) attracted a substantial group of young Americans, more than 3,000 in all, who formed the "Abraham Lincoln brigade" and traveled to Spain to join in the fight. About a third of its members died in combat, but those who survived remembered the experience with pride, as one of the great moments of their lives.

Instrumental in creating the Lincoln brigade, and directing many of its activities, was the American Communist Party. Its membership reached perhaps 100,000 at its peak in the mid-1930s. One reason for its growth was the party's shift in tactics beginning in 1935, when it dropped its insistence on working completely apart from other organizations and began to advocate a democratic alliance of all antifascist groups in the United States, a "Popular Front." Communists began to praise Franklin Roosevelt and John L. Lewis, a powerful (and strongly anticommunist) labor leader. The party adopted the slogan "Communism is twentieth-century Americanism."

The American Communist Party was active in organizing the unemployed in the early 1930s and staged a hunger march in Washington, D.C., in 1931. Party members were among the most effective union organizers in some industries. And the party was one of the few political organizations to take a firm stand in favor of racial justice; its active defense of the Scotts-boro defendants was but one example of its efforts to ally itself with the aspirations of African Americans. It also helped organize a union of black sharecroppers in Alabama, which resisted—in several instances violently—efforts of white landowners and authorities to displace its members from their farms.

But despite its progressive achievements and its efforts to appear a patriotic organization, the American Communist Party was always under the close and rigid supervision of the Soviet Union. Its leaders took their orders from the Comintern in Moscow. Most members obediently followed the "party line." The subordination of the party leadership to the Soviet Union was most clearly demonstrated in 1939, when Stalin signed a nonaggression pact with Nazi Germany. Moscow then sent orders to the American Communist Party to abandon the Popular Front idea and return to its old stance of harsh criticism of American liberals; and the leaders in the United States immediately obeyed—although thousands of disillusioned members left the party as a result.

The Socialist Party of America, now under the leadership of Norman Thomas, also cited the economic crisis as evidence of the failure of capitalism and sought vigorously to win public support for its own political program. Among other things, it attempted to mobilize support among the rural poor. The Southern Tenant Farmers Union (STFU), supported by the party, attempted to create a biracial coalition of sharecroppers, tenant farmers, and others to demand economic reform. Neither the STFU nor the party itself, however, made any real progress toward establishing socialism as a major force in American politics. By 1936, in fact, membership in the Socialist Party had fallen below 20,000.

THE ORDEAL OF HERBERT HOOVER

Herbert Hoover began his presidency in March 1929 believing, like most Americans, that the nation faced a bright and prosperous future. For the first six months of his administration, he attempted to expand the policies he had advocated during his eight years as secretary of commerce, policies that would, he believed, complete a stable system of cooperative individualism and sustain a successful economy. The economic crisis that began before the year was out forced the president to deal with a new set of problems, but for most of the rest of his term, he continued to rely on the principles that had always governed his public life.

The Hoover Program

Hoover's first response to the Depression was to attempt to restore public confidence in the economy. "The fundamental business of this country, that is, production and distribution of commodities," he said in 1930, "is on a sound and prosperous basis." He then summoned leaders of business, labor, and agriculture to the White House and urged them to adopt a program of voluntary cooperation for recovery. He implored businessmen not to cut production or lay off workers; he talked labor leaders into forgoing demands for higher wages or better hours. But by mid-1931, economic conditions had deteriorated so much that the structure of voluntary cooperation he had erected collapsed. Frightened industrialists began cutting production, laying off workers, and slashing wages.

Hoover also attempted to use government spending as a tool for fighting the Depression. The president proposed to Congress an increase of $423 million—a significant sum by the standards of the time—in federal public works programs, and he exhorted state and local governments to fund public construction. But the spending was not nearly enough in the face of such devastating problems. And when economic conditions worsened, he became less willing to increase spending, worrying instead about keeping the budget balanced. In 1932, at the depth of the Depression, he proposed a tax increase to help the government avoid a deficit.

Even before the stock market crash, Hoover had begun to construct a program to assist the troubled agricultural economy. In April 1929, he proposed the Agricultural Marketing Act, which established the first major government program to help farmers maintain prices. A federally sponsored Farm Board would make loans to national marketing cooperatives or establish corporations to buy surpluses and thus raise prices. At the same time, Hoover attempted to protect American farmers from international competition by raising agricultural tariffs. The Hawley-Smoot Tariff of 1930 contained increased protection on seventy-five farm products.

Neither the Agricultural Marketing Act nor the Hawley-Smoot Tariff ultimately helped American farmers significantly. The Marketing Act relied on voluntary cooperation among farmers and gave the government no authority to do what the agricultural economy most badly needed: limit production. Prices continued to fall despite its efforts. The Hawley-Smoot Tariff provoked foreign governments to enact trade restrictions of their own in reprisal, further diminishing the market for American agricultural goods.

By the spring of 1931, Herbert Hoover's political position had deteriorated considerably. In the 1930 congressional elections, Democrats won control of the House and made substantial inroads in the Senate by promising increased government assistance to the economy. Many Americans held the president personally to blame for the crisis and began calling the shantytowns that unemployed people established on the outskirts of cities "Hoovervilles." Democrats urged the president to support more vigorous programs of relief and public spending. Hoover, instead, seized on a slight improvement in economic conditions early in 1931 as proof that his policies were working.

The international financial panic of the spring of 1931 destroyed the illusion that the economic crisis was coming to an end. Throughout the 1920s, European nations had depended on loans from American banks to allow them to make payments on their debts. After 1929, when they could no longer get such loans, the financial fabric of several European nations began to unravel. In May 1931, the largest bank in Austria collapsed. Over the next several months, panic gripped the financial institutions of neighboring countries. The American economy rapidly declined to new lows.

By the time Congress convened in December 1931, conditions had grown so desperate that Hoover supported a series of measures designed to keep endangered banks afloat and protect homeowners from foreclosure on their mortgages. More important was a bill passed in January 1932 establishing the Reconstruction Finance Corporation (RFC), a government agency whose purpose was to provide federal loans to troubled banks, railroads, and other businesses. It even made funds available to local governments to support public works projects and assist relief efforts. Unlike some earlier Hoover programs, it operated on a large scale. In 1932, the RFC had a budget of $1.5 billion for public works alone.

Nevertheless, the new agency failed to deal directly or forcefully enough with the real problems of the economy to produce any significant recovery. The RFC lent funds only to financial institutions with sufficient collateral, and so much of its money went to large banks and corporations. At Hoover's insistence, it helped finance only those public works projects that promised ultimately to pay for themselves (toll bridges, public housing, and others). Above all, the RFC did not have enough money to make any real impact on the Depression, and it did not even spend all the money it had. Of the $300 million available to support local relief efforts, the RFC lent out only $30 million in 1932. Of the $1.5 billion public works budget, it released only about 20 percent.

Popular Protest

For the first several years of the Depression, most Americans were either too stunned or too confused to raise any effective protest. By the middle of 1932, however, dissident voices began to be heard.

In the summer of 1932, a group of unhappy farm owners gathered in Des Moines, Iowa, to establish a new organization: the Farmers' Holiday Association, which endorsed the withholding of farm products from the market—in effect a farmers' strike. The strike began in August in western Iowa, spread briefly to a few neighboring areas, and succeeded in blockading several markets, but in the end it dissolved in failure. The scope of the effort was too modest to affect farm prices, and many farmers in the region refused to cooperate in any case. Nevertheless, the uprising created considerable consternation in state governments in the farm belt and even more in Washington, where the president and much of Congress were facing a national election.

A more celebrated protest movement emerged from American veterans. In 1924, Congress had approved the payment of a $1,000 bonus to all those who had served in World War I, the money to be paid beginning in 1945.

THE BONUS MARCH The 1932 march on Washington by the so-called Bonus Army ended in violent disarray. But it began in high spirits and something close to military precision—as this march along Independence Avenue suggests.

By 1932, however, many veterans were demanding that the bonus be paid immediately. Hoover, concerned about balancing the budget, rejected their appeal. In June, more than 20,000 veterans, members of the self-proclaimed Bonus Expeditionary Force, or "Bonus Army," marched into Washington, built crude camps around the city, and promised to stay until Congress approved legislation to pay the bonus. Some of the veterans departed in July, after Congress had voted down their proposal. Many, however, remained where they were.

Their continued presence in Washington was an embarrassment to Herbert Hoover. Finally, in mid-July, he ordered police to clear the marchers out of several abandoned federal buildings in which they had been staying. A few marchers threw rocks at the police, and someone opened fire; two veterans fell dead. Hoover called the incident evidence of violence and radicalism. He ordered the United States Army to assist the police in clearing out the buildings.

General Douglas MacArthur, the army chief of staff, carried out the mission himself (with the assistance of his aide, Dwight D. Eisenhower) and greatly exceeded the president's orders. He led the Third Cavalry (under the command of George S. Patton), two infantry regiments, a machine-gun detachment, and six tanks down Pennsylvania Avenue in pursuit of the Bonus Army. The veterans fled in terror. MacArthur followed them across the Anacostia River, where he ordered the soldiers to burn their tent city to the ground. More than 100 marchers were injured. One baby died.

The incident served as perhaps the final blow to Hoover's already battered political standing. Hoover's own cold and gloomy personality reinforced the public image of him as aloof and unsympathetic to distressed people. The Great Engineer, the personification of the optimistic days of the 1920s, had become a symbol of the nation's failure to deal effectively with its startling reversal of fortune.

The Election of 1932

As the 1932 presidential election approached, few people doubted the outcome. The Republican Party dutifully renominated Herbert Hoover for a second term in office, but the gloomy atmosphere of the convention made it clear that few delegates believed he could win. The Democrats, in the meantime, gathered jubilantly in Chicago to nominate the governor of New York, Franklin Delano Roosevelt.

Roosevelt had been a well-known figure in the party for many years already. A Hudson Valley aristocrat, a distant cousin of Theodore Roosevelt

ROOSEVELT AND SMITH Franklin Roosevelt, the 1932
Democratic presidential nominee, and Al Smith, the 1928
candidate, appear together at a rally for Roosevelt at the
Brooklyn Academy of Music in the fall of 1932. The two
men had once been close political allies; but by 1932, they
were already at odds. Not long after Roosevelt became
president, Smith turned against him publicly and remained
an outspoken critic.

(a connection strengthened by his marriage in 1904 to the president's niece,
Eleanor), and a handsome, charming young man, he progressed rapidly: from
a seat in the New York State legislature to a position as assistant secretary
of the navy under Woodrow Wilson during World War I to his party's vice
presidential nomination in 1920 on the ill-fated ticket with James M. Cox.
Less than a year later, he was stricken with polio. Although he never regained
use of his legs (and could walk only by using crutches and braces), he built
up sufficient physical strength to return to politics in 1928. When Al Smith
received the Democratic nomination for president that year, Roosevelt was
elected to succeed him as governor. In 1930, he easily won reelection.

Roosevelt worked no miracles in New York, but he did initiate enough

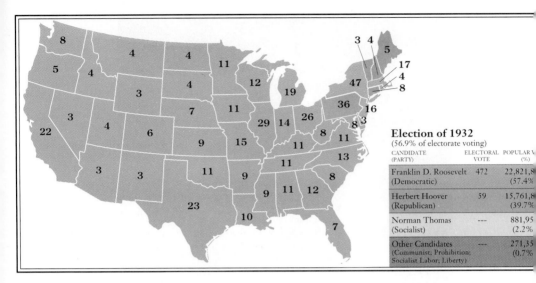

Election of 1932
(56.9% of electorate voting)

CANDIDATE (PARTY)	ELECTORAL VOTE	POPULAR VOTE (%)
Franklin D. Roosevelt (Democratic)	472	22,821,8 (57.4%
Herbert Hoover (Republican)	59	15,761,8 (39.7%
Norman Thomas (Socialist)	---	881,95 (2.2%
Other Candidates (Communist; Prohibition; Socialist Labor; Liberty)	---	271,35 (0.7%

positive programs of government assistance to be able to present himself as a more energetic and imaginative leader than Hoover. In national politics, he avoided such divisive cultural issues as religion and prohibition and emphasized the economic grievances that most Democrats shared. He was able as a result to assemble a broad coalition within the party and win his party's nomination. In a dramatic break with tradition, he flew to Chicago to address the convention in person and accept the nomination.

In the course of his acceptance speech, Roosevelt aroused the delegates with his ringing promise: "I pledge you, I pledge myself, to a new deal for the American people," giving his future program a name that would long endure. Neither then nor in the subsequent campaign did Roosevelt give much indication of what that program would be. But Herbert Hoover's unpopularity virtually ensured Roosevelt's election.

In November, to the surprise of no one, Roosevelt won by a landslide. He received 57.4 percent of the popular vote to Hoover's 39.7. In the electoral college, the result was even more overwhelming. Hoover carried Pennsylvania, Connecticut, Vermont, New Hampshire, and Maine. Roosevelt won everything else. Democrats won majorities in both houses of Congress. It was a broad and convincing mandate, but it was not yet clear what Roosevelt intended to do with it.

The "Interregnum"

The period between the election and the inauguration (which in the early 1930s lasted more than four months) was a season of growing economic crisis. Presidents-elect traditionally do not involve themselves directly in government. But in a series of brittle exchanges with Roosevelt in the months following the election, Hoover tried to exact from the president-elect a pledge to maintain policies of economic orthodoxy. Roosevelt genially refused.

In February, only a month before the inauguration, a new crisis developed when the collapse of the American banking system suddenly and rapidly accelerated. Public confidence in the banks was ebbing; depositors were withdrawing their money in panic; and one bank after another was closing its doors and declaring bankruptcy. In mid-February, the governor of Michigan, one of the states hardest hit by the panic, ordered all banks temporarily closed. Other states soon followed, and by the end of the month banking activity was restricted drastically in every state but one. Hoover again asked Roosevelt to give prompt public assurances that there would be no tinkering with the currency, no heavy borrowing, no unbalancing of the budget. Roosevelt again refused.

March 4, 1933, was, therefore, a day of both economic crisis and considerable personal bitterness. On that morning, Herbert Hoover, convinced that the United States was headed for disaster, rode glumly down Pennsylvania Avenue with a beaming, buoyant Franklin Roosevelt, who would shortly be sworn in as the thirty-second president of the United States.

CHAPTER TWENTY-SIX

The New Deal

Launching the New Deal ~ *The New Deal in Transition*
The New Deal in Disarray ~ *Limits and Legacies of the New Deal*

RANKLIN ROOSEVELT SERVED longer as president than anyone else before or since, and during his twelve years in office he became more central to the life of the nation than any chief executive had ever been. Most important, his administration constructed a series of programs that permanently altered the federal government and its relationship to society.

By the end of the 1930s, the New Deal (as the Roosevelt administration was called) had created many of the broad outlines of the political world we know today. It had constructed the beginnings of a modern welfare system. It had extended federal regulation over new areas of the economy. It had presided over the birth of the modern labor movement. It had made the government a major force in the agricultural economy. It had created a powerful coalition within the Democratic Party that would dominate American politics for most of the next thirty years. And it had produced the beginnings of a new liberal ideology that would govern reform efforts for several decades after the war. One thing the New Deal had not done, however, was end the Great Depression. It helped stabilize the economy in 1933, and there was a limited, if erratic, recovery after that. But by the end of 1939, many of the basic problems of the Depression remained unsolved.

LAUNCHING THE NEW DEAL

Roosevelt's first task upon taking office was to alleviate the panic that was threatening to create chaos in the financial system. He did so in part by force of personality and in part by constructing very rapidly an ambitious and diverse program of legislation.

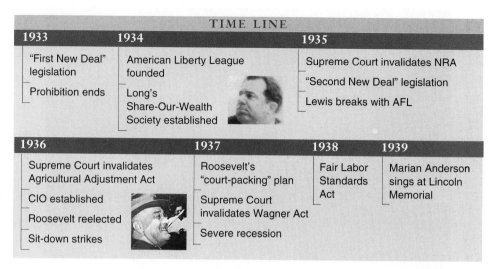

TIME LINE

1933	1934	1935
"First New Deal" legislation	American Liberty League founded	Supreme Court invalidates NRA
Prohibition ends	Long's Share-Our-Wealth Society established	"Second New Deal" legislation
		Lewis breaks with AFL

1936	1937	1938	1939
Supreme Court invalidates Agricultural Adjustment Act	Roosevelt's "court-packing" plan	Fair Labor Standards Act	Marian Anderson sings at Lincoln Memorial
CIO established	Supreme Court invalidates Wagner Act		
Roosevelt reelected	Severe recession		
Sit-down strikes			

Restoring Confidence

Much of Roosevelt's early success was a result of his ebullient personality. He was the first president to make regular use of the radio; and his friendly "fireside chats," during which he explained his programs and plans to the people, helped build public confidence in the administration. Roosevelt held frequent informal press conferences and won both the respect and the friendship of most reporters.

But Roosevelt could not rely on image alone. On March 6, two days after taking office, he issued a proclamation closing all American banks for four days until Congress could meet in special session to consider banking reform legislation. So great was the panic about bank failures that the "bank holiday," as the president euphemistically described it, created a general sense of relief and hope.

Three days later, Roosevelt sent to Congress the Emergency Banking Act, a generally conservative bill (much of it drafted by holdovers from the Hoover administration) designed primarily to protect the larger banks from being dragged down by the weakness of smaller ones. The bill provided for Treasury Department inspection of all banks before they would be allowed to reopen, for federal assistance to some troubled institutions, and for a thorough reorganization of those banks in the greatest difficulty. A confused and frightened Congress passed the bill within a few hours of its introduction. Whatever else the new law accomplished, it helped dispel the panic. Three-quarters of the banks in the Federal Reserve system reopened within the next

THE ROOSEVELT SMILE The battered hat, the uptilted cigarette holder, the jaunty smile—all were hallmarks of Franklin Roosevelt's ebullient public personality. In part, at least, the president's hearty optimism was a deliberate pose, adopted to distract attention from the paralysis that had denied him the use of his legs since 1921.

three days, and $1 billion in hoarded currency and gold flowed back into them within a month. The immediate banking crisis was over.

On the morning after passage of the Emergency Banking Act, Roosevelt sent to Congress another measure—the Economy Act—designed to convince the public (and especially the business community) that the federal government was in safe, responsible hands. The act proposed to balance the federal budget by cutting the salaries of government employees and reducing pensions to veterans by as much as 15 percent. Otherwise, the president warned, the nation faced a $1 billion deficit. Like the banking bill, this one passed through Congress almost instantly—despite heated protests from some congressional progressives. Later that spring, Roosevelt signed the Glass-Steagall Act of June 1933, which gave the government authority to curb irresponsible speculation by banks. More important, perhaps, it established the Federal Deposit Insurance Corporation, which guaranteed all bank deposits up to $2,500. In other words, even if a bank should fail, small depositors would be able to recover their money. (Later, in 1935, Congress passed a major banking act that transferred much of the authority once wielded by the regional Federal Reserve banks to the Federal Reserve Board in Washington.)

To restore confidence in the stock market, Congress passed the so-called Truth in Securities Act of 1933, requiring corporations issuing new securities to provide full and accurate information about them to the public. Another act, of June 1934, established the Securities and Exchange Commission (SEC) to police the stock market.

Roosevelt also moved in his first days in office to put to rest one of the divisive issues of the 1920s. He supported and then signed a bill to legalize the manufacture and sale of beer with a 3.2 percent alcohol content—an interim measure pending the repeal of prohibition, for which a constitutional amendment (the Twenty-first) was already in process. The amendment was ratified later in 1933.

Agricultural Adjustment

These initial actions were largely stopgaps, to buy time for more comprehensive programs. The first such program was the Agricultural Adjustment Act, which Congress passed in May 1933. Its most important feature was its provision for reducing crop production to end agricultural surpluses and halt the downward spiral of farm prices.

Under the "domestic allotment" system of the act, producers of seven basic commodities (wheat, cotton, corn, hogs, rice, tobacco, and dairy products) would decide on production limits for their crops. The government, through the Agricultural Adjustment Administration (AAA), would then tell individual farmers how much they should produce and would pay them subsidies for leaving some of their land idle. A tax on food processing (for example, the milling of wheat) would provide the funds for the new payments. Farm prices were to be subsidized up to the point of parity.

The AAA helped bring about a rise in prices for farm commodities in the years after 1933. Gross farm income increased by half in the first three years of the New Deal, and the agricultural economy as a whole emerged from the 1930s much more stable and prosperous than it had been in many years. The AAA did, however, favor larger farmers over smaller ones, particularly since local administration of its programs often fell into the hands

706 ～ THE UNFINISHED NATION

of the most powerful producers in a community. By distributing payments to landowners, not those who worked the land, the government did little to discourage planters who were reducing their acreage from evicting tenants and sharecroppers and firing field hands.

In January 1936, the Supreme Court struck down the crucial provisions of the Agricultural Adjustment Act, arguing that the government had no constitutional authority to require farmers to limit production. But within a few weeks the administration had secured passage of new legislation (the Soil Conservation and Domestic Allotment Act), which permitted the government to pay farmers to reduce production so as to "conserve soil," prevent erosion, and accomplish other secondary goals. The Court did not interfere with the new laws.

The new legislation also attempted to correct one of the injustices of the original act: its failure to protect sharecroppers and tenant farmers. It required landlords to share the payments they received for cutting back production with those who worked their land. (The new requirements were, however, largely evaded.) The administration launched other efforts to assist poor farmers as well. The Resettlement Administration, established in 1935, and its successor, the Farm Security Administration, created in 1937, provided loans to help farmers cultivating submarginal soil to relocate on better lands. But the programs never moved more than a few thousand farmers. More effective was the Rural Electrification Administration, created in 1935, which worked to make electric power available for the first time to thousands of farmers through utility cooperatives.

Industrial Recovery

The Roosevelt administration considered rescuing the industrial economy from the spiraling deflation of the early 1930s at least as important as rescuing agriculture. Ever since 1931, leaders of the United States Chamber of Commerce and many others had been urging the government to adopt an antideflation scheme that would permit trade associations to cooperate in stabilizing prices within their industries. Existing antitrust laws clearly forbade such practices, and Herbert Hoover had refused to endorse suspension of the laws. The Roosevelt administration was more receptive. In exchange for relaxing antitrust provisions, however, New Dealers insisted on other provisions. Businesspeople would have to make important concessions to labor—recognize the workers' right to bargain collectively through unions—to ensure that the incomes of workers would rise along with prices. And to help create jobs and increase consumer buying power, the administration

THE BLUE EAGLE The leaders of the National Recovery Administration, one of the first great New Deal experiments, believed that public support for the project was as important as the particular policies it pursued. As a result, they encouraged even the smallest businesses to sign an NRA "code" and to display the agency's symbol—a blue eagle above the phrase "We Do Our Part"—in their windows. The owners of this tailor shop proudly complied.

added a major program of public works spending. The result of these and many other impulses was the National Industrial Recovery Act, which Congress passed in June 1933.

At first, the new program appeared to work miracles. At its center was a new federal agency, the National Recovery Administration (NRA), under the direction of the flamboyant and energetic Hugh S. Johnson. Johnson called on every business establishment in the nation to accept a temporary "blanket code": a minimum wage of between 30 and 40 cents an hour, a maximum workweek of thirty-five to forty hours, and the abolition of child labor. Adherence to the code, he claimed, would raise consumer purchasing power and increase employment. At the same time, Johnson negotiated another, more specific set of codes with leaders of the nation's major industries. These industrial codes set floors below which no company would lower prices or wages in its search for a competitive advantage, and they included provisions for maintaining employment and production. He quickly won agreements from almost every major industry in the country.

From the beginning, however, the NRA encountered serious difficulties. The codes themselves were hastily and often poorly written. Administering them was beyond the capacities of federal officials with no prior experience in running so vast a program. Large producers consistently dominated the code-writing process and ensured that the new regulations would work to their advantage and to the disadvantage of smaller firms. And the codes at times did more than simply set floors under prices; they actively and artificially raised them—sometimes to levels higher than the market could sustain.

Other NRA goals did not progress as quickly as the efforts to raise prices. Section 7(a) of the National Industrial Recovery Act promised workers the right to form unions and engage in collective bargaining and encouraged many workers to join unions for the first time. But Section 7(a) contained no enforcement mechanisms. Hence recognition of unions by employers (and thus the significant wage increases the unions were committed to winning) did not follow. The Public Works Administration (PWA), established to administer the National Industrial Recovery Act's spending programs, only gradually allowed the $3.3 billion in public works funds to trickle out. Not until 1938 was the PWA budget pumping an appreciable amount of money into the economy.

Perhaps the clearest evidence of the NRA's failure was that industrial production actually declined in the months after the agency's establishment—from an index of 101 in July 1933 to 71 in November—despite the rise in prices that the codes had helped to create. By the spring of 1934, the NRA was besieged by criticism, and businessmen were flaunting many of its provisions. That fall, Roosevelt pressured Johnson to resign and established a new board of directors to oversee the NRA. Then in 1935, the Supreme Court intervened.

The constitutional basis for the NRA had been Congress's power under the Constitution to regulate interstate commerce, a power the administration had interpreted very broadly. In 1935, a case came before the Court involving alleged NRA code violations by the Schechter brothers, who operated a wholesale poultry business confined to Brooklyn, New York. The Court ruled unanimously that the Schechters were not engaged in interstate commerce and, further, that Congress had unconstitutionally delegated legislative power to the president to draft the NRA codes. The justices struck down the legislation establishing the agency. Roosevelt denounced the justices for their "horse-and-buggy" interpretation of the interstate commerce clause. He was rightly concerned, for the reasoning in the Schechter case threatened many other New Deal programs as well. But the Court's destruction of the NRA itself gave the New Deal a convenient excuse for ending a failed experiment.

Regional Planning

The AAA and the NRA largely reflected the beliefs of New Dealers who favored economic planning but wanted private interests (farmers or business leaders) to dominate the planning process. Other reformers believed that the government itself should be the chief planning agent in the economy. Their most conspicuous success, and one of the most celebrated accomplishments of the New Deal, was an unprecedented experiment in regional planning: the Tennessee Valley Authority (TVA).

The TVA had its roots in a political controversy of the 1920s. Progressive reformers had agitated for years for public development of the nation's water resources as a source of cheap electric power. In particular, they had urged completion of a great dam at Muscle Shoals on the Tennessee River in Alabama—a dam begun during World War I but left unfinished when the war ended. But opposition from the utilities companies had been too powerful to overcome.

In 1932, however, one of the great utility empires—that of the electricity magnate Samuel Insull—collapsed spectacularly, amid widely publicized exposés of corruption. Hostility to the utilities soon grew so intense that the companies were no longer able to block the public power movement. The result was legislation supported by the president and enacted by Congress in May 1933 creating the Tennessee Valley Authority. The TVA was authorized not only to complete the dam at Muscle Shoals and build others in the region, and not only to generate and sell electricity from them to the public at reasonable rates. It was also intended to be an agent for a comprehensive redevelopment of the entire region: for stopping the disastrous flooding that had plagued the Tennessee Valley for centuries, for encouraging the development of local industries, for supervising a substantial program of reforestation, and for helping farmers improve productivity.

Opposition by conservatives within the administration ultimately blocked many of the ambitious social planning projects proposed by the more visionary TVA administrators, but the Authority revitalized the region in numerous ways. It improved water transportation. It virtually eliminated flooding in the region. It provided electricity to thousands who had never before had it. Throughout the country, largely because of the "yardstick" provided by the TVA's cheap production of electricity, private power rates declined. Still, the Authority worked no miracles. The Tennessee Valley remained a generally impoverished region despite its efforts. And like many other New Deal programs, it made no serious effort to challenge local customs and racial prejudices.

The Growth of Federal Relief

Millions of Americans were unemployed and in desperate need of assistance in 1933, and the relief efforts of private organizations and state and local governments were unable to meet the demand. The Roosevelt administration did not consider relief its most important task, but it recognized the necessity of doing something to help impoverished Americans survive until the government could revive the economy to the point where relief might not be necessary.

Among Roosevelt's first acts as president was the establishment of the Federal Emergency Relief Administration (FERA), which provided cash grants to states to prop up bankrupt relief agencies. To administer the program, he chose the director of the New York State relief agency, Harry Hopkins, who disbursed the FERA grants widely and rapidly. But both Hopkins and Roosevelt had misgivings about establishing a government "dole."

They felt somewhat more comfortable with another form of government assistance: work relief. Thus when it became clear that the FERA grants were not enough, the administration established a second program: the Civil Works Administration (CWA). Between November 1933 and April 1934, it put more than 4 million people to work on temporary projects. Some of the projects were of lasting value, such as the construction of roads, schools, and parks; others were little more than make-work. To Hopkins, however, the important thing was pumping money into an economy badly in need of it and providing assistance to people with nowhere else to turn.

Roosevelt's favorite relief project was the Civilian Conservation Corps (CCC). Established in the first weeks of the new administration, the CCC was designed to provide employment to the millions of young men who could find no jobs in the cities and who many feared might become a source of urban crime and violence. At the same time, it was intended to advance the work of conservation and reforestation—goals Roosevelt had long cherished. The CCC created camps in national parks and forests and in other rural and wilderness settings. There young men (women were excluded from the program) worked in a semimilitary environment on such projects as planting trees, building reservoirs, developing parks, and improving agricultural irrigation. CCC camps were segregated by race. The vast majority of them were restricted to whites, but a few were reserved for blacks, Mexicans, and Indians.

Mortgage relief was a pressing need for millions of farm owners and homeowners. The Farm Credit Administration, which within two years refinanced one-fifth of all farm mortgages in the United States, was one response to that problem. The Frazier-Lemke Farm Bankruptcy Act of 1933 was another. It enabled some farmers to regain their land even after the foreclosure of their mortgages. Despite such efforts, however, 25 percent of all American farm owners had lost their land by 1934. Homeowners were similarly troubled, and in June 1933 the administration established the Home Owners' Loan Corporation, which by 1936 had refinanced the mortgages of more than 1 million householders. A year later, Congress established the Federal Housing Administration to insure mortgages for new construction and home repairs.

THE NEW DEAL IN TRANSITION

Seldom has an American president enjoyed such remarkable popularity as Franklin Roosevelt did during his first two years in office. But by early 1935, with no end to the Depression yet in sight, the New Deal found itself the target of fierce public criticism. In the spring of 1935, partly in response to these growing attacks, Roosevelt launched an ambitious new program of legislation that has often been called the "Second New Deal."

Critics of the New Deal

Some of the most strident attacks on the New Deal came from critics on the right. Roosevelt had tried for a time to conciliate conservatives and business leaders. By the end of 1934, however, it was clear that the American right in general, and much of the corporate world in particular, had become irreconcilably hostile to the New Deal. In August 1934, a group of the most fervent (and wealthiest) Roosevelt opponents, led by members of the Du Pont family, formed the American Liberty League, designed specifically to arouse public opposition to the New Deal's "dictatorial" policies and its supposed attacks on free enterprise. But the new organization was never able to expand its constituency much beyond the northern industrialists who had founded it.

Roosevelt's critics on the far left also managed to produce alarm among some supporters of the administration, but like the conservatives, they proved to have only limited strength. The Communist Party, the Socialist Party, and other radical and semiradical organizations were at times harshly critical of the New Deal. But they too failed ever to attract genuine mass support.

More menacing to the New Deal than either the far right or the far left was a group of dissident political movements that defied easy ideological classification. Some gained substantial public support within particular states and regions. And three men succeeded in mobilizing genuinely national followings. Dr. Francis E. Townsend, an elderly California physician, rose from obscurity to lead a movement of more than 5 million members with his plan for federal pensions for the elderly. According to the Townsend Plan, all Americans over the age of sixty would receive monthly government pensions of $200, provided they retired (thus freeing jobs for younger, unemployed Americans) and spent the money in full each month (which would pump needed funds into the economy). By 1935, the Townsend Plan had attracted the support of many older men and women. And while the plan itself made little progress in Congress, the public sentiment behind it helped build support for the Social Security system, which Congress did approve in 1935.

Father Charles E. Coughlin, a Catholic priest in the Detroit suburb of Royal Oak, Michigan, achieved even greater renown through his weekly sermons broadcast nationally over the radio. He proposed a series of monetary reforms—remonetization of silver, issuing of greenbacks, and nationalization of the banking system—that he insisted would restore prosperity and ensure economic justice. At first a warm supporter of Franklin Roosevelt, by late 1934 he had become disheartened by what he claimed was the president's failure to deal harshly enough with the "money powers." In the spring of 1935, he established his own political organization, the National Union for Social Justice. He was widely believed to have one of the largest regular radio audiences of anyone in America.

Most alarming of all to the administration was the growing national popularity of Senator Huey P. Long of Louisiana. Long had risen to power in his home state through his strident attacks on the banks, oil companies, and utilities and on the conservative political oligarchy allied with them. Elected governor in 1928, he launched an assault on his opponents so thorough and forceful that they were soon left with virtually no political power whatever. Many claimed that he had, in effect, become a dictator. But he also maintained the overwhelming support of the Louisiana electorate, in part because of his flamboyant personality and in part because of his solid record of conventional progressive accomplishment: building roads, schools, and hospitals; revising the tax codes; distributing free textbooks; lowering utility rates.

HUEY LONG Few public speakers could arouse a crowd
more effectively than Huey Long of Louisiana, known to
many as "the Kingfish" (a nickname borrowed from the
popular radio show *Amos 'n Andy*). It was Long's effective
use of radio, however, that contributed most directly to his
spreading national popularity in the early 1930s.

Barred by law from succeeding himself as governor, he ran in 1930 for a seat
in the United States Senate and won easily.

Long, like Coughlin, supported Franklin Roosevelt for president in
1932. But within six months of Roosevelt's inauguration he had broken with
the president. As an alternative to the New Deal, he advocated a drastic program of wealth redistribution, a program he ultimately named the Share-
Our-Wealth Plan. The government, he claimed, could end the Depression
easily by using the tax system to confiscate the surplus riches of the wealthiest men and women in America and distribute these surpluses to the rest of
the population. That would, he claimed, allow the government to guaran-

tee every family a minimum "homestead" of $5,000 and an annual wage of $2,500. In 1934, Long established his own national organization: the Share-Our-Wealth Society, which soon attracted a large following through much of the nation. A poll by the Democratic National Committee in the spring of 1935 disclosed that Long might attract more than 10 percent of the vote if he ran as a third-party candidate, enough to tip a close election to the Republicans.

Members of the Roosevelt administration considered dissident movements—and the broad popular discontent they represented—a genuine threat to the president. An increasing number of advisers were warning Roosevelt that he would have to do something dramatic to counter their strength.

The "Second New Deal"

Roosevelt launched the so-called Second New Deal in the spring of 1935 in response both to the growing political pressures and to the continuing economic crisis. The new proposals represented, if not a new direction, at least a shift in the emphasis of New Deal policy. Perhaps the most conspicuous change was in the administration's attitude toward big business. Symbolically at least, the president was now willing to attack corporate interests openly. In March, for example, he proposed to Congress an act designed to break up the great utility holding companies, and he spoke harshly of monopolistic control of their industry. The Holding Company Act of 1935 was the result, although furious lobbying by the utilities led to amendments that sharply limited its effects.

Equally alarming to affluent Americans was a series of tax reforms proposed by the president in 1935, a program conservatives quickly labeled a "soak-the-rich" scheme. Apparently designed to undercut the appeal of Huey Long's Share-Our-Wealth Plan, the Roosevelt proposals called for establishing the highest and most progressive peacetime tax rates in history—although the actual impact of these rates was limited, and many wealthy people found ways to escape them altogether.

The Supreme Court decision in 1935 to invalidate the National Industrial Recovery Act meant that Section 7(a) of the now defunct act, which had guaranteed workers the right to organize and bargain collectively, was now gone. A group of progressives in Congress led by Senator Robert E. Wagner of New York introduced what became the National Labor Relations Act of 1935. The new law, popularly known as the Wagner Act, provided workers with more federal protection than Section 7(a) of the National Industrial Recovery Act had offered. It created a crucial enforcement mechanism, the National Labor Relations Board (NLRB), which would have power to compel employers to recognize and bargain with legitimate unions. The president was not entirely happy with the bill, but he signed it anyway. That was in large part because American workers themselves had by 1935 become so important and vigorous a force that Roosevelt realized his own political future would depend in part on responding to their demands.

Labor Militancy

The emergence of a powerful trade union movement in the 1930s was one of the most important social and political developments of the decade. It occurred partly in response to government efforts to enhance the power of unions, but it was also a result of the increased militancy of American workers and their leaders. During the 1920s, most workers had displayed relatively little militancy in challenging employers or demanding recognition of their unions. In the 1930s, however, many of the factors that had impeded militancy vanished or grew weaker. Business leaders and industrialists lost (at least temporarily) the ability to control government policies. Both Section 7(a) of the National Industrial Recovery Act of 1933 and the Wagner Act of 1935 were passed over the strong objections of most (although not all) corporate leaders. Equally important, new and more militant labor organizations emerged to challenge the established, relatively conservative unions.

The growing militancy first became obvious in 1934, when newly organized workers (many of them inspired by the collective bargaining provisions of the National Industrial Recovery Act) demonstrated an assertiveness and at times radicalism seldom seen in recent years. Some became involved in violent confrontations with employers and local authorities. Despite the new militancy, however, it was clear that without stronger legal protection, most organizing drives would end in frustration. Once the Wagner Act became law, the search for more effective forms of organization rapidly gained strength in labor ranks.

The American Federation of Labor remained committed to the idea of the craft union: organizing workers on the basis of their skills. But that concept had little to offer unskilled laborers, who now constituted the bulk of the industrial work force. During the 1930s, therefore, a newer concept of labor organization challenged the craft union ideal: industrial unionism. Advocates of this approach argued that all the workers in a particular industry should be organized in a single union, regardless of what functions the workers performed. All autoworkers should be in a single automobile union; all steelworkers should be in a single steel union. United in this way, workers would greatly increase their power.

Leaders of the AFL craft unions for the most part opposed the new concept. But industrial unionism found a number of important advocates, most prominent among them John L. Lewis, the talented, flamboyant, and eloquent leader of the United Mine Workers. At first, Lewis and his allies attempted to work within the AFL, but friction between the new industrial organizations Lewis was promoting and the older craft unions grew rapidly. At the 1935 AFL convention, Lewis became embroiled in a series of angry confrontations (and one celebrated fistfight) with craft union leaders before finally walking out. A few weeks later, he created the Committee on Industrial Organization—a body officially within the AFL but unsanctioned by its leadership. After a series of bitter jurisdictional conflicts, the AFL finally expelled the new committee from its ranks, and along with it all the industrial unions it represented. In response, Lewis renamed the committee the Congress of Industrial Organizations (CIO), established it in 1936 as an organization directly rivaling the AFL, and became its first president. The schism clearly weakened the labor movement in many ways. But by freeing the advocates of industrial unionism from the restrictive rules of the AFL, it gave impetus to the creation of powerful new organizations.

The CIO also expanded the constituency of the labor movement. It was more receptive to women and to blacks than the AFL had been, in part because women and blacks were more likely to be relegated to unskilled jobs and in part because CIO organizing drives targeted previously unorganized industries (textiles, laundries, tobacco factories, and others) where women and minorities constituted much of the work force. The CIO was also a more militant organization than the AFL. By the time of the 1936 schism, it was already engaged in major organizing battles in the automobile and steel industries.

Organizing Battles

Out of several competing auto unions, the United Auto Workers (UAW) was gradually emerging preeminent in the early and mid-1930s. But although it was gaining recruits, it was making little progress in winning recognition from the corporations. In December 1936, however, autoworkers employed a controversial and effective new technique for challenging corporate opposition: the sit-down strike. Employees in several General Motors plants in Detroit simply sat down inside the plants, refusing either to work or to leave, thus preventing the company from using strikebreakers. The tactic spread to other locations, and by February 1937 strikers had occupied seventeen GM plants. The strikers ignored court orders and local police efforts to force them to vacate the buildings. When Michigan's governor, Frank Murphy, a liberal Democrat, refused to call up the National Guard to clear out the strikers, and when the federal government also refused to intervene on behalf of employers, General Motors relented. In February 1937, it became the first major manufacturer to recognize the UAW; other automobile companies soon did the same. The sit-down strike proved effective for rubber workers and others as well, but it survived only briefly as a labor technique. Its apparent illegality aroused so much public opposition that labor leaders soon abandoned it.

In the steel industry, the battle for unionization was less easily won. In 1936, the Steel Workers' Organizing Committee (SWOC; later the United Steelworkers of America) began a major organizing drive involving thousands of workers and frequent, at times bitter, strikes. These conflicts were notable not only for the militancy of the (predominantly male) steelworkers themselves but for the involvement of thousands of women (many of them wives or relatives of workers), who provided important logistical support for the strikers and who at times took direct action by creating a buffer between strikers and the police.

In March 1937, to the surprise of almost everyone, United States Steel, the giant of the industry, recognized the union rather than risk a costly strike at a time when it sensed itself on the verge of recovery from the Depression. But the smaller companies (known collectively as "Little Steel") were less accommodating. On Memorial Day 1937, a group of striking workers from Republic Steel gathered with their families for a picnic and demonstration in South Chicago. When they attempted to march peacefully (and legally) toward the steel plant, police opened fire on them. Ten demonstrators were killed; another ninety were wounded. Despite a public outcry against the "Memorial Day Massacre," the harsh tactics of Little Steel succeeded. The 1937 strike failed.

But the victory of Little Steel was one of the last gasps of the kind of brutal strikebreaking that had proved so effective in the past. In 1937 alone, there were 4,720 strikes—over 80 percent of them settled in favor of the unions. By the end of the year, more than 8 million workers were members of unions recognized as official bargaining units by employers (as compared with 3 million in 1932). By 1941, that number had expanded to 10 million and included the workers of Little Steel, whose employers had finally recognized the SWOC.

Social Security

From the first moments of the New Deal, important members of the administration, most notably Secretary of Labor Frances Perkins, had been lobbying for a system of federally sponsored social insurance for the elderly and the unemployed. In 1935, Roosevelt gave public support to what became the Social Security Act, which Congress passed the same year. It established several distinct programs. For the elderly, there were two types of assistance. Those who were presently destitute could receive up to $15 a month in federal assistance. More important for the future, many Americans presently working were incorporated into a pension system, to which they and their employers would contribute by paying a payroll tax; it would provide them with an income on retirement. Pension payments would not begin until 1942 and even then would provide only $10 to $85 a month to recipients. And broad categories of workers (including domestic servants and agricultural laborers, occupations with disproportionate numbers of blacks and women) were excluded from the program. But the act was a crucial first step in building the nation's most important social program for the elderly.

In addition, the Social Security Act created a system of unemployment insurance, which employers alone would finance and which made it possible for workers laid off from their jobs to receive temporary government assistance. It also established a system of federal aid to disabled people and a program of aid to dependent children.

The framers of the Social Security Act wanted to create a system of "insurance," not "welfare." And the largest programs (old-age pensions and unemployment insurance) were in many ways similar to private insurance programs, with contributions from participants and benefits available to all. But the act also provided considerable direct assistance based on need—to the elderly poor, to the disabled, to dependent children and their mothers. These groups were widely perceived to be small and genuinely unable to support themselves. But in later generations the programs for these groups would expand until they assumed dimensions that the planners of Social Security had neither foreseen nor desired.

The distinction built into the Social Security Act between "insurance" and "public assistance" reflected a set of cultural assumptions that would continue to influence the politics of welfare for the rest of the twentieth century. New Dealers, like most other Americans, believed that some people had "earned" social protection—either because they (or their employers) had contributed to the programs from which they drew, as was the case with old-age pensions and unemployment insurance, or because they had performed some special service to the nation, as had been the case in the past for Civil War and World War I veterans. Other people (many of them women) "needed" benefits because they were incapable of supporting themselves; and while New Dealers (and progressive reformers before them) were willing to provide such benefits, they did so less generously than they did for those they believed had earned them. Whatever its limits, however, it is clear that the 1935 act was the most important single piece of social welfare legislation in American history.

New Directions in Relief

Social Security was designed primarily to fulfill long-range goals. But millions of unemployed Americans had immediate needs. To help meet them, the administration established in 1935 the Works Progress Administration (WPA). Like the Civil Works Administration and other earlier efforts, the WPA established a system of work relief for the unemployed. But it was much bigger than the earlier agencies, both in the size of its budget ($5 billion at first) and in the energy and imagination of its operations.

Under the direction of Harry Hopkins, the WPA was responsible for building or renovating 110,000 public buildings (schools, post offices, government office buildings) and for constructing almost 600 airports, more than 500,000 miles of roads, and over 100,000 bridges. In the process, the WPA kept an average of 2.1 million workers employed and pumped needed money into the economy.

The WPA also displayed remarkable flexibility and imagination in offering assistance to those whose occupations did not fit into any traditional category of relief. The Federal Writers Project of the WPA, for example, gave unemployed writers a chance to do their work and receive a government salary. The Federal Arts Project, similarly, helped painters, sculptors, and others to continue their careers. The Federal Music Project and the Federal Theater Project oversaw the production of concerts and plays, creating work for unemployed musicians, actors, and directors. Other relief agencies emerged alongside the WPA. The National Youth Administration (NYA) provided work and scholarship assistance to high-school and college-age men and women. The Emergency Housing Division of the Public Works Administration began federal sponsorship of public housing.

WPA ART The Federal Art Project of the Works Progress Administration funded many kinds of projects, but it was probably best known for the striking murals it commissioned for post offices and other government buildings. Here, FAP artist Lucile Lloyd works on a mural portraying the history of California, which she painted for a government office building in Los Angeles.

The hiring practices of the WPA, the NYA, and other work-relief programs revealed another important, if at the time largely unrecognized, feature of the New Deal welfare system. Men and women alike were in distress in the 1930s (as in all difficult times). But the new welfare system dealt with members of the two sexes in very different ways. For men, the government concentrated mainly on work relief—on such programs as the CCC, the CWA, and the WPA, all of which were overwhelmingly male. The principal government aid to women was not work relief but cash assistance—most notably through the Aid to Dependent Children program of Social Security, which was designed largely to assist single mothers. This disparity in treatment reflected a widespread assumption that men constituted the bulk of the paid work force and that women needed to be treated within the context of the family. In fact, millions of women were already employed by the 1930s.

The 1936 "Referendum"

The presidential election of 1936, it was clear from the start, was to be a national referendum on Franklin Roosevelt and the New Deal. And while in 1935 there had been reason to question the president's political prospects, by the middle of 1936—with the economy visibly reviving—there could be little doubt that he would win a second term. The Republican Party nominated the moderate governor of Kansas, Alf M. Landon, who waged a generally pallid campaign. Republican conservatives seemed impotent even within their own party. Roosevelt's dissident challengers now appeared similarly powerless. One reason was the violent death of their most effective leader, Huey Long, who was assassinated in Louisiana in September 1935. Another reason was the ill-fated alliance among Father Coughlin, Dr. Townsend, and Gerald L. K. Smith (an intemperate henchman of Huey Long), who joined forces that summer to establish a new political movement—the Union Party, which nominated an undistinguished North Dakota congressman, William Lemke, for president.

The result was the greatest landslide in American history to that point. Roosevelt polled just under 61 percent of the vote to Landon's 36 percent and carried every state except Maine and Vermont. The Democrats increased their already large majorities in both houses of Congress. The Union Party received fewer than 900,000 votes.

The election results demonstrated the party realignment that the New Deal had produced. The Democrats now controlled a broad coalition of western and southern farmers, the urban working classes, the poor and unemployed, and the black communities of northern cities, as well as traditional progressives and committed new liberals—a coalition that constituted a substantial majority of the electorate. It would be decades before the Republican Party could again create a lasting majority coalition of its own.

THE NEW DEAL IN DISARRAY

Roosevelt emerged from the 1936 election at the zenith of his popularity. Within months, however, the New Deal was mired in serious new difficulties—a result of continuing opposition, the president's own political errors, and major economic setbacks.

The Court Fight and the "Purge"

The 1936 mandate, Franklin Roosevelt believed, made it possible for him to do something about the problem of the Supreme Court. No program of reform, he had become convinced, could long survive the obstructionist justices, who had already struck down the NRA and the AAA and threatened to invalidate even more legislation.

In February 1937, Roosevelt sent a surprise message to Capitol Hill proposing a general overhaul of the federal court system; included among the many provisions was one to add up to six new justices to the Supreme Court. The courts were "overworked," he claimed, and needed additional manpower and younger blood to enable them to cope with their increasing burdens. But Roosevelt's real purpose was to give himself the opportunity to appoint new, liberal justices and change the ideological balance of the Court.

Conservatives were outraged at the "Court-packing plan," and even many Roosevelt supporters were disturbed by what they considered evidence of the president's hunger for power. Still, Roosevelt might well have persuaded Congress to approve at least a compromise measure had not the Supreme Court itself intervened. Four justices consistently opposed the New Deal, and three generally supported it. Of the remaining two, Chief Justice Charles Evans Hughes often sided with the progressives and Associate Justice Owen J. Roberts usually voted with the conservatives. On March 29, 1937, Roberts, Hughes, and the three progressive justices voted together to uphold a state minimum-wage law—in the case of *West Coast Hotel* v. *Parrish*—thus reversing a 5-to-4 decision of the previous year invalidating a similar law. Two weeks later, again by a 5-to-4 margin, the Court upheld the Wagner Act, and in May it validated the Social Security Act. The Court had prudently moderated its position to make the Court-packing bill unnecessary. Congress ultimately defeated it.

On one level, the affair was a significant victory for Franklin Roosevelt. The Court was no longer an obstacle to New Deal reforms, particularly after the older justices began to retire, to be replaced by Roosevelt appointees. But the Court-packing episode did lasting political damage to the administration. From 1937 on, southern Democrats and other conservatives voted against his measures much more often than they had in the past.

A year later, the president's political situation deteriorated further. Roosevelt was determined to regain the initiative in his legislative battles, and in several primary campaigns in spring 1938 he openly spoke against members of his own party who had opposed his programs. Not only was he unable to unseat any of the five Democratic senators against whom he campaigned, but his "purge" efforts drove an even deeper wedge between the administration and its conservative opponents.

Retrenchment and Recession

By the summer of 1937, the national income, which had dropped from $82 billion in 1929 to $40 billion in 1932, had risen to nearly $72 billion. Other economic indices showed similar advances. Roosevelt seized on these improvements as an excuse to try to balance the federal budget, convinced by Treasury secretary Henry Morgenthau and many economists that the real danger now was no longer depression but inflation. Between January and August 1937, for example, he cut the WPA in half, laying off 1.5 million relief workers. A few weeks later, the fragile boom collapsed. The index of industrial production dropped from 117 in August 1937 to 76 in May 1938. Four million additional workers lost their jobs. Economic conditions were soon almost as bad as they had been in the bleak days of 1932–1933.

The recession of 1937 was a result of many factors. But to many observers at the time (including, apparently, Roosevelt), it seemed to be a direct result of the administration's unwise decision to reduce spending. And so the new crisis forced a reevaluation of policies. The advocates of government spending as an antidote to the Depression stood vindicated, it seemed; and the notion of using government deficits to stimulate the economy established a timid foothold in American public policy. In April 1938, the president asked Congress for an emergency appropriation of $5 billion for public works and relief programs, and government funds soon began pouring into the economy once again. Within a few months, another tentative recovery seemed to be under way, and the advocates of spending pointed to it as proof of the validity of their approach.

At the same time, a group of younger liberals in the administration who saw the recession as the result of excessively concentrated corporate power were urging the president to launch a new assault on monopoly. In April 1938, Roosevelt sent a stinging message to Congress, vehemently denouncing what he called an "unjustifiable concentration of economic power" and asking for the creation of a commission to examine that concentration with an eye to major reforms in the antitrust laws. In response, Congress established the Temporary National Economic Committee (TNEC), whose members included representatives of both houses of Congress and officials from several executive agencies. At about the same time, Roosevelt appointed a new head of the antitrust division of the Justice Department:

Thurman Arnold, a Yale Law School professor who soon proved to be the most vigorous director ever to serve in that office.

By the end of 1938, however, it was becoming clear that these ambitious new goals faced an uncertain future. For the New Deal had by then essentially come to an end. Congressional opposition now made it difficult for the president to enact any major new programs. But more important, perhaps, the threat of world crisis hung heavy in the political atmosphere, and Roosevelt was gradually growing more concerned with persuading a reluctant nation to prepare for war than with pursuing new avenues of reform.

LIMITS AND LEGACIES OF THE NEW DEAL

The New Deal made major changes in American government, some of them still controversial today. It also left important problems unaddressed.

African Americans and the New Deal

One group the New Deal did relatively little to assist was African Americans. The administration was not hostile to black aspirations. On the contrary, the New Deal was probably more sympathetic to them than any previous government of the twentieth century had been. Eleanor Roosevelt spoke throughout the 1930s on behalf of racial justice and put continuing pressure on her husband and others in the federal government to ease discrimination against blacks. The president himself appointed a number of blacks to significant second-level positions in his administration, creating an informal network of officeholders that became known as the "Black Cabinet." Eleanor Roosevelt, Interior secretary Harold Ickes, and WPA director Harry Hopkins all made efforts to ensure that New Deal relief programs did not exclude blacks, and by 1935 an estimated 30 percent of all African Americans were receiving some form of government assistance. One result was a historic change in black electoral behavior. As late as 1932, most American blacks were voting Republican, as they had been doing since the Civil War. By 1936, more than 90 percent of them were voting Democratic—the beginnings of a political alliance that would endure for many decades.

Blacks supported Franklin Roosevelt because they knew he was not their enemy. But they had few illusions that the New Deal represented a millennium in American race relations. The president was, for example, never will-

ELEANOR ROOSEVELT AND MARY MCLEOD BETHUNE Mrs. Roosevelt was a leading champion of racial equality within her husband's administration, and her commitment had an important impact on the behavior of the government even though she held no official post. She is seen here meeting in 1937 with Aubrey Williams, executive director of the National Youth Administration, and Mary McLeod Bethune, the agency's Director of Negro Affairs.

ing to risk losing the support of southern Democrats by supporting legislation to make lynching a federal crime or to ban the poll tax, one of the most potent tools by which white southerners kept blacks from voting.

New Deal relief agencies did not challenge, and indeed reinforced, existing patterns of discrimination. The Civilian Conservation Corps established separate black camps. The NRA codes tolerated paying blacks less than whites doing the same jobs. African Americans were largely excluded from employment in the TVA. The Federal Housing Administration refused to provide mortgages to blacks moving into white neighborhoods, and the first public housing projects financed by the federal government were racially segregated. The WPA routinely relegated black and Hispanic workers to the least skilled and lowest-paying jobs; when funding ebbed, African Americans, like women, were among the first to be dismissed.

The New Deal was not hostile to black Americans, and it made some contributions to their progress. But it refused to make the issue of race a significant part of its agenda.

The New Deal and the "Indian Problem"

New Deal policy toward the Indian tribes marked a significant break from the approach in the years before Roosevelt, largely because of the efforts of the extraordinary commissioner of Indian affairs in the 1930s, John Collier. Collier was greatly influenced by the work of twentieth-century anthropologists who advanced the idea of cultural relativism—the theory that every culture should be accepted and respected on its own terms and that no culture is inherently superior to another. Cultural relativism was a challenge to the three-centuries-old assumption among white Americans that Indians were "savages" and that white society was inherently superior and more "civilized."

Collier favored legislation that would, he hoped, reverse the pressures on Native Americans to assimilate and allow them to remain Indians. Not all tribal leaders agreed with Collier. Indeed, his belief in the importance of preserving Indian culture would not find its greatest support among the tribes until the 1960s. Nevertheless, Collier effectively promoted legislation—which became the Indian Reorganization Act of 1934—to advance his goals. Among other things, it restored to the tribes the right to own land collectively (reversing the allotment policy adopted in 1887, which encouraged the breaking up of tribal lands into individually owned plots) and to elect tribal governments. In the thirteen years after passage of the 1934 bill, tribal land increased by nearly 4 million acres, and Indian agricultural income increased dramatically (from under $2 million in 1934 to over $49 million in 1947).

Even with the redistribution of lands under the 1934 act, however, Indians continued to possess, for the most part, only territory whites did not want—much of it arid, some of it desert. And as a group, they continued to constitute the poorest segment of the population. The efforts of the 1930s did not solve, or even greatly alleviate, what some called the "Indian problem." They did, however, provide Indians with some tools for rebuilding the viability of the tribes.

Women and the New Deal

Symbolically, at least, the New Deal marked a breakthrough in the role of women in public life. Roosevelt appointed the first female member of the cabinet in the nation's history, Secretary of Labor Frances Perkins. He also named more than 100 other women to positions at lower levels of the federal bureaucracy. But New Deal support for women operated within limits.

Even many of the women in the administration were concerned not so much about achieving gender equality as about obtaining special protections for women.

The New Deal generally supported the belief (not always matched by practice) that in hard times women should withdraw from the workplace to open up more jobs for men. Frances Perkins, for example, spoke out against what she called the "pin-money worker"—the married woman working to earn extra money for the household. New Deal relief agencies offered relatively little employment for women. The NRA sanctioned sexually discriminatory wage practices. The Social Security program excluded domestic servants, waitresses, and other predominantly female occupations.

As with African Americans, so also with women: The New Deal was not actively hostile to feminist aspirations; in many ways, it was unprecedentedly supportive. It did, however, accept prevailing cultural norms. There was not yet sufficient political pressure from women themselves to persuade the administration to do otherwise. Indeed, some of the most important supporters of policies that reinforced traditional gender roles (such as Social Security) were themselves women.

The New Deal and the West

One part of American society that did receive special attention from the New Deal was the American West, which benefited disproportionately from federal relief and public works programs. The West received more government funds per capita through New Deal relief programs than any other region.

Most westerners were eager for the assistance New Deal agencies provided, but their political leaders were not always as supportive. In Colorado, for example, the state legislature refused to provide the required matching funds for FERA relief in 1933. When, in response, Harry Hopkins cut Colorado off from the program, unemployed people rioted in Denver and looted food stores. Only then did the legislature reverse course and provide funding.

Just as in the South locally administered relief programs did not challenge prevailing racial norms, so in the West New Deal programs sustained existing racial and ethnic prejudices. In several states, relief agencies paid different groups at different rates: white Anglos received the most generous aid; blacks, Indians, and Mexican Americans received lower levels of support. In the CCC camps in New Mexico, Hispanics and Anglos sometimes worked in the same camps, but there were frequent tensions and occasional conflicts between them.

But the main reason for the New Deal's particular impact on the West was that conditions in the region made the government's programs especially important. Federal agricultural programs had an enormous impact on the West because farming remained so much more central to the economy of the region than it did in much of the East. The largest New Deal public works programs—the great dams and power stations—were mainly in the West, both because the best locations for such facilities were there and because the West had the most need for new sources of water and power. The Grand Coulee dam on the Columbia River was the largest public works project in American history to that point, and it provided cheap electric power for much of the Northwest. Its construction, and the construction of other, smaller dams and water projects, created a basis for economic development in the region.

Without this enormous public investment by the federal government, much of the economic growth that transformed the West after World War II would have been much more difficult, if not impossible, to achieve. For generations after the Great Depression, the federal government maintained a much greater and more visible bureaucratic presence in the West than in any other region.

The New Deal and the Economy

The most frequent criticisms of the New Deal involve its failure genuinely to revive or reform the American economy. New Dealers never fully recognized the value of government spending as a vehicle for recovery, and their efforts along other lines never succeeded in ending the Depression. The economic boom sparked by World War II, not the New Deal, finally ended the crisis. Nor did the New Deal substantially alter the distribution of power within American capitalism, and it had only a small impact on the distribution of wealth among the American people.

Nevertheless, the New Deal did have a number of important and lasting effects on both the behavior and the structure of the American economy. It helped elevate new groups—workers, farmers, and others—to positions from which they could at times effectively challenge the power of the corporations. It increased the regulatory functions of the federal government in ways that helped stabilize previously troubled areas of the economy: the stock market, the banking system, and others. And the administration helped establish the basis for new forms of federal fiscal policy, which in the postwar years would give the government tools for promoting and regulating economic growth.

The New Deal also created the rudiments of the American welfare state, through its many relief programs and above all through the Social Security system. The conservative inhibitions New Dealers brought to this task ensured that the welfare system that ultimately emerged would be limited in its impact (at least in comparison with the systems of other industrial nations), would reinforce some traditional patterns of gender and racial discrimination, and would be expensive and cumbersome to administer. But for all its limits, the new system marked a historic break with the nation's traditional reluctance to offer any public assistance whatever to its neediest citizens.

The New Deal and American Politics

Perhaps the most dramatic effect of the New Deal was its impact on the structure and behavior of American government and on the character of American politics. Franklin Roosevelt helped enhance the power of the federal government as a whole. By the end of the 1930s, state and local governments were clearly of secondary importance to the government in Washington; in the past, that had not always been clear. Roosevelt also established the presidency as the preeminent center of authority within the federal government. Not for many years would Congress wield as much independent power as it had in the years before the New Deal.

Finally, the New Deal had a profound impact on how the American people defined themselves politically. It took a weak, divided Democratic Party, which had been a minority force in American politics for many decades, and turned it into a mighty coalition that would dominate national party competition for more than thirty years. It turned the attention of many voters away from some of the cultural issues that had preoccupied them in the 1920s and awakened in them an interest in economic matters of direct importance to their lives. And it created among the American people greatly increased expectations of government—expectations that the New Deal itself did not always fulfill but that survived for generations to become the basis of new liberal crusades in the postwar era.

D E B A T I N G   T H E   P A S T

The New Deal

C ONTEMPORARIES OF FRANKLIN ROOSEVELT debated the impact of the New Deal with ferocious intensity: conservatives complaining of a menacing tyranny of the state, liberals celebrating the New Deal's progressive achievements, people on the left charging that the reforms of the 1930s were largely cosmetic and ignored the nation's fundamental problems. Although the conservative critique has found relatively little scholarly expression since Roosevelt's death, the liberal and left positions continued for many years to shape the way historians described the Roosevelt administration.

The dominant view from the beginning was an approving liberal interpretation, and its most important early voice was that of Arthur M. Schlesinger, Jr. He argued in the three volumes of *The Age of Roosevelt* (1957–1960) that the New Deal marked a continuation of the long struggle between public power and private interests, a struggle Roosevelt had moved to a new level as the unconstrained influence of business elites finally encountered an effective challenge. Workers, farmers, consumers and others now had much more protection than they had enjoyed in the past.

At almost the same time, however, other historians were offering more qualified assessments of the New Deal, even if ones that remained securely within the liberal framework. Richard Hofstadter argued in 1955 that the New Deal was a "drastic new departure . . . different from anything that had yet happened in the United States"; that it gave American liberalism a "social-democratic tinge that had never before been present in American reform movements"; but that its highly pragmatic approach lacked a central, guiding philosophy. James MacGregor Burns argued in 1956 that Roosevelt failed to make full use of his potential as a leader and had accommodated himself unnecessarily to existing patterns of power.

William Leuchtenburg's *Franklin D. Roosevelt and the New Deal* (1963) was the first systematic "revisionist" interpretation. Leuchtenburg was a sympathetic critic, arguing that most of the limitations of the New Deal were the result of political and ideological constraints over which Roosevelt had little control. But he challenged the views of earlier scholars who had proclaimed the New Deal a "revolution" in social policy. Leuchtenburg could muster only enough enthusiasm to call it a "halfway revolution," one that helped some previously disadvantaged groups (most notably farmers and workers) but that did little or nothing for many others (blacks, sharecroppers, the urban poor).

Harsher criticisms soon emerged. Barton Bernstein in a 1968 essay compiled a dreary chronicle of missed opportunities and inadequate responses to problems and concluded that the New Deal had saved capitalism, but at the expense of the least powerful. Ronald Radosh, Paul Conkin, and, more recently, Thomas Ferguson and Colin Gordon expanded on these criticisms; the New Deal, they contended, was part of the twentieth-century tradition of "corporate liberalism"—a tradition in which reform is closely wedded to the needs and interests of capitalism.

Most scholars in the 1980s and 1990s, however, seemed largely to have accepted the revised liberal view: that the New Deal was a significant (and most agree valuable) chapter in the history of reform, but one that worked within rigid, occasionally crippling limits. Much of the recent work on the New Deal, therefore, has focused on the constraints it faced. Some scholars (notably the sociologist Theda Skocpol) have emphasized the issue of "state capacity"—the absence of a government bureaucracy with sufficient strength and expertise to shape or administer many programs. James T. Patterson, Barry Karl, Mark Leff, and others have emphasized the political constraints the New Deal encountered—the conservative inhibitions about government that remained strong in Congress and among the public. Frank Freidel, Ellis Hawley, Herbert Stein, and many others point as well to the ideological constraints affecting Franklin Roosevelt and his supporters, the limits of their own understanding of their time. Alan Brinkley, in *The End of Reform* (1995), described an ideological shift within New Deal liberalism that marginalized older concerns about wealth and monoply power.

The phrase "New Deal liberalism" has come in the postwar era to seem synonymous with modern ideas of aggressive federal management of the economy, elaborate welfare systems, a powerful bureaucracy, and large-scale government spending. But many historians of the New Deal would argue that the modern idea of New Deal liberalism bears only a limited relationship to the ideas that New Dealers themselves embraced.

CHAPTER TWENTY-SEVEN

The Global Crisis, 1921–1941

The Diplomacy of the New Era ∼ *Isolationism and Internationalism*
From Neutrality to Intervention

ENRY CABOT LODGE of Massachusetts, chairman of the Senate
Foreign Relations Committee and one of the most powerful figures in the Republican Party, led the fight against ratification of the Treaty
of Versailles in 1918 and 1919. In part because of his efforts, the treaty was
defeated. The United States failed to join the League of Nations; and American foreign policy embarked on an independent course that for the next two
decades would attempt, but ultimately fail, to expand American influence and
maintain international stability without committing the United States to any
lasting relationships with other nations.

Lodge was not an isolationist. He recognized that America had emerged
from World War I the most powerful nation in the world. He believed the
United States should exert its influence internationally. But he believed, too,
that America's expanded role in the world should reflect the nation's own
interests and its own special virtues; the United States should remain unfettered with obligations to anyone else. He said in 1919:

> We are a great moral asset of Christian civilization. . . . How did we get
> there? By our own efforts. Nobody led us, nobody guided us, nobody con-
> trolled us. . . . I would keep America as she has been—not isolated, not pre-
> vent her from joining other nations for . . . great purposes—but I wish her
> to be master of her own fate.

In the end, the limited American internationalism of the interwar years
proved insufficient to protect the interests of the United States, to create
global stability, or to keep the nation from becoming involved in the most
catastrophic war in human history.

TIME LINE

1924	1928	1931	1933	1937
Dawes Plan	Kellogg-Briand Pact	Japan invades Manchuria	U.S. recognizes Soviet Union Good Neighbor Policy	Roosevelt's "quarantine" speech

1938	1939	1940	1941
Munich Conference	Nazi-Soviet nonaggression pact World War II begins	Tripartite Pact America First Committee founded Roosevelt reelected Destroyers-for-bases deal	Lend-lease plan Atlantic Charter Japan attacks Pearl Harbor U.S. enters World War II

THE DIPLOMACY OF THE NEW ERA

Critics of American foreign policy in the 1920s often described it with a single word: isolationism. But in reality, the United States played a more active role in world affairs in the 1920s than it had at almost any previous time in its history.

Replacing the League

By the time the Harding administration took office in 1921, American membership in the League of Nations was no longer a realistic possibility. But Secretary of State Charles Evans Hughes wanted to find something with which to replace the League as a guarantor of world peace and stability. He embarked on a series of efforts to build safeguards against future wars—safeguards, however, that would not hamper American freedom of action in the world.

The most important of such efforts was the Washington Conference of 1921—an attempt to prevent a destabilizing naval armaments race among the United States, Britain, and Japan. Hughes proposed a plan for dramatic reductions in the fleets of all three nations and a ten-year moratorium on the construction of large warships. To the surprise of almost everyone, the conference ultimately agreed to accept most of Hughes's terms. The Five-Power Pact of February 1922 established limits for total naval tonnage and a ratio of armaments among the signatories. For every 5 tons of American and British warships, Japan would maintain 3 and France and Italy 1.75 each.

The Washington Conference began the New Era effort to protect world peace (and the international economic interests of the United States) without accepting international obligations. The Kellogg-Briand Pact of 1928 concluded it. When the French foreign minister, Aristide Briand, asked the United States in 1927 to join an alliance against Germany, Secretary of State Frank Kellogg (who had replaced Hughes in 1925) proposed instead a multilateral treaty outlawing war as an instrument of national policy. Fourteen nations signed the agreement in Paris on August 27, 1928, amid great solemnity and wide international acclaim. Forty-eight other nations later joined the pact. It contained no instruments of enforcement.

Debts and Diplomacy

The first responsibility of diplomacy, Hughes, Kellogg, and others agreed, was to ensure that American overseas trade faced no obstacles. Preventing a dangerous and expensive armaments race and reducing the possibility of war were two steps to that end. So were new financial arrangements to deal with international debts. The Allied powers of Europe were struggling to repay $11 billion in loans they had contracted with the United States during and shortly after the war. At the same time, Germany was attempting to pay the reparations levied by the Allies. With the financial structure of Europe on the brink of collapse as a result, the United States stepped in with a solution.

Charles G. Dawes, an American banker, negotiated an agreement in 1924 among France, Britain, Germany, and the United States under which American banks would provide enormous loans to the Germans, enabling them to meet their reparations payments; in return, Britain and France would agree to reduce the amount of those payments. The Dawes Plan became the source of a troubling circular pattern in international finance. The United States would lend money to Germany, which would use that money to pay reparations to France and England, which would in turn use those funds (as well as large loans they themselves were receiving from American banks) to repay war debts to the United States. The flow was able to continue only by virtue of the enormous debts Germany and the other European nations were acquiring to American banks and corporations. Some in the American government warned that the reckless expansion of overseas loans and investments threatened disaster—that the United States was becoming too dependent on unstable European economies. Such warnings fell, for the most part, on deaf ears, and the American economic involvement in Europe continued to expand until the worldwide depression shattered the system in 1931.

The government felt even fewer reservations about assisting American economic expansion in Latin America. During the 1920s, American military forces maintained a presence in Nicaragua, Panama, and several other countries in the region, while United States investments in Latin America more than doubled. American banks were offering large loans to Latin American governments, just as they were in Europe; and just as in Europe, the Latin Americans were having difficulty earning the money to repay them in the face of the formidable United States tariff barrier.

Hoover and the World Crisis

After the relatively placid international climate of the 1920s, the diplomatic challenges facing the Hoover administration must have seemed bewildering. The world financial crisis that had begun in 1929 and greatly intensified after 1931 was producing a dangerous nationalism in Europe, toppling some existing political leaders and replacing them with powerful, belligerent governments committed to expansion as a solution to their economic problems. An expansionist government in Japan was creating similar problems in Asia. Hoover was confronted with the beginning of a process that would ultimately lead to war.

In Latin America, Hoover tried to repair some of the damage earlier American policies had created. He made a ten-week good-will tour through the region before his inauguration. Once in office, he generally abstained from intervening in the internal affairs of neighboring nations and moved to withdraw American troops from Nicaragua and Haiti. When economic distress led to the collapse of several Latin American regimes, Hoover announced a new policy: America would grant diplomatic recognition to any sitting government in the region without questioning the means it had used to obtain power. He even repudiated the Roosevelt corollary to the Monroe Doctrine by refusing to permit American intervention when several Latin American countries defaulted on debt obligations to the United States in October 1931.

In Europe, the administration enjoyed few successes in its efforts to promote economic stability. When Hoover's proposed moratorium on debts failed to attract broad support or produce financial stability, he refused to cancel all war debts to the United States as many economists advised him to do. Several European nations promptly went into default. Efforts to extend the 1921 limits on naval construction fell victim to French and British fears of German and Japanese militarism. And the World Disarmament Conference in Geneva in 1932 similarly ended in frustration.

HITLER AND MUSSOLINI The German and Italian dictators, shown here reviewing troops together in Berlin in the mid-1930s, acted publicly as if they were equals. Privately, however, Hitler viewed Mussolini with contempt, and the Italian dictator complained frequently of being treated as a junior partner by his ally.

The ineffectiveness of American diplomacy in Europe was particularly troubling in light of the new governments on the Continent. Benito Mussolini's Fascist Party had been in control of Italy since the early 1920s and had become increasingly nationalistic and militaristic. Still more ominous was the growing power of the National Socialist (or Nazi) Party in Germany. By the late 1920s, the Weimar Republic, the nation's government since the end of World War I, had been largely discredited by, among other things, a ruinous inflation. Adolf Hitler, the leader of the Nazis, was growing rapidly in popular favor and would take power in 1933. Hitler believed in the genetic superiority of the Aryan (German) people and in extending German territory to provide Lebensraum (living space) for the German "master race." He also displayed a pathological anti-Semitism and a passionate militarism.

More immediately alarming to the Hoover administration was a major crisis in Asia—another early step toward World War II. The Japanese, suffering from an economic depression of their own, were concerned about the increasing power of the Soviet Union and of Chiang Kai-shek's nationalist China. In particular, they were alarmed at Chiang's insistence on expanding his government's power in Manchuria, which remained officially a part of China but over which the Japanese had maintained informal economic control since 1905. In 1933, Japan's military leaders staged what was, in effect, a coup and took control of the government in Tokyo. Weeks later, they launched an invasion of northern Manchuria. They had conquered the region by the end of the year. Hoover permitted Secretary of State Henry Stimson to issue stern warnings to the Japanese but barred him from cooperating with the League of Nations to impose economic sanctions against them. Early in 1932, Japan expanded its aggression further into China, attacking the city of Shanghai and killing thousands of civilians.

By the time Hoover left office, early in 1933, the international system the United States had attempted to create in the 1920s—a system based on voluntary cooperation among nations and on an American refusal to commit itself to any collective obligations—had collapsed. The United States faced a choice. It could adopt a more energetic form of internationalism and enter into firmer and more meaningful associations with other nations. It could resort to nationalism and try to deal with international problems alone. Or it could ignore global problems altogether. For the next six years, it experimented with elements of all three approaches.

ISOLATIONISM AND INTERNATIONALISM

The administration of Franklin Roosevelt faced a dual challenge as it entered office in 1933. It had to deal with the worst economic crisis in the nation's history, and it had to deal as well with the effects of a decaying international structure. The two problems were not unrelated, for it was the Depression itself that was producing much of the political chaos throughout the world.

Depression Diplomacy

Perhaps Roosevelt's sharpest break with the policies of his predecessor was on the question of American economic relations with Europe. Hoover had argued that only by resolving the question of war debts and reinforcing the gold standard could the American economy hope to recover. He had, therefore, agreed to participate in the World Economic Conference, to be held in London in June 1933, to attempt to resolve these issues. By the time the conference assembled, however, Roosevelt had already become convinced that the gold value of the dollar had to be allowed to fall in order for American goods to be able to compete in world markets. Shortly after the conference convened, he released what became known as the "bombshell message," repudiating the orthodox views of most of the delegates and rejecting any agreement on currency stabilization. The conference quickly dissolved without reaching agreement.

At the same time, Roosevelt abandoned the commitments of the Hoover administration to settle the issue of war debts through international agreement. In April 1934 he signed a bill that prohibited American banks from making loans to any nation in default on its debts. The legislation ended the old, circular system by which debt payments continued only by virtue of increasing American loans; within months, war-debt payments from every nation except Finland stopped for good.

The United States and Russia had viewed each other with mistrust and even hostility since the Bolshevik Revolution of 1917, and the American government still had not officially recognized the Soviet regime in 1933. But a growing number of influential Americans were urging a change in policy—largely because the Soviet Union appeared to be a possible source of trade. The Russians, for their part, were hoping for American cooperation in containing Japan. In November 1933, the United States and the Soviet Union agreed to open formal diplomatic relations.

Despite this promising beginning, however, relations with the Soviet Union soon soured once again. American trade failed to establish a foothold in Russia, disappointing hopes in the United States; and the American government did little to reassure the Soviets that it was interested in stopping Japanese expansion in Asia, dousing expectations in Russia. By the end of 1934, the Soviet Union and the United States were once again viewing each other with considerable mistrust. And the Soviet leader, Josef Stalin, was beginning to consider making agreements of his own with the fascist governments of Japan and Germany.

The Good Neighbor Policy

The United States succeeded during the 1930s in increasing both its exports to and its imports from Latin America by over 100 percent. At the same time, the Roosevelt administration was taking a new approach toward Latin America, an approach which became known as the "Good Neighbor Policy" and which expanded on the changes the Hoover administration had made. At the Inter-American Conference in Montevideo, Uruguay, in December 1933, Secretary of State Cordell Hull signed a formal convention declaring: "No state has the right to intervene in the internal or external affairs of another." By repudiating military intervention, Roosevelt, like Hoover, eased tensions between the United States and its neighbors considerably. But the Good Neighbor Policy did little to stem the growing American domination of the Latin American economy.

The Rise of Isolationism

With the international system of the 1920s now decayed beyond repair, the United States faced a choice between more active efforts to stabilize the world and more energetic attempts to isolate itself from it. Most Americans unhesitatingly chose the latter. Support for isolationism emerged from many quarters. Some Wilsonian internationalists had grown disillusioned with the League of Nations and its inability to stop Japanese aggression in Asia. Other Americans were listening to the argument that powerful business interests—Wall Street, munitions makers, and others—had tricked the United States into participating in World War I. An investigation by a Senate committee chaired by Senator Gerald Nye of North Dakota claimed to have produced evidence of exorbitant profiteering and tax evasion by many corporations during the war, and it suggested that bankers had pressured Wilson to intervene in the war so as to protect their loans abroad. (Few historians now lend much credence to these charges.)

Roosevelt himself was sympathetic to some of the isolationist arguments. But he continued to hope for at least a modest American role in maintaining world peace. In 1935, he proposed to the Senate a treaty to make the United States a member of the World Court—a largely symbolic gesture. Nevertheless, isolationists such as Father Coughlin and William Randolph Hearst aroused popular opposition to the agreement, and the Senate voted it down. The president would not soon again attempt to challenge the isolationist tide.

In the summer of 1935, it became clear that Mussolini's Italy was preparing to invade Ethiopia. Fearing the invasion would provoke a new European war, American legislators began to design legal safeguards to prevent the United States from being dragged into the conflict. The result was the Neutrality Act of 1935, followed by additional acts in 1936 and 1937. The 1935 law established a mandatory arms embargo against both sides in any military conflict and directed the president to warn American citizens against traveling on the ships of warring nations. Thus, isolationists believed, the "protection of neutral rights" could not again become an excuse for American intervention in war. The 1936 Neutrality Act renewed these provisions, and the 1937 law added new ones, establishing the so-called cash-and-carry policy, by which belligerents could purchase only nonmilitary goods from the United States and could do so only by paying cash and shipping their purchases themselves.

Isolationist sentiment showed its strength again in 1936–1937 in response to the civil war in Spain. The Falangists of General Francisco Franco, a group much like the Italian fascists, revolted in July 1936 against the existing republican government. Hitler and Mussolini supported Franco, both vocally and with weapons and supplies. Some individual Americans traveled to Spain to assist the republican cause, but the United States government joined with Britain and France in an agreement to offer no assistance to either side.

Roosevelt, however, was slowly becoming convinced that the course of international events required some more forceful American response. Particularly disturbing was the deteriorating situation in Asia. In the summer of 1937, Japan intensified its six-year-old assault on Manchuria and attacked China's five northern provinces. Roosevelt responded in a speech in Chicago in October 1937. He warned of the dangers of the Japanese actions and argued that aggressors should be "quarantined" by the international community to prevent the contagion of war from spreading. He was deliberately vague about what such a "quarantine" would mean. Even so, public response to the speech was disturbingly hostile, and Roosevelt drew back. On December 12, 1937, Japanese aviators bombed and sank the United States gunboat *Panay*, almost certainly deliberately, as it sailed the Yangtze River in China. But so reluctant was the Roosevelt administration to antagonize the isolationists that the United States eagerly seized on Japanese claims that the bombing had been an accident, accepted Japan's apologies, and overlooked the attack.

The Failure of Munich

In 1936, Hitler had moved the revived German army into the Rhineland, rearming an area that France had, in effect, controlled since World War I. In March 1938, German forces marched into Austria, and Hitler proclaimed a union (or *Anschluss*) between Austria, his native land, and Germany, his adopted one. Neither in America nor in most of Europe was there much more than a murmur of opposition.

The Austrian invasion, however, soon created another crisis, for Germany had by now occupied territory surrounding three sides of western Czechoslovakia, a region Hitler dreamed of annexing. In September 1938, he demanded that Czechoslovakia cede him part of that region, the Sudetenland, an area in which many ethnic Germans lived. Although Czechoslovakia was prepared to fight to stop Hitler, it needed assistance from other nations. But most Western governments, including the United States, were willing to pay almost any price to settle the crisis peacefully. On September 29, Hitler met with the leaders of France and Great Britain at Munich in an effort to resolve the crisis. The French and British agreed to accept the German demands in Czechoslovakia in return for Hitler's promise to expand no farther.

The Munich agreement, which Roosevelt applauded at the time, was the

THE BLITZ, LONDON The German Luftwaffe terrorized London and other British cities in 1940–1941 and again late in the war by bombing civilian areas indiscriminately in an effort to break the spirit of the English people. The effort failed, and the fortitude of the British did much to arouse support for their cause in the United States.

most prominent element of a policy that came to be known as "appeasement" and that came to be identified (not altogether fairly) largely with British Prime Minister Neville Chamberlain. Whoever was to blame, the policy was a failure. In March 1939, Hitler occupied the remaining areas of Czechoslovakia, violating the Munich agreement unashamedly. And in April, he began issuing threats against Poland.

At that point, both Britain and France gave assurances to the Polish government that they would come to its assistance in case of an invasion; they even tried, too late, to draw the Soviet Union into a mutual defense agreement. But Stalin, who had not even been invited to the Munich Conference, had already decided he could expect no protection from the West. He signed a nonaggression pact with Hitler in August 1939, freeing the Germans for the moment from the danger of a two-front war. Shortly after that, Hitler staged an incident on the Polish border to allow him to claim that Germany had been attacked, and on September 1, 1939, he launched a full-scale invasion of Poland. Britain and France, true to their pledges, declared war on Germany two days later. World War II had begun.

FROM NEUTRALITY TO INTERVENTION

"This nation will remain a neutral nation," the president declared shortly after the hostilities began in Europe, "but I cannot ask that every American remain neutral in thought as well." There was never any question that both he and the majority of the American people favored Britain, France, and the other Allied nations in the contest. The question was how much the United States was prepared to do to assist them.

Neutrality Tested

At the very least, Roosevelt believed, the United States should make armaments available to the Allied armies to help them counter the military advantage the large German munitions industry gave Hitler. In September 1939, he asked Congress to revise the Neutrality Acts and lift the arms embargo against any nation engaged in war. Powerful isolationist opposition forced Congress to maintain the prohibition on American ships entering war zones. But the 1939 law did permit belligerents to purchase arms on the same cash-and-carry basis that the earlier Neutrality Acts had established for the sale of nonmilitary materials.

For a time, it was possible to believe that little more would be necessary. After the German armies quickly subdued Poland, the war in Europe settled into a long, quiet lull that lasted through the winter and spring—a "phony war," some called it. (In the meantime, the Soviet Union overran the small Baltic republics of Latvia, Estonia, and Lithuania and then, in late November, established effective control over Finland. The United States responded with nothing more than an ineffective "moral embargo" on the shipment of armaments to Russia.)

Whatever illusions Americans had harbored about the war in western Europe were shattered in the spring of 1940 when Germany launched a massive invasion to the west—first attacking Denmark and Norway, sweeping next across the Netherlands and Belgium, and driving finally deep into the heart of France. Allied efforts proved futile against the Nazi blitzkrieg. One western European stronghold after another fell into German hands. On June 10, Mussolini invaded France from the south as Hitler was attacking from the north. On June 22, finally, France fell, and Nazi troops marched into Paris. A new collaborationist French regime assembled in Vichy; and in all Europe, only the shattered remnants of the British and French armies, rescued from the beaches of Dunkirk, remained to oppose the Axis forces.

On May 16, in the midst of the offensive, Roosevelt asked Congress for an additional $1 billion for defense and received it quickly. That was one day after Winston Churchill, the new British prime minister, had sent Roosevelt the first of many long lists of requests for armaments, without which, he insisted, England could not long survive. Some Americans (including the United States ambassador to London, Joseph P. Kennedy) argued that the British plight was already hopeless, that any aid to the English was a wasted effort. But the president was determined to make war materials available to Britain. He even circumvented the cash-and-carry provisions of the Neutrality Acts by giving England fifty American destroyers (most of them left over from World War I) in return for the right to build American bases on British territory in the Western Hemisphere, and he returned to the factories a number of new airplanes purchased by the American government so that the British could buy them instead.

Roosevelt was able to take such steps in part because of a major shift in American public opinion. By July 1940, more than 66 percent of the public (according to opinion polls) believed that Germany posed a direct threat to the United States. Congress was, therefore, more willing to permit expanded American assistance to the Allies. Congress was also becoming more concerned about the need for internal preparations for war, and in September it approved the Burke-Wadsworth Act, inaugurating the first peacetime military draft in American history.

But the isolationists were far from finished. A powerful new isolationist lobby—the America First Committee, whose members included such prominent Americans as Charles Lindbergh and Senators Gerald Nye and Burton Wheeler—joined the debate over American policy toward the war. The lobby had at least the indirect support of a large proportion of the Republican Party. The debate was a bitter one. Through the summer and fall of 1940, moreover, it was complicated by a presidential campaign.

The biggest political question of 1940 was whether Franklin Roosevelt would break with tradition and run for an unprecedented third term. The president himself did not reveal his own wishes. But by refusing to withdraw from the contest, he made it impossible for any rival Democrat to establish a claim to the nomination. And when, just before the Democratic Convention in July, he let it be known that he would accept a "draft" from his party, the issue was virtually settled. The Democrats quickly renominated him and even reluctantly swallowed his choice for vice president: Agriculture secretary Henry A. Wallace, a man too liberal and too controversial for the taste of many party leaders.

The Republicans, again uncertain how to oppose Roosevelt effectively, nominated for president a politically inexperienced Indiana businessman, Wendell Willkie, who benefited from a powerful grassroots movement. Both the candidate and the party platform took positions little different from Roosevelt's: they would keep the country out of war but would extend generous assistance to the Allies. Willkie was an appealing figure and a vigorous campaigner, and he managed to evoke more public enthusiasm than any Republican candidate in decades. The election was closer than in either 1932 or 1936, but Roosevelt still won decisively. He received 55 percent of the popular vote to Willkie's 45 percent, and he won 449 electoral votes to Willkie's 82.

Neutrality Abandoned

In the last months of 1940, with the election behind him and with the situation in Europe deteriorating, Roosevelt began to make subtle but profound changes in the American role in the war. Great Britain was virtually bankrupt and could no longer meet the cash-and-carry requirements imposed by the Neutrality Acts. The president, therefore, proposed a new system for supplying Britain: "lend-lease." It would allow the government not only to sell but to lend or lease armaments to any nation deemed pivotal to the defense of the United States." In other words, America could funnel weapons to England on the basis of no more than Britain's promise to return them when the war was over. Isolationists attacked the measure bitterly, but Congress enacted the bill by wide margins.

With lend-lease established, Roosevelt soon faced another serious problem. Attacks by German submarines had made shipping lanes in the Atlantic extremely dangerous. The British navy was losing ships more rapidly than it could replace them and was finding it difficult to transport materials across the Atlantic from America. Secretary of War Henry Stimson (who had been Hoover's secretary of state and who returned to the cabinet at Roosevelt's request in 1940) argued that the United States should itself convoy vessels to England; but Roosevelt took a more limited approach. He argued that the western Atlantic was a neutral zone and the responsibility of the American nations. By July 1941, therefore, American ships were patrolling the ocean as far east as Iceland.

At first, Germany did little to challenge these obviously hostile American actions. By September 1941, however, the situation had changed. Nazi forces had invaded the Soviet Union in June of that year. When the Soviets did not surrender, as many had predicted they would, Roosevelt persuaded Congress to extend lend-lease privileges to them. Now American industry was providing vital assistance to Hitler's foes on two fronts, and the American navy was protecting the flow of those goods to Europe. In September, Nazi submarines began a concerted campaign against American vessels. Roosevelt ordered American ships to fire on German submarines "on sight." In October, Nazi submarines hit two American destroyers and sank one of them, the *Reuben James*, killing many American sailors. Congress now voted to allow the United States to arm its merchant vessels and to sail all the way into belligerent ports. The United States had, in effect, launched a naval war against Germany.

In August 1941, Roosevelt met with Churchill aboard a British vessel off the coast of Newfoundland. The president made no military commitments, but he did join with the prime minister in releasing a document that became known as the Atlantic Charter, in which the two nations set out "certain common principles" on which to base "a better future for the world." It called openly for "the final destruction of the Nazi tyranny" and for a new world order in which every nation controlled its own destiny. It was, in effect, a statement of war aims.

The Road to Pearl Harbor

Japan, in the meantime, was taking advantage of events in Europe to extend its empire in the Pacific. In September 1940, the Japanese signed the Tripartite Pact, a loose defensive alliance with Germany and Italy (although in reality, the European Axis powers never developed a very strong relationship with Japan). In July 1941, imperial troops moved into Indochina and seized the capital of Vietnam, a colony of France. The United States, having broken Japanese codes, knew their next target would be the Dutch East Indies; and when Tokyo failed to respond to Roosevelt's stern warnings, the president froze all Japanese assets in the United States, severely limiting Japan's ability to purchase needed American supplies.

Tokyo now faced a choice. Either it would have to repair relations with the United States to restore the flow of supplies or it would have to find those supplies elsewhere, most notably by seizing British and Dutch possessions

PEARL HARBOR Virtually no one in authority in Hawaii or Washington imagined that the Japanese were capable of launching an attack on a place as far from Japan as Pearl Harbor. That is one reason why intelligence experts failed to predict the attack, despite the many clues they received from deciphering secret Japanese messages. It also helps to explain why so many ships remained bunched together helplessly in the harbor, easy prey to the Japanese bombers.

in the Pacific. At first, the Tokyo government seemed willing to negotiate. But in October, militants in Tokyo forced the moderate prime minister out of office and replaced him with the leader of the war party, General Hideki Tojo. There seemed little alternative now to war.

For several weeks, the Tojo government maintained a pretense of wanting to continue negotiations. But Tokyo had already decided it would not yield on the question of China, and Washington had made clear that it would accept nothing less than a reversal of that policy. By late November, the State Department had given up on the possibility of a peaceful settlement. American intelligence, meanwhile, had decoded Japanese messages that made clear a Japanese attack was imminent. But Washington did not know where the attack would take place. Most officials continued to believe that the Japanese would move first not against American territory but against British or Dutch possessions to the south. A combination of confusion and miscalculation caused the government to overlook indications that Japan intended a direct attack on American forces.

At 7:55 A.M. on Sunday, December 7, 1941, a wave of Japanese bombers attacked the United States naval base at Pearl Harbor in Hawaii. A second wave came an hour later. Within two hours, the United States lost 8 battleships, 3 cruisers, 4 other vessels, 188 airplanes, and several vital shore installations. More than 2,400 soldiers and sailors died, and another 1,000 were injured. The Japanese suffered only light losses.

American forces were now greatly diminished in the Pacific (although by a fortunate accident, no American aircraft carriers—the heart of the Pacific fleet—had been at Pearl Harbor on December 7). Nevertheless, the raid on Hawaii unified the American people behind war. On December 8, after a stirring speech by the president, the Senate voted unanimously and the House voted 388 to 1 to approve a declaration of war against Japan. Three days later, Germany and Italy, Japan's European allies, declared war on the United States; on the same day, December 11, Congress reciprocated without a dissenting vote.

CHAPTER TWENTY-EIGHT

America in a World at War

War on Two Fronts ～ *The American People in Wartime*
The Defeat of the Axis

HE ATTACK ON PEARL Harbor had thrust the United States into
the greatest and most terrible war in the history of humanity.
World War I had destroyed centuries-old European social and political institutions. But World War II created unprecedented carnage and horror, not only in Europe but around much of the rest of the globe. And in the end, it changed the world as profoundly as any event of the twentieth century, perhaps any century.

But World War II also transformed the United States in profound, if not always readily visible, ways. The story of American involvement in the war, therefore, is the story of the creation of a new world, both abroad and at home.

WAR ON TWO FRONTS

Whatever political disagreements and social tensions there may have been among the American people during World War II, there was striking unity of opinion about the conflict itself. But both unity and confidence faced severe tests in the first, troubled months of 1942.

Containing the Japanese

Ten hours after the strike at Pearl Harbor, Japanese airplanes attacked the American airfields at Manila in the Philippines, destroying much of America's remaining air power in the Pacific. Three days later Guam, an American possession, fell to Japan; Wake Island and Hong Kong followed. The

TIME LINE

1942	1943	1944	1945
Battle of Midway	Americans capture Guadalcanal	Allies invade Normandy	Roosevelt dies; Truman becomes president
Campaign in Northern Africa		Roosevelt reelected	Germany surrenders
Japanese-Americans interned	Allied invasion of Italy	Americans capture Philippines	U.S. drops atomic bombs on Hiroshima, Nagasaki
Manhattan Project begins			
CORE founded			Japan surrenders
	Soviet victory at Stalingrad		

great British fortress of Singapore in Malaya surrendered in February 1942, the Dutch East Indies in March, Burma in April. In the Philippines, exhausted Filipino and American troops gave up their defense of the islands on May 6.

American strategists planned two broad offensives to turn the tide against the Japanese. One, under the command of General Douglas MacArthur, would move north from Australia, through New Guinea, and eventually to the Philippines. The other, under Admiral Chester Nimitz, would move west from Hawaii toward major Japanese island outposts in the central Pacific. Ultimately, strategists predicted, the two offensives would come together to invade Japan itself.

The Allies achieved their first important victory in the Battle of the Coral Sea, just northwest of Australia, on May 7–8, 1942, when American forces turned back the previously unstoppable Japanese. A month later, there was an even more important turning point northwest of Hawaii. An enormous battle raged for four days, June 3–6, 1942, near the small American outpost at Midway Island, at the end of which the United States, despite great losses, was clearly victorious. The American navy destroyed four Japanese aircraft carriers and lost only one of its own; the action regained control of the central Pacific for the United States.

The Americans took the offensive for the first time several months later in the southern Solomon Islands, to the east of New Guinea. In August 1942, American forces assaulted three of the islands: Gavutu, Tulagi, and Guadalcanal. A struggle of terrible ferocity developed at Guadalcanal and contin-

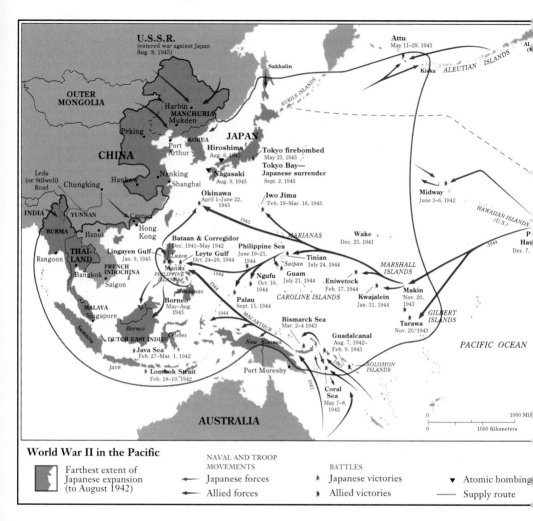

World War II in the Pacific

Farthest extent of
Japanese expansion
(to August 1942)

NAVAL AND TROOP
MOVEMENTS

⟵ Japanese forces

⟵ Allied forces

BATTLES

✷ Japanese victories

✷ Allied victories

▼ Atomic bombing

⎯ Supply route

ued for six months, inflicting heavy losses on both sides. In the end, however, the Japanese were forced to abandon the island—and with it their last
chance of launching an effective offensive to the south. In both the southern and the central Pacific, therefore, the initiative had shifted to the United
States by mid-1943. The Japanese advance had been halted. The Americans,
with aid from the Australians and the New Zealanders, now began the slow,
arduous process of moving toward the Philippines and Japan itself.

GUADALCANAL The battle of Guadalcanal, in the Solomon Islands, was the scene of some of the bloodiest and most protracted combat of the Pacific war. United States Marines are shown here charging ashore in August 1942, in the first stages of what became a six-month campaign.

Holding Off the Germans

In the European war, the United States was fighting in cooperation with, among others, Britain and the exiled "Free French" forces in the west; and it was trying also to conciliate its new ally, the Soviet Union, which was now fighting Hitler in the east. The army chief of staff, General George C. Marshall, supported a plan for a major Allied invasion of France across the English Channel in the spring of 1943, and he placed a hitherto little-known general, Dwight D. Eisenhower, in charge of planning the operation. But the American plan faced challenges from the other Allies. The Soviet Union, which was absorbing the brunt of the German war effort (as it would through most of the conflict), wanted the Allied invasion to begin at the earliest possible moment. The British, on the other hand, wanted first to launch a series of Allied offensives around the edges of the Nazi empire—in northern Africa and southern Europe—before undertaking the major invasion of France.

Roosevelt was torn, but he ultimately decided to support the British plan—in part because he was eager to get American forces into combat quickly and feared that a cross-Channel invasion would take a long time to prepare. At the end of October 1942, the British opened a counteroffensive against Nazi forces in North Africa under General Erwin Rommel, who was threatening the Suez Canal. In a major battle at El Alamein, they forced the Germans to retreat from Egypt. On November 8, Anglo-American forces landed at Oran and Algiers in Algeria and at Casablanca in Morocco—areas under the Nazi-controlled French government at Vichy—and began moving east toward Rommel. The Germans threw the full weight of their forces in Africa against the inexperienced Americans and inflicted a serious defeat on them at the Kasserine Pass in Tunisia. General George S. Patton, however, regrouped the American troops and began an effective counteroffensive. With the help of Allied air and naval power and of British forces attacking from the east under Field Marshall Bernard Montgomery (the hero of El Alamein), the American offensive finally drove the last Germans from Africa in May 1943.

The North African campaign had tied up a large proportion of the Allied resources. That was one reason why the planned May 1943 cross-Channel invasion of France had to be postponed, despite angry complaints from the Soviet Union. By now, however, the threat of a Soviet collapse seemed much diminished, for during the winter of 1942–1943, the Red Army had successfully held off a major German assault at Stalingrad in southern Russia. Hitler had committed such enormous forces to the battle, and had suffered such appalling losses, that he could not continue his eastern offensive.

The Soviet successes persuaded Roosevelt to agree, in a January 1943 meeting with Churchill in Casablanca, to a British plan for an Allied invasion of Sicily. Churchill argued that the operation in Sicily might knock Italy out of the war and tie up German divisions that might otherwise be stationed in France. On the night of July 9, 1943, American and British armies landed in southeast Sicily; thirty-eight days later, they had conquered the island and were moving onto the Italian mainland. In the face of these setbacks, Mussolini's government collapsed and the dictator himself fled north toward Germany. Although Mussolini's successor, Pietro Badoglio, quickly committed Italy to the Allies, Germany moved eight divisions into the country and established a powerful defensive line south of Rome. The Allied offensive on the Italian peninsula, which began on September 3, 1943, soon bogged down. Not until May 1944 did the Allies break through the German defenses to resume their northward advance. On June 4, 1944, they captured Rome.

The invasion of Italy contributed to the Allied war effort in several important ways. But it contributed to postponing the invasion of France by as

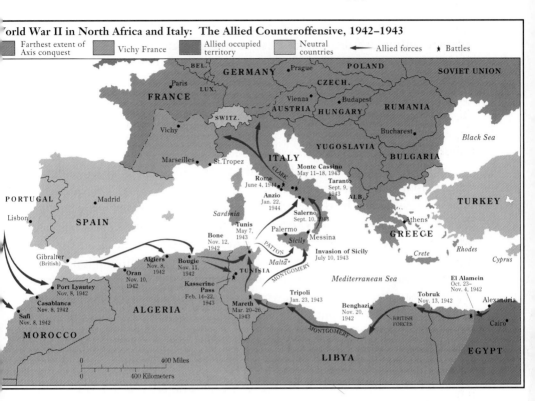

World War II in North Africa and Italy: The Allied Counteroffensive, 1942–1943

much as a year, deeply embittering the Soviet Union and giving the Soviets time to begin moving toward the countries of eastern Europe.

America and the Holocaust

In the midst of this intensive fighting, the leaders of the American government found themselves confronted with one of history's great tragedies: the Nazi campaign to exterminate the Jews of Europe—the Holocaust. As early as 1942, high officials in Washington had incontrovertible evidence that Hitler's forces were rounding up Jews and others (including Poles, homosexuals, and communists) from all over Europe, transporting them to concentration camps in eastern Germany and Poland, and systematically murdering them. (The death toll would ultimately reach 6 million Jews and at least 4 million others.) News of the atrocities was reaching the public as well, and pressure began to build for an Allied effort to end the killing or at least to rescue some of the surviving Jews.

The American government consistently resisted almost all such entreaties. Although Allied bombers were flying missions within a few miles of the most notorious death camp, at Auschwitz in Poland, the War Department rejected pleas that the planes try to destroy the crematoria at the camp as militarily unfeasible. American officials also refused requests that the Allies try to destroy railroad lines leading to the camp. And the United States resisted pleas that it admit large numbers of the Jewish refugees attempting to escape Europe.

After 1941, there was probably little American leaders could have done, other than defeat Germany in the war, to save most of Hitler's victims. But more forceful action by the United States (and Britain, which was even less amenable to Jewish requests for assistance) might well have saved at least some lives. That they did not take such action, it seems clear in retrospect, constituted a considerable moral failure. But policymakers found it possible to justify ignoring pleas to help the Jews by insisting that they needed to focus exclusively on the larger goal of winning the war. Any diversion of energy and attention to other purposes, they apparently believed, would distract them from the overriding goal of victory.

THE AMERICAN PEOPLE IN WARTIME

Not since the Civil War had the United States been involved in so prolonged and consuming a military experience as World War II. American armed forces engaged in combat around the globe for nearly four years. American society, in the meantime, experienced changes that reached into virtually every corner of the nation.

Prosperity and the Rights of Labor

World War II had its most profound impact on American domestic life by ending the Great Depression at last. By the middle of 1941, the economic problems of the 1930s—unemployment, deflation, industrial sluggishness—had virtually vanished before the great wave of wartime industrial expansion.

The most important agent of the new prosperity was government spending, which after 1939 was pumping more money into the economy each year than all the New Deal relief agencies combined had done. In 1939, the federal budget had been $9 billion; by 1945, it had risen to $100 billion. Largely as a result, the gross national product soared: from $91 billion in 1939 to $166 billion in 1945. Personal incomes in some regions grew by as much as

100 percent or more. The demands of wartime production created a shortage of consumer goods, so many wage earners diverted much of their new affluence into savings, which would later help keep the economic boom alive in the postwar years.

The impact of government spending was perhaps most dramatic in the West. The West Coast, naturally, became the launching point for most of the naval war against Japan, and the government created large manufacturing facilities in California and elsewhere to serve the needs of its military. Altogether, the government made almost $40 billion worth of capital investments (factories, military and transportation facilities, highways, power plants) in the West during the war, more than in any other region. Ten percent of all the money the federal government spent between 1940 and 1945 went to California alone. By the end of the war, the economy of the Pacific Coast and, to a lesser extent, other areas of the West had been transformed. The Pacific Coast had become the center of the growing American aircraft industry. New yards in southern California, Washington State, and elsewhere made the West a center of the shipbuilding industry. Los Angeles, formerly a medium-sized city notable chiefly for its film industry, now became a major industrial center as well.

Instead of the prolonged and debilitating unemployment that had been the most troubling feature of the Depression economy, the war created a serious labor shortage. The armed forces took over 15 million men and women out of the civilian work force at the same time that the demand for labor was rising rapidly. Nevertheless, the civilian work force increased by almost 20 percent during the war. The 7 million who had previously been unemployed accounted for some of the increase; the employment of many people previously considered inappropriate for the work force—the very young, the elderly, minorities, and, most important, several million women—accounted for the rest of it.

The war gave an enormous boost to union membership, which rose from about 10.5 million in 1941 to over 3 million in 1945. But it also created important new restrictions on the ability of unions to fight for their members' demands. The government was principally interested in keeping production moving without disruption and preventing inflation. It managed to win two important concessions from union leaders toward those ends. One was the "no-strike" pledge, by which unions agreed not to stop production in wartime. Another was the so-called Little Steel formula, which set a 15 percent limit on wage increases. In return, the government provided labor with a "maintenance-of-membership" agreement, which ensured that the thousands of new workers pouring into unionized defense plants would be automatically enrolled in the unions. The agreement guaranteed the continued health of the union organizations, but in return workers had to give up the right to demand major gains during the war.

Despite the no-strike pledge, there were nearly 15,000 work stoppages during the war, mostly wildcat strikes (strikes unauthorized by the union leadership), many protesting harsh working conditions and high levels of stress. When the United Mine Workers defied the government by striking in May 1943, Congress reacted by passing, over Roosevelt's veto, the Smith-Connally Act (War Labor Disputes Act), which required that unions wait thirty days before striking and which empowered the president to seize a struck war plant. In the meantime, public animosity toward labor rose rapidly, and many states passed laws to limit union power.

Stabilizing the Boom and Mobilizing Production

The fear of deflation, the central concern of the 1930s, gave way during the war to a fear of inflation, particularly after prices rose 25 percent in the two years before Pearl Harbor. In October 1942, Congress grudgingly responded to the president's request and passed the Anti-Inflation Act, which gave the administration authority to freeze agricultural prices, wages, salaries, and rents throughout the country. Enforcement of these provisions was the task of the Office of Price Administration (OPA), led first by Leon Henderson and then by Chester Bowles. In part because of its success, inflation was a much less serious problem during World War II than it had been during World War I. Even so, the OPA was never popular. There was widespread resentment of its controls over wages and prices. And there was only grudging acquiescence to its complicated system of rationing scarce consumer goods: coffee, sugar, meat, butter, canned goods, shoes, tires, gasoline, and fuel oil. Black-marketing and overcharging grew in proportions far beyond OPA policing capacity.

From 1941 to 1945, the federal government spent a total of $321 billion—twice as much as it had spent in the entire 150 years of its existence to that point, and ten times as much as the cost of World War I. The national debt rose from $49 billion in 1941 to $259 billion in 1945. The government borrowed about half the revenues it needed by selling $100 billion worth of bonds. Much of the rest it raised by radically increasing income-tax rates, through the Revenue Act of 1942. To simplify collection, Congress enacted a withholding system of payroll deductions in 1943.

The search for an effective mechanism to mobilize the economy for war began as early as 1939 and continued for nearly four years. One failed agency after another attempted to bring order to the mobilization effort. Finally, in January 1942, the president responded to widespread criticism by creating the War Production Board (WPB), under the direction of former Sears Roebuck executive Donald Nelson. In theory, the WPB was to be a "superagency," with broad powers over the economy. In fact, it never had as much authority as its World War I equivalent, the War Industries Board.

Throughout its troubled history, the WPB found itself constantly outmaneuvered and frustrated. It was never able to win complete control over military purchases; the army and navy often circumvented the board entirely in negotiating contracts with producers. It was never able to satisfy the complaints of small business, which charged (correctly) that most contracts were going to large corporations. Gradually, the president transferred much of the WPB's authority to a new office located within the White House: the Office of War Mobilization (OWM). But the OWM was only slightly more successful than the WPB.

Despite the administrative problems, however, the war economy managed to meet almost all of the nation's critical war needs. By the beginning of 1944, American factories were, in fact, producing more than the government needed. Their output was twice that of all the Axis countries combined.

African Americans and the War

During World War I, many African Americans had eagerly seized the chance to serve in the armed forces, believing that their patriotic efforts would win them an enhanced position in postwar society. They had been cruelly disappointed. As World War II approached, blacks were again determined to use the conflict to improve the position of their race—this time, however, not by currying favor but by making demands.

In the summer of 1941, A. Philip Randolph, president of the Brotherhood of Sleeping Car Porters, an important union with a primarily black membership, began to insist that the government require companies receiving defense contracts to integrate their work forces. To mobilize support for the demand, Randolph planned a massive march on Washington. Roosevelt finally persuaded Randolph to cancel the march in return for a promise to establish what became the Fair Employment Practices Commission (FEPC) to investigate discrimination against blacks in war industries. The FEPC's enforcement powers, and thus its effectiveness, were limited, but its creation was a rare symbolic victory for African American demands of the government.

The need for labor in war plants greatly increased the migration of blacks from the rural areas of the South into industrial cities. The migration bettered the economic condition of many African Americans, but it also created urban tensions and occasionally violence. The most serious conflict occurred in Detroit in 1943, when racial friction in the city produced a major riot in which thirty-four people died, twenty-five of them blacks.

Despite such tensions, the leading black organizations redoubled their efforts during the war to challenge the system of segregation. The Congress of Racial Equality (CORE), organized in 1942, mobilized mass popular resistance to discrimination in a way that the older, more conservative organizations had never done. Randolph, Bayard Rustin, James Farmer, and other, younger black leaders helped organize sit-ins and demonstrations in segregated theaters and restaurants. Their defiant public spirit would survive into the 1950s and help produce the civil rights movement.

Pressure for change was also growing within the military. At first, the armed forces maintained their traditional practice of limiting blacks to the most menial assignments, keeping them in segregated training camps and units, and barring them entirely from the Marine Corps and the Army Air Force. Gradually, however, military leaders were forced to make adjustments—in part because of public and political pressures, but also because they recognized that these forms of segregation were wasting manpower. By the end of the war, the number of black servicemen had increased sevenfold, to 700,000; some training camps were being at least partially integrated; blacks were being allowed to serve on ships with white sailors; and more black units were being sent into combat. But tensions remained. In some of the partially integrated army bases—Fort Dix, New Jersey, for example—riots occasionally broke out when blacks protested having to serve in segregated divisions. Substantial discrimination survived in all the services until well after the war. But within the military, as within society at large, the traditional pattern of race relations was slowly eroding.

Indians and the War

Approximately 25,000 Indians performed military service during World War II. Many Native Americans served in combat. Others (mostly Navajos) became "code-talkers," working in military communications and speaking their own language (which enemy forces would be unlikely to understand) over the radio and the telephones. The war had important effects on the Indians who served in the military. It brought them into intimate contact (often for the first time) with white society, and it awakened among some of them a taste for the material benefits of life in capitalist America that they would retain after the war. Some never returned to the reservations, but chose to remain in the non-Indian world and assimilate to its ways.

The war had important effects, too, on those Native Americans who stayed on the reservations. Little war work reached the tribes. Government subsidies dwindled. Talented young people left the reservations to serve in the military or work in war production, creating manpower shortages in some tribes. The wartime emphasis on national unity undermined support for the revitalization of tribal autonomy that the Indian Reorganization Act of 1934 had launched. New pressures emerged to eliminate the reservation system and require the tribes to assimilate into white society—pressures so severe that John Collier, the energetic director of the Bureau of Indian Affairs who had done so much to promote the reinvigoration of the reservations, resigned in 1945.

Mexican-American War Workers

Large numbers of Mexican workers entered the United States during the war in response to labor shortages on the Pacific coast and in the Southwest. The American and Mexican governments agreed in 1942 to a program by which *braceros* (contract laborers) would be admitted to the United States for a limited time to work at specific jobs, and American employers in some parts of the Southwest began actively recruiting Hispanic workers. During the Depression, many Mexican farmworkers had been deported to make room for desperate white workers. The wartime labor shortage caused farm owners to begin hiring them again. More important, however, Mexicans were able for the first time to find significant numbers of factory jobs. They formed the second-largest group of migrants (after blacks) to American cities in the 1940s. They were concentrated mainly in the West, but there were significant Mexican communities in Chicago, Detroit, and other industrial cities in the Midwest and East.

The sudden expansion of Mexican-American neighborhoods created tensions and occasionally conflict in some American cities. White residents of Los Angeles became alarmed at the activities of Mexican-American teenagers, many of whom were joining street gangs *(pachucos)*. The youths were particularly distinctive because of their style of dress, which some whites considered outrageous. They wore long, loose jackets with padded shoulders, baggy pants tied at the ankles, long watch chains, broad-brimmed hats, and greased, ducktail hairstyles. The outfit was known as a "zoot suit."

In June 1943, animosity toward the "zoot-suiters" produced a four-day riot in Los Angeles, during which white sailors stationed at a base in Long Beach invaded Mexican-American communities and attacked zoot-suiters (in response to alleged attacks by them on servicemen). The police did little to restrain the sailors, who grabbed Hispanic teenagers, tore off and burned their clothes, cut off their ducktails, and beat them. When Mexicans tried to fight back, the police moved in and arrested them. In the aftermath of the "zoot-suit riots," Los Angeles passed a law prohibiting the wearing of zoot suits.

Women and Children in Wartime

The war drew increasing numbers of women into roles from which they had previously been largely barred by custom or law. The number of women in the work force increased by nearly 60 percent, as many women took indus-

WOMEN WORKERS DURING WORLD WAR II Women—including many who had never worked for pay before—took over a broad range of traditionally male industrial jobs during World War II, replacing men serving in the armed forces. Some did so as a patriotic duty, some because they needed the money. But most also came to enjoy the independence paid employment provided, one reason why the number of women in the work force did not decline dramatically after the war.

trial jobs to replace male workers serving in the military. And these wage-earning women were more likely to be married and were on the whole older than most of those who had entered the work force in the past.

But while economic and military necessity eroded some of the popular objections to women in the workplace, obstacles remained. Many factory owners continued to categorize jobs by gender, reserving the most lucrative positions for men. (Female work, like male work, was also categorized by race: black women were usually assigned more menial tasks, and paid at a lower rate, than their white counterparts.) Still, women did make important inroads in industrial employment during the war. Women had been working in industry for over a century, but some began now to take on heavy industrial jobs that had long been considered "men's work." The famous wartime image of "Rosie the Riveter" symbolized the new importance of the female industrial worker. Women joined unions in substantial numbers, and they helped erode at least some of the prejudice, including the prejudice against mothers working, that had previously kept many of them from paid employment.

In the end, however, most women workers during the war were employed not in factories but in service-sector jobs. Above all, they worked for the government, whose bureaucratic needs expanded dramatically alongside its military and industrial needs. Even within the military, which enlisted substantial numbers of women as WAACs (army) and WAVEs (navy), most female work was clerical.

The new opportunities produced new problems. Many mothers whose husbands were in the military had to combine working with caring for their children. The scarcity of child-care facilities or other community services meant that some women had no choice but to leave young children—often known as "latchkey children" or "eight-hour orphans"—at home alone (or sometimes locked in cars in factory parking lots) while they worked.

Perhaps in part because of the family dislocations the war produced, juvenile crime rose markedly in the war years. Young boys were arrested at rapidly increasing rates for car theft and other burglary, vandalism, and vagrancy. The arrest rate for prostitutes, many of whom were teenage girls, rose too, as did the incidence of venereal disease. For many children, however, the distinctive experience of the war years was not crime but work. More than a third of all teenagers between the ages of fourteen and eighteen were employed late in the war, causing some reduction in high-school enrollments.

The return of prosperity helped increase the marriage rate and lower the age at which people married, but many marriages were unable to sur-

A M E R I C A N   V O I C E S

SARAH KILLINGSWORTH

An African-American Woman Encounters the Wartime Industrial Boom

THE WAR STARTED and jobs kinda opened up for women that the men had. . . . They started takin' applications at Douglas, to work in a defense plant. I was hired.

I didn't want a job on the production line. I heard so many things about accidents. . . . I was frightened. All I wanted to do was get in the factory, because they were payin' more than what I'd been makin'. . . . I got the job workin' nights in the ladies' rest room, which wasn't hard. . . .

I do know one thing, this place was very segregated when I first come here. Oh, Los Angeles, you just couldn't go and sit down like you do now. You had certain places you went. You had to more or less stick to the restaurants and hotels where black people were. It wasn't until the war that it really opened up. 'Cause when I come out here it was awful, just like bein' in the South. . . .

For a person that grew up and knew nothin' but hard times to get out on my own at eighteen years old and make a decent livin' and still make a decent person outa myself, I really am proud of me. . . .

In ways it was too bad that so many lives were lost. But I think it was for a worthy cause, because it did make a way for us. And we were able to really get out.

SOURCE: Studs Terkel, *The Good War*, pp. 113–116. Copyright © 1984 by Studs Terkel. Reprinted by permission of Pantheon Books.

vive the pressures of wartime separation. The divorce rate rose rapidly. The rise in the birth rate that accompanied the increase in marriages was the first sign of what would become the great postwar "baby boom."

The Internment of the Japanese Americans

During World War I, popular prejudice against the German people—and against German Americans—had run high. No such passions emerged against Germans, Italians, or Americans of German and Italian descent during World War II. The same could not be said, however, about the Japanese. After the attack on Pearl Harbor, government propaganda and popular culture combined to create an image of the Japanese as a devious, malign, and savage people.

Predictably, this racial animosity soon extended to Americans of Japanese descent. There were not many Japanese Americans in the United States—only about 127,000, most of them concentrated in a few areas in California. About a third of them were unnaturalized, first-generation immigrants (Issei); two-thirds were naturalized or native-born citizens of the United States (Nisei). Because they generally kept to themselves and preserved traditional Japanese cultural patterns, it was possible for others to imagine that the Japanese Americans were engaged in conspiracies on behalf of their ancestral homeland. (There is no evidence to suggest that they actually were.) Public pressure to remove the "threat" grew steadily.

Finally, in February 1942, in response to pressure from military officials and political leaders on the West Coast and recommendations from the War Department, the president authorized the army to "intern" the Japanese Americans. More than 100,000 people (Issei and Nisei alike) were rounded up, told to dispose of their property however they could (which often meant simply abandoning it), and taken to what the government euphemistically termed "relocation centers" in the "interior." In fact, they were facilities little different from prisons, many of them located in the western mountains and desert. Conditions in the internment camps were not brutal, but they were harsh and uncomfortable. More important, loyal, hardworking people (many of them citizens of the United States) were forced to spend up to three years in grim, debilitating isolation, barred from lucrative employment, provided with only minimal medical care, and deprived of decent schools for their children. (In Hawaii, by contrast, residents of Japanese descent encountered little harassment, perhaps because they were more numerous and more crucial to the economy of the islands.) The Supreme Court upheld the evacuation in a 1944 decision; and although most of the Japanese Americans were released later that year, they were largely unable to win any compensation for their losses until Congress finally acted to redress the wrongs in the late 1980s.

The Retreat from Reform

Late in 1943, Franklin Roosevelt publicly suggested that "Dr. New Deal," as he called it, had served its purpose and should now give way to "Dr. Win-the-War." The statement reflected the president's own genuine shift in concern: victory was now more important than reform. But it reflected, too, the political reality that had emerged during the first two years of war. Liberals in government were finding themselves unable to enact new programs. They were even finding it difficult to protect existing ones from conservative assault.

The greatest assault on New Deal reforms came from conservatives in Congress, who seized on the war as an excuse to do what many had wanted to do in peacetime: dismantle many of the achievements of the New Deal. They were assisted by the end of mass unemployment, which decreased the need for such relief programs as the Civilian Conservation Corps and the Works Progress Administration (both of which Congress abolished). They were assisted, too, by their own increasing numbers. In the congressional elections of 1942, Republicans gained 47 seats in the House and 10 in the Senate.

Republicans approached the 1944 election determined to exploit what they believed was resentment of wartime regimentation and unhappiness with Democratic reform. They nominated as their candidate the young and vigorous governor of New York, Thomas E. Dewey. Roosevelt was unopposed within his party, but Democratic leaders pressured him to abandon Vice President Henry Wallace, an advanced New Dealer and hero of the CIO, and replace him with a more moderate figure. Roosevelt reluctantly acquiesced in the selection of Senator Harry S. Truman of Missouri, who had won acclaim as chairman of the Senate War Investigating Committee (known as the Truman Committee). It had compiled an impressive record uncovering waste and corruption in wartime production.

The conduct of the war was not an issue in the campaign. Instead, the election revolved around domestic economic issues and, indirectly, the president's health. The president was, in fact, gravely ill, suffering from, among other things, arteriosclerosis. It is not too much to say that he was dying. But the campaign seemed momentarily to revive him. He made several strenuous public appearances late in October, which dispelled popular doubts about his health and ensured his reelection. He captured 53.5 percent of the popular vote to Dewey's 46 percent. (It was a substantial margin of victory, but the lowest percentage of his four campaigns). He won 432 electoral votes to Dewey's 99. Democrats lost 1 seat in the Senate, gained 20 in the House, and maintained control of both.

THE DEFEAT OF THE AXIS

By the middle of 1943, America and its allies had succeeded in stopping the Axis advance both in Europe and in the Pacific. In the next two years, the Allies themselves seized the offensive and launched a series of powerful drives that rapidly led the way to victory.

The Liberation of France

By early 1944, American and British bombers were attacking German industrial installations and other targets almost around the clock, drastically cutting production and impeding transportation. Especially devastating was the massive bombing of such German cities as Leipzig, Dresden, and Berlin. A February 1945 incendiary raid on Dresden created a great firestorm that destroyed three-fourths of the previously undamaged city and killed approximately 135,000 people, almost all civilians. The morality of such attacks has been much debated in the years since the war; but at the time, few Americans questioned the claims of military leaders that the bombing cleared the way for the great Allied invasion of France in the late spring.

An enormous offensive force had been gathering in England for two years before the spring of 1944: almost 3 million troops, and perhaps the greatest array of naval vessels and armaments ever assembled in one place. On the morning of June 6, 1944, this vast invasion force moved into action. The landing came not at the narrowest part of the English Channel, where the Germans had expected and prepared for it, but along sixty miles of the Cotentin Peninsula on the coast of Normandy. While airplanes and battleships offshore bombarded the Nazi defenses, 4,000 vessels landed troops and supplies on the beaches. (Three divisions of paratroopers had been dropped behind the German lines the night before.) Fighting was intense along the beach, but the superior manpower and equipment of the Allied forces gradually prevailed. Within a week, the German forces had been dislodged from virtually the entire Normandy coast.

For the next month, further progress remained slow. But in late July in the Battle of Saint-Lô, General Omar Bradley's First Army smashed through

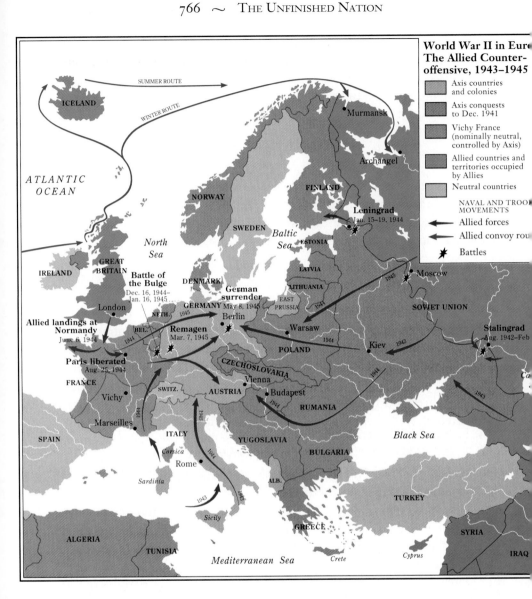

the German lines. George S. Patton's Third Army, spearheaded by heavy tank attacks, then moved through the hole Bradley had created and began a drive into the heart of France. On August 25, Free French forces arrived in Paris and liberated the city from four years of German occupation. By mid-September the Allied armies had driven the Germans almost entirely out of France and Belgium.

The great Allied drive came to a halt, however, at the Rhine River against a firm line of Nazi defenses. In mid-December, German forces struck in desperation along fifty miles of front in the Ardennes Forest. In the Battle of the Bulge (named for a large bulge that appeared in the American lines as the Germans pressed forward), they drove fifty-five miles toward Antwerp before they were finally stopped at Bastogne. It was the last major battle on the western front.

While the Allies were fighting their way through France, Soviet forces were sweeping westward into central Europe and the Balkans. In late January 1945, the Russians launched a great offensive toward the Oder River, inside Germany. By early spring, they were ready to launch a final assault against Berlin. General Omar Bradley, in the meantime, was pushing toward the Rhine from the west. Early in March, his forces captured the city of Cologne, on the river's west bank. The next day, he discovered and seized an undamaged bridge over the river at Remagen; Allied troops were soon

A VICTORY CELEBRATION IN SAN FRANCISCO Soldiers and sailors in San Francisco react jubilantly to the news that the war in Europe has ended. But the news they celebrate was, in fact, one of the many false rumors of surrender circulating in the spring of 1945. The actual V-E Day occurred several weeks later.

pouring across the Rhine. In the following weeks the British commander, Montgomery, with a million troops, pushed into Germany in the north while Bradley's army, sweeping through central Germany, completed the encirclement of 300,000 German soldiers in the Ruhr.

The German resistance was now broken on both fronts. American forces were moving eastward faster than they had anticipated and could have beaten the Russians to Berlin and Prague. The American and British high commands decided, instead, to halt the advance along the Elbe River in central Germany to await the Russians. That decision enabled the Soviets to occupy eastern Germany and Czechoslovakia.

On April 30, with Soviet forces on the outskirts of Berlin, Adolf Hitler killed himself in his bunker in the capital. And on May 8, 1945, the remaining German forces surrendered unconditionally. V-E (Victory in Europe) Day prompted great celebrations in western Europe and in the United States, tempered by the knowledge of the continuing war against Japan.

The Pacific Offensive

In February 1944, American naval forces under Admiral Chester Nimitz won a series of victories in the Marshall Islands and cracked the outer perimeter of the Japanese Empire. Within a month, the navy had destroyed other vital Japanese bastions. American submarines, in the meantime, were decimating Japanese shipping and crippling Japan's domestic economy.

A more frustrating struggle was in progress in the meantime on the Asian mainland. In 1942, the Japanese had forced General Joseph H. Stilwell of the United States out of Burma and had moved their own troops as far west as the mountains bordering on India. For a time, Stilwell supplied the isolated Chinese forces still fighting Japan with an aerial ferry over the Himalayas. In 1943, finally, he led Chinese, Indian, and a few American troops back through northern Burma, constructing a road and pipeline across the mountains into China (the Burma Road, also known as the Ledo Road or Stilwell Road); the road opened in the fall of 1944.

By then, however, the Japanese had launched a major counteroffensive and had driven so deep into the Chinese interior that they threatened the terminus of the Burma Road and the center of Chinese government at Chungking. The Japanese offensive precipitated a long-simmering feud between General Stilwell and Premier Chiang Kai-shek of China. Stilwell was indignant because Chiang was using many of his troops to maintain an armed frontier against the Chinese communists and would not deploy those troops against the Japanese.

The decisive battles of the war against Japan, however, occurred in the Pacific. In mid-June 1944, an enormous American armada struck the heavily fortified Mariana Islands and, after some of the bloodiest operations of the war, captured Tinian, Guam, and Saipan, 1,350 miles from Tokyo. In September, American forces landed on the western Carolines. And on October 20, General MacArthur's troops landed on Leyte Island in the Philippines. The Japanese now employed virtually their entire fleet against the Allied invaders in three major encounters—which together constituted the decisive Battle of Leyte Gulf, the largest naval engagement in history. American forces held off the Japanese onslaught and sank four Japanese carriers, all but destroying Japan's capacity to continue a serious naval war. Nevertheless, as American forces advanced closer to the Japanese mainland early in 1945, the imperial forces seemed only to increase their resistance. In February 1945, American marines seized the tiny volcanic island of Iwo Jima, only 750 miles from Tokyo, but only after the costliest battle in the history of the Marine Corps.

The battle for Okinawa, an island only 370 miles south of Japan, was further evidence of the strength of the Japanese resistance in these last desperate days. Week after week, the Japanese sent kamikaze (suicide) planes against American and British ships, sacrificing 3,500 of them while inflicting great damage. Japanese troops on shore launched desperate nighttime attacks on the American lines. The United States and its allies suffered nearly 50,000 casualties before finally capturing Okinawa in late June 1945. Over 100,000 Japanese died in the siege.

It seemed that the same kind of bitter fighting would await the Americans when they invaded Japan. But there were signs early in 1945 that such an invasion might not be necessary. The Japanese had almost no ships or planes left with which to fight. The firebombing of Tokyo in May, in which American bombers dropped napalm on the city and created a firestorm in which over 80,000 people died, further weakened the Japanese will to resist. Moderate Japanese leaders, who had long since concluded the war was lost, were increasing their power within the government and were looking for ways to bring the fighting to an end, although they continued to face powerful opposition from military leaders. Whether the moderates could ultimately have prevailed is a question about which historians and others continue to disagree. In any case, their efforts became superfluous in August 1945, when the United States made use of a terrible new weapon it had been developing throughout the war.

The Manhattan Project and Atomic Warfare

Reports had reached the United States in 1939 that Nazi scientists had taken the first step toward the creation of an atomic bomb, a weapon more powerful than any ever previously devised. The United States and Britain immediately began a race to develop the weapon before the Germans did.

Over the next three years, the government secretly poured nearly $2 billion into the so-called Manhattan Project—a massive scientific effort conducted at hidden laboratories in Oak Ridge, Tennessee; Los Alamos, New Mexico; and other sites. (The name of the project had emerged earlier, when many of the atomic physicists had been working at Columbia University in New York.) The scientists pushed ahead much faster than anyone had predicted. Even so, the war in Europe ended before they were ready to test the first bomb. Just before dawn on July 16, 1945, in the desert near Alamogordo, New Mexico, the scientists gathered to witness the first atomic explosion in history: a blinding flash of light brighter than any ever seen on earth, and a huge, billowing mushroom cloud.

News of the explosion reached President Harry S. Truman (who had taken office in April on the death of Roosevelt) in Potsdam, Germany, where he was attending a conference of Allied leaders. He issued an ultimatum to the Japanese (signed jointly by the British) demanding that they surrender by August 3 or face utter devastation. When the Japanese failed to meet the deadline, Truman ordered the air force to use the new atomic weapons against Japan.

Controversy has continued for decades over whether Truman's decision to use the bomb was justified and what his motives were. Some have argued that the atomic attack was unnecessary—that had the United States agreed to the survival of the emperor (which it ultimately did agree to in any case), or had it waited only a few more weeks, the Japanese would have surrendered. Others argue that nothing less than the atomic bombs could have persuaded the Japanese to surrender without a costly American invasion. Some critics of the decision, including some of the scientists involved in the Manhattan Project, have argued that whatever the Japanese intentions, the United States, as a matter of morality, should not have used the terrible new weapon.

The nation's military and political leaders, however, showed little concern about such matters. Truman, who had not even known of the existence of the Manhattan Project until he became president, was, apparently, making what he believed to be a simple military decision. A weapon was available that would end the war quickly; he could see no reason not to use it.

On August 6, 1945, an American B-29, the *Enola Gay*, dropped an atomic

HIROSHIMA AFTER THE BOMB Where once a bustling city stood, only rubble remains. This photograph shows the center of Hiroshima shortly after it was devastated by the first of two atomic bombs the United States dropped on Japan in the last days of World War II.

weapon on the Japanese industrial center at Hiroshima. With a single bomb, the United States completely incinerated a four-square-mile area at the center of the previously undamaged city. More than 80,000 civilians died, according to later American estimates. Many more survived to suffer the crippling effects of radioactive fallout or to pass those effects on to their children in the form of birth defects.

The Japanese government, stunned by the attack, was at first unable to agree on a response. Two days later, on August 8, the Soviet Union declared war on Japan. And the following day, another American plane dropped another atomic weapon—this time on the city of Nagasaki—inflicting 100,000 deaths and horrible damage on yet another unfortunate community. Finally, the emperor intervened to break the stalemate in the cabinet, and on August 14 the government announced that it was ready to give up. On September 2, 1945, on board the American battleship *Missouri*, anchored in Tokyo Bay, Japanese officials signed the articles of surrender.

The greatest war in the history of mankind had come to an end, and the United States had emerged from it not only victorious but in a position of unprecedented power, influence, and prestige. It was a victory, however, that few could greet with unambiguous joy. Fourteen million combatants had died in the struggle. Many more civilians had perished. The United States had suffered only light casualties in comparison with some other nations, but the cost had still been high: 322,000 dead, another 800,000 injured. And despite the sacrifices, the world continued to face an uncertain future, menaced by the threat of nuclear warfare and by an emerging antagonism between the world's two strongest nations—the United States and the Soviet Union—that would darken the peace for many decades to come.

CHAPTER TWENTY-NINE

America and the Cold War

Origins of the Cold War ~ *The Collapse of the Peace*
America After the War ~ *The Korean War*
The Crusade Against Subversion

VEN BEFORE WORLD WAR II ended, there were signs of tension
between the United States and the Soviet Union. Once the hostilities were over, those tensions quickly grew to create what became known
as the "Cold War"—a tense and dangerous rivalry between the two former
allies that would cast its shadow over international affairs for decades. The
Cold War also had profound effects on American domestic life, ultimately
producing the most corrosive outbreak of antiradical hysteria of the century.
America in the postwar years was both powerful and prosperous, but it was
also for a time troubled and uncertain about its future.

ORIGINS OF THE COLD WAR

No issue in twentieth-century American history has aroused more debate
than the question of the origins of the Cold War. (See "Debating the Past,"
pp. 801–802.) Some have claimed that Soviet duplicity and expansionism created the international tensions, others that American provocations and imperial ambitions were at least equally to blame. Most historians agree, however, that wherever the preponderance of blame may lie, both the United
States and the Soviet Union contributed to the atmosphere of hostility and
suspicion that quickly clouded the peace.

Sources of Soviet-American Tension

At the heart of the rivalry between the United States and the Soviet Union
in the 1940s was a fundamental difference in the ways the great powers envisioned the postwar world. One vision was that of many people in the

TIME LINE			
1945	**1946**	**1947**	**1948**
Yalta and Potsdam Conferences	Atomic Energy Commission established	Truman Doctrine	Berlin blockade
		Marshall Plan proposed	Truman elected president
	Iran crisis	National Security Act	
		Taft-Hartley Act	Hiss case begins
United Nations founded			
1949	**1950**	**1951**	**1952**
NATO established	NSC-68	Truman fires MacArthur	American occupation of Japan ends
Soviet Union explodes A-bomb	Korean War begins		
	McCarthy's anticommunism campaign begins		Eisenhower elected president

United States. First openly outlined in the Atlantic Charter in 1941, it was a vision of a world in which nations abandoned their traditional belief in military alliances and spheres of influence and governed their relations with one another through democratic processes, with an international organization serving as the arbiter of disputes and the protector of every nation's right of self-determination.

The other vision was that of the Soviet Union and to some extent, it gradually became clear, of Great Britain. Both Stalin and Churchill had signed the Atlantic Charter. But Britain had always been uneasy about the implications of the self-determination ideal for its own enormous empire. And the Soviet Union was determined to create a secure sphere for itself in Central and Eastern Europe as protection against possible future aggression from the West. Both Churchill and Stalin, therefore, tended to envision a postwar structure in which the great powers would control areas of strategic interest to them, in which something vaguely similar to the traditional European balance of power would reemerge.

By the end of the war Roosevelt was able to win at least the partial consent of Winston Churchill to his principles; but although he believed at times that Stalin would similarly relent, he never managed to steer the Soviets from their determination to control Central and Eastern Europe and from their vision of a postwar order in which each of the great powers would dominate its own sphere. Gradually, the differences between these two positions would turn the peacemaking process into a form of warfare.

Wartime Diplomacy

Serious strains had already begun to develop in the alliance with the Soviet Union in January 1943, when Roosevelt and Churchill met in Casablanca, Morocco, to discuss Allied strategy. (Stalin had declined Roosevelt's invitation to attend.) The two leaders could not accept Stalin's most important demand—the immediate opening of a second front in western Europe. But they tried to reassure Stalin by announcing that they would accept nothing less than the unconditional surrender of the Axis powers. It was a signal that the Americans and British would not negotiate a separate peace with Hitler and leave the Soviets to fight on alone.

In November 1943, Roosevelt and Churchill traveled to Teheran, Iran, for their first meeting with Stalin. By now, however, Roosevelt's most effective bargaining tool—Stalin's need for American assistance in his struggle against Germany—had been largely removed. The German advance against Russia had been halted; Soviet forces were now launching their own westward offensive. Meanwhile, new tensions had emerged in the alliance as a result of the refusal by the British and Americans to allow any Soviet participation in the creation of a new Italian government following the fall of Mussolini.

Nevertheless, the Teheran Conference seemed in most respects a success. Roosevelt and Stalin established a cordial personal relationship. Stalin agreed to an American request that the Soviet Union enter the war in the Pacific soon after the end of hostilities in Europe. Roosevelt, in turn, promised that an Anglo-American second front would be established within six months. All three leaders agreed in principle to a postwar international organization and to efforts to prevent a resurgence of German expansionism.

On other matters, however, the origins of future disagreements were already visible. Most important was the question of the future of Poland. Roosevelt and Churchill were willing to agree to a movement of the Soviet border westward, allowing Stalin to annex some historically Polish territory. But on the nature of the postwar government in the portion of Poland that would remain independent, there were sharp differences. Roosevelt and Churchill supported the claims of the Polish government-in-exile that had been functioning in London since 1940; Stalin wished to install another, pro-communist exiled government that had spent the war in Lublin, in the Soviet Union. The three leaders avoided a bitter conclusion to the Teheran Conference only by leaving the issue unresolved.

Yalta

For more than a year after Teheran, the Grand Alliance among the United States, Britain, and the Soviet Union alternated between high tension and warm amicability. In February 1945, Roosevelt joined Churchill and Stalin for a great peace conference in the Soviet city of Yalta. On a number of issues, the Big Three reached mutually satisfactory agreements. In return for Stalin's renewed promise to enter the Pacific war, Roosevelt agreed that the Soviet Union should receive some of the territory in the Pacific that Russia had lost in the 1904 Russo-Japanese War.

The negotiators also agreed to accept a plan for a new international organization, a plan that had been hammered out the previous summer at a conference in Washington, D.C., at the Dumbarton Oaks estate. The new United Nations would contain a General Assembly, in which every member would be represented, and a Security Council, with permanent representatives of the five major powers (the United States, Britain, France, the Soviet Union, and China), each of which would have veto power. The Security Council would also have temporary delegates from several other nations. These agreements became the basis of the United Nations charter, drafted at a conference of fifty nations beginning April 25, 1945, in San Fran-

YALTA, 1945 Churchill *(left)* and Stalin *(right)* were shocked at the physical appearance of Franklin Roosevelt *(center)* when he arrived for their critical meeting at Yalta. Roosevelt had enough energy to perform capably at the conference, but he was in fact gravely ill. Two months later, not long after he gave Congress what turned out to be an unrealistically optimistic report of the prospects for postwar peace, he died.

cisco. The United States Senate ratified the charter in July by a vote of 80 to 2 (a striking contrast to the slow and painful defeat it had administered to the charter of the League of Nations twenty-five years before).

On other issues, however, the Yalta Conference produced no real accord. Basic disagreement remained about the postwar Polish government. Stalin, whose armies now occupied Poland, had already installed a government composed of the pro-communist "Lublin" Poles. Roosevelt and Churchill insisted that the pro-Western "London" Poles must be allowed a place in the Warsaw regime. Roosevelt envisioned a government based on free, democratic elections—which both he and Stalin recognized the pro-Western forces would win. Stalin agreed only to a vague compromise by which an unspecified number of pro-Western Poles would be granted a place in the government. He reluctantly consented to hold "free and unfettered elections" in Poland, but he made no commitment to a date for them. They did not take place for more than forty years.

Nor was there agreement about the future of Germany. Roosevelt seemed to want a reconstructed and reunited Germany—one that would be permitted to develop a prosperous, modern economy while remaining under the careful supervision of the Allies. Stalin wanted to impose heavy reparations on Germany and to ensure a permanent dismemberment of the nation. The final agreement was, like the Polish accord, vague and unstable. The decision on reparations would be referred to a future commission. The United States, Great Britain, France, and the Soviet Union would each control its own "zone of occupation" in Germany—the zones to be determined by the position of troops at the end of the war. Berlin, the German capital, was already well inside the Soviet zone, but because of its symbolic importance it would itself be divided into four sectors, one for each nation to occupy. At an unspecified date, Germany would be reunited; but there was no agreement on how the reunification would occur. As for the rest of Europe, the conference produced a murky accord on the establishment of interim governments "broadly representative of all democratic elements." They would be replaced ultimately by permanent governments "responsible to the will of the people" and created through free elections. Once again, no specific provisions or timetables accompanied the agreements.

The Yalta accords, in other words, were less a settlement of postwar issues than a set of loose principles that sidestepped the most divisive questions. Roosevelt, Churchill, and Stalin returned home from the conference each apparently convinced that he had signed an important agreement. But the Soviet interpretation of the accords differed so sharply from the Anglo-American interpretation that the illusion endured only briefly. In the weeks following the Yalta Conference, Roosevelt watched with growing alarm as the Soviet Union moved systematically to establish pro-communist governments in one Central or Eastern European nation after another and as Stalin refused to make the changes in Poland that the president believed he had promised.

But Roosevelt did not abandon hope. Still believing the differences could be settled, he left Washington early in the spring for a vacation at his retreat in Warm Springs, Georgia. There, on April 12, 1945, he suffered a sudden, massive stroke and died.

THE COLLAPSE OF THE PEACE

Harry S. Truman, who succeeded Roosevelt in the presidency, had almost no familiarity with international issues. Nor did he share Roosevelt's faith in the flexibility of the Soviet Union. Roosevelt had believed that Stalin was, essentially, a reasonable man with whom an ultimate accord could be reached. Truman, in contrast, sided with those in the government (and there were many) who considered the Soviet Union fundamentally untrustworthy and viewed Stalin himself with suspicion and even loathing.

The Failure of Potsdam

Truman had been in office only a few days before he decided to "get tough" with the Soviet Union. Stalin had made what the new president considered solemn agreements with the United States at Yalta. The United States should insist that the Soviets honor them. Truman met on April 23 with Soviet Foreign Minister Molotov and sharply chastised him for violations of the Yalta accords.

In fact, Truman had only limited leverage by which to compel the Soviet Union to carry out its agreements. Russian forces already occupied Poland and much of the rest of Central and Eastern Europe. Germany was already divided among the conquering nations. The United States was still engaged in a war in the Pacific and was neither able nor willing to enter into a second conflict in Europe. Truman insisted that the United States should be able to get "85 percent" of what it wanted, but he was ultimately forced to settle for much less.

He conceded first on Poland. When Stalin made a few minor concessions to the pro-Western exiles, Truman recognized the Warsaw government, hoping that noncommunist forces might gradually expand their influence there. Until the 1980s, they did not. Other questions remained, above all the question of Germany. To settle them, Truman met in July at Potsdam, in Russian-occupied Germany, with Churchill (who, after elections in Britain, was replaced as prime minister by Clement Attlee in the midst of the negotiations) and Stalin. Truman reluctantly accepted adjustments of the Polish-German border that Stalin had long demanded; he refused, however, to permit the Russians to claim any reparations from the American, French, and British zones of Germany. This stance effectively confirmed that Germany would remain divided, with the western zones united into one nation, friendly to the United States, and the Russian zone surviving as another nation, with a pro-Soviet, communist government. Soon, the Soviet Union was siphoning between $1.5 and $3 billion a year out of its zone of occupation.

The China Problem

Central to American hopes for an open, peaceful world "policed" by the great powers was a strong, independent China. But even before the war ended, the American government was aware that those hopes faced a major, perhaps insurmountable obstacle: the Chinese government of Chiang Kai-shek. Chiang was generally friendly to the United States, but he had few other virtues. His government was corrupt and incompetent. His popular legitimacy was feeble. And Chiang himself lived in a world of almost surreal isolation, unable or unwilling to face the problems that were threatening to engulf him. Ever since 1927, the nationalist government he headed had been engaged in a prolonged and bitter rivalry with the communist armies of Mao Zedong. So successful had the communist challenge grown that Mao was in control of one-fourth of the population by 1945.

At Potsdam, Truman had managed to persuade Stalin to recognize Chiang as the legitimate ruler of China; but Chiang was rapidly losing his grip on his country. Some Americans urged the government to try to find a "third force" to support as an alternative to either Chiang or Mao. A few argued that the United States should try to reach some accommodation with Mao. Truman, however, decided reluctantly that he had no choice but to continue supporting Chiang. For the next several years, as the long struggle between the nationalists and the communists erupted into a full-scale civil war, the United States continued to pump money and weapons to Chiang, even as it was becoming clear that the cause was lost. But Truman was not prepared to intervene militarily to save the nationalist regime.

Instead, the American government was beginning to consider an alternative to China as the strong, pro-Western force in Asia: a revived Japan.

Abandoning the strict occupation policies of the first years after the war (when General Douglas MacArthur had governed the nation), the United States lifted all restrictions on industrial development and encouraged rapid economic growth in Japan. The vision of an open, united world was giving way in Asia, as it was in Europe, to an acceptance of a divided world with a strong, pro-American sphere of influence.

The Containment Doctrine

By the end of 1945, the Grand Alliance was a shambles. With its passing went any realistic hope of a postwar world constructed according to the Atlantic Charter ideals Roosevelt and others had supported. Instead, a new American policy was slowly emerging. It became known as containment. Rather than attempting to create a unified, "open" world, the West would work to "contain" the threat of further Soviet expansion. The United States would be the leading force in that effort.

The new doctrine emerged in part as a response to events in Europe in 1946. In Turkey, Stalin was trying to win some control over the vital sea lanes to the Mediterranean. In Greece, communist forces were again threatening the pro-Western government; the British had announced they could no longer provide assistance. Faced with these challenges, Truman decided to enunciate a firm new policy. In doing so, he drew from the ideas of the influential American diplomat George F. Kennan, who had warned not long after the war that in the Soviet Union the United States faced "a political force committed fanatically to the belief that with the U.S. there can be no permanent modus vivendi," and that the only answer was "a long-term, patient but firm and vigilant containment of Russian expansive tendencies." On March 12, 1947, Truman appeared before Congress and used Kennan's warnings as the basis of what became known as the Truman Doctrine. "I believe," he argued, "that it must be the policy of the United States to support free peoples who are resisting attempted subjugation by armed minorities or by outside pressures." In the same speech he requested $400 million— part of it to bolster the armed forces of Greece and Turkey, another part to provide economic assistance to Greece. Congress quickly approved the measure.

The American commitment ultimately helped ease Soviet pressure on Turkey and helped the Greek government defeat the communist insurgents. More important, it established a basis for American foreign policy that would survive for more than thirty years. On the one hand, the Truman Doctrine was a way of accommodating the status quo: it accepted that there was no immediate likelihood of overturning the communist governments Stalin had established in Eastern Europe. On the other hand, it was a strategy for the future: communism was an innately expansionist force, and it must be contained within its present boundaries.

The Marshall Plan

An integral part of the containment policy was a proposal to aid in the economic reconstruction of Western Europe. There were many motives: humanitarian concern for the European people; a fear that Europe would re-

THE MARSHALL PLAN, 1950 Workers in West Berlin rebuild the war-damaged city with the aid of money funneled to them from the United States through the European Recovery Program, better known as the Marshall Plan. This photograph shows repair work in progress on Titania Palace, Berlin's biggest concert hall.

main an economic drain on the United States if it could not quickly rebuild and begin to feed itself; a desire for a strong European market for American goods. But above all, American policymakers believed that unless something could be done to strengthen the shaky pro-American governments in Western Europe, those governments might fall under the control of rapidly growing domestic communist parties.

In June 1947, therefore, Secretary of State George C. Marshall announced a plan to provide economic assistance to all European nations (including the Soviet Union) that would join in drafting a program for recovery. Although Russia and its Eastern satellites quickly and predictably rejected the plan, sixteen Western European nations eagerly participated. Whatever domestic opposition there was in the United States largely vanished after a sudden coup in Czechoslovakia in February 1948 that established a Soviet-dominated communist government there. In April, Congress approved the creation of the Economic Cooperation Administration, the agency that would administer the Marshall Plan, as it became known. And over the next three years, the Marshall Plan channeled over $12 billion of American aid into Europe, helping to spark a substantial economic revival. By the end of 1950, European industrial production had risen 64 percent, communist strength in the member nations was declining, and opportunities for American trade had revived.

Mobilization at Home

That the United States had fully accepted a continuing commitment to the containment policy became clear in 1947 and 1948 through a series of measures designed to maintain American military power at near wartime levels. In 1948, at the president's request, Congress approved a new military draft and revived the Selective Service System. In the meantime, the United States, having failed to reach agreement with the Soviet Union on international control of nuclear weapons, redoubled its own efforts in atomic research, elevating nuclear weaponry to a central place in its military arsenal. The Atomic Energy Commission, established in 1946, became the supervisory body charged with overseeing all nuclear research, civilian and military alike. And in 1950, the Truman administration approved the development of the new hydrogen bomb, a nuclear weapon far more powerful than the bombs the United States had used in 1945.

Particularly important was the National Security Act of 1947, which reshaped the nation's major military and diplomatic institutions. A new Department of Defense would oversee all branches of the armed services, com-

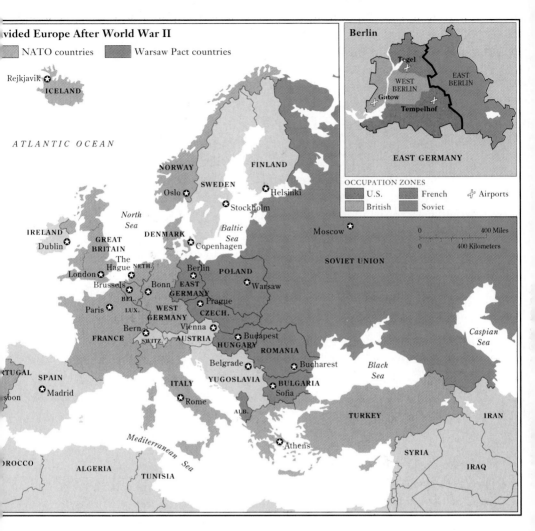

Divided Europe After World War II

■ NATO countries ■ Warsaw Pact countries

Berlin

OCCUPATION ZONES
U.S. | French ✈ Airports
British | Soviet

bining functions previously performed separately by the War and Navy departments. A National Security Council (NSC), operating out of the White House, would govern foreign and military policy. A Central Intelligence Agency (CIA) would replace the wartime Office of Strategic Services and would be responsible for collecting information through both open and covert methods; as the Cold War continued, it would also engage secretly in political and military operations on behalf of American goals. The National Security Act, in other words, gave the president expanded powers with which to pursue the nation's international goals.

The Road to NATO

At about the same time, the United States was moving to strengthen the military capabilities of Western Europe. Convinced that a reconstructed Germany was essential to the hopes of the West, Truman reached an agreement with England and France to merge the three western zones of occupation into a new West German republic (which would include the American, British, and French sectors of Berlin, even though that city lay well within the Soviet zone). Stalin responded quickly. On June 24, 1948, he imposed a tight blockade around the western sectors of Berlin. If Germany was to be officially divided, he was implying, then the country's Western government would have to abandon its outpost in the heart of the Soviet-controlled eastern zone. Truman refused to do so. Unwilling to risk war through a military response to the blockade, he ordered a massive airlift to supply the city with food, fuel, and other needed goods. The airlift continued for more than ten months, transporting nearly 2.5 million tons of material, keeping a city of 2 million people alive, and transforming West Berlin into a symbol of the West's resolve to resist communist expansion. In the spring of 1949, Stalin lifted the now ineffective blockade. And in October, the division of Germany into two nations—the Federal Republic in the west and the Democratic Republic in the East—became official.

The crisis in Berlin accelerated the consolidation of what was already in effect an alliance among the United States and the countries of Western Europe. On April 4, 1949, twelve nations signed an agreement establishing the North Atlantic Treaty Organization (NATO) and declaring that an armed attack against one member would be considered an attack against all. The NATO countries would, moreover, maintain a standing military force in Europe to defend against what many believed was the threat of a Soviet invasion. The American Senate quickly ratified the treaty, which fused European nations that had been fighting one another for centuries into a strong and enduring alliance. The formation of NATO spurred the Soviet Union to create an alliance of its own with the communist governments in Eastern Europe—an alliance formalized in 1955 by the Warsaw Pact.

Reevaluating Cold War Policy

For a time, some American leaders believed that these initial achievements had turned the tide of the battle against communism. But a series of events in 1949 eroded that confidence and propelled the Cold War in new directions. An announcement in September that the Soviet Union had successfully exploded its first atomic weapon, years earlier than predicted, shocked and frightened many Americans. So did the collapse of Chiang Kai-shek's nationalist government in China, which occurred with startling speed in the last months of 1949. Chiang fled with his political allies and the remnants of his army to the offshore island of Formosa (Taiwan), and the entire Chinese mainland came under the control of a communist government that many Americans believed to be an extension of the Soviet Union. Few policymakers shared the belief of the so-called China lobby that the United States should now commit itself to the rearming of Chiang Kai-shek. But neither would the United States recognize the new communist regime. The Chinese mainland would remain almost entirely closed to the West for a generation. The United States, in the meantime, would devote increased attention to the revitalization of Japan as a buffer against Asian communism, ending the American occupation in 1952.

In this atmosphere of escalating crisis, Truman called for a thorough review of American foreign policy. The result was a National Security Council report, issued in 1950 and commonly known as NSC-68, which outlined a shift in the American position. The first statements of the containment doctrine—the writings of George Kennan, the Truman Doctrine speech—had made at least some distinctions between areas of vital interest to the United States and areas of less importance to the nation's foreign policy. They also had viewed containment as a commitment shared among the United States and its allies. But the April 1950 document argued that the United States could no longer rely on other nations to take the initiative in resisting communism. It must itself establish firm and active leadership of the noncommunist world. And it must move to stop communist expansion virtually anywhere it occurred, regardless of the intrinsic strategic or economic value of the lands in question. Among other things, the report called for a major expansion of American military power, with a defense budget almost four times the previously projected figure.

AMERICA AFTER THE WAR

The crises overseas were not the only frustrations the American people encountered after the war. The nation also faced serious, if short-lived, economic difficulties in adapting to the peace. And it suffered from an exceptionally heated political climate that produced a new wave of insecurity and repression.

The Problems of Reconversion

Despite predictions that the end of the war would return America to Depression conditions, economic growth continued after 1945. Pent-up consumer demand from workers who had accumulated substantial savings during the war helped spur the boom. So did a $6 billion tax cut. The Servicemen's Readjustment Act of 1944, better known as the GI Bill of Rights, provided housing, education, and job training subsidies to veterans and increased spending even further.

This flood of consumer demand ensured that there would be no new depression, but it contributed to more than two years of serious inflation, during which prices rose at rates of 14 to 15 percent annually. In the summer of 1946, the president vetoed an extension of the authority of the wartime Office of Price Administration, thus eliminating price controls. (He was opposed not to the controls but to congressional amendments that had weakened the OPA.) Inflation soared to 25 percent before he relented a month later and signed a bill little different from the one he had rejected.

Compounding the economic difficulties was a sharp rise in labor unrest, driven in part by the impact of inflation. By the end of 1945, there had already been major strikes in the automobile, electrical, and steel industries. In April 1946, John L. Lewis led the United Mine Workers out on strike, shutting down the coal fields for forty days. Fears grew rapidly that without vital coal supplies, the entire nation might virtually grind to a halt. Truman finally forced coal production to resume by ordering government seizure of the mines. But in the process, he pressured mine owners to grant the union most of its demands, which he had earlier denounced as inflationary. Almost simultaneously, the nation's railroads suffered a total shutdown—the first in the nation's history—as two major unions walked out on strike. By threatening to use the army to run the trains, Truman pressured the strikers back to work after only a few days.

Reconversion was particularly difficult for the millions of women and minorities who had entered the work force during the war. With veterans returning home and looking for jobs in the industrial economy, employers tended to push women, blacks, Hispanics, and others out of the plants to make room for white males. Some of the war workers, particularly women, left the work force voluntarily, out of a desire to return to their former domestic lives. But as many as 80 percent of women workers, and virtually all black and Hispanic males, wanted to continue working. The postwar inflation, the pressure to meet the growing expectations of a high-consumption society, the rising divorce rate (which left many women responsible for their own economic well-being)—all combined to create a high demand for paid employment among women. As they found themselves excluded from industrial jobs, therefore, women workers moved increasingly into other areas of the economy (above all, the service sector).

The Fair Deal Rejected

Days after the Japanese surrender, Truman submitted to Congress a twenty-one-point domestic program outlining what he later termed the "Fair Deal." It called for expansion of Social Security benefits, the raising of the legal minimum wage from 40 to 65 cents an hour, a program to ensure full employment through aggressive use of federal spending and investment, a permanent Fair Employment Practices Act, public housing and slum clearance, long-range environmental and public works planning, and government promotion of scientific research. Weeks later he added other proposals: federal aid to education, government health insurance, prepaid medical care, funding for the St. Lawrence Seaway, and nationalization of atomic energy. The president was declaring an end to the wartime moratorium on liberal reform.

But the Fair Deal programs fell victim to the same public and congressional conservatism that had crippled the last years of the New Deal. Indeed, that conservatism seemed to be intensifying, as the November 1946 congressional elections suggested. Using the simple but devastating slogan "Had Enough?" the Republican Party won control of both houses of Congress. The new Republican Congress quickly moved to reduce government spending and chip away at New Deal reforms. Its most notable action, perhaps, was its assault on the Wagner Act of 1935. Conservatives had always resented the new powers the legislation had granted unions, and in response to the labor difficulties during and after the war, such resentments intensified sharply. The result was the Labor-Management Relations Act of 1947, better known as the Taft-Hartley Act. It made illegal the closed shop (a workplace in which no one can be hired without first being a member of a union). And although it continued to permit the creation of union shops (in which workers must join a union after being hired), it permitted states to pass "right-to-work" laws prohibiting even that. This provision, the controversial Section 14(b), remained a target of the labor movement for decades. The Taft-Hartley Act also empowered the president to call for a ten-week "cooling-off" period before a strike by issuing an injunction against any work stoppage that endangered national safety or health. Outraged workers and union leaders denounced the measure as a "slave labor bill." Truman vetoed it. But both houses easily overruled him the same day. The Taft-Hartley Act did not destroy the labor movement, as many union leaders had predicted. But it did damage weaker unions in relatively lightly organized industries such as chemicals and textiles, and it made much more difficult the organizing of workers who had never been union members at all, especially in the South and West.

The Election of 1948

Truman and his advisers believed that the American public was not ready to abandon the achievements of the New Deal, despite the 1946 election results. As they planned strategy for the 1948 campaign, therefore, they placed their hopes in an appeal to enduring Democratic loyalties. Throughout 1948, Truman proposed one reform measure after another (including, on February 2, the first major civil rights bill of the century). To no one's surprise, Congress ignored or defeated them all. The president was building campaign issues for the fall.

There remained, however, the problem of Truman's personal unpopularity—the assumption among much of the electorate that he lacked stature and that his administration was weak and inept—and the deep divisions within the Democratic Party. At the Democratic Convention that summer, two factions abandoned the party altogether. Southern conservatives were angered by Truman's proposed civil rights bill and by the approval at the convention of a civil rights plank in the platform (engineered by Hubert Humphrey, the reform mayor of Minneapolis). They walked out and formed the States' Rights (or "Dixiecrat") Party, with Governor Strom Thurmond of South Carolina as its nominee. At the same time, some members of the party's left wing joined the new Progressive Party, whose candidate was Henry A. Wallace. Wallace supporters objected to what they considered the slow and ineffective domestic policies of the Truman administration, but they resented even more the president's confrontational stance toward the Soviet Union.

Many Democratic liberals who were unhappy with Truman were unwilling to leave the party. They attempted instead to replace the president as the party's nominee in 1948. The Americans for Democratic Action (ADA), a coalition of liberals, tried to entice Dwight D. Eisenhower, the popular war hero, to contest the nomination. Only after Eisenhower had refused did liberals bow to the inevitable and concede the nomination to Truman. The Republicans, in the meantime, had once again nominated Governor Thomas E. Dewey of New York, whose substantial reelection victory in 1946 had made him one of the nation's leading political figures. Austere, dignified, and competent, he seemed to offer an unbeatable alternative to the president.

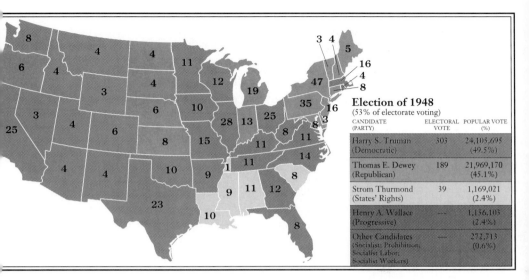

Election of 1948
(53% of electorate voting)

CANDIDATE (PARTY)	ELECTORAL VOTE	POPULAR VOTE (%)
Harry S. Truman (Democratic)	303	24,105,695 (49.5%)
Thomas E. Dewey (Republican)	189	21,969,170 (45.1%)
Strom Thurmond (States' Rights)	39	1,169,021 (2.4%)
Henry A. Wallace (Progressive)	---	1,156,103 (2.4%)
Other Candidates (Socialist; Prohibition; Socialist Labor; Socialist Workers)	---	272,713 (0.6%)

Only Truman, it seemed, believed he could win. As the campaign gathered momentum, he became ever more aggressive, turning the fire away from himself and toward Dewey and the "do-nothing, good-for-nothing" Republican Congress, which was, he told the voters, responsible for fueling inflation and abandoning workers and common people. To dramatize his point, he called Congress into special session in July to give it a chance, he said, to enact the liberal measures the Republicans had recently written into their platform. Congress met for two weeks and, predictably, did almost nothing.

The president traveled nearly 32,000 miles and made 356 speeches, delivering blunt, extemporaneous attacks. He had told Alben Barkley, his running mate, "I'm going to fight hard. I'm going to give them hell." He called for repeal of the Taft-Hartley Act, increased price supports for farmers, and strong civil rights protection for African Americans. (He was the first president to campaign in Harlem since it had become a predominantly black community.) He sought, in short, to re-create much of Franklin Roosevelt's New Deal coalition. To the surprise of virtually everyone, he succeeded. On election night, he won a narrow but decisive victory: 49.5 percent of the popular vote to Dewey's 45.1 percent (with the two splinter parties dividing the small remainder evenly between them), and an electoral margin of 303 to 189. Democrats, in the meantime, had regained both houses of Congress by substantial margins. It was perhaps the most dramatic comeback in the history of presidential elections.

The Fair Deal Revived

Despite the Democratic victories, the Eighty-first Congress was no more hospitable to Truman's Fair Deal reform than its Republican predecessor had been. Truman did win some important victories, to be sure. Congress raised the legal minimum wage from 40 cents to 75 cents an hour. It approved an important expansion of the Social Security system, increasing benefits by 75 percent and extending them to 10 million additional people. And it passed the National Housing Act of 1949, which provided for the construction of 810,000 units of low-income housing accompanied by long-term rent subsidies. (Inadequate funding plagued the program for years, and the initial goal was reached only in 1972.)

But on other issues—national health insurance and aid to education among them—Truman made little progress. Nor was he able to persuade Congress to accept the civil rights legislation he proposed in 1949, legislation that would have made lynching a federal crime, provided federal protection of black voting rights, abolished the poll tax, and established a new Fair Employment Practices Commission to curb discrimination in hiring. Southern Democrats filibustered to kill the bill.

Truman did proceed on his own to battle several forms of racial discrimination. He ordered an end to discrimination in the hiring of government employees. He began to dismantle segregation within the armed forces. And he allowed the Justice Department to become actively involved in court battles against discriminatory statutes. The Supreme Court, in the meantime, signaled its own growing awareness of the issue by ruling, in *Shelley* v. *Kraemer* (1948), that the courts could not be used to enforce private "covenants" meant to bar blacks from residential neighborhoods. The achievements of the Truman years made only minor dents in the structure of segregation, but they were the tentative beginnings of a federal commitment to confront the problem of race.

THE KOREAN WAR

On June 24, 1950, the armies of communist North Korea swept across their southern border and invaded the pro-Western half of the Korean peninsula to the south. Within days, they had occupied much of South Korea, including Seoul, its capital. Almost immediately, the United States committed itself to the conflict. It was the first American military engagement of the Cold War.

The Divided Peninsula

The Korean conflict was the result of several years of tension within the peninsula. By the summer of 1945, both the United States and the Soviet Union had sent troops into Korea against the Japanese. When World War II ended, neither the Americans nor the Soviets were willing to leave. Instead, they divided the nation, supposedly temporarily, along the 38th par-

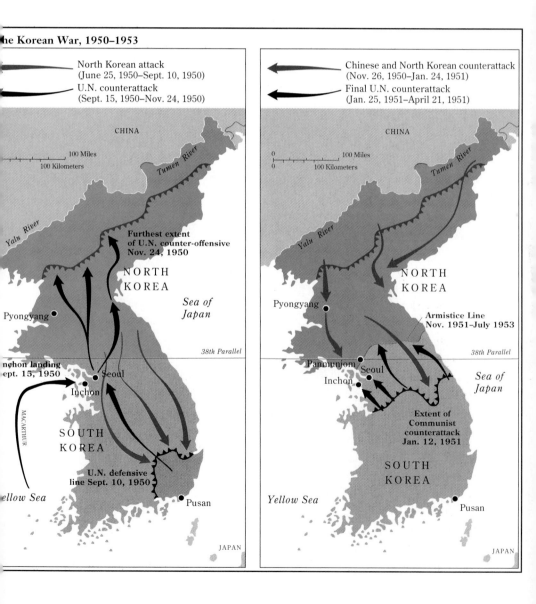

The Korean War, 1950–1953

North Korean attack
(June 25, 1950–Sept. 10, 1950)

U.N. counterattack
(Sept. 15, 1950–Nov. 24, 1950)

Chinese and North Korean counterattack
(Nov. 26, 1950–Jan. 24, 1951)

Final U.N. counterattack
(Jan. 25, 1951–April 21, 1951)

CHINA

100 Miles

100 Kilometers

Tumen River

Yalu River

Furthest extent
of U.N. counter-offensive
Nov. 24, 1950

NORTH
KOREA

Sea of
Japan

Pyongyang

38th Parallel

Inchon landing
Sept. 15, 1950

Seoul

Inchon

MACARTHUR

SOUTH
KOREA

U.N. defensive
line Sept. 10, 1950

Yellow Sea

Pusan

JAPAN

CHINA

0   100 Miles

0   100 Kilometers

Tumen River

Yalu River

NORTH
KOREA

Pyongyang

Armistice Line
Nov. 1951–July 1953

38th Parallel

Panmunjom   Seoul

Inchon

Sea of
Japan

Extent of
Communist
counterattack
Jan. 12, 1951

SOUTH
KOREA

Yellow Sea

Pusan

JAPAN

allel. The Russians finally departed in 1949, leaving behind a communist government in the north with a strong, Soviet-equipped army. The Americans left a few months later, handing control to the pro-Western government of Syngman Rhee, anticommunist but only nominally democratic. He had a relatively small military, which he used primarily to suppress internal opposition.

The relative weakness of the south offered a strong temptation to nationalists in the North Korean government who wanted to reunite the country. The temptation grew stronger when the American government implied that it did not consider South Korea within its own "defense perimeter." The role of the Soviet Union remains unclear; there is some reason to believe that the North Koreans acted without Stalin's approval. But the Soviets supported the offensive once it began.

MACARTHUR IN KOREA, 1950 General Douglas MacArthur visits Marines along the fighting front in Korea in September 1950. Revered by those who fought under him, MacArthur was nevertheless a persistent irritant to policymakers in Washington with his demands for widening the conflict—demands that grew more frequent and more public after the Chinese entered the war about two months after this photograph was taken.

The Truman administration responded quickly. On June 27, 1950, the president ordered limited American military assistance to South Korea, and on the same day he appealed to the United Nations to intervene. The Soviet Union was boycotting the Security Council at the time (to protest the council's refusal to recognize the new communist government of China) and was thus unable to exercise its veto power. As a result, American delegates were able to win UN agreement to a resolution calling for international assistance to the Rhee government. On June 30, the United States ordered its own ground forces into Korea, and Truman appointed General Douglas MacArthur to command the UN operations there. (Several other nations provided assistance and troops, but the "UN" armies were, in fact, overwhelmingly American.)

The intervention in Korea was the first expression of the newly expansive American foreign policy outlined in NSC-68. But the administration quickly went beyond NSC-68. It decided that the war would be an effort not simply at containment but also at "liberation." After a surprise American invasion at Inchon in September had routed the North Korean forces from the south and sent them fleeing back across the 38th parallel, Truman gave MacArthur permission to pursue the communists into their own territory. His aim, as an American-sponsored UN resolution proclaimed in October, was to create "a unified, independent and democratic Korea."

From Invasion to Stalemate

For several weeks, MacArthur's invasion of North Korea proceeded smoothly. On October 19, the capital, Pyongyang, fell to the UN forces. Victory seemed near—until the Chinese government, alarmed by the movement of American forces toward its border, intervened. By November 4, eight divisions of the Chinese army had entered the war. The UN offensive stalled and then collapsed. Through December 1950, outnumbered American forces fought a bitter, losing battle against the Chinese divisions, retreating at almost every juncture. Within weeks, communist forces had pushed the Americans back below the 38th parallel once again and had recaptured the South Korean capital of Seoul. By mid-January 1951 the rout had ceased; and by March the UN armies had managed to regain much of the territory they had recently lost, taking back Seoul and pushing the communists north of the 38th parallel for the second time. But with that, the war degenerated into a protracted stalemate.

From the start, Truman had been determined to avoid a direct conflict with China, which he feared might lead to a new world war. Once China entered the war, he began seeking a negotiated solution to the struggle; and for the next two years, he insisted that there be no wider war. But he faced a formidable opponent in General MacArthur, who resisted any limits on his military discretion. The United States was really fighting the Chinese, MacArthur argued. It should, therefore, attack China itself, if not through an actual invasion, then at least by bombing communist forces massing north of the Chinese border. In March 1951, he indicated his unhappiness in a public letter to House Republican leader Joseph W. Martin that concluded: "There is no substitute for victory." His position had wide popular support.

The Martin letter came after nine months during which MacArthur had resisted Truman's decisions. More than once, the president had warned the general to keep his objections to himself. The release of the Martin letter, therefore, struck the president as intolerable insubordination. On April 11, 1951, he relieved MacArthur of his command.

There was a storm of public outrage. Sixty-nine percent of the American people supported MacArthur, a Gallup poll reported. When the general returned to the United States later in 1951, he was greeted with wild enthusiasm. Public criticism of Truman finally abated somewhat when a number of prominent military figures, including General Omar Bradley, publicly supported the president's decision. But substantial hostility toward Truman remained.

In the meantime, the Korean stalemate continued. Negotiations between the opposing forces began at Panmunjom in July 1951, but the talks—and the war—dragged on until 1953.

Limited Mobilization

Just as the war in Korea produced only a limited American military commitment abroad, so it created only a limited economic mobilization at home. Still, the government did try to control the wartime economy in several important ways.

First, Truman set up the Office of Defense Mobilization to fight inflation by holding down prices and discouraging high union wage demands. When these cautious regulatory efforts failed, the president took more drastic action. Railroad workers walked off the job in 1951, and Truman, who considered the workers' demands inflationary, ordered the government to seize control of the railroads. That helped keep the trains running, but it had no effect on union demands. Workers ultimately got most of what they had demanded. In 1952, during a nationwide steel strike, Truman seized the steel mills, citing his powers as commander in chief. But in a 6-to-3 decision, the

Supreme Court ruled that the president had exceeded his authority, and Truman was forced to relent.

The Korean War gave a significant boost to economic growth by pumping new government funds into the economy at a point when many believed it was about to decline. But the war had other, less welcome effects. It came at a time of rising insecurity about America's position in the world and intensified anxiety about communism. As the long stalemate continued, producing 140,000 American dead and wounded, frustration turned to anger. The United States, which had recently won the greatest war in history, seemed unable to conclude what many Americans considered a minor border skirmish in a small country. Many began to believe that something must be deeply wrong—not only in Korea but within the United States as well. Such fears contributed to the rise of the second major campaign of the century against domestic communism.

THE CRUSADE AGAINST SUBVERSION

Why did the American people develop a growing fear of internal communist subversion—a fear that by the early 1950s had reached the point of near hysteria? There are many possible answers, but no single definitive explanation.

One factor was obvious. Communism was not an imagined enemy in the 1950s. It had tangible shape, in Josef Stalin and the Soviet Union. Adding to the concern were the setbacks America had encountered in its battle against communism: the Korean stalemate, the "loss" of China, the Soviet development of an atomic bomb. Searching for someone to blame, many were attracted to the idea of a communist conspiracy within American borders. But there were other factors as well, rooted in events in American domestic politics.

HUAC and Alger Hiss

Much of the anticommunist furor emerged out of the search by the Republican Party for an issue with which to attack the Democrats, and out of the efforts of the Democrats to take that issue away from them. Beginning in 1947, the House Un-American Activities Committee (HUAC) held widely publicized investigations to prove that, under Democratic rule, the government had tolerated (if not actually encouraged) communist subversion. The committee turned first to the movie industry, arguing that communists had

AMERICAN VOICES

WHITTAKER CHAMBERS

The Hiss Case

 I BELIEVED THAT I was not meant to be spared from testifying [against Alger Hiss]. I sensed, with a force greater than any fear or revulsion, that it was for this that my whole life had been lived. For this I had been a Communist, for this I had ceased to be a Communist. . . . This challenge was the terrible meaning of my whole life, of all that I had done that was evil, of all that I had sought that was good, of my weakness and my strength. . . .

For the moment had arrived when some man must be a witness. . . . The danger to the nation from Communism had now grown acute, both within its own house and abroad. Its existence was threatened. And the nation did not know it. For the first time, the [House Unamerican Activities] Committee's subpoena gave me an opportunity to tell what I knew about that danger. . . .

I did not wish to harm, more than was unavoidable, those whom I must testify against. . . . But I must testify that they had been concealed Communists and that an underground had existed in the Government. . . . They and I must stand up in face of the nation and confess what we had been that it might take alarm, throw off its apathy and skepticism, see that the enemy really was embedded in its midst, and be given time to act and save itself. That was the least that we could do in atonement.

SOURCE: Whittaker Chambers, *Witness*, pp. 533–534. Copyright © 1952 by Whittaker Chambers. Reprinted by permission of Random House, Inc.

infiltrated Hollywood and tainted American films with propaganda. Writers and producers, some of them former communists, were called to testify; and when some of them ("the Hollywood Ten") refused to answer questions about their own political beliefs and those of their colleagues, they were sent to jail for contempt. Others were barred from employment in the industry when Hollywood, attempting to protect its public image, adopted a "blacklist" of those of "suspicious loyalty."

More alarming to the public was HUAC's investigation into charges of disloyalty leveled against a former high-ranking member of the State Department: Alger Hiss. In 1948, Whittaker Chambers, a self-avowed former communist agent, now a conservative editor at *Time* magazine, told the

ALGER HISS No single figure did more to polarize opinion about the dangers of domestic communism than Alger Hiss, the respected diplomat accused in 1948 of having been a spy in the 1930s for the Soviet Union and later convicted of perjury for testifying falsely before a congressional committee. Even half a century later, opinions remain sharply divided about Hiss's guilt.

committee that Hiss had passed classified State Department documents to him in 1937 and 1938. When Hiss sued him for slander, Chambers produced microfilms of the documents (called the "pumpkin papers," because Chambers had kept them hidden in a pumpkin in his vegetable garden). Hiss could not be tried for espionage because of the statute of limitations (a law that protects individuals from prosecution for most crimes after seven years have passed). But largely because of the relentless efforts of Richard M. Nixon, a freshman Republican congressman from California and a member of HUAC, Hiss was convicted of perjury and served several years in prison. The Hiss case not only discredited a prominent young diplomat; it cast suspicion on a generation of liberal Democrats and made it possible for the public to believe that communists had actually infiltrated the government. It also transformed Nixon into a national figure and helped him win a seat in the United States Senate in 1950.

The Federal Loyalty Program and the Rosenberg Case

Partly to protect itself against Republican attacks, partly to encourage support for the president's foreign policy initiatives, the Truman administration in 1947 initiated a widely publicized program to review the "loyalty" of federal employees. In August 1950, the president authorized some agencies to fire people deemed no more than "bad security risks." By 1951, more than 2,000 government employees had resigned under pressure and 212 had been dismissed.

The employee loyalty program became a signal throughout the executive branch to launch a major assault on subversion. The attorney general established a widely cited list of supposedly subversive organizations. The director of the Federal Bureau of Investigation (FBI), J. Edgar Hoover, investigated and harassed alleged radicals. The anticommunist frenzy quickly grew so intense that even a Democratic Congress felt obliged to bow to it. In 1950, Congress passed the McCarran Internal Security Act, which, among other restrictions on "subversive" activity, required that all communist organizations register with the government and publish their records. Truman vetoed the bill. Congress easily overrode his veto.

The successful Soviet detonation of an atomic bomb in 1949, earlier than generally expected, suggested to some people that there had been a conspiracy to pass American atomic secrets to the Russians. In 1950, Klaus Fuchs, a young British scientist, seemed to confirm those fears when he testified that he had delivered to the Russians details of the manufacture of the bomb. The case ultimately settled on an obscure New York couple, Julius and Ethel Rosenberg, members of the Communist Party. The government claimed the Rosenbergs had received secret information from Ethel's brother, a machinist on the Manhattan Project in New Mexico, and had passed it on to the Soviet Union through other agents (including Fuchs). The Rosenbergs were convicted and, on April 5, 1951, sentenced to death. After two years of appeals and public protests, they died in the electric chair on June 19, 1953, proclaiming their innocence to the end.

All these factors—the HUAC investigations, the Hiss trial, the loyalty investigations, the McCarran Act, the Rosenberg case—combined with other concerns by the early 1950s to create a fear of communist subversion that seemed to grip the entire country. State and local governments, the judiciary, schools and universities, labor unions—all sought to purge themselves of real or imagined subversives. A pervasive fear settled on much of the country—not only the fear of communist infiltration but the fear of being suspected of communism. It was a climate that made possible the rise of an extraordinary public figure, whose behavior at any other time might have been dismissed as preposterous.

McCarthyism

Joseph McCarthy was an undistinguished, first-term Republican senator from Wisconsin when, in February 1950, he suddenly burst into national prominence. In the midst of a speech in Wheeling, West Virginia, he lifted up a sheet of paper and claimed to "hold in my hand" a list of 205 known communists currently working in the American State Department. No person of comparable stature had ever made so bold a charge against the federal government; and in the weeks to come, as McCarthy repeated and expanded on his accusations, he emerged as the nation's most prominent leader of the crusade against domestic subversion.

Within weeks of his charges against the State Department, McCarthy was leveling accusations at other agencies. After 1952, with the Republicans in control of the Senate and McCarthy the chairman of a special subcommittee, he conducted highly publicized investigations of subversion in many areas of the government. McCarthy never produced conclusive evidence that any federal employee was a Communist. But a growing constituency adored him nevertheless for his coarse, "fearless" assaults on a government establishment that many considered arrogant, effete, even traitorous. Republicans, in particular, rallied to his claims that the Democrats had been responsible for "twenty years of treason" and that only a change of parties could rid the country of subversion. McCarthy, in short, provided his followers with an issue into which they could channel a wide range of resentments: fear of communism, animosity toward the country's "eastern establishment," and frustrated partisan ambitions. For a time, McCarthy intimidated all but a few people from opposing him. Even the highly popular Dwight D. Eisenhower, running for president in 1952, did not speak out against him, although he disliked McCarthy's tactics and was outraged at, among other things, McCarthy's attacks on General George Marshall.

The Republican Revival

Public frustration over the stalemate in Korea and popular fears of internal subversion combined to make 1952 a bad year for the Democratic Party. Truman, whose own popularity had diminished almost to the vanishing point, wisely withdrew from the presidential contest. The party united instead behind Governor Adlai E. Stevenson of Illinois. Stevenson's dignity, wit, and eloquence made him a beloved figure to many liberals and intellectuals. But those same qualities seemed only to fuel Republican charges that Stevenson lacked the strength or the will to combat communism sufficiently.

Stevenson's greatest problem, however, was the Republican candidate opposing him. Rejecting the efforts of conservatives to nominate Robert Taft or Douglas MacArthur, the Republicans turned to a man who had no previous identification with the party: General Dwight D. Eisenhower—military hero, commander of NATO, president of Columbia University in New York—who won nomination on the first ballot. He chose as his running mate the young California senator who had gained national prominence through his crusade against Alger Hiss: Richard M. Nixon.

In the fall campaign, Eisenhower attracted support through his geniality and his statesmanlike pledges to settle the Korean conflict. Nixon (after surviving early accusations of financial improprieties, which he effectively neutralized in a famous television address, the "Checkers speech") exploited the issue of domestic anticommunism by attacking the Democrats for "cowardice" and "appeasement." The response at the polls was overwhelming. Eisenhower won both a popular and an electoral landslide: 55 percent of the popular vote to Stevenson's 44 percent, 442 electoral votes to Stevenson's 89. Republicans gained control of both houses of Congress for the first time since 1946. The election of 1952 ended twenty years of Democratic dominance. And while it might not have seemed so at the time, it also signaled the end of some of the worst turbulence of the postwar era.

DEBATING THE PAST

The Cold War

 OR MORE than a decade after the beginning of the Cold War, few historians saw any reason to challenge the official American interpretation of its origins. The breakdown of relations between the United States and the Soviet Union was, most agreed, a direct result of Soviet expansionism and of Stalin's violation of the wartime agreements forged at Yalta and Potsdam. The Soviet imposition of communist regimes in Eastern Europe was part of a larger ideological design to spread communism throughout the world. American policy was the logical and necessary response: a firm commitment to oppose Soviet expansionism and to keep American forces in a continual state of readiness.

Disillusionment with the official justifications for the Cold War began to find expression even in the late 1950s, when anticommunist sentiment in America remained strong and pervasive. William Appleman Williams's *The Tragedy of American Diplomacy* (1959) insisted that the Cold War was simply the most recent version of a consistent American effort in the twentieth century to preserve an "open door" for American trade in world markets. The confrontation with the Soviet Union, he argued, was less a response to Soviet aggressive designs than an expression of the American belief in the necessity of capitalist expansion.

As the Vietnam War grew larger and more unpopular in the 1960s, the scholarly critique of the Cold War quickly gained intensity. Walter LaFeber's *America, Russia, and the Cold War*, first published in 1967, maintained that America's supposedly idealistic internationalism at the close of

(continued on next page)

the war was in reality an effort to ensure a postwar order shaped in the American image—with every nation open to American influence (and to American trade). That was why the United States was so apt to misinterpret Soviet policy, much of which reflected a perfectly reasonable commitment to ensure the security of the Soviet Union itself, as part of a larger aggressive design. Important to many revisionist arguments has been the American decision to use atomic weapons against Japan in 1945. Gar Alperovitz's *Atomic Diplomacy* (1965) and *The Decision to Use the Atomic Bomb* (1995) expanded on arguments that had begun to appear as early as 1948 and claimed that American decision makers used the bombs not to win the war (for Japan was already effectively defeated) but to impress and intimidate the Soviet Union. In fact, Alperovitz argued, this atomic diplomacy had the opposite effect: it convinced the Soviet Union of America's hostile intentions and helped speed the onset of the Cold War.

The revisionist interpretations of the Cold War ultimately produced a reaction of their own: what has come to be known as "postrevisionist" scholarship. The most important works in this school have attempted to strike a balance between orthodoxy and revisionism and to identify areas of blame and patterns of misconception on both sides of the conflict. Thomas G. Patterson, John Lewis Gaddis, Melvin Leffler, and others have presented a picture of two nations—each with a highly inadequate understanding of the other—struggling to preserve a wartime alliance that had in fact temporarily disguised a basic difference in outlook and interests. "The United States and the Soviet Union were doomed to be antagonists," Ernest May wrote in 1984. "There probably was never any real possibility that the post-1945 relationship could be anything but hostility verging on conflict."

The collapse of Soviet communism and the dissolution of the Soviet empire will undoubtedly stimulate new interpretations of the Cold War and will (by facilitating the opening of Soviet archives) cast new light on many contested issues. For the moment, however, the dominant scholarly view is one that de-emphasizes the question of who is to blame and emphasizes the ways in which both sides learned to manage a conflict that neither could easily have avoided.

CHAPTER THIRTY

The Affluent Society

Abundance and Society ～ *The Other America*
The Rise of the Civil Rights Movement ～ *Eisenhower Republicanism*
Eisenhower, Dulles, and the Cold War

I F AMERICA EXPERIENCED a golden age in the 1950s and early 1960s, as many Americans believed at the time and many continue to believe today, it was largely a result of two developments. One was a booming national prosperity, which profoundly altered the social, economic, and even physical landscape of the United States, as well as the way many Americans thought about their lives and their world. The other was the continuing struggle against communism, a struggle that created considerable anxiety but that also encouraged Americans to look even more approvingly at their own society.

But if these powerful forces created a widespread sense of national purpose and self-satisfaction, they also helped blind many Americans to serious problems plaguing large groups of the population. More than 30 million Americans, according to some estimates, continued to live in poverty in the 1950s. And significant minorities—most prominently the 10 percent of the American people who were black, but also Hispanics, Asians, Indians, gays and lesbians—continued to suffer social, political, and economic discrimination. Many American women, too, were chafing at obstacles to personal and professional fulfillment. The very things that made America seem so successful in the 1950s also contributed, in the end, to making the nation's social problems more difficult to avoid.

ABUNDANCE AND SOCIETY

Perhaps the most striking feature of American society in the 1950s and early 1960s was the booming, almost miraculous economic growth that made even the heady 1920s seem pale by comparison. It was a better-balanced and

TIME LINE

1947	1952	1953	1954	1955
Levittown construction begins	Eisenhower elected	Korean War ends	*Brown* v. *Board of Education* Army-McCarthy hearings	Montgomery bus boycott

1956	1957	1959	1960	1961	1969
Federal Highway Act Eisenhower reelected Suez crisis	Sputnik launched Kerouac's *On the Road* Little Rock desegregation crisis	Castro seizes power in Cuba	U-2 incident	First American in space	Americans land on moon

more widely distributed prosperity than that of thirty years earlier. It was not, however, as universal as some Americans liked to believe.

Economic Growth

By 1949, despite the continuing problems of postwar reconversion, an economic expansion had begun that would continue with only brief interruptions for almost twenty years. Between 1945 and 1960, the gross national product grew by 250 percent, from $200 billion to over $500 billion. Unemployment, which during the Depression had averaged between 15 and 25 percent, remained at about 5 percent or lower throughout the 1950s and early 1960s. Inflation, in the meantime, hovered around 3 percent a year or less.

The causes of this growth were varied. Government spending, which had ended the Depression in the 1940s, continued to stimulate growth through public funding of schools, housing, veterans' benefits, welfare, and interstate highways. Above all, there was military spending. Economic growth was at its peak during the first half of the 1950s, when military spending was highest because of the Korean War. In the late 1950s, with spending on armaments in decline, the rate of growth declined by half.

The national birth rate reversed a long pattern of decline with the so-called baby boom, which had begun during the war and peaked in 1957. The nation's population rose almost 20 percent in the decade, from 150 million in 1950 to 179 million in 1960. The baby boom meant increased consumer demand and expanding economic growth.

The rapid expansion of suburbs—whose population grew 47 percent in the 1950s—helped stimulate growth in several important sectors of the economy. The number of privately owned cars (more essential for suburban than for urban living) more than doubled in a decade, sparking a great boom in the automobile industry. Demand for new homes helped sustain a vigorous housing industry. The construction of roads, which was both a cause and a result of the growth of suburbs, stimulated the economy as well.

These forces helped the American economy to grow nearly ten times as fast as the population in the thirty years after the war. And while that growth was far from equally distributed, it affected most of society. The average American in 1960 had over 20 percent more purchasing power than in 1945, and more than twice as much as during the prosperous 1920s. The American people had achieved the highest standard of living of any society in the history of the world.

The Rise of the Modern West

No region of the country experienced more dramatic changes as a result of the new economic growth than the American West. Its population expanded dramatically; its cities boomed; its industrial economy flourished. Before World War II, most of the West had been, economically at least, an appendage of the great industrial economy of the East—providing it with raw materials and agricultural goods. By the 1960s, some parts of the West were among the most important (and populous) industrial and cultural centers of the nation in their own right.

As during World War II, much of the growth of the West was a result of federal spending and investment—on the dams, power stations, highways, and other infrastructure projects that made economic development possible; and on the military contracts that continued to flow disproportionately to factories in California and Texas, many of them built with government funds during the war. But other factors played a role as well. The enormous increase in automobile use after World War II—a result, among other things, of suburbanization and improved highway systems—gave a large stimulus to the petroleum industry and contributed to the rapid growth of oil fields in Texas and Colorado and of the metropolitan centers serving them: Houston, Dallas, and Denver. State governments in the West invested heavily in their universities. The University of Texas and University of California systems, in particular, became among the nation's largest and best;

as centers of research, they helped attract technology-intensive industries to the region. Climate also contributed. Once they had the infrastructure (and, most important, the water supplies) to sustain large populations, southern California, Nevada, and Arizona, in particular, attracted many migrants from the East because of their warm, dry climates. The growth of Los Angeles after World War II was a remarkable phenomenon: more than 10 percent of all new businesses in the United States between 1945 and 1950 began in Los Angeles. Its population rose by over 50 percent between 1940 and 1960.

Capital and Labor

There were more than 4,000 corporate mergers in the 1950s. To a greater extent than ever before, a relatively small number of large-scale organizations controlled an enormous proportion of the nation's economic activity. By the end of the decade, half of the net corporate income in the nation was going to only slightly more than 500 firms, or one-tenth of 1 percent of the total number of corporations.

A similar consolidation was occurring in the agricultural economy. Increasing mechanization reduced the need for farm labor, and the agricultural work force declined by more than half in the two decades after the war. Mechanization also endangered one of the most cherished American institutions: the family farm. By the 1960s, relatively few individuals could any longer afford to buy and equip a modern farm, and much of the nation's most productive land had been purchased by financial institutions and corporations.

Corporations enjoying booming growth were reluctant to allow strikes to interfere with their operations; and since the most important labor unions were now so large and entrenched that they could not easily be suppressed or intimidated, leaders of large businesses made important concessions to them. As early as 1948, Walter Reuther, president of the United Automobile Workers, obtained a contract from General Motors that included a built-in "escalator clause"—an automatic cost-of-living increase pegged to the consumer price index. In 1955, Reuther received a guarantee from Ford Motor Company that it would continue wages to autoworkers even during layoffs. A few months later, steelworkers in several corporations won a guaranteed annual salary. By the mid-1950s, factory wages in all industries had risen substantially, to an average of $80 per week.

The labor movement enjoyed significant success in winning better wages and benefits for workers already organized in strong unions. For the majority of laborers who were as yet unorganized, however, there were fewer advances. Total union membership remained relatively stable, at about 16 million, throughout the 1950s; and while this was in part a result of a shift in the work force from blue-collar to white-collar jobs, it was also a result of new obstacles to organization. The Taft-Hartley Act and the state right-to-work laws that the act spawned made it more difficult to create new unions powerful enough to demand recognition from employers.

The economic successes of the 1950s helped pave the way for a reunification of the labor movement. In December 1955, the American Federation of Labor and the Congress of Industrial Organizations ended their twenty-year rivalry and merged to create the AFL-CIO, under the leadership of George Meany.

But success also bred stagnation and corruption in some union bureaucracies. In 1957, the powerful Teamsters Union became the subject of a congressional investigation, and its president, David Beck, was charged with the misappropriation of union funds. Beck ultimately stepped down to be replaced by Jimmy Hoffa, whom government investigators pursued for nearly a decade before finally winning a conviction against him (for tax evasion) in 1967. The United Mine Workers, similarly, became tainted by violence and charges of corruption.

Consumerism and Suburbanization

Among the most striking social developments of the immediate postwar era was the rapid extension of a middle-class lifestyle and outlook to an expanding portion of the population. The American middle class was becoming a larger, more powerful, and more self-conscious force than it had ever been before.

At the center of middle-class culture in the 1950s was a growing absorption with consumer goods. That was a result of increased prosperity, of the increasing variety and availability of products, and of the adeptness of advertisers in creating a demand for those products. It was also a result of the growth of consumer credit, which increased by 800 percent between 1945 and 1957 through the development of credit cards, revolving charge accounts, and easy-payment plans. Prosperity fueled such longtime consumer crazes as the automobile, and Detroit responded to the boom with ever-flashier styling and accessories. Consumers also responded eagerly to the development of such new products as dishwashers, garbage disposals, televisions, and high-fidelity and stereo record players.

A third of the nation's population lived in suburbs by 1960. The growth

of suburbs was a result not only of increased affluence but of important innovations in home building, which made single-family houses affordable to
millions of new people. The most famous of the suburban developers,
William Levitt, came to symbolize the new suburban growth with his use of
mass-production techniques to construct large housing developments, the
first of which was on Long Island, near New York City. The houses sold for
under $10,000. Young couples—often newly married war veterans eager to
start a family rushed to purchase the inexpensive homes, not only in the
"Levittowns" but in the many other relatively inexpensive developments that
soon began appearing throughout the country.

Why did so many Americans want to move to the suburbs? One reason
was the enormous importance postwar Americans placed on family life after
five years of war during which families had often been separated or otherwise disrupted. Suburbs provided families with larger homes than they could
find (or afford) in the cities, and thus made it easier to raise larger numbers
of children. They provided privacy. They also provided a sense of security

LEVITTOWN BEFORE THE TREES A section of the Levittown on
Long Island in New York, photographed in July 1948 a few months
after the first families moved in. The Levitt family pioneered
techniques in constructing mass-produced housing that made
possible the proliferation of similar inexpensive suburbs in many
areas of the country.

from the noise and dangers of urban living. They offered space for the new consumer goods—the appliances, cars, boats, outdoor furniture, and other products that middle-class Americans craved.

For many Americans, suburban life also helped provide a sense of community that was sometimes difficult to develop in large, crowded, impersonal urban areas. In later years, the suburbs would come under attack for their supposed conformity, homogeneity, and isolation. But in the 1950s, many people were attracted by the idea of living in a community populated largely by people of similar age and background, and they found it easier to form friendships and social circles there than in the city. Women in particular often valued the presence of other nonworking mothers living nearby to share the tasks of child raising.

Another factor motivating white Americans to move to the suburbs was race. Most suburbs were restricted to white inhabitants—both because relatively few blacks could afford to live in them and because formal and informal barriers kept even prosperous blacks out of all but a few. In an era when the black population of most cities was rapidly growing, many white families fled to the suburbs to escape the integration of urban neighborhoods and schools.

The Suburban Family

For professional men (who tended to work in the city, at some distance from their homes), suburban life generally meant a rigid division between their working and personal worlds. For many middle-class women, it meant an increased isolation from the workplace. The enormous cultural emphasis on family life in the 1950s strengthened popular prejudices against women entering the professions or occupying any paid job at all. Many middle-class husbands considered it demeaning for their wives to be employed. And many women themselves shied away from the workplace when they could afford to, in part because of prevailing ideas about motherhood (popularized by such widely consulted books as Dr. Benjamin Spock's *Baby and Child Care*, first published in 1946) that instructed women to stay at home with their children.

Affluent women, then, faced heavy pressures—both externally and internally imposed—to remain in the home and concentrate on raising their children. Some women, however, had to balance these pressures against other, contradictory ones. As expectations of material comfort rose, many middle-class families needed a second income to maintain the standard of living they desired. As a result, the number of married women working out-

THE BABY BOOM IN THE SUBURBS Mothers of young children cluster outside a shopping center in Levittown, New York in the spring of 1949, during the peak of the postwar "baby boom." The rapid population growth the "baby boom" produced, and the massive movement of middle-class families into suburbs that accompanied it, were among the most important demographic trends of the postwar era.

side the home actually increased in the postwar years—even as the social pressure for them to stay out of the workplace grew. By 1960, nearly a third of all married women were part of the paid work force.

The Birth of Television

Television, perhaps the most powerful medium of mass communication in history, was central to the culture of the postwar era. Experiments in broadcasting pictures (along with sound) had begun as early as the 1920s, but commercial television began only shortly after World War II. It experienced a phenomenally rapid growth. In 1946, there were only 17,000 television sets in the country; by 1957, there were 40 million sets in use—almost as many sets as there were families. More people had television sets, according to one report, than had refrigerators.

The impact of television on American life was rapid, pervasive, and profound. By the late 1950s, television news had replaced newspapers, magazines, and radios as the nation's most important vehicle of information. Television advertising helped create a vast market for new fashions and products. Televised athletic events gradually made professional and college sports one of the important sources of entertainment (and one of the biggest businesses) in America. Television entertainment programming, almost all of it controlled by the three national networks (and their corporate sponsors), replaced movies and radio as the principal source of diversion for American families.

Much of the programming of the 1950s and early 1960s created a relatively uniform image of American life—an image that was predominantly white, middle-class, and suburban, an image epitomized by such popular situation comedies as *Ozzie and Harriet* and *Leave It to Beaver*. But television

THE MICKEY MOUSE CLUB In an early example of the highly integrated marketing for which it is now famous, the Walt Disney Corporation created this successful television program for children in the mid-1950s. It coincided with, and helped to promote, the opening in 1955 of Disneyland—the company's enormously profitable theme park near Los Angeles.

also conveyed other images: the gritty, urban working-class families in Jackie Gleason's *The Honeymooners;* the childless show-business family of the early *I Love Lucy;* the unmarried professional women in *Our Miss Brooks* and *My Little Margie.* Television not only sought to create an idealized image of a homogeneous suburban America. It also sought to convey experiences at odds with that image in warm, unthreatening terms—taking social diversity and cultural conflict and domesticating them, turning them into something benign and even comic.

Yet television also, inadvertently, created conditions that could accentuate social conflict. Even those unable to share in the affluence of the era could, through television, acquire a vivid picture of how the rest of their society lived. At the same time that television was reinforcing the homogeneity of the white middle class, therefore, it was also contributing to the sense of alienation and powerlessness among groups excluded from the world it portrayed. And when social conflict began to accelerate, television made that conflict seem vivid and immediate to a far-flung audience and helped it to spread.

Science and Space

In 1961, *Time* magazine chose as its "man of the year" not a specific person but "the American Scientist." The choice was an indication of the widespread fascination with which Americans in the age of atomic weapons viewed science and technology. Major medical advances accounted for much of that fascination. Jonas Salk's vaccine to prevent polio was provided free to the public by the federal government beginning in 1955, and within a few years it (and the Sabin vaccine that soon followed) had virtually eliminated the much feared polio from American life. Other dread diseases such as diphtheria and tuberculosis also all but vanished from society as new drugs and treatments were discovered. Infant mortality and the death rate among young children both declined significantly in the first twenty-five years after the war (although less than in Western Europe). Average life expectancy in that same period rose by five years, to seventy-one.

But Americans were at least equally attracted to other scientific and technological innovations: the jet plane, the computer, synthetics, new types of commercially prepared foods. And nothing better illustrated the nation's veneration of scientific expertise than the popular enthusiasm for the American space program.

The program began in large part because of the Cold War. When the Soviet Union announced in 1957 that it had launched a satellite—*Sputnik*—

into outer space, the American government (and much of society) reacted with alarm, as if the Soviet achievement was also a massive American failure. Federal policy began encouraging (and funding) strenuous efforts to improve scientific education in the schools, to create more research laboratories, and, above all, to speed the development of America's own exploration of outer space. The centerpiece of that exploration was the manned space program, established in 1958 with the selection of the first American space pilots, or "astronauts," who quickly became the nation's most revered heroes. On May 5, 1961, Alan Shepard became the first American launched into space (several months after a Soviet "cosmonaut," Yuri Gagarin, had made a similar, if longer, flight). On February 2, 1962, John Glenn (later a United States senator) became the first American to orbit the globe (again, only after Gagarin had already done so).

Interest in the space program remained high in the summer of 1969, when Neil Armstrong and Edwin Aldrin became the first men to walk on the surface of the moon. Not long after that, however, the government began to cut the funding for future missions, and popular enthusiasm for the program began to wane.

Organized Society and Its Detractors

Large-scale organizations and bureaucracies increased their influence over American life in the postwar era, as they had been doing for many decades before. White-collar workers came to outnumber blue-collar laborers for the first time, and an increasing proportion of them worked in corporate settings with rigid hierarchical structures. Industrial workers also confronted large bureaucracies both in the workplace and in their own unions.

As in earlier eras, Americans reacted to these developments with ambivalence, often hostility. The debilitating impact of bureaucratic life on the individual slowly became one of the central themes of popular and scholarly debate. William H. Whyte, Jr., produced one of the most widely discussed books of the decade: *The Organization Man* (1956), which attempted to describe the special mentality of the worker in a large, bureaucratic setting. Self-reliance, Whyte claimed, was losing place to the ability to "get along" and "work as a team" as the most valuable trait in the modern character. The sociologist David Riesman made similar observations in *The Lonely Crowd* (1950), in which he argued that the traditional "inner-directed man," who judged himself on the basis of his own values and the esteem of his family, was giving way to a new "other-directed man," more concerned with winning the approval of the larger organization or community.

The most derisive critics of bureaucracy, and of middle-class society generally, were a group of young poets, writers, and artists known as the "beats" (or, by derisive critics, as "beatniks"). They wrote harsh critiques of what they considered the sterility and conformity of American life, the meaninglessness of American politics, and the banality of popular culture. Allen Ginsberg's dark, bitter poem *Howl* (1955) decried the "Robot apartments! invincible suburbs! skeleton treasuries! blind capitals! demonic industries!" of modern life. Jack Kerouac produced what may have been the central document of the Beat Generation in his novel *On the Road* (1957), an account of a cross-country automobile trip that depicted the rootless, iconoclastic lifestyle of Kerouac and his friends. Other, less starkly alienated writers—among them Saul Bellow, J. D. Salinger, John Updike, and John Cheever—also used their work to express misgivings about the enormity, the impersonality, and what they considered the hollowness of modern society.

THE OTHER AMERICA

It was relatively easy for white, middle-class Americans in the 1950s to believe that the world they knew—a world of economic growth, personal affluence, and cultural homogeneity—was the world virtually all Americans knew, that the values and assumptions they shared were ones that most other Americans shared too. But such beliefs were false. Even within the middle class, there was considerable restiveness—among women, intellectuals, young people, and others who found the middle-class consumer culture somehow unsatisfying, even stultifying. More importantly, large groups of Americans remained outside the circle of abundance and shared neither in the affluence of the middle class nor in many of its values.

On the Margins of the Affluent Society

In 1962, the socialist writer Michael Harrington published a celebrated book called *The Other America*, in which he chronicled the continuing existence of poverty in the United States. The conditions he described were not new. Only the attention he was bringing to them was.

The great economic expansion of the postwar years reduced poverty dramatically but did not eliminate it. In 1960, at any given moment, more than a fifth of all American families (over 30 million people) continued to live below what the government defined as the poverty line (down from a third of all families fifteen years before). Many millions more lived just above the official poverty line, but with incomes that gave them little comfort and no security.

Most of the poor—up to 80 percent—experienced poverty intermittently and temporarily. But approximately 20 percent of the poor were people for whom poverty was a continuous, debilitating reality from which there was no easy escape. That included approximately half the nation's elderly and a significant proportion of African Americans and Hispanics. Native Americans constituted the single poorest group in the country, a result in part of government policies that had undermined the economies of the reservations and driven many Indians into cities, where—unprepared for urban life— some lived in a poverty worse than that they had left.

This "hard-core" poverty rebuked the assumptions of those who argued that economic growth would eventually lead everyone into prosperity— that, as many claimed, "a rising tide lifts all boats." It was a poverty that the growing prosperity of the postwar era seemed to affect hardly at all, a poverty, as Harrington observed, that appeared "impervious to hope."

Rural Poverty

Among those on the margins of the affluent society were many rural Americans. In 1948, farmers had received 8.9 percent of the national income; in 1956, they received only 4.1 percent. In part, this decline reflected the steadily shrinking farm population; in 1956 alone, nearly 10 percent of the rural population moved into or was absorbed by cities. But it also reflected declining farm prices. Because of enormous surpluses in basic staples, prices fell 33 percent in those years, even though national income as a whole rose 50 percent at the same time. Even most farmers who managed to survive experienced substantial losses of income at the same time that the prices of many consumer goods rose.

Not all farmers were poor. Some were quite affluent. But the agrarian economy did produce substantial numbers of genuinely impoverished people. Black sharecroppers and tenant farmers continued to live at or below subsistence level throughout the rural South—in part because of the mechanization of cotton picking beginning in 1944, in part because of the development of synthetic fibers that reduced demand for cotton generally. (Two-thirds of the cotton acreage of the South went out of production between 1930 and 1960.) Migrant farmworkers, a group concentrated especially in the West and Southwest and containing many Mexican-American and Asian-American workers, lived in similarly dire circumstances. In rural areas without much commercial agriculture—such as the Appalachian region in the

818 ~ THE UNFINISHED NATION

East, where the decline of the coal economy reduced the one significant source of support for the region—whole communities lived in desperate poverty, increasingly cut off from the market economy. All these groups were vulnerable to malnutrition and even starvation.

The Inner Cities

As prospering white families moved from cities to suburbs in vast numbers, more and more inner-city neighborhoods became repositories for the poor, "ghettoes" from which there was no easy escape. The growth of these neighborhoods owed much to a vast migration of African Americans out of the countryside (where the cotton economy was in decline) and into industrial cities. Not all these migrants were poor, and many found in the city some of the same routes to economic progress that many whites were finding. But African Americans were substantially more likely to live in poverty than most other groups, in part because of the persistence of historic patterns of discrimination that denied them any real opportunities.

More than 3 million black men and women moved from the South to northern cities between 1940 and 1960, many more than had made the same journey in the Great Migration during and after World War I. Chicago, Detroit, Cleveland, New York, and other eastern and midwestern industrial cities experienced a major expansion of their black populations—both in absolute numbers and, even more, as a percentage of the whole, since so many whites were leaving at the same time.

Similar migrations from Mexico and Puerto Rico expanded poor Hispanic neighborhoods in many American cities at the same time. Between 1940 and 1960, nearly a million Puerto Ricans moved into American cities (the largest group to New York). Mexican workers crossed the border into Texas and California and swelled the already substantial Latino communities of such cities as San Antonio, Houston, San Diego, and Los Angeles (which by 1960 had the largest Mexican-American population of any city, approximately 500,000 people).

Why these inner-city communities, populated largely by racial and ethnic minorities, remained so poor in the midst of growing affluence has been the subject of considerable, and very heated, debate. But it is indisputable that inner cities were filling up with poor minority residents at the same time that the unskilled industrial jobs they were seeking were diminishing. Employers were moving factories and mills from old industrial cities to new locations in suburbs, smaller cities, and even abroad—places where the cost of labor or other things were lower. Even in the factories that remained, automation was reducing the number of unskilled jobs. The economic opportunities that had helped earlier immigrant groups to rise up from poverty were unavailable to many of the postwar migrants. Nor can there be any doubt that historic patterns of racial discrimination in hiring, education, and housing doomed many members of these communities to continuing, and in some cases increasing, poverty.

One result of inner-city poverty was a rising rate of juvenile crime. Indeed, "juvenile delinquency" was one of the few results of poverty that middle-class Americans discussed and worried about with any consistency. A 1955 book, *One Million Delinquents*, called juvenile crime a "national epidemic" and described a troubling subculture of inner-city youth—embittered, rebellious adolescents with no hope of advancement and no sense of having a stake in the structure of their society.

THE RISE OF THE CIVIL RIGHTS MOVEMENT

After decades of skirmishes, an open battle began in the 1950s against racial segregation and discrimination, a battle that would prove to be one of the longest and most difficult social struggles of the century. White Americans played an important role in the civil rights movement. But pressure from African Americans themselves was the crucial element in raising the issue of race to prominence.

The Brown *Decision and "Massive Resistance"*

On May 17, 1954, the Supreme Court announced one of the most important decisions in its history in the case of *Brown* v. *Board of Education of Topeka*. In considering the legal segregation of a Kansas public school system, the Court rejected its own 1896 *Plessy* v. *Ferguson* decision, which had ruled that communities could provide blacks with separate facilities as long as the facilities were equal to those of whites. The *Brown* decision unequivocally declared the segregation of public schools on the basis of race unconstitutional. The justices argued that school segregation inflicted unacceptable damage on those it affected, regardless of the relative quality of the separate schools. Chief Justice Earl Warren explained the unanimous opinion of his colleagues: "We conclude that in the field of public education the doctrine of 'separate but equal' has no place. Separate educational facilities are inherently unequal." The following year, the Court issued another decision (known as *Brown II*) to provide rules for implementing the 1954 order. It ruled that communities must work to desegregate their schools "with all deliberate speed," but it set no timetable and left specific decisions up to lower courts.

In some communities, for example, Washington, D.C., compliance came relatively quickly and quietly. More often, however, strong local opposition (what came to be known in the South as "massive resistance") produced long delays and bitter conflicts. Some school districts ignored the ruling altogether. Others attempted to circumvent it with purely token efforts to integrate. More than 100 southern members of Congress signed a "manifesto" in 1956 denouncing the *Brown* decision and urging their constituents to defy it. Southern governors, mayors, local school boards, and nongovernmental pressure groups (including hundreds of White Citizens' Councils) all worked to obstruct desegregation. By the fall of 1957, only 684 of 3,000 affected

CONFRONTATION IN LITTLE ROCK, 1957 After the governor of Arkansas, Orval Faubus, refused to call the National Guard to enforce court-ordered integration of Central High School in Little Rock, President Eisenhower federalized the troops and ordered them to protect the nine black students who were attempting to begin school. Conflicts over school integration would continue into the 1970s and beyond.

school districts in the South had even begun to desegregate their schools. The *Brown* decision, far from ending segregation, had launched a prolonged battle between federal authority and state and local governments.

The Eisenhower administration was not eager to commit itself to that battle. But in September 1957, it faced a case of direct state defiance of federal authority and felt compelled to act. Federal courts had ordered the desegregation of Central High School in Little Rock, Arkansas. An angry white mob tried to block implementation of the order by blockading the entrances to the school, and Governor Orval Faubus refused to do anything to stop the obstruction. President Eisenhower finally responded by sending federal troops to Little Rock to keep the peace and ensure that the court orders would be obeyed. Only then did Central High School admit its first black students.

The Expanding Movement

The *Brown* decision helped spark a growing number of popular challenges to segregation in the South. On December 1, 1955, Rosa Parks, an African-American woman, was arrested in Montgomery, Alabama, when she refused to give up her seat on a Montgomery bus to a white passenger (as required by the Jim Crow laws that regulated race relations in the city and throughout most of the South). Parks, an active civil rights leader in the community, had apparently decided spontaneously to resist the order to move. The arrest of this admired woman produced outrage in the city's African-American community, which organized a boycott of the bus system to demand an end to segregated seating.

Once launched, the boycott was almost completely effective. It put economic pressure not only on the bus company (a private concern) but on many Montgomery merchants, because the bus boycotters found it difficult to get to downtown stores and tended to shop instead in their own neighborhoods. Even so, the boycott might well have failed had it not been for a Supreme Court decision late in 1956, inspired in part by the protest, that declared segregation in public transportation to be illegal. The buses in Montgomery abandoned their discriminatory seating policies, and the boycott came to a close.

Perhaps the most important accomplishments of the Montgomery boycott were the legitimization of a new form of racial protest and the elevation to prominence of a new figure in the movement for civil rights. The man chosen to lead the boycott movement once it was launched was a local

Baptist pastor, Martin Luther King, Jr., the son of a prominent Atlanta minister, a powerful orator, and a gifted leader. King's approach to black protest was based on the doctrine of nonviolence—that is, of passive resistance even in the face of direct attack. And he produced an approach to racial struggle that captured the moral high ground for his supporters. For the next thirteen years—as leader of the Southern Christian Leadership Conference (SCLC), an interracial group he founded shortly after the bus boycott—he was the most influential and most widely admired black leader in the country. The popular movement he came to represent soon spread throughout the South and throughout the country.

EISENHOWER REPUBLICANISM

Dwight D. Eisenhower was the least experienced politician to serve in the White House in the twentieth century. He was also among the most popular and politically successful presidents of the postwar era. At home, he pursued essentially moderate policies, avoiding most new initiatives but accepting the work of earlier reformers. Abroad, he continued and even intensified American commitments to oppose communism but brought to some of those commitments a measure of restraint that his successors did not always match.

"What's Good for . . . General Motors"

The first Republican administration in twenty years staffed itself with men drawn from the same quarter as those who had staffed Republican administrations in the 1920s: the business community. But many in the American business community had acquired a very different social and political outlook by the 1950s from that of their predecessors of earlier decades. Above all, many of the nation's leading businessmen and financiers had reconciled themselves to at least the broad outlines of the Keynesian welfare state the New Deal had launched. Indeed, some corporate leaders had come to see it as something that actually benefited them—by helping maintain social order, by increasing mass purchasing power, and by stabilizing labor relations.

To his cabinet, Eisenhower appointed wealthy corporate lawyers and business executives who were not apologetic about their backgrounds. Charles Wilson, president of General Motors, assured senators considering his nomination for secretary of defense that he foresaw no conflict of interest because he was certain that "what was good for our country was good for General Motors, and vice versa." But missing from most members of this business-oriented administration was the deep hostility to "government interference" that had so dominated corporate attitudes three decades before.

Eisenhower's consistent inclination was to limit federal activities and encourage private enterprise. He supported the private rather than public development of natural resources (and once talked about selling the Tennessee Valley Authority to a private company). To the chagrin of farmers, he lowered federal support for farm prices. He also removed the last limited wage and price controls maintained by the Truman administration. He opposed the creation of new social service programs such as national health insurance. He strove constantly to reduce federal expenditures (even during the recession of 1958) and balance the budget. He ended 1960, his last full year in office, with a $1 billion budget surplus.

The president took few new initiatives in domestic policy, but he resisted pressure from the right wing of his party to dismantle those welfare policies of the New Deal that had survived the conservative assaults of the war years and after. Indeed, during his term, he agreed to extend the Social Security system to an additional 10 million people and unemployment compensation to an additional 4 million people, and he agreed to increase the minimum hourly wage from 75 cents to $1. Perhaps the most significant legislative accomplishment of the Eisenhower administration was the Federal Highway Act of 1956, which authorized $25 billion for a ten-year effort to construct over 40,000 miles of interstate highways. The program was to be funded through a highway "trust fund," whose revenues would come from new taxes on the purchase of fuel, automobiles, trucks, and tires.

In 1956, Eisenhower ran for a second term, even though he had suffered a serious heart attack the previous year. With Adlai Stevenson opposing him once again, he won by another, even greater landslide, receiving nearly 57 percent of the popular vote and 457 electoral votes to Stevenson's 73. Still, Democrats retained the control of both houses of Congress they had won back in 1954. And in 1958—during a serious recession—they increased that control by substantial margins.

The Decline of McCarthyism

The Eisenhower administration did little in its first years in office to discourage the anticommunist furor that had gripped the nation. Indeed, in many ways it helped sustain it. The president intensified the search for sub-

THE ARMY-McCARTHY HEARINGS Senator Joseph McCarthy uses a map
to show the supposed distribution of communists throughout the
United States during the televised 1954 Senate hearings to mediate
the dispute between McCarthy and the U.S. Army. Joseph Welch,
chief counsel for the army, remains conspicuously unimpressed.

versives in the government, which Truman had begun several years earlier.
More than 2,220 federal employees resigned or were dismissed as a result
of security investigations.

By 1954, however, such policies were beginning to produce significant
popular opposition—an indication that the anticommunist passion of several years earlier was beginning to abate. The clearest signal of that change
was the political demise of Senator Joseph McCarthy.

During the first year of the Eisenhower administration, McCarthy continued to operate with impunity. But McCarthy finally overreached himself
in January 1954 when he attacked Secretary of the Army Robert Stevens and
the armed services in general. At that point, the administration and influential members of Congress organized a special investigation of the charges,
which became known as the Army-McCarthy hearings. They were among
the first congressional hearings to be nationally televised.

The result was devastating to McCarthy. Watching McCarthy in
action—bullying witnesses, hurling groundless (and often cruel) accusations, evading issues—much of the public began to see him as a villain, and
even a buffoon. In December 1954, the Senate voted 67 to 22 to condemn

him for "conduct unbecoming a senator." Three years later, with little public support left, he died—a victim, apparently, of complications arising from alcoholism.

EISENHOWER, DULLES, AND THE COLD WAR

The threat of nuclear war with the Soviet Union created a sense of high anxiety in international relations in the 1950s. But the nuclear threat had another effect as well. With the potential devastation of an atomic war so enormous, both superpowers began to edge away from direct confrontations. The attention of both the United States and the Soviet Union began to turn to the rapidly escalating instability in the nations of the Third World.

Dulles and "Massive Retaliation"

Eisenhower's secretary of state, and (except for the president himself) the dominant figure in the nation's foreign policy in the 1950s, was John Foster Dulles, an aristocratic corporate lawyer with a stern moral revulsion to communism. He entered office denouncing the containment policies of the Truman years as excessively passive, arguing that the United States should pursue an active program of "liberation," which would lead to a "rollback" of communist expansion. Once in power, however, he had to defer to the far more moderate views of the president himself, and he began to develop a new set of doctrines that reflected the impact of nuclear weapons on the world.

The most prominent of those doctrines was the policy of "massive retaliation," which Dulles announced early in 1954. The United States would, he explained, respond to communist threats to its allies not by using conventional forces in local conflicts (a policy that had led to so much frustration in Korea) but by relying on "the deterrent of massive retaliatory power" (by which he clearly meant nuclear weapons).

In part, the new doctrines reflected Dulles's inclination for tense confrontations, an approach he once defined as "brinksmanship"—pushing the Soviet Union to the brink of war in order to exact concessions. But the real force behind the massive-retaliation policy was economics. With pressure growing both in and out of government for a reduction in American military expenditures, an increasing reliance on atomic weapons seemed to promise, as some advocates put it, "more bang for the buck."

France, America, and Vietnam

What had been the most troubling foreign policy concern of the Truman years—the war in Korea—plagued the Eisenhower administration only briefly. On July 27, 1953, negotiators at Panmunjom finally signed an agreement ending the hostilities. Each antagonist was to withdraw its troops a mile and a half from the existing battle line, which ran roughly along the 38th parallel, the prewar border between North and South Korea. A conference in Geneva was to consider means by which to reunite the nation peacefully—although in fact the 1954 meeting produced no agreement and left the cease-fire line as the apparently permanent border between the two countries.

Almost simultaneously, however, the United States was being drawn into a long, bitter struggle in Southeast Asia. Ever since 1945, France had been attempting to restore its authority over Vietnam, its one-time colony, which it had to abandon to the Japanese towards the end of World War II. Opposing the French, however, were the powerful nationalist forces of Ho Chi Minh, determined to win independence for their nation. Ho had hoped for American support in 1945, on the basis of the anticolonial rhetoric of the Atlantic Charter and Franklin Roosevelt's speeches, and also because he had received support from American intelligence forces during World War II while he was fighting the Japanese. But he was then, as he had been for many years, not only a committed nationalist but a committed communist. The Truman administration ignored him and supported the French, one of America's most important Cold War allies.

By 1954, Ho was receiving aid from communist China and the Soviet Union. America, in the meantime, had been paying most of the costs of France's ineffective military campaign in Vietnam since 1950. Early in 1954, 12,000 French troops became surrounded in a disastrous siege at the city of Dien Bien Phu. Only American intervention, it was clear, could prevent the total collapse of the French military effort. Yet despite the urgings of Secretary of State Dulles, Vice President Nixon, and others, Eisenhower refused to permit direct American military intervention in Vietnam, claiming that neither Congress nor America's other allies would support such action.

Without American aid, the French defense of Dien Bien Phu finally collapsed on May 7, 1954, and France quickly agreed to a settlement of the conflict at the same conference in Geneva that summer that was considering the Korean settlement. The Geneva accords on Vietnam of July 1954, to which the United States was not a direct party, established a supposedly temporary division of Vietnam along the 17th parallel. The north would be governed by Ho Chi Minh, the south by a pro-Western regime. Democratic elections would be the basis for uniting the nation in 1956. The agreement marked the end of the French commitment to Vietnam and the beginning of an expanded American presence there. The United States helped establish a pro-American government in the south, headed by Ngo Dinh Diem, a member of his country's Roman Catholic minority. Diem, it was clear, would not permit the 1956 elections, which he knew he would lose. He felt secure in his refusal because the United States had promised to provide him with ample military assistance against any attack from the north. (There is some evidence that the Soviet Union, eager to avoid a confrontation with the United States at this point, was at the same time pressuring Ho and his regime not to press for an election.)

Cold War Crises

American foreign policy in the 1950s rested on a reasonably consistent foundation: the containment policy, as revised by the Eisenhower administration. But the nation's leaders spent much of their time reacting to both real and imagined crises in far-flung areas of the world. Among them were a series of crises in the Middle East, a region in which the United States had been little involved until after World War II.

On May 14, 1948, after years of Zionist efforts and a dramatic decision by the new United Nations, the nation of Israel proclaimed its independence. President Truman recognized the new Jewish homeland the next day. But the creation of Israel, while it resolved some conflicts, created others. Palestinian Arabs, unwilling to accept being displaced from what they considered their own country, fought determinedly against the new state in 1948—the first of several Arab-Israeli wars.

Committed as the American government was to Israel, it was also concerned about the stability and friendliness of the Arab regimes in the oil-rich region, in which American petroleum companies had major investments. Thus the United States reacted with alarm as it watched Mohammed Mossadegh, the nationalist prime minister of Iran, begin to resist the presence of Western corporations in his nation in the early 1950s. In 1953, the American CIA joined forces with conservative Iranian military leaders to engineer a coup that drove Mossadegh from office. To replace him, the CIA helped elevate the young Shah of Iran, Mohammed Reza Pahlevi, from his position as token constitutional monarch to that of virtually absolute ruler. The Shah remained closely tied to the United States for the next twenty-five years.

American policy was less effective in dealing with the nationalist government of Egypt, under the leadership of General Gamal Abdel Nasser, which began to develop a trade relationship with the Soviet Union in the early 1950s. In 1956, to punish Nasser for his friendliness toward the communists, Dulles withdrew American offers to assist in building the great Aswan Dam across the Nile. A week later, Nasser retaliated by seizing control of the Suez Canal from the British, saying that he would use the income from it to build the dam himself.

On October 29, 1956, Israeli forces attacked Egypt. The next day the British and French landed troops in the Suez to drive the Egyptians from the canal. Dulles and Eisenhower feared that the Suez crisis would drive the Arab states toward the Soviet Union and precipitate a new world war. By refusing to support the invasion, and by joining in a United Nations denunciation of it, the United States helped pressure the French and British to withdraw and helped persuade Israel to agree to a truce with Egypt.

Cold War concerns affected American relations in Latin America as well. In 1954, the Eisenhower administration ordered the CIA to help topple the new, leftist government of Jacobo Arbenz Guzmán in Guatemala, a regime that Dulles (responding to the entreaties of the United Fruit Company, a major investor in Guatemala fearful of Arbenz) argued was potentially communist.

No nation in the region had been more closely tied to America than Cuba. Its leader, Fulgencio Batista, had ruled as a military dictator since 1952, when with American assistance he had toppled a more moderate government. Cuba's relatively prosperous economy had become a virtual fiefdom of American corporations, which controlled almost all the island's natural resources and had cornered over half the vital sugar crop. American organized-crime syndicates controlled much of Havana's lucrative hotel and nightlife business. In 1957, a popular movement of resistance to the Batista regime began to gather strength under the leadership of Fidel Castro. On January 1, 1959, with Batista having fled to exile in Spain, Castro marched into Havana and established a new government.

Castro soon began implementing drastic policies of land reform and expropriating foreign-owned businesses and resources. Cuban-American relations deteriorated rapidly as a result. When Castro began accepting assistance from the Soviet Union in 1960, the United States cut back the "quota" by which Cuba could export sugar to America at a favored price. Early in 1961, as one of its last acts, the Eisenhower administration severed diplomatic relations with Castro. Isolated by the United States, Castro soon cemented an alliance with the Soviet Union.

Europe and the Soviet Union

Although the problems of the Third World were moving slowly toward the center of American foreign policy, the direct relationship with the Soviet Union and the effort to resist communist expansion in Europe remained the principal concerns of the Eisenhower administration. In 1955, Eisenhower and other NATO leaders met with the Soviet premier, Nikolai Bulganin, at a cordial summit conference in Geneva. But when a subsequent conference of foreign ministers met to try to resolve specific issues, they could find no basis for agreement. Relations between the Soviet Union and the West soured further in 1956 in response to the Hungarian Revolution. Hungarian dissidents had launched a popular uprising in November to demand democratic reforms. Before the month was out, Soviet tanks and troops entered Budapest to crush the uprising and restore an orthodox, pro-Soviet regime. The Eisenhower administration refused to intervene. But the suppression of the uprising convinced many American leaders that Soviet policies had not softened.

The U-2 Crisis

In November 1958, Nikita Khrushchev, who had succeeded Bulganin as Soviet premier and Communist Party chief earlier that year, renewed the demands of his predecessors that the NATO powers abandon West Berlin. When the United States and its allies predictably refused, Khrushchev suggested that he and Eisenhower discuss the issue personally, both in visits to each other's countries and at a summit meeting in Paris in 1960. The United States agreed. Khrushchev's 1959 visit to America produced a cool but polite public response. Plans proceeded for the summit conference and for Eisenhower's visit to Moscow shortly thereafter. Only days before the scheduled beginning of the Paris meeting, however, the Soviet Union announced that it had shot down an American U-2, a high-altitude spy plane, over Russian territory. Its pilot, Francis Gary Powers, was in captivity. Khrushchev lashed back angrily, breaking up the Paris summit almost before it could begin and withdrawing his invitation to Eisenhower to visit the Soviet Union. But the U-2 incident may have been only a pretext. By the spring of 1960, Khrushchev was under pressure from hard-liners in the Kremlin to toughen his stance toward the West; he also knew that no agreement was possible on the Berlin issue. The U-2 incident may simply have been an excuse to avoid what he believed would be fruitless negotiations.

The events of 1960 provided a somber backdrop for the end of the Eisenhower administration. After eight years in office, Eisenhower had failed to eliminate, and in some respects had actually increased, the tensions between the United States and the Soviet Union. Yet Eisenhower had brought to the Cold War his own sense of the limits of American power. He had resisted military intervention in Vietnam. And he had placed a measure of restraint on those who urged the creation of an enormous American military establishment. In his farewell address in January 1961, he warned of the "unwarranted influence" of a vast "military-industrial complex." His caution, in both domestic and international affairs, stood in marked contrast to the attitudes of his successors, who argued that the United States must act more boldly and aggressively on behalf of its goals at home and abroad.

CHAPTER THIRTY-ONE

The Ordeal of Liberalism

Expanding the Liberal State ∼ *The Battle for Racial Equality*
"Flexible Response" and the Cold War ∼ *Vietnam*
The Traumas of 1968

 Y THE LATE 1950s, a growing restlessness was becoming visible beneath the apparently placid surface of American society. Anxiety about America's position in the world, growing pressures from African Americans and other minorities, the increasing visibility of poverty, the rising frustrations of women, and other long-suppressed discontents were beginning to make themselves felt in the nation's public life. Ultimately, that restlessness would make the 1960s one of the most turbulent and divisive eras of the twentieth century. But at first, it contributed to a bold and confident effort by political leaders to attack social and international problems within the framework of conventional liberal politics.

EXPANDING THE LIBERAL STATE

Those who yearned for a more active government in the late 1950s and who accused the Eisenhower administration of allowing the nation to "drift" looked above all to the presidency for leadership. The two men who served in the White House through most of the 1960s—John Kennedy and Lyndon Johnson—seemed for a time to be the embodiment of these liberal hopes.

John Kennedy

The campaign of 1960 produced two young candidates who claimed to offer the nation active leadership. The Republican nomination went almost uncontested to Vice President Richard Nixon, who promised moderate reform. The Democrats, in the meantime, emerged from a spirited primary cam-

TIME LINE			
1960	**1961**	**1962**	**1963**
Kennedy elected president	Freedom rides Bay of Pigs Berlin Wall erected	Cuban missile crisis	March on Washington Kennedy assassinated; Johnson becomes president
1964	**1965**	**1967**	**1968**
Johnson launches war on poverty Civil Rights Act Gulf of Tonkin Resolution Johnson elected president	Malcolm X assassinated Voting Rights Act U.S. troops in Vietnam	Antiwar movement grows	Tet offensive Martin Luther King, Jr. assassinated Robert Kennedy assassinated Nixon elected president

paign united, somewhat uneasily, behind John Fitzgerald Kennedy, an attractive and articulate senator from Massachusetts who had narrowly missed being the party's vice presidential candidate in 1956.

John Kennedy was the son of the wealthy, powerful, and highly controversial Joseph P. Kennedy, former American ambassador to Britain. But while he had grown up in a world of ease and privilege, he became a spokesman for energy and sacrifice. He premised his campaign, he said, "on the single assumption that the American people are uneasy at the present drift in our national course." But his appealing public image was at least as important as his political positions in attracting popular support. He overcame doubts about his youth (he turned forty-three in 1960) and religion (he was a Catholic) to win with a tiny plurality of the popular vote—49.9 percent to Nixon's 49.6 percent and only a slightly more comfortable electoral majority—303 to 219.

Kennedy had campaigned promising a set of domestic reforms more ambitious than any since the New Deal, a program he described as the "New Frontier." But his thin popular mandate and a Congress dominated by a coalition of Republicans and conservative Democrats frustrated many of his hopes. As a result, the president had to look elsewhere for opportunities to display positive leadership. One area where he believed he could do that was the economy. Economic growth was sluggish in 1961 when Kennedy entered the White House, with unemployment hovering at about 6 percent of the work force. Kennedy initiated a series of tariff negotiations with foreign governments—the "Kennedy Round"—in an effort to stimulate American

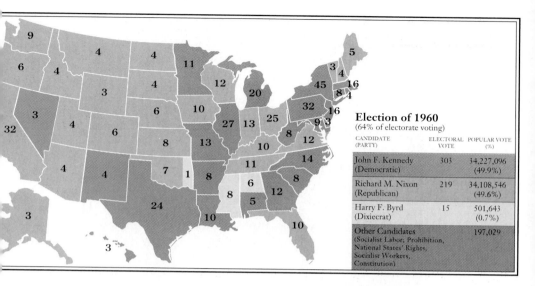

Election of 1960
(64% of electorate voting)

CANDIDATE (PARTY)	ELECTORAL VOTE	POPULAR VOTE (%)
John F. Kennedy (Democratic)	303	34,227,096 (49.9%)
Richard M. Nixon (Republican)	219	34,108,546 (49.6%)
Harry F. Byrd (Dixiecrat)	15	501,643 (0.7%)
Other Candidates (Socialist Labor; Prohibition, National States' Rights, Socialist Workers, Constitution)		197,029

exports. He began to consider an expanded use of Keynesian fiscal and monetary tools—culminating in his 1962 proposal for a substantial federal tax cut to stimulate the economy.

He also used his personal prestige to battle inflation. In 1962, several steel companies, led by U.S. Steel, announced that they were raising their prices by $6 a ton, a move certain to trigger similar action by the rest of the industry. Kennedy put heavy pressure on U.S. Steel president Roger Blough and other steel executives to rescind the increase. The companies soon relented. But it was a fleeting victory, which permanently strained Kennedy's relationship with the corporate community. A few months later the steel companies quietly raised prices again. The president did not protest.

More than any other president of the century (except perhaps the two Roosevelts and, later, Ronald Reagan), Kennedy made his own personality an integral part of his presidency and a central focus of national attention. Nothing illustrated that more clearly than the popular reaction to the tragedy of November 22, 1963. Kennedy had traveled to Texas with his wife and Vice President Lyndon Johnson for a series of political appearances. While the presidential motorcade rode slowly through the streets of Dallas, shots rang out. Two bullets struck the president—one in the throat, the other in the head. He was sped to a nearby hospital, where minutes later he was pronounced dead. Lee Harvey Oswald, who appeared to be a confused and embittered Marxist, was arrested for the crime later that day, and then mysteriously murdered by a Dallas nightclub owner, Jack Ruby, two days later as he was being moved from one jail to another. The popular assumption at

JOHN F. KENNEDY AND HIS ADVISERS Kennedy meets in the
White House with Robert McNamara and General Maxwell
Taylor, two men who would play important roles in the
process that would lead to full-scale American military
intervention in Vietnam.

the time was that both Oswald and Ruby had acted alone, assumptions endorsed by a federal commission, chaired by Chief Justice Earl Warren, that
was appointed to investigate the assassination. In later years, however, many
Americans came to believe that the Warren Commission report had ignored evidence of a wider conspiracy behind the murders.

Lyndon Johnson

The Kennedy assassination was a national trauma—a defining event for almost everyone old enough to be aware of it. At the time, however, much of
the nation took comfort in the personality and performance of Kennedy's
successor in the White House, Lyndon Baines Johnson. Johnson was a native of the poor "hill country" of west Texas and had risen to become majority leader of the U.S. Senate by dint of extraordinary, even obsessive ef-

fort and ambition. Having failed to win the Democratic nomination for president in 1960, he surprised many who knew him by agreeing to accept the second position on the ticket with Kennedy. The events in Dallas thrust him into the White House.

Johnson's rough-edged, even crude personality could hardly have been more different from Kennedy's. But like Kennedy, Johnson was a man who believed in the active use of power. And he proved, in the end, more effective than his predecessor in translating his goals into reality. Between 1963 and 1966, he compiled the most impressive legislative record of any president since Franklin Roosevelt. He was aided by the tidal wave of emotion that followed the death of President Kennedy, which helped win support for many New Frontier proposals. But Johnson constructed a remarkable reform program of his own, one that he ultimately labeled the "Great Society." And he won approval of much of it through the same sort of skillful lobbying in Congress that had made him an effective majority leader.

Johnson envisioned himself as a great "coalition builder." He wanted the support of everyone, and for a time he very nearly got it. His first year in office was, by necessity, dominated by the campaign for reelection. There was little doubt that he would win—particularly after the Republican Party fell under the sway of its right wing and nominated the conservative Senator Barry Goldwater of Arizona. In the November election, the president received a larger plurality, over 61 percent, than any candidate before or since. Goldwater managed to carry only his home state of Arizona and five states in the Deep South. Record Democratic majorities in both houses of Congress, many of whose members had been swept into office only because of the margin of Johnson's victory, ensured that the president would be able to fulfill many of his goals.

The Assault on Poverty

For the first time since the 1930s, the federal government took steps in the 1960s to create important new social welfare programs. The most important of these, perhaps, was Medicare: a program to provide federal aid to the elderly for medical expenses. Its enactment in 1965 came at the end of a bitter, twenty-year debate between those who believed in the concept of national health assistance and those who denounced it as "socialized medicine." But the program as it went into effect placated many critics. For one thing, it avoided the stigma of "welfare" by making Medicare benefits available to all elderly Americans, regardless of need (just as Social Security had done with pensions). That created a large middle-class constituency for the program. The program also defused the opposition of the medical community by allowing doctors serving Medicare patients to practice privately and to charge their normal fees; Medicare simply shifted responsibility for paying those fees from the patient to the government. In 1966, Johnson steered to passage the Medicaid program, which extended federal medical assistance to welfare recipients and other indigent people of all ages.

Medicare and Medicaid were the first steps in a much larger assault on poverty—one that Kennedy had been planning in the last months of his life and that Johnson launched only weeks after taking office. The centerpiece of this "war on poverty," as Johnson called it, was the Office of Economic Opportunity (OEO), which created an array of new educational, employment, housing, and health-care programs. But the OEO was controversial from the start, in part because of its commitment to the idea of "community action."

Community action was an effort to involve members of poor communities themselves in the planning and administration of the programs designed to help them. The Community Action programs provided jobs for many poor people and gave them valuable experience in administrative and political work. Many men and women who went on to significant careers in politics or community organizing, including many black and Hispanic politicians, as well as many Indians, got their start in Community Action programs.

But despite its achievements, the Community Action approach proved impossible to sustain. Many programs fell victim to mismanagement or to powerful opposition from the local governments with which they were at times competing. Some activists in Community Action agencies employed tactics that mainstream politicians considered frighteningly radical. The apparent excesses of a few agencies damaged the popular image of the Community Action programs, and indeed the war on poverty, as a whole.

The OEO spent nearly $3 billion during its first two years of existence, and it helped reduce poverty in some areas. But it fell far short of eliminating poverty altogether. That was in part because of the weaknesses of the programs themselves and in part because funding for them, inadequate from the beginning, dwindled as the years passed and a costly war in Southeast Asia became the nation's first priority.

Cities, Schools, and Immigration

Closely tied to the antipoverty program were federal efforts to promote the revitalization of decaying cities and to strengthen the nation's schools. The Housing Act of 1961 offered $4.9 billion in federal grants to cities for the preservation of open spaces, the development of mass-transit systems, and the subsidization of middle-income housing. In 1966, Johnson established a new cabinet agency, the Department of Housing and Urban Development (whose first secretary, Robert Weaver, was the first African American ever to serve in the cabinet). Johnson also inaugurated the Model Cities program, which offered federal subsidies for urban redevelopment.

Kennedy had long fought for federal aid to public education, but he had failed to overcome two important obstacles: Many Americans feared that aid to education was the first step toward federal control of the schools, and Catholics insisted that federal assistance must extend to parochial as well as public schools. Johnson managed to circumvent both objections with the Elementary and Secondary Education Act of 1965 and a series of subsequent measures. The bills extended aid to both private and parochial schools and based the aid on the economic conditions of the students, not on the needs of the schools themselves. Total federal expenditures for education and technical training rose from $5 billion to $12 billion between 1964 and 1967.

The Johnson administration also supported the Immigration Act of 1965, one of the most important pieces of legislation of the 1960s, even if largely unnoticed at the time. The law maintained a strict limit on the number of newcomers admitted to the country each year (170,000), but it eliminated the "national origins" system established in the 1920s, which gave preference to immigrants from northern Europe over those from other parts of the world. It continued to restrict immigration from some parts of Latin America, but it allowed people from all parts of Europe, Asia, and Africa to enter the United States on an equal basis. By the early 1970s, the character of American immigration had changed, with members of new national groups—and particularly large groups of Asian—entering the United States and changing the character of the American population.

Legacies of the Great Society

Taken together, the Great Society reforms meant a significant increase in federal spending. For a time, rising tax revenues from the growing economy nearly compensated for the new expenditures. In 1964, Johnson managed to win passage of the $11.5 billion tax cut that Kennedy had first proposed in 1962. The cut increased the federal deficit, but it helped produce substantial economic growth over the next several years that made up for much of the revenue initially lost. As Great Society programs began to multiply, however, and particularly as they began to compete with the escalating costs of America's military ventures, the federal budget rapidly outpaced increases in revenues. In 1961, the federal government had spent $94.4 billion. By 1970, that sum had risen to $196.6 billion.

The high costs of the Great Society programs and the inability of the government to find the revenues to pay for them contributed to a growing disillusionment in later years with the idea of federal efforts to solve social problems. By the 1980s, many Americans had become convinced that the Great Society efforts had not worked and that, indeed, government programs to solve social problems could not work. But the Great Society was far from a failure. It significantly reduced hunger in America. It made medical care available to millions of elderly and poor people who would otherwise have had great difficulty affording it. And it contributed to the greatest reduction in poverty in American history. In 1959, according to the most widely accepted estimates, 21 percent of the American people lived below the officially established poverty line. By 1969, only 12 percent remained below that line. The improvements affected blacks and whites in about the same proportion: 56 percent of the black population had lived in poverty in 1959, while only 32 percent did so ten years later—a 42 percent reduction; 18 percent of all whites had been poor in 1959, but only 10 percent were poor a decade later—a 44 percent reduction. Much of that progress was a result of economic growth, but some of it was a result of Great Society programs.

THE BATTLE FOR RACIAL EQUALITY

The nation's most important domestic initiative in the 1960s was the effort to provide justice and equality to African Americans. It was the most difficult commitment, the one that produced the severest strains on American society. But it was one that could not be avoided. African Americans were themselves ensuring that the nation would have to deal with the problem of race.

Expanding Protests

John Kennedy had long been sympathetic to the cause of racial justice, but he was hardly a committed crusader. Like presidents before him, he feared alienating southern Democratic voters and powerful southern Democrats in Congress. His administration hoped to contain the racial problem by expanding enforcement of existing laws and supporting litigation to overturn existing segregation statutes.

But the pressure for change could not long be contained. In February 1960, black college students in Greensboro, North Carolina, staged a sit-in at a segregated Woolworth's lunch counter; and in the following months, such demonstrations spread throughout the South, forcing many merchants to integrate their facilities. In the fall of 1960, some of those who had participated in the sit-ins formed the Student Nonviolent Coordinating Committee (SNCC)—a student branch of Martin Luther King, Jr.'s Southern Christian Leadership Council; SNCC worked to keep the spirit of resistance alive.

In 1961, an interracial group of students, working with the Congress of Racial Equality (CORE), began what they called "freedom rides." Traveling by bus throughout the South, they tried to force the desegregation of bus stations. They were met in some places with such savage violence on the part of whites that the president finally dispatched federal marshals to help keep the peace and ordered the integration of all bus and train stations.

Events in the Deep South in 1963 helped bring the growing movement to something of a climax. In April, Martin Luther King, Jr., helped launch a series of nonviolent demonstrations in Birmingham, Alabama, a city unsurpassed in the strength of its commitment to segregation. Police Commissioner Eugene "Bull" Connor personally supervised a brutal effort to break up the peaceful marches, arresting hundreds of demonstrators and using attack dogs, tear gas, electric cattle prods, and fire hoses—at times even against small children—as much of the nation watched televised reports in horror. Two months later, Governor George Wallace stood in the doorway of a building at the University of Alabama to prevent the court-ordered enrollment of several black students. Only after the arrival of federal marshals did he give way. The same night, NAACP official Medgar Evers was murdered in Mississippi.

A National Commitment

The events in Alabama and Mississippi were a warning to the president that he could not any longer contain or avoid the issue of race. In an important television address the night of the University of Alabama confrontation, Kennedy spoke eloquently of the "moral issue" facing the nation. Days later, he introduced a series of new legislative proposals prohibiting segregation in "public accommodations" (stores, restaurants, theaters, hotels), barring discrimination in employment, and increasing the power of the government to file suits on behalf of school integration.

To generate support for the legislation, and to dramatize the power of

THE MARCH ON WASHINGTON, 1963 Martin Luther King, Jr. waves to the vast crowd spreading out from the Lincoln Memorial shortly after delivering his famous "I Have a Dream" speech—the centerpiece of the March on Washington. Initially envisioned as a broad and militant protest against discrimination, it became in the end a moderate, interracial demonstration of support for the civil rights bill President Kennedy had recently proposed to Congress, which passed in 1964.

the growing movement, more than 200,000 demonstrators marched down the Mall in Washington, D.C., in August 1963 and gathered before the Lincoln Memorial for the largest civil rights demonstration in the nation's history. Martin Luther King, Jr., in one of the greatest speeches of his distinguished oratorical career, aroused the crowd with a litany of images prefaced again and again by the phrase "I have a dream."

The assassination of President Kennedy three months later gave new impetus to the battle for civil rights legislation. The ambitious measure that Kennedy had proposed in June 1963 was stalled in the Senate after having passed through the House of Representatives with relative ease. Early in 1964, after Johnson had applied both public and private pressure, supporters of the measure finally mustered the two-thirds majority necessary to close debate and end a filibuster by southern senators; and the Senate passed the most comprehensive civil rights bill in the history of the nation.

The Battle for Voting Rights

Having won a significant victory in one area, the civil rights movement shifted its focus to another: voting rights. During the summer of 1964, thousands of civil rights workers, black and white, northern and southern, spread out through the South, but primarily in Mississippi, to work on behalf of black voter registration and participation. The campaign was known as "Freedom Summer," and it produced a violent response from some southern whites. Three of the first freedom workers to arrive in the South—two whites, Andrew Goodman and Michael Schwerner, and one black, James Chaney—were murdered. Local law enforcement officials were involved in the crime.

The "Freedom Summer" also produced the Mississippi Freedom Democratic Party (MFDP), an integrated alternative to the regular state party organization. Under the leadership of Fannie Lou Hamer and others, the MFDP challenged the regular party's right to its seats at the Democratic National Convention that summer. President Johnson, with King's help, managed to broker a compromise by which members of the MFDP could be seated as observers, with promises of party reforms later on, while the regular party retained its official standing. Many MFDP members rejected the agreement and left the convention embittered.

A year later, in March 1965, King helped organize a major demonstration in Selma, Alabama, to press the demand for the right of blacks to register to vote. Selma sheriff Jim Clark led local police in a brutal attack on the demonstrators—which, as in Birmingham, was televised to a horrified nation. Two northern whites participating in the Selma march were murdered in the course of the effort there—one, a minister, beaten to death in the streets of the town; the other, a Detroit housewife, shot as she drove along a highway at night. The national outrage that followed the events in Alabama helped push Lyndon Johnson to propose and win passage of the Civil Rights Act of 1965, which provided federal protection to African Americans attempting to exercise their right to vote. But important as such gains were, they failed to satisfy the rapidly rising expectations of American blacks, as the focus of the movement began to move from political to economic issues.

The Changing Movement

For decades, the nation's African-American population had been undergoing a major demographic shift. By 1966, 69 percent of American blacks were living in metropolitan areas and 45 percent outside the South. Although the economic condition of much of American society was improving, in many of the poor urban communities in which much of the black population was becoming concentrated, things were getting significantly worse. More than half of all American nonwhites lived in poverty at the beginning of the 1960s; black unemployment was twice that of whites.

By the mid-1960s, therefore, the issue of race was moving out of the South and into the rest of the nation. The legal battle for school integration was moving beyond the issue of formal, legal segregation to an attack on the informal practices that often sustained separation of the races. That carried the fight into northern cities, which had no Jim Crow laws but much segregation. Many African-American leaders (and their white supporters) were demanding, similarly, that the battle against job discrimination move to a new level. They argued that the only way for employers to prove that they were not discriminating against African Americans was for them to demonstrate that they were hiring minorities. If necessary, they should adopt positive measures to recruit minorities. Lyndon Johnson gave his support to the concept of "affirmative action" in 1965. Over the next decade, affirmative action guidelines gradually extended to virtually all institutions doing business with or receiving funds from the federal government (including schools and universities)—and to many others as well.

A symbol of the movement's new direction, and of the problems it would cause, was a major campaign in the summer of 1966 in Chicago, in which King played a prominent role. Organizers of the Chicago campaign hoped to direct national attention to housing and employment discrimination in northern industrial cities in much the same way that similar campaigns had exposed legal racism in the South. But the Chicago campaign not only evoked vicious and at times violent opposition from white residents of that city; it failed to attract wide attention or support in the way events in the South had done.

Urban Violence

Well before the Chicago campaign, the problem of urban poverty had thrust itself into national prominence when riots broke out in black neighborhoods in major cities. There were a few scattered disturbances in the summer of 1964, most notably in New York City's Harlem. The first large race riot since the end of World War II occurred the following summer in the Watts section of Los Angeles. In the midst of a traffic arrest, a white police officer struck a protesting black bystander with his club. The incident triggered a storm of anger and a week of violence. Thirty-four people died during the uprising, which was eventually quelled by the National Guard. In the summer of 1966, there were forty-three additional outbreaks, the most serious of them in Chicago and Cleveland. And in the summer of 1967, there were eight major riots, including the largest of them all—a racial clash in Detroit in which forty-three people died.

Televised reports of the violence alarmed millions of Americans and created both a new sense of urgency and a growing sense of doubt among some whites who had embraced the cause of racial justice only a few years before. A special Commission on Civil Disorders, created by the president in response to the riots, issued a celebrated report in the spring of 1968 recommending massive spending to eliminate the abysmal conditions of the ghettoes. To many white Americans, however, the lesson of the riots was the need for stern measures to stop violence and lawlessness.

Black Power

Disillusioned with the ideal of peaceful change through cooperation with whites, an increasing number of African Americans were turning to a new approach to the racial issue: the philosophy of "black power." Black power could mean many different things. But in all its forms, it suggested a shift away from the goal of assimilation and toward increased awareness of racial distinctiveness.

Perhaps the most enduring impact of the black-power ideology was a social and psychological one: instilling racial pride in African Americans who had been taught by their nation's dominant culture to think of themselves as somehow inferior to whites. But black power took political forms as well, and it created a deep schism within the civil rights movement. Traditional black organizations that emphasized cooperation with sympathetic whites— groups such as the NAACP, the Urban League, and King's Southern Christian Leadership Conference—now faced competition from more radical groups. The Student Nonviolent Coordinating Committee and the Congress of Racial Equality had both begun as relatively moderate, interracial organizations. By the mid-1960s, however, these and other groups were calling for more radical and occasionally even violent action against the racism of white society and were openly rejecting the approaches of older, more established black leaders.

The most radical expressions of the black-power idea came from such revolutionary organizations as the Black Panthers, based in Oakland, California, and the separatist group, the Nation of Islam, which denounced whites as "devils" and appealed to blacks to embrace the Islamic faith and

A M E R I C A N   V O I C E S

MALCOLM X

The Angriest Negro in America

 THEY CALLED me "the angriest Negro in America." I wouldn't deny that charge. I spoke exactly as I felt. "I *believe* in anger. The Bible says there is a *time* for anger." They called me "a teacher, a fomentor of violence." I would say point blank, "That is a lie. I'm not for wanton violence, I'm for justice. I feel that if white people were attacked by Negroes—if the forces of law prove unable, or inadequate, or reluctant to protect those whites from those Negroes—then those white people should protect and defend themselves from those Negroes, using arms if necessary. And I feel that when the law fails to protect Negroes from whites' attack, then those Negroes should use arms, if necessary, to defend themselves." . . .

What was wrong with that? I'll tell you what was wrong. I was a black man talking about physical defense against the white man. The white man can lynch and burn and bomb and beat Negroes—that's all right: "Have patience" . . . "The customs are entrenched" . . . "Things are getting better."

Well, I believe it's a crime for anyone who is being brutalized to continue to accept that brutality without doing something to defend himself. . . . I don't go for non-violence if it also means a delayed solution. To me a delayed solution is a non-solution.

SOURCE: *The Autobiography of Malcolm X*, pp. 366–367. © 1964 by Alex Haley and Malcolm X, © 1965 by Malcolm X and Betty Shabazz. Reprinted by permission of Ballantine Books.

work for complete racial separation. The most celebrated of the Black Muslims, as whites often termed them, was Malcolm Little, who had adopted the name Malcolm X ("X" to denote his lost African surname). He died in 1965 when black gunmen, presumably under orders from rivals within the Nation of Islam, assassinated him. But he remained a major figure in many black communities long after his death—as important to and revered by many African Americans as Martin Luther King, Jr.

"FLEXIBLE RESPONSE" AND THE COLD WAR

In international affairs as much as in domestic reform, the optimistic liberalism of the Kennedy and Johnson administrations dictated a more active and aggressive approach to dealing with the nation's problems than that of the 1950s.

Diversifying Foreign Policy

The Kennedy administration entered office convinced that the United States needed to be able to counter communist aggression in more flexible ways than the atomic weapons–oriented defense strategy of the Eisenhower years permitted. In particular, Kennedy was unsatisfied with the nation's ability to meet communist threats in "emerging areas" of the Third World—the areas in which, Kennedy believed, the real struggle against communism would be waged in the future. He gave enthusiastic support to the expansion of the Special Forces (or "Green Berets," as they were soon known)—soldiers trained specifically to fight guerrilla conflicts and other limited wars.

Kennedy also favored expanding American influence through peaceful means. To repair the badly deteriorating relationship with Latin America, he proposed an "Alliance for Progress": a series of projects for peaceful development and stabilization of the nations of that region. Kennedy also inaugurated the Agency for International Development (AID) to coordinate foreign aid. And he established what became one of his most popular innovations: the Peace Corps, which sent young American volunteers abroad to work in developing areas.

Among the first foreign policy ventures of the Kennedy administration was a disastrous assault on the Castro government in Cuba. The Eisenhower administration had launched the project; and by the time Kennedy took office, the CIA had been working for months to train a small army of anti-

The United States in Latin Amer[ica]
1954–1996

- U.S. possessions
- U.S. interventions

0 — 400 Miles
0 — 400 Kilometers

UNITED STATES
- Houston
- New Orleans
- *Gulf of Mexico*

ATLANTIC OCEAN

- Miami

BAHAMAS

CUBA
1959: Batista overthrown and Castro installed
1961: Unsuccessful anti-Castro invasion backed by CIA
1962: U.S. blockade of Cuba during missile crisis
1994–1995: U.S. and Cuba agree on limiting legal immigration into U.S. from Cuba

- Havana

Guantanamo (U.S.-leased naval base)

DOMINICAN REPUBLIC
1965–1966: Occupation by U.S. forces following overthrow of Trujillo

- Santo Domingo
- San Juan

VIRGIN ISLANDS

PUERTO RICO

MEXICO
- Mexico City

GUATEMALA
1954: U.S.-backed overthrow of socialist government
1954–1976, 1981–1995: military support
1995: U.S. cuts off aid in response to failure to punish crimes committed by military in civil war

- Guatemala City

BELIZE

HONDURAS
1981–present: U.S. military and economic aid

- Tegucigalpa

JAMAICA

Caribbean Sea

HAITI
1986 U.S. flies J.-C. Duvalier into exile
1994: U.S. military force secures return of elected president Aristide

GRENADA
1983: Invasion by U.S. and regional allies; restoration of pro-Western government

NICARAGUA
1979: Overthrow of Somoza followed by U.S. aid to *Contras*
1981–1990: U.S. military and economic support for anti-Sandinista forces

- Managua

PACIFIC OCEAN

EL SALVADOR
1980–present: Increased military and economic support to government during civil war

- San Salvador

COSTA RICA
U.S. military and economic aid

PANAMA
1978: Canal Zone Treaty—control returned to Panama, U.S. retains control of canal operation to 1999
1989: U.S. troops ensure ouster of Noriega
1990: U.S. troops help stop pro-Noriega rebellion

- Panama City

COLOMBIA

- Caracas

VENEZUELA
1958 Anti-Nixon riots

Castro Cuban exiles in Central America. On April 17, 1961, with the approval of the new president, 2,000 of the armed exiles landed at the Bay of Pigs in Cuba, expecting first American air support and then a spontaneous uprising by the Cuban people on their behalf. They received neither. At the last minute, as it became clear that things were going badly, Kennedy withdrew the air support, fearful of involving the United States too directly in the invasion. The expected uprising did not occur. Instead, well-armed Castro forces easily crushed the invaders, and within two days the entire mission had collapsed.

Confrontations with the Soviet Union

In the grim aftermath of the Bay of Pigs, Kennedy traveled to Vienna in June 1961 for his first meeting with Soviet Premier Nikita Khrushchev. Their frosty exchange of views did little to reduce tensions between the two nations. Nor did Khrushchev's veiled threat of war unless the United States ceased to support a noncommunist West Berlin in the heart of East Germany.

Khrushchev was particularly unhappy about the mass exodus of residents of East Germany to the West through the easily traversed border in the center of Berlin. But he ultimately found a method short of war to stop it. Before dawn on August 13, 1961, the East German government, complying with directives from Moscow, constructed a wall between East and West Berlin. Guards fired on those who continued to try to escape. For nearly thirty years, the Berlin Wall served as the most potent physical symbol of the conflict between the communist and noncommunist worlds.

The rising tensions culminated the following October in the most dangerous and dramatic crisis of the Cold War. During the summer of 1962, American intelligence agencies had become aware of the arrival of a new wave of Soviet technicians and equipment in Cuba and of military construction in progress. On October 14, aerial reconnaissance photos produced clear evidence that the Soviets were constructing sites on the island for offensive nuclear weapons. To the Soviets, placing missiles in Cuba probably seemed a reasonable—and relatively inexpensive—way to counter the presence of American missiles in Turkey (and a way to deter any future American invasion of Cuba). But to Kennedy and most other Americans, the missile sites represented an act of aggression by the Soviets toward the United States. Almost immediately, the president decided that the weapons could not be allowed to remain. On October 22, he ordered a naval and air blockade around Cuba, a "quarantine" against all offensive weapons. Preparations were under way for an American air attack on the missile sites when, late in the evening of October 26, Kennedy received a message from Khrushchev implying that the Soviet Union would remove the missile bases in exchange for an American pledge not to invade Cuba. Ignoring other, tougher Soviet messages, the president agreed. The crisis was over.

Johnson and the World

Lyndon Johnson entered the presidency lacking even John Kennedy's limited prior experience with international affairs. He was eager, therefore, not only to continue the policies of his predecessor but to prove quickly that he too was a strong and forceful leader.

An internal rebellion in the Dominican Republic gave him an early opportunity to do so. A 1961 assassination had toppled the repressive dictatorship of General Rafael Trujillo, and for the next four years various factions in the country had struggled for dominance. In the spring of 1965, a conservative military regime began to collapse in the face of a revolt by a broad range of groups on behalf of the left-wing nationalist Juan Bosch. Arguing (without any evidence) that Bosch planned to establish a pro-Castro, communist regime, Johnson dispatched 30,000 American troops to quell the disorder. Only after a conservative candidate defeated Bosch in a 1966 election were the forces withdrawn.

From Johnson's first moments in office, however, his foreign policy was almost totally dominated by the bitter civil war in Vietnam and by the expanding involvement of the United States there.

VIETNAM

George Kennan, who helped devise the containment doctrine in the name of which America went to war in Vietnam, once called the conflict "the most disastrous of all America's undertakings over the whole 200 years of its history." In retrospect, few would now wholly disagree. Yet at first, the conflict in Vietnam seemed simply one more Third World struggle on the periphery of the Cold War.

The First Indochina War

Vietnam had been a colony of France since the mid-nineteenth century. And like other European possessions in Asia, it fell under the control of Japan during World War II. After the defeat of Japan, the question arose of what was to happen to Vietnam in the postwar world. The French wanted to reassert their control over Vietnam. Challenging them was a powerful nationalist movement within Vietnam committed to creating an independent nation. The nationalists were organized into a political party, the Vietminh, which had been created in 1941 and led ever since by Ho Chi Minh, a communist educated in Paris and Moscow, and a fervent believer in Vietnamese independence. The Vietminh had fought against Japan throughout World War II (unlike the French colonial officials who had remained in Vietnam until the last year of the war—as representatives of the Vichy regime—and had collaborated with the Japanese). In the fall of 1945, after the collapse of Japan and before the Western powers had time to return, the Vietminh declared Vietnam an independent nation and set up a government under Ho Chi Minh in Hanoi.

Ho had worked closely during the war with American intelligence forces in Indochina in fighting the Japanese; he apparently considered the United

States something like an ally. When the war ended in 1945, he began writing President Truman asking for support in his struggle against the French. He received no reply to his letters, probably because no one in the State Department had heard of him. At the same time, Truman was under heavy pressure from both the British and the French to support France in its effort to reassert its control over Vietnam. The French argued that without Vietnam, their domestic economy would collapse. And since the economic revival of Western Europe was quickly becoming one of the Truman administration's top priorities, the United States did nothing to stop (although, at first, also relatively little to encourage) the French as they moved back into Vietnam in 1946 and began a struggle with the Vietminh to regain control over the country.

At first, the French had little difficulty reestablishing control. They drove Ho Chi Minh out of Hanoi. But the Vietminh continued to challenge the French-dominated regime and slowly increased its control over large areas of the countryside. The French appealed to the United States for support, and in February 1950, the Truman administration agreed to provide them with direct military and economic aid.

For the next four years, during what has become known as the First Indochina War, Truman and then Eisenhower continued to support the French military campaign against the Vietminh; by 1954, by some calculations, the United States was paying 80 percent of France's war costs. But the war went badly for the French anyway. Finally, late in 1953, Vietminh forces surrounded the French during a major battle in the far northwest corner of the country, at Dien Bien Phu. The result was a prolonged siege, with the French position steadily deteriorating. It was at this point that the Eisenhower administration decided not to intervene to save the French (see p. 824). The defense of Dien Bien Phu soon collapsed, and the French government decided the time had come to get out. The First Indochina War had come to an end.

Geneva and the Two Vietnams

An international conference at Geneva, planned many months before to settle the Korean dispute and other controversies, now took up the fate of Vietnam as well. The United States was only indirectly involved in the Vietnam phase of the Geneva Conference and never signed the accords. Even so, the Geneva Conference produced an agreement to end the Vietnam conflict. There would be an immediate cease-fire in the war; Vietnam would be temporarily partitioned along the 17th parallel, with the Vietminh in control of

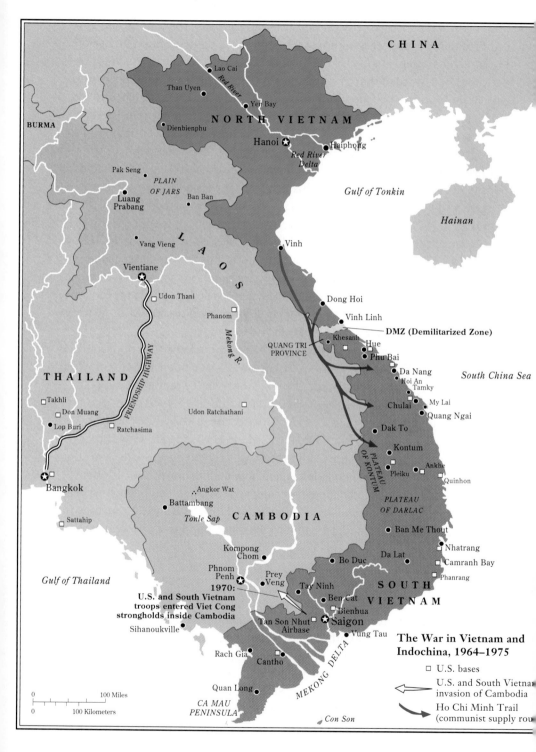

CHINA

Lao Cai

Than Uyen

Yen Bay

Red River

NORTH VIETNAM

Dienbienphu

Hanoi ✪   Haiphong

Red River Delta

BURMA

Pak Seng

PLAIN OF JARS

Luang Prabang

Ban Ban

Gulf of Tonkin

Vang Vieng

Hainan

Vientiane ✪

Udon Thani

L A O S

Phanom

Vinh

Mekong R.

Dong Hoi

Vinh Linh

DMZ (Demilitarized Zone)

QUANG TRI PROVINCE   Khesanh

Khesanh   Hue   Phu Bai

THAILAND

Takhli

Don Muang

Lop Buri

Ratchasima

Udon Ratchathani

Da Nang

Hoi An

Tamky

South China Sea

Chulai   My Lai

Quang Ngai

Dak To

Kontum

Bangkok ✪

Battambang

Angkor Wat

Tonle Sap   CAMBODIA

PLATEAU OF KONTUM

Pleiku   Ankhe

Quinhon

PLATEAU OF DARLAC

Sattahip

Ban Me Thout

Kompong Chom

Gulf of Thailand

Phnom Penh ✪

1970:
U.S. and South Vietnam
troops entered Viet Cong
strongholds inside Cambodia

Sihanoukville

Prey Veng

Tay Ninh

Bo Duc

Da Lat

Nhatrang

Camranh Bay

Phanrang

SOUTH VIETNAM

Ben Cat

Bienhua

Tan Son Nhut Airbase   Saigon

Rach Gia

Cantho

MEKONG DELTA

Vung Tau

The War in Vietnam and Indochina, 1964–1975

□ U.S. bases

⇨ U.S. and South Vietnam
invasion of Cambodia

➤ Ho Chi Minh Trail
(communist supply rou

Quan Long

CA MAU PENINSULA

Con Son

0   100 Miles

0   100 Kilometers

FRIENDSHIP HIGHWAY

North Vietnam, and a pro-Western regime in control of South Vietnam. In 1956, elections would be held to reunite the country under a single government.

The partition of Vietnam was, therefore, an essentially artificial one. But there were, in fact, real and important differences between North and South Vietnam. North Vietnam, the area now to be controlled by the Vietminh, was the heart of traditional Vietnamese society, the area where French influence had been the weakest. It had remained a reasonably stable, reasonably homogeneous culture, most of whose people lived in very close-knit, traditional villages. Northern Vietnam was also the poorest and most populous region of the country.

South Vietnam, by contrast, was a much more recently settled area. Even in the 1950s, most of its people had been there only three generations or less. It was a looser, more heterogeneous, more individualistic society than that of the north. It was highly factionalized—religiously, politically, and ethnically—with powerful sects (and even a powerful mafia) all competing for dominance, which made it a very difficult region to unite and govern. It was also more prosperous and fertile than the north. South Vietnam had no legacy of strong commitment to the Vietminh and a much less fervent commitment than did the north to national unification. It was the area where the influence of the French had been strongest and where there was a substantial, westernized middle class.

America and Diem

As soon as the Geneva accords established the partition, the French left Vietnam altogether. The United States almost immediately stepped into the vacuum and became the principal benefactor of the new government in the south, led by Ngo Dinh Diem.

Diem was an aristocratic Catholic from central Vietnam, an outsider in the south. But he was also a nationalist, uncontaminated by collaboration with the French. And he was, for a time, apparently successful. With the help of the American CIA, Diem waged an effective campaign against some of the powerful religious sects and the South Vietnamese mafia, which had challenged the authority of the central government. As a result, the United States came to regard Diem as a powerful and impressive alternative to Ho Chi Minh.

The American government supported Diem's refusal in 1956 to permit the elections called for by the Geneva accords, reasoning, almost certainly correctly, that Ho Chi Minh would easily win any such election. In the meantime, the United States poured military and economic aid into South Vietnam. By 1956, it was the second-largest recipient of American military aid in the world, after Korea.

Diem's early successes in suppressing the sects in Vietnam led him in 1959 to begin a similar campaign to eliminate the Vietminh supporters who had stayed behind in the south after the partition. That campaign persuaded Ho Chi Minh and his supporters to resume his armed struggle for national unification. In 1959, the Vietminh cadres in the south created the National Liberation Front (NLF), known to many Americans as the Viet Cong—an organization closely allied with the North Vietnamese government. It was committed to overthrowing the "puppet regime" of Diem and reuniting the nation. In 1960, under orders from Hanoi, and with both material and manpower support from North Vietnam, the NLF began military operations in the south. This marked the beginning of the Second Indochina War.

By 1961, NLF forces had established effective control over many areas of the countryside. Diem was also by now losing the support of many other groups in South Vietnam, and he was even losing support within his own military. In 1963, the Diem regime precipitated a major crisis by trying to discipline and repress the South Vietnamese Buddhists in an effort to make Catholicism the dominant religion of the country. The Buddhists began to stage enormous antigovernment demonstrations, during which several monks doused themselves with gasoline, sat cross-legged in the streets of downtown Saigon, and set themselves on fire—in view of photographers and television cameras.

American officials pressured Diem to reform his now tottering government, but the president made no significant concessions. As a result, in the fall of 1963, Kennedy gave his tacit approval to a plot by a group of South Vietnamese generals to topple Diem. In early November 1963, the generals staged the coup, assassinated Diem and his brother and principal adviser, Ngo Dinh Nhu (killings the United States had not wanted or expected), and established the first of a series of new governments, which were, for over three years, even less stable than the one they had overthrown. A few weeks after the coup, John Kennedy too was dead.

From Aid to Intervention

Lyndon Johnson, therefore, inherited what was already a substantial American commitment to the survival of an anticommunist South Vietnam. During his first months in office, he expanded the American involvement in Vietnam only slightly, sending an additional 5,000 military advisers there and preparing to send 5,000 more. Then, early in August 1964, the president announced that American destroyers on patrol in international waters in the Gulf of Tonkin had been attacked by North Vietnamese torpedo boats. Later information raised serious doubts as to whether the administration reported the attacks accurately. At the time, however, virtually no one questioned Johnson's portrayal of the incident as a serious act of aggression or his insistence that the United States must respond. By a vote of 416 to 0 in the House and 88 to 2 in the Senate, Congress hurriedly passed the Gulf of Tonkin Resolution, which authorized the president to "take all necessary measures" to protect American forces and "prevent further aggression" in

ON PATROL IN VIETNAM, JUNE 1965 Several weeks before
President Johnson announced that American ground troops
would enter the Vietnam War, United States soldiers were
already engaged in combat. These marines, patrolling the area
around the American base at Da Nang, were ambushed by
communist guerrillas moments after this photograph was taken.
One marine was killed and three were wounded.

Southeast Asia. The resolution became, in Johnson's view at least, an open-ended legal authorization for escalation of the conflict.

With the South Vietnamese leadership still in disarray and the communist military pressure on the south growing stronger, more and more of the burden of opposition to the Viet Cong fell on the United States. In February 1965, after communist forces attacked an American military base at Pleiku, Johnson ordered American bombings of the north, in an attempt to destroy the depots and transportation lines responsible for the flow of North Vietnamese soldiers and supplies into South Vietnam. The bombing continued intermittently until 1972. A month later, in March 1965, two battalions of American marines landed at Da Nang in South Vietnam. There were now more than 100,000 American troops in Vietnam.

Four months later, the president finally admitted that the character of the war had changed. American soldiers would now, he announced, begin playing an active combat role in the conflict. By the end of the year, there were more than 180,000 American combat troops in Vietnam; in 1966, that number doubled; and by the end of 1967, there were over 500,000 American soldiers there. In the meantime, the air war had intensified until the tonnage of bombs dropped ultimately exceeded that in all theaters during World War II. And American casualties were mounting. By the spring of 1966, more than 4,000 Americans had been killed.

The Quagmire

For more than seven years, American combat forces remained bogged down in a war that the United States was never able either to win or fully to understand. Combating a foe whose strength lay less in weaponry than in its infiltration of the population, the United States responded with heavy-handed technological warfare designed for conventional battles against conventional armies.

Central to the American war effort was the strategy known to the military as "attrition," one premised on the belief that the United States could inflict more damage on the enemy than the enemy could absorb. But the attrition strategy failed because the North Vietnamese were willing to commit many more soldiers and resources to the conflict than the United States had expected.

It failed, too, because the United States relied so heavily on its bombing of the north to eliminate the communists' war-making capacity. American bombers attacked almost every identifiable strategic target in North Vietnam as well as jungle areas in Cambodia and Laos thought to shelter the "Ho Chi Minh Trail," by which Hanoi sent troops and supplies into the south. But North Vietnam was not a modern industrial society, and it had relatively few of the sorts of targets against which bombing is effective. And the North Vietnamese responded to the bombing with great ingenuity: creating a network of underground tunnels, shops, and factories; securing substantial aid from the Soviet Union and China; and continually moving the Ho Chi Minh Trail to make it elusive to American bombers. Far from breaking the north's resolve, the bombing seemed actually to strengthen popular commitment to the war.

Another important part of the American strategy was the "pacification" program, whose purpose was to push the Viet Cong from particular regions and then "pacify" those regions by winning the "hearts and minds" of the people. Routing the Viet Cong was often possible, but the subsequent pacification was more difficult. American forces were not adept at establishing rapport with provincial Vietnamese, and the American military never gave that part of the program a very high priority in any case. Gradually, the pacification program gave way to the more heavy-handed relocation strategy, through which American troops uprooted villagers from their homes, sent them fleeing to refugee camps or into the cities (producing by 1967 more than 3 million refugees), and then destroyed the vacated villages and surrounding countryside.

As the war dragged on and victory remained elusive, some American officers and officials began to urge the president to expand the military efforts. But the Johnson administration resisted—in part because it was beginning to encounter obstacles and frustrations at home.

The War at Home

Few Americans, and even fewer influential ones, had protested the American involvement in Vietnam as late as the end of 1965. But as the war dragged on and came to seem increasingly futile, political support for it began to erode.

By the end of 1967, American students opposed to the war had become a significant political force. Enormous peace marches in New York, Washington, D.C., and other cities drew broad public attention to the antiwar movement. In the meantime, a growing number of journalists, particularly reporters who had spent time in Vietnam, helped sustain the movement with their frank revelations about the brutality and apparent futility of the war.

The growing chorus of popular protest helped stimulate opposition to the war from within the government. Senator J. William Fulbright of

Arkansas, chairman of the powerful Senate Foreign Relations Committee, turned against the war and in January 1966 began to stage highly publicized and occasionally televised congressional hearings to air criticisms of it. Other members of Congress joined Fulbright in opposing Johnson's policies—including, in 1967, Robert F. Kennedy, brother of the slain president, now a senator from New York. Even within the administration, the consensus seemed to be crumbling. Robert McNamara, who had done much to help extend the American involvement in Vietnam, quietly left the government, disillusioned, in 1968. His successor as secretary of defense, Clark Clifford, became a quiet but powerful voice within the administration on behalf of a cautious scaling down of the commitment.

In the meantime, the American economy was beginning to suffer. Johnson's commitment to fighting the war while continuing his Great Society reforms helped cause a rise in the inflation rate, from the 2 percent level it had occupied through most of the early 1960s to 3 percent in 1967, 4 percent in 1968, and 6 percent in 1969. In August 1967, Johnson asked Congress for a tax increase to avoid even more ruinous inflation. In return, congressional conservatives demanded and received a $6 billion reduction in the funding for Great Society programs.

THE TRAUMAS OF 1968

By the end of 1967, the twin crises of the war in Vietnam and the deteriorating racial situation at home had produced great social and political tensions. In the course of 1968, those tensions seemed suddenly to burst to the surface and threaten national chaos.

The Tet Offensive

On January 31, 1968, the first day of the Vietnamese New Year (Tet), communist forces launched an enormous, concerted attack on American strongholds throughout South Vietnam. A few cities, most notably Hue, fell temporarily to the communists. Others suffered major disruptions. But what made the Tet offensive so shocking to the American people, who saw vivid reports of it on television, was the sight of communist forces in the heart of Saigon, setting off bombs, shooting down South Vietnamese officials and troops, and holding down fortified areas (including, briefly, the grounds of

JOHNSON AND HUMPHREY, MARCH 27, 1968 Four days before
announcing he would not run for reelection, a grim and tired Lyndon
Johnson, accompanied by Vice President Hubert Humphrey, receives a
briefing on the military situation in Vietnam.

the American embassy). The Tet offensive also suggested to the American
public something of the brutality of the fighting in Vietnam. In the midst of
the fighting, television cameras recorded the sight of a South Vietnamese
officer shooting a captured Viet Cong soldier in the head in the streets of
Saigon.

American forces soon dislodged the Viet Cong from most of the positions they had seized, and the Tet offensive in the end cost the communists
such appalling casualties that they were significantly weakened for months
to come. Indeed, the Tet defeats permanently depleted the ranks of the NLF
and forced North Vietnamese troops to take on a much larger share of the
subsequent fighting. But all that had little impact on American opinion. Tet
may have been a military victory for the United States, but it was a political
defeat for the administration, a defeat from which it would never fully recover.

In the following weeks, opposition to the war grew substantially. Leading newspapers and magazines, television commentators, and mainstream
politicians began taking public stands in favor of de-escalation of the conflict. Within weeks of the Tet offensive, public opposition to the war had

almost doubled. And Johnson's personal popularity rating had slid to 35 percent, the lowest of any president since Harry Truman.

The Political Challenge

Beginning in the summer of 1967, dissident Democrats tried to mobilize support behind an antiwar candidate who would challenge Lyndon Johnson in the 1968 primaries. When Robert Kennedy turned them down, they recruited Senator Eugene McCarthy of Minnesota. A brilliantly orchestrated campaign by young volunteers in the New Hampshire primary produced a startling showing by McCarthy in March; he nearly defeated the president.

A few days later, Robert Kennedy finally entered the campaign, embittering many McCarthy supporters but bringing his own substantial strength among blacks, poor people, and workers to the antiwar cause. Polls showed the president trailing badly in the next scheduled primary, in Wisconsin. On March 31, 1968, Johnson went on television to announce a limited halt in the bombing of North Vietnam—his first major concession to the antiwar forces—and, much more surprising, his withdrawal from the presidential contest.

Robert Kennedy quickly established himself as the champion of the Democratic primaries, winning one election after another. In the meantime, however, Vice President Hubert Humphrey, with the support of President Johnson, entered the contest and began to attract the support of party leaders and of the many delegations that were selected not by popular primaries but by state party organizations. He soon appeared to be the front-runner in the race.

The King Assassination

On April 4, Martin Luther King, Jr., who had traveled to Memphis, Tennessee, to lend his support to striking black sanitation workers in the city, was shot and killed while standing on the balcony of his motel. The assassin, James Earl Ray, who was captured days later in London, had no apparent motive. Subsequent evidence suggested that he had been hired by others to do the killing, but he himself never revealed the identity of his employers.

King's tragic death produced a great outpouring of grief. Among American blacks, it also produced anger. In the days after the assassination, major riots broke out in more than sixty American cities. Forty-three people died; more than 3,000 suffered injuries; as many as 27,000 people were arrested.

The Kennedy Assassination and Chicago

Late in the night of June 6, Robert Kennedy appeared in the ballroom of a Los Angeles hotel to acknowledge his victory in that day's California primary. As he left the ballroom after his victory statement, Sirhan Sirhan, a young Palestinian apparently enraged by pro-Israeli remarks Kennedy had recently made, emerged from a crowd and shot him in the head. Early the next morning, Kennedy died. The shock of this second tragedy in two months cast a deep pall over the remainder of the presidential campaign.

When the Democrats finally gathered in Chicago in August, for a convention in which Hubert Humphrey was now the only real contender, even the most optimistic observers were predicting turbulence. Inside the hall, delegates bitterly debated an antiwar plank in the party platform that both Kennedy and McCarthy supporters favored. Miles away, in a downtown park, thousands of antiwar protesters were staging demonstrations. On the third night of the convention, as the delegates were beginning their balloting on the now virtually inevitable nomination of Hubert Humphrey, demonstrators and police clashed in a bloody riot in the streets of Chicago. Hundreds of protesters were injured as police attempted to disperse them with tear gas and billy clubs. Aware that the violence was being televised to the nation, the demonstrators taunted the authorities with the chant, "The whole world is watching!" And Hubert Humphrey, who had spent years dreaming of becoming his party's candidate for president, received a nomination that night which appeared at the time to be almost worthless.

The Conservative Response

The turbulent events of 1968 persuaded many observers that American society was in the throes of revolutionary change. In fact, however, the response of most Americans to the turmoil was a conservative one.

The most visible sign of the conservative backlash was the surprising success of the campaign of George Wallace for the presidency. Wallace had established himself in 1963 as one of the leading spokesmen for the defense of segregation when, as governor of Alabama, he had attempted to block the admission of black students to the University of Alabama. In 1968, he became a third-party candidate for president, basing his campaign on a host of conservative grievances. He denounced the forced busing of students, the proliferation of government regulations and social programs, and the permissiveness of authorities toward crime, race riots, and antiwar demonstrations. There was never any serious chance that Wallace would win the election, but his standing in the polls rose at times to over 20 percent.

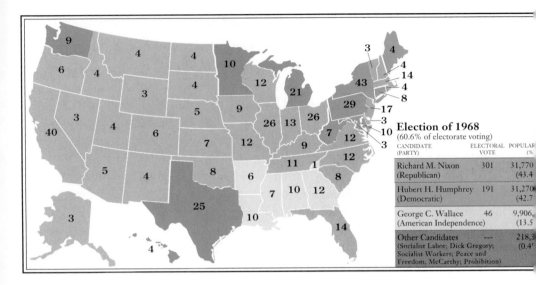

Election of 1968
(60.6% of electorate voting)

CANDIDATE (PARTY)	ELECTORAL VOTE	POPULAR (%
Richard M. Nixon (Republican)	301	31,770 (43.4
Hubert H. Humphrey (Democratic)	191	31,270 (42.7
George C. Wallace (American Independence)	46	9,906 (13.5
Other Candidates (Socialist Labor; Dick Gregory; Socialist Workers; Peace and Freedom; McCarthy; Prohibition)	---	218,3 (0.4'

A more effective effort to mobilize the conservative middle in favor of order and stability was under way within the Republican Party. Richard Nixon, whose political career had seemed at an end after his losses in the presidential race of 1960 and a California gubernatorial campaign two years later, reemerged as the preeminent spokesman for what he sometimes called the "silent majority." Nixon recognized that many Americans were tired of hearing about their obligations to the poor, tired of hearing about the sacrifices necessary to achieve racial justice, tired of judicial reforms that seemed designed to help criminals. By offering a vision of stability, law and order, government retrenchment, and "peace with honor" in Vietnam, he easily captured the nomination of his party for the presidency. And despite a last-minute surge by Humphrey, he hung on to eke out a victory almost as narrow as his defeat in 1960. He received 43.4 percent of the popular vote to Humphrey's 42.7 percent (a margin of only about 500,000 votes), and 301 electoral votes to Humphrey's 191. George Wallace, who like most third-party candidates faded in the last weeks of the campaign, still managed to poll 13.5 percent of the popular vote and to carry five southern states with a total of 46 electoral ballots. Nixon had hardly won a decisive personal mandate. But the election made clear that a majority of the American electorate was more interested in restoring stability than in promoting social change.

D E B A T I N G   T H E   P A S T

The Vietnam Commitment

T HE DEBATE over why the United States became involved in the conflict in Vietnam (which is only one of many debates about the meaning of the war) has centered on two different, if related, questions. One is
an effort to assess the broad objectives Americans believed they were pursuing in Vietnam. The other is an effort to explain how and why policymakers made the specific decisions that led the United States to a military
commitment in Indochina.

Scholars and writers such as Norman Podhoretz, Guenter Lewy, and R.
B. Smith, echoing elements of the official government explanation of American intervention in the war, have argued that the communist aggression
in Vietnam was part of a Chinese and Soviet design to spread revolution
throughout Asia. America, therefore, was not only protecting Vietnam,
although that was an important part of its mission; it was also defending
the rest of Asia, which would soon be threatened by communism if Vietnam fell. The intervention in Vietnam was a rational and even necessary expression of America's legitimate security interests and its belief in democracy.

Most scholars, however, have been more skeptical. Historians on the left
argue that America's intervention in Vietnam was a form of imperialism—
part of a larger effort by the United States after World War II to impose a
particular political and economic order on the world. "The Vietnam War,"
Gabriel Kolko wrote in 1985, "was for the United States the culmination of
its frustrating postwar effort to merge its arms and politics to halt and re-

(continued on next page)

verse the emergence of states and social systems opposed to the international order Washington sought to establish." Others argued that the United States fought in Vietnam to serve the domestic economic interests that had a stake in the region or in the arms production the war stimulated. Other, more moderate critics blame the Vietnam intervention on the myopia of a foreign policy elite unwilling to question its own unreflective commitment to containing communism everywhere and unable to distinguish between international aggression and domestic insurgency.

Those who have looked less at the nation's broad objectives than at the workings of the policymaking process have also produced competing explanations. David Halberstam's *The Best and the Brightest* (1972) argued that policymakers deluded themselves into thinking they could achieve their goals in Vietnam by ignoring, suppressing, or dismissing information that should have suggested that they were wrong; because of arrogance or ideological rigidity, they simply refused to consider that victory was beyond their grasp.

Larry Berman, writing in 1982, offered a different view. Neither Johnson nor his advisers were unaware of the obstacles to success in Vietnam. Almost everyone suspected that victory would be difficult, even impossible, to attain. The president was not misled or misinformed. But Johnson committed troops to the war anyway, because he feared that allowing Vietnam to fall would ruin him politically and destroy his hopes for building his "Great Society" at home. Leslie Gelb and Richard Betts made a related argument in 1979. Vietnam, they claimed, was the logical, perhaps inevitable result of a political and bureaucratic order shaped by the ideology of the Cold War. However costly the intervention in Vietnam, policymakers concluded, the costs of not intervening and allowing South Vietnam to fall always seemed higher. The war escalated in the 1960s not because American aims changed but because the situation in Vietnam deteriorated to the point where nothing short of intervention would prevent defeat. Only when the national and international political situation itself shifted in the late 1960s and early 1970s—only when it became clear that the political costs of staying in Vietnam were higher than the political costs of getting out—was it possible for the United States to begin disengaging.

CHAPTER THIRTY-TWO

The Crisis of Authority

The Turbulent Society ∼ *The Mobilization of Minorities* ∼ *The New Feminism*
Nixon, Kissinger, and the War ∼ *Nixon, Kissinger, and the World*
Politics and Economics in the Nixon Years ∼ *The Watergate Crisis*

T HE ELECTION OF Richard Nixon in 1968 was the result of more than the unpopularity of Lyndon Johnson and the war. It was the result, too, of a broad popular reaction against what many Americans considered a dangerous assault on the foundations of their society and culture. In Richard Nixon they found a man who seemed perfectly to match their mood. Himself a product of a hardworking, middle-class family, he projected an image of stern dedication to traditional values. Yet the presidency of Richard Nixon, far from returning calm and stability to American politics, coincided with, and helped to produce, more years of crisis.

THE TURBULENT SOCIETY

Perhaps most alarming to many conservatives in the 1960s and 1970s was a pattern of social and cultural protest by younger Americans, who were giving vent to two related impulses. One was the impulse, emerging from the political left, to create a great new community of "the people," which would rise up to break the power of elites and force the nation to end the war, pursue racial and economic justice, and transform its political life. The other, at least equally powerful impulse was related to, but not entirely compatible with, the first: the vision of personal "liberation." It found expression in part through the efforts of many groups—African Americans, Indians, Hispanics, women, gay people, and others—to define and assert themselves and make demands on the larger society. It also found expression through the efforts of individuals to create a new culture—one that would allow them to escape from what some considered the dehumanizing pressures of the modern "technocracy."

861

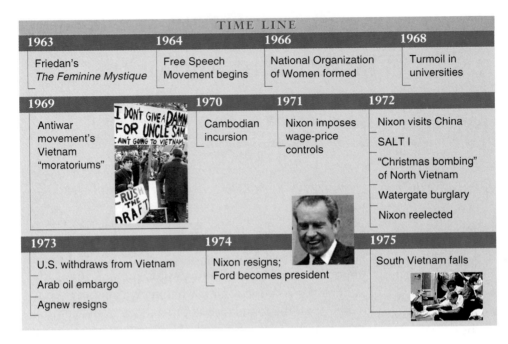

TIME LINE

1963	1964	1966	1968
Friedan's *The Feminine Mystique*	Free Speech Movement begins	National Organization of Women formed	Turmoil in universities

1969	1970	1971	1972
Antiwar movement's Vietnam "moratoriums"	Cambodian incursion	Nixon imposes wage-price controls	Nixon visits China SALT I "Christmas bombing" of North Vietnam Watergate burglary Nixon reelected

1973	1974	1975
U.S. withdraws from Vietnam Arab oil embargo Agnew resigns	Nixon resigns; Ford becomes president	South Vietnam falls

The New Left

Among the products of the racial crisis and the war in Vietnam was a radicalization of many American students, who in the course of the 1960s formed what became known as the New Left. The New Left emerged from many sources, but from nothing so much as the civil rights movement, in which many idealistic young white Americans had become involved in the early 1960s. Within a few years, some white civil rights activists were beginning to consider broader political commitments. In 1962, a group of students (most of them white) gathered in Michigan to form an organization to give voice to their demands: Students for a Democratic Society (SDS). Their declaration of beliefs, the Port Huron Statement, expressed their disillusionment with the society they had inherited and their determination to build a new politics. In the following years, SDS became the leading organization of student radicalism.

Since most members of the New Left were students, much of their radicalism centered for a time on issues related to the modern university. A 1964 dispute at the University of California at Berkeley over the rights of students to engage in political activities on campus—the Free Speech Movement—was the first outburst of what was to be nearly a decade of campus turmoil.

Students at Berkeley and elsewhere protested the impersonal character of the modern university, and they denounced the role of educational institutions in sustaining what they considered corrupt or immoral public policies. The antiwar movement greatly inflamed and expanded the challenge to the universities; and beginning in 1968, campus demonstrations, riots, and building seizures became almost commonplace. At Columbia University in New York, students seized the offices of the president and other members of the administration and occupied them for several days until local police forcibly ejected them. Over the next several years, hardly any major university was immune to some level of disruption. Small groups of especially dogmatic radicals—among them the "Weathermen," an offshoot of SDS—were responsible for a few cases of arson and bombing that destroyed campus buildings and claimed several lives.

Not many people ever accepted the radical political views that lay at the heart of the New Left. But many supported the position of SDS and other groups on particular issues, and above all on the Vietnam War. Between 1967 and 1969, student activists organized some of the largest political demonstrations in American history—in Washington, D.C., and around the country—to protest the war. They helped thrust the issue of Vietnam into the center of American politics.

Closely related to opposition to the war—and another issue that helped fuel the antiwar movement—was opposition to the military draft. The gradual abolition of many traditional deferments—for graduate students, teachers, husbands, fathers, and others—swelled the ranks of those faced with conscription (and thus likely to oppose it). Draft card burnings became common features of antiwar rallies on college campuses. Many draft-age Americans simply refused induction, accepting what were occasionally long terms in jail as a result. Thousands of others fled to Canada, Sweden, and elsewhere (where they were joined by many deserters from the armed forces) to escape conscription. Not until 1977, when President Jimmy Carter issued a general pardon to draft resisters and a far more limited amnesty for deserters, did the Vietnam exiles begin to return to the country in substantial numbers.

The Counterculture

Closely related to the New Left was a new youth culture openly scornful of the values and conventions of middle-class society. The most visible characteristic of the counterculture, as it became known, was a change in lifestyle. As if to display their contempt for conventional standards, young Americans flaunted long hair, shabby or flamboyant clothing, and a rebellious disdain

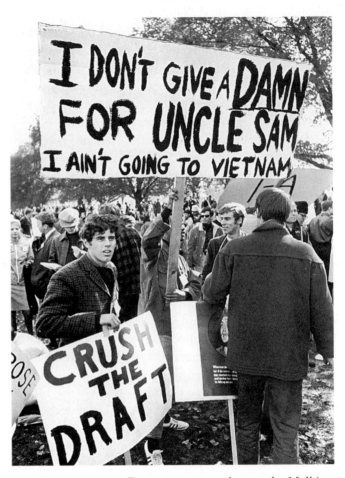

THE WAR AT HOME Demonstrators gather on the Mall in
Washington in the fall of 1967 for one of the first of the
great antiwar demonstrations of the late 1960s. Over time,
the antiwar movement helped erode the national
consensus on the conflict in Vietnam. But the principal
basis for opposing the war was never the moral or
economic arguments of the left; it was simply the
frustration among many Americans of seeing a war
continuing too long and too inconclusively.

for traditional speech and decorum. Central to the counterculture were drugs: marijuana smoking—which after 1966 became almost as common a youthful diversion as beer drinking had once been—and the use of other, more potent hallucinogens, such as LSD. There was also a new, more permissive view of sex.

The counterculture's iconoclasm and hedonism sometimes obscured the philosophy behind it, which offered a fundamental challenge to the American middle-class mainstream. Like the New Left, with which it in many ways overlapped, the counterculture challenged the structure of modern American society, attacking its banality, its hollowness, its artificiality, its isolation from nature. The most committed adherents of the counterculture—the hippies, who came to dominate the Haight-Ashbury neighborhood of San Francisco and other places, and the social dropouts, many of whom retreated to rural communes—rejected modern society altogether and attempted to find refuge in a simpler, more "natural" existence. But even those whose commitment to the counterculture was less intense shared a commitment to the idea of personal fulfillment through rejecting the inhibitions and conventions of middle-class culture and giving fuller expression to personal instinct and desire. The first responsibility of the individual, the counterculture seemed to suggest, is cultivation of the self, the unleashing of one's own full potential for pleasure and fulfillment.

The counterculture was in many ways only an exaggerated expression of impulses that were coursing through the larger society. A new set of social norms emerged among many young people (and some adults) whose links to the counterculture were otherwise negligible. Long hair and freakish clothing became the badge not only of hippies and radicals but of an entire generation. The use of marijuana, the freer attitudes toward sex, the iconoclastic (and often obscene) language—all spread far beyond the realm of the true devotees of the counterculture. And perhaps the most pervasive element of the new youth society was one that even the least radical members of the generation embraced: rock music. Rock's driving rhythms, its undisguised sensuality, its often harsh and angry tone—all made it an appropriate vehicle for expressing the social and political restlessness of the late 1960s.

THE MOBILIZATION OF MINORITIES

The growth of black protest, and of a significant white response to it, both preceded the political and cultural upheavals of the 1960s and helped to produce them. It also encouraged other minorities to assert themselves and demand redress of their grievances. For Indians, Hispanic Americans, gay men and lesbians, and others, the late 1960s and 1970s were a time of growing self-expression and political activism.

Seeds of Indian Militancy

Few minorities had deeper or more justifiable grievances against the prevailing culture than American Indians—or Native Americans, as some began defiantly to call themselves in the 1960s. Indians were the least prosperous, least healthy, and least stable group in the nation. Average annual family income for Indians was $1,000 less than that for blacks. The Native American unemployment rate was ten times the national rate. Joblessness was particularly high on the reservations, where nearly half of all Indians lived. But even most Indians living in cities were victims of limited education and training and could find only menial jobs. Life expectancy among Indians was more than twenty years less than the national average. Suicides among Indian youths were a hundred times more frequent than among white youths. And while black Americans attracted the attention (for good or for ill) of many whites, Indians for many years remained largely ignored.

For much of the postwar era, and particularly after the resignation of John Collier as commissioner of Indian affairs in 1945, federal policy toward the tribes had been shaped by a determination to incorporate Indians into mainstream American society whether Indians wanted to assimilate or not. Two laws passed in 1953 established the basis of a new policy, which became known as "termination." Through termination, the federal government withdrew all official recognition of the tribes as legal entities, administratively separate from state governments, and made them subject to the same local jurisdictions as white residents. At the same time, the government encouraged Indians to assimilate into the white world and worked to funnel Native Americans into cities, where, presumably, they would adapt themselves to the larger society and lose their cultural distinctiveness.

To some degree, the termination and assimilation policies achieved their objectives. The tribes grew weaker as legal and political entities. Many Native Americans adapted to life in the cities, at least to a degree. On the whole, however, the new policies were a disastrous failure. Indians themselves fought so bitterly against them that in 1958 the Eisenhower administration barred further "terminations" without the consent of the affected tribes. In the meantime, the struggle against termination had mobilized a new generation of Indian militants and had breathed life into the principal

Native American organization, the National Congress of American Indians, which had been created in 1944.

The Democratic administrations of the 1960s did not disavow the termination policy, but neither did they make any effort to revive it. Instead, they made modest efforts to restore at least some degree of tribal autonomy. The funneling of OEO money to tribal organizations through the Community Action program was one prominent example. In the meantime, the tribes themselves were beginning to fight for self-determination—partly in response to the black civil rights movement and partly in response to other social and cultural changes (among them, the expanding mobility and rising educational levels of younger Indians, who were becoming more aware of the world around them and of their own anomalous place within it). The new militancy also benefited from the rapid increase in the Indian population, which was growing much faster than that of the rest of the nation (nearly doubling between 1950 and 1970 to a total of about 800,000).

The Indian Civil Rights Movement

In 1961, more than 400 members of 67 tribes gathered in Chicago to discuss ways of bringing all Indians together in an effort to redress common wrongs. The manifesto they issued, the Declaration of Indian Purpose, stressed the "right to choose our own way of life" and the "responsibility of preserving our precious heritage."

The 1961 meeting was only one example of a growing Indian self-consciousness. The National Indian Youth Council, created in the aftermath of the 1961 Chicago meeting, promoted the idea of Indian nationalism and intertribal unity. In 1968, a group of young, militant Indians established the American Indian Movement (AIM), which drew its greatest support from those Indians who lived in urban areas but which soon established a significant presence on the reservations as well.

The new activism had some immediate political results. In 1968, Congress passed the Indian Civil Rights Act, which guaranteed reservation Indians many of the protections accorded other citizens by the Bill of Rights but which also recognized the legitimacy of tribal laws within the reservations. But leaders of AIM and other insurgent groups were not satisfied and turned increasingly to direct action. In 1968, Indian fishermen, citing old treaty rights, clashed with Washington State officials on the Columbia River and in Puget Sound. The following year, members of several tribes occupied the abandoned federal prison on Alcatraz Island in San Francisco Bay, claiming the site "by right of discovery."

WOUNDED KNEE In 1890, Wounded Knee, South Dakota, had been the site of a bloody conflict between white troops and Sioux Indians, a conflict that turned into a notorious massacre in which over 300 Indians died. In 1973, the American Indian Movement chose the same place as a site for a militant protest against conditions on the Pine Ridge Indian reservation.

In response to the growing pressure, the new Nixon administration appointed Louis Bruce, a Mohawk-Sioux, to the position of commissioner of Indian affairs in 1969; and in 1970 the president promised both increased tribal self-determination and an increase in federal aid. But the protests continued. In November 1972, nearly a thousand demonstrators, most of them Lakota (or Sioux) Indians, forcibly occupied the building of the Bureau of Indian Affairs in Washington for six days. A more celebrated protest occurred later that winter at Wounded Knee, South Dakota, the site of the 1890 massacre of Sioux by federal troops. In February 1973, members of AIM seized and occupied the town of Wounded Knee for two months, demanding radical changes in the administration of the reservation and insisting that the government honor its long-forgotten treaty obligations. A brief clash between the occupiers and federal forces left one Indian dead and another wounded. Shortly thereafter the siege came to an end.

The Indian civil rights movement, like other civil rights movements of the same time, fell far short of winning full justice and equality for Native

Americans. But it helped the tribes win a series of new legal rights and protections that, together, gave them a stronger position than they had enjoyed at any previous time in the twentieth century. It also helped many Indians gain a renewed awareness of and pride in their identity as Indians and as part of a distinct community within the larger United States.

Hispanic-American Activism

More numerous and more visible than Indians were Hispanic Americans (sometimes known as Latinos), the fastest-growing minority group in the United States. Large numbers of Mexicans had entered the country during World War II in response to the wartime labor shortage, and many had remained in the cities of the Southwest and the Pacific Coast. By 1960, there were substantial Mexican-American neighborhoods (or barrios) in American cities from El Paso to Detroit. The largest (with more than 500,000 people, according to census figures) was in Los Angeles, which by then had a bigger Mexican population than anyplace except Mexico City.

But the greatest expansion in the Hispanic population of the United States was yet to come. In 1960, the census reported slightly more than 3 million Hispanics living in the United States. By 1970, that number had grown to 9 million and by 1990 to 20 million. Hispanics constituted more than a third of all legal immigrants to the United States after 1960. Since there was also an uncounted but very large number of illegal immigrants in those years (estimates ranged from 7 million to 12 million), the real percentage of Hispanic immigrants was undoubtedly much larger.

Large numbers of Puerto Ricans (who were entitled to American citizenship by birth) migrated to eastern urban areas, particularly New York, where they formed one of the poorest communities in the city. South Florida's substantial Cuban population began with a wave of middle-class refugees fleeing the Castro regime in the early 1960s. These first Cuban migrants quickly established themselves as a successful and highly assimilated part of Miami's middle class. In 1980, a second, much poorer wave of Cuban immigrants—the so-called Marielietos, named for the port from which they left Cuba—arrived in Florida when Castro temporarily relaxed exit restrictions. (This group included a large number of criminals, whom Castro had, in effect, expelled from the country.) This second wave was less welcomed by the government (and the existing Cuban community) and less easily assimilated. Later in the 1980s, large numbers of immigrants (both legal and illegal) began to arrive from Central and South America—from Guatemala, Nicaragua, El Salvador, Peru, and other countries. The most numerous

Hispanic group, however, remained the Mexican Americans, who were concentrated in the Southwest and California but who were also spreading throughout the nation's interior.

Many Hispanic Americans were affluent and successful people. But most of the newer immigrants were less well educated than either "Anglo" or black Americans and hence less well prepared for high-paying jobs. The fact that many spoke English poorly or not at all further limited their employment prospects. As a result, they found themselves concentrated in poorly paid service jobs.

Like blacks and Indians, many Hispanic Americans responded to the highly charged climate of the 1960s by strengthening their ethnic identification and by organizing for political and economic power. Affluent Hispanics in Miami filled influential positions in the professions and local government; in the Southwest, they elected Mexican Americans to seats in Congress and to governorships. A Mexican-American political organization, La Raza Unida, exercised influence in southern California and elsewhere in the Southwest in the 1970s and beyond.

One of the most visible efforts to organize Hispanics occurred in California, where an Arizona-born farmworker of Mexican descent, César Chávez, created an effective union of itinerant farmworkers: the United Farm Workers (UFW), a largely Hispanic organization. For most Hispanics, however, the path to economic and political power was more difficult. Partly because of language barriers, partly because of ineffective organization, and partly because of discrimination, Mexican Americans and others were slow to develop political influence in proportion to their numbers. In the meantime, Hispanics formed one of the poorest segments of the United States population.

Challenging the "Melting Pot" Ideal

The efforts of blacks, Hispanics, Indians, and others to forge a clearer group identity challenged a longstanding premise of liberal political thought—the idea of the "melting pot." Older, European immigrant groups liked to believe that they had advanced in American society by adopting the values and accepting the rules of the world to which they had moved and by advancing within it on its own terms. The more militant ethnic groups of the 1960s were less willing to accept the standards of the larger society and more likely to demand recognition of their own ethnic identity. African Americans, Indians, and Hispanics all challenged the assimilationist idea and advocated instead a culturally pluralist society, in which racial and ethnic groups would preserve not only a sense of their heritage (which older, more "assimilationist" ethnic groups did as well) but also their own social and cultural norms.

To a large degree, the advocates of cultural pluralism succeeded. Recognition of the special character of particular groups was embedded in federal law through a wide range of affirmative action programs, which extended not only to blacks but to Indians, Hispanics, and others as well. Ethnic studies programs proliferated in schools and universities. Eventually, this impulse led to an even more assertive (and highly controversial) cultural movement that in the 1980s and 1990s became known as "multiculturalism," which challenged the "Eurocentric" basis of American education and culture and demanded that non-European civilizations be accorded at least equal attention.

Gay Liberation

The last important liberation movement to emerge in the 1960s, and the most unsettling to some Americans, was the effort by gay men and lesbians to win political and economic rights and, more important, social acceptance. Homosexuality has been a generally unacknowledged reality through most of American history. Nonheterosexual men and women were forced for generations either to suppress their sexual preferences, to exercise them surreptitiously, or to live within isolated and often persecuted communities. But by the late 1960s, the liberating impulses that had affected other groups helped mobilize gay men and lesbians to fight for their own rights.

On June 27, 1969, police officers raided the Stonewall Inn, a gay nightclub in New York City's Greenwich Village, and began arresting patrons simply for frequenting the place. The raid was not unusual, but the response was. Gay onlookers taunted the police and then attacked them. Someone started a blaze in the Stonewall Inn itself, almost trapping the policemen inside. Rioting continued throughout Greenwich Village (the center of New York's gay community) through much of the night.

The "Stonewall Riot" marked the beginning of the gay liberation movement—one of the most controversial challenges to traditional values and assumptions of its time. New organizations—among them the Gay Liberation Front, founded in New York in 1969—sprang up around the country. Public discussion and media coverage of homosexuality, long subject to an unofficial taboo, quickly and dramatically increased. Gay activists were having some success in challenging the longstanding assumption that homosexuality was aberrant behavior and were arguing that no sexual preference was any more normal than another.

Most of all, however, the gay liberation movement transformed the outlook of many gay men and lesbians themselves. It helped them to "come out," to express their preferences openly and unapologetically, and to demand from society a recognition that gay relationships could be as significant and worthy of respect as heterosexual ones. Some gays advocated not only an acceptance of homosexuality as a valid and "normal" preference but a change in the larger society as well: a redefinition of personal identity to give much greater importance to erotic impulses. There was much resistance to such efforts. But by the early 1980s, the gay liberation movement had made remarkable strides. Even the ravages of the AIDS epidemic, which, in the beginning at least, affected the gay community more disastrously than it affected any other group, failed to halt the growth of gay liberation. In many ways, it strengthened it.

By the early 1990s, gay men and lesbians were achieving many of the same milestones that other oppressed minorities had attained in earlier decades. Openly gay politicians were winning election to public office. Universities were establishing gay and lesbian studies programs. And laws prohibiting discrimination on the basis of sexual preference were making slow, halting progress at the state and local levels. But gay liberation produced a powerful backlash as well, as became evident in 1993 when President Bill Clinton's effort to end the ban on gay men and lesbians serving in the military met a storm of criticism from members of Congress and within the military itself. At the same time, voters in some cities and states were approving referendum questions on their ballots outlawing civil rights protections for gay men and lesbians.

THE NEW FEMINISM

American women constitute over 50 percent of the population. But during the 1960s and 1970s, many women began to identify with minority groups as they renewed demands for a liberation of their own. Sexual discrimination was so deeply embedded in the fabric of society that when feminists first began to denounce it, many men (and even many women) responded with bafflement and anger. By the mid-1970s, however, public awareness of the issue had increased greatly, and the role of women in American life was changing more rapidly and dramatically than that of any other group in the nation.

The Rebirth

Feminism had been a weak and often embattled force in American life for more than forty years after the adoption of the woman suffrage amendment in 1920. A few determined women kept feminist political demands alive in the National Woman's Party and other organizations. Many more women expanded the acceptable bounds of female activity by entering new areas of the workplace or engaging in political activities. Nevertheless, through the 1950s and early 1960s, active feminism was often difficult to detect.

The 1963 publication of Betty Friedan's *The Feminine Mystique* is often cited as the first event of contemporary women's liberation. Friedan, who had been a writer for women's magazines in the 1950s, traveled around the country interviewing the women who had graduated with her from Smith College in 1947. Most of these women were living out the dream that postwar American society had created for them: they were affluent wives and mothers living in comfortable suburbs. And yet many of them were deeply frustrated and unhappy, with no outlets for their intelligence, talent, and education. By chronicling their unhappiness and frustration, Friedan's book had a powerful impact. But it did not so much cause the revival of feminism as help give voice to a movement that was already stirring.

By the time *The Feminine Mystique* appeared, John Kennedy had established the President's Commission on the Status of Women, which brought national attention to sexual discrimination and helped create important networks of feminist activists who would lobby for legislative redress. Also in 1963, the Kennedy administration helped win passage of the Equal Pay Act, which barred the pervasive practice of paying women less than men for equal work. A year later, Congress incorporated into the Civil Rights Act of 1964 an amendment—Title VII—that extended to women many of the same legal protections against discrimination that were being extended to blacks.

In 1966, Friedan joined with other feminists to create the National Organization for Women (NOW), which was to become the nation's largest and most influential feminist organization. NOW reflected the varying constituencies of the emerging feminist movement. It responded to the complaints of the women Friedan's book had examined—affluent suburbanites with no outlet for their interests—by demanding greater educational opportunities for women and denouncing the domestic ideal and the traditional concept of marriage. But the heart of the movement, at least in the beginning, was directed toward the needs of women in the workplace. NOW denounced the exclusion of women from professions, from politics, and from countless other areas of American life.

Women's Liberation

By the late 1960s, new and more radical feminist demands were also attracting a large following, especially among younger, white, educated women. Many of them drew inspiration from the New Left and the counterculture. Some were involved in the civil rights movement, others in the antiwar crusade. Many had found that even within those movements, they faced discrimination and exclusion and were subordinated to male leaders.

In its most radical form, the new feminism rejected the whole notion of marriage, family, and even heterosexual intercourse (a vehicle, some women claimed, of male domination). Not many women, not even many feminists, embraced such extremes. But by the early 1970s large numbers of women were coming to see themselves as an exploited group banding together against oppression and developing a culture of their own. The women's liberation movement inspired the creation of grassroots organizations and activities through which women not only challenged sexism and discrimination but created communities of their own. In cities and towns across the country, feminists opened women's bookstores, bars, and coffee shops. They founded feminist newspapers and magazines. They created centers to assist victims of rape and abuse, women's health clinics (and, particularly after 1973, abortion clinics), and day-care centers.

Expanding Achievements

By the early 1970s, the public and private achievements of the women's movement were already substantial. In 1971, the government extended its affirmative action guidelines to include women—linking sexism with racism as an officially acknowledged social problem. Women were making rapid progress, in the meantime, in their efforts to move into the economic and political mainstream. The nation's major all-male educational institutions began to open their doors to women. (Princeton and Yale did so in 1969, and most others soon did the same.) Some women's colleges, in the meantime, began accepting male students.

Women were also becoming an important force in business and the professions. Nearly half of all married women held jobs by the mid-1970s, and almost 90 percent of all women with college degrees worked. The two-career family, in which both the husband and the wife maintained active professional lives, was becoming a widely accepted middle-class norm. (It had been common within the working class for decades.) Some middle-class women were postponing marriage or motherhood for the sake of their careers. There were also important symbolic changes, such as the refusal of many women to adopt their husbands' names when they married and the use of the term "Ms." in place of "Mrs." or "Miss" to denote the irrelevance of a woman's marital status in the professional world.

In politics, women began to compete effectively with men for both elected and appointive positions in the 1970s. By the mid-1980s, women were serving in both houses of Congress, on the Supreme Court, in numerous federal cabinet positions, as governors of several states, and in many other political positions. In 1981, Ronald Reagan named the first female Supreme Court justice, Sandra Day O'Connor; in 1993, Bill Clinton named the second, Ruth Bader Ginsburg. In 1984, the Democratic Party chose a woman, Representative Geraldine Ferraro of New York, as its vice presidential candidate. In academia, women were expanding their presence in traditional scholarly fields; they were also creating new fields—women's and gender studies, which in the 1980s and 1990s were among the fastest-growing areas of American scholarship.

In 1972, Congress approved the Equal Rights Amendment (ERA) to the Constitution, which some feminists had been promoting since the 1920s, and sent it to the states. For a while ratification seemed almost certain. By the late 1970s, however, the momentum behind the amendment had died. The ERA was in trouble not because of indifference but because of a rising chorus of objections to it from people (including many antifeminist women) who feared that it would disrupt traditional social patterns. In 1982, the amendment finally died when the ten years allotted for ratification expired.

The Abortion Controversy

A major element of American feminism since the 1920s has been the effort by women to win greater control of their own sexual and reproductive lives. In its least controversial form, this impulse helped produce an increasing awareness in the 1960s and 1970s of the problems of rape, sexual abuse, and wife beating. There continued to be some controversy over the dissemination of contraceptives and birth-control information, but that issue, at least, seemed to have lost much of the explosive character it had once possessed. A related issue, however, stimulated as much popular passion as any question of its time: abortion.

Abortion had once been legal in much of the United States, but by the beginning of the twentieth century it was banned by statute in most of the country and remained so into the 1960s (although many abortions continued to be performed quietly, and often dangerously, out of sight of the law).

The women's movement created strong new pressures on behalf of the legalization of abortion. Several states had abandoned restrictions on abortion by the end of the 1960s. And in 1973, the Supreme Court's decision in *Roe v. Wade*, based on a new theory of a constitutional "right to privacy" first recognized by the Court only a few years earlier, invalidated all laws prohibiting abortion during the "first trimester"—the first three months of pregnancy. The issue, it seemed, was finally settled. But it soon became clear that it was not.

In many ways, feminism was much like other "liberation" movements of the 1960s and 1970s. But it differed from them in one fundamental respect: its success. The women's movement may not have fulfilled all its goals. But it achieved fundamental and permanent changes in the position of women in American life, and it promised to do much more.

NIXON, KISSINGER, AND THE WAR

Richard Nixon assumed office in 1969 committed not only to restoring stability at home but to creating a new and more stable order in the world. Central to Nixon's hopes for international stability was a resolution of the stalemate in Vietnam. Yet the new president felt no freer than his predecessor to abandon the American commitment there.

Vietnamization

Despite Nixon's own deep interest in international affairs, he brought with him into government a man who seemed to overshadow the president himself at times in the conduct of diplomacy: Henry Kissinger, a Harvard professor whom Nixon appointed as his special assistant for national security affairs. Kissinger quickly established dominance over the secretary of state, William Rogers, and the secretary of defense, Melvin Laird, who were both more experienced in public life. That was in part a result of Nixon's passion for concentrating decision making in the White House. But Kissinger's keen intelligence, his bureaucratic skills, his penchant for secrecy, and his success in handling the press were at least equally important. Together, Nixon and Kissinger set out to find an acceptable solution to the stalemate in Vietnam.

The new Vietnam policy moved along several fronts. One was an effort to limit domestic opposition to the war so as to give the administration more political space in which to maneuver. The administration moved, therefore, to "Vietnamize" the war—that is, to train and equip the South

Vietnamese military to assume the burden of combat in place of American forces. In the fall of 1969, Nixon announced the withdrawal of 60,000 American ground troops from Vietnam, the first reduction in United States troop strength since the beginning of the war. The withdrawals continued steadily for more than three years, so that by the fall of 1972 relatively few American soldiers remained in Indochina. From a peak of more than 540,000 in 1969, the number had dwindled to about 60,000.

Vietnamization (and the decreased draft calls it produced) did help quiet domestic opposition to the war for a time. It did nothing, however, to break the stalemate in the negotiations with the North Vietnamese in Paris. The new administration quickly decided that new military pressures would be necessary to do that.

Escalation

By the end of their first year in office, Nixon and Kissinger had decided that the most effective way to tip the military balance in America's favor was to destroy the bases in Cambodia and Laos from which the American military believed the North Vietnamese were launching many of their attacks. Very early in his presidency, Nixon ordered the air force to begin bombing Cambodian and Laotian territory to destroy the enemy sanctuaries. He kept the raids secret from Congress and the public. In the spring of 1970, and many believed with American encouragement and support, conservative military leaders overthrew the neutral government of Cambodia and established a new, pro-American regime under General Lon Nol. Lon Nol quickly gave his approval to American incursions into his territory; and on April 30, Nixon went on television to announce that he was ordering American troops across the border into Cambodia to "clean out" the bases that the enemy had been using for its "increased military aggression."

Literally overnight, the Cambodian invasion restored the dwindling antiwar movement to vigorous life. The first days of May saw the most widespread and vocal antiwar demonstrations ever. A mood of crisis was already mounting when, on May 4, four college students were killed and nine others injured after members of the National Guard opened fire on antiwar demonstrators at Kent State University in Ohio. Ten days later, police killed two black students at Jackson State University in Mississippi during a demonstration there.

The clamor against the war spread into the government and the press. Congress angrily repealed the Gulf of Tonkin Resolution in December, stripping the president of what had long served as the legal basis for the war.

Nixon ignored the action. Then, in June 1971, first the *New York Times* and later other newspapers began publishing excerpts from a secret study of the war prepared by the Defense Department during the Johnson administration. The so-called Pentagon Papers, leaked to the press by former Defense official Daniel Ellsberg, confirmed what many had long believed: the government had been dishonest, both in reporting the military progress of the war and in explaining its own motives for American involvement. The administration went to court to suppress the documents, but the Supreme Court ruled that the press had the right to publish them.

Particularly troubling, both to the public and to the government itself, were signs of decay within the American military itself. Morale and discipline among American troops in Vietnam, who had been fighting a savage and inconclusive war for more than five years, were rapidly deteriorating. The trial and conviction in 1971 of Lieutenant William Calley, who was charged with overseeing a massacre of more than 100 unarmed South Vietnamese civilians in 1968 near the village of My Lai, attracted wide public attention to the dehumanizing impact of the war on those who fought it—and to the terrible consequences for the Vietnamese people of that dehumanization. Less publicized were other, more widespread problems among American troops in Vietnam: desertion, drug addiction, racial bias, refusal to obey orders, even the killing of unpopular officers by enlisted men.

The continuing carnage, the increasing savagery, and the social distress at home had largely destroyed public support for the war. By 1971, nearly two-thirds of those interviewed in public opinion polls were urging American withdrawal from Vietnam. President Nixon, however, was determined to resist, and if possible destroy, his critics, convinced that a defeat in Vietnam would cause unacceptable damage to the nation's (and his own) credibility. The FBI, the CIA, the White House itself, and other federal agencies increased their efforts to discredit and harass antiwar and radical groups, often through illegal means.

In Indochina, meanwhile, the fighting raged on. In February 1971, the president ordered the air force to assist the South Vietnamese army in an invasion of Laos—a test, as he saw it, of his Vietnamization program. Within weeks, the South Vietnamese scrambled back across the border in defeat. American bombing in Vietnam and Cambodia increased, despite its apparent ineffectiveness. In March 1972, the North Vietnamese mounted their biggest offensive since 1968 (the so-called Easter offensive). American and South Vietnamese forces managed to halt the communist advance, but it was clear that without American support the South Vietnamese would not have succeeded. At the same time, Nixon ordered American planes to bomb targets near Hanoi, the capital of North Vietnam, and Haiphong, its principal port, and called for the mining of seven North Vietnamese harbors (including Haiphong).

"Peace with Honor"

As the 1972 presidential election approached, the administration stepped up its effort to produce a breakthrough in negotiations with the North Vietnamese. In April 1972, the president dropped his longtime insistence on a removal of North Vietnamese troops from the south before any American withdrawal. Meanwhile, Henry Kissinger was meeting privately in Paris with the North Vietnamese foreign secretary, Le Duc Tho, to work out terms for a cease-fire. On October 26, only days before the presidential election, Kissinger announced that "peace is at hand."

Several weeks later (after the election), negotiations broke down once again. Although both the American and the North Vietnamese governments were ready to accept the Kissinger-Tho plan for a cease-fire, President Nguyen Van Thieu of South Vietnam balked, still insisting on a full withdrawal of North Vietnamese forces from the south. Kissinger tried to win additional concessions from the communists to meet Thieu's objections, but on December 16 talks broke off.

The next day, December 17, American B-52s began the heaviest and most destructive air raids of the entire war on Hanoi, Haiphong, and other North Vietnamese targets. Civilian casualties were high. And fifteen American B-52s were shot down by the North Vietnamese; in the entire war to that point, the United States had lost only one of the giant bombers. On December 30, Nixon terminated the "Christmas bombing." The United States and the North Vietnamese returned to the conference table. And on January 27, 1973, they signed an "agreement on ending the war and restoring peace in Vietnam." Nixon claimed that the Christmas bombing had forced the North Vietnamese to relent. At least equally important, however, was the enormous American pressure on Thieu to accept the cease-fire.

The terms of the Paris accords were little different from those Kissinger and Tho had accepted in principle a few months before. There would be an immediate cease-fire. The North Vietnamese would release several hundred American prisoners of war, whose fate had become an emotional issue of great importance within the United States. The Thieu regime would survive for the moment, but North Vietnamese forces already in the south would remain there. An undefined committee would work out a permanent settlement.

Defeat in Indochina

American forces were hardly out of Indochina before the Paris accords collapsed. In March 1975, finally, the North Vietnamese launched a full-scale offensive against the now greatly weakened forces of the south. Thieu appealed to Washington for assistance. The president (now Gerald Ford) appealed to Congress for additional funding; Congress refused. Late in April 1975, communist forces marched into Saigon, shortly after officials of the Thieu regime and the staff of the American embassy had fled the country in humiliating disarray. The communist forces quickly occupied the capital, renamed it Ho Chi Minh City, and began the process of reuniting Vietnam under the harsh rule of Hanoi. At about the same time, the Lon Nol regime in Cambodia fell to the murderous forces of the Khmer Rouge—whose brutal policies led to the death of more than a third of the country's people over the next several years.

Such were the dismal results of more than a decade of direct American military involvement in Vietnam. More than 1.2 million Vietnamese soldiers had died in combat, along with countless civilians throughout the region. A

THE FALL OF SAIGON The chaotic evacuation of Americans from Saigon in the spring of 1975, only hours before victorious North Vietnamese troops entered the city, was a humiliating spectacle. Desperate South Vietnamese soldiers and officials fought with American soldiers and diplomats for space on the few airplanes and helicopters available.

beautiful land had been ravaged, its agrarian economy left in ruins; until an economic revival began in the early 1990s, Vietnam remained one of the poorest and most politically oppressive nations in the world. The United States had paid a heavy price as well. The war had cost the nation almost $150 billion in direct costs and much more indirectly. It had resulted in the deaths of over 57,000 young Americans and the injury of 300,000 more. And the nation had suffered a blow to its confidence and self-esteem from which it would not soon recover.

NIXON, KISSINGER, AND THE WORLD

The continuing war in Vietnam provided a dismal backdrop to what Nixon considered his larger mission in world affairs: the construction of a new international order. The president had become convinced that the old assumptions of a "bipolar" world—in which the United States and the Soviet Union were the only real great powers—were now obsolete. America must adapt to the new "multipolar" international structure, in which China, Japan, and Western Europe were becoming major, independent forces. Nixon and Kissinger believed it was possible to construct something like the "balance of power" that had permitted nineteenth-century Europe to enjoy nearly a century of relative stability. To do so, however, required a major change in several longstanding assumptions of American foreign policy.

The China Initiative and Détente

For more than twenty years, ever since the fall of Chiang Kai-shek in 1949, the United States had treated China, the second-largest nation on earth, as if it did not exist. Instead, America recognized the forlorn regime-in-exile on Taiwan as the legitimate government of mainland China. Nixon and Kissinger wanted to forge a new relationship with the Chinese communists—in part to strengthen them as a counterbalance to the Soviet Union. The Chinese, for their part, were eager to forestall the possibility of a Soviet-American alliance against China and to end China's own isolation from the international arena.

On July 1971, Nixon sent Henry Kissinger on a secret mission to Beijing. When Kissinger returned, the president made the startling announcement that he would visit China himself within the next few months. That fall, with American approval, the United Nations admitted the communist government of China and expelled the representatives of the Taiwan regime. Finally, in February 1972, Nixon paid a formal visit to China and, in a single stroke, erased much of the deep American animosity toward the Chinese communists. Nixon did not yet formally recognize the communist regime, but in 1972 the United States and China began low-level diplomatic relations.

The initiatives in China coincided with (and probably assisted) an effort by the Nixon administration to improve relations with the Soviet Union. In 1969, American and Soviet diplomats met in Helsinki, Finland, to begin talks on limiting nuclear weapons. In 1972, they produced the first Strategic Arms Limitation Treaty (SALT I), which froze some nuclear missiles (ICBMs) of both sides at present levels. In May of that year, the president traveled to Moscow to sign the agreement. The next year, the Soviet premier, Leonid Brezhnev, visited Washington.

DÉTENTE AT HIGH TIDE The visit of Soviet Premier Leonid Brezhnev to Washington in 1973 was a high-water mark in the search for détente between the two nations. Here, Brezhnev and Nixon share friendly words on the White House balcony.

A M E R I C A N   V O I C E S

RICHARD NIXON

The China Trip, 1972

ON FEBRUARY 17, 1972, at 10:35 A.M. we left Andrews Air Force Base for Peking. . . . We stopped briefly in Shanghai . . . ; an hour and a half later we prepared to land in Peking. I looked out the window. It was winter, and the countryside was drab and gray. The small towns and villages looked like pictures I had seen of towns in the Middle Ages. . . .

Chou En-lai stood at the foot of the ramp, hatless in the cold. Even a heavy overcoat did not hide the thinness of his frail body. When we were about halfway down the steps, he began to clap. I paused for a moment and then returned the gesture, according to the Chinese custom.

I knew that Chou had been deeply insulted by Foster Dulles's refusal to shake hands with him at the Geneva Conference in 1954. When I reached the bottom step, therefore, I made a point of extending my hand as I walked toward him. When our hands met, one era ended and another began. . . .

I stood on Chou's left while the band played the anthems. "The Star-Spangled Banner" had never sounded so stirring to me as on that windswept runway in the heart of Communist China. . . .

Chou and I rode into the city in a curtained car. As we left the airport, he said, "Your handshake came over the vastest ocean in the world—twenty-five years of no communication." When we came into Tienamen Square at the center of Peking . . . I noticed that the streets were empty.

SOURCE: *RN: The Memoirs of Richard Nixon*, pp. 559–560. Copyright © 1978 by Richard Nixon. Reprinted by permission of Warner Books, Inc.

The Problems of Multipolarity

The policies of rapprochement with communist China and détente with the Soviet Union reflected Nixon's and Kissinger's belief in the importance of stable relationships among the great powers. But great-power relationships could not alone ensure international stability, for the Third World remained the most volatile and dangerous source of international tension.

Central to the Nixon-Kissinger policy toward the Third World was the effort to maintain the status quo without involving the United States too deeply in local disputes. In 1969 and 1970, the president described what became known as the Nixon Doctrine, by which the United States would "participate in the defense and development of allies and friends" but would leave the "basic responsibility" for the future of those "friends" to the nations themselves. In practice, the Nixon Doctrine meant a declining American interest in contributing to Third World development; a growing contempt for the United Nations, where underdeveloped nations were gaining influence through their sheer numbers; and increasing support to authoritarian regimes attempting to withstand radical challenges from within.

In 1970, for example, the CIA poured substantial funds into Chile to help support the established government against a communist challenge. When the Marxist candidate for president, Salvador Allende, came to power anyway through an open election, the United States began funneling more money to opposition forces in Chile to help destabilize the new government. In 1973, a military junta seized power from Allende, who was subsequently murdered. The United States developed a friendly relationship with the new, repressive military government of General Augusto Pinochet.

In the Middle East, conditions grew more volatile in the aftermath of the 1967 war, in which Israel had occupied substantial new territories. Palestinian Arabs continued to claim the lands now controlled by Israel; many of them had been dislodged from their homes, and the refugees were a source of considerable instability in Jordan, Lebanon, and the other surrounding countries into which they moved.

In October 1973, on the Jewish high holy day of Yom Kippur, Egyptian and Syrian forces attacked Israel. For ten days, the Israelis struggled to recover from the surprise attack; finally, they launched an effective counteroffensive against Egyptian forces in the Sinai. At that point, the United States intervened, placing heavy pressure on Israel to accept a cease-fire rather than press its advantage.

The imposed settlement of the Yom Kippur War demonstrated the growing dependence of the United States and its allies on Arab oil. Permitting Israel to continue its drive into Egypt might have jeopardized the ability of the United States to purchase needed petroleum from the Arab states. A brief but painful embargo by the Arab governments on the sale of oil to America in 1973 provided an ominous warning of the costs of losing access to the region's resources. The lesson of the Yom Kippur War, therefore, was that the United States could not ignore the interests of the Arab nations in its efforts on behalf of Israel.

A larger lesson of 1973 was that the nations of the Third World could no longer be expected to act as passive, cooperative "client states." And the United States could not depend on cheap, easy access to raw materials as it had in the past.

POLITICS AND ECONOMICS IN THE NIXON YEARS

For a time in the late 1960s, it had seemed to many Americans that forces of chaos and radicalism were taking control of the nation. The domestic policy of the Nixon administration was, the president claimed, an attempt to restore order. In the end, however, economic and political crises sharply limited the administration's ability to fulfill its domestic goals.

Domestic Initiatives

Many of Nixon's domestic policies were a response to what he believed to be the demands of his constituency—conservative, middle-class people, the "silent majority" who he believed wanted to reduce federal "interference" in local affairs. He tried, unsuccessfully, to persuade Congress to pass legislation prohibiting school desegregation through the use of forced busing. He forbade the Department of Health, Education, and Welfare to cut off federal funds from school districts that had failed to comply with court orders to integrate. At the same time, he began to reduce or dismantle many of the social programs of the Great Society and the New Frontier. In 1973, he abolished the Office of Economic Opportunity, the centerpiece of the antipoverty program of the Johnson years.

Yet Nixon's domestic policies had progressive and creative elements as well. He signed legislation creating the Environmental Protection Agency and establishing the most stringent environmental regulations in the nation's history. He ordered the first affirmative action program for workers on federally funded projects. One of the administration's boldest efforts was an attempt to overhaul the nation's enormous welfare system. Nixon proposed replacing the existing system, which almost everyone agreed was cumbersome, expensive, and inefficient, with what he called the Family Assistance Plan (FAP). It would in effect have created a guaranteed annual income for all Americans: $1,600 in federal grants, which could be supplemented by outside earnings up to $4,000. The FAP won approval in the House in 1970, but concerted attacks by welfare recipients (who considered the benefits inadequate), members of the welfare bureaucracy (whose own influence stood to be sharply diminished by the bill), and conservatives (who opposed a guaranteed income on principle) helped kill it in the Senate.

From the Warren Court to the Nixon Court

Of all the liberal institutions that aroused the enmity of the "silent majority" in the 1950s and 1960s, none evoked more anger and bitterness than the Supreme Court. Not only did its rulings on racial matters disrupt traditional social patterns in both the North and the South, but its staunch defense of civil liberties directly contributed, in the eyes of many Americans, to the increase in crime, disorder, and moral decay. In *Engel* v. *Fitak* (1962), the Court ruled that prayers in public schools were unconstitutional, sparking outrage among religious fundamentalists and others. In *Roth* v. *United States* (1957), the Court had sharply limited the authority of local governments to curb pornography. In a series of other decisions, the Court greatly strengthened the civil rights of criminal defendants and, many Americans believed, greatly weakened the power of law enforcement officials to do their jobs. For example, in *Gideon* v. *Wainwright* (1963), the Court ruled that every felony defendant was entitled to a lawyer regardless of his or her ability to pay. In *Escobedo* v. *Illinois* (1964), it ruled that a defendant must be allowed access to a lawyer before questioning by police. In *Miranda* v. *Arizona* (1966), the Court confirmed the obligation of authorities to inform a criminal suspect of his or her rights. By 1968, the Warren Court had become the target of Americans of all kinds who felt the balance of power in the United States had shifted too far toward the poor, the dispossessed, and the criminal at the expense of the middle class.

Nixon was determined to use his judicial appointments to give the Court a more conservative cast. When Chief Justice Earl Warren resigned early in 1969, Nixon replaced him with a federal appeals court judge of known conservative leanings, Warren Burger. A few months later, Associate Justice Abe Fortas resigned his seat after the disclosure of a series of alleged financial improprieties. To replace him, Nixon named Clement F. Haynsworth, a respected federal circuit court judge from South Carolina. But Haynsworth came under fire from Senate liberals, black organizations, and labor unions for his conservative record on civil rights and for what some claimed was a conflict of interest in several of the cases on which he had sat. The Senate rejected him. Nixon's next choice was G. Harrold Carswell, a judge of the Florida federal appeals court almost entirely lacking in distinction and widely considered unfit for the Supreme Court. The Senate rejected his nomination too.

Nixon angrily denounced the votes. But he was careful thereafter to choose men of standing within the legal community to fill vacancies on the Supreme Court: Harry Blackmun, a moderate jurist from Minnesota; Lewis E. Powell, Jr., a respected judge from Virginia; and William Rehnquist, a member of the Nixon Justice Department. In the process, he transformed the Court.

The new Court, however, fell short of what the president and many conservatives had expected. Rather than retreating from its commitment to social reform, the Court in many areas actually moved further toward it. In *Swann v. Charlotte-Mecklenburg Board of Education* (1971), it ruled in favor of the use of forced busing to achieve racial balance in schools. Not even the intense and occasionally violent opposition of local communities as diverse as Boston and Louisville, Kentucky, was able to weaken the judicial commitment to integration. In *Furman* v. *Georgia* (1972), the Court overturned existing capital punishment statutes and established strict new guidelines for such laws in the future. In *Roe* v. *Wade* (1973), it struck down laws forbidding abortions.

In other decisions, however, the Burger Court did demonstrate a more conservative temperament than the Warren Court had shown. Although the justices approved busing as a tool for achieving integration, they rejected, in *Milliken* v. *Bradley* (1974), a plan to transfer students across district lines (in this case, between Detroit and its suburbs) to achieve racial balance. While the Court upheld the principle of affirmative action in its celebrated 1978 decision in *Bakke* v. *Board of Regents of California*, it established restrictive new guidelines for such programs in the future. In *Stone* v. *Powell* (1976), the Court agreed to certain limits on the right of a defendant to appeal a state conviction to the federal judiciary.

The Election of 1972

However unsuccessful the Nixon administration may have been in achieving some of its specific goals, Nixon entered the presidential race in 1972 with a substantial reserve of strength. The events of that year improved his position immeasurably. His energetic reelection committee collected enormous sums of money to support the campaign. The president himself used the powers of incumbency to strengthen his political standing in strategic areas.

Nixon was most fortunate in 1972, however, in his opposition. George Wallace, partly at Nixon's urging, entered the Democratic primaries and helped divide the party until a would-be assassin shot the Alabama governor during a rally at a Maryland shopping center in May. Paralyzed from the waist down, Wallace was unable to continue campaigning. In the meantime, the most liberal factions of the party were succeeding in establishing their candidate, Senator George S. McGovern of South Dakota, as the frontrunner for the nomination. An outspoken critic of the war, a forceful advocate of advanced liberal positions on virtually every social and economic issue, McGovern profited greatly from party reforms (which he himself had helped to draft) that gave increased influence to women, blacks, and young people in the selection of the Democratic ticket. But in the process, the McGovern campaign came to be associated with aspects of the turbulent 1960s that many middle-class Americans were eager to reject.

On election day, Nixon won reelection by one of the largest margins in history: 60.7 percent of the popular vote compared with 37.5 percent for the forlorn McGovern, and an electoral margin of 520 to 17. The Democratic candidate had carried only Massachusetts and the District of Columbia. But serious problems, some beyond the president's control and some of his own making, were already lurking in the wings.

The Troubled Economy

Although it was political scandal that would ultimately destroy the Nixon presidency, the most important national crisis of the early 1970s was the beginning of a long-term transformation of the American economy. For three decades, that economy had been the envy of the world. It had produced as much as a third of the world's industrial goods and had dominated international trade. The American dollar had been the strongest currency in the world, and the American standard of living had risen steadily and consistently from its already substantial heights, improving the lives of the vast majority of the nation's citizens. Most Americans had come to assume that this remarkable prosperity was the normal condition of their society. In fact, however, it rested in part on several artificial conditions that were by the late 1960s rapidly disappearing.

The most immediate change was the end of the nation's easy access to

cheap raw materials, a change that became a major cause of the serious inflation that plagued the economy through much of the 1970s. Large increases
in federal deficit spending in the 1960s were responsible for some of the inflation. But at least equally important was the rising price of energy.

More than any nation on earth, the United States based its economy on
the easy availability of cheap and plentiful fuels. No society was more dependent on the automobile; none was more wasteful in its use of oil and gas
in its homes, schools, and factories. Domestic petroleum reserves were no
longer sufficient to meet this demand, and the nation was growing increasingly dependent on imports from the Middle East and Africa.

For many years, the Organization of Petroleum Exporting Countries
(OPEC) had operated as an informal bargaining unit for the sale of oil by
Third World nations but had seldom managed to exercise any real strength.
But in the early 1970s, OPEC began to assert itself, to use its oil both as an
economic tool and as a political weapon. In 1973, in the midst of the Yom
Kippur War, Arab members of OPEC announced that they would no longer
ship petroleum to nations supporting Israel—that is, to the United States
and its allies in Western Europe. At about the same time, the OPEC nations
agreed to raise their prices 500 percent (from \$3 to \$15 a barrel). These twin
shocks produced momentary economic chaos in the West. The United
States suffered its first fuel shortage since World War II. And although the
crisis eased a few months later, the price of energy continued to skyrocket.

The energy crisis eventually subsided, but another, longer-term change
in the American economy was the transformation of the nation's manufacturing sector. Ever since World War II, American industry had enjoyed relatively little competition from the rest of the world in its search for export
markets and even less competition in its domination of the American domestic market. By the end of the 1960s, however, both Western Europe and
Japan had recovered from the damage their manufacturing sectors had absorbed during World War II; by the early 1970s, they were providing stiff
competition to American firms in the sale of automobiles, steel, and many
other products both in world markets and, more importantly at first, within
the United States. Many American corporations responded to these new conditions at first with confusion and bewilderment. Gradually, however, some
of the nation's major industries restructured themselves to become more
competitive again in world markets. In the process, they closed many older
plants and eliminated hundreds of thousands of once-lucrative manufacturing jobs. The high-wage, high-employment industrial economy that had
been a central fact of American life since the 1940s was gradually disappearing.

The Nixon Response

Nixon's initial answer to these mounting economic problems was a conventional anti-inflationary one. He reduced spending and raised taxes. But those policies produced both congressional and popular protest, and Nixon turned increasingly to an economic tool more readily available to him: control of the currency. Placing conservative economists at the head of the Federal Reserve Board, he ensured sharply higher interest rates and a contraction of the money supply. But the tight money policy did little to curb inflation. The cost of living rose a cumulative 15 percent during Nixon's first two and a half years in office. Economic growth, in the meantime, declined. The United States was encountering a new and puzzling dilemma: "stagflation," a combination of rising prices and general economic stagnation.

In the summer of 1971, Nixon imposed a ninety-day freeze on all wages and prices at their existing levels. Then, in November, he launched Phase II of his economic plan: mandatory guidelines for wage and price increases, to be administered by a federal agency. Inflation subsided temporarily, but the recession continued. Fearful that the recession would be more damaging than inflation in an election year, the administration reversed itself late in 1971: interest rates were allowed to drop sharply, and government spending increased—producing the largest budget deficit since World War II. The new tactics helped revive the economy in the short term, but inflation rose substantially—particularly after the administration abandoned the strict Phase II controls and replaced them with a set of voluntary, and almost entirely ineffective, guidelines. In 1973, prices rose 9 percent; in 1974, after the Arab oil embargo and the OPEC price increases, they rose 12 percent—the highest rate since shortly after World War II. The value of the dollar continued to slide, and the nation's international trade continued to decline. The new energy crisis, in the meantime, was quickly becoming a national preoccupation. But while Nixon talked often about the need to achieve "energy independence," he offered few concrete proposals.

The erratic economic programs of the Nixon administration were a sign of a broader national confusion about the longer-term causes of American economic decline. The Nixon pattern—of lurching from a tight money policy to curb inflation at one moment to a spending policy to cure recession at the next—repeated itself during the two administrations that followed. Nowhere was there any serious attempt to address the deeper problems that lay at the heart of the erosion of the American economy.

THE WATERGATE CRISIS

Although economic problems greatly concerned the American people in the 1970s, another stunning development almost entirely preoccupied the nation beginning early in 1973: the fall of Richard Nixon. The president's demise was a result in part of his own personality. Defensive, secretive, resentful of his critics, he brought to his office an element of mean-spiritedness that helped undermine even his most important accomplishments. But the larger explanation for the crisis lay in Nixon's view of American society and the world, and of his own role in both. The president believed the United States faced grave dangers from the radicals and dissidents who were challenging his policies. He came increasingly to consider any challenge to his policies a threat to "national security." By identifying his own political fortunes with those of the nation, Nixon was creating a climate in which he and those who served him could justify almost any tactics to stifle dissent and undermine opposition.

The Scandals

Nixon's approach to his office was in part a culmination of long-term changes in the presidency. Public expectations of the president had increased dramatically in the years since World War II, yet the constraints on the authority of the office had grown as well. In response, a succession of presidents had sought new methods for exercising power, often stretching the law, occasionally breaking it.

Nixon not only continued but greatly accelerated these trends. Facing a Democratic Congress hostile to his goals, he attempted to find ways to circumvent the legislature whenever possible. Saddled with a federal bureaucracy unresponsive to his wishes, he constructed a hierarchy of command in which virtually all executive power became concentrated in the White House. Operating within a rigid, even autocratic staff structure, the president became a solitary, brooding figure, whose contempt for his opponents and impatience with obstacles to his policies festered and grew. Unknown to all but a few intimates, he also became mired in a pattern of illegalities and abuses of power that late in 1972 began to break through to the surface.

Early on the morning of June 17, 1972, police arrested five men who had broken into the offices of the Democratic National Committee in the Watergate office building in Washington, D.C. Two others were seized a short time later and charged with supervising the break-in. When reporters for the *Washington Post* began researching the backgrounds of the culprits, they discovered that among those involved in the burglary were former employees of the Committee for the Re-Election of the President (CRP). One of them had worked in the White House itself. They had, moreover, been paid for the break-in from a secret fund of the reelection committee, a fund controlled by, among others, members of the White House staff.

Public interest in the disclosures grew slowly in the last months of 1972. Early in 1973, however, the Watergate burglars went on trial; and under prodding from federal judge John J. Sirica, one of the defendants, James W. McCord, agreed to cooperate both with the grand jury and with a special Senate investigating committee recently established under Senator Sam J. Ervin of North Carolina. McCord's testimony opened a floodgate of confessions, and for months a parade of White House and campaign officials exposed one illegality after another. Foremost among them was a member of the inner circle of the White House, John Dean, counsel to the president, who leveled allegations against Nixon himself.

Two different sets of scandals were emerging from the investigations. One was a general pattern of abuses of power involving both the White House and the Nixon campaign committee, which included, but was not limited to, the Watergate break-in. The other scandal, and the one that became the major focus of public attention for nearly two years, was the way in which the administration tried to manage the investigations of the Watergate break-in and other abuses—a pattern of behavior that became known as the "cover-up." There was never any conclusive evidence that the president had planned or approved the burglary in advance. But there was mounting evidence that he had been involved in illegal efforts to obstruct investigations of and withhold information about the episode. As interest in the case grew to something approaching a national obsession, the investigation focused increasingly on a single question: in the words of Senator Howard Baker of Tennessee, a member of the Ervin Committee, "What did the President know and when did he know it?"

Nixon accepted the departure of those members of his administration implicated in the scandals. But the president continued to insist on his own innocence. There the matter might have rested had it not been for the disclosure during the Senate hearings of a White House taping system that had recorded virtually every conversation in the president's office during the period in question. All those investigating the scandals sought access to the tapes; Nixon, pleading "executive privilege," refused to release them. A special prosecutor appointed by the president to handle the Watergate cases, Harvard law professor Archibald Cox, took Nixon to court in October 1973 in an effort to force him to relinquish the recordings. Nixon, now clearly growing desperate, fired Cox and suffered the humiliation of watching both Attorney General Elliot Richardson and his deputy resign in protest. This "Saturday night massacre" made the president's predicament much worse. Not only did public pressure force him to appoint a new special prosecutor, Texas attorney Leon Jaworski, who proved just as determined as Cox to subpoena the tapes; but the episode precipitated an investigation by the House of Representatives into the possibility of impeachment.

The Fall of Richard Nixon

Nixon's situation deteriorated further in the following months. Late in 1973, Vice President Spiro Agnew became embroiled in a scandal of his own when evidence surfaced that he had accepted bribes and kickbacks while serving as governor of Maryland and even as vice president. In return for a Justice Department agreement not to press the case, Agnew pleaded no contest to a lesser charge of income-tax evasion and resigned from the government. With the controversial Agnew no longer in line to succeed to the presidency, the prospect of removing Nixon from the White House became less worrisome to his opponents. The new vice president (the first appointed under the terms of the Twenty-fifth Amendment, which had been adopted in 1967) was House Minority Leader Gerald Ford, an amiable and popular Michigan congressman.

The impeachment investigation quickly gathered momentum. In April 1974, in an effort to head off further subpoenas of the tapes, the president released transcripts of a number of relevant conversations, claiming that they proved his innocence. Investigators and much of the public felt otherwise. Even these edited tapes seemed to suggest Nixon's complicity in the cover-up. In July, the crisis reached a climax. First the Supreme Court ruled unanimously, in *United States* v. *Richard M. Nixon*, that the president must relinquish the tapes to Special Prosecutor Jaworski. Days later, the House Judiciary Committee voted to recommend three articles of impeachment.

Even without additional evidence, Nixon might well have been impeached by the full House and convicted by the Senate. Early in August, however, he provided at last the "smoking gun"—the concrete proof of his guilt—that his defenders had long contended was missing from the case against him. Among the tapes that the Supreme Court compelled Nixon to relinquish were several that offered apparently incontrovertible evidence of his involvement in the Watergate cover-up. Only three days after the burglary, the recordings disclosed, the president had ordered the FBI to stop investigating the break-in. Impeachment and conviction now seemed inevitable.

For several days, Nixon brooded in the White House, on the verge, some claimed, of a breakdown. Finally, on August 8, 1974, he announced his resignation—the first president in American history ever to do so. At noon the next day, while Nixon and his family were flying west to their home in California, Gerald Ford took the oath of office as president.

Many Americans expressed relief and exhilaration that, as the new president put it, "our long national nightmare is over." They were relieved to be rid of Richard Nixon, who had lost the great popularity that had won him

---

DEBATING THE PAST

Women's History

THE REVIVAL OF feminism as a powerful social and political force in the 1960s and 1970s brought with it a dramatic rise of interest in, and a transformation of, women's history.

Both men and women have been writing histories of women for centuries, but during much of the twentieth century, women's history remained in the shadows of other fields. However, as modern feminism began to sweep across society in the 1960s and 1970s, interest in women's history revived as well. For a time, the new women's history replicated the pattern of earlier studies of women. Much of the early work was in the "contributionist" tradition, revealing ways in which women had contributed more to American history than scholars had previously recognized. Other work stressed ways in which women had been victimized by their subordination to men and by their powerlessness within the industrial economy.

Many historians developed their feminist sensibilities under the influence of the civil rights movement; and in the 1960s and 1970s they tended to emphasize the artificiality of gender distinctions, just as early civil rights activists emphasized the artificiality of racial distinctions. The difference between women and men in the public world, they argued, was "socially constructed," not inherent in the biological differences between the sexes. Much of the history of women was, therefore, the history of how men (with the

his landslide reelection victory only two years before. And they were exhilarated that, as some boasted, "the system had worked." But the wave of good feeling could not obscure the deeper and more lasting damage of the Watergate crisis. In a society in which distrust of leaders and institutions of authority was already widespread, the fall of Richard Nixon confirmed for many Americans their most cynical assumptions about the character of American public life.

---

unwitting help of many women) had created and maintained a set of fictions about women's capacities that late-twentieth-century women were now attempting to shatter.

By the late 1970s, however, some feminists were beginning to argue that there were basic differences between women and men—not just biological differences, but differences in values, sensibilities, and culture. These differences were not evidence of women's incapacities. Instead, feminist historians argued, they were evidence of an alternative female culture capable of challenging (and improving) the male-dominated world. Historians of women, therefore, began exploring areas of female experience that revealed the special character of women's culture and values: family, housework, motherhood, women's clubs and organizations, female literature, the social lives of working-class women, women's sexuality, and many other subjects that suggested "difference" more than "contributions" or "victimization." Partly in response, some historians began to make the same argument about men—that understanding "masculinity" and its role in shaping men's lives is as important as understanding notions of "femininity" in explaining the history of women.

The notion of gender as a source of social and cultural difference was responsible for the most powerful challenge women's history raised to the way in which scholars viewed the past. Gender, they argued, is a critical element of the explanation for many kinds of historical experiences, not just women's experiences. Historians in all fields need to incorporate gender into their "categories of analysis" and make it stand alongside such other categories as race, class, ethnicity, religion, and region as a major element of any historical explanation.

CHAPTER THIRTY-THREE

The Age of Limits

Politics and Diplomacy After Watergate
The Rise of the American Right ～ *The "Reagan Revolution"*

HE FRUSTRATIONS OF the early 1970s—the defeat in Vietnam, the Watergate crisis, the decay of the American economy—inflicted damaging blows to the confident, optimistic nationalism that had characterized so much of the postwar era. At first some Americans responded to these problems by announcing the arrival of an "age of limits," in which America would have to learn to live with increasingly constricted expectations. By the end of the decade, however, the contours of another response to the challenges had become visible in both American culture and American politics. It was a response that combined a conservative retreat from some of the heady visions of the 1960s with a reinforced commitment to the idea of economic growth, international power, and American exceptionalism.

POLITICS AND DIPLOMACY
AFTER WATERGATE

In the aftermath of Richard Nixon's ignominious departure from office, many wondered whether faith in the presidency, and in the government as a whole, could easily be restored. The administrations of the two presidents who succeeded Nixon did little to answer those questions.

The Ford Custodianship

Gerald Ford inherited the presidency under unenviable circumstances. He had to try to rebuild confidence in government after the Watergate scandals. And he had to try to restore prosperity in the face of unprecedented

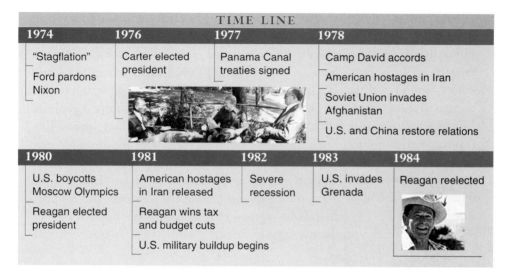

TIME LINE

1974	1976	1977	1978
"Stagflation"	Carter elected president	Panama Canal treaties signed	Camp David accords
Ford pardons Nixon			American hostages in Iran
			Soviet Union invades Afghanistan
			U.S. and China restore relations

1980	1981	1982	1983	1984
U.S. boycotts Moscow Olympics	American hostages in Iran released	Severe recession	U.S. invades Grenada	Reagan reelected
Reagan elected president	Reagan wins tax and budget cuts			
	U.S. military buildup begins			

domestic and international challenges to the American economy. He enjoyed some success in the first of these efforts but very little in the second.

The new president's effort to establish himself as a symbol of political integrity suffered a setback only a month after he took office, when he granted Richard Nixon "a full, free, and absolute pardon" for any crimes he may have committed during his presidency. Ford explained that he was attempting to spare the nation the ordeal of years of litigation and to spare Nixon himself any further suffering. But much of the public suspected a secret deal with the former president. The pardon caused a decline in Ford's popularity from which he never fully recovered. Nevertheless, most Americans considered Ford a decent man; his honesty and amiability did much to reduce the bitterness and acrimony of the Watergate years.

The Ford administration enjoyed less success in its effort to solve the problems of the American economy. In his attempts to curb inflation, the president rejected the idea of wage and price controls and called instead for largely ineffective voluntary efforts. After supporting high interest rates, opposing increased federal spending (through liberal use of his veto power), and resisting pressures for a tax reduction, Ford had to deal with a serious recession in 1974 and 1975. Central to the economic problems was the continuing energy crisis. In the aftermath of the Arab oil embargo of 1973, the OPEC cartel began to raise the price of oil—by 400 percent in 1974 alone. Even so, American dependence on OPEC supplies continued to grow—one of the principal reasons why inflation reached 11 percent in 1976.

At first it seemed that the foreign policy of the new administration would differ little from that of its predecessor. The new president retained Henry Kissinger, whom Nixon had appointed secretary of state in 1973, and continued the general policies of the Nixon years. Late in 1974, Ford met with Leonid Brezhnev at Vladivostok in Siberia and signed an arms control accord that was to serve as the basis for SALT II, thus achieving a goal the Nixon administration had long sought. The following summer, after a European security conference in Helsinki, Finland, the Soviet Union and Western nations agreed to ratify the borders that had divided Europe since 1945; and the Soviets pledged to increase respect for human rights within their own country. In the Middle East, in the meantime, Henry Kissinger helped produce a new accord by which Israel agreed to return large portions of the occupied Sinai to Egypt; the two nations pledged not to resolve future differences by force.

Nevertheless, as the 1976 presidential election approached, Ford's policies were coming under attack from both the right and the left. In the Republican primary campaign, Ford faced a powerful challenge from former California governor Ronald Reagan, leader of the party's conservative wing, who spoke for many on the right who were unhappy with any conciliation of communists. The president only barely survived the assault to win his party's nomination. The Democrats, in the meantime, were gradually uniting behind a new and, before 1976, almost entirely unknown candidate:

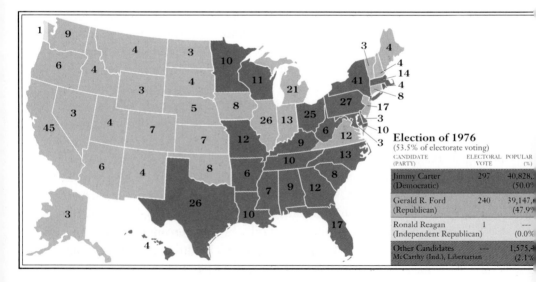

Election of 1976
(53.5% of electorate voting)

CANDIDATE (PARTY)	ELECTORAL VOTE	POPULAR VOTE (%)
Jimmy Carter (Democratic)	297	40,828, (50.0%
Gerald R. Ford (Republican)	240	39,147, (47.9%
Ronald Reagan (Independent Republican)	1	--- (0.0%
Other Candidates McCarthy (Ind.), Libertarian	---	1,575,4 (2.1%

Jimmy Carter, a former governor of Georgia who organized a brilliant primary campaign and appealed to the general unhappiness with Washington by offering honesty, piety, and an outsider's skepticism of the federal government. And while Carter's mammoth lead dwindled to almost nothing by election day, unhappiness with the economy and a general disenchantment with Ford enabled the Democrat to hold on for a narrow victory. Carter emerged with 50 percent of the popular vote to Ford's 47.9 percent and 297 electoral votes to Ford's 240.

The Trials of Jimmy Carter

Like Ford, Jimmy Carter assumed the presidency at a moment when the nation faced problems of staggering complexity and difficulty. Perhaps no leader could have thrived in such inhospitable circumstances. But Carter seemed at times to make his predicament worse by a style of leadership that many considered self-righteous and inflexible. He left office in 1981 as one of the least popular presidents of the century.

Carter had campaigned for the presidency as an "outsider," representing Americans suspicious of entrenched bureaucracies and complacent public officials. He carried much of that suspiciousness with him to Washington. He surrounded himself in the White House with a group of close-knit associates from Georgia, and in the beginning, at least, he seemed deliberately to spurn assistance from more experienced political figures.

Carter devoted much of his time to the problems of energy and the economy. Entering office in the midst of a recession, he moved first to reduce unemployment by raising public spending and cutting federal taxes. Unemployment declined, but inflation soared—less because of Carter's fiscal policies than because of the escalating cost of oil. During Carter's last two years in office, prices rose at an annual rate of well over 10 percent. Like Nixon and Ford before him, Carter responded with a combination of tight money and calls for voluntary restraint. He appointed first G. William Miller and then Paul Volcker, conservative economists, to head the Federal Reserve Board, thus ensuring a policy of high interest rates and reduced currency supplies. By 1980, interest rates had risen to the highest levels in American history; at times, they exceeded 20 percent.

The problem of energy also grew steadily more troublesome in the Carter years. In the summer of 1979, instability in the Middle East produced a second major fuel shortage in the United States. In the midst of the crisis, OPEC announced another major price increase, clouding the economic picture still further. Faced with increasing pressure to act (and with public opinion polls showing his approval rating at a dismal 26 percent), Carter withdrew to Camp David, the presidential retreat in the Maryland mountains. Ten days later, he emerged to deliver a remarkable television address. It included a series of proposals for resolving the energy crisis. But it was most notable for Carter's bleak assessment of the national condition. Speaking with unusual fervor, he complained of a "crisis of confidence" that had struck "at the very heart and soul of our national will." The address became known as the "malaise" speech (although Carter himself had never used that word), and it helped fuel attacks that the president was trying to blame his own problems on the American people. Carter's sudden firing of several members of his cabinet a few days later deepened his political problems.

Human Rights and National Interests

Among Jimmy Carter's most frequent campaign promises was a pledge to build a new basis for American foreign policy, one in which the defense of "human rights" would replace the pursuit of "selfish interests." Carter spoke out sharply and often about violations of human rights in many countries (including, most prominently, the Soviet Union). Beyond that general commitment, the Carter administration focused on several more traditional concerns. Carter completed negotiations begun several years earlier on a pair of treaties to turn over control of the Panama Canal to the government of Panama. Domestic opposition to the treaties was intense, especially among conservatives who viewed the new arrangements as part of a general American retreat from international power. But the administration argued that relinquishing the canal was the best way to improve relations with Latin America and avoid violence in Panama. After an acrimonious debate, the Senate ratified the treaties by 68 to 32, only one vote more than the necessary two-thirds.

Far more popular, within the United States at least, was Carter's success in arranging a peace treaty between Egypt and Israel—the crowning achievement of his presidency. Middle East negotiations had seemed hopelessly stalled when a dramatic breakthrough occurred in November 1977. The Egyptian president, Anwar Sadat, accepted an invitation from Prime Minister Menachem Begin to visit Israel. In Tel Aviv, Sadat announced that Egypt was now willing to accept the state of Israel as a legitimate political entity. But translating these good feelings into an actual peace treaty proved more difficult.

When talks between Israeli and Egyptian negotiators stalled, Carter invited Sadat and Begin to a summit conference at Camp David in September

FORGING THE CAMP DAVID ACCORDS Probably the greatest achievement of Jimmy Carter's generally frustrating presidency was his success in guiding Israel and Egypt toward a peaceful settlement of their longstanding grievances. While hosting Israeli Prime Minister Menachem Begin *(right)* and Egyptian President Anwar Sadat *(left)* at his Camp David retreat in September 1978, he helped the two leaders reach a historic agreement.

1978, holding them there for two weeks while he and others helped mediate the disputes between them. On September 17, Carter escorted the two leaders into the White House to announce agreement on a framework for an Egyptian-Israeli peace treaty. Carter intervened again several months later, when talks stalled once more, and helped produce a compromise on the most sensitive issue between the two parties: the Palestinian refugee issue. On March 26, 1979, Begin and Sadat returned together to the White House to sign a formal peace treaty between their two nations.

Carter responded eagerly to the overtures of Deng Xiaoping, the new Chinese leader who was attempting to open his nation to the outside world. On December 15, 1978, Washington and Beijing announced the resumption of formal diplomatic relations between the two nations. A few months later, Carter traveled to Vienna to meet with the aging and visibly ailing Brezhnev to finish drafting the new SALT II arms control agreement. The treaty set limits on the number of long-range missiles, bombers, and nuclear warheads on each side. Almost immediately, however, SALT II met with fierce conservative opposition in the United States. Central to the arguments against the treaty was a fundamental distrust of the Soviet Union that nearly a decade of détente had failed to destroy. By the fall of 1979, with the Senate scheduled to begin debate over the treaty shortly, ratification was already in jeopardy. Events in the following months provided a final blow, both to the treaty and to the larger framework of détente.

The Year of the Hostages

Ever since the early 1950s, the United States had provided political support and, more recently, massive military assistance to the government of the Shah of Iran, hoping to make his nation a bulwark against Soviet expansion in the Middle East. By 1979, however, the Shah was in deep trouble with his own people. Iranians resented the repressive, authoritarian tactics through which the Shah had maintained his autocratic rule. At the same time, Islamic clergy (and much of the fiercely religious populace) opposed his efforts to modernize and westernize a fundamentalist society. The combination of resentments produced a powerful revolutionary movement. In January 1979, the Shah fled the country.

The United States made cautious efforts in the first months after the Shah's abdication to establish cordial relations with the succession of increasingly militant regimes that followed. By late 1979, however, revolutionary chaos in Iran was making any normal relationships impossible. What power there was resided with a zealous religious leader, the Ayatollah Ruhollah Khomeini, whose hatred of the West in general and the United States in particular was intense.

In late October 1979, the deposed Shah arrived in New York to be treated for cancer. Days later, on November 4, an armed mob invaded the American embassy in Teheran, seized the diplomats and military personnel inside, and demanded the return of the Shah to Iran in exchange for their freedom. Fifty-three Americans remained hostages in the embassy for over a year. Coming after years of what many Americans considered international humiliations and defeats, the hostage seizure released a deep well of anger and emotion.

Only weeks after the hostage seizure, on December 27, 1979, Soviet troops invaded Afghanistan, the mountainous nation bordering the Soviet Union and Iran. The Soviet Union had, in fact, been a power in Afghanistan for years, and the dominant force since April 1978, when a coup had estab-

THE HOSTAGES ON DISPLAY The holding hostage of American diplomats in Iran for over a year beginning in November 1979 was always as much an effort to generate publicity as a real negotiating tactic. Anti-western Iranians wasted few opportunities to display their grievances against the United States for its long support of the Shah, and they were eager to present the hostages themselves as evidence of their ability to humble the mighty United States. Here a number of the fifty-three hostages sit on display under signs written in English for the American television audience.

lished a Marxist government there with close ties to the Kremlin. Knowledgeable observers argued that the Soviet invasion was a Russian attempt to secure the status quo against a growing rebel movement. Others—most notably the president—claimed that the invasion was a Russian "stepping stone to their possible control over much of the world's oil supplies." It was also the "gravest threat to world peace since World War II." Carter angrily imposed a series of economic sanctions on the Russians, canceled American participation in the 1980 summer Olympic Games in Moscow, and announced the withdrawal of SALT II from Senate consideration.

The combination of domestic economic troubles and international crises created widespread anxiety, frustration, and anger in the United States—damaging President Carter's already low standing with the public, and giving added strength to an alternative political force that had already made great strides.

THE RISE OF THE AMERICAN RIGHT

The jarring public events of the 1960s and 1970s, and the broader changes in the character of America's economy, society, and culture, disillusioned many liberals, perplexed the already weakened left, and provided the right with its most important opportunity in generations to seize a position of authority in American life.

The Sunbelt and Its Politics

One of the major demographic events of the 1970s was the rise of what became known as the "Sunbelt," a group of regions that included some of the most dynamically growing parts of the country. The Sunbelt included the Southeast (particularly Florida), the Southwest (particularly Texas), and above all, California, which became the nation's most populous state in 1964. By 1980, more people lived in the Sunbelt than lived in the industrial regions of the North and East.

Among other things, the rise of the Sunbelt helped produce a change in the political climate. The strong populist traditions in the South and the West—and the high emphasis on individual liberty in particular—were capable of producing progressive and even radical politics; but more often in the late twentieth century, they produced a strong opposition to the growth of government, and to government regulations in particular. Many federal regulations and restrictions—environmental laws, land-use restrictions, even the fifty-five-mile-per-hour speed limit created during the energy crisis to force motorists to conserve fuel—affected the West more than any other region.

The so-called Sagebrush Rebellion, which emerged in parts of the West in the late 1970s, mobilized conservative opposition to environmental laws and restrictions on development. It also sought to portray the West (which had probably benefited more than any other region from federal investment) as a victim of government control. Its members complained about the very large amounts of land the federal government owned in many western states and demanded that they be opened for development.

The South as a whole was considerably more conservative than other parts of the nation, and its growth served to increase the power of the right in the 1960s and 1970s. The West had not, on the whole, been more conservative than other regions historically; but in the postwar period, the West produced some of the most numerous and powerful conservative movements in the nation—particularly in southern California, where Orange

County (a large suburban area south of Los Angeles) emerged as one of the most important centers of right-wing politics in the country.

Religious Revivalism

The United States experienced the beginning of a major religious revival in the 1970s which continued in various forms into the 1990s. Some of the new religious enthusiasm found expression in the rise of cults and pseudo-faiths: the Church of Scientology; the Unification Church of the Reverend Sun Myung Moon; even the tragic People's Temple, whose members committed mass suicide in their jungle retreat in Guyana in 1978. But the most important impulse of the religious revival was the growth of evangelical Christianity. Evangelicism is the basis of many forms of Christian faith. But evangelicals have in common a belief in personal conversion through direct communication with God.

For many years, the evangelicals had gone largely unnoted by much of the media and the secular public, which had dismissed them as a limited, provincial phenomenon. By the late 1970s, it was no longer possible to do so. Earlier in the century, many (although never all) evangelicals had been relatively poor rural people. But the great capitalist expansion after World War II had lifted many of these people out of poverty and into the middle class, where they were more visible and more assertive. Over 70 million Americans now described themselves as "born-again" Christians—men and women who had established a "direct personal relationship with Jesus." Christian evangelicals owned their own newspapers, magazines, radio stations, and television networks. They operated their own schools and universities. One of them occupied the White House itself—Jimmy Carter, who during the 1976 campaign had talked proudly of his own "conversion experience" and who continued openly to proclaim his "born-again" Christian faith during his years in office.

For Jimmy Carter and for some others, evangelical Christianity had formed the basis for a commitment to racial justice and world peace. But many evangelicals in the 1970s became active on the political and cultural right. They were alarmed by what they considered the spread of immorality and disorder in American life; and they were concerned about the way a secular and, as they saw it, godless culture was intruding into their communities and families—through popular culture, through the schools, and through government policies. Particularly alarming to them were Supreme Court decisions eliminating prayer from schools and, later, guaranteeing women the right to an abortion.

By the late 1970s, the "Christian right" had become a visible and increasingly powerful political force. Jerry Falwell, a fundamentalist minister in Virginia with a substantial television audience, launched a movement he called the Moral Majority, which attacked the rise of "secular humanism" in American culture. The Moral Majority and other, similar organizations denounced abortion, divorce, feminism, and homosexuality, defended unrestricted free enterprise, and supported a strong American posture in the world. Some evangelicals reopened issues that had long seemed closed. For example, many fundamentalist Christians denied the scientific doctrine of evolution and instead urged the teaching in schools of the biblical story of the Creation. Others advocated various forms of censorship of books, films, plays, and other works of art whose content they considered immoral.

The New Right

Evangelical Christians were an important part, but only a part, of what became known as the New Right—a diverse but powerful movement that enjoyed rapid growth in the 1970s and early 1980s. It had begun to take shape after the 1964 election, in which Barry Goldwater had suffered his shattering defeat. Richard Viguerie, a remarkable conservative activist and organizer, took a list of 12,000 contributors to the Goldwater campaign and used it to develop a formidable conservative communications and fund-raising organization. By the mid-1970s, he had gathered a list of 4 million contributors and 15 million supporters. Gradually these direct-mail operations helped create a much larger conservative infrastructure, designed to match and even exceed what the right saw as the powerful liberal infrastructure. By the late 1970s, there were right-wing think tanks, consulting firms, lobbyists, foundations, and scholarly centers. Another factor in the revival of the right was the emergence of credible leadership. Chief among this new generation of conservative leaders was Ronald Reagan, once a moderately successful film actor, who had become deeply involved in right-wing politics in California and, in 1966, won election as governor of the state. His engaging, self-assured demeanor and his smooth, eloquent speeches in defense of individual freedom and private enterprise won him increasing national recognition.

The presidency of Gerald Ford also played an important role in the rise of the right, by destroying the fragile equilibrium that had enabled the right wing and the moderate wing of the Republican Party to coexist. Ford appointed as vice president Nelson Rockefeller, the liberal Republican governor of New York and an heir to one of America's great fortunes; many conservatives had been demonizing Rockefeller and his family for more than twenty years. Ford proposed an amnesty program for draft resisters, embraced and even extended the hated Nixon-Kissinger policies of détente, presided over the fall of Vietnam, and agreed to cede the Panama Canal to Panama. When Reagan challenged Ford in the 1976 Republican primaries, the president survived, barely, only by dropping Nelson Rockefeller from the ticket and agreeing to a platform largely written by one of Reagan's principal allies, Senator Jesse Helms of North Carolina. Reagan hailed that platform by saying that the party "must raise a banner of no pale pastels, but bold colors which make it unmistakably clear where we stand on all the issues troubling the people."

The Tax Revolt

At least equally important to the success of the new right was a new and potent conservative issue: the tax revolt. It had its public beginnings in 1978, when Howard Jarvis, a conservative activist, launched a successful tax revolt in California with Proposition 13, a referendum question on the state ballot rolling back property-tax rates. Similar antitax movements soon began in other states and eventually spread to national politics.

For more than thirty years after the New Deal, Republican conservatives had struggled to halt and even reverse the growth of the federal government. But during most of those years, as right-wing politicians from Robert Taft to Barry Goldwater discovered, attacking government programs did not succeed in attracting majority support. Every federal program had a political constituency, and the biggest and most expensive programs had the broadest support. Proposition 13 and similar initiatives gave members of the right a better way to undermine government than by attacking specific programs: attacking taxes. By separating the issue of taxes from the issue of what taxes supported, the right found a way to achieve the most controversial elements of its own agenda (eroding the government's ability to launch new ventures and even to sustain old ones) without openly antagonizing the millions of voters who supported specific programs. Virtually no one liked to pay taxes, and as the economy grew weaker and the relative burden of paying taxes grew heavier, that resentment naturally rose. The right exploited that resentment and, in the process, expanded its constituency far beyond anything it had known before. The 1980 presidential election propelled it to a historic victory.

The Campaign of 1980

By the time of the crises in Iran and Afghanistan, Jimmy Carter was in desperate political trouble. His standing in popularity polls was lower than that of any president in history. Senator Edward Kennedy, younger brother of John and Robert Kennedy, was preparing to challenge him in the primaries. For a short while, the seizure of the hostages and the stern American response to the Soviet invasion revived Carter's candidacy. But as the hostage crisis dragged on, public impatience grew. Kennedy won a series of victories over the president in the later primaries. And while Carter managed in the end to stave off Kennedy's challenge and win his party's nomination, it was an unhappy convention that heard the president's listless call to arms.

The Republican Party, in the meantime, had rallied enthusiastically behind Ronald Reagan, a man whom, not many years before, many Americans had considered a frightening reactionary. But he now emerged not just as a poised and articulate campaigner but as a spokesman for the public's growing discontent with its leadership and its government.

On election day 1980, the anniversary of the seizure of the hostages in Iran, Reagan swept to victory with 51 percent of the vote to 41 percent for Jimmy Carter and 7 percent for John Anderson—a moderate Republican congressman from Illinois who had mounted an independent campaign. Carter carried only five states and the District of Columbia, for a total of 49 electoral votes to Reagan's 489. The Republican Party won control of the

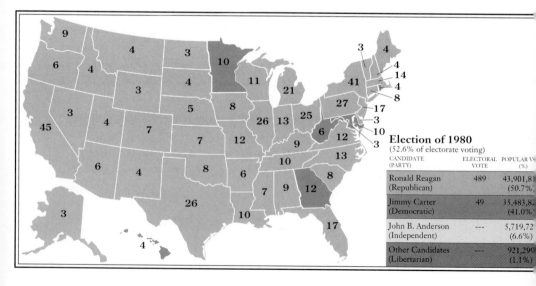

Election of 1980
(52.6% of electorate voting)

CANDIDATE (PARTY)	ELECTORAL VOTE	POPULAR VOTE (%)
Ronald Reagan (Republican)	489	43,901,8 (50.7%)
Jimmy Carter (Democratic)	49	35,483,8 (41.0%)
John B. Anderson (Independent)	---	5,719,72 (6.6%)
Other Candidates (Libertarian)	---	921,290 (1.1%)

Senate for the first time since 1952; and although the Democrats retained a narrow majority in the House, the lower chamber too seemed firmly in the hands of conservatives.

On the day of Reagan's inauguration, the American hostages in Iran were released after their 444-day ordeal, as a result of negotiations Jimmy Carter had concluded in the last hours of his presidency. Americans welcomed the hostages home with demonstrations of euphoria and patriotism not seen since the end of World War II. But while the celebration in 1945 had marked a great American triumph, the euphoria in 1981 marked something quite different—a troubled nation grasping for reassurance. Ronald Reagan set out to provide it.

THE "REAGAN REVOLUTION"

Ronald Reagan assumed the presidency in January 1981 promising a change in government more profound than any since the New Deal of fifty years before. His eight years in office produced a significant shift in public policy, but they brought nothing so fundamental as many of his supporters had hoped or his opponents had feared. There was, however, no ambiguity about his administration's purely political achievements. Ronald Reagan succeeded brilliantly in making his own engaging personality the central fact of American politics in the 1980s.

Reagan in the White House

Even many people who disagreed with the president's policies found themselves drawn to his attractive and carefully honed public image. Reagan was a master of television and a gifted public speaker. He was the oldest man ever to serve as president, but he seemed vigorous, resilient, even youthful. When he was wounded in an assassination attempt in 1981, he joked with doctors on his way into surgery and appeared to bounce back from the ordeal with remarkable speed. Four years later, he seemed to rebound from cancer surgery with similar zest. He had few visible insecurities. Even when things went wrong, as they often did, the blame seemed seldom to attach to Reagan himself (inspiring some Democrats to begin referring to him as "the Teflon president").

Reagan was not much involved in the day-to-day affairs of running the government; he surrounded himself with tough, energetic administrators who insulated him from many of the pressures of the office and apparently

THE REAGANS IN SANTA BARBARA In the weeks before the 1980
Republican convention, at which he was nominated for the
presidency, Ronald Reagan and his wife Nancy spent time
relaxing, very publicly, at their ranch near Santa Babara,
California. Reagan returned often to his ranch during his
presidency and, indeed, spent more days vacationing than any
president in decades.

relied on him largely for general guidance, not specific decisions. But Reagan did make active use of his office to generate support for his administration's programs, by appealing repeatedly to the public over television and by fusing his proposals with a highly nationalistic rhetoric.

"Supply-Side" Economics

Reagan's 1980 campaign for the presidency had promised, among other things, to restore the economy to health by a bold experiment that became known as "supply-side" economics or, to some, "Reaganomics." Supply-side economics operated from the assumption that the woes of the American economy were in large part a result of excessive taxation, which left inadequate capital available to investors to stimulate growth. The solution, therefore, was to reduce taxes, with particularly generous benefits to corporations and wealthy individuals, in order to encourage new investments. The result would be a general economic revival that would help everyone. Because a tax cut would reduce government revenues (at least at first), it would also be necessary to reduce government expenses. Another cornerstone of the Reagan economic program, therefore, was a dramatic cut in the federal budget, which would, the administration promised, bring it into balance within a few years.

In its first months in office, accordingly, the new administration hastily assembled a legislative program based on the supply-side idea. It proposed $40 billion in budget cuts and managed to win congressional approval of almost all of them. In addition, the president proposed a bold, three-year rate reduction on both individual and corporate taxes. In the summer of 1981, Congress passed it too. Not since Lyndon Johnson had a president compiled so impressive a legislative record in his first months in office.

By early 1982, the nation had sunk into the most severe recession since the 1930s. The Reagan economic program was not directly to blame for the problems, but critics claimed that the administration's policies were doing nothing to improve the situation. In fact, however, the economy recovered more rapidly and impressively than almost anyone had expected. By the middle of 1983, unemployment (which had reached nearly 11 percent in 1982, the highest level in over forty years) had fallen to 8.2 percent. The gross national product had grown 3.6 percent, the largest increase since the mid-1970s. Inflation had fallen below 5 percent. The economy continued to grow, and both inflation and unemployment remained low (at least by the new and more pessimistic standards the nation seemed now to have accepted) through most of the decade.

The recovery was a result of many things. Years of tight money policies by the Federal Reserve Board had helped lower inflation. A worldwide "energy glut," the virtual collapse of the OPEC cartel, and the deregulation of natural-gas production had produced at least a temporary end to the inflationary pressures of spiraling fuel costs. And staggering federal budget deficits were pumping billions of dollars into the flagging economy but also, many warned, threatening ultimately to destroy the recovery they were helping to create.

The Fiscal Crisis

By the mid-1980s, the growing fiscal crisis had become one of the central issues in American politics. Having entered office promising a balanced budget within four years, Reagan presided over record budget deficits and accumulated more debt in his eight years in office than the American government had accumulated in its entire previous history. Before the 1980s, the highest single-year budget deficit in American history had been $66 billion (in 1976). Throughout the 1980s, the annual budget deficit consistently exceeded $100 billion (and in 1986 peaked at $221 billion). The national debt rose from $907 billion in 1980 to nearly $3 trillion by 1990.

The enormous deficits had many causes, some of them stretching back over decades of American public policy decisions. In particular, the budget suffered from enormous increases in the costs of "entitlement" programs (especially Social Security and Medicare), a result of the aging of the population and dramatic increases in the cost of health care. But some of the causes of the deficit lay in the policies of the Reagan administration. The 1981 tax cuts, the largest in American history, sharply eroded the revenue base of the federal government and accounted for a large percentage of the deficit. The massive increase in military spending (a proposed $1.6 trillion over five years) on which the Reagan administration insisted added more to the federal budget than its cuts in domestic spending removed.

In the face of these deficits, the administration refused to consider raising income taxes (although it did agree to a major increase in the Social Security tax). It would not agree to reductions in military spending. It was not willing to take the unpopular steps necessary to reduce the costs of entitlement programs, and it could do nothing to reduce interest payments on the massive (and growing) debt. Its answer to the fiscal crisis, therefore, was further cuts in "discretionary" domestic spending, which included many programs aimed at the poorest (and politically weakest) Americans. There were reductions in funding for food stamps; a major cut in federal subsidies for low-income housing; strict new limitations on Medicare and Medicaid payments; reductions in student loans, school lunches, and other educational programs; and an end to many forms of federal assistance to the states and cities—which helped precipitate years of local fiscal crises as well.

By the end of Reagan's third year in office, funding for domestic programs had been cut nearly as far as Congress (and, apparently, the public) was willing to tolerate. Congress responded with the Gramm-Rudman-Hollings Act, passed late in 1985, which mandated major deficit reductions over five years and provided for automatic budget cuts in all areas of government spending should the president and Congress fail to agree on an alternative solution. Under Gramm-Rudman-Hollings, the budget deficit did decline for several years from its 1983 high. But much of that decline was a result of a substantial surplus in the Social Security trust fund (which the sharply increased Social Security taxes had produced), not of any larger fiscal successes.

Reagan and the World

Reagan encountered a similar combination of triumphs and difficulties in international affairs. Determined to restore American pride and prestige in the world, he argued that the United States should once again become active and assertive in opposing communism and supporting friendly governments whatever their internal policies.

Relations with the Soviet Union, which had been steadily deteriorating in the last years of the Carter administration, grew still more chilly in the first years of the Reagan presidency. The president spoke harshly of the Soviet regime (which he once called the "evil empire"), accusing it of sponsoring world terrorism and declaring that any armaments negotiations must be linked to negotiations on Soviet behavior in other areas. Relations with the Russians deteriorated further after the government of Poland (under strong pressure from Moscow) imposed martial law on the country in the winter of 1981 to crush a growing challenge from an independent labor organization, Solidarity.

Although the president had long denounced the SALT II arms control treaty as unfavorable to the United States, he continued to honor its provisions. But the Reagan administration at first made little progress toward arms control in other areas, despite the growing political power of a popular antinuclear movement in both Europe and the United States. In fact, the president proposed the most ambitious new military program in many years: the Strategic Defense Initiative (SDI), widely known as "Star Wars" (after a popular science-fiction movie). Reagan claimed that SDI, through the use of lasers and satellites, could provide an effective shield against incoming missiles and thus make nuclear war obsolete. The Soviet Union claimed that the new program would elevate the arms race to new and more dangerous levels and insisted that any arms control agreement begin with an American abandonment of SDI.

At the same time, the Reagan administration began, rhetorically at least, to support opponents of communism anywhere in the world, whether or not the regimes they were challenging were directly allied to the Soviet Union. This policy became known as the Reagan Doctrine, and it meant, above all, a new American activism in the Third World. The most conspicuous examples of the new activism came in Latin America. In October 1983, the administration sent American soldiers and marines to the tiny Caribbean island of Grenada to oust an anti-American Marxist regime that was forging a relationship with the Soviet Union. In El Salvador, where first a repressive military regime and later a moderate civilian one were engaged in murderous struggles with left-wing revolutionaries (who were supported, according to the Reagan administration, by Cuba and the Soviet Union), the president provided increased military and economic assistance. In neighboring Nicaragua, a pro-American dictatorship had fallen to the revolutionary "Sandinistas" in 1979; the new government had grown increasingly anti-American (and increasingly Marxist) throughout the early 1980s. The administration gave both rhetorical and material support to the so-called contras, a guerrilla movement drawn from several antigovernment groups and fighting (without great success) to topple the Sandinista regime. Indeed, support of the contras became a mission of special importance to the president, and later the source of some of his greatest difficulties.

In other parts of the world, the administration's bellicose rhetoric seemed to hide an instinctive restraint. In June 1982, the Israeli army launched an invasion of Lebanon in an effort to drive guerrillas of the Palestinian Liberation Organization from the country. The United States supported the Israelis rhetorically but also worked to permit PLO forces to leave Lebanon peacefully. An American peacekeeping force entered Beirut to supervise the evacuation. American marines then remained in the city, apparently to protect the fragile Lebanese government, which was embroiled in a vicious civil war. Now identified with one faction in the struggle, Americans themselves became the targets; a 1983 terrorist bombing of a United States military barracks in Beirut left 241 marines dead. Rather than become more deeply involved in the Lebanese struggle, Reagan withdrew the American forces.

The Election of 1984

Reagan approached the campaign of 1984 at the head of a united Republican Party firmly committed to his candidacy. The Democrats, as had become their custom, followed a more fractious course. In the end, however, former vice president Walter Mondale withstood a series of vigorous challenges to capture the nomination. He brought momentary excitement to the Democratic Convention in San Francisco that summer by selecting a woman, Representative Geraldine Ferraro of New York, to be his running mate and the first female candidate ever to appear on a major-party national ticket.

The Republican Party, in the meantime, rallied comfortably behind its revered leader, whose triumphant campaign that fall scarcely took note of his opponents. Reagan's victory in 1984 was decisive. He won approximately 59 percent of the vote, and he carried every state except Mondale's native Minnesota and the District of Columbia. But Reagan was stronger than his party. Democrats gained a seat in the Senate and maintained only slightly reduced control of the House of Representatives.

The triumphant reelection of Ronald Reagan was the high-water mark up to that point of conservative, and Republican, fortunes in the postwar era. It reflected satisfaction with the impressive performance of the economy under the Republican economic program, and pride in the new assertiveness the United States was showing in the world. To many Reagan supporters, the 1984 election seemed to be the dawn of a new conservative era. Few anticipated that it also coincided with the beginning of a revolutionary change in the world order, and the United States' place in it. The election of 1984 was less the first of a new era than the last of the old one. It was the final campaign of the Cold War.

CHAPTER THIRTY-FOUR

Beyond the Cold War

America and the Waning of the Cold War ~ *Modern Times*

O N NOVEMBER 8, 1989, East German soldiers stood guard at the Berlin Wall—keeping westerners out and easterners in—as they had done every day for more than twenty-eight years. The next day they were gone. Within hours, thousands of citizens of both sides of the divided city were swarming over the wall in celebration. Within weeks, bulldozers were tearing it down. Within a year, East and West Germany—divided by the Cold War for forty-five years—had reunited.

The breaching of the Berlin Wall and the reunification of Germany were among the most dramatic of a series of changes between 1986 and 1991 that radically transformed the world order. The Cold War, which as late as 1985 had seemed a permanent fact of international life, came to an end. A new world order, the outlines of which were still only dimly visible, was in the process of being born.

The Cold War had shaped the foreign policy and many aspects of the domestic life of the United States for nearly half a century. Its sudden end changed the character of national politics, economics, and culture. But America in the late 1980s and early 1990s was also encountering a series of other important social and economic changes, many of them unrelated to the Cold War. As the end of the twentieth century approached, most Americans were uncertain whether the changes would bring a better, safer world or a harsher and more dangerous one.

AMERICA AND THE WANING
OF THE COLD WAR

Many factors contributed to the collapse of the Soviet empire. The long, stalemated war in Afghanistan proved at least as disastrous to the Soviet Union as the Vietnam War had been to America. The government in Mos-

TIME LINE

1979	1981	1985	1986
Three Mile Island nuclear accident	AIDS first reported in U.S.	Reagan and Gorbachev meet Crack cocaine appears in U.S. cities	U.S. bombs Libya Iran-Contra scandal revealed

1987	1988	1989	1990
Gorbachev visits U.S. Stock market falls	Bush elected president	Berlin Wall dismantled Communist regimes collapse American troops in Panama	Iraq invades Kuwait

1991	1992	1993
Collapse of Soviet regime Persian Gulf War	Los Angeles race riots Clinton elected president	North American Free Trade Agreement ratified Health care reform fails

cow had failed to address a long-term economic decline in the Soviet republics and the Eastern-bloc nations. Restiveness with the heavy-handed policies of communist police states was growing throughout much of the Soviet empire. But the most visible factor at the time was the emergence of a single man: Mikhail Gorbachev, who succeeded to the leadership of the Soviet Union in 1985 and, to the surprise of almost everyone (including, perhaps, himself), very quickly became the most revolutionary figure in world politics in at least four decades.

The Fall of the Soviet Union

Gorbachev quickly transformed Soviet politics with two dramatic new initiatives. The first he called *glasnost* (openness): the dismantling of many of the repressive mechanisms that had been conspicuous features of Soviet life for over half a century. The other policy Gorbachev called *perestroika* (reform): an effort to restructure the rigid and unproductive Soviet economy by introducing, among other things, such elements of capitalism as private ownership and the profit motive. He also began to transform Soviet foreign policy.

The severe economic problems at home evidently convinced Gorbachev that the Soviet Union could no longer sustain its extended commitments

SMASHING THE WALL Once it became clear in November 1989 that the East German government was no longer defending the wall that had divided Berlin for nearly thirty years, Germans on both sides of the divide swarmed over it in celebration. Here, a West German takes a sledgehammer to the already battered wall as East German border guards passively look on.

around the world. As early as 1987, he began reducing Soviet influence in Eastern Europe. And in 1989, in the space of a few months, every communist state in Europe—Poland, Hungary, Czechoslovakia, Bulgaria, Romania, East Germany, Yugoslavia, and Albania—either overthrew its government or forced it to transform itself into an essentially noncommunist (and in some cases, actively anticommunist) regime. The Communist Parties of Eastern Europe all but collapsed. Gorbachev and the Soviet Union actively encouraged the changes.

The challenges to communism were not successful everywhere. In May 1989, students in China launched a mass movement calling for greater democratization. But in June, hard-line leaders seized control of the government and sent military forces to crush the uprising. The result was a bloody massacre on June 3, 1989, in Tiananmen Square in Beijing, in which a still-unknown number of demonstrators died. The assault crushed the democracy movement and restored the hard-liners to power. It did not, however, stop China's efforts to modernize and even westernize its economy.

But China was an exception to the worldwide movement toward democratization, which even extended to parts of the world far removed from the Soviet empire. Early in 1990, the government of South Africa, long an international pariah for its rigid enforcement of "apartheid" (a system designed to protect white supremacy) began a cautious retreat from its traditional policies. Among other things, it legalized the chief black party in the nation, the African National Congress (ANC), which had been banned for decades; and on February 11, 1990, it released from prison the leader of the ANC, and a revered hero to black South Africans, Nelson Mandela, who had been in jail for twenty-seven years. Over the next several years, the South African government repealed its apartheid laws. And in 1994, there were national elections in which all South Africans could participate. As a result, Nelson Mandela became the first black president of South Africa.

In 1991, communism began to collapse at the site of its birth: the Soviet Union itself. An unsuccessful coup by hard-line Soviet leaders on August 19 precipitated a dramatic unraveling of communist power. Within days, the coup itself collapsed in the face of resistance from the public and, more important, crucial elements within the military. Mikhail Gorbachev returned to power, but it soon became evident that the legitimacy of both the Communist Party and the central Soviet government had been fatally injured. By the end of August, almost every republic in the Soviet Union had declared independence; the Soviet government was clearly powerless to stop the fragmentation. Gorbachev himself finally resigned as leader of the now virtually powerless Communist Party and Soviet government, and the Soviet Union ceased to exist.

Reagan and Gorbachev

The last years of the Reagan administration coincided with the first years of the Gorbachev regime; and while Reagan was skeptical of Gorbachev at first, he gradually became convinced that the Soviet leader was sincere in his desire for reform. At a summit meeting with Reagan in Reykjavik, Iceland, in 1986, Gorbachev proposed reducing the nuclear arsenals of both sides by 50 percent or more, although continuing disputes over Reagan's commitment to the SDI program derailed agreements. But in 1988, after Reagan and Gorbachev exchanged cordial visits to each other's capital, the two superpowers signed a treaty eliminating American and Soviet intermediate-range nuclear forces (INF) from Europe—the most significant arms control agreement of the nuclear age. At about the same time, Gorbachev ended the Soviet Union's long and frustrating military involvement in Afghanistan, removing one of the principal irritants in the relationship between Washington and Moscow.

The Fading of the Reagan Revolution

For a time, the dramatic changes around the world and Reagan's personal popularity deflected attention from a series of scandals that might well have destroyed another administration. There were revelations of illegality, corruption, and ethical lapses in the Environmental Protection Agency, the CIA, the Department of Defense, the Department of Labor, the Department of Justice, and the Department of Housing and Urban Development. A more serious scandal emerged within the savings and loan industry, which the Reagan administration had helped deregulate in the early 1980s. Many savings banks had responded by rapidly, often recklessly, and sometimes corruptly, expanding. By the end of the decade the industry was in chaos, and the government was forced to step in to prevent a complete collapse. Government insurance covered the assets of most savings and loan depositors; the cost of the debacle to the public eventually ran to more than half a trillion dollars.

But the most politically damaging scandal of the Reagan years came to light in November 1986, when the White House conceded that it had sold weapons to the revolutionary government of Iran as part of a largely unsuccessful effort to secure the release of several Americans being held hostage by radical Islamic groups in the Middle East. Even more damaging was the revelation that some of the money from the arms deal with Iran had been covertly and illegally funneled into a fund to aid the contras in Nicaragua.

In the months that followed, aggressive reporting and a highly publicized series of congressional hearings exposed a widespread pattern of covert activities orchestrated by the White House and dedicated to advancing the administration's foreign policy aims through secret and at times illegal means. The principal figure in this covert world appeared at first to be an obscure marine lieutenant colonel assigned to the staff of the National Security Council, Oliver North. But gradually it became clear that North was acting in concert with other, more powerful figures in the administration. The Iran-contra scandal, as it became known, did serious damage to the Reagan presidency—even though the investigations were never able decisively to tie the president himself to the most serious violations of the law.

The Election of 1988

The fraying of the Reagan administration helped the Democrats regain control of the United States Senate in 1986 and fueled hopes in the party for a presidential victory in 1988. Even so, several of the most popular figures in the Democratic Party refused to run, and the nomination finally went to a previously little-known figure: Michael Dukakis, a three-term governor of Massachusetts. Dukakis was a dry, even dull campaigner. But Democrats were optimistic about their prospects in 1988, largely because of the identity of their opponent, Vice President George Bush, who had captured the Republican nomination without great difficulty but had failed to spark any real public enthusiasm. He entered the last months of the campaign well behind Dukakis.

Beginning at the Republican Convention, however, Bush staged a remarkable turnaround by making his campaign a long, relentless attack on Dukakis, tying him to all the unpopular social and cultural stances Americans had come to identify with "liberals." Indeed, the Bush campaign was almost certainly the most savage of the twentieth century. It was also, apparently, one of the most effective, although the listless, indecisive character of the Dukakis effort contributed to the Republican cause as well. Bush won a substantial victory in November: 54 percent of the popular vote to Dukakis's 46, and 426 electoral votes to Dukakis's 112. But Bush carried few Republicans into office with him; the Democrats retained secure majorities in both houses of Congress.

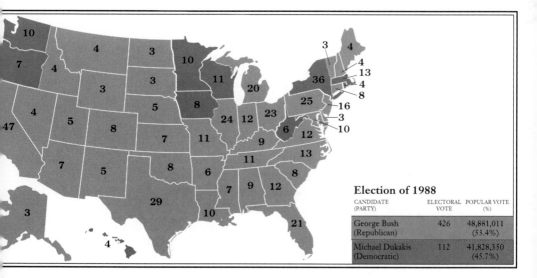

Election of 1988

CANDIDATE (PARTY)	ELECTORAL VOTE	POPULAR VOTE (%)
George Bush (Republican)	426	48,881,011 (53.4%)
Michael Dukakis (Democratic)	112	41,828,350 (45.7%)

The Bush Presidency

The Bush presidency was notable for a series of dramatic developments in international affairs and an almost complete absence of initiatives or ideas on domestic issues. For a time, Bush's achievements in foreign policy managed to obscure the absence of a domestic agenda. By early 1992, however, with the nation in the second year of a serious recession, the president's popularity had begun to fray.

The broad popularity Bush enjoyed during his first three years in office was partly because of his subdued, unthreatening public image. But it was primarily because of the wonder and excitement with which Americans viewed the dramatic events in the rest of the world.

Bush moved cautiously at first in dealing with the changes in the Soviet Union. But like Reagan, he eventually embraced Gorbachev and reached a series of significant agreements with the Soviet Union in its waning years. In the three years after the INF agreement in 1988, the United States and the Soviet Union moved rapidly toward even more far-reaching arms reduction agreements, including major troop reductions in Europe and the dismantling of new categories of strategic weapons.

On domestic issues, the Bush administration was less successful—partly because the president himself seemed to have little interest in promoting a domestic agenda and partly because he faced serious obstacles. His administration inherited a staggering burden of debt and a federal deficit that had been out of control for nearly a decade. Any domestic agenda that required significant federal spending was, therefore, incompatible with the president's pledge to reduce the deficit and his 1988 campaign promise of "no new taxes." Bush faced a Democratic Congress with an agenda very different from his own. And he was constantly concerned about the right wing of his own party and, in his eagerness to ingratiate himself with it, took divisive positions on such cultural issues as abortion and affirmative action that further damaged his ability to work with Congress.

Despite this political stalemate, Congress and the White House managed on occasion to agree on significant measures. They cooperated in producing a plan to salvage the floundering savings and loan industry. In 1990, the president bowed to congressional pressure and agreed to a significant tax increase as part of a multiyear "budget package" designed to reduce the deficit. In 1991, after almost two years of acrimonious debate, the president and Congress agreed on a civil rights bill to combat job discrimination.

But the most serious domestic problem facing the Bush administration was one to which neither the president nor Congress had any answer: a recession that began late in 1990 and slowly increased its grip on the national economy in 1991 and 1992. Because of the enormous level of debt that corporations (and individuals) had accumulated in the 1980s, the recession caused an unusual number of bankruptcies. It also created growing fear and frustration among middle- and working-class Americans and increasing pressure on the government to address such problems as the rising cost of health care.

The Gulf War

The events of 1989–1991 had left the United States in the unanticipated position of being the only real superpower in the world. The Bush administration, therefore, had to consider what to do with America's formidable political and military power in a world in which the major justification for that power—the Soviet threat—was now gone.

The events of 1989–1991 suggested two possible answers, both of which had some effect on policy. One was that the United States would reduce its military strength dramatically and concentrate its energies and resources on pressing domestic problems. And, indeed, there was considerable movement in that direction both in Congress and within the administration. The other was that America would continue to use its power actively, not to fight communism but to defend its regional and economic interests. In 1989, that led the administration to order an invasion of Panama, which overthrew the unpopular military leader Manuel Noriega (under indictment in the United States for drug trafficking) and replaced him with an elected, pro-American regime. And in 1990, that same impulse drew the United States into the turbulent politics of the Middle East.

On August 2, 1990, the armed forces of Iraq invaded and quickly overwhelmed their small, oil-rich neighbor, the emirate of Kuwait. Saddam Hussein, the militaristic leader of Iraq, soon announced that he was annexing Kuwait and set out to entrench his forces there. After some initial indecision, the Bush administration agreed to join with other nations to force Iraq out of Kuwait—through the pressure of economic sanctions if possible, through military force if necessary. Within a few weeks, Bush had persuaded virtually every important government in the world, including the Soviet Union and almost all the Arab and Islamic states, to join in a United Nations–sanctioned trade embargo of Iraq.

At the same time, the United States and its allies (including the British, French, Egyptians, and Saudis) began deploying a massive military force along the border between Kuwait and Saudi Arabia, a force that ultimately reached 690,000 troops (425,000 of them American) and that assembled the largest and most sophisticated collection of military technology ever used in warfare. On November 29, the United Nations, at the request of the United States, voted to authorize military action to expel Iraq from Kuwait if Iraq did not leave by January 15, 1991. On January 12, both houses of Congress voted to authorize the use of force against Iraq, although many Democrats opposed the resolution, arguing that sanctions should be given more time to work. And on January 16, American and allied air forces began a massive bombardment of Iraqi forces in Kuwait and of military and industrial installations in Iraq itself.

The allied bombing continued for six weeks, meeting only token resistance from the small Iraqi air force and ground defenses. And on February 23, allied (primarily American) forces under the command of General Norman Schwarzkopf began a major ground offensive—not primarily against the heavily entrenched Iraqi forces along the Kuwait border, as expected, but into Iraq itself. The allied armies encountered almost no resistance and suffered only light casualties (141 fatalities). There were no reliable figures for the number of Iraqi military casualties, but some estimated the deaths (most as a result of the bombing) to be 100,000 or more. There were also a significant, if unverifiable, number of civilian casualties. On February 28, Iraq announced its acceptance of allied terms for a cease-fire, and the brief war came to an end.

The quick and (for America) relatively painless victory over Iraq was highly popular in the United States. But the longer-range results of the Gulf War were more difficult to assess. The tyrannical regime of Saddam Hussein survived, in a weakened form but showing few signs of retreat from its militaristic ambitions. And Kuwait returned to the control of its prewar government, an undemocratic monarchy increasingly unpopular with its own people.

The Election of 1992

President Bush's popularity reached a record high in the immediate aftermath of the Gulf War. But the glow of that victory faded quickly as the recession worsened in late 1991, and as the administration declined to propose any policies for combating it. The president's popularity soon eroded.

Because the early maneuvering for the 1992 presidential election occurred when President Bush's popularity remained high, many leading Democrats declined to run. That gave Bill Clinton, the young five-term governor of Arkansas, an opportunity to emerge early as the front-runner, as a result of a skillful campaign that emphasized broad economic issues instead of the racial and cultural questions that had so divided the Democrats in the past. Clinton survived a bruising primary campaign and a series of damaging personal controversies to win his party's nomination. And George Bush withstood an embarrassing primary challenge from the conservative journalist Pat Buchanan to become the Republican nominee again.

Complicating the campaign was the emergence of Ross Perot, a blunt, forthright Texas billionaire who became an independent candidate by tapping popular resentment of the federal bureaucracy and by promising tough, uncompromising leadership to deal with the fiscal crisis and other problems of government. Particularly appealing to many voters were Perot's attacks on corruption in the political system and his insistence that his own campaign (funded by his personal fortune, not by special-interest lobbies) was a pure reflection of the will of the people. At several moments in the spring, Perot led both Bush and Clinton in public opinion polls. In July, as he began to face hostile scrutiny from the media, he abruptly withdrew from the race. But early in October, he reentered and soon regained much (although never all) of his early support.

After a campaign in which the economy and the president's unpopularity were the principal issues, Clinton won a clear, but hardly overwhelming, victory over Bush and Perot. He received 43 percent of the vote in the three-way race, to the president's 38 percent and Perot's 19 percent (the best

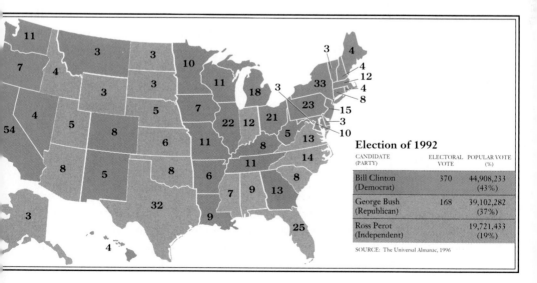

Election of 1992

CANDIDATE (PARTY)	ELECTORAL VOTE	POPULAR VOTE (%)
Bill Clinton (Democrat)	370	44,908,233 (43%)
George Bush (Republican)	168	39,102,282 (37%)
Ross Perot (Independent)		19,721,433 (19%)

SOURCE: The Universal Almanac, 1996

showing for a third-party or independent candidate since Theodore Roosevelt in 1912). Clinton won 370 electoral votes to Bush's 168; Perot won none. Democrats retained control of both houses of Congress.

Launching the Clinton Presidency

Bill Clinton was the first Democratic president since Jimmy Carter and the first real activist to be president since Lyndon Johnson. He entered office carrying the extravagant expectations of liberals who had spent a generation in exile and with a domestic agenda more ambitious than that of any president since Lyndon Johnson. But Clinton also had significant political weaknesses. Having won the votes of well under half the electorate, he enjoyed no powerful mandate. Democratic majorities in Congress were frail, and Democrats in any case had grown unaccustomed to bowing to presidential leadership. The Republican leadership in Congress was highly adversarial and opposed the president with unusual unanimity on many issues.

The new administration compounded its problems with a series of missteps and misfortunes in its first months. The president's effort to end the longtime ban on gay men and lesbians serving in the military met with ferocious resistance from the armed forces themselves and from many conservatives in both parties. He was forced to settle for a pallid compromise. Several of his early appointments—to the Justice Department, in particular— became so controversial that he had to withdraw them. A longtime friend of the president from Arkansas serving in the office of the White House counsel committed suicide in the summer of 1993. His death helped spark an escalating inquiry into some banking and real estate ventures involving the President and his wife in the early 1980s; and the clumsy actions of some administration officials raised suspicions that the White House was attempting to interfere with the investigation into what became known as the Whitewater affair. A special prosecutor began examining these issues in 1993, and several congressional committees began hearings that continued into 1996.

Despite its many problems, the Clinton administration could boast of some significant achievements in its first year. The president narrowly (by a single vote in the Senate) won approval of a budget that marked a significant turn away from the policies of the Reagan-Bush years. It included a substantial tax increase on the wealthiest Americans, a significant reduction in many areas of government spending, and a major expansion of tax credits to low-income working people, designed to help lift many struggling families out of poverty. And after a long and difficult battle against, among others,

Ross Perot, the AFL-CIO, and many Democrats in Congress, he won approval of the North American Free Trade Agreement, which eliminated most trade barriers among the United States, Canada, and Mexico.

But the administration's substantial achievements were overshadowed by a large failure. The president's most important and ambitious initiative—the project that he hoped would define his presidency—was a major reform of the nation's health-care system. Early in 1993, he appointed a task force chaired by his wife, Hillary Rodham Clinton, which proposed a sweeping reform designed to guarantee coverage to every American and hold down the costs of medical care. (In the process of heading the task force, Mrs. Clinton emerged as the most powerful first lady in American history). The Clinton plan relied heavily on existing institutions, most notably private insurance companies, and some critics from the left complained that the new system would rely too heavily on an unreliable market. But the most substantial opposition came from those who believed the reform would transfer too much power to the government; and that opposition—combined with the determination of Republican leaders to deny the president any kind of victory on this potent issue—doomed the plan. There was particular opposition to the proposed tax on employers to finance the plan, a tax that small businesses claimed would be too burdensome for them. But there were complaints, too, from doctors, drug companies, insurance companies, and many people who were content with their existing insurance plans and feared the new system would treat them less favorably. In September 1994, after a series of compromises failed to attract majorities, Congress abandoned the health reform effort—a tremendous blow to the president's, and the Democratic party's, political fortunes.

The foreign policy of the Clinton administration was at first cautious and even tentative—a reflection, perhaps, of the president's relative inexperience in international affairs, but also of the rapidly changing character of the world order. Clinton presided over (although his administration had played a small role in creating) a historic agreement between Israel and the Palestinian Liberation Organization to end their long struggle over the lands Israel had occupied in 1967. His administration reached an agreement with Ukraine for an elimination of the nuclear weapons that had been positioned there when the republic had been part of the Soviet Union. And the president helped broker an agreement that led to the departure of a brutal military government from Haiti; American troops arrived to help preserve order as the elected president of Haiti returned from exile and established a new civilian regime.

The most troubling international question of the early 1990s emerged in eastern Europe. Yugoslavia, a nation created after World War I out of a group of small Balkan countries formerly part of the Austro-Hungarian Empire, dissolved into several new nations in the wake of the collapse of communism in Europe after 1989. Bosnia was among the new nations, and it quickly became embroiled in a bloody civil war between its two major ethnic groups: one Muslim, the other Serbian and Christian. All efforts by the other European nations and the United States to negotiate an end to the struggle failed until 1995, when the American negotiator Richard Holbrooke finally brought the warring parties together and crafted an agreement to partition Bosnia. The United States was among the nations to send peacekeeping troops to Bosnia to police the fragile settlement.

The Republican Resurgence

The trials of the Clinton administration, and the failure of the health-care reform in particular, proved enormously damaging to the Democratic Party as it faced the congressional elections of 1994. Few doubted that the Republicans would make significant gains that year, but almost everyone was surprised by the dimensions of their victory. Every Republican incumbent won reelection. Democrats lost in droves. For the first time in forty years, Republicans seized control of both houses of Congress.

Several months before the election, Representative Newt Gingrich of Georgia released a set of campaign promises signed by almost all Republican candidates for the House and called it the "Contract with America." It called for dramatic changes in federal spending to produce a balanced budget, tax reductions, and a host of other measures consistent with the longtime goals of the Republican Party's conservative wing. Opinion polls suggested that few voters in 1994 were aware of the "Contract" at the time they voted. But Gingrich and the new Republican congressional leadership nevertheless interpreted the election results as a mandate for their program.

Throughout 1995, the Republican Congress worked at a sometimes feverish pace to construct one of the most ambitious and even radical legislative programs in modern times. The leaders proposed a series of measures to transfer important powers from the federal government to the states (including a proposal to abolish welfare as it had existed since the 1930s and replace it with block grants to state governments). They proposed dramatic reductions in federal spending, including a major restructuring of the oncesacrosanct Medicare program to reduce costs. They attempted to scale back a wide range of federal regulatory functions. In all these efforts, they could count on an unprecedentedly disciplined Republican majority in the House

CLINTON AND THE NEW CONGRESSIONAL LEADERSHIP In the aftermath of the dramatic Republican victories in the 1994 congressional elections, President Clinton vowed to cooperate with the new leaders of the House and Senate. He meets here, on January 5, 1995, with Speaker of the House Newt Gingrich, who spearheaded the campaign that put Congress in Republican hands for the first time in forty years, and Senate Majority Leader Robert Dole, who was already preparing to challenge President Clinton in the 1996 election.

and an only slightly less united Republican majority in the Senate. The Republican agenda, if successfully enacted, would represent the most substantial shift in the distribution of public authority in at least fifty years.

President Clinton responded to the 1994 election results by shifting his own agenda conspicuously to the center and calling for his own plan to cut taxes and balance the budget. Indeed, the gap between the Democratic White House and the Republican Congress on most major issues was relatively small. But because the legislative politics of 1995 was becoming part of the presidential politics of 1996, compromise between the president and Congress became very difficult. In November 1995 and again in January 1996, the federal government literally shut down because the president and Congress could not agree on a budget. By early 1996, public opinion seemed to be turning against much of the Republican agenda—and against the man most clearly identified with it. Gingrich was one of the most unpopular political leaders in the nation, while Clinton was slowly improving his standing in the polls. Even so, the events of 1994 and 1995 marked a remarkable change in American politics—a culmination, of sorts, of nearly thirty years of conservative efforts. Whatever the extent of the Republican legislative victories, it was clear that American politics had moved into a new era, the full outlines of which remained undefined.

MODERN TIMES

The widespread popular suspicion of politics and government that characterized American life in the 1980s and 1990s was in part a result of decades of crises and scandals in public life. But it reflected, too, a series of major changes in the character and behavior of the American economy and American society, changes more rapid—and more jarring—than those of any since at least the 1930s.

The Two-Tiered Economy

Foremost among these changes was the dramatic transformation of the American economy, a transformation that had begun in earnest in the early 1970s and that continued unabated in the mid-1990s. The new economy created dazzling new miracles of technology that transformed the lives of almost everyone. It created enormous new wealth that enriched those talented, or lucky, enough to profit from the areas of growth. And it produced enormous disparities in income, wealth, and opportunity that contributed to deep and increasingly corrosive divisions in American society.

The jarring changes in America's relationship to the world economy that had begun in the 1970s—the loss of cheap and easy access to raw materials, the penetration of the American market by foreign competitors, the restructuring of American heavy industry so that it produced fewer jobs and paid lower wages—continued and in some respects accelerated through the last decades of the century. Economic growth continued, but at a slower rate than before. In the twenty years after World War II, the gross national product grew, on average, by 3.8 percent a year. In the 1970s and 1980s, the GNP grew by an average of less than 2.6 percent. Productivity grew 2.6 percent a year in the 1950s and 1960s; in the 1970s and 1980s it grew by less than 1 percent. The national savings rate—the rate at which individuals and institutions saved income, which then became available for investment—peaked at around 10 percent between 1948 and 1973. The highest single-year rate in the 1980s was 3.2 percent.

For many families and individuals, the results of these contractions were jarring. In the first twenty years after World War II, it was possible for many, perhaps most, Americans to sustain themselves on a single (usually male) income. In later years, more and more families required two incomes to maintain their standards of living, and even that was often not enough. In the 1950s and 1960s, most Americans could expect to live more comfortably as adults than their parents had; in the 1980s and 1990s, increasing numbers of Americans were finding it impossible even to live as well as the generation before them. From 1973 to 1989, median family income increased less than 2 percent after inflation (from $33,656 a year to $34,213 in constant dollars), even though many families added a second income in those years.

Poverty in America had declined steadily and at times dramatically in the years after World War II, so that by the mid-1970s the percentage of people living in poverty had dropped to 12.3 percent (from 22.2 percent in 1960). By the early 1980s, the poverty rate was beginning to rise, and it reached 15 percent in 1993. As always, this increase in poverty affected women, children, and minorities far more than any other groups.

The increasingly unequal distribution of wealth and income in the United States accentuated these changes. Over 94 percent of the new wealth created by the American economy in the 1980s went to the wealthiest 20 percent of the population; over 50 percent went to the top 1 percent. In the meantime, the middle 40 percent of the population experienced an actual decline in wealth. Forty-seven percent of the total income in the United States in 1993 went to the wealthiest 20 percent of the population, and over 20 percent to the wealthiest 5 percent. Less than 30 percent of the income went to the bottom 60 percent of families, and only 4 percent to the bottom 20 percent. It was little wonder that the economic anxieties of the working and middle classes became one of the central issues in American politics in the late 1980s and early 1990s.

The new economy caused a real decline in the standard of living of most working-class Americans and even of many members of the middle class. But it created enormous rewards for others. The most dramatic area of growth in the 1980s and 1990s was technology, a field in which the United States continued to be highly competitive internationally. Biotechnology—which included pioneering new areas of medical research—was one sector of the economy that produced a bonanza. Even more important were computers, whose impact on American life exploded beginning in the 1980s and showed no signs of slowing as the century neared its close. Many of the greatest fortunes of the late twentieth century went to those men and women who capitalized on the growing market for computers and the services they provided.

The wealthiest man in America in the mid-1990s was William Gates, the founder and president of Microsoft—the software company whose operating systems served the vast majority of the world's computers. But Gates was only the most fabulously successful of large numbers of people who earned great wealth through technology and, in the process, created flourishing new areas of the national and international economies.

It became a cliché of public rhetoric that the new economy rewarded education, skills, and knowledge; but like many clichés, this one was largely true. Older sectors that relied on heavy machinery, large labor forces, and big corporate organizations did not disappear; in many cases, they restructured themselves and became more profitable—although often at the expense of their workers. But the "knowledge-based economy" was creating a disproportionate amount of the wealth and the bulk of the highly paid jobs of the 1990s.

The result was what many began to call a "two-tiered economy"—an increasingly affluent group at the top, constituting a quarter of the population or less; a struggling middle class faced with stagnating incomes and increasing insecurity; and an impoverished bottom, at times approaching a quarter of the population, with decreasing prospects for advancement in a world in which unskilled and semiskilled labor had much less value than in the past.

"Globalization"

Perhaps the most important change, and certainly the one whose impact was the most difficult to gauge, was what became known as the "globalization" of the economy. The great prosperity of the 1950s and 1960s had rested on, among other things, the relative insulation of the United States from the pressures of international competition. As late as 1970, only 9 percent of the goods made in America were exported. More important, fewer than a third of the goods produced in America faced competition from abroad for the domestic market. The United States was an important participant in international trade. But in 1970, international trade still played a relatively small role in the American economy as a whole, which thrived on the basis of the huge domestic market in North America.

By the end of the 1970s, the world had intruded into the American economy in profound ways, and that intrusion increased unabated for the next twenty years. Exports rose, both in absolute numbers and as a percentage of goods produced: from just under $43 billion in 1970 to nearly $513 billion in 1994. More important, imports rose even more dramatically:

from just over $40 billion in 1970 to over $663 billion in 1994. As early as 1980, over 70 percent of American products faced foreign competition inside the United States, most notably some of the products whose role in creating and sustaining prosperity was especially important: steel and automobiles. America had made 76 percent of the world's automobiles in 1950 and 48 percent in 1960. By 1990, that share had dropped to 20 percent; and in 1994, even after a substantial revival of the automobile industry, the American share had risen only to 25 percent.

America was the largest exporter in the world in the 1980s and 1990s, and yet it had a huge trade imbalance (meaning it was importing much more than it was exporting). That was a reflection of how many competitors it faced and how deeply they had penetrated the United States market. The first American trade imbalance in the postwar era was in 1971; only twice since then, in 1973 and 1975, has the balance been favorable.

Globalization brought many benefits for the American consumer: new and more varied products, and lower prices for many of them. Most economists, and most national leaders, welcomed the process and worked to encourage it through lowering trade barriers. The North American Free Trade Agreement (NAFTA), ratified by the United States Senate in 1993, and the General Agreement on Tariffs and Trade (GATT), ratified a year later, were the boldest of a long series of treaties lowering trade barriers stretching back to the 1960s. But globalization was also enormously destabilizing. It was particularly hard on industrial workers, who were affected in two important ways. First, American workers lost industrial jobs as American companies lost market share. As foreign, especially Japanese, competition cut into steel, automobiles, and other heavy industries in the 1970s and beyond, the work forces in those industries declined. Second, American workers lost jobs as American companies began exporting work: building plants in Mexico, Asia, and other lower-wage countries to avoid having to pay the high wages workers had won in America. More than half of the production costs of making American cars were spent outside the United States by the 1990s. That was one reason for the rising unpopularity of free trade among many working-class people—an unpopularity effectively exploited by such self-proclaimed "populist" politicians as Ross Perot and Pat Buchanan, the conservative Republican who was running for president in 1996, and whose surprising victory in the New Hampshire primary thrust trade issues into the center of Republican Party debate for a time.

Globalization was also visible in the increasing presence of non-American investors and corporations within the American economy. Japanese and German automobile companies built new plants in the United

States. European and Asian corporations established large presences in America and sometimes bought major American companies. A group of Japanese investors bought the Columbia motion picture studio in 1989, and foreign companies purchased American corporations as large and visible as RCA, Goodyear, and Pillsbury.

The Graying of America

After decades of steady growth, the nation's birth rate began to decline in the 1970s and remained low through the 1980s and early 1990s. In 1970, there were 18.4 births for every 1,000 people in the population. By 1975, the rate had declined to 14.6, the lowest in the twentieth century. And despite a modest increase in the 1980s, the rate remained below 16 in the mid-1990s. The declining birth rate and a significant rise in life expectancy produced a substantial increase in the proportion of elderly citizens. There were 17 million Americans over sixty-five years old in 1960 and 33 million in 1994. Over 12 percent of the population was more than sixty-five years old by 1990, as compared with 8 percent in 1970. That figure was projected to rise to over 20 percent by the end of the century as the members of the postwar baby boom began to enter old age. In 1994 the median age was thirty-four years, as compared with twenty-eight in 1970.

The aging of the population had important political and economic implications. It was a cause of the increasing costliness of Social Security pensions, and of steadily rising payroll taxes to sustain the system. It helped cause dramatic increases in health costs, both for the federal Medicare and Medicaid systems and for private hospitals and insurance companies. One of the reasons for the enormous federal deficits that came to dominate American political life in the late twentieth century was the rapidly rising cost of these pensions and medical programs for the elderly. But the changing demography also ensured that the aged, who already formed one of the most powerful interest groups in America, would remain politically formidable well into the twenty-first century.

The Changing Profile of Immigration

Perhaps the most striking demographic change in America in the 1980s and 1990s, and one of those likely to have the farthest-reaching consequences, was the enormous change in both the extent and the character of immigration. Immigration had steadily declined for sixty years until the 1970s, when it began to increase sharply. In the 1970s, more than 4 million legal immigrants entered the United States. In the 1980s and early 1990s, the number rose to more than 6 million. (In 1994 alone, over 800,000 legal immigrants entered the United States.) When the uncounted but very large numbers of illegal immigrants in those years are included, the wave of immigration in the quarter-century after 1970 is almost certainly the largest of the twentieth century. In 1994, 8.7 percent of the American population was foreign-born—the largest percentage since 1940 and an 80 percent increase from 1970.

Equally striking was the character of the new immigration. The Immigration Reform Act of 1965 (see p. 835) had eliminated quotas based on national origin; from then on, newcomers from regions other than Latin America were generally admitted on a first-come, first-served basis. In 1965, 90 percent of the immigrants to the United States came from Europe. Twenty years later, only 10 percent of the new arrivals were Europeans. The three largest groups of foreign-born Americans in 1994 were, in order, Mexicans, Filipinos, and Cubans. The extent and character of the new immigration was causing a dramatic change in the composition of the American population. Already by the early 1990s, people of white European background constituted under 80 percent of the population (as opposed to 90 percent a half-century before). It seemed likely that by the middle of the twenty-first century, whites of European heritage would constitute less than 50 percent of the population.

Particularly important to the new immigration were two groups: Hispanics and Asians. Both had been significant segments of the American population for many decades—Hispanics since the very beginning of the nation's history, Asians since the waves of Chinese and Japanese immigration in the nineteenth century. But both groups experienced enormous, indeed unprecedented, growth after 1965.

People from Latin America—from Cuba, El Salvador, the Dominican Republic, and above all Mexico—constituted more than a third of the total number of legal immigrants to the United States in every year after 1965—and a much larger proportion of the total number of illegal immigrants. In California and the Southwest, in particular, they became an increasingly important presence. There were also substantial Hispanic populations in Illinois, New York, and Florida. High birth rates among Hispanic communities already in the United States further increased their numbers. In the 1980 census, 6 percent of the population was listed as being of Hispanic origin. The 1990 census showed an increase to 9 percent—or 20 million people. (Twenty years earlier, the number had been 7 million.) Economic problems and political repression in Mexico and other Latin American and Caribbean nations propelled the new immigrants to the United States; but in most of the areas to which they moved, opportunities were hard to find. Mexican Americans had an official poverty rate of 20 percent in 1990 (and a real poverty rate that was probably much higher, given the number of illegal immigrants who evaded official statistics). The poverty rate among Puerto Ricans was 30 percent. For illegal immigrants, conditions were particularly dire. Because they were subject to deportation if they came to the attention of the government, they had no legal recourse to being exploited by employers. Most worked for subsistence wages in menial jobs, constantly fearful of exposure.

The growing Hispanic presence became a political issue of increasing importance in the 1980s and 1990s, both to "Anglos" and, of course, to Hispanics themselves. The Immigration Reform and Control (or Simpson-Mazzoli) Act of 1987 reflected the political power of both groups. Its principal goal was to respond to the demands of whites in the Southwest and California by stemming the flow of illegal immigrants (mostly from Mexico). To that end, it placed the burden on employers for the first time to confirm the legal status of their employees. Those who failed to do so faced economic and even criminal penalties. Hispanics charged that the bill would increase discrimination in hiring, and in the first years after its passage there was considerable evidence that such charges were well founded. At the same time, the act responded to the growing political influence of Hispanics by offering amnesty to all undocumented workers who had entered the country before 1982. By the early 1990s, however, it seemed clear that the law was failing. Illegal immigration from Mexico and elsewhere was continuing at near-record levels.

White residents of areas in which the Hispanic populations were growing rapidly often reacted with alarm, fearing that they would soon become a minority in what they considered their own cities. Such fears lay behind efforts to bar the use of the Spanish language in public schools and other measures to force Hispanic immigrants to assimilate more quickly and completely.

In the 1980s and early 1990s, Asian immigrants arrived in numbers almost equal to those of Hispanics. Over 6 million of the foreign-born in America in 1994 were from Asian nations (most notably the Philippines, China, Korea, Vietnam, and India). They swelled the already substantial Chinese communities in California and elsewhere. And they created substantial new communities of immigrants from other areas of Asia. By 1990, there were more than 7 million Asian Americans in the United States, more than twice the number of ten years before. Like Hispanics, they were concentrated mainly in large cities and in the West.

A M E R I C A N   V O I C E S

A Vietnamese Immigrant Describes Her Life in America, 1984

HERE IN AMERICA, I just remain. I don't change my traditional ways. . . . My children have adapted to American customs in hair styles and dress. . . . The older women don't change much, and most of the older men don't change either.

Over here, for older people, we receive money from the government; if not, we would die of starvation because we are older and don't know what to do. In Vietnam, we have less fear of survival, but over here, I'm afraid that when I get older I'll have to go into a nursing home to stay there, because all of my children are working. . . . Old age here is scary. . . .

The difference is that over here children do not obey their parents; in Vietnam, they obeyed us more. Over here, whenever we say something, they like to argue about it. . . . Things we consider to be right they consider wrong. Like a wife they select whom we don't like. They argue with us, against it, saying that it's right for them and that they will take the responsibility for it. They claim it's their *right* and that we don't have the right to tell them what to do. It is just like we are strangers; they won't let us interfere. . . . Our children do not keep the old traditions. They live apart from one another.

SOURCE: Reprinted from *Hearts of Sorrow: Vietnamese-American Lives*, by James M. Freeman, with the permission of the publisher, Stanford University Press. © 1989 by the Board of Trustees of the Leland Stanford Junior University.

Like most new immigrant groups, Asian Americans found adjustment to the very different culture of the United States difficult and disorienting. They also experienced resentment and discrimination. Whites feared Asian competition in economic activities that they had been accustomed to controlling. For example, there were heated disputes between white and Vietnamese shrimpers on the Gulf Coast in Texas, Mississippi, and Louisiana. Some African Americans resented the success of Asian merchants in black neighborhoods (as the black filmmaker Spike Lee noted in his 1989 film *Do the Right Thing.*) In New York, racial tensions led to a black boycott of some Korean grocery stores in African American neighborhoods in 1990.

Resentment of Asian Americans may also have been a result, in part, of their remarkable success. Indeed, some Asian groups (most notably Indians, Japanese, and Chinese) were by the 1980s earning larger average annual incomes than whites. Chinese and Japanese Americans consistently ranked at or near the top of high-school and college classes in the 1980s. That was in part because Asian-American communities contained significant numbers of people who had been involved in business and the professions before coming to America and had arrived with a high degree of expertise. They also placed an unusually high value on education.

Black America in the Postliberal Era

The vast political and economic changes of the years after the civil rights movement had contrasting effects on African Americans. On the one hand, there were increased opportunities for advancement available to those in a position to take advantage of them. On the other hand, as industrial employment declined and government services dwindled, there was a growing sense of helplessness and despair among the large groups of nonwhites who continued to find themselves barred from upward mobility.

For the black middle class, which by the late 1970s constituted nearly a third of the entire black population of America, the progress was at times astonishing. Economic disparities between black and white professionals did not vanish, but they diminished substantially. Black families moved into more affluent urban communities and, in many cases, into suburbs—at times as neighbors of whites, more often into predominantly black communities. The number of blacks attending college rose by 350 percent in the decade following the passage of the civil rights acts (in contrast to a 150 percent increase among whites); African Americans made up 12 percent of the college population in 1990 (up from 5 percent twenty-five years earlier), although by 1994 that figure had declined to just over 10 percent. The percentage of black high-school graduates going on to college was by then virtually the same as that of white high-school graduates (although a far smaller proportion of blacks than whites managed to complete high school). And African Americans were making rapid strides in many professions from which, a generation earlier, they had been barred or within which they had been segregated. They were becoming partners in major law firms and joining the staffs of major hospitals and the faculties of major universities. Nearly half of all employed blacks in the United States had white-collar jobs. There were few areas of American life from which blacks were any longer entirely excluded. Middle-class blacks, in other words, had realized great gains from the legislation of the 1960s, from the changing national mood on race, from the creation of controversial affirmative action programs, and from their own educational and professional efforts.

But the rise of a black middle class also accentuated (and perhaps even helped cause) the increasingly desperate plight of other black Americans, whom many of the liberal programs of the 1960s had never reached. This growing "underclass" made up about a third of the nation's black population. It felt the impact of the economic troubles of the 1970s and 1980s with special force. And as more successful blacks moved out of the inner cities, the poor were left virtually alone in their decaying neighborhoods. A third of all black families lived in poverty in 1993; at the same time, just over 12 percent of white families could be officially classified as poor. Fewer than half of young inner-city blacks finished high school; more than 60 percent were unemployed.

The black family structure suffered as well from the dislocations of urban poverty. There was a radical increase in the number of single-parent, female-headed black households in the 1970s and 1980s. In the early 1990s, over 60 percent of all black children were born into single-parent families, as opposed to only 15 percent of white children (also a substantial increase over earlier eras). In 1960, only 20 percent of black children had lived in single-parent homes.

Nonwhites faced many disadvantages in the changing social and economic climate of the 1980s and 1990s. Among them was a growing impatience with affirmative action and other programs designed to advance their fortunes, as symbolized by the *Bakke* case in 1978 and by a growing reluctance among federal officials after 1980 to move aggressively to enforce affirmative action guidelines. By the mid-1990s, the white assault on affirmative action had gained so much momentum that there was real doubt as to whether very much of it would survive. Nonwhites suffered as well from a steady decline in the number of unskilled jobs in the economy. They suffered from the long, steady deterioration of urban public education and of other social services, which made it more difficult for them to find opportunities for advancement. And they suffered, in some cases, from a sense of futility and despair, born of years of entrapment in brutal urban ghettoes.

By the early 1990s, whole generations of nonwhites had grown to maturity living in destitute neighborhoods where welfare, drug dealing, and other crimes were virtually the only means of support for many people. Violence was increasingly a part of daily life. While rates of violent crime were declining nationally in the late 1980s and early 1990s, violence (much of it entirely random) was escalating in many inner-city communities—a result of the drug trade, gang wars, and the proliferation of guns.

The anger and despair such conditions were creating among inner-city residents became clear in the summer of 1992 in Los Angeles. The previ-

LOS ANGELES, APRIL 1992 An aerial view of a section of south central Los Angeles in the immediate aftermath of the great riot of 1992. The decision of an all-white jury to acquit Los Angeles police officers accused of brutalizing a black suspect (a beating recorded by a bystander on video tape) created widespread outrage and crystallized a frustration that residents of this poor, crime-plagued community had been feeling for years.

ous year, a bystander had videotaped several Los Angeles police officers beating an apparently helpless black man whom they had captured after an auto chase. Broadcast repeatedly around the country, the tape evoked outrage among whites and blacks alike. But an all-white jury in a suburban community just outside Los Angeles acquitted the officers when they were tried for assault. Black residents of South Central Los Angeles, one of the poorest communities in the city, erupted in anger—precipitating the largest racial disturbance of the twentieth century. There was widespread looting and arson. More than fifty people died. In the 1960s, urban uprisings had helped produce a major (if ultimately inadequate) government effort to deal with the problems of the inner city. But in the fiscally starved 1990s, the Los Angeles riot produced no such response.

What Americans had long called "race relations," the way in which white and black Americans viewed each other, grew increasingly sour in these difficult years. White impatience with black demands grew, as did a willingness to listen to old and long-discredited arguments about genetic differences between the races. A controversial book by two social scientists, *The Bell Curve*, published in 1994, helped reopen this bitter debate about the innate capacities of members of different races. Many African Americans, for their part, developed an intensified mistrust of the institutions of white society—of the government, the corporations, the universities, and perhaps above all the system of law enforcement.

Nowhere was this mutual suspicion more evident than in the celebrated trial of the former football star O. J. Simpson, an African American, who was accused of murdering his former wife and a young man, both of whom were white, in Los Angeles in 1994. The long and costly "O. J. trial" was an enormous media sensation for over a year, and throughout the proceedings, opinions about Simpson's guilt broke down along strikingly racial lines. A vast majority of whites believed he was guilty, and a vast majority of blacks believed he was innocent. Simpson's acquittal in the fall of 1995 caused great celebrations in many black communities and a quiet disgust among many whites.

Modern Plagues: Drugs, AIDS, and Homelessness

Poor African Americans, new immigrants, and many others found themselves clustered, often trapped, in cities being ravaged not just by economic decline but by two new and deadly epidemics. One was a dramatic increase in drug use, which penetrated nearly every community in the nation. The enormous demand for drugs, and particularly for "crack" cocaine, spawned what was in effect a multibillion-dollar industry, and those reaping the enormous profits of the illegal trade fought strenuously and often savagely to protect their positions.

Political figures of both parties spoke heatedly about the need for a "war on drugs," but in the absence of significant funding for such programs and clear ideas about what they should accomplish, government efforts appeared to be having little effect. Drug use declined significantly among middle-class people beginning in the late 1980s, but the epidemic showed no signs of abating in the poor urban neighborhoods where it was doing the most severe damage.

The drug epidemic was directly related to another scourge of the 1980s and 1990s: the epidemic spread of a new and lethal disease first documented in 1981 and soon named AIDS (acquired immune deficiency syndrome). AIDS is the product of the HIV virus, which is transmitted by the exchange of bodily fluids (blood or semen). The virus gradually destroys the body's immune system and makes its victims highly vulnerable to a number of diseases (particularly to various forms of cancer and pneumonia) to which they would otherwise have a natural resistance. Although many of those infected with the virus (i.e., people who are "HIV positive") live for many years without developing AIDS, once they do become ill they are virtually certain to die. The first American victims of AIDS (and in the early 1990s the group among whom cases remained the most numerous) were homosexual men. But by the late 1980s, as the gay community began to take preventive measures, the most rapid increase in the spread of the disease occurred among heterosexuals, many of them intravenous drug users, who spread the virus by sharing contaminated hypodermic needles. By the early 1990s, United States government agencies were estimating that between 1 and 1.5 million Americans were infected with the HIV virus. (Worldwide, the figure was over 10 million.) Over 400,000 Americans had actually contracted AIDS, and over 280,000 had died by the mid-1990s.

A large research effort produced a wealth of new knowledge about the virus and developed several drugs that could delay or limit the effects of AIDS. But neither a cure nor a vaccine seemed imminent. Governments and private groups, in the meantime, began promoting AIDS awareness in increasingly visible and graphic ways—urging young people, in particular, to avoid "unsafe sex" through abstinence or the use of latex condoms.

The spread of AIDS had a chilling effect on the sexual revolution that had transformed behavior beginning in the 1960s. Fear of infection caused many people to avoid casual sexual relations; but the more puritanical sexual standards against which many Americans had rebelled in the 1960s—and that some conservative Americans hoped to restore—did not return.

The increasing scarcity of housing for low-income people contributed to another urban crisis of the 1980s and 1990s: homelessness. There had always been homeless men and women in most major cities, but their numbers were clearly growing at an alarming rate in the face of rising housing costs, severe cutbacks in federal support for public housing, reduced welfare assistance, deinstitutionalization of the mentally ill, the declining availability of unskilled jobs, and the increasing weakness of family structures. The phenomenon of tens of thousands of homeless people at large in the cities put pressure on municipal governments to provide shelter and assistance for the indigent, but in an age of fiscal stringency and greatly reduced federal aid, cities found it difficult to respond adequately to the dimensions of the crisis.

Battles Against Feminism and Abortion

Among the principal goals of the New Right as it became more powerful and assertive in the 1980s and 1990s was to challenge feminism and its achievements. Leaders of the New Right had campaigned successfully against the proposed Equal Rights Amendment to the Constitution. And they played a central role in the most divisive issue of the late 1980s and early 1990s: the controversy over abortion rights.

For those who favored allowing women to choose to terminate unwanted pregnancies, the Supreme Court's decision in *Roe* v. *Wade* (1973) had seemed to settle the question. By the 1980s, abortion was the most commonly performed surgical procedure in the country. But at the same time, opposition to abortion was creating a powerful grassroots movement. The right-to-life movement, as it called itself, found its most fervent supporters among Catholics; and indeed, the Catholic Church itself lent its institutional authority to the battle against legalized abortion. Religious doctrine also motivated the antiabortion stance of Mormons, fundamentalist Christians, and other groups. The opposition of some other antiabortion activists had less to do with religion than with their commitment to traditional notions of family and gender relations. To them, abortion was a particularly offensive part of a much larger assault by feminists on the role of women as wives and mothers. It was also, many foes contended, a form of murder. Fetuses, they claimed, were human beings who had a "right to life" from the moment of conception.

Although the right-to-life movement was persistent in its demand for a reversal of *Roe* v. *Wade* or, barring that, a constitutional amendment banning abortion, it also attacked abortion in more limited ways, at its most vulnerable points. In the 1970s, Congress and many state legislatures began barring the use of public funds to pay for abortions, thus making them almost inaccessible for many poor women. The Reagan and Bush administrations imposed further restrictions on federal funding and even on the right of doctors in federally funded clinics to give patients any information on abortion. Extremists in the right-to-life movement began picketing, occupying, and at times bombing abortion clinics. One antiabortion activist murdered a doctor in Florida who performed abortions; other physicians were subject to campaigns of terrorism and harassment—part of an effort to force them to abandon serving women who wanted abortions.

The changing composition of the Supreme Court in the 1980s to early 1990s (when five new conservative justices were named by Presidents Reagan and Bush) renewed the right-to-life movement's hopes for a reversal of *Roe* v. *Wade*. In *Webster* v. *Reproductive Health Services* (1989), the Court upheld a Missouri law that forbade any institution receiving state funds from performing abortions, whether or not those funds were used to finance the abortions. But the Court stopped short of overturning its 1973 decision.

Through much of the 1970s and 1980s, defenders of abortion had remained confident that *Roe* v. *Wade* protected their right to choose abortion and that the antiabortion movement was unlikely to prevail. But the changing judicial climate of the late 1980s and early 1990s mobilized defenders of abortion as never before. They called themselves the "pro-choice" movement, because they were defending not so much abortion itself as every woman's right to choose whether and when to bear a child. It quickly became clear that the pro-choice movement was in many parts of the country at least as strong as, and in some areas much stronger than, the right-to-life movement. With the election of President Clinton in 1992, the immediate threat to *Roe* v. *Wade* seemed to fade. In his first two years in office, Clinton named two pro-choice justices to the Court—Ruth Bader Ginsburg and Stephen Breyer. But the increasing strength of the Republican right, as demonstrated in the 1994 congressional elections, suggested that the issue was far from closed.

At times the pro-choice campaign overshadowed other efforts by feminists to protect and expand the rights of women. But such efforts continued. Women's organizations and many individual women worked strenuously in the 1980s and 1990s to improve access to child care for poor women and to win the right to caregiver leaves for parents. They also worked to raise awareness of sexual harassment in the workplace, with considerable success. Colleges, universities, government agencies, even many corporations established strict new standards of behavior for their employees in dealing with members of the opposite sex and created grievance procedures for those who believed they had been harassed. Both the achievements and the limits of their progress on this issue were evident in the sensational controversy in 1991 over Judge Clarence Thomas, President Bush's nominee for a seat on the Supreme Court. Late in the confirmation proceedings, accusations of sexual harassment from Anita Hill, a law professor and former employee of Thomas, became public. Hill's testimony before the Senate Judiciary Committee dramatically polarized both the Senate and the nation. Feminists and others tended to believe the accusations and hailed the accuser for drawing national attention to the issue of harassment; but many Americans (and most members of the virtually all-male Senate) apparently did not believe her— or at least concluded that the alleged activities should not disqualify Thomas from serving on the Court. Thomas was ultimately confirmed by a narrow margin.

The Changing Left and the New Environmentalism

The New Left of the 1960s and early 1970s did not disappear after the end of the war in Vietnam, but it faded rapidly. Many of the students who had fought in its battles grew up, left school, and entered conventional careers. Some radical leaders, disillusioned by the unresponsiveness of American society to their demands, resignedly gave up the struggle and chose instead to work "within the system." Radical ideas continued to flourish in some academic circles, but to much of the public they came to appear dated and irrelevant—particularly as, beginning in 1989, Marxist governments collapsed in disrepute.

Yet a left of sorts did survive, giving evidence in the process of how greatly the nation's political climate had changed. Where 1960s activists had rallied to protest racism, poverty, and war, their counterparts in the 1980s and 1990s more often fought to stop the proliferation of nuclear weapons and power plants, to save the wilderness, to protect endangered species, to limit reckless economic development, and otherwise to protect the environment.

Public concerns about the environment had arisen intermittently since the beginning of the industrial era and had been growing in intensity since 1962, when the publication of Rachel Carson's *Silent Spring* aroused widespread public concern about the effect of insecticides on the natural world.

Several highly visible environmental catastrophes in the 1960s and 1970s greatly increased that concern. Among them were a major oil spill off Santa Barbara, California, in 1969; the discovery of large deposits of improperly disposed toxic wastes in a residential community in upstate New York in 1978; and a frightening accident at the nuclear power plant on Three Mile Island, Pennsylvania, in 1979. These and other revelations of the extent to which human progress threatened the natural world helped produce a major popular movement.

In the spring of 1970, a nationwide "Earth Day" signaled the beginning of the modern environmental movement. It differed markedly from the "conservation" movements of earlier years. Modern environmentalists shared the concerns of such earlier figures as John Muir and Gifford Pinchot about preserving the wilderness or carefully managing the exploitation of resources. But the new activists went much further, basing their positions on the developing field of ecology, the study of the interconnections among all components of an environment. Toxic wastes, air and water pollution, the destruction of forests, the extinction of species—these were not separate, isolated problems. All elements of the earth's environment were intimately and delicately linked, ecologists claimed. Damaging any one of those elements risked damaging all the others. Only by adopting a new social ethic, in which economic growth became less important than ecological health, or a new economics, in which environmental costs were factored into economic analyses, could the human race hope to survive in a healthy world.

In the twenty years after the first Earth Day, environmental issues gained increasing attention and support. Although the federal government often displayed limited interest in the subject, environmentalists won a series of significant battles, mostly at the local level. They blocked the construction of roads, airports, and other projects (including American development of the supersonic transport airplane, or SST) that they claimed would be ecologically dangerous. By the end of the decade, the sense of urgency had grown, as scientists began warning that the release of certain industrial pollutants (most notably chlorofluorocarbons) into the atmosphere was depleting the ozone layer of the earth's atmosphere, which protects the globe from the sun's most dangerous rays. They warned, too, of the related danger of global warming, a rise in the earth's temperature as a result of emissions from the burning of fossil fuels (coal and oil).

The concern for the environment, the opposition to nuclear power, the resistance to economic development—all were reflections of a more fundamental characteristic of the post-Vietnam left. In a sharp break from the nation's long commitment to growth and progress, many dissidents argued that only by limiting growth and curbing traditional forms of progress could society hope to survive. Some of these critics of the "idea of progress" expressed a gloomy resignation, urging a lowering of social expectations and predicting an inevitable deterioration in the quality of life. Other advocates of restraint believed that change did not require decline: human beings could live more comfortably and more happily if they learned to respect the limits imposed on them by their environment. But in either case, such arguments evoked strong opposition from conservatives and others, who ridiculed the no-growth ideology as an expression of defeatism and despair. Ronald Reagan, in particular, made an attack on the idea of "limits" central to his political success.

The rising popularity of environmental issues reflected another important shift both in the character of the American left and in the tone of American public life generally. Through much of the first half of the twentieth century, American politics had been preoccupied with debates over economic power and disparities of wealth. In the late twentieth century, with concentrations of wealth and power reaching unprecedented levels, such debates had largely ceased. There were, of course, economic implications to environmentalism and other no-growth efforts. But what drove such movements was less a concern about class than a concern about the quality of individual and community life.

The "Culture Wars"

As class-based controversies ceased to shape American public life, cultural battles gradually took their place. Indeed, few issues attracted more attention in the 1990s than the battle over what became known as "multiculturalism." Multiculturalism meant different things to different people, but at its core was an effort to legitimize the cultural pluralism of the rapidly diversifying American population. That meant acknowledging that "American culture," which had long been defined primarily by white males of European descent, also included other traditions: female, African American, Indian, and increasingly in the late twentieth-century Hispanic and Asian. Although such demands were often controversial, especially when they became the basis of assaults on traditional academic curricula, much greater acrimony emerged out of efforts by some revisionists to portray traditional Western culture as inherently racist and imperialistic. A prolonged, if somewhat muted, dispute over how to commemorate the 500th anniversary of Columbus's first voyage to the "New World" illustrated how sharply ideas of multiculturalism had changed the way Americans discussed their past. In

1892, the Columbian anniversary had been the occasion of boisterous national celebration—and a great world's fair in Chicago. In 1992, it produced agonizing debates over the impact of the European discovery on native peoples. The only world's fairs were in Italy and Spain.

Debates over multiculturalism and related issues helped produce an increasingly strained climate in academia and in the larger American intellectual world. People on the left complained that the ascendancy of conservative politics placed new and intolerable limits on freedom of expression, as efforts to restrict National Endowment for the Arts grants to controversial artists suggested. Many on the right complained equally vigorously of a

THE "NET" By the mid 1990s, the Internet—a communications system that made available vast amounts of information and entertainment through a worldwide computer network—had become something like an obsession to many Americans. Many predicted that the Internet would soon become one of the nation's primary forms of communication. Already by the mid-1990s, many people were using e-mail (electronic mail) transmitted through the Internet more often than they were using the telephone or the postal system. Access to the Internet was available at first only to employees of large institutions that had their own computer networks. But commercial services such as America Online—whose "home page" appears here—soon began to offer connections to individual consumers through their telephone lines.

tyranny of "political correctness," by which feminists, cultural radicals, and others introduced a new form of intolerance into public discourse in the name of defending the rights of women and minorities.

The controversies surrounding multiculturalism and "political correctness" were illustrations of a painful change in the character of American society. Traditional patterns of authority faced challenges from women, minorities, and others. The liberal belief in tolerance and assimilation was fraying in the face of the growing cultural separatism of members of some ethnic and racial groups. Confidence in the nation's future was declining, and with it confidence in the capacity of American society to provide justice and opportunity to all its citizens.

The American Future

The American people approached the end of the twentieth century filled with anxieties, doubts, and resentments. Faith in the nation's institutions—most notably government—was at its lowest point in many decades. Confidence in the nation's leaders had all but vanished. Deep economic anxieties, which few Americans seemed able to translate into a coherent economic agenda, increased the nation's growing discontent.

And yet the United States in the 1990s, despite its many problems, remained a remarkably successful society—and one that had made dramatic strides in improving the lives of its citizens and dealing with many of its social problems since the end of World War II. The crisis of confidence that seemed to darken the nation's public life in the waning years of the century was not irrational, to be sure. There were many reasons for concern, even alarm, about the national condition. But crisis and division are hardly new to America's long, turbulent history. Conflict and uncertainty are, in fact, more characteristic of the national experience than the stability and consensus that many Americans believed they could restore.

The American people have seldom, if ever, been wholly content about the condition of their nation. But they have also been extraordinarily resilient—and through much of their history they have been possessed with the belief that if they tried hard enough, they could improve their world. Recovering that faith—a faith at the heart of most of the many traditions that have shaped American history—is one of the challenges of our time.

APPENDICES

CANADA

Lake of the Woods

ional Falls

Duluth

NESOTA

Lake Superior

Sault Ste. Marie

MICHIGAN

Lake Huron

St. Paul

eapolis

WISCONSIN

Green Bay

Mississippi River

Lake Michigan

Bay City

Grand Rapids

Flint

Lansing

MAINE

Bangor

Augusta

VERMONT

Montpelier

NEW HAMPSHIRE

Portland

Concord

Portsmouth

Boston

Lake Ontario

Rochester

Buffalo

Syracuse

Schenectady

Albany

Springfield

MASSACHUSETTS

Providence

RHODE ISLAND

Milwaukee

Waterloo

IOWA

Madison

Kalamazoo

Rockford

Cedar

Des

Rapids

oines

a

Davenport

Chicago

Aurora

Gary

Illinois River

Peoria

Livonia

Sterling Heights

Detroit

Ann Arbor

Cleveland

Lake Erie

South Bend

Fort Wayne

Toledo

Akron

Erie

Scranton

NEW YORK

White Plains

Paterson

Newark

Hudson River

Hartford

Connecticut R.

New Haven

CONNECTICUT

Stamford

New York

Youngstown

Allentown

NEW JERSEY

Trenton

Philadelphia

ILLINOIS

INDIANA

OHIO

Columbus

Muncie

Dayton

PENNSYLVANIA

Pittsburgh

Harrisburg

Baltimore

Dover

DELAWARE

St. Joseph

Springfield

Kansas City

Independence

Indianapolis

Cincinnati

Wabash River

Frankfort

Louisville

Evansville

Lexington/

Fayette

WEST VIRGINIA

Charleston

Washington, D.C.

Alexandria

Annapolis

MARYLAND

Potomac R.

Chesapeake Bay

Jefferson

City

St. Louis

Ohio River

KENTUCKY

VIRGINIA

Richmond

Newport News

Hampton

Norfolk

Portsmouth

Chesapeake

ATLANTIC

OCEAN

MISSOURI

Springfield

Roanoke

Lynchburg

Durham

Greensboro

Raleigh

Cape Hatteras

ARKANSAS

Nashville/

Davidson

Knoxville

NORTH CAROLINA

Arkansas River

Fort

Smith

Little

Rock

Tennessee R.

Memphis

Chattanooga

TENNESSEE

Huntsville

Charlotte

Greenville

Columbia

Wilmington

Cape Fear

Myrtle Beach

d

ite

Texarkana

Monroe

Yazoo River

Birmingham

Atlanta

Augusta

SOUTH CAROLINA

Charleston

MISSISSIPPI

ALABAMA

Macon

Shreveport

Vicksburg

Jackson

Selma

Columbus

Montgomery

GEORGIA

Savannah

LOUISIANA

Mississippi River

Mobile

Albany

Jacksonville

ont

Baton Rouge

Lafayette

Pensacola

Tallahassee

St. Augustine

uston

adena

Lake Charles

New Orleans

FLORIDA

Daytona Beach

alveston

Orlando

Cape Canaveral

Gulf of Mexico

St. Petersburg

Sarasota

Tampa

Lake Okeechobee

Fort Myers

Fort Lauderdale

Hollywood

Hialeah

Miami

0   300 Miles

0   400 Kilometers

Key West

The United States in 1996

⭐ National Capital

★ State Capitals

URBAN POPULATION CENTERS

◼ Over 5,000,000

◼ 3,000,000–5,000,000

● 1,000,000–3,000,000

◻ 500,000–1,000,000

○ 100,000–500,000

• Less than 100,000 (selected)

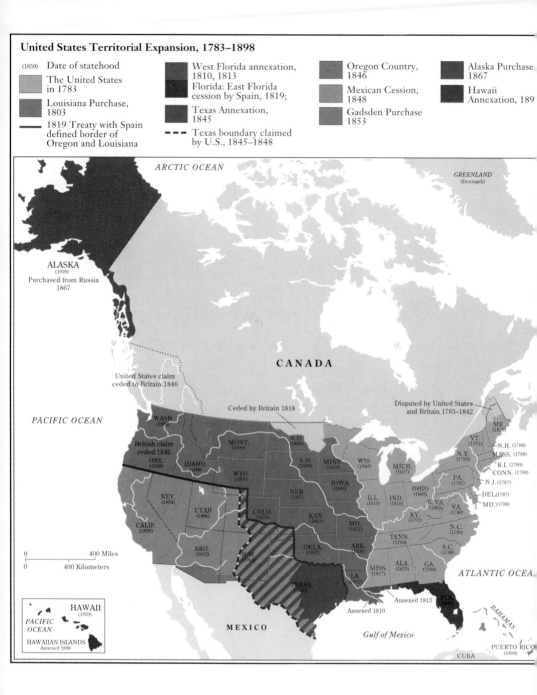

United States Territorial Expansion, 1783–1898

(1859) Date of statehood

The United States in 1783

Louisiana Purchase, 1803

1819 Treaty with Spain defined border of Oregon and Louisiana

West Florida annexation, 1810, 1813

Florida: East Florida cession by Spain, 1819;

Texas Annexation, 1845

- - - Texas boundary claimed by U.S., 1845–1848

Oregon Country, 1846

Mexican Cession, 1848

Gadsden Purchase 1853

Alaska Purchase 1867

Hawaii Annexation, 189

ARCTIC OCEAN

GREENLAND
(Denmark)

ALASKA
(1959)
Purchased from Russia
1867

CANADA

United States claim
ceded to Britain 1846

Ceded by Britain 1818

Disputed by United States
and Britain 1783–1842

PACIFIC OCEAN

WASH.
(1889)

British claim
ceded 1846

ORE.
(1859)

IDAHO
(1890)

MONT.
(1889)

N.D.
(1889)

S.D.
(1889)

MINN.
(1858)

WIS.
(1848)

MICH.
(1837)

ME.
(1820)

VT.
(1791)

N.H. (1788)

MASS. (1788)

N.Y.
(1788)

R.I. (1790)

CONN. (1788)

PA.
(1787)

N.J. (1787)

WYO.
(1890)

IOWA
(1846)

OHIO
(1803)

IND.
(1816)

ILL.
(1818)

DEL (1787)

MD. (1788)

NEV.
(1864)

UTAH
(1896)

NEB.
(1867)

COLO.
(1876)

KAN.
(1861)

MO.
(1821)

KY.
(1792)

W.VA.
(1863)

VA.
(1788)

CALIF.
(1850)

ARIZ.
(1912)

N.M.
(1912)

OKLA.
(1907)

ARK.
(1836)

TENN.
(1796)

N.C.
(1789)

S.C.
(1788)

ALA.
(1819)

GA.
(1788)

MISS.
(1817)

LA.
(1812)

TEXAS
(1845)

Annexed 1813

FLA.
(1845)

ATLANTIC OCEA

BAHAMAS

0   400 Miles

0   400 Kilometers

Annexed 1810

MEXICO

Gulf of Mexico

PUERTO RICO
(1898)

CUBA

HAWAII
(1959)

PACIFIC
OCEAN

HAWAIIAN ISLANDS
Annexed 1898

A–4

Documents and Tables

THE DECLARATION OF INDEPENDENCE

In Congress, July 4, 1776,

When, in the course of human events, it becomes necessary for one people to dissolve the political bands which have connected them with another, and to assume, among the powers of the earth, the separate and equal station to which the laws of nature and of nature's God entitle them, a decent respect to the opinions of mankind requires that they should declare the causes which impel them to the separation.

We hold these truths to be self-evident, that all men are created equal; that they are endowed by their Creator with certain unalienable rights; that among these, are life, liberty, and the pursuit of happiness. That, to secure these rights, governments are instituted among men, deriving their just powers from the consent of the governed; that, whenever any form of government becomes destructive of these ends, it is the right of the people to alter or to abolish it, and to institute a new government, laying its foundation on such principles, and organizing its powers in such form, as to them shall seem most likely to effect their safety and happiness. Prudence, indeed, will dictate that governments long established, should not be changed for light and transient causes; and, accordingly, all experience hath shown, that mankind are more disposed to suffer, while evils are sufferable, than to right themselves by abolishing the forms to which they are accustomed. But, when a long train of abuses and usurpations, pursuing invariably the same object, evinces a design to reduce them under absolute despotism, it is their right, it is their duty, to throw off such government and to provide new guards for their future security. Such has been the patient sufferance of these colonies, and such is now the necessity which constrains them to alter their former systems of government. The history of the present King of Great Britain is a history of repeated injuries and usurpations, all having, in direct object, the establishment of an absolute tyranny over these States. To prove this, let facts be submitted to a candid world:

He has refused his assent to laws the most wholesome and necessary for the public good.

He has forbidden his governors to pass laws of immediate and pressing importance, unless suspended in their operation till his assent should be obtained; and, when so suspended, he has utterly neglected to attend to them.

He has refused to pass other laws for the accommodation of large districts of people, unless those people would relinquish the right of representation in the legislature; a right inestimable to them, and formidable to tyrants only.

He has called together legislative bodies at places unusual, uncomfortable, and distant from the depository of their public records, for the sole purpose of fatiguing them into compliance with his measures.

He has dissolved representative houses repeatedly for opposing, with manly firmness, his invasions on the rights of the people.

He has refused, for a long time after such dissolutions, to cause others to be elected; whereby the legislative powers, incapable of annihilation, have returned to the people at large for their exercise; the state remaining, in the meantime, exposed to all the danger of invasion from without, and convulsions within.

He has endeavored to prevent the population of these States; for that purpose, obstructing the laws for naturalization of foreigners, refusing to pass others to encourage their migration hither, and raising the conditions of new appropriations of lands.

He has obstructed the administration of justice, by refusing his assent to laws for establishing judiciary powers.

He has made judges dependent on his will alone, for the tenure of their offices, and the amount and payment of their salaries.

He has erected a multitude of new offices, and sent hither swarms of officers to harass our people, and eat out their substance.

He has kept among us, in time of peace, standing armies, without the consent of our legislatures.

He has affected to render the military independent of, and superior to, the civil power.

He has combined, with others, to subject us to a jurisdiction foreign to our Constitution, and unacknowledged by our laws; giving his assent to their acts of pretended legislation:

For quartering large bodies of armed troops among us:

For protecting them by a mock trial, from punishment, for any murders which they should commit on the inhabitants of these States:

For cutting off our trade with all parts of the world:

For imposing taxes on us without our consent:

For depriving us, in many cases, of the benefit of trial by jury:

For transporting us beyond seas to be tried for pretended offences:

For abolishing the free system of English laws in a neighboring province, establishing therein an arbitrary government, and enlarging its boundaries, so as to render it at once an example and fit instrument for introducing the same absolute rule into these colonies:

For taking away our charters, abolishing our most valuable laws, and altering, fundamentally, the powers of our governments:

For suspending our own legislatures, and declaring themselves invested with power to legislate for us in all cases whatsoever.

He has abdicated government here, by declaring us out of his protection, and waging war against us.

He has plundered our seas, ravaged our coasts, burnt our towns, and destroyed the lives of our people.

He is, at this time, transporting large armies of foreign mercenaries to complete the works of death, desolation, and tyranny, already begun, with circumstances of cruelty and perfidy scarcely paralleled in the most barbarous ages, and totally unworthy the head of a civilized nation.

He has constrained our fellow citizens, taken captive on the high seas, to bear arms against their country, to become the executioners of their friends, and brethren, or to fall themselves by their hands.

He has excited domestic insurrections amongst us, and has endeavored to bring on the inhabitants of our frontiers, the merciless Indian savages, whose known rule of warfare is an undistinguished destruction of all ages, sexes, and conditions.

In every stage of these oppressions, we have petitioned for redress, in the most humble terms; our repeated petitions have been answered only by repeated injury. A prince, whose character is thus marked by every act which may define a tyrant, is unfit to be the ruler of a free people.

Nor have we been wanting in attention to our British brethren. We have warned them, from time to time, of attempts made by their legislature to extend an unwarrantable jurisdiction over us. We have reminded them of the circumstances of our emigration and settlement here. We have appealed to their native justice and magnanimity, and we have conjured them, by the ties of our common kindred, to disavow these usurpations, which would inevitably interrupt our connections and correspondence. They, too, have been deaf to the voice of justice and consanguinity. We must, therefore, acquiesce in the necessity which denounces our separation, and hold them as we hold the rest of mankind, enemies in war, in peace, friends.

We, therefore, the representatives of the United States of America, in general Congress assembled, appealing to the Supreme Judge of the world for the rectitude of our intentions, do, in the name, and by the authority of the good people of these colonies, solemnly publish and declare, that these united colonies are, and of right ought to be, free and independent states: that they are absolved from all allegiance to the British Crown, and that all political connection between them and the state of Great Britain is, and ought to be, totally dissolved; and that, as free and independent states, they have full power to levy war, conclude peace, contract alliances, establish commerce, and to do all other acts and things which independent states may of right do. And, for the support of this declaration, with a firm reliance on the protection of Divine Providence, we mutually pledge to each other our lives, our fortunes, and our sacred honor.

The foregoing Declaration was, by order of Congress, engrossed, and signed by the following members:

John Hancock

New Hampshire
Josiah Bartlett
William Whipple
Matthew Thornton

Massachusetts Bay
Samuel Adams
John Adams
Robert Treat Paine
Elbridge Gerry

Rhode Island
Stephen Hopkins
William Ellery

Connecticut
Roger Sherman
Samuel Huntington
William Williams
Oliver Wolcott

New York
William Floyd
Philip Livingston
Francis Lewis
Lewis Morris

New Jersey
Richard Stockton
John Witherspoon
Francis Hopkinson
John Hart
Abraham Clark

Pennsylvania
Robert Morris
Benjamin Rush
Benjamin Franklin
John Morton
George Clymer
James Smith
George Taylor
James Wilson
George Ross

Delaware
Caesar Rodney
George Read
Thomas M'Kean

Maryland
Samuel Chase
William Paca
Thomas Stone
Charles Carroll,
    of Carrollton

Virginia
George Wythe
Richard Henry Lee
Thomas Jefferson
Benjamin Harrison
Thomas Nelson, Jr.
Francis Lightfoot Lee
Carter Braxton

North Carolina
William Hooper
Joseph Hewes
John Penn

South Carolina
Edward Rutledge
Thomas Heyward, Jr.
Thomas Lynch, Jr.
Arthur Middleton

Georgia
Button Gwinnett
Lyman Hall
George Walton

Resolved, That copies of the Declaration be sent to the several assemblies, conventions, and committees, or councils of safety, and to the several commanding officers of the continental troops; that it be proclaimed in each of the United States, at the head of the army.

THE CONSTITUTION
OF THE UNITED STATES[1]

We the People of the United States, in Order to form a more perfect Union, establish Justice, insure domestic Tranquility, provide for the common defence, promote the general Welfare, and secure the Blessings of Liberty to ourselves and our Posterity, do ordain and establish this CONSTITUTION for the United States of America.

Article I

Section 1.

All legislative Powers herein granted shall be vested in a Congress of the United States, which shall consist of a Senate and House of Representatives.

Section 2.

The House of Representatives shall be composed of Members chosen every second Year by the People of the several States, and the Electors in each State shall have the Qualifications requisite for Electors of the most numerous Branch of the State Legislature.

No Person shall be a Representative who shall not have attained to the Age of twenty-five Years, and been seven Years a Citizen of the United States, and who shall not, when elected, be an Inhabitant of that State in which he shall be chosen.

[Representatives and direct Taxes[2] shall be apportioned among the several States which may be included within this Union, according to their respective Numbers, which shall be determined by adding to the whole Number of free Persons, including those bound to Service for a Term of Years, and excluding Indians not taxed, three fifths of all other Persons.][3] The actual Enumeration shall be made within three Years after the first Meeting of the Congress of the United States, and within every subsequent Term of ten Years, in such Manner as they shall by Law direct. The Number of Representatives shall not exceed one for every thirty Thousand, but each State shall have at Least one Representative; and until such enumeration shall be made, the State of New Hampshire shall be entitled to chuse three, Massachusetts eight, Rhode-Island and Providence Plantations one, Connecticut five, New York six, New Jersey four, Pennsylvania eight, Delaware one,

---

[1] This version, which follows the original Constitution in capitalization and spelling, was published by the United States Department of the Interior, Office of Education, in 1935.
[2] Altered by the Sixteenth Amendment.
[3] Negated by the Fourteenth Amendment.

Maryland six, Virginia ten, North Carolina five, South Carolina five, and Georgia three.

When vacancies happen in the Representation from any State, the Executive Authority thereof shall issue Writs of Election to fill such Vacancies.

The House of Representatives shall chuse their Speaker and other Officers; and shall have the sole Power of Impeachment.

Section 3.

The Senate of the United States shall be composed of two Senators from each State, chosen by the Legislature thereof, for six Years; and each Senator shall have one Vote.

Immediately after they shall be assembled in Consequence of the first Election, they shall be divided as equally as may be into three Classes. The Seats of the Senators of the first Class shall be vacated at the Expiration of the second Year, of the second Class at the Expiration of the fourth Year, and of the third Class at the Expiration of the sixth Year, so that one-third may be chosen every second Year; and if Vacancies happen by Resignation, or otherwise, during the Recess of the Legislature of any State, the Executive thereof may make temporary Appointments until the next Meeting of the Legislature, which shall then fill such Vacancies.

No Person shall be a Senator who shall not have attained to the Age of thirty Years, and been nine Years a Citizen of the United States, and who shall not, when elected, be an Inhabitant of that State for which he shall be chosen.

The Vice President of the United States shall be President of the Senate, but shall have no vote, unless they be equally divided.

The Senate shall chuse their other Officers, and also a President pro tempore, in the absence of the Vice President, or when he shall exercise the Office of President of the United States.

The Senate shall have the sole Power to try all Impeachments. When sitting for that purpose they shall be on Oath or Affirmation. When the President of the United States is tried, the Chief Justice shall preside: And no person shall be convicted without the Concurrence of two thirds of the Members present.

Judgment in Cases of Impeachment shall not extend further than to removal from Office, and disqualification to hold and enjoy any Office of honor, Trust, or Profit under the United States: but the Party convicted shall nevertheless be liable and subject to Indictment, Trial, Judgment, and Punishment, according to Law.

Section 4.

The Times, Places and Manner of holding Elections for Senators and Representatives, shall be prescribed in each State by the Legislature thereof; but the Congress may at any time by Law make or alter such Regulations, except as to the Places of Chusing Senators.

The Congress shall assemble at least once in every Year, and such Meeting shall be on the first Monday in December, unless they shall by Law appoint a different Day.

Section 5.

Each House shall be the Judge of the Elections, Returns and Qualifications of its own Members, and a Majority of each shall constitute a Quorum to do Business; but a smaller number may adjourn from day to day, and may be authorized to compel the Attendance of absent Members, in such Manner, and under such Penalties, as each House may provide.

Each House may determine the Rules of its Proceedings, punish its Members for disorderly Behaviour, and, with the Concurrence of two thirds, expel a Member.

Each House shall keep a Journal of its Proceedings, and from time to time publish the same, excepting such Parts as may in their Judgment require Secrecy; and the Yeas and Nays of the Members of either House on any question shall, at the Desire of one fifth of those Present, be entered on the Journal.

Neither House, during the Session of Congress, shall, without the Consent of the other, adjourn for more than three days, nor to any other Place than that in which the two Houses shall be sitting.

Section 6.

The Senators and Representatives shall receive a Compensation for their Services, to be ascertained by Law, and paid out of the Treasury of the United States. They shall in all Cases, except Treason, Felony, and Breach of the Peace, be privileged from Arrest during their Attendance at the Session of their respective Houses, and in going to and returning from the same; and for any Speech or Debate in either House, they shall not be questioned in any other Place.

No Senator or Representative shall, during the Time for which he was elected, be appointed to any civil Office under the Authority of the United States, which shall have been created, or the Emoluments whereof shall have been increased, during such time; and no Person holding any Office under the United States shall be a Member of either House during his continuance in Office.

Section 7.

All Bills for raising Revenue shall originate in the House of Representatives; but the Senate may propose or concur with Amendments as on other bills.

Every Bill which shall have passed the House of Representatives and the Senate, shall, before it become a Law, be presented to the President of the United States; If he approve he shall sign it, but if not he shall return it, with his Objections, to that House in which it shall have originated, who shall enter the Objections at large on their Journal, and proceed to reconsider it. If after such Reconsideration two thirds of that House shall agree to pass the bill, it shall be sent, together with the objections, to the other House, by which it shall likewise be reconsidered, and if approved by two thirds of that House, it shall become a Law. But in all such Cases the Votes of both Houses shall be determined by Yeas and Nays, and the Names of the Persons voting for and against the Bill shall be entered on the Journal of each House respectively. If any Bill shall not be returned by the President within ten Days (Sundays excepted) after it shall have been presented to him, the Same shall be a Law, in like Manner as if he had signed it, unless the Congress by their Adjournment prevent its Return, in which Case it shall not be a Law.

Every Order, Resolution, or Vote to which the Concurrence of the Senate and House of Representatives may be necessary (except on a question of Adjournment) shall be presented to the President of the United States; and before the Same shall take Effect, shall be approved by him, or being disapproved by him, shall be repassed by two thirds of the Senate and House of Representatives, according to the Rules and Limitations prescribed in the Case of a Bill.

Section 8.
The Congress shall have Power To lay and collect Taxes, Duties, Imposts and Excises, to pay the Debts and provide for the common Defence and general Welfare of the United States; but all Duties, Imposts and Excises shall be uniform throughout the United States;

To borrow money on the credit of the United States;

To regulate Commerce with foreign Nations, and among the several States, and with the Indian Tribes;

To establish an uniform rule of Naturalization, and uniform Laws on the subject of Bankruptcies throughout the United States;

To coin Money, regulate the Value thereof, and of foreign Coin, and fix the Standard of Weights and Measures;

To provide for the Punishment of counterfeiting the Securities and current Coin of the United States;

To establish Post Offices and post Roads;

To promote the Progress of Science and useful Arts, by securing for limited Times to Authors and Inventors the exclusive Right to their respective Writings and Discoveries;

To constitute Tribunals inferior to the Supreme Court;

To define and punish Piracies and Felonies committed on the high Seas, and Offenses against the Law of Nations;

To declare War, grant Letters of Marque and Reprisal, and make Rules concerning Captures on Land and Water;

To raise and support Armies, but no Appropriation of Money to that Use shall be for a longer Term than two Years;

To provide and maintain a Navy;

To make Rules for the Government and Regulation of the land and naval forces;

To provide for calling forth the Militia to execute the Laws of the Union, suppress Insurrections and repel Invasions;

To provide for organizing, arming, and disciplining the Militia, and for governing such Part of them as may be employed in the Service of the United States, reserving to the States respectively, the Appointment of the Officers, and the Authority of training the Militia according to the discipline prescribed by Congress;

To exercise exclusive Legislation in all Cases whatsoever, over such District (not exceeding ten Miles square) as may, by Cession of particular States, and the acceptance of Congress, become the Seat of the Government of the United States, and to exercise like Authority over all Places purchased by the Consent of the Legislature of the State in which the Same shall be, for the Erection of Forts, Magazines, Arsenals, Dock-yards, and other needful Buildings;—And

To make all Laws which shall be necessary and proper for carrying into Execution the foregoing Powers, and all other Powers vested by this Constitution in the Government of the United States, or in any Department or Officer thereof.

Section 9.

The Migration or Importation of such Persons as any of the States now existing shall think proper to admit, shall not be prohibited by the Congress prior to the Year one thousand eight hundred and eight, but a tax or duty may be imposed on such Importation, not exceeding ten dollars for each Person.

The privilege of the Writ of Habeas Corpus shall not be suspended, unless when in Cases of Rebellion or Invasion the public Safety may require it.

No bill of Attainder or ex post facto Law shall be passed.

No capitation, or other direct, Tax shall be laid unless in Proportion to the Census or Enumeration herein before directed to be taken.

No Tax or Duty shall be laid on Articles exported from any State.

No Preference shall be given by any Regulation of Commerce or Revenue to the Ports of one State over those of another: nor shall Vessels bound to, or from, one State, be obliged to enter, clear, or pay Duties in another.

No Money shall be drawn from the Treasury, but in Consequence of Appropriations made by Law; and a regular Statement and Account of the Receipts and Expenditures of all public Money shall be published from time to time.

No Title of Nobility shall be granted by the United States: And no Person holding any Office of Profit or Trust under them, shall, without the Consent of the Congress, accept of any present, Emolument, Office, or Title, of any kind whatever, from any King, Prince, or foreign State.

Section 10.

No State shall enter into any Treaty, Alliance, or Confederation; grant Letters of Marque and Reprisal; coin Money; emit Bills of Credit; make any Thing but gold and silver Coin a Tender in Payment of Debts; pass any Bill of Attainder, ex post facto Law, or Law impairing the Obligation of Contracts, or grant any Title of Nobility.

No State shall, without the Consent of the Congress, lay any Imposts or Duties on Imports or Exports, except what may be absolutely necessary for executing its inspection Laws; and the net Produce of all Duties and Imposts, laid by any State on Imports or Exports, shall be for the use of the Treasury of the United States; and all such Laws shall be subject to the Revision and Control of the Congress.

No state shall, without the Consent of Congress, lay any duty of Tonnage, keep Troops, or Ships of War in time of Peace, enter into any Agreement or Compact with another State, or with a foreign Power, or engage in War, unless actually invaded, or in such imminent Danger as will not admit of delay.

Article II

Section 1.
The executive Power shall be vested in a President of the United States of America. He shall hold his Office during the Term of four years, and, together with the Vice President, chosen for the same Term, be elected, as follows:

Each State shall appoint, in such Manner as the Legislature thereof may direct, a Number of Electors, equal to the whole Number of Senators and Representatives to which the State may be entitled in the Congress: but no Senator or Representative, or Person holding an Office of Trust or Profit under the United States, shall be appointed an Elector.

[The Electors shall meet in their respective States, and vote by Ballot for two persons, of whom one at least shall not be an Inhabitant of the same State with themselves. And they shall make a List of all the Persons voted for, and of the Number of Votes for each; which List they shall sign and certify, and transmit sealed to the Seat of the Government of the United States, directed to the President of the Senate. The President of the Senate shall, in the Presence of the Senate and House of Representatives, open all the Certificates, and the Votes shall then be counted. The Person having the greatest Number of Votes shall be the President, if such Number be a Majority of the whole Number of Electors appointed; and if there be more than one who have such Majority, and have an equal Number of Votes, then the House of Representatives shall immediately chuse by Ballot one of them for President; and if no Person have a Majority, then from the five highest on the List the said House shall in like Manner chuse the President. But in chusing the President, the Votes shall be taken by States, the Representation from each State having one Vote; a quorum for this Purpose shall consist of a Member or Members from two-thirds of the States, and a Majority of all the States shall be necessary to a Choice. In every Case, after the Choice of the President, the Person having the greatest Number of Votes of the Electors shall be the Vice President. But if there should remain two or more who have equal votes, the Senate shall chuse from them by Ballot the Vice President.][4]

The Congress may determine the Time of chusing the Electors, and the Day on which they shall give their Votes; which Day shall be the same throughout the United States.

No person except a natural-born Citizen, or a Citizen of the United States, at the time of the Adoption of this Constitution, shall be eligible to the Office of President; neither shall any Person be eligible to that Office who shall not have attained

[4] Revised by the Twelfth Amendment.

to the Age of thirty-five years, and been fourteen Years a Resident within the United States.

In Case of the Removal of the President from Office, or of his Death, Resignation, or Inability to discharge the Powers and Duties of the said Office, the same shall devolve on the Vice President, and the Congress may by Law provide for the Case of Removal, Death, Resignation, or Inability, both of the President and Vice President, declaring what Officer shall then act as President, and such Officer shall act accordingly, until the disability be removed, or a President shall be elected.

The President shall, at stated Times, receive for his Services a Compensation, which shall neither be increased nor diminished during the Period for which he shall have been elected, and he shall not receive within that Period any other Emolument from the United States, or any of them.

Before he enter on the execution of his Office, he shall take the following Oath or Affirmation:—"I do solemnly swear (or affirm) that I will faithfully execute the Office of President of the United States, and will, to the best of my Ability, preserve, protect, and defend the Constitution of the United States."

Section 2.

The President shall be Commander in Chief of the Army and Navy of the United States, and of the Militia of the several States, when called into the actual Service of the United States; he may require the Opinion, in writing, of the principal Officer in each of the executive Departments, upon any subject relating to the Duties of their respective Offices, and he shall have Power to Grant Reprieves and Pardons for Offenses against the United States, except in Cases of Impeachment.

He shall have Power, by and with the Advice and Consent of the Senate, to make Treaties, provided two-thirds of the Senators present concur; and he shall nominate, and by and with the Advice and Consent of the Senate, shall appoint Ambassadors, other public Ministers and Consuls, Judges of the supreme Court, and all other Officers of the United States, whose Appointments are not herein otherwise provided for, and which shall be established by Law: but the Congress may by Law vest the Appointment of such inferior Officers, as they think proper, in the President alone, in the Courts of Law, or in the Heads of Departments.

The President shall have Power to fill up all Vacancies that may happen during the Recess of the Senate, by granting Commissions which shall expire at the End of their next Session.

Section 3.

He shall from time to time give to the Congress Information of the State of the Union, and recommend to their Consideration such Measures as he shall judge necessary and expedient; he may, on extraordinary occasions, convene both Houses, or either of them, and in Case of Disagreement between them, with respect to the Time of Adjournment, he may adjourn them to such Time as he shall think proper; he shall receive Ambassadors and other public Ministers; he shall take care that the Laws be faithfully executed, and shall Commission all the Officers of the United States.

Section 4.
The President, Vice President and all civil Officers of the United States, shall be removed from Office on Impeachment for, and Conviction of, Treason, Bribery, or other high Crimes and Misdemeanors.

Article III

Section 1.
The judicial Power of the United States, shall be vested in one supreme Court, and in such inferior Courts as the Congress may from time to time ordain and establish. The Judges, both of the supreme and inferior Courts, shall hold their Offices during good Behaviour, and shall, at stated Times, receive for their Services, a Compensation, which shall not be diminished during their Continuance in Office.

Section 2.
The judicial Power shall extend to all Cases, in Law and Equity, arising under this Constitution, the Laws of the United States, and Treaties made, or which shall be made, under their Authority;—to all Cases affecting ambassadors, other public ministers and consuls;—to all cases of admiralty and maritime Jurisdiction;—to Controversies to which the United States shall be a Party;—to Controversies between two or more States;—between a State and Citizens of another State;[5]—between Citizens of different States—between Citizens of the same State claiming Lands under Grants of different States, and between a State, or the Citizens thereof, and foreign States, Citizens, or Subjects.

In all Cases affecting Ambassadors, other public Ministers and Consuls, and those in which a State shall be Party, the supreme Court shall have original Jurisdiction. In all the other Cases before mentioned, the supreme Court shall have appellate Jurisdiction, both as to Law and Fact, with such Exceptions, and under such Regulations as the Congress shall make.

The trial of all Crimes, except in Cases of Impeachment, shall be by Jury; and such Trial shall be held in the State where the said Crimes shall have been committed; but when not committed within any State, the Trial shall be at such Place or Places as the Congress may by Law have directed.

Section 3.
Treason against the United States, shall consist only in levying War against them, or in adhering to their Enemies, giving them Aid and Comfort. No Person shall be convicted of Treason unless on the Testimony of two Witnesses to the same overt Act, or on Confession in open Court.

The Congress shall have power to declare the Punishment of Treason, but no Attainder of Treason shall work Corruption of Blood, or Forfeiture except during the Life of the Person attained.

---

[5] Qualified by the Eleventh Amendment.

Article IV

Section 1.

Full Faith and Credit shall be given in each State to the public Acts, Records, and judicial Proceedings of every other State. And the Congress may by general Laws prescribe the Manner in which such Acts, Records and Proceedings shall be proved, and the Effect thereof.

Section 2.

The Citizens of each State shall be entitled to all Privileges and Immunities of Citizens in the several States.

A Person charged in any State with Treason, Felony, or other Crime, who shall flee from Justice, and be found in another State, shall on demand of the executive Authority of the State from which he fled, be delivered up, to be removed to the State having Jurisdiction of the crime.

No Person held to Service or Labour in one State, under the Laws thereof, escaping into another, shall, in Consequence of any Law or Regulation therein, be discharged from such Service or Labour, but shall be delivered up on Claim of the Party to whom such Service or Labour may be due.

Section 3.

New States may be admitted by the Congress into this Union; but no new State shall be formed or erected within the Jurisdiction of any other State; nor any State be formed by the Junction of two or more States, or parts of States, without the Consent of the Legislatures of the States concerned as well as of the Congress.

The Congress shall have Power to dispose of and make all needful Rules and Regulations respecting the Territory or other Property belonging to the United States; and nothing in this Constitution shall be so construed as to Prejudice any Claims of the United States, or of any particular State.

Section 4.

The United States shall guarantee to every State in this Union a Republican Form of Government, and shall protect each of them against Invasion; and on Application of the Legislature, or of the Executive (when the Legislature cannot be convened) against domestic Violence.

Article V

The Congress, whenever two-thirds of both Houses shall deem it necessary, shall propose Amendments to this Constitution, or, on the Application of the Legislatures of two-thirds of the several States, shall call a Convention for proposing Amendments, which, in either Case, shall be valid to all Intents and Purposes, as part of this Constitution, when ratified by the Legislatures of three-fourths of the several States, or by Conventions in three-fourths thereof, as the one or the other Mode of Ratification may be proposed by the Congress; Provided that no Amendment which may be made prior to the Year One thousand eight hundred and eight shall in any Manner affect the first and fourth Clauses in the Ninth Section of the first Article; and that no State, without its Consent, shall be deprived of its equal Suffrage in the Senate.

Article VI

All Debts contracted and Engagements entered into, before the Adoption of this Constitution, shall be as valid against the United States under this Constitution, as under the Confederation.

This Constitution, and the Laws of the United States which shall be made in Pursuance thereof; and all Treaties made, or which shall be made, under the Authority of the United States, shall be the supreme Law of the Land; and the Judges in every State shall be bound thereby, any Thing in the Constitution or Laws of any State to the Contrary notwithstanding.

The Senators and Representatives before mentioned, and the Members of the several State Legislatures, and all executive and judicial Officers, both of the United States and of the several States, shall be bound by Oath or Affirmation to support this Constitution; but no religious Tests shall ever be required as a qualification to any Office or public Trust under the United States.

Article VII

The Ratification of the Conventions of nine States shall be sufficient for the Establishment of this Constitution between the States so ratifying the same.

Done in Convention by the Unanimous Consent of the States present the Seventeenth Day of September in the Year of our Lord one thousand seven hundred and Eighty seven, and of the Independence of the United States of America the Twelfth. In Witness whereof We have hereunto subscribed our Names.[6]

George Washington
President and deputy and deputy from Virginia

New Hampshire	*Pennsylvania*	*Virginia*
John Langdon	Benjamin Franklin	John Blair
Nicholas Gilman	Thomas Mifflin	James Madison, Jr.
	Robert Morris	
Massachusetts	George Clymer	*North Carolina*
Nathaniel Gorham	Thomas FitzSimons	William Blount
Rufus King	Jared Ingersoll	Richard Dobbs
	James Wilson	Spaight
	Gouverneur Morris	Hugh Williamson

[6] These are the full names of the signers, which in some cases are not the signatures on the document.

Connecticut
William Samuel Johnson
Roger Sherman

New York
Alexander Hamilton

New Jersey
William Livingston
David Brearley
William Paterson
Jonathan Dayton

Delaware
George Read
Gunning Bedford, Jr.
John Dickinson
Richard Bassett
Jacob Broom

Maryland
James McHenry
Daniel of
   St. Thomas Jenifer
Daniel Carroll

South Carolina
John Rutledge
Charles Cotesworth
   Pinckney
Charles Pinckney
Pierce Butler

Georgia
William Few
Abraham Baldwin

Articles in Addition to, and Amendment of, the Constitution of the United States of America, Proposed by Congress, and Ratified by the Legislatures of the Several States, Pursuant to the Fifth Article of the Original Constitution.[7]

[Article I]

Congress shall make no law respecting an establishment of religion, or prohibiting the free exercise thereof; or abridging the freedom of speech, or of the press; or the right of the people peaceably to assemble, and to petition the Government for a redress of grievances.

[Article II]

A well regulated Militia, being necessary to the security of a free State, the right of the people to keep and bear Arms shall not be infringed.

[Article III]

No Soldier shall, in time of peace, be quartered in any house, without the consent of the Owner, nor in time of war, but in a manner to be prescribed by law.

[Article IV]

The right of the people to be secure in their persons, houses, papers, and effects, against unreasonable searches and seizures, shall not be violated, and no Warrants shall issue, but upon probable cause, supported by Oath or affirmation, and

[7] This heading appears only in the joint resolution submitting the first ten amendments.

particularly describing the place to be searched, and the persons or things to be seized.

[Article V]

No person shall be held to answer for a capital or otherwise infamous crime, unless on a presentment or indictment of a Grand Jury, except in cases arising in the land or naval forces, or in the Militia, when in actual service in time of War or public danger; nor shall any person be subject for the same offence to be twice put in jeopardy of life or limb; nor shall be compelled in any criminal case to be a witness against himself, nor be deprived of life, liberty, or property, without due process of law; nor shall private property be taken for public use, without just compensation.

[Article VI]

In all criminal prosecutions, the accused shall enjoy the right to a speedy and public trial, by an impartial jury of the State and district wherein the crime shall have been committed, which district shall have been previously ascertained by law, and to be informed of the nature and cause of the accusation; to be confronted with the witnesses against him; to have compulsory process for obtaining witnesses in his favour, and to have the Assistance of Counsel for his defense.

[Article VII]

In suits at common law, where the value in controversy shall exceed twenty dollars, the right of trial by jury shall be preserved, and no fact tried by a jury, shall be otherwise reexamined in any Court of the United States, than according to the rules of the common law.

[Article VIII]

Excessive bail shall not be required, nor excessive fines imposed, nor cruel and unusual punishments inflicted.

[Article IX]

The enumeration of the Constitution, of certain rights, shall not be construed to deny or disparage others retained by the people.

[Article X]

The powers not delegated to the United States by the Constitution, nor prohibited by it to the States, are reserved to the States respectively, or to the people.
[Amendments I–X, in force 1791.]

[Article XI][8]

The Judicial power of the United States shall not be construed to extend to any suit in law or equity, commenced or prosecuted against one of the United States by Citizens of another State, or by Citizens or Subjects of any Foreign State.

[Article XII][9]

The Electors shall meet in their respective States and vote by ballot for President and Vice-President, one of whom, at least, shall not be an inhabitant of the same State with themselves; they shall name in their ballots the person voted for as President, and in distinct ballots the person voted for as Vice-President, and they shall make distinct lists of all persons voted for as President, and of all persons voted for as Vice-President, and of the number of votes for each, which lists they shall sign and certify, and transmit sealed to the seat of the government of the United States, directed to the President of the Senate;—The President of the Senate shall, in the presence of the Senate and House of Representatives, open all the certificates and the votes shall then be counted;—The person having the greatest number of votes for President, shall be the President, if such number be a majority of the whole number of Electors appointed; and if no person have such majority, then from the persons having the highest numbers not exceeding three on the list of those voted for as President, the House of Representatives shall choose immediately, by ballot, the President. But in choosing the President, the votes shall be taken by states, the representation from each state having one vote; a quorum for this purpose shall consist of a member or members from two-thirds of the states, and a majority of all the states shall be necessary to a choice. And if the House of Representatives shall not choose a President whenever the right of choice shall devolve upon them, before the fourth day of March next following, then the Vice-President shall act as President, as in the case of the death or other constitutional disability of the President.—The person having the greatest number of votes as Vice-President, shall be the Vice-President, if such number be a majority of the whole number of Electors appointed, and if no person have a majority, then from the two highest numbers on the list, the Senate shall choose the Vice-President; a quorum for the purpose shall consist of two-thirds of the whole number of Senators, and a majority of the whole number shall be necessary to a choice. But no person constitutionally in-

[8] Adopted in 1798.
[9] Adopted in 1804.

eligible to the office of President shall be eligible to that of Vice-President of the United States.

[Article XIII][10]

Section 1.
Neither slavery nor involuntary servitude, except as a punishment for crime whereof the party shall have been duly convicted, shall exist within the United States, or any place subject to their jurisdiction.

Section 2.
Congress shall have power to enforce this article by appropriate legislation.

[Article XIV][11]

Section 1.
All persons born or naturalized in the United States, and subject to the jurisdiction thereof, are citizens of the United States and of the State wherein they reside. No State shall make or enforce any law which shall abridge the privileges or immunities of citizens of the United States; nor shall any State deprive any person of life, liberty, or property, without due process of law; nor deny to any person within its jurisdiction the equal protection of the laws.

Section 2.
Representatives shall be apportioned among the several States according to their respective numbers, counting the whole number of persons in each State, excluding Indians not taxed. But when the right to vote at any election for the choice of electors for President and Vice-President of the United States, Representatives in Congress, the Executive and Judicial officers of a State, or the members of the Legislature thereof, is denied to any of the male inhabitants of such State, being twenty-one years of age, and citizens of the United States, or in any way abridged, except for participation in rebellion, or other crime, the basis of representation therein shall be reduced in the proportion which the number of such male citizens shall bear to the whole number of male citizens twenty-one years of age in such State.

Section 3.
No person shall be a Senator or Representative in Congress, or elector of President and Vice-President, or hold any office, civil or military, under the United States, or under any State, who, having previously taken an oath, as a member of Congress, or as an officer of the United States, or as a member of any State legislature, or as

[10] Adopted in 1865.
[11] Adopted in 1868.

an executive or judicial officer of any State, to support the Constitution of the United States, shall have engaged in insurrection or rebellion against the same, or given aid or comfort to the enemies thereof. But Congress may by a vote of two-thirds of each House, remove such disability.

Section 4.
The validity of the public debt of the United States, authorized by law, including debts incurred for payment of pensions and bounties for services in suppressing insurrection or rebellion, shall not be questioned. But neither the United States nor any State shall assume or pay any debts or obligation incurred in aid of insurrection or rebellion against the United States, or any claim for the loss or emancipation of any slave; but all such debts, obligations, and claims shall be held illegal and void.

Section 5.
The Congress shall have the power to enforce, by appropriate legislation, the provisions of this article.

[Article XV][12]

Section 1.
The right of citizens of the United States to vote shall not be denied or abridged by the United States or by any State on account of race, color, or previous condition of servitude—

Section 2.
The Congress shall have power to enforce this article by appropriate legislation.

[Article XVI][13]

The Congress shall have power to lay and collect taxes on incomes, from whatever source derived, without apportionment among the several States, and without regard to any census or enumeration.

[Article XVII][14]

The Senate of the United States shall be composed of two Senators from each State, elected by the people thereof, for six years; and each Senator shall have one vote. The electors in each State shall have the qualifications requisite for electors of the most numerous branch of the State legislatures.

[12] Adopted in 1870.
[13] Adopted in 1913.
[14] Adopted in 1913.

When vacancies happen in the representation of any State in the Senate, the executive authority of such State shall issue writs of election to fill such vacancies: *Provided*, That the legislature of any State may empower the executive thereof to make temporary appointments until the people fill the vacancies by election as the legislature may direct.

This amendment shall not be so construed as to affect the election or term of any Senator chosen before it becomes valid as part of the Constitution.

[Article XVIII][15]

Section 1.
After one year from the ratification of this article the manufacture, sale, or transportation of intoxicating liquors within, the importation thereof into, or the exportation thereof from the United States and all territory subject to the jurisdiction thereof for beverage purposes is hereby prohibited.

Section 2.
The Congress and the several States shall have concurrent power to enforce this article by appropriate legislation.

Section 3.
This article shall be inoperative unless it shall have been ratified as an amendment to the Constitution by the legislatures of the several States, as provided in the Constitution, within seven years from the date of the submission hereof to the States by the Congress.

[Article XIX][16]

The right of citizens of the United States to vote shall not be denied or abridged by the United States or by any State on account of sex.

Congress shall have power to enforce this article by appropriate legislation.

[Article XX][17]

Section 1.
The terms of the President and Vice-President shall end at noon on the 20th day of January, and the terms of Senators and Representatives at noon on the 3d day of January, of the years in which such terms would have ended if this article had not been ratified; and the terms of their successors shall then begin.

[15] Adopted in 1918.
[16] Adopted in 1920.
[17] Adopted in 1933.

Section 2.

The Congress shall assemble at least once in every year, and such meeting shall begin at noon on the 3d day of January, unless they shall by law appoint a different day.

Section 3.

If, at the time fixed for the beginning of the term of the President, the President elect shall have died, the Vice-President elect shall become President. If a President shall not have been chosen before the time fixed for the beginning of his term or if the President elect shall have failed to qualify, then the Vice-President elect shall act as President until a President shall have qualified; and the Congress may by law provide for the case wherein neither a President elect nor a Vice-President elect shall have qualified, declaring who shall then act as President, or the manner in which one who is to act shall be selected, and such person shall act accordingly until a President or Vice-President shall have qualified.

Section 4.

The Congress may by law provide for the case of the death of any of the persons from whom the House of Representatives may choose a President whenever the right of choice shall have devolved upon them, and for the case of the death of any of the persons from whom the Senate may choose a Vice-President whenever the right of choice shall have devolved upon them.

Section 5.

Sections 1 and 2 shall take effect on the 15th day of October following the ratification of this article.

Section 6.

This article shall be inoperative unless it shall have been ratified as an amendment to the Constitution by the legislatures of three-fourths of the several States within seven years from the date of its submission.

[Article XXI] [18]

Section 1.

The eighteenth article of amendment to the Constitution of the United States is hereby repealed.

Section 2.

The transportation or importation into any State, Territory, or possession of the United States for delivery or use therein of intoxicating liquors, in violation of the laws thereof, is hereby prohibited.

[18] Adopted in 1933.

Section 3.

This article shall be inoperative unless it shall have been ratified as an amendment to the Constitution by conventions in the several States, as provided in the Constitution, within seven years from the date of the submission hereof to the States by the Congress.

[Article XXII][19]

No person shall be elected to the office of the President more than twice, and no person who has held the office of President, or acted as President, for more than two years of a term to which some other person was elected President shall be elected to the office of the President more than once.

But this Article shall not apply to any person holding the office of President when this Article was proposed by the Congress, and shall not prevent any person who may be holding the office of President, or acting as President, during the term within which this Article becomes operative from holding the office of President or acting as President during the remainder of such term.

This article shall be inoperative unless it shall have been ratified as an amendment to the Constitution by the legislatures of three-fourths of the several states within seven years from the date of its submission to the states by the Congress.

[Article XXIII][20]

Section 1.

The District constituting the seat of Government of the United States shall appoint in such manner as the Congress may direct:

A number of electors of President and Vice-President equal to the whole number of Senators and Representatives in Congress to which the District would be entitled if it were a State, but in no event more than the least populous State; they shall be in addition to those appointed by the States, but they shall be considered, for the purposes of the election of President and Vice-President, to be electors appointed by a State; and they shall meet in the District and perform such duties as provided by the twelfth article of amendment.

Section 2.

The Congress shall have power to enforce this article by appropriate legislation.

[19] Adopted in 1961.
[20] Adopted in 1961.

[Article XXIV][21]

Section 1.
The right of citizens of the United States to vote in any primary or other election for President or Vice President, for electors for President or Vice President, or for Senator or Representative in Congress, shall not be denied or abridged by the United States or any state by reason of failure to pay any poll tax or other tax.

Section 2.
The Congress shall have the power to enforce this article by appropriate legislation.

[Article XXV][22]

Section 1.
In case of the removal of the President from office or of his death or resignation, the Vice President shall become President.

Section 2.
Whenever there is a vacancy in the office of the Vice President, the President shall nominate a Vice President who shall take office upon confirmation by a majority vote of both Houses of Congress.

Section 3.
Whenever the President transmits to the President Pro Tempore of the Senate and the Speaker of the House of Representatives his written declaration that he is unable to discharge the powers and duties of his office, and until he transmits to them a written declaration to the contrary, such powers and duties shall be discharged by the Vice President as Acting President.

Section 4.
Whenever the Vice President and a majority of either the principal officers of the executive departments or of such other body as Congress may by law provide, transmit to the President Pro Tempore of the Senate and the Speaker of the House of Representatives their written declaration that the President is unable to discharge the powers and duties of his office, the Vice President shall immediately assume the powers and duties of the office as Acting President.

Thereafter, when the President transmits to the President Pro Tempore of the Senate and the Speaker of the House of Representatives his written declaration that no inability exists, he shall resume the powers and duties of his office unless the Vice President and a majority of either the principal officers of the executive departments or of such other body as Congress may by law provide, transmit within four days to

[21] Adopted in 1964.
[22] Adopted in 1967.

the President Pro Tempore of the Senate and the Speaker of the House of Representatives their written declaration that the President is unable to discharge the powers and duties of his office. Thereupon Congress shall decide the issue, assembling within forty-eight hours for that purpose if not in session. If the Congress, within twenty-one days after receipt of the latter written declaration, or, if Congress is not in session, within twenty-one days after Congress is required to assemble, determines by two-thirds vote of both Houses that the President is unable to discharge the powers and duties of his office, the Vice President shall continue to discharge the same as Acting President; otherwise, the President shall resume the powers and duties of his office.

[Article XXVI][23]

Section 1.
The right of citizens of the United States, who are eighteen years of age or older, to vote shall not be denied or abridged by the United States or by any State on account of age.

Section 2.
The Congress shall have power to enforce this article by appropriate legislation.

[Article XXVII][24]

No law varying the compensation for the services of the Senators and Representatives shall take effect until an election of Representatives shall have intervened.

[23] Adopted in 1971.
[24] Adopted in 1992.

PRESIDENTIAL ELECTIONS

Year	Candidates	Parties	Popular Vote	Percentage of Popular Vote	Electoral Vote	Percentage of Voter Participation
1789	**GEORGE WASHINGTON (Va.)***				69	
	John Adams				34	
	Others				35	
1792	**GEORGE WASHINGTON (Va.)**				132	
	John Adams				77	
	George Clinton				50	
	Others				5	
1796	**JOHN ADAMS (Mass.)**	Federalist			71	
	Thomas Jefferson	Democratic-Republican			68	
	Thomas Pinckney	Federalist			59	
	Aaron Burr	Dem.-Rep.			30	
	Others				48	
1800	**THOMAS JEFFERSON (Va.)**	Dem.-Rep.			73	
	Aaron Burr	Dem.-Rep.			73	
	John Adams	Federalist			65	
	C. C. Pinckney	Federalist			64	
	John Jay	Federalist			1	
1804	**THOMAS JEFFERSON (Va.)**	Dem.-Rep.			162	
	C. C. Pinckney	Federalist			14	
1808	**JAMES MADISON (Va.)**	Dem.-Rep.			122	
	C. C. Pinckney	Federalist			47	
	George Clinton	Dem.-Rep.			6	

Year	Candidate	Party	Popular Vote	% Popular Vote	% Voter Participation	Electoral Vote
1812	**JAMES MADISON (Va.)**	Dem.-Rep.				128
	De Witt Clinton	Federalist				89
1816	**JAMES MONROE (Va.)**	Dem.-Rep.				183
	Rufus King	Federalist				34
1820	**JAMES MONROE (Va.)**	Dem.-Rep.				231
	John Quincy Adams	Dem.-Rep.				1
1824	**JOHN Q. ADAMS (Mass.)**	Dem.-Rep.	108,740	30.5	26.9	84
	Andrew Jackson	Dem.-Rep.	153,544	43.1		99
	William H. Crawford	Dem.-Rep.	46,618	13.1		41
	Henry Clay	Dem.-Rep.	47,136	13.2		37
1828	**ANDREW JACKSON (Tenn.)**	Democratic	647,286	56.0	57.6	178
	John Quincy Adams	National Republican	508,064	44.0		83
1832	**ANDREW JACKSON (Tenn.)**	Democratic	687,502	55.0	55.4	219
	Henry Clay	National Republican	530,189	42.4		49
	John Floyd	Independent				11
	William Wirt	Anti-Mason	33,108	2.6		7
1836	**MARTIN VAN BUREN (N.Y.)**	Democratic	765,483	50.9	57.8	170
	W. H. Harrison	Whig				73
	Hugh L. White	Whig	739,795	49.1		26
	Daniel Webster	Whig				14
	W. P. Magnum	Independent				11

* State of residence at time of election.

PRESIDENTIAL ELECTIONS *(cont.)*

Year	Candidates	Parties	Popular Vote	Percentage of Popular Vote	Electoral Vote	Percentage of Voter Participation
1840	**WILLIAM H. HARRISON (Ohio)**	Whig	1,274,624	53.1	234	80.2
	Martin Van Buren	Democratic	1,127,781	46.9	60	
	J. G. Birney	Liberty	7,069		—	
1844	**JAMES K. POLK (Tenn.)**	Democratic	1,338,464	49.6	170	78.9
	Henry Clay	Whig	1,300,097	48.1	105	
	J. G. Birney	Liberty	62,300	2.3		
1848	**ZACHARY TAYLOR (La.)**	Whig	1,360,967	47.4	163	72.7
	Lewis Cass	Democratic	1,222,342	42.5	127	
	Martin Van Buren	Free-Soil	291,263	10.1	—	
1852	**FRANKLIN PIERCE (N.H.)**	Democratic	1,601,117	50.9	254	69.6
	Winfield Scott	Whig	1,385,453	44.1	42	
	John P. Hale	Free-Soil	155,825	5.0	—	
1856	**JAMES BUCHANAN (Pa.)**	Democratic	1,832,955	45.3	174	78.9
	John C. Frémont	Republican	1,339,932	33.1	114	
	Millard Fillmore	American	871,731	21.6	8	
1860	**ABRAHAM LINCOLN (Ill.)**	Republican	1,865,593	39.8	180	81.2
	Stephen A. Douglas	Democratic	1,382,713	29.5	12	
	John C. Breckinridge	Democratic	848,356	18.1	72	
	John Bell	Union	592,906	12.6	39	
1864	**ABRAHAM LINCOLN (Ill.)**	Republican	2,213,655	55.0	212	73.8
	George B. McClellan	Democratic	1,805,237	45.0	21	
1868	**ULYSSES S. GRANT (Ill.)**	Republican	3,012,833	52.7	214	78.1
	Horatio Seymour	Democratic	2,703,249	47.3	80	

Year	Candidate	Party	Popular Vote	%	Electoral Vote	% Voter Participation
1872	**ULYSSES S. GRANT (Ill.)**	Republican	3,597,132	55.6	286	71.3
	Horace Greeley	Democratic; Liberal Republican	2,834,125	43.9	66	
1876	**RUTHERFORD B. HAYES (Ohio)**	Republican	4,036,298	48.0	185	81.8
	Samuel J. Tilden	Democratic	4,300,590	51.0	184	
1880	**JAMES A. GARFIELD (Ohio)**	Republican	4,454,416	48.5	214	79.4
	Winfield S. Hancock	Democratic	4,444,952	48.1	155	
1884	**GROVER CLEVELAND (N.Y.)**	Democratic	4,874,986	48.5	219	77.5
	James G. Blaine	Republican	4,851,981	48.2	182	
1888	**BENJAMIN HARRISON (Ind.)**	Republican	5,439,853	47.9	233	79.3
	Grover Cleveland	Democratic	5,540,309	48.6	168	
1892	**GROVER CLEVELAND (N.Y.)**	Democratic	5,556,918	46.1	277	74.7
	Benjamin Harrison	Republican	5,176,108	43.0	145	
	James B. Weaver	People's	1,041,028	8.5	22	
1896	**WILLIAM McKINLEY (Ohio)**	Republican	7,104,779	51.1	271	79.3
	William J. Bryan	Democratic-People's	6,502,925	47.7	176	
1900	**WILLIAM McKINLEY (Ohio)**	Republican	7,207,923	51.7	292	73.2
	William J. Bryan	Dem.-Populist	6,358,133	45.5	155	
1904	**THEODORE ROOSEVELT (N.Y.)**	Republican	7,623,486	57.9	336	65.2
	Alton B. Parker	Democratic	5,077,911	37.6	140	
	Eugene V. Debs	Socialist	402,283	3.0	—	
1908	**WILLIAM H. TAFT (Ohio)**	Republican	7,678,908	51.6	321	65.4
	William J. Bryan	Democratic	6,409,104	43.1	162	
	Eugene V. Debs	Socialist	420,793	2.8	—	

PRESIDENTIAL ELECTIONS (cont.)

Year	Candidates	Parties	Popular Vote	Percentage of Popular Vote	Electoral Vote	Percentage of Voter Participation
1912	**WOODROW WILSON (N.J.)**	Democratic	6,293,454	41.9	435	58.8
	Theodore Roosevelt	Progressive	4,119,538	27.4	88	
	William H. Taft	Republican	3,484,980	23.2	8	
	Eugene V. Debs	Socialist	900,672	6.0	—	
1916	**WOODROW WILSON (N.J.)**	Democratic	9,129,606	49.4	277	61.6
	Charles E. Hughes	Republican	8,538,221	46.2	254	
	A. L. Benson	Socialist	585,113	3.2	—	
1920	**WARREN G. HARDING (Ohio)**	Republican	16,152,200	60.4	404	49.2
	James M. Cox	Democratic	9,147,353	34.2	127	
	Eugene V. Debs	Socialist	919,799	3.4	—	
1924	**CALVIN COOLIDGE (Mass.)**	Republican	15,725,016	54.0	382	48.9
	John W. Davis	Democratic	8,386,503	28.8	136	
	Robert M. LaFollette	Progressive	4,822,856	16.6	13	
1928	**HERBERT HOOVER (Calif.)**	Republican	21,391,381	58.2	444	56.9
	Alfred E. Smith	Democratic	15,016,443	40.9	87	
	Norman Thomas	Socialist	267,835	0.7	—	
1932	**FRANKLIN D. ROOSEVELT (N.Y.)**	Democratic	22,821,857	57.4	472	56.9
	Herbert Hoover	Republican	15,761,841	39.7	59	
	Norman Thomas	Socialist	881,951	2.2	—	
1936	**FRANKLIN D. ROOSEVELT (N.Y.)**	Democratic	27,751,597	60.8	523	61.0
	Alfred M. Landon	Republican	16,679,583	36.5	8	
	William Lemke	Union	882,479	1.9	—	

Year	Candidate	Party	Popular Vote	Percent	Electoral Vote	Percent
1940	**FRANKLIN D. ROOSEVELT (N.Y.)**	Democratic	27,244,160	54.8	449	62.5
	Wendell L. Willkie	Republican	22,305,198	44.8	82	
1944	**FRANKLIN D. ROOSEVELT (N.Y.)**	Democratic	25,602,504	53.5	432	55.9
	Thomas E. Dewey	Republican	22,006,285	46.0	99	
1948	**HARRY S. TRUMAN (Mo.)**	Democratic	24,105,695	49.5	304	53.0
	Thomas E. Dewey	Republican	21,969,170	45.1	189	
	J. Strom Thurmond	State-Rights Democratic	1,169,021	2.4	38	
	Henry A. Wallace	Progressive	1,156,103	2.4	—	
1952	**DWIGHT D. EISENHOWER (N.Y.)**	Republican	33,936,252	55.1	442	63.3
	Adlai E. Stevenson	Democratic	27,314,992	44.4	89	
1956	**DWIGHT D. EISENHOWER (N.Y.)**	Republican	35,575,420	57.6	457	60.6
	Adlai E. Stevenson	Democratic	26,033,066	42.1	73	
	Other	—	—		1	
1960	**JOHN F. KENNEDY (Mass.)**	Democratic	34,227,096	49.9	303	62.8
	Richard M. Nixon	Republican	34,108,546	49.6	219	
	Other	—	—		15	
1964	**LYNDON B. JOHNSON (Tex.)**	Democratic	43,126,506	61.1	486	61.7
	Barry M. Goldwater	Republican	27,176,799	38.5	52	
1968	**RICHARD M. NIXON (N.Y.)**	Republican	31,770,237	43.4	301	60.6
	Hubert H. Humphrey	Democratic	31,270,533	42.7	191	
	George Wallace	American In-dependent	9,906,141	13.5	46	

PRESIDENTIAL ELECTIONS (cont.)

Year	Candidates	Parties	Popular Vote	Percentage of Popular Vote	Electoral Vote	Percentage of Voter Participation
1972	RICHARD M. NIXON (N.Y.)	Republican	47,169,911	60.7	520	55.2
	George S. McGovern	Democratic	29,170,383	37.5	17	
	Other	—			1	
1976	JIMMY CARTER (Ga.)	Democratic	40,828,587	50.0	297	53.5
	Gerald R. Ford	Republican	39,147,613	47.9	241	
	Other	—	1,575,459	2.1	—	
1980	RONALD REAGAN (Calif.)	Republican	43,901,812	50.7	489	52.6
	Jimmy Carter	Democratic	35,483,820	41.0	49	
	John B. Anderson	Independent	5,719,722	6.6	—	
	Ed Clark	Libertarian	921,188	1.1	—	
1984	RONALD REAGAN (Calif.)	Republican	54,455,075	59.0	525	53.3
	Walter Mondale	Democratic	37,577,185	41.0	13	
1988	GEORGE BUSH (Texas)	Republican	47,946,422	54.0	426	50.2
	Michael S. Dukakis	Democratic	41,016,429	46.0	112	
1992	BILL CLINTON (Ark.)	Democratic	43,728,375	43.0	370	55.0
	George Bush	Republican	38,167,416	38.0	168	
	Ross Perot	Independent	19,237,247	19.0	0	

POPULATION OF THE UNITED STATES, 1790–1994

Year	Population	Percent Increase	Population per Square Mile	Percent Urban/ Rural	Percent White/ Nonwhite	Median Age
1790	3,929,214		4.5	5.1/94.9	80.7/19.3	NA
1800	5,308,483	35.1	6.1	6.1/93.9	81.1/18.9	NA
1810	7,239,881	36.4	4.3	7.3/92.7	81.0/19.0	NA
1820	9,638,453	33.1	5.5	7.2/92.8	81.6/18.4	16.7
1830	12,866,020	33.5	7.4	8.8/91.2	81.9/18.1	17.2
1840	17,069,453	32.7	9.8	10.8/89.2	83.2/16.8	17.8
1850	23,191,876	35.9	7.9	15.3/84.7	84.3/15.7	18.9
1860	31,443,321	35.6	10.6	19.8/80.2	85.6/14.4	19.4
1870	39,818,449	26.6	13.4	25.7/74.3	86.2/13.8	20.2
1880	50,155,783	26.0	16.9	28.2/71.8	86.5/13.5	20.9
1890	62,947,714	25.5	21.2	35.1/64.9	87.5/12.5	22.0
1900	75,994,575	20.7	25.6	39.6/60.4	87.9/12.1	22.9
1910	91,972,266	21.0	31.0	45.6/54.4	88.9/11.1	24.1
1920	105,710,620	14.9	35.6	51.2/48.8	89.7/10.3	25.3
1930	122,775,046	16.1	41.2	56.1/43.9	89.8/10.2	26.4
1940	131,669,275	7.2	44.2	56.5/43.5	89.8/10.2	29.0
1950	150,697,361	14.5	50.7	64.0/36.0	89.5/10.5	30.2
1960	179,323,175	18.5	50.6	69.9/30.1	88.6/11.4	29.5
1970	203,302,031	13.4	57.4	73.5/26.5	87.6/12.4	28.0
1980	226,545,805	11.4	64.0	73.7/26.3	86.0/14.0	30.0
1990	248,709,873	9.9	70.3	77.5/22.5	80.3/19.7	32.9
1994	260,340,990	4.7*	NA	79.7/20.3	NA	34.0†

NA = Not available.
*Since 1990.
†Projected.

EMPLOYMENT, 1870–1994

Year	Number of Workers (in millions)	Male/Female Employment Ratio	Percentage of Workers in Unions
1870	12.5	85/15	—
1880	17.4	85/15	—
1890	23.3	83/17	—
1900	29.1	82/18	3
1910	38.2	79/21	6
1920	41.6	79/21	12
1930	48.8	78/22	7
1940	53.0	76/24	27
1950	59.6	72/28	25
1960	69.9	68/32	26
1970	82.1	63/37	25
1980	108.5	58/42	23
1985	108.9	57/43	19
1988	114.9	55/45	17
1990	124.8	54/46	16
1994	131.1	NA	15.5

NA = Not available.

PRODUCTION, TRADE, AND FEDERAL SPENDING/DEBT, 1790–1994

Year	Gross National Product (GNP) (in billions $)	Balance of Trade (in millions $)	Federal Budget (in billions $)	Federal Surplus/Deficit (in billions $)	Federal Debt (in billions $)
1790	—	−3	.004	+0.00015	.076
1800	—	−20	.011	+0.0006	.083
1810	—	−18	.008	+0.0012	.053
1820	—	−4	.018	−0.0004	.091
1830	—	+3	.015	+0.100	.049
1840	—	+25	.024	−0.005	.004
1850	—	−26	.040	+0.004	.064
1860	—	−38	.063	−0.01	.065
1870	7.4	−11	.310	+0.10	2.4
1880	11.2	+92	.268	+0.07	2.1
1890	13.1	+87	.318	+0.09	1.2
1900	18.7	+569	.521	+0.05	1.2
1910	35.3	+273	.694	−0.02	1.1
1920	91.5	+2,880	6.357	+0.3	24.3
1930	90.7	+513	3.320	+0.7	16.3
1940	100.0	−3,403	9.6	−2.7	43.0
1950	286.5	+1,691	43.1	−2.2	257.4
1960	506.5	+4,556	92.2	+0.3	286.3
1970	992.7	+2,511	196.6	+2.8	371.0
1980	2,631.7	+24,088	579.6	−59.5	914.3
1990	5,465.1	−100,997.1	1,251.8	−220.3	3,223.3
1994	6,726.9	−150,629.2	1,460.6	−203.4	4,692.8

Suggested Readings

CHAPTER 15 RECONSTRUCTION AND THE NEW SOUTH

Reconstruction: General Studies. E. Merton Coulter, *The South During Reconstruction* (1947); W. E. B. Du Bois, *Black Reconstruction* (1935); William A. Dunning, *Reconstruction, Political and Economic, 1865–1877* (1907); Eric Foner, *Reconstruction: America's Unfinished Revolution, 1863–1877* (1988); John Hope Franklin, *Reconstruction After the Civil War* (1961); Rembert Patrick, *The Reconstruction of the Nation* (1967); Kenneth M. Stampp, *The Era of Reconstruction, 1865–1877* (1965).

Early Reconstruction. Richard H. Abbott, *The First Southern Strategy: The Republican Party and the South, 1855–1877* (1986); Herman Belz, *Reconstructing the Union* (1969); Louis S. Gerteis, *From Contraband to Freedman* (1973); William B. Hesseltine, *Lincoln's Plan of Reconstruction* (1960); Willie Lee Rose, *Rehearsal for Reconstruction: The Port Royal Experiment* (1964); Brooks D. Simpson, *Let Us Have Peace: Ulysses S. Grant and the Politics of War and Reconstruction, 1861–1868* (1991).

Congressional Reconstruction. Howard K. Beale, *The Critical Year: A Study of Andrew Johnson and Reconstruction* (1930); Herman Belz, *A New Birth of Freedom* (1976), and *Emancipation and Equal Rights* (1978); Michael Les Benedict, *A Compromise of Principle: Congressional Republicans and Reconstruction, 1863–1869* (1974), and *The Impeachment and Trial of Andrew Johnson* (1973); Richard Franklin Bensel, *Yankee Leviathan: The Origins of Central State Authority in America, 1859–1877* (1990); William R. Brock, *An American Crisis* (1963); Fawn Brodie, *Thaddeus Stevens* (1959); LaWanda Cox and John H. Cox, *Politics, Principles, and Prejudice, 1865–1867* (1963); Richard N. Current, *Old Thad Stevens* (1942); David Donald, *Charles Sumner and the Rights of Man* (1970), and *The Politics of Reconstruction* (1965); Charles Fairman, *Reconstruction and Reunion* (1971); William Gillette, *The Right to Vote* (1965); Harold Hyman, *A More Perfect Union* (1973); Stanley Kutler, *The Judicial Power and Reconstruction Politics* (1968); Eric McKitrick, *Andrew Johnson and Reconstruction* (1960); Mark W. Summers, *Railroads, Reconstruction, and the Gospel of Prosperity* (1984); Hans L. Trefousse, *The Radical Republicans* (1963), *The Impeachment of a President* (1975), and *Andrew Johnson: A Biography* (1989).

The South in Reconstruction. Roberta Alexander, *North Carolina Faces the Freedmen: Race Relations During Presidential Reconstruction, 1865–1867* (1985); James D. Anderson, *The Education of Blacks in the South* (1989); George Bentley, *A History of the Freedmen's Bureau* (1955); Dan Carter, *When the War Was Over: The Failure of Self-Reconstruction in the South, 1865–1867* (1985); Richard N. Current, *Those Terrible Carpetbaggers* (1988); Barbara Fields, *Slavery and Freedom on the Middle Ground* (1985); Eric Foner, *Nothing but Freedom: Emancipation and Its Legacy* (1983); William Gillette, *Retreat from Reconstruction, 1869–1879* (1980), and *The Right to Vote: Politics and Passage of the Fifteenth Amendment*

(1969); William C. Harris, *The Day of the Carpetbagger: Republican Reconstruction in Mississippi, 1867–1875* (1979); Robert Higgs, *Competition and Coercion: Blacks in the American Economy, 1865–1914* (1977); Thomas Holt, *Black over White: Negro Political Leadership in South Carolina During Reconstruction* (1977); Elizabeth Jacoway, *Yankee Missionaries in the South* (1979); Jacqueline Jones, *Soldiers of Light and Love: Northern Teachers and Georgia Blacks, 1865–1873* (1980), and *Labor of Love, Labor of Sorrow: Black Women, Work, and the Family from Slavery to the Present* (1985); Peter Kolchin, *First Freedom: The Responses of Alabama's Blacks to Emancipation* (1972); Leon Litwack, *Been in the Storm So Long: The Aftermath of Slavery* (1979); Richard Lowe, *Republicans and Reconstruction in Virginia, 1865–1870* (1991); Peyton McCrary, *Abraham Lincoln and Reconstruction* (1978); William S. McFeely, *Yankee Stepfather: General O. O. Howard and the Freedmen* (1968); Otto Olsen, *Carpetbagger's Crusade: Albion Winegar Tourgé* (1965); Michael Perman, *Reunion Without Compromise* (1973), and *The Road to Redemption: Southern Politics, 1869–1979* (1984); L. N. Powell, *New Masters: Northern Planters During the Civil War and Reconstruction* (1980); Roger L. Ransom and Richard Sutch, *One Kind of Freedom: The Economic Consequences of Emancipation* (1977); C. Peter Ripley, *Slaves and Freedmen in Civil War Louisiana* (1976); James Sefton, *The United States Army and Reconstruction* (1967); Crandall A. Shifflett, *Patronage and Poverty in the Tobacco South: Louisa County, Virginia, 1860–1900* (1982); Joel G. Taylor, *Louisiana Reconstructed* (1974); Allen Trelease, *White Terror: The Ku Klux Klan Conspiracy and Southern Reconstruction* (1967); Michael Wayne, *The Reshaping of Plantation Society: The Natchez District* (1983); Vernon Wharton, *The Negro in Mississippi, 1865–1890* (1965); Sarah Wiggins, *The Scalawag in Alabama Politics, 1865–1881* (1977); Joel Williamson, *After Slavery: The Negro in South Carolina During Reconstruction* (1965).

The Grant Administration. William B. Hesseltine, *U. S. Grant, Politician* (1935); Ari Hoogenboom, *Outlawing the Spoils* (1961); David Loth, *Public Plunder* (1938); William S. McFeely, *Grant* (1981); Allan Nevins, *Hamilton Fish* (1936); K. I. Polakoff, *The Politics of Inertia* (1973); John G. Sproat, *"The Best Men"* (1968); Margaret S. Thompson, *The "Spider Web": Congress and Lobbying in the Age of Grant* (1985); Irwin Unger, *The Greenback Era* (1964); C. Vann Woodward, *Reunion and Reaction* (1951).

The New South. Edward L. Ayers, *The Promise of the New South: Life After Reconstruction* (1992); Paul Buck, *The Road to Reunion* (1937); Orville Vernon Burton, *In My Father's House Are Many Mansions: Family and Community in Edgefield, South Carolina* (1985); Orville Vernon Burton and Robert C. McMath, Jr., eds., *Toward a New South? Studies in Post–Civil War Southern Communities* (1982); W. J. Cash, *The Mind of the South* (1941); Paul Gaston, *The New South Creed* (1970); J. Morgan Kousser and James M. McPherson, eds., *Region, Race, and Reconstruction* (1982); Jonathan Wiener, *Social Origins of the New South: Alabama, 1860–1885* (1978); C. Vann Woodward, *Origins of the New South* (1951), *The Burden of Southern History* (1960), *American Counterpoint* (1971), *Thinking Back* (1986), and *The Future of the Past* (1989).

Politics in the New South. Kenneth E. Davison, *The Presidency of Rutherford B. Hayes* (1972); Carl Degler, *The Other South: Southern Dissenters in the Nineteenth Century* (1974); Vincent P. DeSantis, *Republicans Face the Southern Question: The New Departure Years, 1877–1897* (1959); Sheldon Hackney, *Populism to Progressivism in Alabama* (1959); Stanley P. Hirshson, *Farewell to the Bloody Shirt: Northern Republicans and the Southern Negro* (1962); V. O. Key, Jr., *Southern Politics and the Nation* (1949); J. Morgan Kousser, *The Shaping of Southern Politics: Suffrage Restriction and the Establishment of the One-Party South,*

1880–1910 (1974); Paul Lewinson, *Race, Class, and Party* (1932); David Potter, *The South and the Concurrent Majority* (1972); Francis B. Simkins, *Pitchfork Ben Tillman* (1944); Joseph F. Wall, *Henry Watterson: Reconstructed Rebel* (1956); C. Vann Woodward, *Reunion and Reaction* (1951), and *Tom Watson: Agrarian Rebel* (1938).

Race, Economics, and Social Structure.   Francis Broderick, *W. E. B. DuBois* (1959); W. Fitzhugh Brundage, *Lynching in the New South: Georgia and Virginia, 1880–1930* (1993); David Carlton, *Mill and Town in South Carolina, 1880–1920* (1982); Melvin Greenhut and W. Tate Whitman, eds., *Essays in Southern Economic Development* (1964); Steven Hahn, *The Roots of Southern Populism: Yeoman Farmers and the Transformation of the Georgia Upcountry* (1983); Steven Hahn and Jonathan Prude, eds., *The Countryside in the Age of Capitalist Transformation* (1985); Jacquelyn Dowd Hall et al., *Like a Family: The Making of a Southern Cotton Mill World* (1987); Louis R. Harlan, *Booker T. Washington: The Making of a Black Leader, 1856–1901* (1972), and *Booker T. Washington: The Wizard of Tuskegee: 1901–1915* (1983); Robert Higgs, *Competition and Coercion: Blacks in the American Economy, 1865–1914* (1977); Melton A. McLaurin, *Paternalism and Protest: Southern Cotton Mill Workers and Organized Labor* (1971); James M. McPherson, *The Abolitionist Legacy: From Reconstruction to the NAACP* (1975); August Meier, *Negro Thought in America* (1963); Cynthia Neverdon-Morton, *Afro-American Women of the South and the Advancement of the Race, 1895–1925* (1989); David Oshinsky, *Worse Than Slavery: Parchman Prison and the Ordeal of Jim Crow Justice* (1996); Howard Rabinowitz, *Race Relations in the Urban South, 1865–1890* (1978); Roger Ransom and Richard Sutch, *One Kind of Freedom* (1977); Elliott M. Rudwick, *W. E. B. DuBois: Propagandist of Negro Protest* (1968); Altina L. Waller, *Feud: Hatfields, McCoys, and Social Changes: Appalachia, 1860–1900* (1988); Joel Williamson, *After Slavery* (1965), *The Crucible of Race: Black-White Relations in the American South Since Emancipation* (1985), and *A Rage for Order* (1986), an abridgment of *The Crucible of Race*; C. Vann Woodward, *The Strange Career of Jim Crow*, rev. ed. (1974); Gavin Wright, *Old South, New South: Revolutions in the Southern Economy Since the Civil War* (1986).

CHAPTER 16 THE CONQUEST
OF THE FAR WEST

General Works.   Ray A. Billington and Martin Ridge, *Westward Expansion*, 5th ed. (1982); Thomas D. Clark, *Frontier America* (1959); William Cronon et al., eds., *Under an Open Sky: Rethinking America's Western Past* (1992); Robert V. Hine, *The American West*, 2nd ed. (1984); Patricia Nelson Limerick, *The Legacy of Conquest: The Unbroken Past of the American West* (1987); Patricia Nelson Limerick et al., eds., *Trails: Toward a New Western History* (1992); Frederick Merk, *History of the Westward Movement* (1978); Rodman W. Paul, *The Far West and the Great Plains in Transition, 1859–1900* (1988); Rodman W. Paul and Richard W. Etulain, *The Frontier and the American West* (1977); Richard White, *"It's Your Misfortune and None of My Own": A History of the American West* (1991).

Migrations and Communities.   Gunther Barth, *Bitter Strength: A History of the Chinese in the United States, 1850–1870* (1964); Albert Camarillo, *Chicanos in a Changing Society: From Mexican Pueblos to American Barrios in Santa Barbara and Southern California* (1979); Sucheng Chan, *This Bittersweet Soil: The Chinese in California Agriculture, 1860–1910* (1986); Richard Griswold del Castillo, *La Familia: Chicano Families in the*

Urban Southwest, 1848 to the Present (1984), and *The Los Angeles Barrio, 1850–1890* (1979); Arnold De Leon, *They Called Them Greasers: Anglo Attitudes Toward Mexicans in Texas, 1821–1900* (1983); Sarah Deutsch, *No Separate Refuge: Culture, Class, and Gender on the Anglo-Hispanic Frontier in the Early Southwest, 1880–1940* (1987); Mario T. Garcia, *Desert Immigrants: The Mexicans of El Paso, 1880–1920* (1981); Robert V. Hine, *Community on the American Frontier* (1980); Richard Hogan, *Class and Community in Frontier Colorado* (1979); Howard R. Lamar, *Dakota Territory, 1861–1889* (1956), *The Far Southwest, 1846–1912* (1966), and *Texas Crossings: The Lone Star State and the American Far West, 1836–1986* (1991); Laurie F. Maffly-Kipp, *Religion and Society in Frontier California* (1994); Timothy R. Mahoney, *River Towns in the Great West* (1990); Dean L. May, *Three Frontiers: Family, Land, and Society in the American West, 1850–1900* (1994); Leonard Pitt, *The Decline of the Californios: A Social History of the Spanish-Speaking Californians, 1846–1890* (1960); Earl Pomeroy, *The Pacific Slope: A History of California, Oregon, Washington, Idaho, Utah, and Nevada* (1965); Andrew F. Rolle, *California: A History*, 2nd ed. (1969); Robert J. Rosenbaum, *Mexicano Resistance in the Southwest* (1981); Alexander Saxton, *The Indispensable Enemy: Labor and the Anti-Chinese Movement in California* (1971); Lillian Schlissel, *Women's Diaries of the Westward Journey* (1982); Thomas Sheridan, *Los Tucsonenses: The Mexican Community in Tucson, 1854–1941* (1986); Ronald Takaki, *Strangers from a Different Shore: A History of Asian Americans* (1989); Shih-shan Henry Tsai, *The Chinese Experience in America* (1986); Oscar O. Winther, *The Transportation Frontier: The Trans-Mississippi West, 1865–1890* (1964).

Miners and Cattlemen.   Andy Adams, *The Log of a Cowboy* (1927); Lewis Atherton, *The Cattle Kings* (1961); Gunther Barth, *Instant Cities* (1975); Edward E. Dale, *The Range Cattle Industry*, rev. ed. (1969); Philip Durham and Everett L. Jones, *The Negro Cowboys* (1965); Robert R. Dykstra, *The Cattle Towns* (1968); Odie B. Faulk, *Tombstone: Myth and Reality* (1972); Joe B. Frantz and Julian Choate, *The American Cowboy: The Myth and the Reality* (1955); Marion S. Goldman, *Gold Diggers & Silver Miners: Prostitution and Social Life on the Comstock* (1981); William S. Greever, *Bonanza West: Western Mining Rushes* (1963); Ralph Mann, *After the Gold Rush: Society in Grass Valley and Nevada City, California, 1849–1870* (1982); Ernest E. Osgood, *The Day of the Cattleman* (1929); Rodman W. Paul, *Mining Frontiers of the Far West, 1848–1880* (1963), and *The Far West and the Great Plains in Transition, 1859–1900* (1988); Wilson P. Rodman, *Mining Frontiers of the Far West* (1963); J. M. Skaggs, *The Cattle Trailing Industry* (1973); Richard W. Slatta, *Cowboys of the Americas* (1990); Duane A. Smith, *Rocky Mountain Mining Camps* (1967), and *Mining America: The Industry and the Environment, 1800–1980* (1987); L. Steckmesser, *The Western Hero in History and Legend* (1965); Donald E. Worcester, *The Chisholm Trail* (1980).

Indians.   Ralph K. Andrist, *The Long Death: The Last Days of the Plains Indians* (1964); Robert F. Berkhofer, Jr., *The White Man's Indian* (1978); Donald J. Berthrong, *The Southern Cheyennes* (1963); Dee Brown, *Bury My Heart at Wounded Knee: An Indian History of the American West* (1970); Margret Coel, *Chief Left Hand: Southern Arapaho* (1981); Angie Debo, *Geronimo* (1976); Richard Drinnon, *Facing West: The Metaphysics of Indian-Hating and Empire-Building* (1980); Thomas W. Dunlay, *Wolves for the Blue Soldiers* (1982); Loretta Fowler, *Arapahoe Politics, 1851–1978: Symbols in Crisis of Authority* (1982); William T. Hagan, *The Indian Rights Association: The Herbert Welsh Years, 1882–1904* (1985), and *American Indians* (1961); Howard L. Harrod, *Renewing the World: Plains Indians Religion and Morality* (1987); Dwight L. Hoover, *The Red and the Black* (1976); Frederick E. Hoxie,

A Final Promise: The Campaign to Assimilate the Indians, 1880–1920 (1984), and *The Crow* (1989); Peter Inverson, *The Navajos* (1990); Robert Mardock, *Reformers and the American Indian* (1971); Janet A. McDonnell, *The Dispossession of the American Indian, 1887–1934* (1991); John G. Neihardt, *Black Elk Speaks* (1932); James C. Olson, *Red Cloud and the Sioux Problem* (1965); Theda Perdue, *The Cherokee* (1989); John Powell, *People of the Sacred Mountain: A History of the Northern Cheyenne Chiefs and Warrior Societies, 1830–1879*, 2 vols. (1981); Francis P. Prucha, *American Indian Policy in Crisis* (1976), and *The Great White Father: The United States Government and the American Indians* (1984); David Roberts, *Once They Moved Like the Wind: Cochise, Geronimo, and the Apache Wars* (1993); Willard H. Rollings, *The Comanche* (1989); Mari Sandoz, *Crazy Horse* (1961); Edwin R. Sweeney, *Cochise: Chiricahua Apache Chief* (1991); Robert M. Utley, *Last Days of the Sioux Nation* (1963), *Frontiersmen in Blue: The United States Army and the Indian, 1848–1865* (1967), *Frontier Regulars: The United States Army and the Indian* (1973), *The Indian Frontier of the American West, 1846–1890* (1984), and *The Lance and the Shield: The Life and Times of Sitting Bull* (1993); Wilcomb E. Washburn, *The Indian in America* (1975), and *Red Man's Land/White Man's Law* (1971); Richard White, *The Roots of Dependency: Subsistence, Environment, and Social Change Among the Choctaws, Pawnees, and Navajos* (1983); Charles F. Wilkinson, *American Indians, Time, and the Law: Native Societies in a Modern Constitutional Democracy* (1987).

Western Women.   Susan Armitage and Elizabeth Jameson, eds., *The Women's West* (1987); John Mack Faragher, *Women and Men on the Overland Trail* (1979); Elizabeth Hampsten, *Read This Only to Yourself: The Private Writings of Midwestern Women, 1880–1910* (1982); Dolores Janiewski, *Sisterhood Denied* (1985); Julie Jeffrey, *Frontier Women: The Trans-Mississippi West, 1840–1880* (1979); Polly Welts Kaufman, *Women Teachers on the Frontier* (1984); Ruth Moynihan, *Rebel for Rights: Abigail Scott Dunaway* (1983); Sandra L. Myres, *Westering Women and the Frontier Experience, 1800–1915* (1982); Peggy Pascoe, *Relations of Rescue: The Search for Female Moral Authority in the American West, 1874–1939* (1990); Linda Peavy and Ursula Smith, *Women in Waiting in the Westward Movement: Life on the Home Frontier* (1994); Glenda Riley, *Women and Indians on the Frontier, 1825–1915* (1984), and *A Place to Grow* (1992); Joanna L. Stratton, *Pioneer Women: Voices from the Kansas Frontier* (1981).

Western Agriculture.   Allan Bogue, *From Prairie to Corn Belt* (1963); Everett Dick, *The Sod-House Frontier* (1937); John Mack Faragher, *Sugar Creek: Life on the Illinois Prairie* (1986); Gilbert Fite, *The Farmer's Frontier, 1865–1900* (1966); Paul W. Gates, *History of Public Land Development* (1968); Norris Hundley, Jr., *The Great Thirst: Californians and Water, 1770s–1990s* (1992); D. Aidan McQuillen, *Prevailing over Time: Ethnic Adjustment on the Kansas Prairies, 1875–1925* (1990); Nell Irvin Painter, *Exodusters: Black Migration to Kansas After Reconstruction* (1976); Fred A. Shannon, *The Farmer's Last Frontier, 1860–1897* (1945); Walter Prescott Webb, *The Great Plains* (1931); Thomas A. Woods, *Knights of the Plow: Oliver H. Kelley and the Origins of the Grange in Republican Ideology* (1991). (See also Suggested Readings for Chapter 19.)

The Idea and the Environment of the West.   Ray A. Billington, *Frederick Jackson Turner* (1973); William Cronon, *Nature's Metropolis: Chicago and the Great West* (1991); John Mack Faragher, *Daniel Boone* (1992); Richard Slotkin, *The Fatal Environment: The Myth of the Frontier in the Age of Industrialization* (1985), and *Gunfighter Nation* (1992); Henry Nash Smith, *Virgin Land* (1950); Frederick Jackson Turner, *The Frontier in Amer-*

ican History (1920); Donald Worster, *Under Western Skies: Nature and History in the American West* (1992), and *Rivers of Empire* (1985).

CHAPTER 17 INDUSTRIAL SUPREMACY

General Histories. Daniel Boorstin, *The Americans: The Democratic Experience* (1973); Thomas C. Cochran and William Miller, *The Age of Enterprise* (1942); Carl Degler, *The Age of the Economic Revolution* (1977); John A. Garraty, *The New Commonwealth* (1968); Ray Ginger, *The Age of Excess* (1963); Samuel P. Hays, *The Response to Industrialism, 1885–1914* (1957); Robert L. Heilbroner, *The Economic Transformation of America* (1977); Robert Higgs, *The Transformation of the American Economy, 1865–1914* (1971); Edward C. Kirkland, *Industry Comes of Age: Business, Labor, and Public Policy, 1860–1897* (1961); Alan Trachtenberg, *The Incorporation of America: Culture and Society in the Gilded Age* (1982); Robert Wiebe, *The Search for Order, 1877–1920* (1968).

Technology. Robert W. Bruce, *Bell* (1973); Roger Burlingame, *Engines of Democracy: Inventions and Society in Mature America* (1940), and *Henry Ford* (1957); Robert Conot, *A Streak of Luck* (1979); Richard N. Current, *The Typewriter and the Men Who Made It* (1954); George Daniels, *Science and Society in America* (1971); Frank E. Hill, *Ford* (1954); Thomas P. Hughes, *Networks of Power: Electrification in Western Society, 1880–1930* (1983); Judith McGaw, *Most Wonderful Machine: Mechanization and Social Change in Berkshire Paper Making, 1801–1885* (1988); Martin V. Melosi, *Coping with Abundance: Energy and Environment in Industrial America* (1985); Elting E. Morison, *Men, Machines, and Modern Times* (1966); Lewis Mumford, *Technics and Civilization* (1934); Allan Nevins, *Ford*, 3 vols. (1954–1962); David F. Noble, *America by Design: Science, Technology, and the Rise of Corporate Capitalism* (1977); Leonard S. Reich, *The Making of American Industrial Research: Science and Business at GE and Bell, 1876–1926* (1985); Nathan Rosenberg, *Technology and American Economic Growth* (1972); Peter Temin, *Steel in Nineteenth Century America* (1964); Wyn Wachhorst, *Thomas Alva Edison: An American Myth* (1981); Frederick A. White, *American Industrial Research Laboratories* (1961).

Railroads. Lee Benson, *Merchants, Farmers, and Railroads* (1955); Edward G. Campbell, *The Reorganization of the American Railroad System* (1938); Thomas C. Cochran, *Railroad Leaders* (1953); Robert Fogel, *Railroads and American Economic Growth* (1964); Edward C. Kirkland, *Men, Cities, and Transportation*, 2 vols. (1948); Gabriel Kolko, *Railroads and Regulation, 1877–1916* (1965); George H. Miller, *Railroads and the Granger Laws* (1971); Richard C. Overton, *Burlington West* (1941), and *Gulf to Rockies* (1953); John F. Stover, *The Life and Decline of the American Railroad* (1970), and *The Railroads of the South, 1865–1900* (1955); George R. Taylor and I. D. Neu, *The American Railroad Network, 1861–1890* (1956); Anthony F. C. Wallace, *St. Clair: A Nineteenth-Century Coal Town's Experience with a Disaster-Prone Industry* (1987).

The Corporation. Alfred D. Chandler, Jr., *Strategy and Structure: Chapters in the History of the American Industrial Enterprise* (1962), *Pierre S. DuPont and the Making of the Modern Corporation* (1971), *The Visible Hand: The Managerial Revolution in American Business* (1977), and *Scale and Scope: The Dynamics of Industrial Capitalism* (1990); David F. Hawkes,

John D.: The Founding Father of the Rockefellers (1980); Matthew Josephson, *The Robber Barons* (1934); Maury Klein, *The Life and Legend of Jay Gould* (1986); Norma R. Lamoreaux, *The Great Merger Movement in American Business, 1895–1904* (1985); Harold C. Livesay, *Andrew Carnegie and the Rise of Big Business* (1975); Allan Nevins, *Study in Power: John D. Rockefeller*, 2 vols. (1953); Glenn Porter and Harold C. Livesay, *Merchants and Manufacturers* (1971); Joseph Wall, *Andrew Carnegie* (1970); Bernard Weisberger, *The Dream Maker* (1979); Olivier Zunz, *Making America Corporate, 1870–1920* (1990).

Ideologies. Charles A. Baker, *Henry George* (1955); Robert C. Bannister, *Social Darwinism: Science and Myth in Anglo-American Social Thought* (1967); Samuel Chugerman, *Lester F. Ward: The American Aristotle* (1939); Sidney Fine, *Laissez Faire and the General Welfare State: A Study of Conflict in American Thought, 1865–1901* (1956); Louis Galambos, *The Public Image of Big Business in America, 1880–1940* (1975); Richard Hofstadter, *Social Darwinism in American Thought*, rev. ed. (1955); Edward C. Kirkland, *Dream and Thought in the Business Community, 1860–1900* (1956); T. J. Jackson Lears, *No Place of Grace: Antimodernism and the Transformation of American Culture, 1880–1920* (1981); Robert G. McCloskey, *American Conservatism in the Age of Enterprise* (1951); Arthur E. Morgan, *Edward Bellamy* (1944); Daniel T. Rodgers, *The Work Ethic in Industrial America, 1850–1920* (1978); David Thelen, *Paths of Resistance: Tradition and Dignity in Industrializing Missouri* (1986); John L. Thomas, *Alternative America: Henry George, Edward Bellamy, Henry Demarest Lloyd, and the Adversary Tradition* (1983); Irvin G. Wylie, *The Self-Made Man in America* (1954).

Labor. Paul Avrich, *The Haymarket Tragedy* (1984); John Bodnar, *Immigration and Industrialization: Ethnicity in an American Mill Town* (1977); Stanley Buder, *Pullman* (1967); John T. Cumbler, *Working-Class Community in Industrial America* (1979); Henry David, *The Haymarket Affair* (1936); Ileen A. DeVault, *Sons and Daughters of Labor: Class and Clerical Work in Turn-of-the-Century Pittsburgh* (1990); Melvyn Dubofsky, *Industrialism and the American Worker, 1865–1920* (1975); Melvyn Dubofsky and Warren Van Tine, eds., *Labor Leaders in America* (1987); P. K. Edwards, *Strikes in the United States, 1881–1974* (1981); Leon Fink, *Workingmen's Democracy: The Knights of Labor and American Politics* (1983); Samuel Gompers, *Seventy Years of Life and Labor*, 2 vols. (1975); David M. Gordon, Richard Edwards, and Michael Reich, *Segmented Work, Divided Workers: The Historical Transformation of Labor in the United States* (1982); Brian Greenberg, *Worker and Community: Response to Industrialization in a Nineteenth-Century American City, Albany, New York, 1850–1884* (1985); Herbert G. Gutman, *Work, Culture, and Society in Industrializing America* (1976); William F. Hartford, *Working People of Holyoke: Class and Ethnicity in a Massachusetts Mill Town, 1850–1960* (1990); Stuart Kaufman, *Samuel Gompers and the Origins of the American Federation of Labor* (1978); Alexander Keyssar, *Out of Work: The First Century of Unemployment in Massachusetts* (1986); S. J. Kleinberg, *The Shadow of the Mills: Working-Class Families in Pittsburgh, 1870–1907* (1989); David Montgomery, *Beyond Equality* (1975), *Workers' Control in America: Studies in the History of Work, Technology, and Labor Struggles* (1979), and *The Fall of the House of Labor: The Workplace, the State, and American Labor Activism, 1865–1925* (1987); Daniel Nelson, *Managers and Workers: Origins of the New Factory System in the United States, 1880–1920* (1975); Richard J. Oestreicher, *Solidarity and Fragmentation: Working People and Class Consciousness: Detroit, 1875–1900* (1986); Henry Pelling, *American*

Labor (1960); Peter Rachleff, *Black Labor In Richmond, 1865–1890* (1984); Roy Rosen-zweig, *"Eight Hours for What We Will": Workers and Leisure in an Industrial City, 1870–1920* (1983); Steven J. Ross, *Workers on the Edge: Work, Leisure, and Politics in In-dustrializing Cincinnati, 1788–1890* (1985); Peter R. Shergold, *Working Class Life* (1982); Sheldon Stromquist, *A Generation of Boomers: The Pattern of Railroad Labor Conflict in Nineteenth-Century America* (1987); Philip Taft, *The A. F. of L. in the Time of Gompers*, 2 vols. (1957–1959); Kim Voss, *The Making of American Exceptionalism: The Knights of Labor and Class Formation in the Nineteenth Century* (1993); Daniel J. Walkowitz, *Worker City, Company Town: Iron and Cotton Workers Protest in Troy and Cohoes, New York, 1855–1884* (1978); Leon Wolff, *Lockout: The Story of the Homestead Strike of 1892* (1965).

Women. Mary Blewett, *Men, Women, and Work Culture: Class, Gender, and Protest in the New England Shoe Industry* (1988); Patricia Cooper, *Once a Cigar Maker: Men, Women, and Work Culture in American Cigar Factories, 1900–1919* (1987); Tamara Hareven, *Fam-ily Time and Industrial Time: The Relationship Between the Family and Work in a New Eng-land Industrial Community* (1982); Paula Hyman, Charlotte Baum, and Sonya Michel, *The Jewish Woman in America* (1975); Susan E. Kennedy, *If All We Did Was to Weep at Home: A History of White Working-Class Women in America* (1979); Alice Kessler-Harris, *Out to Work: A History of Wage-Earning Women in the United States* (1982); Susan Levine, *Labor's True Women: Carpet Weavers, Industrialization, and Labor Reform in the Gilded Age* (1984); Elizabeth Anne Payne, *Reform, Labor, and Feminism* (1988); Barbara Wertheimer, *We Were There: The Story of Working Women in America* (1977).

The Left. Mari Jo Buhle, *Women and American Socialism, 1870–1920* (1981); Melvyn Dubofsky, *We Shall Be All: A History of the Industrial Workers of the World* (1969); Gerald N. Grob, *Workers and Utopia* (1961); J. H. M. Laslett, *Labor and the Left* (1970); Mar-garet M. Marsh, *Anarchist Women: 1870–1920* (1981); Nick Salvatore, *Eugene V. Debs: Citizen and Socialist* (1982).

CHAPTER 18 THE AGE OF THE CITY

General Histories. Howard Chudacoff, *The Evolution of American Urban Society*, rev. ed. (1981); Charles N. Glaab and Andrew T. Brown, *A History of Urban America* (1967); Constance M. Green, *The Rise of Urban America* (1965); Blake McKelvey, *The Urbaniza-tion of America* (1963); Lewis Mumford, *The Culture of the Cities* (1938), and *The City in History* (1961); Arthur M. Schlesinger, *The Rise of the City, 1878–1898* (1933); Jon C. Teaford, *City and Suburb: The Political Fragmentation of Urban America* (1979), and The *Twentieth-Century American City: Problem, Promise, and Reality* (1986); Sam Bass Warner, Jr., *The Urban Wilderness* (1972), and *Streetcar Suburbs* (1962).

Mobility and Race. Howard Chudacoff, *Mobile Americans: Residential and Social Mo-bility in Omaha, 1880–1920* (1972); Michael Frisch, *Town into City* (1972); Clyde Griffen and Sally Griffen, *Natives and Newcomers* (1977); Gerald D. Jaynes, *Branches Without Roots: Genesis of the Black Working Class in the American South, 1862–1882* (1986); Philip Kasinitz, *Caribbean New York: Black Immigrants and the Politics of Race* (1992); David M. Katzman, *Before the Ghetto* (1966); Kenneth L. Kusmer, *A Ghetto Takes Shape* (1976); Roger Lane, *The Roots of Black Violence in Philadelphia, 1860–1900* (1986); Gilbert Osofsky, *Harlem:*

The Making of a Ghetto (1966); Richard Sennett, *Families Against the City* (1970); Allan H. Spear, *Black Chicago* (1967); Stephan Thernstrom, *Poverty and Progress* (1964), and *The Other Bostonians* (1973); Stephan Thernstrom and Richard Sennett, eds., *Nineteenth Century Cities* (1969); Olivier Zunz, *The Changing Face of Inequality: Urbanization, Industrial Development, and Immigrants in Detroit, 1880–1920* (1982).

Immigration. Thomas J. Archdeacon, *Becoming American: An Ethnic History* (1983); Josef Barton, *Peasants and Strangers: Italians, Rumanians, and Slovaks in an American City* (1975); John Bodnar, *The Transplanted: A History of Immigrants in America* (1985), and *Immigration and Industrialization* (1977); John W. Briggs, *An Italian Passage* (1978); Jack Chen, *The Chinese of America* (1980); Robert D. Cross, *The Church and the City* (1967); Leonard Dinnerstein and David Reimers, *Ethnic Americans: A History of Immigration and Assimilation* (1975); John B. Duff, *The Irish in the United States* (1971); Elizabeth Ewen, *Immigrant Women in the Land of Dollars: Life and Culture on the Lower East Side, 1890–1925* (1985); Lawrence H. Fuchs, *The American Kaleidoscope: Race, Ethnicity, and the Civic Culture* (1990); Mario T. Garcia, *Desert Immigrants: The Mexicans of El Paso, 1880–1920* (1981); Nathan Glazer and Daniel P. Moynihan, *Beyond the Melting Pot* (1963); Susan A. Glenn, *Daughters of the Shtetl: Life and Labor in the Immigrant Generation* (1990); Milton M. Gordon, *Assimilation in American Life* (1964); Victor Greene, *For God and Country: The Rise of Polish and Lithuanian Ethnic Consciousness in America* (1975); Oscar Handlin, *The Uprooted*, rev. ed. (1973); Marcus Hansen, *The Immigrant in American History* (1940); John Higham, *Strangers in the Land* (1955), and *Send These To Me: Jews and Other Immigrants in Urban America* (1975); John Higham, ed., *Ethnic Leadership in America* (1978); Bill Ong Hing, *Making and Remaking Asian America Through Immigration Policy* (1993); Francis L. K. Hsu, *The Challenge of the American Dream: The Chinese in the United States* (1971); Maldwyn A. Jones, *American Immigration* (1960); Edward R. Kantowicz, *Polish-American Politics in Chicago* (1975); Thomas Kessner, *The Golden Door: Italian and Jewish Immigrant Mobility* (1977); Harry Kitano, *Japanese-Americans: The Evolution of a Subculture* (1969); Alan M. Kraut, *The Huddled Masses: The Immigrant in American Society, 1880–1921* (1982), and *Silent Travelers: Germs, Genes, and the "Immigrant Menace"* (1994); Matt S. Maier and Feliciano Rivera, *The Chicanos: A History of Mexican-Americans* (1972); Gwendolyn Mink, *Old Labor and New Immigrants in American Political Development: Union, Party, and State, 1875–1920* (1986); Ewa Morawska, *For Bread and Butter: The Life-Worlds of East Central Europeans in Johnstown, Pennsylvania, 1890–1940* (1985); Stanley Nadel, *Ethnicity, Religion, and Class in New York City, 1845–1880* (1990); Humbert S. Nelli, *The Italians of Chicago* (1970); Moses Rischin, *The Promised City: New York's Jews* (1962); Barbara Solomon, *Ancestors and Immigrants* (1965); Thomas Sowell, *Ethnic America* (1981); Philip Taylor, *The Distant Magnet: European Emigration to the U.S.A.* (1971); David Ward, *Cities and Immigrants* (1965); Mark Wyman, *Round-Trip to America: The Immigrants Return to Europe, 1880–1900* (1993); Virginia Yans-McLaughlin, *Family and Community: Italian Immigrants in Buffalo, 1880–1930* (1977).

Urban Poverty and Reform. Robert H. Bremner, *From the Depths* (1956); Stephan F. Brumberg, *Going to America, Going to School* (1986); James H. Cassedy, *Charles V. Chapin and the Public Health Movement* (1962); Allen F. Davis, *Spearheads for Reform* (1967); Barbara Gutmann Rosencrantz, *Public Health and the State* (1972); Marvin Lazerson, *Origins of the Urban School* (1971); James T. Patterson, *America's Struggle Against Poverty* (1981); Thomas L. Philpott, *The Slum and the Ghetto* (1978); James F. Richardson, *The New York Police* (1970); Jacob Riis, *How the Other Half Lives* (1890), *Children of the Poor* (1892), and

The Battle with the Slum (1902); Selwyn K. Troen, *The Public and the Schools* (1975); David B. Tyack, *The One Best System: A History of American Urban Education* (1974).

Urban Politics. John M. Allswang, *Bosses, Machines and Urban Voters* (1977); Alexander B. Callow, *The Tweed Ring* (1966); Brian J. Cudahy, *Cash, Tokens, and Transfers: A History of Urban Mass Transit in North America* (1990); Lyle Dorsett, *The Pendergast Machine* (1968); Lori Ginzberg, *Women and the Work of Benevolence: Morality, Politics, and Class in the Nineteenth-Century United States* (1990); Roger Lane, *Policing the City: Boston, 1822–1885* (1967); Seymour Mandelbaum, *Boss Tweed's New York* (1965); Christine M. Rosen, *The Limits of Power: Great Fires and the Process of City Growth in America* (1986); John Sproat, *"The Best Men": Liberal Reformers in the Gilded Age* (1968); Zane L. Miller, *Boss Cox's Cincinnati: Urban Politics in the Progressive Era* (1968).

Social Thought and Urban Culture. Martha Banta, *Imaging American Women: Idea and Ideals in Cultural History* (1987); Stuart Blumin, *The Emergence of the Middle Class: Social Experience in the American City, 1760–1900* (1989); Gunther Barth, *City People: The Rise of Modern City Culture in Nineteenth-Century America* (1980), and *Instant Cities: Urbanization and the Rise of San Francisco and Denver* (1975); Susan Porter Benson, *Counter Cultures: Saleswomen, Managers, and Customers in American Department Stores, 1890–1940* (1986); Henry C. Binford, *The First Suburbs: Residential Communities on the Boston Periphery, 1815–1860* (1985); Paul Boyer, *Urban Masses and Moral Order in America, 1820–1920* (1978); Marc Carnes, *Secret Ritual and Manhood in Victorian America* (1989); Clifford E. Clark, *The American Family Home, 1800–1960* (1986); Lawrence Cremin, *The Transformation of the School* (1961); Perry Duis, *The Saloon: Public Drinking in Chicago and Boston, 1880–1920* (1983); Lewis A. Erenberg, *Steppin' Out: New York Nightlife and the Transformation of American Culture, 1890–1930* (1981); Charles V. Forcey, *The Crossroads of Liberalism* (1961); Timothy J. Gilfoyle, *City of Eros: New York City, Prostitution, and the Commercialization of Sex, 1790–1920* (1992); Eliot Gorn, *The Manly Art: Bare-Knuckle Prize Fighting in America* (1986); Harvey Green, *Fit for America: Fitness, Sport, and American Society* (1986); Allen Guttmann, *A Whole New Ball Game: An Interpretation of American Sports* (1988); Karen Halttunen, *Confidence Men and Painted Women: A Study of Middle-Class Culture in America, 1830–1870* (1982); Neil Harris, *Cultural Excursions: Marketing Appetites and Cultural Tastes in Modern America* (1990); Marilyn Wood Hill, *Their Sisters' Keepers: Prostitution in New York City, 1830–1870* (1993); Daniel Horowitz, *The Morality of Spending: Attitudes Toward the Consumer Society in America, 1875–1940* (1985); Kenneth T. Jackson, *The Crabgrass Frontier: The Suburbanization of the United States* (1985); John F. Kasson, *Amusing the Million: Coney Island at the Turn of the Century* (1978), and *Rudeness and Civility: Manners in Nineteenth-Century Urban America* (1990); William Leach, *True Love and Perfect Union: The Feminist Reform of Sex and Society* (1980), and *Land of Desire: Merchants, Power, and the Rise of a New American Culture* (1993); T. J. Jackson Lears, *No Place of Grace: Antimodernism and the Transformation of American Culture, 1880–1920* (1981); T. J. Jackson Lears and Richard Wightman Fox, eds., *The Culture of Consumption* (1983); Godfrey M. Lebhar, *Chain Stores in America* (1962); Lawrence Levine, *Highbrow/Lowbrow: The Emergence of a Cultural Hierarchy in America* (1988); John A. Lucas and Ronald Smith, *Saga of American Sport* (1978); D. W. Marcell, *Progress and Pragmatism* (1974); Jay Martin, *Harvests of Change* (1967); Martin V. Melosi, ed., *Pollution and Reform in American Cities* (1980); Steven Mintz and Susan Kellogg, *Domestic Revolutions: A Social History of American Family Life* (1988); Frank Luther Mott, *American Jour-*

nalism, rev. ed. (1962); Donald R. Mrozek, *Sport and American Mentality, 1880–1910* (1983); Lewis Mumford, *The Brown Decades* (1931); David Nasaw, *Going Out: The Rise and Fall of Public Amusements* (1993), and *Schooled to Order: A Social History of Public Schooling in the United States* (1979); James D. Norris, *Advertising and the Transformation of American Society, 1865–1920* (1990); Kathy Peiss, *Cheap Amusements: Working Women and Leisure in Turn-of-the-Century New York* (1986); Roy Rosenzweig and Elizabeth Blackmar, *The Park and the People: A History of Central Park* (1992); Alexander Saxton, *The Rise and Fall of the White Republic: Class Politics and Mass Culture in Nineteenth-Century America* (1990); Robert W. Snyder, *The Voice of the City: Vaudeville and Popular Culture in New York* (1989); Dale Somers, *The Rise of Sports in New Orleans* (1972); Susan Strasser, *Satisfaction Guaranteed: The Making of the American Mass Market* (1989); William R. Taylor, *In Pursuit of Gotham: Culture and Commerce in New York* (1992); Christopher Tunnard and H. H. Reed, *American Skyline* (1955); Alexander Von Hoffman, *Local Attachments: The Making of an American Urban Neighborhood, 1850–1920* (1994); Morton White, *Social Thought in America* (1949); Larzer Ziff, *The American 1890s: Life and Times of a Lost Generation* (1966).

CHAPTER 19 FROM STALEMATE TO CRISIS

General Histories. Sean Dennis Cashman, *America and the Gilded Age* (1984); Carl N. Degler, *The Age of the Economic Revolution, 1876–1900*, 2nd ed. (1977); John H. Dobson, *Politics in the Gilded Age* (1972); Harold U. Faulkner, *Politics, Reform, and Expansion* (1959); John A. Garraty, *The New Commonwealth* (1969); Samuel P. Hays, *The Response to Industrialism, 1885–1914* (1957); Nell Irvin Painter, *Standing at Armageddon: The United States, 1877–1919* (1987); Alan Trachtenberg, *The Incorporation of America: Culture and Society in the Gilded Age* (1982); Robert Wiebe, *The Search for Order, 1877–1920* (1967); R. Hal Williams, *Years of Decision: American Politics in the 1890s* (1978).

Politics, Reform, and the State. Geoffrey Blodgett, *The Gentle Reformers* (1966); Ruth Bourdin, *Women and Temperance: The Quest for Power and Liberty, 1873–1900* (1980); James Bryce, *The American Commonwealth*, 2 vols. (1888); Tony Freyer, *Regulating Big Business: Antitrust in Great Britain and America, 1880–1990* (1992); Ari Hoogenboom, *Outlawing the Spoils: The Civil Service Movement* (1961); Richard Jensen, *The Winning of the Midwest: Social and Political Conflict, 1888–1896* (1971); Matthew Josephson, *The Politicos* (1963); Morton Keller, *Affairs of State* (1977); Paul Kleppner, *The Cross of Culture: A Social Analysis of Midwestern Politics, 1850–1900* (1970), and *The Third Electoral System, 1853–1892* (1979); J. Morgan Kousser, *The Shaping of Southern Politics: Suffrage Restriction and the Establishment of the One-Party South, 1880–1910* (1974); Michael P. Malone, *The Battle for Butte: Mining and Politics on the Northern Frontier, 1864–1906* (1981); Robert D. Marcus, *Grand Old Party* (1971); Gerald W. McFarland, *Mugwumps, Morals, and Politics, 1884–1920* (1975); Michael E. McGerr, *The Decline of Popular Politics* (1986); H. Wayne Morgan, *From Hayes to McKinley* (1969); Walter T. K. Nugent, *Money and American Society, 1865–1880* (1968); David J. Rothman, *Politics and Power: The United States Senate, 1869–1901* (1966); Martin J. Sklar, *The Corporate Reconstruction of American Capitalism, 1890–1916* (1988); Theda Skocpol, *Protecting Soldiers and Mothers: The Political Origins of Social Policy in the United States* (1992); Stephen Skowronek, *Building a New American State: The Expansion of National*

Administrative Capacities, 1877–1920 (1982); John Sproat, *"The Best Men": Liberal Reformers in the Gilded Age* (1968); Tom E. Terrill, *The Tariff, Politics, and American Foreign Policy, 1874–1901* (1973); Irwin Unger, *The Greenback Era* (1964); Leonard D. White, *The Republican Era* (1958).

Party Leaders. Harry Barnard, *Rutherford B. Hayes and His America* (1954); Herbert Croly, *Marcus Alonzo Hanna* (1912); Kenneth Davison, *The Presidency of Rutherford B. Hayes* (1972); Lewis L. Gould, *The Presidency of William McKinley* (1981); David Jordan, *Roscoe Conkling of New York* (1971); Margaret Leech, *In the Days of McKinley* (1959); Margaret Leech and Harry J. Brown, *The Garfield Orbit* (1978); Horace Samuel Merrill, *Bourbon Leader: Grover Cleveland and the Democratic Party* (1957); H. Wayne Morgan, *William McKinley and His America* (1963); Allan Nevins, *Grover Cleveland: A Study in Courage* (1933); Allan Peskin, *Garfield* (1978); Thomas C. Reeves, *Gentleman Boss: The Life of Chester Alan Arthur* (1975); Nick Salvatore, *Eugene V. Debs: Citizen and Socialist* (1982); Harry J. Sievers, *Benjamin Harrison*, 3 vols. (1952–1968).

The Depression. Ray Ginger, *Altgeld's America* (1958), and *The Bending Cross* (1949); Almot Lindsey, *The Pullman Strike* (1942); Donald McMurray, *Coxey's Army* (1929); Samuel McSeveney, *The Politics of Depression* (1972); Carlos A. Schwantes, *Coxey's Army* (1955).

Populism. Peter Argersinger, *Populism and Politics: William Alfred Peffer and the People's Party* (1974); O. Gene Clanton, *Populism: The Humane Preference in America, 1890–1900* (1991), and *Kansas Populism: Ideas and Men* (1969); Robert F. Durden, *The Climax of Populism: The Election of 1896* (1965); Lawrence Goodwyn, *Democratic Promise* (1976), and *The Populist Moment* (1978), an abridgment of *Democratic Promise*; Sheldon Hackney, *Populism to Progressivism in Alabama* (1969); Steven Hahn, *The Roots of Southern Populism: Yeoman Farmers and the Transformation of the Georgia Upcountry, 1850–1890* (1983); John D. Hicks, *The Populist Revolt* (1931); Richard Hofstadter, *The Age of Reform* (1954); Robert McMath, *Populist Vanguard* (1975), and *American Populism: A Social History, 1877–1898* (1993); Theodore R. Mitchell, *Political Education in the Southern Farmers Alliance, 1887–1900* (1987); Walter T. K. Nugent, *The Tolerant Populists* (1960); Bruce Palmer, *Man over Money* (1980); Stanley Parsons, *The Populist Context: Rural Versus Urban Power on a Great Plains Frontier* (1973); Norman Pollack, *The Populist Response to Industrial America* (1962), and *The Just Polity: Populism, Law, and Human Welfare* (1987); Martin Ridge, *Ignatius Donnelly: Portrait of a Politician* (1962); Theodore Saloutos, *Farmer Movements in the South, 1865–1933* (1960); Fred Shannon, *The Farmer's Last Frontier* (1945); Barton C. Shaw, *The Wool-Hat Boys: Georgia's Populist Party* (1984); Francis B. Simkins, *Pitchfork Ben Tillman* (1944); Allan Weinstein, *Prelude of Populism: Origins of the Silver Issue* (1970); C. Vann Woodward, *Origins of the New South* (1972), and *Tom Watson, Agrarian Rebel* (1938); James E. Wright, *The Politics of Populism: Dissent in Colorado* (1974).

The "Battle of the Standards" and the Election of 1896. Paolo Coletta, *William Jennings Bryan*, 3 vols., (1964–1969); Milton Friedman and Anna J. Schwartz, *A Monetary History of the United States* (1963); Paul Glad, *McKinley, Bryan, and the People* (1964), and *The Trumpet Soundeth* (1960); J. Rogers Hollingsworth, *The Whirligig of Politics: The Democracy of Cleveland and Bryan* (1963); Stanley Jones, *The Presidential Election of 1896* (1964).

CHAPTER 20 THE IMPERIAL REPUBLIC

General Histories.   Robert L. Beisner, *From the Old Diplomacy to the New, 1865–1900,* 2nd ed. (1986); Charles S. Campbell, *The Transformation of American Foreign Relations, 1865–1900* (1976); John Dobson, *America's Ascent: The United States Becomes a Great Power, 1880–1914* (1978); Foster Rhea Dulles, *Prelude to World Power, 1865–1900* (1965); J. A. S. Grenville and George Berkeley Young, *Politics, Strategy and American Diplomacy: Studies in Foreign Policy, 1873–1917* (1966); David F. Healy, *U.S. Expansionism: Imperialist Urge in the 1890s* (1970); Walter LaFeber, *The Cambridge History of American Foreign Relations,* vol. 2: *The Search for Opportunity, 1865–1913* (1993), and *The New Empire* (1963); Ernest May, *Imperial Democracy* (1961), and *American Imperialism: A Speculative Essay* (1968); H. Wayne Morgan, *America's Road to Empire* (1965); Milton Plesur, *America's Outward Thrust: Approaches to Foreign Affairs, 1865–1890* (1971); David M. Pletcher, *The Awkward Years: American Foreign Relations Under Garfield and Arthur* (1962); Julius W. Pratt, *Expansionists of 1898* (1936); Emily S. Rosenberg, *Spreading the American Dream: American Economic and Cultural Expansion, 1890–1945* (1982); Albert K. Weinberg, *Manifest Destiny: A Study in Nationalist Expansion in American History* (1935); William Appleman Williams, *The Tragedy of American Diplomacy,* rev. ed. (1972).

The Spanish-American War.   Richard Challener, *Admirals, Generals, and American Foreign Policy, 1889–1914* (1973); Graham A. Cosmas, *An Army for Empire: The United States Army in the Spanish-American War* (1971); Philip S. Foner, *The Spanish-Cuban-American War and the Birth of American Imperialism,* 2 vols. (1972); Frank Freidel, *The Splendid Little War* (1958); Willard B. Gatewood, Jr., *Black Americans and the White Man's Burden, 1898–1903* (1975), and *"Smoked Yankees": Letters from Negro Soldiers, 1898–1902* (1971); Gerald F. Linderman, *The Mirror of War: American Society and the Spanish-American War* (1974); Walter Millis, *The Martial Spirit* (1931); Joyce Milton, *The Yellow Journalists* (1989); Edmund Morris, *The Rise of Theodore Roosevelt* (1979); John L. Offner, *An Unwanted War: The Diplomacy of the United States and Spain over Cuba, 1895–1898* (1992); Louis A. Perez, Jr., *Cuba Between Empires, 1868–1902* (1983); Hyman Rickover, *How the Battleship Maine Was Destroyed* (1976); David F. Trask, *The War with Spain in 1898* (1981); Richard S. West, Jr., *Admirals of the American Empire* (1948).

Imperialism and Anti-Imperialism.   Robert L. Beisner, *Twelve Against Empire* (1968); Kendrick A. Clements, *William Jennings Bryan* (1983); James H. Hitchman, *Leonard Wood and Cuban Independence, 1898–1902* (1971); Frederick Merk, *Manifest Destiny and Mission in American History* (1963); Thomas J. Osborne, *"Empire Can Wait": American Opposition to Hawaiian Annexation, 1893–1898* (1891); William J. Pomeroy, *American Neo-Colonialism: Its Emergence in the Philippines and Asia* (1970); Julius W. Pratt, *America's Colonial Empire* (1950); Robert Seager II, *Alfred Thayer Mahan* (1977); E. Berkeley Tompkins, *Anti-Imperialism in the United States, 1890–1920: The Great Debate* (1970).

The Pacific Empire.   H. W. Brands, *Bound to Empire: The United States and the Philippines* (1992); John Morgan Gates, *Schoolbooks and Krags: The United States Army in the Philippines, 1898–1902* (1971); Stanley Karnow, *In Our Image: America's Empire in the Philippines* (1989); Paul M. Kennedy, *The Samoan Tangle* (1974), Glenn A. May, *Social Engineering in the Philippines* (1980); Stuart Creighton Miller, *"Benevolent Assimilation": The American Conquest of the Philippines, 1899–1903* (1982); Daniel B. Schirmer, *Republic or Empire? American Resistance to the Philippine War* (1972); Peter Stanley, *A Nation in the*

Making: The Philippines and the United States (1974); Merze Tate, *The United States and the Hawaiian Kingdom* (1965); Richard E. Welch, Jr., *Response to Imperialism: The United States and the Philippine-American War, 1899–1902* (1979); Leon Wolff, *Little Brown Brother* (1961).

America and Asia. Warren Cohen, *America's Response to China*, rev. ed. (1980), and *East Asian Art and American Culture: A Study in International Relations* (1992); Kenton Clymer, *John Hay: Gentleman as Diplomat* (1975); Patricia Hill, *The World Their Household: The American Women's Foreign Mission Movement and Cultural Transformation* (1985); Michael Hunt, *The Making of a Special Relationship: The United States and China to 1914* (1983); Jane Hunter, *The Gospel of Gentility: American Women Missionaries in Turn-of-the-Century China* (1984); Akira Iriye, *Across the Pacific* (1967), and *Pacific Estrangement: Japanese and American Expansion* (1972); Robert McClellan, *The Heathen Chinese: A Study of American Attitudes Toward China* (1971); Thomas J. McCormick, *China Market: America's Quest for Informal Empire, 1893–1901* (1967); Charles Neu, *The Troubled Encounter* (1975); James C. Thomsen, Jr., Peter W. Stanley, and John Curtis Perry, *Sentimental Imperialists: The American Experience in East Asia* (1981); Paul Varg, *The Making of a Myth: The United States and China, 1897–1912* (1968), and *Missionaries, Chinese and Diplomats* (1958); Marilyn B. Young, *The Rhetoric of Empire: American China Policy, 1895–1901* (1968).

CHAPTER 21 THE RISE OF PROGRESSIVISM

Progressivism: Overviews. John D. Buenker, John C. Burnham, and Robert M. Crunden, *Progressivism* (1977); John W. Chambers II, *The Tyranny of Change: America in the Progressive Era, 1900–1917* (1980); John Milton Cooper, *The Pivotal Decades: The United States, 1900–1920* (1990); Alan Dawley, *Struggles for Justice: Social Responsibility and the Liberal State* (1991); Richard Hofstadter, *The Age of Reform: From Bryan to FDR* (1955); Gabriel Kolko, *The Triumph of Conservatism: A Reinterpretation of American History* (1963); Arthur S. Link and Richard L. McCormick, *Progressivism* (1983); Nell Irvin Painter, *Standing at Armageddon: The United States, 1877–1919* (1987); James Weinstein, *The Corporate Ideal in the Liberal State, 1900–1918* (1969); Robert Wiebe, *The Search for Order, 1877–1920* (1967).

The Muckrakers. David Chalmers, *The Social and Political Ideas of the Muckrakers* (1964); Louis Filler, *The Muckrakers*, rev. ed. (1980); Leon Harris, *Upton Sinclair* (1975); Justin Kaplan, *Lincoln Steffens* (1974); C. C. Regier, *The Era of the Muckrakers* (1932); Harold S. Wilson, *McClure's Magazine and the Muckrakers* (1970).

Progressive Thought. Richard Abrams, *The Burdens of Progress* (1978); Carl N. Degler, *In Search of Human Nature: The Decline and Revival of Darwinism in American Social Thought* (1991); Arthur Ekirch, *Progressivism in America* (1974); Charles V. Forcey, *The Crossroads of Liberalism: Croly, Weyl, Lippmann* (1961); Sudhir Kakar, *Frederick Taylor* (1970); D. W. Marcell, *Progress and Pragmatism: James, Dewey, Beard and the American Idea of Progress* (1974); David W. Noble, ed., *The Progressive Mind*, rev. ed. (1981); Jean B. Quandt, *From the Small Town to the Great Community: The Social Thought of Progressive Intellectuals* (1970); Robert Westbrook, *John Dewey and American Democracy* (1991); Morton White, *Social Thought in America* (1949).

Social Work and the Social Gospel.   Jane Addams, *Twenty Years at Hull House* (1910); Paul Boyer, *Urban Masses and Moral Order, 1820–1920* (1978); Mina Carson, *Settlement Folk: Social Thought and the American Settlement Movement, 1885–1930* (1990); Robert M. Crunden, *Ministers of Reform: The Progressives' Achievement in American Civilization, 1889–1920* (1982); Susan Curtis, *A Consuming Faith: The Social Gospel and Modern American Culture* (1991); Allen F. Davis, *Spearheads of Reform: The Social Settlements and the Progressive Movement, 1890–1914* (1968), and *American Heroine: The Life and Legend of Jane Addams* (1973); C. H. Hopkins, *The Rise of the Social Gospel in American Protestantism* (1940); William R. Hutchinson, *The Modernist Impulse in American Protestantism* (1982); Rivka Shpak Lissak, *Pluralism and Progressives: Hull House and the New Immigrants, 1890–1919* (1989); Roy Lubove, *The Progressives and the Slums: Tenement House Reform in New York City* (1962); Henry May, *Protestant Churches and Industrial America* (1949); Timothy Miller, *Following in His Steps: A Biography of Charles M. Sheldon* (1987).

Education and the Professions.   Clyde W. Barrow, *Universities and the Capitalist State: Corporate Liberalism and the Reconstruction of American Higher Education, 1894–1928* (1990); Burton Bledstein, *The Culture of Professionalism* (1976); Lawrence A. Cremin, *The Transformation of the Schools: Progressivism in American Education, 1876–1957* (1971); Lynn D. Gordon, *Gender and Higher Education in the Progressive Era* (1990); Samuel Haber, *The Quest for Authority and Honor in the American Professions, 1750–1900* (1991); Barbara Harris, *Beyond Her Sphere: Women and the Professions in American History* (1978); Thomas L. Haskell, *The Emergence of Professional Social Science* (1977); Morton J. Horwitz, *The Transformation of American Law, 1870–1960: The Crisis of Legal Orthodoxy* (1992); Kenneth M. Ludmerer, *Learning to Heal: The Development of American Medical Education* (1985); Regina Markell Morantz-Sanchez, *Sympathy and Science: Women Physicians in American Medicine* (1985); Barbara Miller Solomon, *In the Company of Educated Women: A History of Women in Higher Education in America* (1985); Paul Starr, *The Social Transformation of American Medicine* (1982); David Tyack and Elizabeth Hansot, *Managers of Virtue: Public School Leadership in America, 1820–1980* (1982); Lawrence Veysey, *The Emergence of the American University* (1970).

Municipal Reform.   John D. Buenker, *Urban Liberalism and Progressive Reform* (1973); James B. Crooks, *Politics and Progress: The Rise of Urban Progressivism in Baltimore* (1968); Oscar Handlin, *Al Smith and His America* (1958); Melvin G. Holli, *Reform in Detroit: Hazen S. Pingree and Urban Politics* (1969); J. Joseph Huthmacher, *Senator Robert F. Wagner and the Rise of Urban Liberalism* (1971); Michael Kazin, *Barons of Labor: The San Francisco Building Trades and Union Power in the Progressive Era* (1981); Zane Miller, *Boss Cox's Cincinnati* (1968); Martin J. Schiesl, *The Politics of Efficiency: Municipal Administration and Reform in America, 1880–1920* (1977).

Women, Reform, and Suffrage.   Paula Baker, *The Moral Frameworks of Public Life: Gender, Politics, and the State in Rural New York, 1870–1930* (1991); Karen Blair, *The Clubwoman as Feminist* (1980); Mari Jo Buhle, *Women and American Socialism* (1983); Norman H. Clark, *Deliver Us from Evil: An Interpretation of American Prohibition* (1976); Mark T. Connelly, *The Response to Prohibition in the Progressive Era* (1980); Nancy Cott, *The Grounding of Modern Feminism* (1987); Ellen C. DuBois, *Feminism and Suffrage: The Emergence of an Independent Women's Movement in America, 1848–1869* (1978); Nancy Shrom Dye, *As Equal as Sisters: Feminism, The Labor Movement, and the Women's Trade*

Union League of New York (1981); Eleanor Flexner, *Century of Struggle* (1959); Linda Gordon, *Woman's Body, Woman's Right: A Social History of Birth Control* (1976); Alan P. Grimes, *The Puritan Ethic and Woman Suffrage* (1967); Jacquelyn Dowd Hall, *The Revolt Against Chivalry* (1979); David M. Kennedy, *Birth Control in America: The Career of Margaret Sanger* (1970); Aileen S. Kraditor, *Ideas of the Woman Suffrage Movement* (1965); Ellen C. Lagemann, *A Generation of Women: Education in the Lives of Progressive Reformers* (1979); Elaine Tyler May, *Great Expectations: Marriage and Divorce in Post-Victorian America* (1980); David Morgan, *Suffragists and Democrats: The Politics of Woman Suffrage in America* (1972); Robyn Muncy, *Creating a Female Dominion in American Reform, 1890–1935* (1991); William O'Neill, *Divorce in the Progressive Era* (1967), and *Everyone Was Brave: The Rise and Fall of Feminism in America* (1969); Ruth Rosen, *The Lost Sisterhood: Prostitutes in America, 1900–1918* (1982); Rosalind Rosenberg, *Beyond Separate Spheres: Intellectual Roots of Modern Feminism* (1982); Elyce J. Rotella, *From Home to Office: U.S. Women and Work, 1870–1930* (1981); Sheila M. Rothman, *Woman's Proper Place* (1978); Anne F. Scott, *Making the Invisible Woman Visible* (1984).

Racial Issues.   John Dittmer, *Black Georgia in the Progressive Era, 1900–1920* (1977); George Frederickson, *The Black Image in the White Mind* (1968); Paula Giddings, *When and Where I Enter: The Impact of Black Women on Race and Sex in America* (1984); Louis Harlan, *Booker T. Washington: The Making of a Black Leader* (1856), and *Booker T. Washington: The Wizard of Tuskegee, 1901–1915* (1983); Charles F. Kellogg, *NAACP* (1970); Jack Temple Kirby, *Darkness at Dawning: Race and Reform in the Progressive South* (1972); David L. Lewis, *W. E. B. DuBois: Biography of a Race, 1868–1919* (1993); William A. Link, *The Paradox of Southern Progressivism, 1880–1930* (1992); Ralph E. Luker, *The Social Gospel in Black and White: American Racial Reform, 1885–1912* (1991); James M. McPherson, *The Abolitionist Legacy: From Reconstruction to the NAACP* (1975); August Meier, *Negro Thought in America, 1880–1915* (1963); Cynthia Neverdon-Morton, *Afro-American Women of the South and the Advancement of the Race, 1885–1925* (1989); Elliott Rudwick, *W. E. B. Du Bois* (1969); Donald Spivey, *Schooling for the New Slavery: Black Industrial Education* (1978); Joel Williamson, *The Crucible of Race: Black-White Relations in the American South Since Emancipation* (1985).

State-Level Reform.   Richard M. Abrams, *Conservatism in a Progressive Era: Massachusetts* (1964); Dewey Grantham, *Southern Progressivism: The Reconciliation of Progress and Tradition* (1983); Sheldon Hackney, *Populism to Progressivism in Alabama* (1969); Robert S. Maxwell, *La Follette and the Rise of Progressivism in Wisconsin* (1944); Richard L. McCormick, *From Realignment to Reform: Political Change in New York State, 1893–1910* (1981); George E. Mowry, *California Progressives* (1951); Russel B. Nye, *Midwestern Progressive Politics* (1951); David P. Thelen, *The New Citizenship: Origins of Progressivism in Wisconsin* (1972), *Robert M. La Follette and the Insurgent Spirit* (1976), and *Paths of Resistance: Tradition and Dignity in Industrializing Missouri* (1986); Robert F. Wesser, *Charles Evans Hughes: Politics and Reform in New York State, 1905–1910* (1967); C. Vann Woodward, *Origins of the New South* (1951), Irwin Yellowitz, *Labor and the Progressive Movement in New York State* (1965).

National Issues.   Ruth Bourdin, *Women and Temperance: The Quest for Power and Liberty, 1873–1900* (1980); Melvyn Dubofsky, *We Shall Be All: A History of the Industrial*

Workers of the World (1969); Sidney Fine, *Laissez Faire and the General Welfare State* (1956); Joseph Gusfield, *Symbolic Crusade: Status Politics and the Temperance Movement* (1963); John Higham, *Strangers in the Land* (1955); Michael E. McGerr, *The Decline of Popular Politics: The American North, 1865–1928* (1986); Bruno Ramirez, *When Workers Organize: The Politics of Industrial Relations in the Progressive Era, 1898–1916* (1978); James T. Timberlake, *Prohibition and the Progressive Movement* (1963); James Weinstein, *The Decline of Socialism in America* (1967); Robert Wiebe, *Businessmen and Reform: A Study of the Progressive Movement* (1962); Olivier Zunz, *Making America Corporate, 1870–1920* (1990).

CHAPTER 22 THE BATTLE FOR NATIONAL REFORM

General Histories. John Milton Cooper, Jr., *The Warrior and the Priest: Woodrow Wilson and Theodore Roosevelt* (1983); Arthur Link, *Woodrow Wilson and the Progressive Era, 1910–1917* (1954); George E. Mowry, *The Era of Theodore Roosevelt* (1958). (See also Suggested Readings for Chapter 21.)

Theodore Roosevelt. John Morton Blum, *The Republican Roosevelt* (1954); G. Wallace Chessman, *Theodore Roosevelt and the Politics of Power* (1969); John A. Garraty, *The Life of George W. Perkins* (1960); Lewis L. Gould, *The Presidency of Theodore Roosevelt* (1991); William H. Harbaugh, *Power and Responsibility* (1961), published in paperback as *The Life and Times of Theodore Roosevelt;* Horace S. Merrill and Marion G. Merrill, *The Republican High Command* (1971); Edmund Morris, *The Rise of Theodore Roosevelt* (1979); Henry F. Pringle, *Theodore Roosevelt* (1931).

William Howard Taft. Donald E. Anderson, *William Howard Taft* (1973); Paolo E. Coletta, *The Presidency of William Howard Taft* (1973); George Mowry, *Theodore Roosevelt and the Progressive Movement* (1946); Henry F. Pringle, *The Life and Times of William Howard Taft*, 2 vols. (1939); Norman Wilensky, *Conservatives in the Progressive Era: The Taft Republicans of 1912* (1965).

Woodrow Wilson. John Morton Blum, *Joseph Tumulty and the Wilson Era* (1951), and *Woodrow Wilson and the Politics of Morality* (1956); Alexander George and Juliette George, *Woodrow Wilson and Colonel House* (1956); L. J. Holt, *Congressional Insurgents and the Party System, 1909–1916* (1967); Arthur S. Link, *Woodrow Wilson*, 5 vols. (1947–1965); Edwin A. Weinstein, *Woodrow Wilson: A Medical and Psychological Biography* (1981).

National Issues. O. E. Anderson, *The Health of a Nation* (1958); Stephen R. Fox, *The American Conservation Movement: John Muir and His Legacy* (1981); Samuel P. Hays, *The Gospel of Efficiency: The Progressive Conservation Movement, 1890–1920* (1962); James Holt, *Congressional Insurgents and the Party System* (1969); John M. Jordan, *Machine Age Ideology: Social Engineering and American Liberalism, 1911–1939* (1994); Susan Kleinberg, *The Shadow of the Mills: Working Class Families in Pittsburgh, 1870–1907* (1989); Naomi Lamoreaux, *The Great Merger Movement in American Business, 1895–1904* (1985); Albro Martin, *Enterprise Denied: Origins of the Decline of the American Railroads, 1897–1917* (1971);

Thomas K. McCraw, ed., *Regulation in Perspective* (1981); Roderick Nash, *Wilderness and the American Mind* (1967); James Penick, Jr., *Progressive Politics and Conservation: The Ballinger-Pinchot Affair* (1968); Harold T. Pinkett, *Gifford Pinchot: Private and Public Forester* (1970); Elmo P. Richardson, *The Politics of Conservation* (1962); David Sarasohn, *The Party of Reform: The Democrats in the Progressive Era* (1989); Martin J. Sklar, *The Corporate Reconstruction of American Capitalism, 1890–1916: The Market, the Law, and Politics* (1988); Peter Temin, *Taking Your Medicine: Drug Regulation in the U.S.* (1980); Melvin I. Urofsky, *Louis D. Brandeis and the Progressive Tradition* (1981); Bernard Weisberger, *The LaFollettes of Wisconsin: Love and Politics in Progressive America* (1994); Craig West, *Banking Reform and the Federal Reserve, 1863–1923* (1977); Robert Wiebe, *Businessmen and Reform: A Study of the Progressive Movement* (1962).

Roosevelt's Foreign Policy. Howard K. Beale, *Theodore Roosevelt and the Rise of America to World Power* (1956); David H. Burton, *Theodore Roosevelt: Confident Imperialist* (1969); Richard Challener, *Admirals, Generals, and American Foreign Policy, 1898–1914* (1973); Raymond A. Esthus, *Theodore Roosevelt and International Rivalries* (1970); Michael H. Hunt, *The Making of a Special Relationship: The United States and China to 1914* (1983); Akira Iriye, *Pacific Estrangement: Japanese and American Expansion, 1897–1911* (1972); Richard Leopold, *Elihu Root and the Conservative Tradition* (1954); Charles E. Neu, *An Uncertain Friendship: Roosevelt and Japan, 1906–1909* (1967); Bradford Perkins, *The Great Rapprochement: England and the United States, 1895–1914* (1968); Julius W. Pratt, *Challenge and Rejection: The United States and World Leadership, 1900–1921* (1967); Charles Vevier, *United States and China* (1955).

America and the Caribbean. P. Edward Haley, *Revolution and Intervention: The Diplomacy of Taft and Wilson with Mexico, 1910–1917* (1975); David Healy, *The United States in Cuba, 1898–1902* (1963); Walter LaFeber, *The Panama Canal* (1978); Lester E. Langley, *The Banana Wars: An Inner History of American Empire, 1900–1934* (1983); David McCullough, *The Path Between the Seas* (1977); Dwight C. Miner, *Fight for the Panama Route* (1966); Dana G. Munro, *Intervention and Dollar Diplomacy in the Caribbean, 1900–1921* (1964); Louis A. Perez, Jr., *Cuba Under the Platt Amendment* (1988); Walter Scholes and Marie Scholes, *The Foreign Policies of the Taft Administration* (1970); John Womack, *Zapata and the Mexican Revolution* (1968).

Wilson's Foreign Policy. Kenneth Grieb, *The United States and Huerta* (1969); David Healy, *Gunboat Diplomacy in the Wilson Era: The U.S. Navy in Haiti, 1915–1916* (1976); Thomas J. Knock, *To End All Wars: Woodrow Wilson and the Quest for a New World Order* (1992); Arthur Link, *Wilson the Diplomatist* (1957), and *Woodrow Wilson: Revolution, War, and Peace* (1979); Dana Munro, *Intervention and Dollar Diplomacy in the Caribbean, 1900–1914* (1964); Robert Quirk, *An Affair of Honor: Woodrow Wilson and the Occupation of Veracruz* (1962), and *The Mexican Revolution, 1914–1915* (1960); James Reed, *The Missionary Mind and America's East Asian Policy, 1911–1915* (1983); Robert Freeman Smith, *The United States and Revolutionary Nationalism in Mexico, 1916–1932* (1972).

CHAPTER 23 AMERICA AND THE GREAT WAR

The Road to War. Thomas A. Bailey and Paul B. Ryan, *The Lusitania Disaster* (1975); John Coogan, *The End to Neutrality* (1981); John Milton Cooper, Jr., *The Vanity of Power:*

American Isolation and the First World War (1969); Patrick Devlin, *Too Proud to Fight: Woodrow Wilson's Neutrality* (1974); Ross Gregory, *The Origins of American Intervention in the First World War* (1971); Manfred Jonas, *The United States and Germany* (1984); C. Roland Marchand, *The American Peace Movement and Social Reform* (1973); Ernest R. May, *The World War and American Isolation* (1959); Emily Rosenberg, *Spreading the American Dream* (1982); Jeffrey J. Sanford, *Wilsonian Maritime Diplomacy* (1978); Daniel Smith, *Robert Lansing and American Neutrality* (1958), and *The Great Departure: The United States and World War I, 1914–1920*, (1965); Barbara M. Tuchman, *The Zimmermann Telegram* (1958), and *The Guns of August* (1962).

Military Histories.   A. E. Barbeau and Florette Henri, *The Unknown Soldiers: Black American Troops in World War I* (1974); Christopher Campbell, *Aces and Aircraft of World War I* (1981); John Whiteclay Chambers, *To Raise an Army* (1987); J. Garry Clifford, *The Citizen Soldiers* (1972); Edward M. Coffman, *The War to End All Wars* (1969); Harvey A. DeWeerd, *President Wilson Fights His War* (1968); Frank Freidel, *Over There: The Story of America's First Great Overseas Crusade* (1964); Robert Jackson, *Fighter Pilots in World War I* (1977); Herbert M. Mason, Jr., *The Lafayette Escadrille* (1964); Donald Smythe, *Pershing* (1986); Lawrence Stallings, *The Doughboys: The Story of the AEF, 1917–1918* (1963); David Trask, *The United States in the Supreme War Council* (1961); Frank E. Vandiver, *Black Jack: The Life and Times of John J. Pershing* (1977); Russell Weigley, *The American Way of War* (1973).

Wartime Diplomacy.   Kathleen Burk, *Britain, America, and the Sinews of War* (1985); W. B. Fowler, *British-American Relations, 1917–1918* (1969); John Lewis Gaddis, *Russia, the Soviet Union and the United States* (1978); George F. Kennan, *Russia Leaves the War* (1956), and *Russia and the West Under Lenin and Stalin* (1961); Carl Parrini, *Heir to Empire: United States Economic Diplomacy, 1916–1923* (1969).

Politics and Government in Wartime.   Ray H. Abrams, *Preachers Present Arms: The Role of the American Churches and Clergy in World Wars I and II* (1969); Daniel R. Beaver, *Newton D. Baker and the American War Effort, 1917–1919* (1966); George T. Blakey, *Historians on the Homefront* (1970); William J. Breen, *Uncle Sam at Home* (1984); Zechariah Chaffee, Jr., *Free Speech in the United States* (1941); Charles Chatfield, *For Peace and Justice: Pacifism in America, 1914–1941* (1971); Edward M. Coffman, *The Hilt of the Sword: The Career of Peyton C. Marsh* (1966); Valerie Jean Conner, *The National War Labor Board* (1983); Alfred E. Conrebise, *War as Advertised: The Four Minute Men and America's Crusade, 1917–1918* (1984); Wayne Cornelius, *Building the Cactus Curtain: Mexican Migration and U.S. Responses from Wilson to Carter* (1980); Robert D. Cuff, *The War Industries Board: Business-Government Relations During World War I* (1973); Charles DeBenedettis, *Origins of the Modern Peace Movement* (1978); Harvey A. DeWeerd, *President Wilson Fights His War* (1968); Charles V. Forcey, *The Crossroads of Liberalism* (1961); Charles Gilbert, *American Financing of World War I* (1970); Otis L. Graham, Jr., *The Great Campaigns* (1971); Ellis W. Hawley, *The Great War and the Search for a Modern Order* (1979); Sondra Herman, *Eleven Against War* (1969); Donald Johnson, *The Challenge to America's Freedoms* (1963); David M. Kennedy, *Over Here* (1980); Seward Livermore, *Politics Is Adjourned* (1966); J. R. Mock and Cedric Larson, *Words That Won the War* (1939); Paul L. Murphy, *World War I and the Origins of Civil Liberties* (1984); George Nash, *The Life of Herbert Hoover: The Humanitarian, 1914–1917* (1990); Harold C. Peterson, *Propaganda for War: The Campaign Against American Neu-*

trality, 1914–1917 (1968); Harold C. Peterson and Gilbert Fite, *Opponents of War, 1917–1918* (1957); Richard Polenberg, *Fighting Faiths: The Abrams Case, the Supreme Court, and Free Speech* (1987); William Preston, Jr., *Aliens and Dissenters: Federal Suppression of Radicals, 1903–1933* (1963); Ronald Schaffer, *America in the Great War: The Rise of the War Welfare State* (1991); Harry N. Scheiber, *The Wilson Administration and Civil Liberties, 1917–1921* (1960); Jordan Schwarz, *The Speculator: Bernard M. Baruch in Washington, 1917–1965* (1981); John A. Thomas, *Reformers and War* (1987); Stephen Vaughn, *Holding Fast the Inner Lines: Democracy, Nationalism, and the Committee on Public Information* (1979); Neil A. Wynn, *From Progressivism to Prosperity: World War I and American Society* (1986).

Wartime Society and Culture. Allan M. Brandt, *No Magic Bullet: A Social History of Venereal Disease in the United States* (1985); Paul Chapman, *Schools as Sorters* (1988); Stanley Cooperman, *World War I and the American Novel* (1970); Alfred W. Crosby, Jr., *Epidemic and Peace, 1918* (1976); Maurine W. Greenwald, *Women, War, and Work* (1980); Carol S. Gruber, *Mars and Minerva* (1975); John Higham, *Strangers in the Land: Patterns of American Nativism* (1955); Michael T. Isenberg, *War on Film* (1981); Frederick C. Luebke, *Bonds of Loyalty: German-Americans and World War I* (1974); Elizabeth Payne, *Reform, Labor, and Feminism: Margaret Dreier Robins and the Women's Trade Union League* (1988); Michael Pearlman, *To Make Democracy Safe for America: Patricians and Preparedness in the Progressive Era* (1984); Barbara J. Steinson, *American Women's Activism in World War I* (1982).

Wilson and the Peace. Lloyd Ambrosius, *Woodrow Wilson and the American Diplomatic Tradition* (1987); John Morton Blum, *Woodrow Wilson and the Politics of Morality* (1956); Robert H. Ferrell, *Woodrow Wilson and World War I* (1985); Peter Filene, *Americans and the Soviet Experiment* (1967); Denna Fleming, *The United States and the League of Nations* (1932); Inga Floto, *Colonel House at Paris* (1980); John L. Gaddis, *Russia, the Soviet Union, and the United States* (1978); Lloyd C. Gardner, *Safe for Democracy: The Anglo-American Response to Revolution, 1913–1923* (1984); John A. Garraty, *Henry Cabot Lodge* (1953); Robert Jackson, *At War with the Bolsheviks: The Allied Intervention into Russia, 1917–1920* (1972); George Kennan, *Decision to Intervene* (1958); Thomas J. Knock, *To End All Wars: Woodrow Wilson and the Quest for a New World Order* (1992); Warren F. Kuehl, *Seeking World Order* (1969); Christopher Lasch, *The American Liberals and the Russian Revolution* (1962); N. Gordon Levin, Jr., *Woodrow Wilson and World Politics* (1968); Arthur S. Link, *Woodrow Wilson,* 5 vols. (1947–1965), *Wilson the Diplomatist* (1957), and *Woodrow Wilson: War, Revolution, and Peace* (1979); Arno Mayer, *Political Origins of the New Diplomacy, 1917–1918* (1963), *Wilson vs. Lenin* (1959), and *Politics and Diplomacy of Peacemaking: Containment and Counterrevolution* (1965); David W. McFadden, *Alternative Paths: Soviets and Americans, 1917–1920* (1993); Charles L. Mee, Jr., *The End of Order: Versailles 1919* (1980); Robert E. Osgood, *Ideals and Self-Interest in American Foreign Relations* (1953); Klaus Schwabe, *Woodrow Wilson, Revolutionary Germany, and Peacemaking, 1918–1919* (1985); Gene Smith, *When the Cheering Stopped* (1964); Ronald Steel, *Walter Lippmann and the American Century* (1980); Ralph Stone, *The Irreconcilables: The Fight Against the League of Nations* (1970); Arthur Walworth, *Wilson and the Peacemakers* (1986); William C. Widenor, *Henry Cabot Lodge and the Search for an American Foreign Policy* (1980).

Postwar America. Wesley M. Bagby, Jr., *The Road to Normalcy* (1962); David Brody, *Steelworkers in America* (1960), and *Labor in Crisis: The Steel Strike of 1919* (1965); Stanley Coben, *A. Mitchell Palmer* (1963); David Cronon, *Black Moses* (1955); Roberta Strauss

Feuerlicht, *Justice Crucified: The Story of Sacco and Vanzetti* (1977); Robert L. Friedheim, *The Seattle General Strike* (1965); Amy J. Garvey, *Garvey and Garveyism* (1963); Robert V. Haynes, *A Night of Violence: The Houston Riot of 1917* (1976); Florette Henri, *Black Migration: Movement Northward, 1900–1920* (1975); Kenneth Kusmer, *A Ghetto Takes Shape* (1976); David Montgomery, *The Fall of the House of Labor: The Workplace, the State, and American Labor Activism, 1865–1921* (1987); Robert K. Murray, *The Red Scare: A Study in National Hysteria, 1919–1920* (1955); Burl Noggle, *Into the Twenties* (1974); Stuart I. Rochester, *American Liberal Disillusionment in the Wake of World War I* (1977); Elliot Rudwick, *Race Riot at East St. Louis* (1964); Francis Russell, *A City in Terror* (1975); Alan Spear, *Black Chicago* (1967). Judith Stein, *The World of Marcus Garvey* (1986); William M. Tuttle, Jr., *Race Riot: Chicago in the Red Summer of 1919* (1970); Theodore Vincent, *Black Power and the Garvey Movement* (1971).

CHAPTER 24 THE NEW ERA

General Studies.   Frederick Lewis Allen, *Only Yesterday* (1931); John Braeman, Robert Bremner, and David Brody, eds., *Change and Continuity in Twentieth Century America: The 1920s* (1968); Ellis Hawley, *The Great War and the Search for a Modern Order* (1979); John D. Hicks, *Republican Ascendancy* (1960); Isabel Leighton, ed., *The Aspirin Age* (1949); William E. Leuchtenburg, *The Perils of Prosperity*, rev. ed. (1994); Donald R. McCoy, *Coming of Age* (1973); Michael Parrish, *Anxious Decades: America in Prosperity and Depression, 1920–1941* (1992); Geoffrey Perrett, *America in the Twenties* (1982); Arthur M. Schlesinger, Jr., *The Crisis of the Old Order* (1957); George Soule, *Prosperity Decade: From War to Depression* (1947).

Labor, Agriculture, and Economic Growth.   Guy Alchon, *The Invisible Hand of Planning: Capitalism, Social Science, and the State in the 1920s* (1985); Irving Bernstein, *The Lean Years: A History of the American Worker, 1920–1933* (1960); David Brody, *Steelworkers in America* (1960), and *Workers in Industrial America* (1980); Alfred Chandler, *Strategy and Structure* (1962); Lisabeth Cohen, *Making a New Deal: Industrial Workers in Chicago, 1919–1939* (1990); Melvyn Dubofsky, *The State and Labor in Modern America* (1994); Gilbert C. Fite, *George Peek and the Fight for Farm Parity* (1954), and *American Farmers: The New Minority* (1981); Louis Galambos, *Competition and Cooperation* (1966); Louis Galambos and Joseph Pratt, *The Rise of the Corporate Commonwealth: U.S. Business and Public Policy in the Twentieth Century* (1988); Peter Gottlieb, *Making Their Own Way: Southern Blacks' Migration to Pittsburgh, 1916–1930* (1987); Jim Potter, *The American Economy Between the Wars* (1974); Theodore Saloutos and John D. Hicks, *Twentieth Century Populism* (1951); George Soule, *Prosperity Decade* (1947); Sharon Hartman Strom, *Beyond the Typewriter: Gender, Class, and the Origins of Modern American Office Work, 1900–1930* (1992); Mira Wilkins, *The Maturing of Multinational Enterprise: American Business Abroad from 1914 to 1970* (1974); Leslie Woodcock, *Wage-Earning Women* (1979); Gerald Zahavi, *Workers, Managers, and Welfare Capitalism* (1988); Robert Zieger, *Republicans and Labor* (1969).

The New Culture.   Erik Barnouw, *A Tower in Babel: A History of American Radio to 1933* (1966); Daniel Boorstin, *The Americans: The Democratic Experience* (1973); Paul Carter, *The Twenties in America* (1968), and *Another Part of the Twenties* (1977); Stanley Coben, *Rebellion Against Victorianism: The Impetus for Cultural Change in 1920s America* (1991); Ed Cray, *Chrome Colossus* (1980); Robert Creamer, *Babe* (1974); Kenneth S. Davis, *The*

Hero: Charles A. Lindbergh (1959); Ann Douglas: *Terrible Honesty: Mongrel Manhattan in the 1920s* (1995); Susan J. Douglas, *Inventing American Broadcasting* (1987); Ronald Edsforth, *Class Conflict and Cultural Consensus: The Making of a Mass Consumer Society: Flint, Michigan* (1987); Melvin Patrick Ely, *The Adventures of Amos 'n' Andy: A Social History of an American Phenomenon* (1991); Stewart Ewen, *Captains of Consciousness* (1976); James J. Flink, *The Car Culture* (1975), and *The Automobile Age* (1988); Stephen Fox, *The Mirror Makers: A History of American Advertising and Its Creators* (1984); Dana Frank, *Purchasing Power: Consumer Organizing, Gender and Seattle Labor Movement, 1919–1929* (1994); Neal Gabler, *An Empire of Their Own: How the Jews Invented Hollywood* (1988); Harvey Green, *Fit for America* (1986); Allen Guttmann, *A Whole New Ball Game* (1988); Sumiko Higashi, *Virgins, Vamps, and Flappers: The American Silent Movie Heroine* (1978); Daniel Horowitz, *The Morality of Spending: Attitudes Toward the Consumer Society in America, 1875–1940* (1985); Jackson Lears, *Fables of Abundance: A Cultural History of Advertising in America* (1994); Robert Lynd and Helen Lynd, *Middletown* (1929); Roland Marchand, *Advertising the American Dream* (1985); Lary May, *Screening Out the Past* (1980); Fred J. McDonald, *Don't Touch That Dial* (1979); Clay McShane, *Down the Asphalt Path: The Automobile and the American City* (1994); Zane Miller, *The Urbanization of America* (1973); William Leach, *Land of Desire: Merchants, Power, and the Rise of a New American Culture* (1993); Kathy H. Ogren, *The Jazz Revolution: Twenties America and the Meaning of Jazz* (1989); Michael Oriard, *Reading Football: How the Popular Press Created an American Spectacle* (1993); Kathy Peiss, *Cheap Amusements: Working Women and Leisure in Turn-of-the-Century New York* (1986); Daniel Pope, *The Making of Modern Advertising* (1983); Randy Roberts, *Jack Dempsey, The Manassa Mauler* (1979); Philip T. Rosen, *The Modern Stentors: Radio Broadcasting and the Federal Government, 1920–1933* (1980); Joan Shelley Rubin, *The Making of Middlebrow Culture* (1992); Robert Sklar, *Movie-Made America* (1975); Susan Smulyan, *Selling Radio: The Commercialization of American Broadcasting, Smithsonian Institution Press* (1994); Susan Strasser, *Satisfaction Guaranteed: The Making of the American Mass Market* (1989); Bernard A. Weisberger, *The Dream Maker* (1979).

Women, Family, and Youth.   W. Andrew Achenbaum, *Shades of Gray: Old Age, American Values, and Federal Policies Since 1920* (1983); Beth L. Bailey, *From Back Porch to Front Seat* (1988); Lois Banner, *American Beauty* (1983); Susan Porter Benson, *Counter Cultures: Saleswomen, Managers, and Customers in American Department Stores, 1890–1940* (1986); William H. Chafe, *The American Woman: Her Changing Social and Political Roles* (1972); Ellen Chesler, *Woman of Valor: Margaret Sanger and the Birth Control Movement in America* (1992); Howard P. Chudacoff, *How Old Are You? Age in American Culture* (1989); Nancy Cott, *The Grounding of American Feminism* (1987); Ruth Schwarz Cowan, *More Work for Mother* (1983); John D'Emilio and Estelle B. Friedman, *Intimate Matters: A History of Sexuality in America* (1988); Paula Fass, *The Damned and Beautiful* (1977); David H. Fischer, *Growing Old in America* (1977); Linda Gordon, *Woman's Body, Woman's Right* (1976); Helen Lefkowitz Horowitz, *Campus Life: Undergraduate Cultures from the End of the Eighteenth Century to the Present* (1987); Alice Kessler-Harris, *Out to Work: A History of Wage-Earning Women in America* (1982); J. Stanley Lemons, *The Woman Citizen: Social Feminism in the 1920s* (1973); Elizabeth Lunbeck, *The Psychiatric Persuasion: Knowledge, Gender, and Power in Modern America* (1994); Sheila Rothman, *Woman's Proper Place* (1978); Lois Scharf, *To Work and to Wed: Female Employment, Feminism, and the Great Depression* (1980); Virginia Scharff, *Taking the Wheel* (1991); Susan Strasser, *Never Done: A History of American Housework* (1982); Winifred Wandersee, *Women's Work and Family Values, 1920–1940* (1981); Renold Wilk, *Henry Ford and Grass Roots America* (1972).

Intellectuals and the Arts. Charles C. Alexander, *Here the Country Lies: Nationalism and the Arts in Twentieth Century America* (1980); Houston Baker, Jr., *Modernism and the Harlem Renaissance* (1987); Loren Baritz, ed., *The Culture of the Twenties* (1970); Cleanth Brooks, *William Faulkner: The Yoknapatawpha Country* (1963); Paul Conkin, *The Southern Agrarians* (1988); Malcolm Cowley, *Exiles Return* (1934); Robert Crunden, *From Self to Society: Transition in American Thought, 1919–1941* (1972); George H. Douglas, *H. L. Mencken* (1978); Frederick J. Hoffman, *The Twenties* (1949); Nathan I. Huggins, *Harlem Renaissance* (1971); Gloria T. Hull, *Color, Sex, and Poetry: Three Women Writers of the Harlem Renaissance* (1987); David L. Lewis, *When Harlem Was in Vogue* (1981); Roderick Nash, *The Nervous Generation: American Thought, 1917–1930* (1969); John Stewart, *The Burden of Time* (1965); Kenneth M. Wheeler and Virginia L. Lussier, eds., *Women, the Arts, and the 1920s in Paris and New York* (1982); Edmund Wilson, *The Twenties* (1975).

Cultural Conflicts. Charles C. Alexander, *The Ku Klux Klan in the Southwest* (1965); Paul Avrich, *Sacco and Vanzetti: The Anarchist Background* (1991); Herbert Asbury, *The Great Illusion* (1950); Kathleen M. Blee, *Women of the Klan: Racism and Gender in the 1920s* (1991); David Chalmers, *Hooded Americanism* (1965); Norman Clark, *Deliver Us from Evil* (1976); Elton C. Fax, *Garvey* (1972); Norman Furniss, *The Fundamentalist Controversy* (1954); Ray Ginger, *Six Days or Forever?* (1958); Joseph Gusfeld, *Symbolic Crusade* (1963); John Higham, *Strangers in the Land* (1963); Kenneth Jackson, *The Ku Klux Klan in the City* (1965); K. Austin Kerr, *Organized for Prohibition: A New History of the Anti-Saloon League* (1985); Don Kirschner, *City and Country: Rural Responses to Urbanization in the 1920s* (1970); Lawrence Levine, *Defender of the Faith, William Jennings Bryan: The Last Decade, 1915–1925* (1965); Nancy MacLean, *Behind the Mask of Chivalry: The Making of the Second Ku Klux Klan* (1994); George M. Marsden, *Fundamentalism and American Culture* (1980); William G. McLoughlin, *Modern Revivalism* (1959); Leonard Moore, *Citizen Klansmen: The Ku Klux Klan in Indiana, 1921–1928* (1991); George J. Sanchez, *Becoming Mexican American: Ethnicity, Culture, and Identity in Chicano Los Angeles, 1900–1945* (1993); Andrew Sinclair, *The Era of Excess* (1962); Richard K. Tucker, *The Dragon and the Cross: The Rise and Fall of the Ku Klux Klan in Middle America* (1991); Theodore Vincent, *Black Power and the Garvey Movement* (1971).

Politics and Government. Kristi Andersen, *The Creation of a Democratic Majority, 1928–1936* (1979); LeRoy Ashby, *Spearless Leader* (1972); Christine Bolt, *American Indian Policy and American Reform* (1987); David Burner, *The Politics of Provincialism* (1967), and *Herbert Hoover* (1979); E. Paula Elder, *Governor Alfred E. Smith: The Politician as Reformer* (1983); Frank Freidel, *Franklin D. Roosevelt: The Ordeal* (1954), and *Franklin D. Roosevelt: The Triumph* (1956); James N. Giglio, *H. M. Daugherty and the Politics of Expediency* (1978); James Gilbert, *Designing the Industrial State* (1972); Oscar Handlin, *Al Smith and His America* (1958); William Harbaugh, *Lawyer's Lawyer* (1973); Ellis Hawley, *Herbert Hoover as Secretary of Commerce: Studies in New Era Thought and Practice* (1974); Robert Herzstein, *Henry R. Luce: A Political Portrait of the Man Who Created the American Century* (1994); Robert F. Himmelberg, *The Origins of the National Recovery Administration: Business, Government, and the Trade Association Issue, 1921–1933* (1976); Morton Keller, *Regulating a New Society: Public Policy and Social Change in America, 1900–1933* (1996); Alan Lichtman, *Prejudice and the Old Politics* (1979); Richard Lowitt, *George W. Norris*, vol. 2 (1971); Carol R. McCann, *Birth Control Politics in the United States, 1916–1945* (1994); Donald R. McCoy, *Calvin Coolidge* (1967); Robert K. Murray, *The Politics of Normalcy* (1973), and *The Harding Era* (1969); Burl Noggle, *Teapot Dome* (1962); Elisabeth Israels Perry, *Belle Moskowitz: Feminine Politics and the Exercise of Power in the Age of Alfred E. Smith* (1987);

Francis Russell, *The Shadow of Blooming Grove* (1968); Andrew Sinclair, *The Available Man* (1965); David P. Thelen, *Robert M. La Follette and the Insurgent Spirit* (1978); George B. Tindall, *The Emergence of the New South* (1967); Eugene Trani and David Wilson, *The Presidency of Warren G. Harding* (1977); G. Edward White, *Justice Oliver Wendell Holmes: Law and the Inner Self* (1993); William Allen White, *A Puritan in Babylon* (1940); John Hoff Wilson, *Herbert Hoover: Forgotten Progressive* (1975).

CHAPTER 25 THE GREAT DEPRESSION

The Coming of the Depression.   Michael Bernstein, *The Great Depression: Delayed Recovery and Economic Change in America, 1929–1939* (1987); Lester V. Chandler, *America's Greatest Depression* (1970); Milton Friedman and Anna Schwartz, *The Great Contraction* (1965), or Chapter 7 of *A Monetary History of the United States* (1963); John Kenneth Galbraith, *The Great Crash* (1954); Susan E. Kennedy, *The Banking Crisis of 1933* (1973); Charles Kindelberger, *The World in Depression* (1973); Broadus Mitchell, *Depression Decade* (1947); Robert Sobel, *The Great Bull Market* (1968); Peter Temin, *Did Monetary Forces Cause the Great Depression?* (1976).

The Impact of the Depression.   Francisco Balerman, *In Defense of La Raza: The Los Angeles Mexican Consulate and the Mexican Community, 1929–1936* (1982); Ann Banks, ed., *First-Person America* (1980); Irving Bernstein, *The Lean Years* (1960); Caroline Bird, *The Invisible Scar* (1966); Glen H. Elder, Jr., *Children of the Great Depression* (1974); Federal Writers' Project, *These Are Our Lives* (1939); James N. Gregory, *American Exodus: The Dust Bowl Migration and Okie Culture in California* (1989); Abraham Hoffman, *Unwanted Mexican-Americans in the Great Depression* (1974); Richard Lowitt and Maurine Beasley, eds., *One-Third of a Nation: Lorena Hickock Reports the Great Depression* (1981); Robert S. McElvaine, ed., *Down and Out in the Great Depression: Letters from the Forgotten Man* (1983); William Mullins, *The Depression and the Urban West Coast, 1929–1933* (1991); Janet Poppendieck, *Breadlines Knee-Deep in Wheat: Food Assistance in the Great Depression* (1986); Udo Sautter, *Three Cheers for the Unemployed: Government and Unemployment Before the New Deal* (1991); Arthur M. Schlesinger, Jr., *The Crisis of the Old Order* (1957); Walter Stein, *California and the Dust Bowl Migration* (1973); Bernard Sternsher, *Hitting Home: The Great Depression in Town and Country* (1970); Catherine McNicol Stock, *Main Street in Crisis: The Great Depression and the Old Middle Class on the Northern Plains* (1992); Studs Terkel, *Hard Times* (1970); Tom Terrill and Jerrold Hirsch, *Such as Us: Southern Voices of the Thirties* (1978); Donald Worster, *Dust Bowl: The Southern Plains in the 1930s* (1979).

Depression-Era Culture and Society.   Charles C. Alexander, *Nationalism in American Thought, 1930–1945* (1969); Frederick Lewis Allen, *Since Yesterday* (1940); Andrew Bergman, *We're in the Money: Depression America and Its Films* (1971); Camille Guerin-Gonzales, *Mexican Workers and American Dreams: Immigration, Repatriation, and California Farm Labor, 1900–1939* (1994); Anthony Heilbut, *Exiled in Paradise: German Refugee Artists and Intellectuals in America from the 1930s to the Present* (1938); Richard Krickus, *Pursuing the American Dream* (1976); Robert Lynd and Helen Merrell Lynd, *Middletown in Transition* (1935); Alice Goldfarb Marquis, *Hopes and Ashes: The Birth of Modern Times, 1929–1939* (1986); Jeffrey Meikle, *Twentieth Century Limited: Industrial Design in America, 1925–1939* (1979); Gilbert Osofsky, *Harlem: The Making of a Ghetto* (1966); Gilman Ostrander, *American Civilization in the First Machine Age* (1970); David P. Peeler, *Hope Among Us Yet: Social Criticism and Social Thought in the Depression Years* (1987); Richard

Pells, *Radical Visions and American Dreams: Culture and Social Thought in the Depression Years* (1973); Thomas Schatz, *The Genius of the System: Hollywood Film Making in the Studio Era* (1988); Ed Sikov, *Screwball: Hollywood's Madcap Romantic Comedies* (1989); Warren Susman, *Culture as History* (1984); (See Suggested Readings at the end of Chapter 26 for more literature on African Americans, Hispanic Americans, Asian Americans, Indians, and labor during the Depression.)

Women and the Depression.   Julia K. Blackwelder, *Women of the Depression: Caste and Culture in San Antonio, 1919–1939* (1984); William Chafe, *The American Woman* (1972); Joan Jensen and Lois Scharf, eds., *Decades of Discontent: The Women's Movement, 1920–1940* (1983); Marjorie Rosen, *Popcorn Venus: Women, Movies, and the American Dream* (1971); Vicki Ruiz, *Cannery Women, Cannery Lives: Mexican Women, Unionization, and the California Food Processing Industry, 1930–1950* (1987); Lois Scharf, *To Work and to Wed: Female Employment, Feminism, and the Great Depression* (1980); Susan Ware, *Holding Their Own: American Women in the 1930s* (1982); Jeane Westin, *Making Do: How Women Survived the '30s* (1976); Patricia Zavella, *Women's Work and Chicano Families* (1987).

The Hoover Presidency.   William J. Barber, *From New Era to New Deal: Herbert Hoover, The Economists, and American Economic Policy, 1921–1933* (1985); David Burner, *Herbert Hoover* (1978); Martin Fausold, *The Presidency of Herbert C. Hoover* (1985); Martin Fausold and George Mazuzun, eds., *The Hoover Presidency* (1974), and *Herbert Hoover, The Great Depression* (1952); James S. Olsen, *Herbert Hoover and the Reconstruction Finance Corporation* (1977), and *Saving Capitalism: The Reconstruction Finance Corporation and the New Deal, 1933–1940* (1988); Albert U. Romasco, *The Poverty of Abundance* (1965); Jordan Schwarz, *The Interregnum of Despair* (1970); Harris Warren, *Herbert Hoover and the Great Depression* (1959); Joan Hoff Wilson, *Herbert Hoover: Forgotten Progressive* (1975).

Politics and Protest.   Gary Dean Best, *FDR and the Bonus Marchers, 1933–1935* (1992); David Burner, *The Politics of Provincialism* (1967); Robert Cohen, *When the Old Left Was Young: Student Radicals and America's First Mass Student Movement, 1929–1941* (1993); Roger Daniels, *The Bonus March* (1971); Frank Freidel, *The Triumph* (1956), and *Launching the New Deal* (1973); Donald Grubbs, *Cry from the Cotton* (1971); Dorothy Healey and Maurice Isserman, *Dorothy Healey Remembers: A Life in the American Communist Party* (1990); Irving Howe and Lewis Coser, *The American Communist Party: A Critical History* (1957); Robin D. G. Kelley, *Hammer and Hoe: Alabama Communists During the Great Depression* (1990); Thomas Kessner, *Fiorello H. La Guardia and the Making of Modern New York* (1989); Harvey Klehr, *The Heyday of American Communism: The Depression Decade* (1984); Donald Lisio, *The President and Protest: Hoover, Conspiracy, and the Bonus Riot* (1974); Mark Naison, *Communists in Harlem During the Depression* (1983); Eliot Rosen, *Hoover, Roosevelt, and the Brains Trust* (1977); Arthur M. Schlesinger, Jr., *The Crisis of the Old Order* (1957); John Shover, *Cornbelt Rebellion* (1965); Rexford G. Tugwell, *The Brains Trust* (1968).

CHAPTER 26 THE NEW DEAL

General and Biographical Studies.   Anthony J. Badger, *The New Deal* (1989); John Braemen et al., eds., *The New Deal*, 2 vols. (1975); James MacGregor Burns, *Roosevelt: The Lion and the Fox* (1956); Blanche Wiesen Cooke, *Eleanor Roosevelt: Volume One,*

1884–1933 (1992); Paul Conkin, *The New Deal*, 2nd ed. (1975); Kenneth Davis, *FDR: The New York Years: 1928–1933* (1985), and *FDR: The New Deal Years, 1933–1937* (1986); Peter Fearon, *War, Prosperity, and Depression* (1987); Steve Fraser and Gary Gerstle, eds., *The Rise and Fall of New Deal Liberalism* (1988); Frank Freidel, *Franklin D. Roosevelt*, 4 vols. (1952–1973), and *Franklin D. Roosevelt: A Rendezvous with Destiny* (1990); Joseph P. Lash, *Eleanor and Franklin* (1971); William E. Leuchtenburg, *Franklin D. Roosevelt and the New Deal* (1963), *In the Shadow of FDR* (1983), and *The FDR Years: On Roosevelt and His Legacy* (1995); Katie Louchheim, *The Making of the New Deal* (1983); Richard Lowitt, *The New Deal and the West* (1984); Robert S. McElvaine, *The Great Depression* (1984); Gerald Nash, *The Great Depression and World War II* (1979); Edgar Robinson, *The Roosevelt Leadership* (1955); Arthur M. Schlesinger, Jr., *The Age of Roosevelt*, 3 vols. (1957–1960); Harvard Sitkoff, ed., *Fifty Years Later: The New Deal Evaluated* (1985); Geoffrey Ward, *Before the Trumpet: Young Franklin Roosevelt, 1882–1905* (1985), and *A First-Class Temperament: The Emergence of Franklin Roosevelt* (1989); J. H. Wilson and Marjorie Lightman, eds., *Without Precedent: The Life and Career of Eleanor Roosevelt* (1984).

New Deal Politics and Programs. Mimi Abramowitz, *Regulating the Lives of Women* (1988); Bernard Bellush, *The Failure of the NRA* (1975); Donald Brand, *Corporatism and the Rule of Law* (1988); William R. Brock, *Welfare, Democracy, and the New Deal* (1987); Searle Charles, *Minister of Relief* (1963); Ralph F. De Bedts, *The New Deal's SEC* (1964); Herbert Feis, *Characters in Crisis* (1966); Sidney Fine, *The Automobile Under the Blue Eagle* (1963); Kenneth Finegold and Theda Skocpol, *State and Party in America's New Deal* (1995); Frank Freidel, *Launching the New Deal* (1973); Gerald H. Gamm, *The Making of New Deal Democrats: Voting Behavior and Realignment in Boston, 1920–1940* (1989); Colin Gordon, *New Deals: Business, Labor, and Politics in America, 1920–1935* (1994); Otis Graham, *Encore for Reform* (1967); Nancy L. Grant, *TVA and Black Americans: Planning for the Status Quo* (1990); Ellis Hawley, *The New Deal and the Problem of Monopoly* (1966); Peter H. Irons, *The New Deal Lawyers* (1982); Mark Leff, *The Limits of Symbolic Reform: The New Deal and Taxation, 1933–1939* (1984); Thomas K. McCraw, *TVA and the Power Fight* (1970); George McJimsey, *Harry Hopkins: Ally of the Poor and Defender of Democracy* (1987); Sidney M. Milkis, *The Presidents and Their Parties: The Transformation of the American Party System Since the End of the New Deal* (1993); Raymond Moley and Eliot Rosen, *The First New Deal* (1966); Michael Parrish, *Securities Regulation and the New Deal* (1970); James T. Patterson, *America's Struggle Against Poverty, 1900–1980* (1981); Albert U. Romasco, *The Politics of Recovery: Roosevelt's New Deal* (1983); John Salmond, *The Civilian Conservation Corps* (1967); Bonnie Fox Schwartz, *The Civil Works Administration, 1933–1934* (1984); Jordan Schwarz, *The New Dealers: Power Politics in the Age of Roosevelt* (1993); Susan Ware, *Beyond Suffrage* (1981), and *Partner and I: Molly Dewson, Feminism, and New Deal Politics* (1987).

Agriculture. Christina Campbell, *The Farm Bureaus* (1962); David Conrad, *The Forgotten Farmers* (1965); Lowell K. Dyson, *Red Harvest: The Communist Party and American Farmers* (1982); Gilbert Fite, *George M. Peek and the Fight for Farm Parity* (1954); David Hamilton, *From New Day to New Deal: American Farm Policy from Hoover to Roosevelt, 1928–1933* (1991); Richard S. Kirkendall, *Social Scientists and Farm Politics in the Age of Roosevelt* (1966); Paul Mertz, *The New Deal and Southern Rural Poverty* (1978); Van L. Perkins, *Crisis in Agriculture* (1969); Bruce Shulman, *From Cotton Belt to Sunbelt* (1991).

Depression Dissidents.   David H. Bennett, *Demagogues in the Depression* (1969); Alan Brinkley, *Voices of Protest: Huey Long, Father Coughlin, and the Great Depression* (1982); Donald Grubbs, *Cry from the Cotton* (1971); William Ivy Hair, *The Kingfish and His Realm: The Life and Times of Huey P. Long* (1991); Glen Jeansonne, *Gerald L. K. Smith: Minister of Hate* (1988); Abraham Holzman, *The Townsend Movement* (1963); R. Alan Lawson, *The Failure of Independent Liberalism* (1971); Donald McCoy, *Angry Voices* (1958); Leo Ribuffo, *The Old Christian Right: The Protestant Far Right from the Great Depression to the Cold War* (1983); Arthur M. Schlesinger, Jr., *The Politics of Upheaval* (1960); Charles J. Tull, *Father Coughlin and the New Deal* (1965); David Warren, *Radio Priest: Charles Coughlin, The Father of Hate Radio* (1996); T. Harry Williams, *Huey Long* (1969); George Wolfskill, *Revolt of the Conservatives* (1962).

The "Second New Deal."   Sidney Baldwin, *Poverty and Politics: The Farm Security Administration* (1968); Edward Berkowitz, *Mr. Social Security: The Life of Wilbur J. Cohen* (1995); Paul Conkin, *Tomorrow a New World* (1971); Linda Gordon, *Pitied But Not Entitled: Single Mothers and the History of Welfare* (1994); J. Joseph Huthmacher, *Senator Robert Wagner and the Rise of Urban Liberalism* (1968); Roy Lubove, *The Struggle for Social Security* (1968); William F. McDonald, *Federal Relief Administration and the Arts* (1968); Jerre Mangione, *The Dream and the Deal* (1972); Jane deHart Matthews, *The Federal Theater* (1967); W. D. Rowley, *M. L. Wilson and the Campaign for Domestic Allotment* (1970).

The Late New Deal.   Leonard Baker, *Back to Back* (1967); Alan Brinkley, *The End of Reform: New Deal Liberalism in Recession and War* (1995); Frank Freidel, *FDR and the South* (1965); Barry Karl, *Executive Reorganization and Reform in the New Deal* (1963); William E. Leuchtenburg, *The Supreme Court Reborn: The Constitutional Revolution in the Age of Roosevelt* (1995); Dean May, *From New Deal to New Economics* (1981); James T. Patterson, *Congressional Conservatism and the New Deal* (1967), and *The New Deal and the States* (1969); Richard Polenberg, *Reorganizing Roosevelt's Government* (1966); Theodore Rosenof, *Dogma and Depression* (1972), and *Patterns of Political Economy in America* (1983); Herbert Stein, *The Fiscal Revolution in America* (1969); Charles Trout, *Boston: The Great Depression and the New Deal* (1977); George Wolfskill and John Hudson, *All But the People* (1969).

Blacks, Hispanics, Indians.   Rodolfo Acuna, *Occupied America*, rev. ed. (1981); Francisco E. Balerman, *In Defense of La Raza* (1982); Thomas Biolsi, *Organizing the Lakota: The Political Economy of the New Deal on the Pine Ridge and Rosebud Reservations* (1992); Ralph Bunche, *The Political Status of the Negro in the Age of FDR* (1973); Dan T. Carter, *Scottsboro* (1969); Vine DeLoria, Jr., *The Nations Within* (1984); Sarah Deutsch, *No Separate Refuge: Culture, Class, and Gender on the Anglo-Hispanic Frontier in the American Southwest, 1880–1940* (1987); John Dollard, *Caste and Class in a Southern Town*, 3rd ed. (1957); Cheryl Lynn Greenberg, *"Or Does It Explode?": Black Harlem in the Great Depression* (1991); Laurence C. Kelly, *The Assault on Assimilation: John Collier and the Origins of Indian Policy Reform* (1983); John B. Kirby, *Black Americans in the Roosevelt Era* (1980); Clifford Lytle, *American Indians, American Justice* (1983); Carey McWilliams, *Factories in the Field* (1939); Donald L. Parman, *The Navajos and the New Deal* (1976); Kenneth R. Philp, *John Collier's Crusade for Indian Reform, 1920–1954* (1977); Harvard Sitkoff, *A New Deal* *for Blacks* (1978); Graham D. Taylor, *The New Deal and American Indian Tribalism* (1980); Nancy Weiss, *Farewell to the Party of Lincoln: Black Politics in the Age of FDR* (1983), and *The National Urban League* (1974); Raymond Wolters, *Negroes and the Great Depression* (1970); Robert L. Zangrando, *The NAACP Crusade Against Lynching* (1980).

Labor.   Jerold Auerbach, *Labor and Liberty* (1966); John Barnard, *Walter Reuther and the Rise of the Auto Workers* (1983); Irving Bernstein, *Turbulent Years* (1970), and *A Caring Society: The New Deal, the Worker, and the Great Depression* (1985); David Brody, *Workers in Industrial America* (1980); Bert Cochran, *Labor and Communism* (1977); Lizabeth Cohen, *Making a New Deal: Industrial Workers in Chicago, 1919–1939* (1990); Melvyn Dubofsky and Warren Van Tine, *John L. Lewis* (1977); Elizabeth Faue, *Community of Suffering and Struggle: Women, Men, and the Labor Movement in Minnesota, 1915–1945* (1991); Sidney Fine, *Sit-Down* (1969); Joshua Freeman, *In Transit: The Transport Workers Union in New York City, 1933–1966* (1989); Peter Friedlander, *The Emergence of a UAW Local* (1975); Gary Gerstle, *Working-Class Americanism: The Politics of Labor in a Textile City 1914–1960* (1989); John W. Hevener, *Which Side Are You On? The Harlan County Coal Miners, 1931–1939* (1978); Nelson Lichtenstein, *The Most Dangerous Man in Detroit: Walter Reuther and the Fate of American Labor* (1995); August Meier and Elliott Rudwick, *Black Detroit and the Rise of the UAW* (1979); David Milton, *The Politics of U.S. Labor: From the Great Depression to the New Deal* (1980); Bruce Nelson, *Workers on the Waterfront: Seamen, Longshoremen, and Unionism in the 1930s* (1988); Daniel Nelson, *American Rubber Workers and Organized Labor, 1900–1941* (1988); Annelise Orleck, *Common Sense and a Little Fire: Women and Working-Class Politics in the United States, 1900–1965* (1995); Paula F. Pfeffer, *A. Philip Randolph, Pioneer of the Civil Rights Movement* (1990); Ronald W. Schatz, *The Electrical Workers* (1983); George G. Suggs, Jr., *Union Busting in the Tristate: The Oklahoma, Kansas, and Missouri Metal Workers Strike of 1935* (1986); Christopher L. Tomlins, *The State and the Unions* (1985); Robert H. Zieger, *John L. Lewis: Labor Leader* (1988), and *American Workers, American Unions, 1920–1985* (1986).

CHAPTER 27 THE GLOBAL CRISIS, 1921–1941

The 1920s.   Thomas Buckley, *The United States and the Washington Conference* (1970); Warren Cohen, *America's Response to China* (1971), and *Empire Without Tears* (1987); Frank Costigliola, *Awkward Dominion: American Political, Economic, and Cultural Relations with Europe, 1919–1933* (1984); Roger Dingman, *Power in the Pacific* (1976); L. Ethan Ellis, *Republican Foreign Policy, 1921–1933* (1968); Robert H. Ferrell, *Peace in Their Time* (1952); Michael J. Hogan, *Informal Entente: The Private Structure of Cooperation in Anglo-American Economic Diplomacy, 1918–1928* (1977); Akira Iriye, *The Cambridge History of American Foreign Relations*, vol. 3: *The Globalizing of America, 1913–1945*, and *After Imperialism* (1965); William Kamman, *A Search for Stability: United States Diplomacy Toward Nicaragua, 1925–1933* (1968); Melvyn P. Leffler, *The Elusive Quest: America's Pursuit of European Stability and French Security, 1919–1933* (1979); Merlo J. Pusey, *Charles Evans Hughes*, 2 vols. (1963); Joseph Tulchin, *The Aftermath of War* (1971); William Appleman Williams, *The Tragedy of American Diplomacy* (1962); Joan Hoff Wilson, *American Business and Foreign Policy, 1920–1933* (1968), and *Ideology and Economics* (1974).

The Hoover Years.   Alexander DeConde, *Hoover's Latin American Policy* (1951); Robert H. Ferrell, *American Diplomacy in the Great Depression* (1970); Elting Morison, *Turmoil* *and Tradition* (1960); Raymond O'Connor, *Perilous Equilibrium* (1962); Armin Rappaport, *Stimson and Japan* (1963).

New Deal Diplomacy. Edward E. Bennett, *Recognition of Russia* (1970); Dorothy Borg, *The United States and the Far Eastern Crisis of 1933–1938* (1964); Robert Browder, *The Origins of Soviet-American Diplomacy* (1953); Bruce J. Calder, *The Impact of Intervention* (1984); Robert Dallek, *Franklin D. Roosevelt and American Foreign Policy, 1932–1945* (1979); Beatrice Farnsworth, *William C. Bullitt and the Soviet Union* (1967); Peter Filene, *Americans and the Soviet Experiment, 1917–1933* (1967); Frank Freidel, *Launching the New Deal* (1973); Lloyd Gardner, *Economic Aspects of New Deal Diplomacy* (1964); Irwin F. Gellman, *Good Neighbor Diplomacy: United States Policies in Latin America, 1933–1945* (1979); David Green, *The Containment of Latin America* (1971); Warren F. Kimball, *The Juggler: Franklin Roosevelt as Wartime Statesman* (1991); Walter LaFeber, *Inevitable Revolutions* (1983); Lorenzo Meyer, *Mexico and the United States in the Oil Controversy* (1977); Bryce Wood, *The Making of the Good Neighbor Policy* (1961).

Isolationism and Pacifism. Selig Adler, *The Uncertain Giant* (1966), and *The Isolationist Impulse* (1957); Charles Chatfield, *For Peace and Justice: Pacifism in America, 1914–1941* (1971); Warren I. Cohen, *The American Revisionists* (1967); Wayne S. Cole, *America First* (1953); *Senator Gerald P. Nye and American Foreign Relations* (1962), *Charles A. Lindbergh and the Battle Against American Intervention in World War II* (1974), and *Roosevelt and the Isolationists, 1932–1945* (1983); Charles DeBenedetti, *Origins of the Modern American Peace Movement, 1915–1929* (1978), and *The Peace Reform in American History* (1980); Robert Divine, *The Reluctant Belligerent* (1965); Thomas N. Guinsburg, *The Pursuit of Isolation in the United States Senate from Versailles to Pearl Harbor* (1982); Manfred Jonas, *Isolationism in America* (1966); Thomas C. Kennedy, *Charles A. Beard and American Foreign Policy* (1975); William Langer and S. Everett Gleason, *The Challenge to Isolation* (1952), and *The Undeclared War* (1953); Richard Lowitt, *George W. Norris*, 3 vols. (1963–1978); John K. Nelson, *The Peace Prophets* (1967); Lawrence Wittner, *Rebels Against War* (1984).

The Coming of World War II. James MacGregor Burns, *Roosevelt: The Soldier of Freedom* (1970); Peter N. Carroll, *Odyssey of the Abraham Lincoln Brigade: Americans in the Spanish Civil War* (1994); Garry Clifford and Samuel R. Spencer, Jr., *The First Peacetime Draft* (1986); Roger Dingman, *Power in the Pacific* (1976); Bernard F. Donahoe, *Private Plans and Public Dangers* (1965); Herbert Feis, *The Road to Pearl Harbor* (1950); Waldo H. Heinrichs, Jr., *Threshold of War* (1988); Akira Iriye, *Across the Pacific* (1967), *After Imperialism: The Search for a New Order in the Far East, 1921–1933* (1965), and *The Origins of the Second World War in Asia and the Pacific* (1987); Manfred Jonas, *The United States and Germany* (1984); Warren Kimball, *The Most Unsordid Act: Lend-Lease, 1939–1941* (1970); Joseph Lash, *Roosevelt and Churchill* (1976); James Leutze, *Bargaining for Supremacy* (1977); Martin V. Melosi, *The Shadow of Pearl Harbor* (1977); Arnold Offner, *The Origins of the Second World War* (1975); Gordon Prange, *At Dawn We Slept* (1981), and *Pearl Harbor* (1986); Michael S. Sherry, *The Rise of American Airpower* (1987); David Reynolds, *The Creation of the Anglo-American Alliance, 1937–1941* (1982); David F. Schmitz, *The United States and Fascist Italy, 1922–1944* (1988); Jonathan Utley, *Going to War with Japan* (1985); Roberta Wohlstetter, *Pearl Harbor: Warning and Decision* (1962); David S. Wyman, *Paper Walls: America and the Refugee Crisis, 1938–1941* (1985).

CHAPTER 28 AMERICA IN A WORLD AT WAR

War and American Society. John Morton Blum, *V Was for Victory* (1976); Lewis A. Erenberg and Susan E. Hirsch, *The War in American Culture: Society and Consciousness During World War II* (1996); Mark J. Harris et al., *The Homefront* (1984); Glen Jeansonne, *Women of the Far Right: The Mothers' Movement and World War II* (1996); Richard R. Lingeman, *Don't You Know There's a War On?* (1970); Gerald D. Nash, *The American West Transformed: The Impact of the Second World War* (1985); Geoffrey Perrett, *Days of Sadness, Years of Triumph: The American People, 1939–1945* (1974); Richard Polenberg, *War and Society* (1972); Studs Terkel, *"The Good War": An Oral History of World War II* (1984).

War Mobilization and Wartime Politics. Oscar E. Anderson, Jr., *The New World* (1962); Ellsworth Barnard, *Wendell Willkie* (1966); Chester Bowles, *Promises to Keep* (1971); Alan Brinkley, *The End of Reform: New Deal Liberalism in Recession and War* (1995); David Brinkley, *Washington Goes to War* (1987); James MacGregor Burns, *Roosevelt: The Soldier of Freedom* (1970); Bruce Catton, *War Lords of Washington* (1946); Lester V. Chandler, *Inflation in the United States, 1940–1948* (1951); Alan Clive, *State of War: Michigan in World War II* (1979); George Q. Flynn, *The Mess in Washington: Manpower Mobilization in World War II* (1979); Doris Kearns Goodwin, *No Ordinary Time: Franklin and Eleanor Roosevelt: The Home Front in World War II* (1994); Leslie R. Groves, *Now It Can Be Told* (1962); Howell John Harris, *The Right to Manage* (1982); Maurice Isserman, *Which Side Were You On? The American Communist Party During World War II* (1982); Eliot Janeway, *Struggle for Survival* (1951); Paul A. C. Koistinen, *The Military-Industrial Complex: A Historical Perspective* (1980); Philip Knightley, *The First Casualty* (1975); Nelson Lichtenstein, *Labor's War at Home: The CIO in World War II* (1982); Donald Nelson, *Arsenal of Democracy* (1946); Joel Seidman, *American Labor from Defense to Reconversion* (1953); Bradley F. Smith, *The Shadow Warriors: The OSS and the Origins of the CIA* (1983); Richard Steele, *Propaganda in an Open Society* (1985); Patrick S. Washburn, *A Question of Sedition: The Federal Government's Investigation of the Black Press During World War II* (1986); Michi Weglyn, *Years of Infamy: The Untold Story of America's Concentration Camps* (1976); Alan M. Winkler, *The Politics of Propaganda; The Office of War Information, 1942–1945* (1978).

The War and Race. Beth Bailey and David Farber, *The First Strange Place: The Alchemy of Race and Sex in World War II Hawaii* (1993); Domenic J. Capeci, Jr., *The Harlem Riot of 1943* (1977), and *Race Relations in Wartime Detroit* (1987); Richard M. Dalfiume, *Desegregation of the U.S. Armed Forces* (1969); Roger Daniels, *The Politics of Prejudice* (1962), *Concentration Camps, USA: Japanese Americans and World War II* (1971), and *Prisoners Without Trial: Japanese Americans in World War II* (1993); John W. Dower, *War Without Mercy: Race and Power in the Pacific War* (1986); Mario T. Garcia, *Mexican-Americans: Leadership, Ideology, and Identity, 1930–1960* (1989); Herbert Garfinkel, *When Negroes March* (1959); Audrie Girdner and Anne Loftis, *The Great Betrayal* (1969); Bill Hosokawa, *Nisei* (1969); Peter Irons, *Justice at War* (1983); Thomas James, *Exiles Within: The Schooling of Japanese-Americans, 1942–1945* (1987); Valerie J. Matsumoto, *Farming the Home Place: A Japanese American Community in California, 1919–1982* (1993); Philip McGuire, ed., *Taps for a Jim Crow Army: Letters from Black Soldiers in World War II* (1982); Mauricio Mazon, *The Zoot-Suit Riots* (1984); August Meier and Elliott Rudwick, *CORE* (1973);

Louis Ruchames, *Race, Jobs, and Politics* (1953); Holly Cowan Shulman, *The Voice of America* (1991); Neil Wynn, *The Afro-American and the Second World War* (1976).

Women and the War. Karen Anderson, *Wartime Women: Sex Roles, Family Relations, and the Status of Women During World War II* (1981); D'Ann Campbell, *Women at War with America* (1984); Sherna B. Gluck, *Rosie the Riveter Revisited* (1987); Susan Hartmann, *The Homefront and Beyond: American Women in the 1940s* (1982); Margaret R. Higgonet et al., *Behind the Lines: Gender and the Two World Wars* (1987); Maureen Honey, *Creating Rosie the Riveter: Class, Gender, and Propaganda During World War II* (1984); Ruth Milkman, *Gender at Work: The Dynamics of Job Segregation by Sex During World War II* (1987); Susan M. Reverby, *Ordered to Care: The Dilemma of American Nursing, 1850–1945* (1987); Leila Rupp, *Mobilizing Women for War* (1978).

Wartime Military and Diplomatic Experiences. Stephen Ambrose, *The Supreme Commander* (1970), *Eisenhower: Soldier, General of the Army, President-Elect* (1983), and *D-Day: June 6, 1944* (1994); Albert Russell Buchanan, *The United States and World War II*, 2 vols. (1962); James MacGregor Burns, *Roosevelt: The Soldier of Freedom* (1970); Winston S. Churchill, *The Second World War*, 6 vols. (1948–1953); Robert Divine, *Roosevelt and World War II* (1969), and *Second Chance* (1967); Dwight D. Eisenhower, *Crusade in Europe* (1948); John S. D. Eisenhower, *Allies: Pearl Harbor to D-Day* (1982); Kenneth Greenfield, *American Strategy in World War II* (1963); Max Hastings, *Overlord: D-Day and the Battle for Normandy* (1984); Patrick Heardon, *Roosevelt Confronts Hitler: American Entry into World War II* (1987); Godfrey Hodgson, *The Colonel: The Life and Wars of Henry Stimson, 1867–1950* (1990); Michael Howard, *The Mediterranean Strategy in World War II* (1968); Margaret Hoyle, *A World in Flames* (1970); D. Clayton James, *A Time for Giants: Politics of the American High Command in World War II* (1987); John Keegan, *Six Armies in Normandy: From D-Day to the Liberation of Paris, June 6–August 25, 1944* (1982); Warren Kimball, *The Juggler: Franklin Roosevelt as Wartime Statesman* (1991); E. J. Kind and W. M. Whitehill, *Fleet Admiral King* (1952); Charles B. McDonald, *The Mighty Endeavor* (1969); William Manchester, *American Caesar* (1979); Samuel Eliot Morison, *Strategy and Compromise* (1958), *History of United States Naval Operations in World War II*, 14 vols. (1947–1960), and *The Two Ocean War* (1963); Geoffrey Perret, *There's a War to Be Won: The United States Army in World War II* (1991); Forrest Pogue, *George C. Marshall*, 2 vols. (1963–1966); Gordon W. Prange, *At Dawn We Slept: The Untold Story of Pearl Harbor* (1981); Fletcher Pratt, *War for the World* (1951); Cornelius Ryan, *The Longest Day* (1959), and *The Last Battle* (1966); Ronald Schaffer, *Wings of Judgment: American Bombing in World War II* (1985); Michael Schaller, *The United States Crusade in China, 1938–1945* (1979); Michael Sherry, *Preparing for the Next War: American Plans for Postwar Defense, 1941–1945* (1977), and *The Rise of American Air Power* (1987); Gaddis Smith, *American Diplomacy During the Second World War* (1964); Ronald H. Spector, *Eagle Against the Sun: The American War with Japan* (1985); Mark A. Stoler, *The Politics of the Second Front: Planning and Diplomacy in Coalition Warfare, 1941–1945* (1977); Christopher Thorne, *Allies of a Kind: The United States, Britain and the War Against Japan, 1941–1945* (1978); John Toland, *The Last Hundred Days* (1966), and *The Rising Sun* (1970); Barbara M. Tuchman, *Stilwell and the American Experience in China* (1971); Russell Weigley, *The American Way of War* (1973), and *Eisenhower's Lieutenants: The Campaign of France and Germany, 1944–1945* (1981); Chester Wilmot, *The Struggle for Europe*

(1952); David S. Wyman, *The Abandonment of the Jews: America and the Holocaust, 1941–1945* (1984).

Atomic Warfare. Gar Alperovitz, *Atomic Diplomacy* (1965); Nuel Davis, *Lawrence and Oppenheimer* (1969); Robert Donovan, *Conflict and Crisis* (1977); Herbert Feis, *The Atomic Bomb and the End of World War II* (1966); Gregg Herken, *The Winning Weapon: The Atomic Bomb in the Cold War* (1980); John Hersey, *Hiroshima* (1946); Robert Jungk, *Brighter Than a Thousand Suns* (1958); Richard Rhodes, *The Making of the Atomic Bomb* (1987); W. S. Schoenberger, *Decision of Destiny* (1969); Martin Sherwin, *A World Destroyed* (1975); Leon V. Sigal, *Fighting to a Finish* (1988).

CHAPTER 29 AMERICA AND THE COLD WAR

Origins of the Cold War. Gar Alperovitz, *Atomic Diplomacy: Hiroshima and Potsdam*, rev. ed. (1985); Stephen Ambrose, *Rise to Globalism*, 5th ed. (1988); Terry H. Anderson, *The United States, Great Britain, and the Cold War, 1944–1947* (1981); H. W. Brands, *Inside the Cold War: Loy Henderson and the Rise of the American Empire, 1918–1961* (1991); Diane Clemens, *Yalta* (1970); Warren I. Cohen, *The Cambridge History of American Foreign Relations*, vol. 4: *America in the Age of Soviet Power, 1945–1991* (1991); Herbert Feis, *Churchill, Roosevelt, and Stalin* (1957), and *Between War and Peace: The Potsdam Conference* (1960); John Lewis Gaddis, *Strategies of Containment* (1982), *The United States and the Origins of the Cold War, 1941–1947* (1972), and *The Long Peace* (1987); Lloyd C. Gardner, *Spheres of Influence: The Great Powers Partition Europe, from Munich to Yalta* (1993); Gregg Herken, *The Winning Weapon: The Atomic Bomb in the Cold War, 1945–1950* (1980); George C. Herring, Jr., *Aid to Russia* (1973); Timothy P. Ireland, *Creating the Entangling Alliance: The Origins of NATO* (1981); Bruce Kuniholm, *The Origins of the Cold War in the Middle East* (1980); Walter LaFeber, *America, Russia, and the Cold War, 1945–1967*, rev. ed. (1980); Melvyn P. Leffler, *A Preponderance of Power: National Security, the Truman Administration, and the Cold War* (1992); William McNeill, *America, Britain, and Russia* (1953); Wilson D. Miscamble, *George F. Kennan and the Making of American Foreign Policy, 1947–1950* (1992); W. L. Neumann, *After Victory* (1969); Thomas G. Paterson, *Soviet-American Confrontation* (1974), *On Every Front: The Making of the Cold War* (1979), and *Meeting the Communist Threat* (1988); Robert A. Pollard, *Economic Security and the Origins of the Cold War* (1985); Martin Sherwin, *A World Destroyed* (1975); Gaddis Smith, *American Diplomacy During the Second World War* (1965), and *Dean Acheson* (1972); John L. Snell, *Illusion and Necessity* (1967); William Taubman, *Stalin's American Policy* (1982); Athan G. Theoharis, *The Yalta Myths* (1970); Adam Ulam, *The Rivals: America and Russia Since World War II* (1971); Bernard Weisberger, *Cold War, Cold Peace* (1984); Lawrence Wittner, *American Intervention in Greece, 1943–1949* (1982); Daniel Yergin, *Shattered Peace* (1977).

Truman's Foreign Policy. Dean Acheson, *Present at the Creation* (1970); Hadley Arkes, *Bureaucracy, the Marshall Plan and National Interest* (1973); Richard J. Barnet, *The Alliance* (1983); Robert M. Blum, *Drawing the Line: The Origin of the American Containment Policy in East Asia* (1982); Russell D. Buhite, *Soviet-American Relations in Asia, 1945–1954* (1982); Warren I. Cohen, *America's Response to China*, rev. ed. (1980); Jeffrey Diefendorf, *American Policy and the Reconstruction of West Germany, 1945–1955* (1993); Robert Donovan, *Conflict and Crisis* (1977), and *Tumultuous Years* (1982); John King

Fairbank, *The United States and China*, rev. ed. (1971); Lloyd Gardner, *Architects of Illusion* (1970); Fraser J. Harbutt, *The Iron Curtain: Churchill, America, and the Origins of the Cold War* (1986); Michael Hogan, *The Marshall Plan* (1987); Akira Iriye, *The Cold War in Asia* (1974); Laurence Kaplan, *The United States and NATO* (1984); George F. Kennan, *American Diplomacy, 1900–1950* (1952), and *Memoirs, 1925–1950* (1967); Joyce Kolko and Gabriel Kolko, *The Limits of Power* (1970); Bruce R. Koniholm, *The Origins of the Cold War in the Middle East* (1980); William R. Louis, *The British Empire in the Middle East* (1984); Gary May, *China Scapegoat* (1979); David Mayer, *George Kennan and the Dilemmas of U.S. Foreign Policy* (1988); Wilson D. Miscamble, *George F. Kennan and the Making of American Foreign Policy, 1947–1950* (1992); Brenda Gayle Plummer, *Black Americans and U.S. Foreign Affairs, 1935–1960* (1996); Edwin O. Reischauer, *The United States and Japan*, rev. ed. (1965); Lisle Rose, *Roots of Tragedy* (1976); Michael Schaller, *The U.S. Crusade in China* (1979), *Communists* (1971), and *The American Occupation of Japan: The Origins of the Cold War in Asia* (1985); Howard Schonberger, *Aftermath of War: Americans and the Remaking of Japan* (1989); Anders Stephanson, *Kennan and the Art of Foreign Policy* (1989); Michael B. Stoff, *Oil, War, and American Security* (1980); Christopher Thorne, *Allies of a Kind* (1978); Imanuel Wexler, *The Marshall Plan Revisited* (1983).

Truman's Domestic Policies. Stephen K. Bailey, *Congress Makes a Law* (1950); Jack S. Ballard, *The Shock of Peace: Military and Economic Demobilization After World War II* (1983); William C. Berman, *The Politics of Civil Rights in the Truman Administration* (1970); Barton J. Bernstein, ed., *Politics and Policies of the Truman Administration* (1970); Allida M. Black, *Casting Her Own Shadow: Eleanor Roosevelt and the Shaping of Postwar Liberalism* (1996); Richard Dalfiume, *Desegregation of the U.S. Armed Forces* (1969); Richard O. Davies, *Housing Reform During the Truman Administration* (1966); John P. Diggins, *The Proud Decades, 1941–1960* (1989); Robert Donovan, *Conflict and Crisis* (1977), and *Tumultuous Years* (1982); Andrew J. Dunar, *The Truman Scandals and the Politics of Morality* (1984); Robert H. Ferrell, *Harry S. Truman and the Modern American Presidency* (1983); Eric Goldman, *The Crucial Decade—and After: America, 1945–1960* (1961); Alonzo Hamby, *Beyond the New Deal: Harry S. Truman and American Liberalism* (1973); Susan Hartmann, *Truman and the 80th Congress* (1971); Roy Jenkins, *Truman* (1986); R. Alton Lee, *Truman and Taft-Hartley* (1967), and *Truman and the Steel Seizure Case* (1977); Arthur F. McClure, *The Truman Administration and the Problems of Postwar Labor* (1969); Donald R. McCoy, *The Presidency of Harry S. Truman* (1984); Donald R. McCoy and Richard Ruetten, *Quest and Response* (1973); David McCullough, *Truman* (1992); Maeva Marcus, *Truman and the Steel Seizure* (1977); Allen J. Matusow, *Farm Policies and Politics in the Truman Years* (1967); Merle Miller, *Plain Speaking* (1980); Richard L. Miller, *Truman: The Rise to Power* (1986); William O'Neill, *American High* (1986); William E. Pemberton, *Harry S. Truman* (1989); Monte S. Poen, *Harry S. Truman Versus the Medical Lobby* (1979); Gary Reichard, *Politics as Usual: The Age of Truman and Eisenhower* (1988); Christopher L. Tomlins, *The State and the Unions* (1985).

Cold War Politics and Culture. H. W. Brands, *The Devil We Knew: Americans and the Cold War* (1993); John P. Diggins, *The Proud Decades, 1941–1960* (1989); Steven M. Gillon, *Politics and Vision: The ADA and American Liberalism, 1947–1985* (1987); David Goldfield, *Black, White, and Southern: Race Relations and Southern Culture* (1990); Maurice Isserman, *If I Had a Hammer . . .: The Death of the Old Left and the Birth of the New Left* (1987); Norman Markowitz, *The Rise and Fall of the People's Century: Henry A. Wal-*

lace and American Liberalism, 1941–1948 (1973); James T. Patterson, *Mr. Republican* (1972); Richard Pells, *The Liberal Mind in a Conservative Age: American Intellectuals in the 1940s and 1950s* (1985); Irwin Ross, *The Loneliest Campaign* (1968); Richard Norton Smith, *Thomas E. Dewey and His Times* (1982); Allan M. Winkler, *Life Under a Cloud: American Anxiety About the Atom* (1993); Allen Yarnell, *Democrats and Progressives* (1974).

The Korean War.   Carl Berger, *The Korean Knot* (1957); Ronald Caridi, *The Korean War and American Politics* (1969); Bruce Cumings, *The Origins of the Korean War* (1980), and ed., *Child of Conflict: The Korean-American Relationship, 1943–1953* (1983); Charles W. Dobbs, *The Unwanted Symbol* (1981); Joseph C. Goulden, *Korea: The Untold Story of the War* (1982); John Halliday and Bruce Cumings, *Korea: The Unknown War* (1980); Robert Leckie, *Conflict* (1962); Glenn D. Paige, *The Korean Decision* (1968); Michael Schaller, *Douglas MacArthur* (1989); Robert R. Simmons, *The Strained Alliance* (1975); John Spanier, *The Truman-MacArthur Controversy* (1959); Allen Whiting, *China Crosses the Yalu* (1960).

Countersubversion.   Michael R. Belknap, *Cold War Political Justice: The Smith Act, the Communist Party, and American Civil Liberties* (1977); Eric Bentley, ed., *Thirty Years of Treason;* David Caute, *The Great Fear* (1978); Larry Ceplair and Steven Englund, *The Inquisition in Hollywood* (1983); Richard Freeland, *The Truman Doctrine and the Origins of McCarthyism* (1971); Richard Fried, *Men Against McCarthy* (1976), and *Nightmare in Red* (1990); Robert Griffith, *The Politics of Fear* (1970); Robert Griffith and Athan Theoharis, eds., *The Specter: Original Essays on the Cold War and the Origins of McCarthyism* (1974); Alan Harper, *The Politics of Loyalty* (1969); Stanley Kutler, *The American Inquisition* (1982); Harvey Levenstein, *Communism, Anticommunism, and the CIO* (1981); Mary Sperling McAuliffe, *Crisis on the Left* (1978); Victor Navasky, *Naming Names* (1980); William O'Neill, *A Better World* (1983); David M. Oshinsky, *A Conspiracy So Immense: The World of Joe McCarthy* (1983); Richard Gid Powers, *Secrecy and Power: The Life of J. Edgar Hoover* (1987); Ronald Radosh and Joyce Milton, *The Rosenberg File* (1983); Thomas C. Reeves, *The Life and Times of Joe McCarthy* (1982); Michael Paul Rogin, *The Intellectuals and McCarthy* (1967); Richard Rovere, *Senator Joe McCarthy* (1959); Walter and Miriam Schneer, *Invitation to an Inquest*, rev. ed. (1983); Ellen Schrecker, *No Ivory Tower* (1986); Edward Shils, *The Torment of Secrecy* (1956); Joseph Starobin, *American Communism in Crisis* (1972); Athan Theoharis, *Seeds of Repression* (1971), and *Spying on Americans* (1978); Athan Theoharis and John Stuart Cox, *The Boss: J. Edgar Hoover and the Great American Inquisition* (1988); Allen Weinstein, *Perjury: The Hiss-Chambers Case* (1978); Stephen J. Whitfield, *The Culture of the Cold War* (1991).

CHAPTER 30 THE AFFLUENT SOCIETY

General Studies.   Numan V. Bartley, *The New South, 1945–1980* (1995); John Brooks, *The Great Leap* (1966); William H. Chafe, *The Unfinished Journey* (1986); Carl Degler, *Affluence and Anxiety* (1968); John P. Diggins, *The Proud Decades, 1941–1960* (1989); Eric Goldman, *The Crucial Decade and After* (1960); David Halberstam, *The Fifties* (1993); Godfrey Hodgson, *America in Our Time* (1976); William Leuchtenburg, *A Troubled Feast* (1979); Douglas T. Miller and Marion Novak, *The Fifties* (1977); William O'Neill,

American High (1986); James T. Patterson, *Grand Expectations: Postwar America, 1945–1974* (1996).

Economy and Labor in Postwar America. David P. Calleo, *The Imperious Economy* (1982); Gilbert C. Fite, *American Farmers* (1981); John K. Galbraith, *The Affluent Society* (1958), and *The New Industrial State* (1967); Mark I. Gelfand, *A Nation of Cities* (1975); Robert Heilbroner, *The Limits of American Capitalism* (1965); John Hutchinson, *The Imperfect Union* (1970); C. Wright Mills, *The Power Elite* (1956); Loren J. Okroi, *Galbraith, Harrington, Heilbroner* (1986); Joel Seidman, *American Labor from Defense to Reconversion* (1953); David Stebenne, *Arthur J. Goldberg: New Deal Liberal* (1996); Harold G. Vatter, *The U.S. Economy in the 1950s* (1963).

Culture and Ideas. Daniel Bell, *The End of Ideology* (1960), and ed., *The Radical Right* (1963); Peter Biskind, *Seeing Is Believing: How Hollywood Taught Us to Stop Worrying and Love the Fifties* (1983); Paul Boyer, *By the Bomb's Early Light* (1986); Howard Brick, *Daniel Bell and the Decline of Intellectual Radicalism* (1986); James L. Baughman, *The Republic of Mass Culture: Journalism, Filmmaking, and Broadcasting in America Since 1941;* Paul A. Carter, *Another Part of the Fifties* (1983); Ann Charters, *Kerouac* (1973); Bruce Cook, *The Beat Generation* (1971); Thomas Cripps, *Making Movies Black: The Hollywood Message Movie from World War II to the Civil Rights Era* (1993); Tom Engelhardt, *The End of Victory Culture: Cold War America and the Disillusioning of a Generation* (1995); Edward J. Epstein, *News from Nowhere* (1973); Herbert Gans, *The Levittowners* (1967); William Graebner, *The Age of Doubt: American Thought and Culture in the 1940s* (1991); David Halberstam, *The Powers That Be* (1979); Jeffrey Hart, *When the Going Was Good: American Life in the Fifties* (1982); Dolores Hayden, *Redesigning the American Dream* (1984); Kenneth T. Jackson, *The Crabgrass Frontier: The Suburbanization of the United States* (1985); Marty Jezer, *The Dark Ages: Life in the U.S., 1945–1960* (1982); Landon Y. Jones, *Great Expectations: America and the Baby Boom Generation* (1980); Neil Jumonville, *Critical Crossings: The New York Intellectuals in Postwar America* (1991); George Lipsitz, *Class and Culture in Cold War America* (1981); Roger W. Lotchin, *Fortress California, 1910–1961: From Warfare to Welfare;* Mary Sperling McAuliffe, *Crisis on the Left* (1978); Walter A. McDougall, *. . . the Heavens and the Earth: A Political History of the Space Age* (1985); Dennis McNally, *Desolate Angel* (1979); Margaret Marsh, *Suburban Lives* (1990); Douglas T. Miller and Marion Novak, *The Fifties* (1977); Zane L. Miller, *Suburb: Neighborhood and Community in Forest Park, Ohio, 1935–1976* (1981); C. Wright Mills, *White Collar* (1956); Richard H. Pells, *The Liberal Mind in a Conservative Age: American Intellectuals in the 1940s and 1950s* (1985); David Potter, *People of Plenty* (1954); David Riesman, *The Lonely Crowd* (1950); Leila Rupp and Verta Taylor, *Survival in the Doldrums* (1987); Arthur M. Schlesinger, Jr., *The Vital Center* (1949); Lynn Spigel, *Make Room for TV* (1992); Walter Sullivan, ed., *America's Race for the Moon* (1962); John Tytell, *Naked Angels* (1976); Alan M. Wald, *The New York Intellectuals* (1987); Stephen J. Whitfield, *The Culture of the Cold War* (1991); William Whyte, *The Organization Man* (1956); Tom Wolfe, *The Right Stuff* (1979); Gwendolyn Wright, *Building the American Dream: A Social History of Housing in America* (1981).

Women and Families. William H. Chafe, *The American Woman: Her Changing Social, Economic, and Political Roles, 1920–1970,* rev. ed. (1988); Ruth Cowan, *More Work for*

Mother: The Irony of Household Technology (1983); Eugenia Kaledin, *Mothers and More: American Women in the 1950s* (1984); Susan Estabrook Kennedy, *If All We Did Was to Weep at Home: A History of White Working-Class Women in America* (1979); Alice Kessler-Harris, *Out to Work: A History of Wage-Earning Women in the United States* (1982); Elaine Tyler May, *Homeward Bound: American Families in the Cold War* (1988); Susan Strasser, *Never Done: A History of American Housework* (1982).

Politics in the Eisenhower Years.   Sherman Adams, *Firsthand Report* (1961); Charles C. Alexander, *Holding the Line* (1975); Stephen Ambrose, *Eisenhower the President* (1984); Jean Baker, *The Stevensons: A Biography of an American Family* (1996); Brian Balogh, *Chain Reaction: Expert Debate and Public Participation in American Nuclear Commercial Power, 1945–1975* (1991); Piers Brendon, *Ike* (1986); Jeff Broadwater, *Eisenhower and the Anti-Communist Crusade* (1992); Robert F. Burk, *Dwight D. Eisenhower* (1986); Barbara B. Clowse, *Brainpower for the Cold War: The Sputnik Crisis and the National Defense Education Act of 1958* (1981); Dwight D. Eisenhower, *The White House Years*, 2 vols. (1963–1965); Fred Greenstein, *The Hidden-Hand Presidency* (1982); Emmet John Hughes, *The Ordeal of Power* (1963); Peter Lyon, *Eisenhower: Portrait of a Hero* (1974); Richard Nixon, *Six Crises* (1962); Herbert S. Parmet, *Eisenhower and the American Crusades* (1972); Nicol C. Rae, *The Decline and Fall of the Liberal Republicans* (1989); Gary Reichard, *The Reaffirmation of Republicanism* (1975), and *Politics as Usual* (1988). David W. Reinhard, *The Republican Right Since 1945* (1983); Elmo Richardson, *The Presidency of Dwight D. Eisenhower* (1979); Mark H. Rose, *Interstate: Express Highway Politics, 1941–1956* (1979); R. L. Rosholt, *An Administrative History of NASA* (1966).

Foreign Policy.   Stephen Ambrose, *Ike's Spies* (1981); David L. Anderson, *Trapped by Success: The Eisenhower Administration and Vietnam, 1953–1961* (1991); Howard Ball, *Justice Downwind: America's Nuclear Testing Program in the 1950s* (1986); Michael Beschloss, *MAYDAY* (1986); Henry W. Brands, *Cold Warriors* (1988), and *The Specter of Neutralism: The United States and the Emergence of the Third World, 1947–1960* (1989); Blanche W. Cooke, *The Declassified Eisenhower* (1981); Chester Cooper, *Lost Crusade* (1970), and *The Lion's Last Roar* (1978); Cecil Currey, *Edward Lansdale: The Unquiet American* (1988); Robert A. Divine, *Foreign Policy and U.S. Presidential Elections*, 2 vols. (1974), and *Blowing in the Wind: The Nuclear Test Ban Debate, 1954–1960* (1978), and *Eisenhower and the Cold War* (1981); William J. Duiker, *U.S. Containment Policy and the Conflict in Indochina* (1992); Frances Fitzgerald, *Fire in the Lake* (1972); Steven Z. Freiberger, *Dawn over Suez: The Rise of American Power in the Middle East, 1953–1957* (1992); Louis Gerson, *John Foster Dulles* (1967); Gregg Herken, *Counsels of War* (1985); George Herring, *America's Longest War* (1979); Richard G. Hewlett and Jack M. Hall, *Atoms for Peace and War, 1953–1961* (1989); Townsend Hoopes, *The Devil and John Foster Dulles* (1973); Richard Immerman, *The CIA in Guatemala* (1982); Burton Kaufman, *The Oil Cartel Case* (1978); Gabriel Kolko, *Confronting the Third World* (1988); Walter LaFeber, *Inevitable Revolutions* (1983); John T. McAlister, Jr., *Vietnam: The Origins of Revolution* (1969); Richard A. Melanson and David A. Mayers, eds., *Reevaluating Eisenhower* (1986); Stephen G. Rabe, *Eisenhower and Latin America* (1988); Kermit Roosevelt, *Counter-Coup* (1980); Andrew Rotter, *The Path to Vietnam* (1987); Richard Smoke, *National Security and the Nuclear Dilemma* (1988); Hugh Thomas, *Suez* (1967); Mira Wilkins, *The Maturing of Multinational Enterprise* (1974).

Legal and Constitutional Issues.   Alexander Bickel, *Politics and the Warren Court* (1965), and *The Supreme Court and the Idea of Progress* (1970); Phillip Kurland, *Politics, the*

Constitution, and the Warren Court (1970); Paul Murphy, *The Constitution in Crisis Times* (1972); Bernard Schwartz, *Super Chief: Earl Warren and His Supreme Court* (1983); Philip Stern, *The Oppenheimer Case* (1969); Michael Straight, *Trial by Television* (1954); John Weaver, *Earl Warren* (1967).

Civil Rights. John W. Anderson, *Eisenhower, Brownell, and the Congress* (1964); Numan V. Bartley, *The Rise of Massive Resistance* (1969); Taylor Branch, *Parting the Waters* (1988); Robert F. Burk, *The Eisenhower Administration and Black Civil Rights* (1984); William H. Chafe, *Civilities and Civil Rights: Greensboro, North Carolina, and the Black Struggle for Freedom* (1980); John Egerton, *Speak Now Against the Day: The Generation Before the Civil Rights Movement in the South* (1994); Kevin Gaines, *Uplifting the Race: Black Leadership, Politics, and Culture in the Twentieth Century* (1996); David Garrow, ed., *The Montgomery Bus Boycott and the Women Who Started It: A Memoir of Jo Ann Gibson Robinson* (1987), and *Bearing the Cross* (1986). Elizabeth Huckaby, *Crisis at Central High* (1980); Martin Luther King, Jr., *Stride Toward Freedom* (1958); Richard H. King, *Civil Rights and the Idea of Freedom* (1992); Richard Kluger, *Simple Justice* (1975); Steven Lawson, *Running for Freedom* (1991); Anthony Lewis, *Portrait of a Decade* (1964); Robert J. Norrell, *Reaping the Whirlwind: The Civil Rights Movement in Tuskegee* (1985); Howell Raines, *My Soul Is Rested* (1977); Harvard Sitkoff, *The Struggle for Black Equality, 1954–1980* (1981); Patricia Sullivan, *Days of Hope: Race and Democracy in the New Deal Era* (1996); Abigail Thernstrom, *Whose Votes Count? Affirmative Action and Minority Voting Rights* (1987); Nancy J. Weiss, *Whitney M. Young, Jr., and the Struggle for Civil Rights* (1989).

Minorities and the Poor. Rodolfo Acuña, *Occupied America: A History of Chicanos* (1981); Larry W. Burt, *Tribalism in Crisis: Federal Indian Policy, 1953–1961* (1982); Donald Fixico, *Termination and Relocation: Federal Indian Policy, 1945–1970* (1986); J. Wayne Flint, *Dixie's Forgotten People: The South's Poor Whites* (1979); Michael Harrington, *The Other America* (1962); Jacqueline Jones, *The Dispossessed: America's Underclasses from the Civil War to the Present* (1992); Nicholas Lemann, *The Promised Land: The Great Black Migration and How It Changed America* (1991); Elena Padilla, *Up from Puerto Rico* (1958); Linda Reed, *Simple Decency and Common Sense* (1992).

CHAPTER 31 THE ORDEAL OF LIBERALISM

General Studies. William Chafe, *The Unfinished Journey: America Since World War II*, rev. ed. (1991); Godfrey Hodgson, *America in Our Time* (1976); Allen J. Matusow, *The Unraveling of America: A History of Liberalism in the 1960s* (1984); Charles R. Morris, *A Time of Passion* (1984); Theodore H. White, *America in Search of Itself* (1982).

Kennedy and Johnson. Vaughn D. Bornet, *The Presidency of Lyndon B. Johnson* (1983); Thomas Brown, *JFK: The History of an Image* (1988); David Burner, *John F. Kennedy and a New Generation* (1988); Robert Caro, *The Years of Lyndon B. Johnson: The Path to Power* (1982), and *Means of Ascent* (1990); Paul K. Conkin, *Big Daddy from the Pedernales* (1986); Robert Dallek, *Lone Star Rising: Lyndon Johnson and His Times, 1908–1960* (1991); Robert A. Divine, *The Johnson Years*, vol. 3: *LBJ at Home and Abroad*; Ronnie Dugger, *The Politician* (1982); Edward J. Epstein, *Inquest* (1966), and *Legend* (1978); Henry Fairlie, *The Kennedy Promise: The Politics of Richard Reeves, President Kennedy: Profile of Power* (1993), and *Expectation* (1973); Eric Goldman, *The Tragedy of Lyndon Johnson* (1968); Richard N.

Goodwin, *Remembering America* (1988); Jim Heath, *Decade of Disillusionment* (1975); Henry Hurt, *Reasonable Doubt* (1985); Lyndon B. Johnson, *Vantage Point* (1971); Doris Kearns, *Lyndon Johnson and the American Dream* (1976); Donald Lord, *John F. Kennedy: The Politics of Confrontation and Conciliation* (1977); William Manchester, *The Death of a President* (1967); Bruce Miroff, *Pragmatic Illusions: The Presidential Politics of JFK* (1976); Lewis Paper, *The Promise and the Performance* (1975); Herbert Parmet, *Jack* (1980), and *JFK* (1983); George Reedy, *The Twilight of the Presidency* (1970); Richard Reeves, *President Kennedy* (1992); Thomas Reeves, *A Question of Character: The Life of John F. Kennedy in Image and Reality* (1991); Arthur M. Schlesinger, Jr., *A Thousand Days* (1965); Theodore Sorensen, *Kennedy* (1965); Anthony Summers, *Conspiracy* (1980); Warren Commission, *The Report of the Warren Commission* (1964); Theodore H. White, *The Making of the President, 1960* (1961); Garry Wills, *The Kennedy Imprisonment* (1982).

Domestic Policies and Politics.   Henry J. Aaron, *Politics and the Professors* (1978); William H. Chafe, *Never Stop Running: Allard Lowenstein and the Struggle to Save American Liberalism;* Greg J. Duncan, *Years of Poverty, Years of Plenty* (1984); Mark Gelfand, *A Nation of Cities* (1975); James Giglio, *The Presidency of John F. Kennedy* (1991); Hugh Davis Graham, *Uncertain Trumpet* (1984); Robert H. Haveman, ed., *A Decade of Federal Antipoverty Programs* (1977); Jim Heath, *John F. Kennedy and the Business Community* (1969); Daniel Knapp and Kenneth Polk, *Scouting the War on Poverty* (1971); Sar Levitan, *The Great Society's Poor Law* (1969); Sar Levitan and Robert Taggart, *The Promise of Greatness* (1976); Allen J. Matusow, *The Unraveling of America: A History of Liberalism in the 1960s* (1984); Charles Morris, *A Time of Passion* (1984); Charles Murray, *Losing Ground* (1984); Victor Navasky, *Kennedy Justice* (1971); James T. Patterson, *America's Struggle Against Poverty, 1900–1980* (1981); Frances Fox Piven and Richard Cloward, *Regulating the Poor* (1971); John E. Schwarz, *America's Hidden Success* (1983); James L. Sundquist, *Politics and Policy: The Eisenhower, Kennedy, and Johnson Years* (1968); Tom Wicker, *JFK and LBJ* (1968).

Race Relations and Civil Rights.   Taylor Branch, *Parting the Waters: America in the King Years* (1988); Carl Brauer, *John F. Kennedy and the Second Reconstruction* (1977); Paul Burstein, *Discrimination, Jobs, and Politics* (1985); James Button, *Black Violence: Political Impact of the 1960s Race Riots* (1978); Stokely Carmichael and Charles Hamilton, *Black Power* (1967); Clayborne Carson, *In Struggle: SNCC and the Black Awakening of the 1960s* (1981); William H. Chafe, *Civilities and Civil Rights: Greensboro, North Carolina, and the Black Struggle for Freedom* (1980); Joe R. Feagin and Harlan Hahn, *Ghetto Revolts* (1973); Robert Fogelson, *Violence as Protest* (1971); David Garrow, *Protest at Selma* (1978); *The FBI and Martin Luther King* (1981), and *Bearing the Cross* (1986); Hugh Davis Graham, *The Civil Rights Era* (1990); Alex Haley, *The Autobiography of Malcolm X* (1966); Martin Luther King, Jr., *Why We Can't Wait* (1964); Steven Lawson, *Black Ballots: Voting Rights in the South, 1966–1969* (1976); Nicholas Lemann, *The Promised Land: The Great Black Migration and How It Changed America* (1991); David L. Lewis, *King: A Critical Biography* (1970); Doug McAdam, *Freedom Summer* (1988); Benjamin Muse, *The American Negro Revolution* (1969); *Report of the National Advisory Commission on Civil Disorders* (1968); Stephen Oates, *Let the Trumpet Sound* (1982); Harvard Sitkoff, *The Struggle for Black Equality, 1954–1992* (1992); James R. Ralph Jr., *Northern Protest: Martin Luther King Jr., Chicago, and the Civil Rights Movement* (1993); Mark Stern, *Calculating Visions: Kennedy, Johnson and Civil Rights* (1992); Abigail Thernstrom, *Whose Votes Count? Affirmative Action and Minority Voting Rights* (1987); Robert Weisbrot, *Freedom Bound: A History of America's Civil Rights Move-*

ment (1990); Harris Wofford, *Of Kennedy and Kings* (1980); Eugene Wolfenstein, *The Victims of Democracy: Malcolm X and the Black Revolution* (1981).

Foreign Policy.   Elie Abel, *The Missile Crisis* (1966); Graham Allison, *Essence of Decision* (1971); Richard Barnet, *Intervention and Revolution* (1968); Michael Bechloss, *The Crisis Years* (1990); McGeorge Bundy, *Danger and Survival* (1989); Warren Cohen, *Dean Rusk* (1980); Herbert Dinerstein, *The Making of a Missile Crisis* (1976); Bernard Firestone, *The Quest for Nuclear Stability* (1982); Louise Fitzsimmons, *The Kennedy Doctrine* (1972); Philip Geyelin, *Lyndon B. Johnson and the World* (1966); John Girling, *America and the Third World* (1980); Trumbull Higgins, *The Perfect Failure: Kennedy, Eisenhower, and the CIA at the Bay of Pigs* (1987); Roger Hilsman, *To Move a Nation* (1965); Haynes Johnson, *The Bay of Pigs* (1964); Robert Kennedy, *Thirteen Days* (1969); Dan Kurzman, *Santo Domingo* (1966); Walter LaFeber, *Inevitable Revolutions: The United States in Central America* (1985); Thomas J. McCormick, *America's Half Century: United States Foreign Policy in the Cold War* (1989); Richard D. Mahoney, *JFK: Ordeal in Africa* (1983); Gerald T. Rice, *The Bold Experiment: JFK's Peace Corps* (1985); Jerome Slater, *Intervention and Negotiation* (1970); Richard Walton, *Cold War and Counterrevolution* (1972); Peter Wyden, *Bay of Pigs* (1969).

Vietnam.   Mark Baker and Christian G. Appy, *Working-Class War: American Combat Soldiers and Vietnam* (1993), and *Nam* (1982); Lawrence Baskir and William Strauss, *Chance and Circumstance* (1978); Larry Berman, *Planning a Tragedy* (1982), and *Lyndon Johnson's War* (1989); Peter Braestrup, *Big Story* (1977; abridged ed., 1978); William Broyles, Jr., *Brothers in Arms: A Journey from War to Peace* (1986); Philip Davidson, *Vietnam at War* (1991); Gloria Emerson, *Winners and Losers* (1976); Frances Fitzgerald, *Fire in the Lake* (1972); John Galloway, *The Gulf of Tonkin Resolution* (1970); Leslie Gelb and Richard Betts, *The Irony of Vietnam: The System Worked* (1979); David Halberstam, *The Best and the Brightest* (1972); Michael Herr, *Dispatches* (1977); George C. Herring, *America's Longest War*, rev. ed. (1986); George McT. Kahin, *Intervention* (1986); Stanley Karnow, *Vietnam* (1983); Alexander Kendrick, *The Wound Within* (1974); Gabriel Kolko, *The Anatomy of a War* (1985); Robert W. Komer, *Bureaucracy at War* (1986); David Levy, *The Debate over Vietnam* (1991); Guenter Lewy, *America in Vietnam* (1978); Don Oberdorfer, *Tet* (1971); Bruce C. Palmer, Jr., *The 25-Year War* (1984); *The Pentagon Papers*, Senator Gravel edition (1975); Norman Podhoretz, *Why We Were in Vietnam* (1982); Thomas Powers, *Vietnam: The War at Home* (1973); Al Santoli, *Everything We Had* (1981); Herbert Schandler, *The Unmaking of a President: Lyndon Johnson and Vietnam* (1977); Neil Sheehan, *A Bright Shining Lie* (1988); R. B. Smith, *An International History of the Vietnam War: The Kennedy Strategy* (1985); Ronald Spector, *Advice and Support* (1983); Col. Harry Summers, *On Strategy* (1981); Wallace Terry, *Bloods* (1984); Thomas C. Thayer, *War Without Fronts* (1985); Wallace J. Thies, *When Governments Collide* (1980); James Thompson, *Rolling Thunder* (1980); Kathleen J. Turner, *Lyndon Johnson's Dual War: Vietnam and the Press* (1981); Irwin Unger, *The Movement* (1974); Marilyn Young, *The Vietnam Wars* (1991).

1968.   Dan T. Carter, *The Politics of Rage: George Wallace, The Origins of the New Conservatism, and the Transformation of American Politics* (1995); David Caute, *The Year of the Barricades* (1988); Lewis Chester, *Godfrey Hodgson, and Lewis Page, American Melodrama* (1969); David Farber, *Chicago '68* (1988); Marshall Frady, *Wallace*, rev. ed. (1976); Godfrey Hodgson, *America in Our Time* (1976); Charles Kaiser, *1968 in America* (1988); Norman Mailer, *Miami and the Siege of Chicago* (1968); Arthur M. Schlesinger, Jr., *Robert*

Kennedy and His Times (1978); Ben Stavis, *We Were the Campaign* (1969); Theodore H. White, *The Making of the President, 1968* (1969).

CHAPTER 32 THE CRISIS OF AUTHORITY

General Studies. John Morton Blum, *Years of Discord: American Politics and Society, 1961–1974* (1991); Peter N. Carroll, It *Seemed Like Nothing Happened* (1982); Allen J. Matusow, *The Unraveling of America: A History of Liberalism in the 1960s* (1984); Kim McQuaid, *The Anxious Years* (1989); William O'Neill, *Coming Apart* (1971).

The New Left and the Counterculture. Edward Bacciocco, Jr., *The New Left in America* (1974); Ronald Berman, *America in the Sixties* (1968); Wini Breines, *Community and Organization in the New Left* (1983); Peter Clecak, *Radical Paradoxes* (1973); Peter Collier and David Horowitz, *Destructive Generation: Second Thoughts About the Sixties* (1989); Margaret Cruikshank, *The Gay and Lesbian Liberation Movement in America* (1992); Morris Dickstein, *Gates of Eden* (1977); Joan Didion, *Slouching Towards Bethlehem* (1967), and *The White Album* (1979); John Diggins, *The American Left in the Twentieth Century* (1973); Sara Evans, *Personal Politics* (1979); Lewis Feuer, *The Conflict of Generations* (1969); Richard Flacks, *Youth and Social Change* (1971); Todd Gitlin, *The Whole World Is Watching* (1981), and *The Sixties: Years of Hope, Days of Rage* (1987); Paul Goodman, *Growing Up Absurd* (1960); David Harris, *Dreams Die Hard* (1983); Maurice Isserman, *"If I Had a Hammer . . .": The Death of the Old Left and the Birth of the New Left* (1987); Joseph Kelner and James Munves, *The Kent State Coverup* (1980); Kenneth Keniston, *Young Radicals* (1968), and *Youth and Dissent* (1971); Richard King, *The Party of Eros* (1972); James Kunen, *The Strawberry Statement* (1968); Lawrence Lader, *Power on the Left* (1979); Klaus Mehnert, *Twilight of the Young* (1978); James Miller, *"Democracy in the Streets": From Port Huron to the Siege of Chicago* (1987); Charles Reich, *The Greening of America* (1970); W. J. Rorabaugh, *Berkeley at War* (1989); Theodore Roszak, *The Making of a Counter Culture* (1969); Kirkpatrick Sale, *SDS* (1973); Irwin Unger, *The Movement* (1974); Milton Viorst, *Fire in the Streets* (1979); Jon Wiener, *Come Together: John Lennon in His Time* (1984).

Indians, Hispanics, Asians. Rodolfo Acuña, *Occupied America*, 2nd ed. (1981); Larry W. Burt, *Tribalism in Crisis: Federal Indian Policy, 1953–1961* (1982); Vine Deloria, Jr., *Behind the Trail of Broken Treaties* (1974), and *Custer Died for Your Sins* (1969); Ronald Dewing, *Wounded Knee: The Meaning and Significance of the Second Incident* (1985); Douglas E. Foley, *From Peones to Politicos: Class and Ethnicity in a South Texas Town, 1900–1987* (1988); Peter Iverson, *The Navajo Nation* (1981); Oscar Lewis, *La Vida* (1969); D'Arcy McNickle, *Native American Tribalism* (1973); Matt Meier and Feliciano Rivera, *The Chicanos* (1972); David M. Reimers, *Still the Golden Door: The Third World Comes to America* (1985); Julian Samora, *Los Mojados* (1971); Stan Steiner, *The New Indians* (1968); Ronald Takaki, *Strangers from a Distant Shore: A History of Asian Americans* (1989), and *A Different Mirror: A History of Multicultural America* (1993); Ronald Taylor, *Chavez and the Farm Workers* (1975); Wilcomb E. Washburn, *Red Man's Land/White Man's Law* (1971); Charles F. Wilkinson, *American Indians, Time, and the Law* (1987).

Feminism. William Chafe, *The American Woman* (1972); Nancy Cott, *The Grounding of Modern Feminism* (1987); Marian Faux, *Roe v. Wade* (1988); Jo Freeman, *The Politics of Women's Liberation* (1975); Betty Friedan, *The Feminine Mystique* (1963); Carol Gilligan,

In A Different Voice (1982); Cynthia Harrison, *On Account of Sex: The Politics of Women's Issues, 1945–1968* (1988); Susan M. Hartmann, *From Margin to Mainstream: Women and American Politics Since 1960* (1989); Alice Kessler-Harris, *Out to Work: A History of Wage-Earning Women in the United States* (1982); Ethel Klein, *Gender Politics* (1984); Kristin Luker, *Abortion and the Politics of Motherhood* (1984); Robin Morgan, ed., *Sisterhood Is Powerful* (1970); Rosalind Petchesky, *Abortion and Women's Choice* (1984); Sheila Rothman, *Woman's Proper Place* (1978); Winifred Wandersee, *On the Move: American Women in the 1970s* (1988); Gayle Yates, *What Women Want* (1975).

Nixon and the World. Seyom Brown, *The Crisis of Power* (1979); Lloyd Gardner, *A Covenant with Power* (1984), and *The Great Nixon Turnaround* (1973); Seymour Hersh, *The Price of Power* (1983); Roger Hilsman, *The Crouching Future* (1975); Arnold Isaacs, *Without Honor: Defeat in Vietnam and Cambodia* (1983); Walter Isaacson, *Kissinger* (1992); Marvin Kalb and Bernard Kalb, *Kissinger* (1974); Henry A. Kissinger, *White House Years* (1979); *Years of Upheaval* (1982), and *Diplomacy* (1994); David Landau, *Kissinger: The Uses of Power* (1972); Robert S. Litwak, *Detente and the Nixon Doctrine: American Foreign Policy and the Pursuit of Stability* (1984); Timothy Lomperis, *The War Nobody Lost—and Won* (1984); Roger Morris, *Uncertain Greatness* (1977); Harland Moulton, *From Superiority to Parity* (1973); John Newhouse, *Cold Dawn* (1973); Michael Oksenberg and Robert Oxnam, eds., *Dragon and Eagle* (1978); Gareth Porter, *A Peace Denied* (1975), and *Vietnam* (1979); Thomas Powers, *The Man Who Kept the Secrets* (1979); William Quandt, *Decade of Decision* (1977); Franz Schurman, *The Foreign Policies of Richard Nixon* (1987); William Shawcross, *Sideshow: Nixon, Kissinger, and the Destruction of Cambodia* (1978); Richard Stevenson, *The Rise and Fall of Detente* (1985); John Stockwell, *In Search of Enemies* (1977); Robert Stookey, *America and the Arab States* (1975); Robert D. Schulzinger, *Henry Kissinger: Doctor of Diplomacy* (1989); Tad Szulc, *The Illusion of Peace* (1978).

Nixon and His Presidency. Stephen Ambrose, *Nixon: The Triumph of a Politician, 1962–1972* (1989); Richard Barnet, *The Lean Years* (1980); Fawn Brodie, *Richard Nixon: The Shaping of His Character* (1981); Vincent Burke and Vee Burke, *Nixon's Good Deed* (1974); John Ehrlichman, *Witness to Power* (1982); John R. Greene, *The Limits of Power: The Nixon and Ford Administrations;* H. R. Haldeman, *The Haldeman Diaries: Inside the Nixon White House* (1994); Joan Hoff, *Nixon Reconsidered* (1994); J. C. Hurewitz, ed., *Oil, the Arab-Israeli Dispute, and the Industrial World* (1976); R. L. Miller, *The New Economics of Richard Nixon* (1972); Daniel P. Moynihan, *The Politics of a Guaranteed Income* (1973); R. P. Nathan et al., *Monitoring Revenue Sharing* (1975); Richard Nixon, *RN: The Memoirs of Richard Nixon* (1978); Herbert Parmet, *Richard Nixon and His America* (1989); Raymond Price, *With Nixon* (1977); James Reichley, *Conservatives in an Age of Change: The Nixon and Ford Administrations* (1981); William Safire, *Before the Fall* (1975); Joan Edelman Spero, *The Politics of International Economic Relations* (1977); Michael Tanzer, *The Energy Crisis* (1974); Theodore H. White, *The Making of the President, 1972* (1973); Bob Woodward and Scott Armstrong, *The Brethren* (1980).

Nixon and Watergate. Fawn Brodie, *Richard Nixon* (1981); Richard Cohen and Jules Witcover, *A Heartbeat Away* (1974); Len Colodny and Robert Gettlin, *Silent Coup* (1991); John Dean, *Blind Ambition* (1976); James Doyle, *Not Above the Law* (1977); Fred Emery, *Watergate: The Corruption of American Politics* (1994); Stanley J. Kutler, *The Wars of Watergate* (1990); J. Anthony Lukas, *Nightmare: The Underside of the Nixon Years* (1976); Bruce Mazlish, *In Search of Nixon* (1972); Richard M. Nixon, *RN: The Memoirs of Richard Nixon*

(1978); Jonathan Schell, *The Time of Illusion* (1975); Arthur M. Schlesinger, Jr., *The Imperial Presidency* (1973); Michael Schudson, *Watergate in American Memory: How We Remember, Forget, and Reconstruct the Past* (1992); William Sirica, *To Set the Record Straight* (1979); Maurice Stans, *The Terrors of Justice* (1984); Theodore H. White, *Breach of Faith* (1975); Garry Wills, *Nixon Agonistes* (1970); Bob Woodward and Carl Bernstein, *All the President's Men* (1974), and *The Final Days* (1976).

CHAPTER 33 THE AGE OF LIMITS

The Ford Presidency.   James M. Cannon, *Time and Chance: Gerald Ford's Appointment with History* (1994), and *Gerald Ford, A Time to Heal* (1979); John R. Greene, *The Limits of Power: The Nixon and Ford Administrations* (1992); Robert T. Hartmann, *Palace Politics* (1980); Gerald Ter Horst, *Gerald Ford* (1975); Richard Reeves, *A Ford Not a Lincoln* (1976); A. James Reichley, *Conservatives in an Age of Change: The Nixon and Ford Administrations* (1981); Edward and Frederick Schapsmeier, *Gerald R. Ford's Date with Destiny: A Political Biography* (1989); James L. Sundquist, *The Decline and Resurgence of Congress* (1981).

The Carter Presidency.   Jack Bass and Walter Devries, *The Transformation of Southern Politics* (1976); James Bill, *The Eagle and the Lion* (1988); Zbigniew Brzezinski, *Power and Principle* (1983); Jimmy Carter, *Why Not the Best?* (1975), and *Keeping Faith* (1982); Rosalynn Carter, *First Lady from Plains* (1984); Steven Gillon, *The Democrats' Dilemma: Walter Mondale and the Liberal Legacy* (1992); Betty Glad, *Jimmy Carter* (1980); Erwin Hargrove, *Jimmy Carter as President* (1989); Steven B. Hunt, *The Energy Crisis* (1978); Haynes Johnson, *In the Absence of Power* (1980); Charles O. Jones, *The Trusteeship Presidency* (1988); Hamilton Jordan, *Crisis* (1982); Walter LaFeber, *Panama Canal* (1978); Clark Mollenhoff, *The President Who Failed* (1980); A. Glenn Mower, Jr., *Human Rights and American Foreign Policy* (1987); William B. Quandt, *Decade of Decisions* (1977), and *Camp David* (1986); Barry Rubin, *Paved with Good Intentions* (1983); Lars Schoultz, *Human Rights and U.S. Policy Toward Latin America* (1981); Gaddis Smith, *Morality, Reason, and Power* (1986); Strobe Talbott, *Endgame* (1979); Jules Witcover, *Marathon* (1977); James Wooten, *Dasher* (1978); Cyrus Vance, *Hard Choices* (1983).

The New Right.   Sidney Blumenthal, *The Rise of the Counter-Establishment* (1986); George Nash, *The Conservative Intellectual Movement in America Since 1945* (1979); Burton Yale Pines, *Back to Basics* (1982); David W. Reinhard, *The Republican Right Since 1945* (1983); Kirkpatrick Sale, *Power Shift: The Rise of the Southern Rim and Its Challenge to the Eastern Establishment* (1975); Peter Steinfels, *The Neo-Conservatives* (1979); John K. White, *The New Politics of Old Values* (1988); Clyde Wilcox, *God's Warriors: The Christian Right in Twentieth Century America* (1992); John Woodridge, *The Evangelicals* (1975).

The Reagan Presidency.   Frank Ackerman, *Reaganomics* (1982); Laurence I. Barrett, *Gambling with History* (1984); Bill Boyarsky, *The Rise of Ronald Reagan* (1968); Paul Boyer, ed., *Reagan as President: Contemporary Views of the Man, His Politics, and His Policies* (1990); William J. Broad, *Teller's War: The Top-Secret Story Behind the Star Wars Deception* (1992); Lou Cannon, *Reagan* (1982), and *President Reagan: The Role of a Lifetime* (1990); Joan Claybrook, *Retreat from Safety: Reagan's Attack on American Health* (1984); Robert Dallek,

Ronald Reagan: The Politics of Symbolism (1984); Ronnie Dugger, *On Reagan* (1983); Thomas Byrne Edsall, *The New Politics of Inequality* (1984); Anne Edwards, *Early Reagan* (1987); Rowland Evans and Robert Novak, *The Reagan Revolution* (1981); Benjamin Friedman, *Day of Reckoning: The Consequences of American Economic Policy Under Reagan and After* (1988); Jack Germond and Jules Witcover, *Blue Smoke and Mirrors: How Reagan Won and Why Carter Lost the Election of 1980* (1981), and *Wake Us When It's Over: Presidential Politics of 1984* (1985); George Gildner, *Wealth and Poverty* (1981); Fred I. Greenstein, ed., *The Reagan Presidency* (1983); William Greider, *The Education of David Stockman and Other Americans* (1982); Haynes Johnson, *Sleepwalking Through History: America in the Reagan Years* (1991); Jonathan Lash, *A Season of Spoils: The Story of the Reagan Administration's Attack on the Environment* (1984); Robert Lekachman, *Greed Is Not Enough: Reaganomics* (1982); Jane Mayer and Doyle McManus, *Landslide: The Unmaking of the President, 1984–1988* (1988); Charles Noble, *Liberalism at Work: The Rise and Fall of OSHA* (1986); Peggy Noonan, *What I Saw at the Revolution: A Political Life in the Reagan Era* (1990); John L. Palmer and Isabel V. Sawhill, eds., *The Reagan Experiment* (1982); Michael J. Piore and Charles F. Sabel, *The Second Industrial Divide* (1984); Frances Fox Piven and Richard A. Cloward, *The New Class War: Reagan's Attack on the Welfare State and Its Consequences* (1982); Nancy Reagan, *My Turn* (1989); Richard Reeves, *The Reagan Detour* (1985); Donald T. Regan, *For the Record* (1988); Michael Rogin, *Ronald Reagan: The Movie* (1987); Michael Schaller, *Reckoning with Reagan: America and Its President in the 1980s* (1992); C. Brant Short, *Ronald Reagan and the Public Lands: America's Conservation Debate, 1979–1984* (1989); Hedrick Smith, *The Power Game* (1988); Hedrick Smith et al., *Reagan: The Man, the President* (1980); David A. Stockman, *The Triumph of Politics* (1986); Sidney Weintraub and Marvin Goodstein, eds., *Reaganomics in the Stagflation Economy* (1983); F. Clifton White and William Gil, *Why Reagan Won* (1982); Theodore H. White, *America in Search of Itself* (1982); Garry Wills, *Reagan's America* (1987).

Reagan and the World. Seweryn Bialer and Michael Mandelbaum, eds., *Gorbachev's Russia and American Foreign Policy* (1988); Raymond Bonner, *Weakness and Deceit: U.S. Policy and El Salvador* (1984); Tom Buckley, *Violent Neighbors* (1984); Steven Emerson, *Secret Warriors: Inside the Covert Military Operations of the Reagan Era* (1988); Thomas L. Friedman, *From Beirut to Jerusalem* (1989); Alexander Haig, *Caveat: Realism, Reagan and Foreign Policy* (1984); Jane Hunter et al., *The Iran-Contra Connection* (1987); David E. Kyvig, ed., *Reagan and the World* (1990); Walter LaFeber, *Inevitable Revolutions: The United States in Central America* (1983); Richard A. Melanson, *Reconstructing Consensus: American Foreign Policy Since the Vietnam War* (1991); John Newhouse, *War and Peace in the Nuclear Age* (1989); Robert O. Pastor, *Condemned to Repetition: The United States and Nicaragua* (1987); Charles D. Smith, *Palestine and the Arab-Israeli Conflict*, 2nd ed. (1992); Strobe Talbott, *Deadly Gambits* (1984), and *The Master of the Game: Paul Nitze and the Nuclear Peace* (1988); Daniel Wirls, *Buildup: The Politics of Defense in the Reagan Era* (1992); Bob Woodward, *Veil: The Secret Wars of the CIA* (1987).

CHAPTER 34 BEYOND THE COLD WAR

The Post Cold-War World. Bernard Gwertzman and Michael T. Kaufman, eds., *The Collapse of Communism* (1990); Paul Kennedy, *The Rise and Fall of the Great Powers* (1987);

Robert Kuttner, *The End of Laissez Faire: National Purpose and the Global Economy After the Cold War* (1991); John Mueller, *Policy and Opinion in the Gulf War* (1994); Henry R. Nau, *The Myth of America's Decline: Leading the World Economy in the 1990s* (1990); Joseph Nye, *Bound to Lead: The Changing Nature of American Power* (1990); H. Norman Schwarzkopf, *It Doesn't Take a Hero* (1992).

Politics After Reagan.   E. J. Dionne, *Why Americans Hate Politics* (1991); Thomas Ferguson and Joel Rogers, *Right Turn* (1986); William Greider, *Who Will Tell the People?* (1992); Robert S. McElvaine, *The End of the Conservative Era: Liberalism After Reagan* (1987); Kevin Phillips, *The Politics of Rich and Poor: Wealth and the American Electorate in the Reagan Aftermath* (1990); Adolph L. Reed, Jr., *The Jesse Jackson Phenomenon* (1986); Bob Woodard, *The Agenda* (1994)

Post-Liberal Culture.   Peter N. Carroll, *It Seemed Like Nothing Happened* (1982); Peter Clecak, *America's Quest for the Ideal Self* (1983); Jim Hougan, *Decadence: Radical Nostalgia, Narcissism, and Decline in the Seventies* (1975); Christopher Lasch, *The Culture of Narcissism* (1978); Edwin Schur, *The Awareness Trap* (1976); Daniel Yankelovich, *New Rules: Search for Self-Fulfillment in a World Turned Upside Down* (1981).

Economy and Society.   Carl Abbott, *The New Urban America: Growth and Politics in the Sunbelt Cities* (1981); Michael A. Bernstein and David E. Adler, *Understanding American Economic Decline* (1994); Barry Bluestone and Bennett Harrison, *The Deindustrializing of America* (1982); Connie Bruck, *The Predator's Ball: The Junk Bond Raiders and the Man Who Staked Them* (1988); Bryan Burroughs and John Helyar, *Barbarians at the Gate: The Fall of RJR Nabisco* (1990); Elizabeth Fee and Daniel M. Fox, eds., *AIDS: The Burdens of History* (1988), and *AIDS: The Making of a Chronic Disease* (1992); Gerald N. Grob, *From Asylum to Community: Mental Health Policy in Modern America* (1991); Robert Heilbroner and Lester Thurow, *Five Economic Challenges* (1983); John Langone, *AIDS: The Facts* (1988); Frank Levy, *Dollars and Dreams: The Changing American Income Distribution* (1987); Michael Lewis, *Liar's Poker* (1989); Eric Marcus, *Making History: The Struggle for Gay and Lesbian Equal Rights, 1945–1990* (1992); Robert Reich, *The Work of Nations: Preparing Ourselves for Twenty-First-Century Capitalism* (1991); Kirkpatrick Sale, *Power Shift* (1975); Jonathan Schell, *The Fate of the Earth* (1982); Arthur M. Schlesinger, Jr., *The Disuniting of America* (1992); Bruce J. Schulman, *From Cotton Belt to Sunbelt: Federal Policy, Economic Development, and the Transformation of the South, 1938–1980* (1991); Randy Shilts, *And the Band Played On: Politics, People, and the AIDS Epidemic* (1987); James B. Stewart, *Den of Thieves* (1991); Studs Terkel, *The Great Divide* (1988); John Woodridge, *The Evangelicals* (1975); Daniel Yergin, *The Prize* (1991).

Gender and Family.   Mary Francis Berry, *Why ERA Failed* (1986); Susan M. Bianchi, *American Women in Transition* (1987); Nancy Caraway, *Segregated Sisterhood: Racism and the Politics of American Feminism* (1991); Andrea Dworkin, *Right-Wing Women* (1983); Barbara Ehrenreich, *The Hearts of Men: American Dreams and the Flight from Commitment* (1983); Jonathan Kozol, *Rachel and Her Children: Homeless Families in America* (1988); Kristin Luker, *Abortion and the Politics of Motherhood* (1984); Jane Mansbridge, *Why We Lost the ERA* (1986); Donald G. Mathews and Jane Sherron De Hart, *Sex, Gender, and the Politics of E.R.A.: A State and the Nation* (1990); Rosalind Pechesky, *Abortion and Woman's Choice* (1984); Harrell R. Rodgers, Jr., *Poor Women, Poor Families* (1986); Hilda

Scott, *Working Your Way to the Bottom: The Feminization of Poverty* (1985); Ruth Sidel, *Women and Children Last* (1986); Suzanne Staggenborg, *The Pro-Choice Movement: Organization and Activism in the Abortion Conflict* (1991); Winifred D. Wandersee, *On the Move: American Women in the 1970s* (1988).

Nonwhites in the 1970s and 1980s. Ken Auletta, *The Underclass* (1981); Frank D. Bean and Marta Tienda, *The Hispanic Population of the United States* (1987); Derrick Bell, *And We Are Not Saved: The Elusive Quest for Racial Justice* (1987); James D. Cockcroft, *Outlaws in the Promised Land: Mexican Immigrant Workers and America's Future* (1986); John Crewden, *The Tarnished Door: The New Immigrants and the Transformation of America* (1983); Vine Deloria, Jr., *American Indian Policy in the Twentieth Century* (1985); Leslie W. Dunbar, ed., *Minority Report* (1984); Marian Wright Edelman, *Families in Peril* (1987); Douglas Glasgow, *The Black Underclass* (1980); Andrew Hacker, *Two Nations: Black and White, Separate, Hostile, Unequal* (1992); Michael Katz, *The Undeserving Poor: From the War on Poverty to the War on Welfare* (1989); Nicholas Lemann, *The Promised Land: The Great Black Migration and How It Changed America* (1989); Carl Nightingale, *On the Edge: A History of Poor Black Children and Their American Dreams* (1993); David M. Reimers, *Still the Golden Door* (1985); Carol B. Stack, *All Our Kin: Strategies for Survival in a Black Community* (1975); William Julius Wilson, *The Truly Disadvantaged* (1987).

Illustration Credits

Index

NOTE: *Page numbers followed by the letter* m *refer to maps.*

About the Author

ALAN BRINKLEY is professor of American history at Columbia University. Educated at Princeton and Harvard, he has served on the faculties of the Massachusetts Institute of Technology, Harvard University, the City University of New York Graduate School, and Princeton University. He is the author of *Voices of Protest: Huey Long, Father Coughlin, and the New Deal,* which won the 1983 National Book Award for History; *The End of Reform: New Deal Liberalism in Recession and War; American History: A Survey;* and the writer of many articles, essays, and reviews in both scholarly and nonscholarly periodicals.

A Note on the Type

The text of this book is a digitized version of Janson, a typeface long thought to have been made by the Dutchman Anton Janson, who was a practicing type founder in Leipzig during the years 1668–1687. However, it has been conclusively demonstrated that this family of type is actually the work of Nicholas Kis (1650–1702), a Hungarian, who most probably learned his trade from the master Dutch type founder Dirk Voskens. Janson is an excellent example of the influential and sturdy Dutch types that prevailed in England up to the time William Caslon developed his own incomparable designs from them.